grow healthy. grow happy.

grow healthy.
grow happy.
the whole baby guide

Becky Cannon, the Founder of i play., Inc.

🪰 Genki Press

Genki Press, LLC
2000 Riverside Drive
Suite 8
Asheville, NC 28804
www.genkipress.com

Distributed in the United States and Canada by i play. Inc.
2000 Riverside Drive
Suite 9
Asheville, NC 28804
www.iplaybaby.com
+1 (800) 876-1574

Ordering Information:
Quantity sales. Special discounts are available on quantity purchases by corporations, associations, and others. For details, contact the distributor at the address above.

Printed in China

Photo Credits

Becky Cannon's family photos from
her personal family album

© Lynne Harty Photography

© BigStock.com

© Shutterstock.com

© Kaelee Denise Photography

© Audrey Goforth Photography

© Keaton Edwards

Designed by Julie Nunnally

Internet addresses given in this book were accurate at the time when it was printed.

The suggestions and ideas in this book are not intended to take the place of professional guidance or treatment; they are meant to complement the advice of your child's health care provider, caretakers, and educators, while offering consolidated information to help you develop your intuition and make choices that fit with your own personal, religious, or spiritual philosophies. There is no guarantee as to the effects of the use of the recommendations and no liabilities can be taken. I believe that you can balance convenience with a conscious and natural lifestyle, and make prioritized decisions to ensure the health and well-being of your child.

Mention of specific companies, organizations, or authorities in this book does not imply endorsement of this book or its author.

Publisher's Cataloging-in-Publication data
Cannon, Becky.
grow healthy. grow happy. The Whole Baby Guide/Becky Cannon
p.   cm.

ISBN 978-0-9916-5390-4
1. Child rearing. 2. Parenting. 3. Child development. I. Title.

Library of Congress Control Number: 2014912447

10 9 8 7 6 5 4 3 2 1

When my mother holds a baby, I see and feel the expression of her love for the baby and the reflection of the baby's essence in her eyes. She naturally knows how to dance with babies—a reciprocal dance and exchange of love.
Like me, she learned this dance from her mother.

I dedicate my book, *Grow Healthy. Grow Happy. The Whole Baby Guide*, to my mother, Dott Cannon. We have shared a reciprocal dance of love since I was born. This experience has taught me to dance, as a mother, with my babies and other ones, as well.

With love and gratitude

Contents at a Glance

Table of Contents

Part 2 Whole Food   323

Essentials to establish your baby's holistic foundation of healthy eating

Preface

MORE THAN 40 YEARS ago, I was introduced to a holistic way of understanding the world that has profoundly influenced how I live, how I eat, and how I have raised my children. Back then, words like *organic*, *holistic*, *locally grown*, and *eco-friendly* were neither mainstream nor commonplace. Today, happily, parents have myriad choices for keeping their children healthy. Many of these choices embrace a nurturing view of parenting and a harmonious, healthy, and environmentally responsible lifestyle. I relied on these principles as I raised my two daughters and as I founded my company, i play., Inc.

I created this guide to help you navigate the maze of information, products, and trends in caring for your baby. The information in *Grow Healthy Grow Happy: The Whole Baby Guide* is based on my background in child development, my decades of experience with the traditional Japanese approach to health and well-being, and my practical experience as both a mother and the founder of my baby products company. This book is designed to be concise, comprehensive, and holistic, with many interrelated parts. All of its content—theories, activities, stories, photos, reference information, charts, recipes, and shopping lists—support the ideal of a natural lifestyle. My intentions are to offer a variety of information; to help you develop your own philosophies and values as a parent; and to assist you in taking an informed, active role in your child's health care, education, learning, and emotional and character development.

Emi, Becky, and Mari

My personal experiences influenced my parenting philosophy. In college I studied child development and was inspired by A. S. Neill, a progressive educator from the UK, and by Rudolf Steiner, the founder of Waldorf education, among others. Their philosophies on the nature of childhood integrate physical, mental, and emotional development in a holistic and experiential way, and that view resonated with me. Burton White, a child-development specialist and the author of *The First Three Years of Life*, also made a significant impression on me. He believed that the time when you can make the greatest impact on your child's development is during the first three years of her life. According to White, by the time a child is three years old, the foundation of her physical, mental, and emotional development has been established. She has learned to smile, eat, crawl, walk, talk, think, and express her feelings, and her birth weight has multiplied by four or five times. She will never learn that much in any other three-year period of her life.

After college, I enrolled in classes in traditional East Asian cooking and philosophy in Boston. The classes focused on Japanese cookery and a philosophy

Dream Window Kindergarten Class

Hideko Yoshida

called the "yin and yang" theory. I explain this theory in depth in the introduction, but basically, yin and yang are two opposite qualities like light and dark, or hot and cold, that support each other and, when in balance, create health and wholeness, like coming home. I found these principles logical and practical as I applied them to my daily life, especially in relation to food choices and preparation. To create balance in my diet, I began eating primarily whole grains and vegetables, which made me feel physically healthy and gave me more energy, clarity, and purpose.

In 1976, I went to Japan and was hired to teach at a preschool, Muso Yochien (Dream Window Kindergarten), which had more than 300 students. Hideko Yoshida, the school's founder and principal, had a primary intention to teach children to be independent and to develop their own judgment while connecting with nature. Under her guidance, I learned about early-childhood education and the traditional Japanese lifestyle. I took classes in Japanese cooking and studied with Takehara-sensei, a Japanese cook who had many years of experience with traditional foods and healing remedies. Her cooking was wholesome and deeply satisfying. She offered a variety of colors, textures, and tastes. She said that traditional Japanese seasoning was like a symphony, with rice as the steady bass notes and different flavors as various notes: vinegar, sweetener, salt, ginger, mustard, soy sauce, and herbs. I enjoyed her simple, fresh, delicious whole-foods cooking—and I lost 30 pounds.

While in Japan, I married Naoki Kubota, an acupuncturist, who had studied the same philosophies of natural healing that I had studied in Boston. Before my pregnancy with Emi, my first daughter, most of the Japanese people I encountered saw me as an outsider. With my curly brown hair, fair and freckled skin, and Mississippi accent, I stood out. The Japanese tend to be polite and accommodating, but they saw me as different. I was a *gaijin*—a foreigner. However, once I became pregnant, I had an entirely new status in Japanese society. I was about to become a mother, which continues to be a highly honored role for a woman in Japan. As my pregnancy became more visible, people on the street greeted me differently. In the shops and on the train, they spoke to me about the joys of pregnancy and parenting. I discovered that the average Japanese person, regardless of gender, knows a great deal about pregnancy and child development because of the cultural emphasis on children and child rearing.

When I was three months pregnant, my obstetrician, Dr. Watanabe, insisted I wear a *hara-obi*, a long cotton cloth that is wrapped around a pregnant woman's belly. It provides support to the growing uterus and helps protect the baby inside. Dr. Watanabe told me to come into his office so that his staff could teach me how to wrap my *hara-obi* on Dog Day, a specific day on the Japanese and Chinese 12-day zodiac cycle. He said that learning to wrap a *hara-obi* on Dog Day is auspicious because dogs have easy births. I was surprised that my scientifically trained medical doctor included folklore in my health care, and I have heard that this is still a custom in Japan today. When I wore the *hara-obi*, I felt snug, warm, and protected. It proved very helpful while I was teaching kindergarten, because I did not have to worry as much about lively five-year-olds bumping into my belly.

After I gave birth to Emi, my pediatrician and other Japanese friends and associates encouraged me to stay in bed for three weeks to allow my body to rest, to heal,

Pregnant Belly Support

A *hara-obi* is a long cotton cloth that can be wrapped around a pregnant belly to provide support and protect the baby inside.

and to produce ample milk to nourish my newborn. Several Japanese women told me that if I rested after giving birth, my milk would be especially sweet and nutritious. They insisted that I eat a variety of strengthening and medicinal foods, such as *mochi*, a nutritious pounded sweet rice that is known for its milk-producing properties. Following their advice, I also ate a healing soup loaded with root vegetables because, as one friend said, "Roots give strength from the earth." Miso soup with wakame sea vegetables was another Japanese staple food recommended to me after childbirth, because it easily assimilates protein and has a rich supply of friendly bacteria that promote healthy digestion. It also has abundant minerals that strengthen the immune system, and promote healing.

Traditional Japanese baby care also influenced how I diapered and carried Emi. I first encountered the wool diaper cover in Japan and found that in combination with a cloth diaper, it was very effective in keeping Emi's bottom dry, while also letting in air for circulation. In the winter, like many other Japanese mothers, I wore a "mama coat"—an overcoat that was big enough to cover us both, with Emi securely nestled in a carrier underneath. My baby and I were warm and cozy.

Far from home, I missed my mother and other family members during my pregnancy and childbirth, but I was comforted by the support

Emi and Becky

of a society that honors and cherishes family, tradition, children, and motherhood. My time in Japan gave me some practical and natural experiences that I was able to use in my daily parenting. I also came to appreciate the high quality and special functions of Japanese baby products that were designed with babies' needs and health in mind. In Japan I discovered items with thoughtful and convenient features, such as flip-pocket bibs, soft cotton muslin wipes, clothes with seams stitched on the outside for comfort, and scissors for cutting toddlers' food.

Mari, our second daughter, was born in 1982, after we moved to the United States. I had some of Emi's hand-me-downs, but I missed the unique baby items that I had bought in Japan. Even though I did not want to live a completely Japanese lifestyle, I appreciated many of their common-sense ways of parenting and integrated them into my Western routine. Traditional Japanese ways of living inspired me to discover natural traditions both from my own heritage and from other cultures. I made Emi and Mari's clothes with natural fibers and prepared their food without preservatives or refined ingredients. I wanted to provide a healthy environment and diet as a foundation, especially during their first three years.

As I blended my Japanese experiences into my parenting principles, I did the same in my career. My first entrepreneurial venture, together with my former husband Naoki, was the East West Center in Asheville, North Carolina. Naoki set up his acupuncture practice in our house and taught martial arts. I held classes in natural-foods cooking and hosted weekly dinners, boardinghouse style. We offered a meal from soup to dessert for three dollars. Together we offered natural-healing consultations and hosted seminars on traditional East Asian medicine and philosophy, including the principles of nature that form the basis of this book.

When I was pregnant with Mari, I often had insomnia and found myself sitting in my spare bedroom in the wee hours of the morning and dreaming up ways to provide natural baby products to other parents. I wanted natural products like those I had found in Japan when Emi had been born—products that were made with the baby's needs in mind. My Japanese mother-in-law sent me wool diaper covers, and I sold them through mail-order from my home. I packed orders for UPS delivery while Mari took her naps and Emi played.

As I developed my business, the first products I sold related to the health, environmental, and economic impacts of cloth diapering. After working for many years with a company that imported diaper covers, I started designing my own products, such as a patented Ultimate Swim Diaper, which is made to support safe swimming. I introduced products made from organic cotton and other natural materials that were not very popular at the time. I researched the dangers of plastic additives, such as polyvinyl chloride (PVC) and bisphenol A (BPA), before others in the industry did, and I developed brochures to educate parents about the dangers of these chemicals.

The business started to grow, and I hired my first employees to help pack orders in laundry baskets in my garage. I gathered a team of women to sew my swim diapers in their homes. At one point, my team made 10,000 swim diapers a week! I experienced firsthand the demands on working mothers. Emi and Mari learned to take care of themselves, yet I was there if they needed me. They helped pack diapers in our living room while UPS waited at the door.

In 1995, I moved the business to an office park, began in-house manufacturing, and shifted from retail to wholesale channels. Because I did not study business in college, the financial, operational, and management aspects of business have always challenged me. However, through trial and error and with help from dedicated, bright people, I have learned how to run a business and make it grow.

My company, i play., Inc. (first called Woolies, and then Family Clubhouse), has grown from a mail-order operation to an international business that now supplies a range of natural baby products, including feeding items, toys, baby care products, apparel, and food.

I started the business as an outgrowth of my commitment to my own children, who inspired me to keep going during challenging times. Even now that my children are adults, we are still working together in my business. Emi, my first daughter, is in a leadership role, and my second daughter, Mari, who is an acupuncturist and natural healer, is a contributor to the wellness section of this book.

our values

Act with intentionality to:
Foster health and happiness
Be honest and fair
Connect with nature
Be open and creative
Nourish compassionate relationships

our mission

We are a values-based and family-oriented company that provides healthy products for babies' early development. Through our collaboration with responsible and open-minded partners, we strive to create a healthier, happier world by sharing our commitment to whole living.

company time line

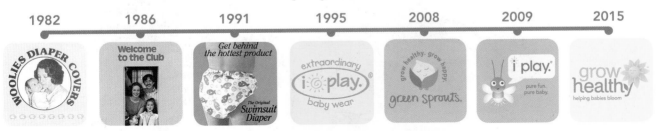

My company was founded with a commitment to researching and carrying the best products and using practices and manufacturing methods that support a life of health and happiness for babies. The information I offer in this book reflects my philosophical commitment to furthering a holistic view of child rearing and parenting.

With a background in child development, I did not intend to go into business, and I was never sure that running a company was my passionate life's work. However, writing this book has helped me integrate my passions and bring purpose and meaning to my business. I appreciate the opportunity to share *Grow Healthy Grow Happy: The Whole Baby Guide* and to help you offer your baby a radiant life.

Introduction

SOAKING UP THE SUN, breathing fresh air, or listening to the birds, your child can easily connect to the wonder of the natural world. When my daughters, Emi and Mari, were small, they enjoyed relaxing into nature's flow by playing in the sand at the beach or throwing rocks in a creek for hours. In nature, your child can experience a "zone" of comfort and peace. As a parent, you can help your child harmonize with the natural world by understanding its principles and by using them as a guide in your care for him.

At Muso Yochien (Dream Window Kindergarten) in Kyoto, Japan, where I worked when I lived in Japan, nature was an integral part of the children's daily life and learning. Hideko Yoshida, the school's principal, believed that the best way to support a young child's physical, mental, and emotional development was to let him spend as much time as possible in the natural world. While I was teaching with Hideko Yoshida, the children often took field trips to dig sweet potatoes, to pick persimmons, and to play in the bamboo forest.

Being surrounded by nature can provide enormous benefits for your baby's health and development. Fresh air and sunshine nourish his body and mind and give him a deep sense of well-being. Animals, plants, and the outdoor world offer endless opportunities to explore and learn. If you live in an urban center, it may be challenging to provide daily experiences with nature. Even if you live in the country, a busy life can pull you away from appreciating the outdoors. However, you can intentionally bring the wonders of the natural world into your child's daily life by providing food, plants, fresh air, and sunshine, and by using nature's principles in your parenting.

Your child's development is a result of the dynamic interaction between nature and nurture. From nature he inherited genetic, instinctual, and biological characteristics that are inherent to his maturation process. Aspects of nurture—your daily care for him, the food he eats, his feelings, his activities, and the environment he lives in—complement his inherited characteristics and influence how he changes and grows. Through the collaboration of nature's principles and the thoughtful and intentional choices that you make to nurture him, your child can learn and adapt to realize his full potential.

Nature's Principles for Whole Parenting

The concept of chi, or vital life energy, is central to traditional East Asian philosophy and medicine. Chi is the life force that infuses all living things, and the yin-yang balance of chi is necessary for their healthy functioning. This invisible force, or energy, is nature's intelligence.

Chi does not require a central nervous system or a brain. Human intelligence is based on the mind's ability to question, think, analyze, and hypothesize. On the other hand, nature's intelligence is based on inherent balance, which it is always seeking. Chi permeates every living thing and is all encompassing. It is generous and abundant, and it supports your baby's individual growth and development with ongoing natural healing energy. For instance, your baby's body knows how to heal an upset stomach or a skinned knee because its natural intelligence seeks wholeness and balance.

As a parent, you instinctively know and understand your baby and his tempo. When you hold him, your innate sense is to carry him close to your body, and he instinctively knows to root and to drink his mother's milk without instructions. His heartbeat, the inhale and exhale of his breath, and all of his biological functions occur rhythmically and naturally. When he is born, he knows how to grow and learn through his natural curiosity and innate developmental process.

I have been influenced by the traditional Japanese view of living in harmony with nature. The principles of nature and the theory of yin and yang have been very helpful in my personal and professional life, and in supporting my children's ability to regulate themselves. I studied and used these principles in East Asian medicine and in macrobiotics philosophy.

The word "macrobiotics" comes from Greek roots meaning "long life," reflecting the goal of long-term health. East Asian medicine and macrobiotic philosophy classify yin and yang slightly differently. My intention is to draw from both schools of thought to provide you with simple ways to navigate your child's growth and development in all areas.

Yin and yang are abstract qualities because they are continually changing and they are relative. However, it is helpful to label something as yin or yang while comparing and developing an understanding of the principles. The yin-yang spectrum is not a dualistic measure of right or wrong. As you observe and think about these principles, you can develop your own understanding and judgment from your experience of how yin and yang work. They are a set of tools that do not necessarily result in solutions; rather, they open up questions that may lead to the unexpected. If you explore and question with curiosity and play with these concepts without taking them too seriously, then you may discover your own insights of how to use yin and yang to create awareness that helps you understand your child.

According to the universal theory, yin and yang express their qualities in every aspect of life: the natural world, activities, behavior, food, and health. Charts throughout this book include a comparison of different categories on a yin-yang spectrum. You can use these charts along with the principles I discuss, as tools, to observe and understand your baby's condition, and then you can guide him through food and activities to make adjustments in his physical, mental, and emotional health.

I describe some principles of yin and yang, along with other principles based on nature's intelligence, which have been most useful to me as a parent. Traditional cultures all over the world have used these principles of nature, and they exist independently of any opinions that people may have. The sun shines, on its own, whether you believe in it or wish for rain. These principles are interrelated, interdependent, and they are foundational to the concepts in this book. I have included examples of how to apply them to assist you in going with the positive flow of nature instead of against it.

The Principle of Complementary Opposites

Both yin and yang are present in all living things, and they exist harmoniously. Specific characteristics have been attributed to opposite poles of a spectrum: yin is calming, yang is energizing; yin is cooling, yang is warming; yin is receptive, yang is active. One cannot exist without the other—day needs night, up needs down, and front needs back in order to have meaning. Pain and pleasure, sadness and joy, fear and security are at different places on the same spectrum. Both polar forces in each of these pairs are essential for your baby's health, just as he needs both exercise and rest in order to achieve balance.

Your baby is small, compact, and full of yang, or active energy. Meanwhile, he expresses his yin side through his vulnerability and dependency on you. Yin is slower and more sensitive and relaxed. Yang is quicker, more focused and strong. Yin and yang apply to parents and other caregivers as well as to babies. For example, when you put your baby to sleep, you get in touch with your gentle, yin feeling for him. Organizing and scheduling your life with your baby develops your yang strength to take care of his daily needs. You need both yin and yang attributes to be sensitive and attuned to your child, and to provide a safe environment in which he can be secure.

The Principle of Relativity

Objects and forces develop meaning—and often shift meaning—only when they are compared to other objects and forces. For example, wood is more yang when compared to water, but when compared to metal, wood is more yin. An apple is more yang compared to a banana but more yin compared to a carrot. Your child may be more yin than one friend but more yang than another friend.

People evaluate situations from their perspective, context, and experience. "Everything is relative" refers to each person's point of view. For instance, you may be ready for your child to go to bed, while he may be energetic and in the mood to play. You and your partner may have different ideas about how to discipline your child based on your respective family histories.

The Principle of Magnetic Attraction

Yin and yang attract and repel each other the way two magnets do. Opposites attract, and likes repel. According to the law of attraction, masculine attracts feminine, an empty stomach seeks to be filled, the heat of a summer day stimulates an urge for something cooling, and activity attracts the need for rest. Throughout a day, your baby moves from one situation to another as his needs are met, and then they are satisfied—attracting and being attracted to people, food, warmth, and other sources of stimulation. He is hungry, and so he eats; he is full, and then he poops; he is restless, and so he moves; he is tired, and so he sleeps; he cries and wants to be held, and then he becomes satisfied and calm with your nurturing, from one attraction to another.

The Principle of Interrelatedness

Everything in the natural world is connected. The yin-yang symbol shows the interrelatedness of yin and yang, with the small dot of color within the white area and the small dot of white within the colored area. A bit of each quality's opposite exists in everything. Ecosystems are an example of this interrelationship in nature. Every ecosystem has producers, consumers, decomposers, and scavengers. If something is added or removed, then the rest of the system adjusts to accommodate and to create balance, if possible.

Likewise, your baby is an ecosystem. His body's systems, brain, and emotions interconnect, work together, and affect each other. According to East Asian medicine and philosophy, the body is a whole with interconnecting parts. Exercise affects your baby's emotions and brain development, while his emotions affect his physical condition. He is also a part of larger ecosystems such as your family, your community, your culture, and the natural environment.

The Principle of Conservation

Animals, plants, and natural resources are limited, and they need conscious attention to prevent them from being depleted. As a parent, you experience the limitations in your family's ecosystem of time, energy, and money, and you recognize the need to conserve these resources every day. To conserve your resources, you need to take care and save some of them for times of unexpected need.

Ecosystem

An ecosystem can be as large as Earth itself or as small as a puddle, where the water, plants, animals, air, light, and soil work together as a balanced system.

The Principle of Stability within Change

The universe is in a state of constant motion and change; never static, it goes through transitions and transformations. The colors of the rainbow fade into each other without clear definition or separation. When yin and yang become out of balance, they affect each other, change proportion, and move to a new balance. Because of the constant change, nothing is completely yin or completely yang. Your baby moves from happy to sad, from clean to dirty, from tired to alert, from healthy to sick, and back again.

Within change are continuity and stability. Even though your child goes through a great deal of transformation in his first three years, he is the same person. His basic constitution, personality, and behavior remain constant and give him a sense of identity.

Which characteristics of your child are likely to endure, and which are likely to change? The stability of your love and support, as well as daily routines, give your child the security and comfort he needs to feel free to explore and learn. Resilience—the ability to be both strong and flexible helps both you and your baby balance change and stability.

Constant change is the only absolute in life—and in parenting. This book offers guidance to help you understand and support your baby's cycles for his first three years so that you can nurture him toward stability and balance through his changes.

The Principle of Balance

Your baby responds to external stimuli by making adjustments that guide him toward equilibrium. Balance is not a permanent state. Your baby reaches out and explores, then returns back to center, like coming home to his essence. The food he eats, his activities, and the environment he lives in all play a role in establishing his balance. When he consumes something cold, the body works to heat the food or drink so that it reaches his body temperature before he can digest it. If he is angry or upset, then he seeks your comforting and soothing, which allow him to relax and to achieve emotional balance. Homeostasis is a dynamic state that the body maintains through continuous adjustments. When your baby's balance is strained by extremes, he requires adjustments to maintain his

balance. If the input becomes too extreme, he could reach the point of overload, with irreparable consequences.

You can either reduce the excessive influence or increase the deficient influence in order to support your child's balance. If you ask the question, "Does my child need more or less yin or yang to restore his balance?" then you can help him make adjustments by encouraging him to raise or to lower his state.

You can also help him restore his balance by feeding him nourishing foods, offering emotional support, or engaging in activities that are moderate on both sides of the yin-yang spectrum, thus reducing the seesaw of alternating extremes. Your child's tastes tell you what he craves and is attracted to. You can help guide him to regulate his state toward balance by adding or subtracting yin or yang influences or by providing moderation to help him maintain an even flow with minimal stress and strain. Throughout this book are ways that you can support your baby's balance, which are marked with:

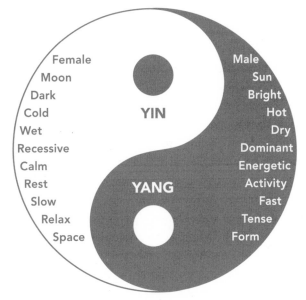

"*If there is yin, there is yang.*
If there is yang, there is yin.
When a mountain is high, then a valley is low."

—*song from Dream Window Kindergarten,*
translated into English

The Principle of Uniqueness

Every person is unique. There is some degree of distinction, no matter how subtle, in each and every thing. Every baby, like every snowflake or autumn leaf, is unique. Your child is an individual with his own needs and gifts, and he came to be who he is by a unique chain of events and circumstances.

Birth order of children within a family affects how each child experiences the world. Genes, gender, geographic region, environmental factors, and the seasons of pregnancy and birth add other dimensions to your child's identity. Every baby has his own essence or spirit that holds the seed of his being and potential.

If you insist that your child participate in team sports when he does not enjoy competition, or force a shy reader to perform in a theater troupe, you can suppress your child's innate sense of self. If you project unfulfilled personal dreams onto your child, it will be a challenge for him to grow into his true self. Instead, by paying close attention to your baby as he grows—as he watches, senses, touches, and listens—you can discover who your baby is and what he needs in order to become and to express his unique self.

The Principle of Cycles of Growth

All of nature shares the life cycles of birth, growth, harvest, and rest. In East Asian medicine, nature has five distinct cycles of change. Winter is a time of hibernation and rest. Spring brings birth and regeneration. Summer supports growth and activity. Late summer is a transition from the peak of summer to the seeds of new beginnings. Autumn becomes cooler again, with harvested crops and changing leaves that signal a transition back to the coldness and quietness of winter. This cycle goes on continuously and involves transformation from beginning to end and back again.

Your child's development is an example of cycles of growth. It may seem as if diapering and sleepless nights will go on forever, but they are part of a cycle in your baby's life that will pass into the next stage of development as he grows. When you watch your baby move through these cycles, you experience the wonders of life. Mother Nature supports his body with the instinctual

knowledge of how to sit up, roll over, crawl, and walk. His brain naturally begins to make connections on its own. When he is one year old, you can take a look at his newborn photos and recognize the changes that happened in a year. Going forward, your baby's development today will biologically evolve and progress into new challenges and growth for him tomorrow.

The Principle of the Integration of Quantity and Quality

Your baby's development is a unified process that integrates his physical, emotional, and mental growth. As he grows, he experiences two interrelated kinds of development: quantitative and qualitative.

Quantitative development can be measured in numbers. It includes weight, height, and vocabulary words that you can measure—for example, "He gained four pounds and one inch in the past year."

Qualitative development relates to the structure or organization of your child's development. Qualitative changes include starting to crawl or walk and beginning to understand cause and effect. They occur when he shifts from throwing a temper tantrum to listening and being reasonable, or when he acquires a new skill, such as reading independently. Qualitative change is more difficult to measure than quantitative development.

Your child grows by integrating and balancing quantity and quality. Too much of a good thing can have a negative effect—too much exercise can cause exhaustion or eating food that is good quality can be unhealthy, if he eats too much. If he eats low-quality food, he can restore balance by eating high-quality food.

Quantitative measurements of development do not always tell the full story. Perhaps your child can recite all 26 letters of the alphabet, but the memorization of letters—or words, for that matter—has no value if he does not understand the meaning behind them. In order to communicate through language in an integrated way, your child first learns a number of vocabulary words (quantitative), and then he attaches meaning to them and gains an understanding of how they fit together to make sentences and thoughts (qualitative). He learns to roll over, to crawl, and to walk by integrating individual experiences into a whole.

The Principle of Attention

Your thoughts, feelings, and energy expand and materialize into your reality. Wherever you focus your attention, your life force, or chi, follows and supports you as you grow, positively or negatively. On the positive side, if you emphasize your blessings and achievements, those blessings and achievements multiply. On the negative side, if you concentrate your energy on fears, failures, obstacles, and mistakes, disappointments become your experience.

Like a plant, your baby thrives on your attention and grows from it. When you take care of his needs and spend time interacting with him, he grows and thrives. Attention is his foundation for a secure attachment and for learning. With your attention, he feels secure and calm, and this allows him to focus his energy and to develop his intelligence. He does not need many material things in order to grow and to be happy, but he does need your presence and attention every day.

The Principle of Cause and Effect

The everyday care of your baby requires a seemingly endless series of cause and effect events. For instance, if you hold your baby upright and bounce him, he calms down; if you forget to change his diaper at bedtime, he wakes up earlier than usual. According to the concept of causality, one event produces a reaction, so that there is a relationship between the two events, with a resulting outcome or consequence. A basic principle of nature is to "sow a garden and reap the harvest."

Cause and effect are not separate, however; they are cyclical. There may be multiple causes for the fact that your baby does not sleep through the night, and these causes may continue for several nights. Observing the flow of your baby's cycles and patterns and how they interact may give you helpful insight into what influences those cycles. In fact, this strategy may be more effective than looking for an isolated cause or effect.

A parent's opportunity

The laws and patterns of nature occur on their own through nature's intelligence, with outcomes that may be significant to your baby, even if you are not aware of them. Your baby's body maintains homeostasis: he sleeps when he is tired, and he grows, learns, and develops on his own. However, you can intervene, question, and challenge reactive patterns that you have learned to offer intentional choices so that your baby can be free to maximize his potential and live a radiant life. By acknowledging nature's intelligence and making informed, proactive choices, you can nurture and guide your baby.

Nurturing Guidelines for Whole Parenting

Your baby came into the world in a state of openness and vulnerability, with the expectation of being cared for. Human babies are among the most fragile of nature's newborns. Within moments of its birth, a foal stands on wobbly legs and finds its way to its mother's breast. But human babies require much more hands-on parental help. They are completely dependent on their caregivers for survival.

Physicians, child psychologists, and other experts say that a baby's brain and other organs are still developing when he enters the world, and this is why the choices you make in your child's first few years matter so much. Your baby's development from birth to age three has tangible and lasting effects on his health, intelligence, and happiness. It is your responsibility to create a foundation for his physical, emotional, and mental health.

Every day, as a parent, you exercise judgment and make choices as you take care of your child. Are you making intentional choices that nourish him, or are you automatically defaulting to patterns that you learned from your parents? By reflecting on the decisions that your parents made for you, you can make deliberate and responsible decisions based on your child's needs, and then actively participate in meeting those needs.

According to Abraham Maslow, an American psychologist who created a hierarchy of needs for psychological health, the realization of a person's potential is built on a specific foundation. Maslow's theory suggests that all people need a safe and nurturing environment in order to learn, to be happy, and to achieve their full potential in society.

The first part of this book is built on an idea similar to Maslow's hierarchy of needs. It begins with meeting your baby's physiological needs and then establishing a secure attachment and connection so that your child feels loved. With this foundation, he has the support and freedom necessary to grow, to learn, to take responsibility, and to reach his full potential.

Following are some guidelines to help you establish a strong foundation for your baby so that he can grow and learn.

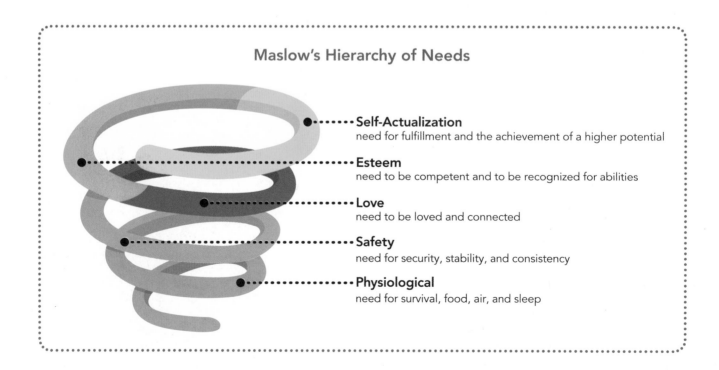

Maslow's Hierarchy of Needs

Self-Actualization
need for fulfillment and the achievement of a higher potential

Esteem
need to be competent and to be recognized for abilities

Love
need to be loved and connected

Safety
need for security, stability, and consistency

Physiological
need for survival, food, air, and sleep

Take Care of Yourself

Once you become a parent, taking time for yourself may seem impossible and selfish. Perhaps you feel guilty for doing something that you enjoy when so many ongoing responsibilities demand your attention. However, when you nourish your own needs, you can refresh and revitalize your core energy to meet the demands of parenting. You also set an example. Modeling self-care is a way of teaching your child to take care of himself. On airplanes, parents are advised to put on their own oxygen masks first before attending to their children's masks. Your child needs you to take care of yourself so that you are available to take care of him.

Provide Nourishment

Daily nourishment for your child includes healthy food for development and energy, comfortable clothing for warmth and protection, and a quiet time and place for him to sleep for restoration and growth. He needs you to take care of him every day by keeping him clean, changing his diapers, washing his clothes, and comforting him if he does not feel well. He also needs fresh air and sunshine—the nourishment of nature.

Provide Safety and Security

Your baby needs you to create a safe environment so that he is protected from accidents and harm. He needs to trust that he will be taken care of so that he can focus on learning and discovering.

Love, Connect, and Be Present

Listening and responding to your baby's needs helps him to develop trust and to be confident that his needs will be met. When you are present and you connect with him through your care, he can relax in knowing that he is loved. You can share your presence with your child as you do activities together—talking, reading, sharing art and music, and laughing. His connection to you will help him learn to regulate his emotions, to be deliberate in his actions, and to develop his intelligence.

See Your Child's Perspective

When you look at your child's vantage point, you can have more compassion and understanding for his needs and meet them more fully. How does it feel to have a wet diaper for a long time? Are his clothes soft or rough next to his skin? Why is he smiling or crying? Imagine how his world looks lying on his back when he looks up at you, the ceiling or sky, without the ability to move and control his world. When he sits up and looks around, crawls, and walks, he gets another viewpoint. What does he see when walking through a crowd of adults and he is knee high? How does he feel when he wants something and cannot communicate?

When you are busy, it may be challenging to see the world from your baby's point of view. Perhaps what may be convenient for you may not be satisfying for him. However, taking time to understand him can be less demanding on you in the long run. If you take care of his true needs early on, he will be more fulfilled as he grows.

Learn and Improve

Since everything is always changing, every moment is an opportunity to reflect and to look for ways to improve your parenting. Sometimes learning comes more from failure than from success. If you are impatient with your child, and you recognize how it affects him, then you may be motivated to stretch to meet his needs the next time he requires your attention. If you pay attention and listen to him, you can understand and learn from the process of parenting.

Listen to Your Intuition

You intuitively know if your baby is tired or hungry because you are in touch with his rhythms and needs. When you acquire knowledge about your child's development, then you can integrate it with your intuition. Pausing and listening helps you hear your inner voice. Then you can trust your intuition and act on it.

Be Mindful

Being in the present moment helps increase your awareness of a situation. Take a few deep breaths to help you stay cool and relaxed when life is hectic. As a parent, you have many responsibilities, but there is a limit to what you can do. Your child has his own strength, resilience, and will. Allowing, accepting, and trusting that he is in the right place at the right time and that he is supported by nature's intelligence can give you the calm and peace to know that not everything is up to you.

Make Intentional Choices

Exercising your judgment calls on your habits, senses, emotions, intelligence, awareness of others, understanding of nature's principles, and intuition. Which sippy cup should you buy? What is for dinner? Which preschool is best for your child? You cannot always make perfect decisions, because you often have to give up one thing to get another. A stainless-steel sippy cup may cost more than a plastic one, so you have to give up some money to buy it. A burger from a fast-food restaurant may be easy and quick in the short term, but the food could compromise your child's health in the long term. The best preschool in town may be far away and inconvenient for your work schedule, so you may choose one that works better logistically for your family. Defining your lifestyle priorities can help you make the many decisions and choices that affect your child. The way you use your resources of time, money, and energy is an expression of your priorities. Developing a clear sense of your priorities can help you be more intentional in the way you nurture your child.

Explore and Play

Babies have a natural curiosity, an openness, and a sense of awe that are infectious. They approach their experiences with a fresh innocence, an adventurous spirit, and an eagerness to explore. You can share the natural world with your child by emulating this "beginner's mind"—using your own curiosity and discovery.

Questioning creates a feeling of wonder. "Why is it this way?" "How does it work?" "Where does it come from?" "How does it grow?" If you question and research an issue for yourself instead of simply following someone else's advice, you may learn more and find your own truth through the process. When you ask a question with sincerity and interest, you create an atmosphere that opens the world of imagination, possibilities, and potential for you and your child to learn together.

Cultivating a sense of appreciation and gratitude for the wonders of nature also maintains a positive mood and enhances emotional well-being. Nature is a teacher that sparks curiosity and creativity through open exploration, while TV, video games, and mechanical toys have limits.

Now, I Understand What Love Really Means

After growing up in Mississippi, my experience of living in Japan, with its very different cultural influences, allowed me to open my mind to new ways of looking at different aspects of life, including parenting. It also inspired me to question my own history and habits, to appreciate my parents and my heritage, and to parent intentionally. In my daily life as a parent and grandparent, and in running my company, I try to maintain a framework of openness and appreciation. When I feel challenged with the pressures of responsibility, I may forget to ask and listen without preconceived ideas or judgments. However, when I do pause, breathe, and take a moment to observe a situation, I can escape my own perspective and become more aware of what is going on around me.

I always wanted Emi and Mari to be independent and imaginative thinkers, to question, to be curious, and to be open to diverse viewpoints. In work and in my personal life, I have found that when I have an inquiring mind, I allow creativity and new ideas to emerge. When my mind is open, I feel the presence of nature's wisdom and support. I hope that you will be open to the ideas in this book, that you will question them and think about them, and that you will develop your own conclusions about a way of parenting that works for you and your family.

While nurturing your child, you will probably make mistakes. You may want the best for your baby, but the reality of life is that many aspects in raising your child will be imperfect, unexpected, and unplanned. Although your daily actions add up and impact him—sometimes positively, sometimes negatively—your individual acts are not what matter most in the long run. The factors central to his wholeness are the knowledge that you love him unconditionally and that your connection with him is secure. With this foundation, he can develop confidence and resilience in the face of challenges.

Parenting is both a responsibility and a privilege. You have the opportunity to share the wonder and joy of your connection with your baby. You can learn and grow along with him as you come to understand the true meaning of love. The following song is for you to enjoy and sing to your baby.

Becky and Zo

"Now, I Understand What Love Really Means"

by the California Honeydrops

Ooh ooh oh how I love my baby
Ooh ooh can't get enough of my baby

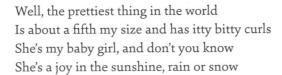

Well, the prettiest thing in the world
Is about a fifth my size and has itty bitty curls
She's my baby girl, and don't you know
She's a joy in the sunshine, rain or snow

Chorus:
You keep growing and growing
From the seeds that we're sowing
And it's all so clear to me
Now, I understand what love really means

Your smile shines a light into my day
And oh how my heart glows to see you laugh and play
With a love in your eyes that's so true
And there ain't nothing I wouldn't do to bring this whole world to you

Chorus:
You keep growing and growing
From the seeds that we're sowing
And it's all so clear to me
Now, I understand what love really means

From the ladybugs in the grass to the deep blue sea
Each day's full of wonders for you and for me
By your side, I slow down the pace
Every moment's the right time, everywhere's the right place

Chorus:
You keep growing and growing
From the seeds that we're sowing
And it's all so clear to me
Now, I understand what love really means, what love really means

 Hear the song at
iplaybaby.com

Children's Bill of Rights

by Farid Gruber, based on the teachings
of Hazrat Inayat Khan

- To be loved, cherished, and protected

- To be valued for being not doing

- To have character and moral education as primary in the school as well as the family

- To be taught the values of stillness, single-mindedness, and concentration

- To learn the interconnectedness of people and the environment

- To be exposed to the music and rhythm of all curricula

- To have spiritual development and faith encouraged

- To have a balance between fun, excitement, and earnestness in all learning

- To be rewarded for personal integrity and truthfulness

- To eat, dance, and pray together

If you accept, honor, and love your child's unique qualities and gifts, and nourish his individual spirit, strength, and power as it unfolds, you can give him the base for a radiant life that optimizes his potential. You can teach your child behaviors, values, and habits that reflect your views, but ultimately, his purpose in life is to discover his own views—and that takes a healthy foundation.

As much as possible, I live my own life, both personal and professional, according to the principles of natural living discussed in this book. These principles have guided the way I maintain my own health, approach the health and development of my children, run my company, and choose the products that we carry. These principles helped form my personal philosophy, and they have inspired the information in this book. I hope that they resonate with you and encourage you to explore a natural approach to living. At the very least, I hope that my book will open your mind to the possibilities that whole, natural living can offer.

My approach is to offer as much information as possible and to provide you with the options to make your own decisions. The suggestions and ideas in this book are not intended to take the place of professional guidance; they are meant to complement the advice of your child's health care providers, caregivers, and educators, while offering consolidated information to help you develop your intuition and make choices that fit with your own personal, religious, or spiritual philosophies. I believe that you can balance convenience with a conscious and natural lifestyle, and make prioritized decisions to ensure your child's health and well-being.

To acknowledge both your sons and your daughters, I have alternated between the pronouns he and she from chapter to chapter.

For more information about the practical aspects of natural parenting and ideas for incorporating fun and creativity into raising your whole child, join our community.

 Join our community at
growhealthygrowhappy.com

Sumi-e

Sumi-e brush painting is a 2,000-year-old Zen Buddhist art form that monks used to develop their clarity and discipline. It continues to be popular in Japan as an artistic expression. Sanae Kubota, Emi and Mari's *obāsan* (grandmother) and my former mother-in-law, was an artist of *sumi-e*. She taught me to appreciate its beauty and meaning. I took enough classes with her to understand how difficult it is to paint simple, smooth strokes. Painting or enjoying *sumi-e* is a way for anyone to connect with nature in daily life.

The goal of *sumi-e* is to capture the *chi* (spirit or life force) of the subject, which is usually an object in nature, such as a flower, an animal, or a landscape. The artist concentrates on the subject, becomes unified with it, and then paints from memory while feeling and expressing the essence of the subject. Throughout this book, *sumi-e* brush paintings offer you inspiration, beauty, and a sense of presence.

Painting by Sanae Kubota

Whole Baby

Whole Baby

YOUR BABY IS NATURALLY a whole human being right from the start. She is more than the sum of her parts. Her physical body, emotions, and mind are all related and interconnected, and her development is an unfolding evolutionary process that has a momentum and energy of its own. She has growth spurts and surges of yin and yang energy as she unfolds her true nature and potential. Part 1, "Whole Baby", offers information about the different aspects of your child's development to assist you as you guide her in meeting her needs, so that she can develop physically, emotionally, and mentally and so that she can reach her full potential.

Each chapter in "Whole Baby" has three sections—the Daily Practices section offers the "what"—simple, practical activities that you can do with your baby everyday. The Theories section provides the "why"—or the reasoning behind her development, so that you can better understand her process. The Essential Skills section includes the "how"—applications for certain circumstances.

❀ Chapter 1—"Wellness and Healing" gives you suggestions on how to support your baby's physical development. Topics included in Daily Practices are food, diapering, sleep, touch, movement, body image, safety, hygiene, and fresh air and temperature. The Theories section offers information about building immunity and principles of natural healing. The Essential Skills section discusses how to diagnose and treat illnesses for natural healing, how to make a natural first-aid kit, and how to choose a health care provider. At the end of the chapter is a reference guide of the Common Illnesses that children face, with suggestions on how you can understand and actively support her when she is sick.

❀ Chapter 2—"Heart and Spirit" is about your baby's emotional development. Daily Practices include things that you can do everyday to help her—being mindful and positive; accepting her feelings; creating a peaceful environment through structure, stress management, food, movement, humor, and traditions; trusting and taking care of yourself; and letting go. The Theories section explains about the importance of establishing a strong attachment and provides information about your baby's individual self, including the aspects of temperament, personality, and gender. The last section, Essential Skills, discusses what you can do to help your baby develop her emotional and social intelligence. Every child is exceptional in some way, as described in this piece. The end of the chapter provides information about choosing a child care provider.

❀ Chapter 3—"Discovery and Learning" provides an overview of your baby's mental, or cognitive, development. Daily Practices includes the areas of food, sleep, sensory stimulation, movement, positive environment, listening, talking, reading, environmental interaction, challenges, media, arts, nature, and finding balance. The Theories section involves your baby's brain development and how she learns. Essential Skills include how parents, teachers, environmental conditions, and tools support learning. I have developed a guide for parents that is called the "Pathways of Whole Learning". When you understand that your baby needs to have experiences in each of these pathways, you can provide opportunities for her. The pathways are: Sensory, Movement, Interactive, Communication, Cognitive, Creative, and Naturalist. At the end of the chapter is information about how to choose a preschool.

CHAPTER 1
Wellness and Healing

Your baby's health and vitality already exist in a seed of her pure energy and potential. All this seed needs is the right nourishment to sprout and grow. When you provide appropriate nourishment, you evoke the power within your baby to thrive, to bloom, and to attain radiant health.

Radiant health stems from a focus on building health and immunity in order to live fully, instead of being concerned merely with the presence, absence, or prevention of disease. For your baby, health is more than an end in itself. It is a necessary foundation for her to live her life wholly and to accomplish her purposes and goals. In his book *Radiant Health: The Ancient Wisdom of the Chinese Tonic Herbs*, master herbalist Ron Teeguarden explains that with the attainment and maintenance of radiant health, the functions of mind, body, and spirit can flourish. In this robust state, body functions cannot easily fall into disharmony or disease, and a person reaches "health beyond danger," which means that she is so internally strong and adaptive that she can adjust to normal stresses and overcome most serious threats to health.

Increasing your knowledge and awareness of how your baby's body develops and functions allows you to play an active role in enhancing her wellness and immunity, aiding her recovery from illness, and maintaining her equilibrium. With the support of your health care provider and your own parental intuition, you can promote your baby's well-being through choices regarding your child's health and general lifestyle.

To maintain my own children's health as they grew, I used a blend of Eastern and Western medicine and found solutions that worked for my family. This chapter contains time-proven practices of Western, Eastern, and alternative medicine that offer natural ways of supporting your child's health and can complement your health care provider's recommendations. Please be aware that I am not a licensed health care professional. I am a mother who raised two children and spent more than 40 years studying and practicing wellness and blending philosophies from the East and the West. The following suggestions are not intended as a substitute for professional advice, diagnosis, or treatment. This chapter offers three sections to help you make the best choices for your child's physical health:

❀ **Daily Practices**—The first section discusses why your child's physical health matters and suggests actions that you can take every day to foster her physical health.

❀ **Theories of Physical Development**—The second section includes information about how your baby's body develops and how to prevent sickness. It also introduces the foundational principles of traditional East Asian medicine.

❀ **Essential Skills for Natural Health**—The third section offers natural-healing diagnosis methods, treatments, and remedies. It also provides information about choosing a health care provider. Finally, it describes your baby's 11 body systems and summarizes common childhood illnesses, along with their symptoms, causes, suggested treatments, and methods of prevention.

As you move through this chapter, remember that your child is unique, with her own constitution and rhythms, and that you intuitively know her better than anyone. With your support, she can grow at her own pace.

Daily Practices

ON MY FIRST TRIP to Emi's pediatrician in Japan the doctor gave me a booklet and instructed me to record her health information. Next, he took out a laminated piece of paper with several photos of babies' bowel movements, each with a different color and consistency. He described the different kinds of bowel movements and said that I should pay attention to Emi's soiled diapers in order to determine her condition and energy as it changed, and to adjust my diet accordingly. He talked about foods I should eat while nursing, as well as foods that I should introduce as Emi's first solids, in order for her to achieve a perfectly balanced bowel movement, which he said was the foundation for Emi's health and chi. Chi is the underlying energy that controls health and vitalizes the physical body. It also links the body, emotions, and mind.

The idea that I could affect my baby's physical health through my daily choices and actions made an impression on me. I realized that the food I ate had a direct effect on the quality of my breast milk, which then influenced my baby's bowel movements, which in turn were an indicator of her health. When I paid attention to my food and observed her condition, I saw the connection. If I ate tomato sauce, oranges, or spicy dishes, her stool was loose and I could smell an acidic odor when I changed her diaper. If I ate very salty food, she became constipated and tense, and she had difficulty sleeping. While nursing, I became even more aware of what I ate than I had been when I was pregnant because I could see the immediate results in the way Emi felt and acted the next day. Based on this experience, I realized that food was not the only area of everyday care that affected my daughter. Through awareness and simple activities, I could easily contribute to her health, wellness, and chi in a proactive way.

Your baby's condition reflects the totality of the actions you take every day. Occasionally giving your baby a piece of cake made with refined sugar will not result in diabetes, but giving her sugary snacks every day could. Healthy habits regarding food, rest, hygiene, exercise, fresh air, and sunshine are the ingredients of a strong physical condition and strong chi. These habits give her fortitude to grow, to feel, to think, to learn, and to achieve her goals.

As her parent, you know your baby's physical condition, responses, and energy levels better than anyone. The responsibility may sometimes seem overwhelming and beyond your knowledge. However, if you trust your intuition, educate yourself, and envision a strong physical constitution and a balanced condition for your child, the right choices for you and your baby will reveal themselves.

You can start by simply recognizing and becoming aware of your child's innate strength, health, and vitality. Her birthright is to be naturally healthy. Next, observe cause and effect relationships regarding your baby's condition. For instance, think about what your baby ate yesterday and how it may account for her behavior and condition today. Notice when she becomes calm or agitated, and reflect on what may have caused these shifts. When you pay attention and listen to your baby's rhythms, you develop your intuition as her caregiver.

Studies indicate that daily care is the single most important factor in developing a pattern of general health. As a parent, you determine your baby's daily care. Your choices regarding food, sleep and rest, diapering, hygiene, air quality, environment, clothing, exercise, and contact with others, among other routine areas of her life, play a major role in her general condition. By taking the time to consider your options in these areas and making informed choices for your baby, you contribute to her wellness and support her inner vitality and strength, as well as helping prevent illness and injury. Your choices in these routine matters lay a permanent foundation for her physical health and functioning.

Nourish with Food Choices

The nutrition in the food that the birth mother eats during pregnancy builds the foundation of a baby's physical makeup. Because of the rapid growth your baby experiences in the first few months after birth, the food she consumes every day through breast milk (whose nutritional content is a direct result of the nursing mother's diet), formula, or solid food has a more powerful effect on her health than what she eats at almost any other time in her life. Therefore, the first year of your baby's life provides you with a special opportunity to enhance her structural health by choosing her food wisely.

After her first year, your baby's basic constitution has been established. As she moves toward her second birthday, her daily foods give her the nourishment to power all the systems of her body. The quality and quantity of the food she eats determine the kind of energy she has and give her body fuel that enables strength, coordination, endurance, agility, speed, and longevity.

Food can also be preventive and healing. A good diet keeps your baby balanced and healthy, helps her build immunity, and acts as medicine to heal her sicknesses. Conversely, a poor diet of foods that are processed and made with synthetic chemicals, refined sugar, and saturated and trans fats can be degenerating and can contribute to both short-term sickness and long-term disease. Whole foods—such as whole grains, vegetables, plant-based protein-rich foods, fruits, fermented foods, and healthy fats—are restorative and strengthening for your baby's physical health today and tomorrow.

Part 2 of this book, Whole Food, focuses on the benefits of whole foods and details how to prepare them for your baby.

Take Care with Diapers

What you find in your baby's diaper serves as an indication of her diet, as well as her overall health. Food goes into her mouth, her digestive system processes it, and the waste comes out through her urine and feces. Although changing poopy diapers may seem unpleasant, it is your opportunity to gather helpful information about the state of your baby's health. Today's poop is the result of yesterday's food, and it shows how her body processed it. By observing your baby's bowel movements on a daily basis, you stay in touch with your baby's ever-changing condition.

If your baby has diarrhea, you can make food adjustments to bring her back toward balance. In the meantime, make sure that she stays hydrated by giving her enough liquids to drink. If diarrhea lasts more than two days, contact your health care provider.

On the other hand, if she is constipated with a stool consistency that is hard, dry, dark, or pellet-like, and her bowel movements are difficult to pass and less frequent than usual, adjustments to food can help loosen her bowels. Note that medications, supplements, and food with dyes can change the color of your baby's stool.

The skin on your baby's bottom is sensitive and delicate. Changing her diaper soon after a bowel movement or urination prevents the acidic residue from rubbing against her skin for a long period of time. Regular application of natural oils, such as sesame and olive, softens and nourishes your baby's bottom. If your baby has a rash, you can leave her diaper off for a while to let her skin breathe and heal.

Diapering

Diapering is a big part of your baby's early life when you consider her comfort and health, your time, and the cost involved. You will change her diaper seven or eight times a day for two to three years. Therefore, the method of diapering you choose will impact the day-to-day life of both you and your baby.

Colors of Poop and Causes

Black—A newborn's first bowel movement, called meconium, is black and sticky.

Bright mustard yellow—For the first few months, the poop of a breast-fed baby has a sweet smell, is a bright mustard yellow color, is loose (sometimes grainy) in texture, and usually is passed about three or four times a day.

Green—If your baby's stools are green and slimy, foul- or putrid-smelling, and frequent, that is a sign of diarrhea, and it needs to be addressed. For a breast-fed baby, green stools could mean that she is getting mostly foremilk and not enough hindmilk. Make sure that one breast is emptied before feeding with the other.

Odd colors—Food with strong colors, such as leafy greens, peas, carrots, beets, and blueberries, can affect the color of your baby's stools. Medications, supplements, and foods with dyes can also change her stool color.

Greenish—After the meconium is passed, stools change to a greenish color for a day or two.

Yellowish brown—A bottle-fed baby passes stools more frequently than a breast-fed baby does, and the stools have a bulkier and firmer texture. The color is usually light brown, yellowish brown, or pale yellow. The smell is stronger, similar to the smell of an adult bowel movement.

Brown—When your baby starts eating solids, the color and consistency of her stools will change, and brown will become the normal daily color.

Red or unexpected—If your baby's stools are red, white, green, yellow, or black, without an apparent reason, it could be a sign of a medical problem, and it is time to check with your health care professional.

I am partial to cloth diapers. I used cloth on both Emi and Mari. Cloth diapers were the first products that I sold in my business. I even started a diaper service and washed the diapers myself—that was a messy business!—I chose cloth diapers for my babies because I wanted to use natural fibers on their skin, because cloth diapers were less expensive than disposables, and because cloth diapers made less of an environmental impact than disposables.

Toilet Training

The best way to support your toddler as she moves from wearing diapers to using the potty is to allow her to set the schedule for this milestone. Toilet training is a developmental process that warrants its own timetable and requires physical and mental readiness. If you try to rush your toddler before she is ready, you both may become frustrated. Trust that your child will use the potty successfully and consistently when she is ready. Most children potty-train between two and three years of age.

Physically, your child's bladder needs the muscle control to hold urine. You will know this has occurred when she has fewer wet diapers during the day. She must also have the fine-motor skills to undress and dress herself.

Mentally, your child needs to be able to recognize and acknowledge the feeling that she has to go. She must be able to follow and remember directions on how to use the potty. Mental readiness also includes showing an interest in using the toilet and in changing from diapers to regular underwear. Children can learn from watching their parents use the toilet.

Once your child demonstrates that she is ready and wants to use the potty, you can support her with directions and positive reinforcement. A daily routine of setting aside a time to sit on the toilet can help build a habit of healthy elimination. Let her lead the way, just as you did when she learned to sit up, talk, and walk. Potty training is a process with false attempts, failures, and progressively more successes. Try to be patient, prepared, and positive.

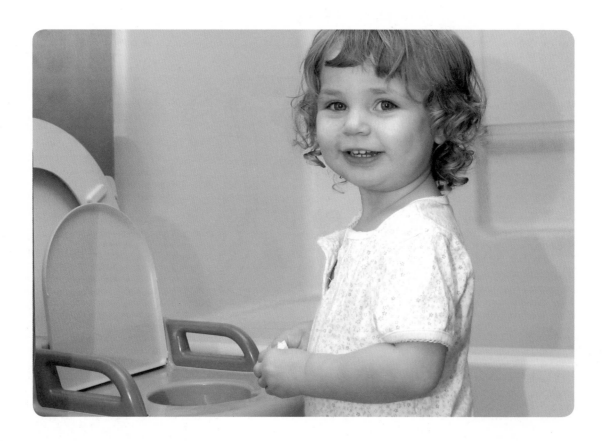

Support Sleep and Rest

Sleep and rest are cornerstones in your baby's physical, emotional, and mental growth and development. They enhance the functioning of her immune system, promote healing, and support her brain development. Sleep is almost as important as food and air. The length and quality of your baby's sleep also play a role in her caregivers' physical, emotional, and mental health. The first few weeks and months of parenting often revolve around ensuring that both baby and parents get enough sleep.

When Emi was born, I placed her crib in a separate room close to ours in our small apartment in Japan. When she awoke at night, I got up from my bed, went to her room, and rocked her back to sleep. By the time I had my second child, Mari, I had discovered an easier way of dealing with nighttime waking and feeding, so that I missed very little sleep. For her first few months, she slept on a small futon on the floor next to ours. Before going to bed, I prepared a clean diaper at the end of her futon. When she woke in the night, I sat up, changed her diaper, and pulled her to my side, and we both fell back asleep as she nursed.

When your baby is born, she does not know the difference between night and day, so her sleeping patterns are random. At six to nine weeks, she may adjust to sleeping cycles, but it could be four or five months before her biological clock matures to the

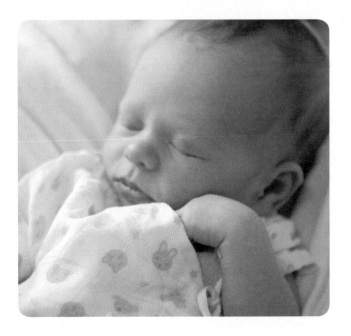

point that she mostly sleeps at night and is mostly awake during the day. Her biological clock is driven by circadian patterns connected to environmental cycles of light and dark, temperature, seasons, and tides.

Your baby's main activity for her first year is sleep. She needs 14 to 15 hours or more each day, generally in two- to three-hour increments. These increments vary, depending on each child's needs, and your baby may require more or less sleep than the average. At times of rapid growth, she will need more sleep, and as she grows and develops, her sleep needs will change. As your baby grows, she experiences two types of sleep.

Rapid Eye Movement (REM) Sleep

In this cycle of sleep, active dreaming occurs, and your baby's brain gets the nourishment it needs for rapid growth and functioning. While in REM sleep, which is a relatively light stage of sleep, your baby's heart rate increases, she may move her arms and legs, her eyes may move under the lids, and she may suck or make sounds. Newborns spend most of their sleep time in this stage because their sleep cycles are shorter due to being awakened by hunger or wet diapers. As your baby grows and her systems mature, often by age two, she will spend only about a quarter of her sleep time in REM sleep, just as adults do.

Amount of Sleep Required for the First Three Years

Age	Required Amount of Sleep
Birth to 6 months	15 to 16 hours
6 to 12 months	14 to 15 hours
1 to 2 years	13 to 14 hours
2 to 3 years	12 to 13 hours

Non-rapid Eye Movement (NREM) Sleep

This is a deeper sleep and starts at around four months old. It includes three cycles of deep sleep and rest, which replenish and strengthen your baby's body. During non-REM sleep, a growth hormone is released, causing your baby to actually grow while sleeping.

Although a newborn sleeps a lot at first, she also wakes up often because her physical systems are not fully developed yet. For instance, her underdeveloped digestive system can cause her to wake up with an upset stomach or gas. Burping your baby after she eats can help prevent her from waking due to gas. Hunger can also disturb her sleep. Your newborn's stomach is small, so it cannot hold much food. In her first few months, she wakes to be fed. Breast-fed babies usually wake more frequently because breast milk is lighter and more easily digested, whereas formula-fed babies tend to sleep for longer stretches since formula is heavier and is more difficult to digest.

When your baby is two to three months old, swaddling may be helpful to settle her down and to make her feel secure so that she can go back to sleep. Swaddling means wrapping your baby in a blanket so that she has the snug feeling of being inside her mother's womb. When she is swaddled, she cannot move her limbs, and this helps her fall asleep. The current school of thought to reduce the risk of sudden infant death syndrome (SIDS) is to make sure that babies are on their back when sleeping. If your baby can roll over on her own, then she should not be swaddled. Note that swaddling too tightly may increase the risk of hip or shoulder dysplasia or dislocation.

As your baby gets older, she can sleep for longer cycles. A soothing, dark environment helps her to distinguish night and day. You can keep her comfortable as she sleeps by providing an extra-absorbent diaper. When using a cloth diaper, use a diaper doubler or a larger size. For a disposable diaper, use a nighttime-absorbency version. In addition, sleep bags (sleeveless wearable blankets that are closed at the bottom), footies, or pajamas in breathable fabrics can help regulate her temperature, so she does not wake up from being too hot or too cold.

The food you eat while breast-feeding, and the food your baby eats in general, can directly affect her sleep quality and quantity. Whole grains provide complex carbohydrates, producing a slow, steady rise in insulin, which helps tryptophan enter her brain and trigger the production of serotonin, which promotes restful sleep. Leafy greens and sesame seeds are sources of calcium, which can also activate tryptophan. Magnesium works in your baby's body as a muscle relaxant. Cherries are rich in melatonin, an antioxidant that helps regulate sleep. Salty or dry foods can create muscle tension, so your baby may have difficulty relaxing, and caffeine and sugary foods can make sleep difficult. In addition, teething, antibiotics, and vaccinations can interrupt sleep.

Going to Sleep

If your baby or toddler has difficulty going to sleep, separation anxiety can be a factor. In response, some parents choose co-sleeping to comfort their babies to sleep, as well as to encourage connection. Others see their baby going to sleep as an opportunity to help their baby learn to self-soothe. They put their baby in a separate bed or a bassinet while still awake and allow her to go to sleep on her own. The goal is that the baby will find that she can calm herself and drift off to sleep independently.

Crib Safety Tips

The Consumer Product Safety Commission (CPSC) recommends a firm crib mattress covered by a fitted sheet (made for crib use) without quilts, toys, or pillows. The CPSC also suggests using a sleep bag, swaddle, or warm pajamas instead of a blanket. Check your baby's crib for lead-based paint. The use of a monitor can be reassuring if your baby sleeps in a room separate from yours.

While some parents believe it is best to let their baby cry it out and learn to self-soothe that way, I could never let my babies cry. To me, it seemed too disruptive to their nervous system and too disturbing to their ability to develop a secure attachment. In addition, I could not bear the pain of hearing them cry. I felt that proactively creating a bedtime routine was the best way to help them develop regular sleep habits.

A bedtime routine, including nursing or a bottle, rocking, massage, soothing music, or a bedtime story, can help your baby develop positive associations with sleep. Older children can also find comfort in rituals, such as sleeping with a special plush toy or blanket or wearing certain pajamas. A warm bath and a massage before bed can help your baby wind down from the day, prepare her for sleep, improve circulation, and remove excess salt from her system.

The bedtime routines that you establish in your child's first years can turn into more age-appropriate bedtime rituals as she grows. For example, reading a book can replace feeding or cuddling. Whatever the age of your child, a positive, firm routine increases her sense of security and helps her sleep well.

A sleep log can help you gather objective data about your baby's sleep patterns and increase awareness of your own activities and behaviors related to her sleep. For her first three to four months, your baby's sleep may be irregular while she adjusts to the many factors that affect her sleep. Over time, she will probably develop more regular patterns and habits. Regularity helps her feel safe because she knows what to expect. It also helps her fall asleep more easily.

How to Swaddle

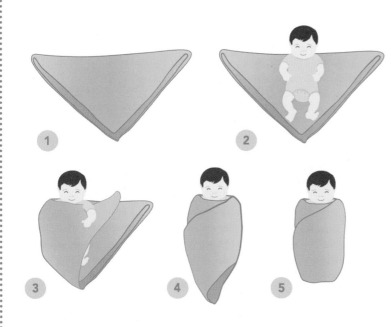

1. Spread a square blanket on a bed or other soft surface, and fold one corner down.

2. Lay your baby on the blanket, with her head faceup above the folded corner.

3. Straighten one of your baby's arms, and wrap the corner on the same side of the blanket over her body. Tuck it between her other arm and the side of her body.

4. Tuck her other arm down, and fold the other corner of the blanket over her body and under her side.

5. Fold the bottom of the blanket loosely, and tuck it under your baby.

6. Make sure the blanket is not too tight. You should be able to place two fingers under each fold without too much difficulty, and your baby's coloring should remain normal.

herself and the power in her own initiative. Then, when you pick her up, she is dependent on you; you are her security.

Your baby's skin is her first medium of communication; touch establishes the foundation for her relationships. When you hold your baby close to you throughout the day, you satisfy her need to be enfolded. Beginning with the secure feeling of your arms around her, she can explore the world of open spaces gradually. Activities such as nursing, holding, rocking, and swaddling create this feeling of security and simultaneously nourish the condition of her skin. Insecurity and prolonged anxiety can actually manifest through skin conditions, such as psoriasis and rashes.

Massage is an easy way to increase skin-to-skin contact with your baby, to get to know her through her body, and to become aware of what is going on with her body on a daily basis. Massage can be an especially valuable activity for mothers who are bottle-feeding, and for fathers and other caregivers who do not have regular skin-to-skin contact with their babies. Massage can help you build your relationship with your baby, as well as your confidence in handling her.

By taking a few extra minutes to massage your baby after a bath or diaper change or before bedtime, you can build a routine that adds to her wellness every day. If you do not have time for a full massage, you can build mini-massages into a few moments each day.

Connect with Touch and Massage

Sometimes I notice a mother holding her baby and unconsciously kissing or touching her child in a way that is so natural to her that she is unaware of her gestures or movements. The mother may not realize that her loving touches do more than nourish her baby emotionally; they help her baby's brain develop and provide tactile stimulation that helps her baby grow and resist disease.

Your baby can live without vision, hearing, taste, and smell, but she needs touch in order to survive. Most parents touch their babies naturally and often. However, an awareness of how touch affects your baby's physical and emotional development can inspire you to pay even more attention to touching her.

Your baby's first way of learning is through touch. If you put your baby on the floor, she experiences contact with the earth and feels secure that she will not fall. Grounded on this foundation, she is independent and free to explore. She naturally begins experimenting with moving her body, while discovering a sense of

Benefits of Massage

🌸 Calms and soothes your baby at bedtime or if she is in pain or unsettled

🌸 Strengthens your baby's body

🌸 Helps develop body awareness

🌸 Builds communication and connection with caregivers

How to Massage Your Baby

Before starting to massage your baby, center yourself by taking some deep breaths, or simply be still and quiet for a few minutes so that any frustrations or worries can leave your body and will not be transferred to your baby.

Make sure your baby is warm, and be sensitive to her feelings and sensations. Use natural oil—sesame is my favorite because of its healing properties. Gently massage her with light, smooth strokes. Listen with your hands as you touch her to get a sense of how she feels and how much pressure is comfortable for her. Her preferences can change from day to day with her condition and age. Too much pressure could be harmful, so observe her reactions; she will let you know what is too much. Relaxing massage uses gentle strokes and is different from acupoint massage, which is focused on a specific point for a therapeutic purpose.

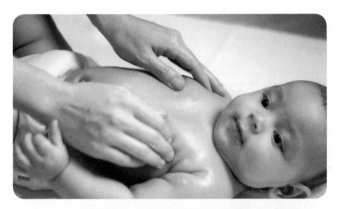

Front—Massage your baby's chest, abdomen, legs, and arms with smooth, even strokes. Light pressure on her stomach or abdomen can be helpful for digestive discomforts.

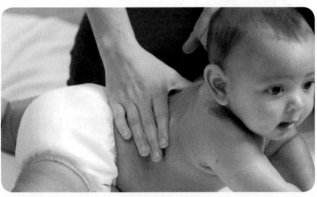

Back—Turn your baby on her stomach and stroke down her back, legs, and arms. Use both hands to move lightly down each side of her spine.

Fingers and toes—My mentor, Hideko Yoshida, told me that the best way to massage babies is to rotate each finger and toe both ways, ten times each—to the right, and then to the left. This can stimulate and awaken your baby's energy flow. "This Little Piggy" is not just a fun game; it also has a real health benefit.

Encourage Movement

Your baby's healthy expressions include spontaneous movements, vocalizations, smiles, and laughter; these are the ways she communicates her vibrant being. Your conscious encouragement of movement, play, and exercise promotes her physical health, as well as her emotional and mental growth and development. At all ages, stretching exercises can increase her circulation, relax tension, and develop her muscle tone. It may be easy to forget that your baby needs exercise when she is an infant, because she cannot crawl or walk on her own. However, she can benefit from a few minutes of daily exercises, such as stretching and tummy time.

As she grows, activities, such as crawling, walking, running, swimming, and dancing, provide cardiovascular and bone strength, in addition to invigorating circulation and developing muscles. Body movements stimulate your baby's brain development and release endorphins to create a positive emotional outlook. Babies and children naturally move when they are awake because they are full of energy, and they need the opportunity to exercise and discharge excess energy every day.

Bonnie Bainbridge Cohen, an occupational and movement therapist, has developed a theory of movement stages in which each step builds on the previous one. In Linda Hartley's *Wisdom of the Body Moving: An Introduction to Body-Mind Centering*, a book about Cohen's theory, Hartley writes, "Development occurs in overlapping waves, with each stage containing elements of all others. Because each previous stage underlies and supports each successive stage, any skipping, interrupting, or failing to complete a stage of development can lead to alignment and movement problems, imbalances within body systems, and problems in perception, sequencing, organization, memory, and creativity." Therefore, if a movement pattern is not expressed, the child's development process may be incomplete and unstable.

People often view the body and the brain as separate and disconnected. According to Cohen, however, the body and the brain communicate when the brain sends messages to muscles to make a movement or when muscles stimulate the brain through movement. In this way, physical movement connects to and supports your baby's brain development. Different areas of the brain correlate to physical, visual, auditory, tactile, manual, and linguistic competencies. As your baby goes through the sequence of movements below, her brain establishes a foundation that builds layer upon layer. As with a building, each block is essential to establish a solid base for the blocks above it.

Your baby naturally develops in the following order:

 She learns to lift her head

 She learns to sit up

 She learns to roll over

 She learns to creep

 She learns to crawl

 She learns to stand and then walk

If you help your baby stand or walk before she is ready, even though she may be able to do it, you are teaching her that she cannot do it by herself, and that she needs your help to achieve it. This deprives her of the satisfaction of pulling herself up onto her own two feet.

As a parent, in your enthusiasm about your child's growth and development, you may encourage her to skip movement stages—to walk before crawling, for example. It may be challenging to step back, put yourself in your child's position, and observe her energy as she moves on her own. Imagine that you are watching a plant grow at fast-forward speed. Like the plant, your baby moves on her own, through internal energy that expresses nature's intelligence. This intelligence is integrated throughout her physical body, her emotions, and her neurological makeup. She intuitively knows how to move and develop. If she has a safe, supportive, encouraging environment in which to move freely, then she can discover the satisfaction of her own initiative, grow naturally, and experience the gratification of her accomplishments.

Your child's body is designed to move. Movement—of body systems, organs, and cells—is a sign of life. Her body's movement transforms and rejuvenates her in cycles of sleep and rest. Physical movement promotes the production of new brain cells. Activities, such as watching television and playing computer games, are the beginnings of a sedentary lifestyle, and they undermine your child's opportunity to participate in the world and to learn with her whole being.

At Muso Yochien (Dream Window Kindergarten) in Japan, I worked with Hideko Yoshida to incorporate movement activities with music and songs in order to help students learn English words. Hideko believed that singing and movement help integrate learning. You can help your baby get in touch with her body through massage, through different kinds of movement and exercise, and through pointing out different parts of her body. To bring awareness to different areas of your baby's body, act out this song by touching the parts of your baby's body:

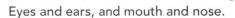

Head, Shoulders, Knees, and Toes

♪ Head, shoulders, knees, and toes.

Head, shoulders, knees, and toes.

Eyes and ears, and mouth and nose.

Head, shoulders, knees, and toes.

Take some time every day to provide the opportunity for your child to move, both indoors and outdoors. She especially needs a safe space to move on her own accord—to roll over, to crawl, and to walk. In your home, you can make a small, safe space by installing safety gates and removing breakable and dangerous objects. An outdoor park or nature reserve can offer a safe environment for her to roam freely.

When your child moves actively from her own initiative, she develops confidence, will, and judgment. Passive movement happens when an outside force initiates the movement for your child, without voluntary action on her part. For example, if you pick her up quickly or unexpectedly, this action can surprise her and diminish her sense of power.

As a parent, you often need to set limits and parameters to ensure the safety of your baby. However, when you encourage your child to

move, to play games, or to dance, try to follow her lead, and support her to move actively rather than passively. When you inspire and guide, instead of managing or forcing, she can discover her own life force and learn to follow it. You can incorporate movement into daily activities while you cook and clean by turning on some fun music and getting your child involved in helping. You may want to dance freely together with or without music.

Swimming is an aerobic exercise, as well as a stretching and muscle-building one. When your baby is born, she has a natural memory of how to swim, and if she does not use that ability, she will forget it over time and need to relearn it. It is easier to teach a one-year-old to swim than it is to teach a four-year-old. An early introduction to swimming provides a positive movement experience before your baby is old enough to crawl or to walk. When you swim with your child, you have the opportunity to interact with her in a playful and active way that bonds you and gives a new dimension to your relationship.

You can start your newborn with swimming lessons in your own bathtub by holding her and bobbing her up and down, floating her on her back, and cuddling in the water. Later, you can swim together in a pool, lake, or ocean. If she swims when she is young, she will feel comfortable in the water later on.

Usually, doctors recommend waiting until your baby is six weeks old before swimming with her in a public pool, and most organizations start offering lessons at four to six months. If your child is sick or has an infectious disease, do not take her swimming in a public pool. This will help keep everyone healthy.

Movement Activities to Do with Your Baby

You can help your baby move and exercise her body by stretching and moving her muscles. Be mindful, and recognize how she feels; if she resists or seems unhappy in any way, then stop the exercises. When you are attuned to and in sync with her, you can read her body and help her respond to your initiatives. You can integrate these movements of gentle stretching, massage, and centering practices into a daily routine. A yoga or fitness ball can also be fun to use for bouncing.

These movements can promote better and longer sleep, improve your baby's digestion, help strengthen her neuromuscular development and immune system, help reduce stress, and increase her body awareness. Toddlers can stretch and have fun by pretending to be a tree, a puppy, a bunny, a kitty, a lion, a snake, or a fish. As each movement stimulates different areas of her brain, each has a unique purpose.

Newborn to 8 Months

At this age your baby is not in a position to initiate her movements consciously. Try to be aware of how she is feeling as you gently and slowly help her stretch and move. Most of these exercises can be done either in her crib or on the floor, with a blanket or mat to provide light cushioning.

Breath sync
Lay your baby on her back. Breathing deeply, synchronize your inhales and exhales with your baby's. Breathe in and out for seven or eight breaths.

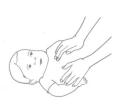

Reiki
Lay your baby on her back. Hold your hand over her belly, close your eyes, relax your thoughts, and focus your attention and love on her belly. Feel energy and warmth moving through your arm, into your hand, and into your baby's belly. Slowly move your hands to her arms, legs, and head, pausing for 5 to 10 seconds at each spot.

Star stretch
Lay your baby on her back. Gently pull her arms and legs out like a starfish. Stretch each finger and toe in a circular motion—clockwise, and then counterclockwise. When your baby is a toddler, she can stretch her own arms and legs and wiggle her own fingers and toes.

Reach for the sky
Lay your baby on her back. Reach your baby's arms up over her head, and gently stretch them. Bring her arms back close to her chest. Repeat three or four times. When your baby is a toddler, she can stretch herself to look like a starfish.

Newborn to 8 Months, continued

Reach up

Lay your baby on her back. Hold a toy above her line of vision and just out of reach. Slowly bring the toy closer as she reaches up and takes it. Repeat with two or three different toys.

Tummy time

Position your baby on her tummy. This practice can help her develop strength in her upper limbs, chest, and back, which are all foundational parts for crawling. Do not leave her alone during this time on her belly. It may be uncomfortable and frustrating because it is difficult for your baby to hold up her heavy head. Start with two to three minutes of tummy time per day when your baby is six weeks old, and gradually increase the amount of time as her neck strength develops. Even when your child is a toddler, she can enjoy tummy time on her own.

Clapping feet

Lay your baby on her back. Gently bring the soles of her feet together, and clap them as you would her hands. Repeat three or four times. When your baby is a toddler, she can do this exercise on her own.

Bicycle

Lay your baby on her back. Gently move her legs back and forth in a bicycle motion. This position helps her release gas and digest food. Bicycle her legs for 30 to 60 seconds. When your baby is a toddler, she can do this exercise on her own.

Roly poly

Lay your baby on her back. Raise her legs up to her stomach, and then help her to hold her feet with her hands. Carefully roll her from side to side. Repeat three or four times. When your baby is a toddler, she can do this exercise on her own.

8 to 12 Months

At this age your child can imitate you and react to you. She can make some movements on her own. You can start with the previous exercises and then continue with these.

Clapping hands

Hold your baby in your lap, or put her in a high chair. Make a clapping-hands motion for her to imitate. Repeat four or five times. When your baby is a toddler, she can do this exercise on her own.

Same-side touch

Lay your baby on the floor on a blanket or mat. Touch her right hand to her right knee and her left hand to her left knee. When your baby is a toddler, she can do this exercise on her own.

Cross-lateral touch

Lay your baby on the floor on a blanket or mat. Touch her right hand to her left knee and her left hand to her right knee. When your baby is a toddler, she can do this exercise on her own.

Crawl

Put your baby on the floor and get down in front of her. Place a toy in front of her in a place that requires her to crawl to get it, and shake the toy. This game is especially exciting when she is learning to crawl, but it can be fun to play as she gets older, too. She can imagine that she is a puppy dog or a snake crawling around.

Blowing bubbles

When your child is in her high chair, in the tub, or in the swimming pool, play the bubbles game with water. Drink water from a cup, blow bubbles in the water, and encourage her to imitate you.

12 to 36 Months

As your baby starts gaining mobility through crawling and then walking, her cognitive functions are growing as well. She can imitate your actions, follow directions, and do activities on her own. Now you can do some of your own movement exercises with her. You can start with the previous exercises and then continue with these.

Child's pose
Place a mat or blanket on the floor for both you and your child. She can imitate you and follow your directions. Get on your hands and knees, and then rest your bottom on your feet while stretching your arms in front of your head. Stay in this position for 10 to 15 seconds.

Downward dog
Place a mat or blanket on the floor for both you and your child. She can imitate you and follow your directions. Get on your hands and knees, and then straighten your legs out while raising your bottom in the air. Stay in this position for 10 to 15 seconds.

Happy baby
Place a mat or blanket on the floor for both you and your child. She can imitate you and follow your directions. Lie on your back and raise your legs into the air. Hold your feet with your hands, and gently rock from side to side. Stay in this position for 10 to 15 seconds.

Tree
Place a mat or blanket on the floor for both you and your child. She can imitate you and follow your directions. Stand on both feet. Lift one foot and place it on the inside of your opposite calf. After 5 to 10 seconds, change feet.

Squat
Place a mat or blanket on the floor for both you and your child. She can imitate you and follow your directions. Stand on your feet, and then squat. This position helps stretch your inner legs and builds stamina. Stay in this position for 10 to 15 seconds.

Namaste
Place a mat or blanket on the floor for both you and your child. She can imitate you and follow your directions. Sit up on your mat with your legs crossed, and hold your hands together in a prayer pose in front of your chest. Bow your head to your child and say, "Namaste," which is a greeting that shows respect for others and acknowledges unity and divinity in others. Stay in this position for 10 to 15 seconds.

Body movements stimulate pathways to your baby's brain and all the sensory information that is related to it. Regular movement strengthens your baby's body, as well as her intellect; in fact, her learning is based on these body-brain patterns. Remember to listen to your baby and be gentle and slow with the movements. One movement session should last around 10 minutes.

Promote a Positive Body Image

Your baby learns about her body in the same way that she learns about everything—through exploration. She moves her body, touches it, tastes it, makes noises, names her body parts, and watches your reactions to it. As she explores what her body can do and realizes it is her own, you can guide her in that exploration and help ensure that she develops a positive body image. Some of this guidance comes from intentionally modeling your own positive body image by developing an internal gauge of your own health and creating an environment in which you accept imperfections.

At birth, your baby's movements and sounds are spontaneous and involuntary. As she grows and gains muscle control, she can begin to explore her body and figure out how she can use it to affect the world around her. At about two months, she finds she can lift her head and move her eyes to follow people and objects. Within another month or so, she sees that she has hands and feet, and she can wave them herself. By four months old, she can use her hands to bring objects to her mouth. As her strength and dexterity increase, she gains the ability to discover what her toes taste like. Through her first year, she explores her body's parts, capabilities, and sensations.

When she is one year old, she begins to recognize and point to her body parts, starting with her eyes, nose, mouth, and hair. Soon she adds her fingers, arms, hands, legs, toes, feet, and tummy to the parts she can identify. By the time she is two years old, she will probably be able to recognize and point out all of these body parts when asked.

As your baby discovers her body, she realizes that it is distinct from other people's bodies. She develops a sense of self. Her image of her body will correlate to her emerging self-esteem and confidence.

Part of your baby's self-image comes from her caregivers' reactions to and acceptance of her movements and explorations. She feels the intention of your touch, she sees your looks of approval or disapproval, and she hears your verbal encouragement or discouragement when she uses her body and tries new things.

To promote your baby's body control and encourage a positive body image, try the following activities.

❀ Provide her with experiences of touch and physical contact. Hold her. Swaddle her. Hug her often. Touch her just for the purpose of connecting. Dance with her in your arms or holding hands.

❀ Encourage her to explore and learn about her body parts. Read books, sing songs, and play games that talk about her body and identify its parts. You can name parts, and she can identify them on herself and then on you.

❀ Provide opportunities for movement, and then provide positive reinforcement for those movements. Put your baby on her tummy, and cheer when she lifts her head or eventually rolls over. Make sure you have steady pieces of furniture available when she is ready to pull up to standing. Show excitement for her when she masters a new physical feat.

❀ Provide toys and objects that stimulate gross and fine-motor activities. For fine-motor skills, provide blocks, crayons, stacking rings, and anything else that requires grasping and manipulating. For gross-motor skills, provide balls, push toys, jumpers, and riding toys. For safety's sake, make sure the toys you offer are appropriate to your baby's age and skill level.

To help your baby form a positive body image, be aware of what you say about your own body in front of your baby. Your baby takes her cues from you. The best way to encourage her to love, respect, and take good care of her body is to model that behavior for her. Show your baby that you honor your body and enjoy your health every day. She will most likely follow suit.

Provide a Safe Environment

A safe environment in which your baby can move and play freely promotes physical development. By staying one step ahead of her with preventive measures, you can minimize potential dangers.

Accidents are the top health hazard that children face today. One of the main challenges of parenting is finding a balance between keeping your child safe and allowing her to explore her abilities. In her first three years, she has three major shifts in her physical development—shifts to crawling, walking, and climbing—which call for three major shifts in child-proofing her environment. While adult supervision is the most effective way to prevent accidents, you can provide your baby freedom of movement by making her surroundings safe.

❀ In the crib—Make sure your baby's crib bars are no more than 2 ³/₈ inches apart. The mattress must be firm, and it must fit snugly in the crib with a tight-fitting mattress pad and sheet. Do not put comforters, pillows, bumper pads, or toys in the crib with your baby. A sleep bag or a lightweight swaddling blanket is best. Place your baby on her back in the crib.

❀ In the bath—Check bathwater to make sure it is not too hot or too cold. Use a rubber mat or seat to prevent slipping. Put a cover over the spout. Never leave your baby alone in the tub.

❀ In the kitchen and at mealtimes—Choking while eating is the biggest safety hazard for babies. Make sure to offer appropriate foods in bite-size pieces.

❀ At play—Choose toys that are age appropriate and made of safe materials. Babies put everything in their mouths, so make sure your baby's toys are large enough that they do not pose a choking hazard. Also, check toys for pointy parts that could harm your baby.

❀ On the go—Install and use your car seat. Never leave your baby unattended in a car. In hot weather, make sure she stays hydrated, protected from the sun, and cool enough.

❀ In case of emergency —Post a list of emergency numbers on your refrigerator door, on your computer desktop, and on your cell phone. Include the numbers of your baby's doctor, a local ambulance service, the nearest hospital emergency room, the poison control center, and the fire and police departments. If an accident happens, you will be prepared and save valuable time.

Childproofing Checklist

To ensure your home is a safe place for your baby, take a look at every room, surface, wall, and closet from the floor to the ceiling. Use this checklist to childproof your home and to ensure it is free of hazards such as the following:

☐ Sharp objects that could cut or hurt

☐ Small objects that could be swallowed and cause choking

☐ Furniture, lamps, bookshelves, or televisions that could topple over

☐ Plastic bags that could cause suffocation

☐ Strings or ropes that could cause strangulation (including ropes for opening and closing blinds; these need to be tied up, out of reach of your baby)

☐ Cabinets, doors, and windows that could be opened (secure them with inexpensive baby locks; even with locks, however, make sure that any cabinet or closet your baby can reach contains no dangerous materials, chemicals, or poisons)

☐ Unprotected outlets and electrical objects that your baby could touch (use inexpensive plugs to fill electrical outlets)

☐ Sources of water, such as open toilets, buckets, or pools, that could cause drowning (toilet lids should be closed, buckets emptied, and pools securely fenced with an alarm)

☐ Hot liquids (do not leave unattended pots on the stove)

☐ Areas where sources of heat could cause burns (create safe barriers around these areas, and never leave your child unattended in a room with a woodstove, fireplace, kerosene heater, or space heater)

☐ Vitamins, supplements, or medicines that could be dangerous when ingested (medicines should be in childproof bottles kept well out of reach of your baby)

☐ Poisonous ingredients or plants that could be dangerous when swallowed

☐ Steps or open spaces that could cause falls (use baby gates to block off such areas)

☐ Smoke or fire hazards that could cause a fire

☐ Harmful chemicals, such as those found in toys and feeding products (harmful plastics), skin care products (parabens), cleaning products (aerosols), and clothing (formaldehyde)

Teach Healthy Hygiene

With the volume of dirty diapers, spit-up, and drool you encounter as a new parent, you may find that your cleanliness standards drop. However, daily hygiene habits for the care of your baby's eyes, ears, nose, nails, mouth and teeth, skin, and clothing are basic to her wellness. Hygiene routines also keep you attuned to your baby's condition.

Eyes

As your newborn begins to adjust to light and new surroundings, her eyes are sensitive, so keep bright lights and sunlight from shining directly into her eyes. Blocked tear ducts, which are common in the first few weeks, may produce a mucus discharge. You can use light massage, along with drops of breast milk or warm water on a clean cloth, to help clear the drainage from her eyes.

Other causes of discharge in a child's eyes include a cold, congestion, and conjunctivitis (pinkeye), most recognizable by redness in her eye. If your baby has a discharge in her eyes, you may choose to limit or eliminate dairy and sugary foods, which can produce mucus. If you notice redness and ongoing discharge, check with your health care provider for natural remedies.

Ears

For daily care, wash the outside of your baby's ears with a soft washcloth and warm water. Earwax protects your baby's ear canal from foreign substances. Swabbing the inside of her ear can increase the risk of infection, irritation, and damage to her eardrum. In addition, swabbing can actually pack a wall of wax against your baby's eardrum, and this can cause earaches. Painful ear infections happen when the Eustachian tube that links the nose, ear, and throat is blocked with fluid. Emi and Mari did have a few moderate earaches, but they did not have regular or serious ear infections that required surgery. Excess dairy, fruit juice, and sugar in the diet can cause ear infections in children.

Because your baby's hearing is very acute and sensitive, irregular noise from televisions, loud music, voices, electronics, and machines can startle her sensitive nerves. White noise or soft music can help mask environmental noise for your baby.

Nose

Except for minimal washing and checking for discharge, there is little to do on a daily basis for care of your child's nose when she is well. When the weather changes, it is natural for your baby to discharge mucus while she adjusts to the new temperatures. Again, dairy, fruit juice, and sugar products can create mucus and contribute to a runny nose. If she has a runny nose, a nasal aspirator designed for babies can suction out the mucus. A steamy bathroom can help break up nasal congestion.

Nails

Your baby's nails protect her fingers and toes. Because her nails are so small and delicate, you may be afraid to trim them at first. Small mitts that minimize scratches are helpful in the first few weeks of life. However, once your baby's nails grow long, they need to be trimmed to prevent her from scratching herself. Start by using a nail file to smooth rough nails, and then trim long nails with infant nail clippers. Leave a little of the white part of her nail so that you do not get too close to her skin. Try cutting your baby's nails when she is sleeping or after a bath when her nails are softer. Fingernails grow faster than toenails and are more likely to scratch, so they need to be cut more frequently.

Hair

It is sufficient to wash your baby's hair two or three times a week because the hair does not get that dirty, and excessive washing can dry her scalp. Shampoo is unnecessary for the first six months, and it can even be harmful because it can wash off the natural, immunity-building healthy bacteria on your baby's skin. You can cleanse her hair with warm water for the first few weeks. Once your baby has some hair, you can use a mild shampoo made with natural ingredients. A soft brush or comb with gentle strokes will help stimulate your baby's scalp and remove old skin.

Your baby's first growth of hair usually sheds within her first two to three months. Red or blond hair sheds before birth, so these babies may have a period of baldness. Dark hair may stay for a while and shed later before new hair comes in. When your child is ready for a haircut, it is easier and more efficient to trim her hair while it is wet. Be careful of barrettes and elastic bands. Tight hair accessories can pull out hair permanently, and loose ones can be a choking hazard. Dressing up a little girl is fun on special occasions, but be aware of hair ornaments that fall out or pull too tightly.

Mouth and teeth

Your baby's mouth has many important functions. Her tongue allows her to taste, her teeth allow her to chew, and her salivary glands start her digestion process. Her mouth forms words for her to talk. It allows air to enter her body. Finally, your baby's mouth is her first tool for exploring the world—she gums and tastes everything to get more information.

At about six or seven months, your baby's teeth start to emerge. Breast-feeding aids in the natural development of her teeth, jaws, and palate, whereas bottles and pacifiers can cause dental concerns. Dental development is dependent on a supply of minerals that can be found in sea vegetables and green leafy vegetables containing calcium, so be sure to include these foods in your diet while nursing your baby and in her diet when she starts to eat solid food.

Teething is a major transition for your baby. The enamel on her teeth is the hardest substance in her body, and cutting teeth is hard work. When your baby's first teeth appear, you can start cleaning her gums with gauze or a soft toothbrush. Toothpaste is not necessary, but if you choose to use toothpaste, check to see that it does not contain fluoride, artificial sweeteners, or potentially harmful chemicals, such as sodium laurel sulfate. While your baby is teething, you can help clean her teeth by letting her chew on a soft silicone toothbrush.

Tooth decay increases with the presence of acidity in your baby's mouth. A diet of sprouted or soaked whole grains and vegetables is alkaline-producing. This helps create a more balanced pH in her mouth, as well as in the rest of her body. By her first birthday, you can take your child to visit the dentist.

Skin

Your baby's skin is the largest organ of her body, and it takes three years to mature. Her skin acts as a protective barrier against air, bacteria, viruses, light, humidity, and pressure. It holds in her body fluids, regulates her temperature, and insulates her internal organs. Even though your baby's skin is external, it is permeable and porous, so substances that come into contact with it can be absorbed and can affect her internal organs and systems.

For her first few months, before your baby is crawling, a daily sponge bath that cleans her face, neck, hands, and bottom is sufficient. It is neither necessary nor particularly healthful to bathe your newborn every day. Her skin stores fat and has more than 1,000 microbes that help build immunity. Daily baths can wash off these oils and beneficial bacteria.

After the umbilical cord site and the circumcision site (if any) have healed, you can immerse your baby in water. You can use a small bathtub or a bath mat that fits in the sink, or you can bathe together in an adult-size bathtub for close skin-to-skin contact. Make sure you have a good grip on your baby in the water.

When preparing for her bath, gather all the necessary equipment before you start bathing, so that you have everything within arm's reach and can keep your eyes on your baby. For convenience, mobility, and safety, use a caddy or an apron to hold your bath supplies—washcloth, wipes, sponge, oils, lotions, diaper supplies, and clean clothing. When your baby is clean and relaxed after her bath, she may enjoy a massage and yoga stretches to help her further unwind before bedtime.

You can clean or bathe your new baby at any time of day. As she grows, a bath before bedtime can establish her routine and help her relax by washing away excess salt from her body and loosening tension in her muscles. Bath time can be an enjoyable, relaxing sensory experience, as well as a bonding time. For older infants and toddlers, playing with toys in the bathtub can become one of the highlights of the day. Never leave your baby alone while bathing.

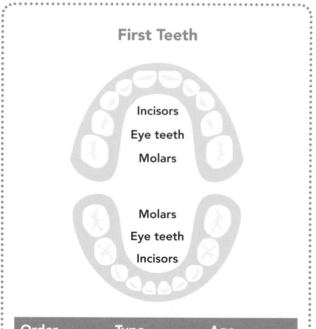

First Teeth

Order	Type	Age
1	Incisors	6–15 months
2 and 3	Incisors	8–10 months
4	Incisors	12–15 months
5 and 6	Molars	12–15 months
7 and 8	Eye teeth	20–30 months
9 and 10	Molars	18–24 months

Eczema (atopic dermatitis) is another common skin condition with many potential causes, including reactions to lotions, soaps, laundry detergents, certain chemicals, dry weather, heat, stress, and certain foods. Eczema runs in families, so if you have a family history of this condition, then your baby may be more prone to it. Use a mild soap on your baby's skin and clothing. While eczema causes itching and can be very uncomfortable, it is treatable and usually disappears before a child reaches adulthood.

Clothing

Clean, comfortable clothes are part of your baby's daily hygiene. They also influence her ability to move about the world. Fibers that are 100 percent cotton or organic cotton are the most breathable and comfortable next to your baby's skin. Cotton is ideal for underwear, sleepwear, first-layer clothing, blankets, diapers, burp cloths, towels, washcloths, sheets, and any other items that contact her skin directly.

Today, partly due to the depletion of the ozone layer, sun protection is an important component of dressing your baby. Even in the shade, the sun's rays penetrate cloud cover and reflect off water and light-colored surfaces. The American Academy of Pediatrics recommends that babies under six months not use sunscreen. Instead, you can protect your baby's delicate skin with lightweight clothing and brimmed hats with a tight weave and special sun-protection treatment. After six months, you can begin using a natural sunscreen. Sunscreen needs to be reapplied every two hours because it loses its strength over time.

When choosing your baby's clothes, try to avoid snaps and zippers made of nickel, because nickel can irritate her skin. Also, try not to dress your baby in tight clothing or in stiff materials—both can cause uncomfortable chafing.

New clothing can contain traces of harmful chemicals involved in the manufacturing process, such as formaldehyde and fabric stiffeners. To reduce the impact of these chemicals, wash new clothes and linens in a mild natural detergent before putting them on your baby.

Some common chemicals in skin care products can remove the natural oils from your baby's skin. When you start using soap on your baby, use mild, fragrance-free soaps, shampoos, lotions, and oils to prevent skin irritation. Unrefined oils with healing properties—such as sesame, coconut, almond, apricot, and avocado oil—are nourishing to her skin and can replenish oils lost in bathing. Add a few drops of oil to her bath, and apply oil directly on her skin after her bath while her pores are open. You can add ground oatmeal or brown rice bran to her bath or put a small amount inside a muslin cloth to rub on your baby's skin to promote daily health or to heal rashes or skin discomforts. It is not necessary to use talc or powder.

The term cradle cap refers to flaky patches of skin on the scalp that resemble dandruff. Common in newborns, cradle cap is caused by oil-producing glands that make skin cells grow faster than they can be shed. Although it is not an infectious skin condition and is neither uncomfortable nor itchy, it is a good idea to address cradle cap in order to prevent a buildup of dry skin on your baby's scalp.

Good hygiene is a preventive measure when it comes to your baby's health. With a few simple daily practices, you can keep your baby clean, keep her skin glowing, and keep her body comfortable so that she can focus on developing and exploring.

Regulate Temperature and Get Fresh Air

You regulate your own temperature by sweating when you are hot and by shivering when you are cold. This process is called thermoregulation. During pregnancy, your body keeps your baby's body temperature fairly constant, independent of the outside environment. Once your baby is in the world, however, it is up to her body to regulate its temperature. At first, she needs your help to do this.

In infancy, your baby's ability to regulate her body temperature is limited. As a newborn, she cannot move very much, and she only has active sweat glands in her head, neck, hands, and feet. Her main source of heat production is her body fat, which requires extra oxygen and glucose. Uncomfortably cold temperatures put stress on her system. If she seems chilly, dress her in warmer clothing such as footed pajamas or a sleep bag. On the other hand, overdressing your baby or keeping your home's temperature too high can cause her to overheat. Check regularly to make sure she does not become too hot or too cold.

When I was living in Japan, Emi's *obāsan* (grandmother) sometimes took care of her. Even on the hottest summer days, she wrapped a towel around Emi's belly before she went to sleep. According to cultural tradition, my mother-in-law believed that Emi's *hara*, or belly, was her body's energy center—the source of chi and the center of her being. (The location of your baby's *hara* is two baby-size finger widths below her belly button and two finger widths inward.) This area, known as the relationship chakra, is connected to the passion for life. *Obāsan* wanted to keep Emi's belly warm in order to keep the temperature of her whole body warm, to allow all her organs to function well, and to allow her blood to flow smoothly. Eventually, *obāsan* gave Emi a *hara-maki*, a stretchy band of cotton fabric to wear around her middle. It was similar to the *hara-obi* that I wore during pregnancy.

Emi

In addition to being a social and cultural concept in Japan, the practice of keeping the belly warm is central to East Asian medicine. If Emi's belly became exposed while we were socializing, a friend or relative would often unconsciously reach over and gently cover her belly with clothing. Samurais wore *hara-makis* beneath their armor. I once saw a construction worker wearing his wool *hara-maki* on a hot, sunny day.

My experiences in Japan led me to keep my children's middle regions warm and covered all year long. I brought several *hara-makis* back to the United States with me and put them on both Emi and Mari during winter months and when they had a cold or fever. When Emi or Mari did not feel well, their father, Naoki, also made sure their feet were covered. He often said, "Warm feet, cool head."

Central heating can be drying for your baby's nose; it can cause the mucous membrane lining her nose to harden. This, in turn, blocks her nasal passages and makes it difficult to breathe. She will most likely be comfortable if you keep the thermostat set between 65°F and 68°F. In addition, you can use a humidifier to add moisture to the air in the room where she sleeps.

Along with a well-regulated temperature, fresh air is an integral part of your baby's physical development. When she breathes, oxygen fills her body and brain and stimulates her growth, so the air she breathes needs to be as clean as possible. In indoor environments, be aware of substances that release toxins that can interfere with growth and may contain hormone disruptors, such as cigarette smoke, fragrances from laundry detergent, fabric softeners, scented hand lotion, perfume, makeup, incense, room fresheners, potpourri, and mothballs. To keep harmful toxins to a minimum, remove these substances from your baby's environment, vacuum frequently, and allow air from the outside to enter your home.

Indoor environments can also produce electromagnetic stress—low-grade tension that comes from prolonged exposure to electromagnetic fields emitted from electronic devices such as televisions and computers. Even when your baby is a few months old, she can benefit from spending one to two hours outside in the fresh air each day. With an infant, make sure the temperature outside is at least 60°F. Older children can enjoy three hours or more a day outside. A natural environment with fresh air can be relaxing and calming to your child's nervous system—and to yours, as well.

In many everyday ways, you can assist your baby's physical development; encourage her as she reaches important milestones; and help her care for, love, and appreciate her own body. Although the responsibility of caregiving may seem overwhelming at first, your baby's physical development is a process, and you can gradually learn to be proficient in your supporting role.

Theories of Physical Development

IN THIS SECTION OF the chapter, I explore the theories behind human physical development and health to give you a general understanding of how your baby's body grows, how it functions when she is healthy, what happens when she becomes physically unbalanced and is not feeling well, and how to help her restore balance.

Your baby has been developing physically since the moment she was conceived. Now that she is in the world, you can watch as her body changes in weight, height, and strength and as her physical senses sharpen. As she grows, her body develops muscle mass, gross- and fine-motor skills, reflexes, senses, and perceptions. According to Novella J. Ruffin, PhD, a child-development and parent-education specialist, physical development typically occurs in the following order:

- **From top to bottom**—Head and neck, shoulders and upper torso, abdomen, hips, legs, and feet

- **Inside to outside**—Torso, arms and legs, hands and feet, fingers and toes

- **Large muscles**—Muscles for running, carrying, climbing, balancing, jumping, and hopping

- **Small muscles**—Muscles involved in wrist and hand activities, such as cutting, drawing, and stringing beads

Your Baby's Physical Development

Your baby's physical development happens in three main areas: muscles, senses, and perception.

Muscle Movement

Your baby's movements involve various muscle groups working together, reflexively at first, and then more consciously as she discovers she has the power to move herself. Movements fall into three main categories.

Reflexes

Reflexes are automatic, involuntary responses to a stimulus. Some reflexes occur only in infancy. The following reflexes indicate normal brain and nerve development in your baby.

Rooting and Sucking Reflex
When an object brushes your baby's face or lips, she begins sucking. This survival reflex helps her find food at birth. It disappears after three weeks.

Moro (Startle) Reflex
When your baby hears a loud noise, sees a sudden movement, or suddenly feels unsupported, her head falls back and her arms and legs curve upward. She may also cry. This reflex disappears after about two months.

Palmar Grasp Reflex
When a finger or toy comes into contact with your baby's palm, she grips the object tightly. This reflex disappears after three or four months.

Babinski Reflex
When you stroke the sole of your baby's foot from her heel to her big toe, her toes fan out and curl, and her foot twists inward. This reflex disappears after one year.

Stepping or Walking Reflex
When you hold your infant so her feet are flat on a surface, she puts one foot in front of the other in a stepping motion. This reflex disappears after two months and reappears at the end of her first year as she begins to walk.

Gross-Motor Skills

These skills involve control of the large muscles in your baby's legs, arms, back, and shoulders. Gross-motor activities include rolling over, sitting, creeping, standing, walking, running, jumping, and climbing.

Fine-Motor Skills

These skills come as your baby masters the small muscles in her fingers and hands. Fine-motor activities include reaching, grasping, holding, releasing, cutting, drawing, and dressing.

Senses

As your baby takes command of her muscles, she is also sharpening her senses. Beginning before your baby was born, senses (touch, taste, smell, hearing, and vision) have been her avenues for taking in information. In utero, she could hear her mother's heartbeat, voice, and grumbling stomach; taste and smell amniotic fluid; and use her hands and feet to touch and feel in the womb.

A baby's eyes typically open at about seven months in utero, and ultrasounds have documented that babies open and close their eyes more often as they approach birth. At birth, your baby's vision is blurry, and her near vision is better than her far vision. She focuses on objects that are 8 to 15 inches in front of her face. She also shows preferences for patterned objects over solids, bold colors over pastels, faces over objects, and smiling faces over faces with other expressions. Her vision develops rapidly, and by three months she can see nearby objects clearly. At about four months, her eyes are working together and can focus equally on objects; she attains binocular vision, three-dimensional vision, depth perception, and the ability to track objects. Within another few months, she can see as well as an adult.

As your baby's sense of sight improves, so does her hearing. Starting at birth, she turns her head toward sounds and reacts to loud noises. She recognizes her mother's voice and finds it soothing. Songs and rhythmic sounds calm her and help her fall sleep. As her hearing matures during her first six months of life, she can hear soft sounds, as well as loud ones, and nearby sounds, as well as distant ones. At one year old, her hearing is comparable to an adult's.

In addition to hearing her mother's voice before birth, a baby tastes and smells her mother's food choices in utero. Fetuses drink several ounces of amniotic fluid a day, and this fluid smells and tastes like the food the mother has consumed. According to studies by Julie Mennella and Gary Beauchamp of the Monell Chemical Senses Center, the foods that a mother eats while pregnant and nursing help form her child's future flavor preferences. So, while you are pregnant and your baby is breast-feeding, you can expose her to a variety of flavors and expand her palate and flavor preferences.

Perception

Perception develops as your baby begins using all her senses to recognize and discriminate among objects, sounds, people, and events. She receives information through her senses from her internal and external environment, and then she filters that information. Her perception improves as her senses sharpen and as she becomes capable of paying attention and focusing enough to distinguish one object or sound from another. In her first year, she develops her visual, depth, and auditory perception, as well as her sound differentiation.

Milestones of Physical Development

As your baby explores and gains control over her body and uses her senses, you can support her achievements by understanding the developmental stage she is in and preparing for the stage she will reach next. For instance, when she sits up at six to eight months, you can be confident that she is progressing typically. Begin taking a second look at your home environment to make sure it is safe and conducive to her next move of pulling herself up to standing.

Milestones of Physical Development

Birth–3 months	3–6 months	6–12 months
• She visually follows a moving object and discriminates among different shapes. • She responds to sounds. • She holds up her head, has body control, and opens and closes her hands. • She moves her arms purposefully and actively kicks her legs. • She holds her arms symmetrically. • She sleeps more soundly.	• She tracks objects due to increased eye-muscle control. • She see objects with very little color contrast. • She is not afraid of everyday sounds. • Her birth weight doubles (usually by four or five months). • She sits unsupported, rolls over, and lifts her head and chest when lying on her stomach. • She waves her hands in the air. • She drools and anticipates the bottle or breast before feeding.	• She enjoys playing with musical toys and toys of varied textures. • She maintains eye contact. • She enjoys various types of movement. • She mouths her toys. • Her birth weight triples (usually by 9 to 12 months). • Her height has increased by 10 inches by her first birthday. • She sits unsupported and walks while holding on to furniture. • She moves around, crawls, points, touches, and pokes.
12–18 months	**18–24 months**	**24–36 months**
• She enjoys banging and playing with musical instruments. • She sits unsupported. • She crawls, pulls up to stand, and begins to walk. • She loses baby fat as she becomes more active. • She may sleep from 11 to 13 hours a night. • She eats solid food.	• She turns her head when someone calls her name. • She points to objects of interest. • She enjoys swinging and movement. • She is very active physically and has increased coordination. • She kicks, throws, and climbs. • By two years of age, she weighs twice as much as at five months. However, her growth rate has slowed to 3 to 5 pounds and 3 to 5 inches in her second year.	• She is interested and aware, and she can maintain eye contact. • She walks up and down steps. • She runs and jumps in place. • She climbs on ladders, slides, and play equipment. • She pedals a tricycle. • Her dexterity increases.

These guidelines for physical development are just that: guidelines. Because development often builds on the completion of previous stages, earlier and faster development is not necessarily better. Each child moves at her own pace; no two children have the same physical growth patterns. However, as a parent, knowledge about the typical timing and sequence of physical development empowers you to assess whether your child is within a healthy range and to seek professional advice if you see that she is not.

Foundations for Health

Childhood is a time for growing naturally, playing and being playful, being spontaneous, expressing feelings freely, learning, and developing imagination. It is also a time for you, as a parent, to delight in the joy and spark of your child's emerging self and to recognize and affirm her strength, vitality, and potential. She is constantly expressing her body's inner intelligence and radiant health. While medical professionals tend to focus on discrete physical health issues, parents have a responsibility to understand their baby's basic and innate health. Nonetheless, there may be times when your baby gets unbalanced and sick, and her energies—and yours—are directed toward restoring her health. There may be times when her everyday activities of exploring the world are put on hold. Physical health is necessary for your baby to progress in her physical, emotional, and intellectual development, and to reach her full potential.

As a parent, a basic understanding of how disease happens gives you insights into ways to help your child build her defenses against illness. Effective defense against disease means not only avoiding germs but also building a strong overall physical constitution, so that when your baby does become sick, her body can fight the illness more efficiently.

Some trends in children's health today show a decrease in disease resistance. Diseases that were once rare in childhood—obesity, heart disease, and type 2 diabetes—are on the rise in children. In addition, an increasing number of children are being diagnosed with and medicated for attention-deficit/hyperactivity disorder (ADHD) and other mood disorders. According to the Centers for Disease Control and Prevention (CDC), more than 10 million children in the United States (nearly 14 percent) take prescription medication on a regular basis.

Researchers are finding that many of these conditions can be reversed or prevented through lifestyle choices. So, while obesity and mood disorders might not be immediate concerns in your baby's first three years of life, the choices you make for her now can set the stage for preventing these conditions in her childhood and throughout her life. For instance, you can help prevent obesity as she grows by providing her with

whole, nutritious foods, daily activity, and plenty of sleep. Furthermore, prevention of obesity is associated with the prevention of type 2 diabetes, prediabetes, and heart and cardiovascular problems.

Those same lifestyle choices—nourishing food, activity, and adequate sleep and rest—help your child's brain function at its steady best and steer clear of triggers for dysfunction. Over the past decade, several studies have demonstrated a connection between certain food additives, such as Butylated hydroxyanisole (BHA), and behavior associated with ADHD. Studies have also shown that refined sugars and highly processed foods aggravate depression and other mood disorders. If your child is diagnosed with ADHD, depression, or another mood disorder, you can avoid (or at least minimize) the need for medication by exploring links between the condition and your lifestyle choices.

By making choices that nourish your baby's health, you provide her with a strong, balanced body that is unlikely to give way to chronic disease in and beyond childhood. However, diseases that are impacted by lifestyle choices are not the only threats to your child's health. Surrounding her are bacteria, viruses, and other pathogens. In addition, her health faces threats from toxins and pollutants. Her best protection against these body invaders is a strong immune system.

Building Defenses

Although a healthy child is naturally resilient and resistant to external factors that can cause imbalance, it is useful to consider the scientific perspective of the "germ theory." According to this view, the majority of challenges to your baby's health come in the form of pathogens—biological agents of disease. The majority of pathogens are called microbes. The term microbe is short for microorganism, meaning "little organism." Millions of these living beings can fit through the eye of a needle. Microbes are the oldest forms of life on the planet.

Microbes are everywhere in the environment. There are microbes in your baby's drinking water and throughout her body, especially in her large intestine, on the surface of her skin, and in her mouth and nose. Microbes create oxygen, make soil fertile, ferment foods, help your baby digest food, and keep your baby well—but they can also make her sick. Of the 50,000 classified species of bacteria, fewer than 100 are linked to disease. Of the 100,000 identified types of fungi, yeasts, and molds, only around 100 affect humans negatively.

Fabric merchant, Antonie van Leeuwenhoek, first described microbes in 1675, after he examined water through a microscope that he built himself. However, it was not until the mid-19th-century work of French chemist, Louis Pasteur, building on the work of others, that people came to accept microbes as agents of fermentation, food spoilage, and eventually disease. Before Pasteur, scientists thought that illness was caused by either contagion or miasma—also known as bad air. The four types of disease-producing microbes are bacteria, viruses, fungi, and protozoa (in the form of parasites).

Bacteria are tiny, single-cell organisms. They eat, grow, and reproduce on their own. Some survive alone, while others link up in chains or clusters. Some bacteria are beneficial and necessary for your baby's body to function and to remain healthy. Others are used to create medicines and vaccines against disease. Yet other bacteria cause illness. Antibiotics and antibacterial soaps and cleaners kill all bacteria they come into contact with—good and bad. Overuse of these products can result in low levels of good bacteria in your baby's body. Over time, infectious bacteria can mutate into stronger bacteria that are untreatable by current antibiotics.

Viruses are much smaller than bacteria. They must have a host in order to reproduce. Once they move into your baby's body, they can spread rapidly. Viruses are responsible for relatively common illnesses, such as colds and the flu. They are also responsible for serious diseases such as smallpox and HIV/AIDS. Antibiotics are useless against viral infections, and antiviral agents have proven effective in treating only a few select viral infections.

Fungi are multicelled organisms. They are plant-like, but they are not plants. Fungi get their nutrition from plants, food, and animals in damp, warm environments. Only a few of the many thousands of species of fungi cause problems for humans. For the most part, fungi-related conditions—athlete's foot, ringworm, yeast infections, and diaper rash—are not serious threats, although they can cause complications in babies and adults with a suppressed immune system.

Parasites live on or in other organisms and take everything they need for survival from their host. Parasite types include protozoa (which cause giardia, malaria, and sleeping sickness), tapeworms (cestodes), roundworms (nematodes), flukes (trematodes), and skin parasites (scabies, bed bugs, and human botflies). Humans usually get parasites by drinking contaminated water, eating undercooked or contaminated food, or getting an insect bite. Antiparasitic agents can rid the body of most parasites.

When any of these destructive microbes or other pathogens enter your baby's body and begin to multiply, her immune system is called into action to protect her.

Your baby's immune system

Your baby was born with innate immunity and barriers to infection. Before and during birth she received antibodies to defend against disease, and if she is breast-fed, she will continue receiving antibodies through breast milk. When she reaches two to three months of age, her body will begin to produce its own antibodies, and at six months, she can produce antibodies that are substantial enough to be effective. Therefore, experts recommend breast-feeding for at least six months, until her immune system has a supply of antibodies, to prevent illness.

Your baby's immune system is her own defense department against illness. Various divisions handle specific tasks. With its coordinated cells, tissues, and organs, her immune system fights invading pathogens, filters toxins, quells infections, and builds defenses against new pathogens. Her skin, tonsils, tears, mucus, saliva, stomach acid, and urine are her primary defenses against illness. Acting as barriers and flushers, and carrying antimicrobial substances, these defenses control the majority of pathogens before they make your baby sick. Additional protection comes from beneficial bacteria and fungi that live on her skin and in her intestines. These microbes eat pathogens and thus eliminate threats to your baby's health.

When a pathogen survives the first lines of defense, your baby's immune system brings out white blood cells. White blood cells come in different types, each of which combats disease in its own way— killing pathogens, warning healthy cells of danger, or searching for and cleaning damaged cells. When your baby has a fever or an inflammation in response to a bug bite, or when the skin around an abrasion begins to heal, her white blood cells are in action. They are part of her innate immunity.

To find and reach pathogens and antigens (toxins) in her body, your baby's white blood cells depend on her lymphatic system for transportation. Her lymphatic system carries lymph—a clear liquid that begins as plasma and contains white blood cells—throughout her body. Along the lymphatic pathway are the spleen, the thymus gland, and the lymph nodes, which all work to cleanse your baby's body and to support her immune functions. The spleen filters blood by removing old red blood cells and pathogens. It also stores reserves of oxygen-rich blood in case the body experiences blood loss. The thymus gland stores immature white blood cells and, when needed, trains them to become T cells—a type of blood cell that protects the body from infection. After producing T cells from prebirth to preadolescence, the thymus gland atrophies. The lymph nodes, which include the tonsils and the adenoids, monitor blood, filter toxins and waste from lymph, and store and create various types of white blood cells. Your baby has 600 to 700 lymph nodes.

Unlike your baby's circulatory system, which moves blood in a loop around her body, her lymphatic system moves lymph along a line. Lymph is collected from places all along her lymphatic pathway, flows upward toward the veins at the base of her neck, and then returns to her bloodstream. Your baby's lymphatic system depends on the movement of her muscles and joints to keep lymph flowing, delivering nutrients, and ridding her body of toxins and pathogens. In addition to supporting immune functions, your baby's lymphatic system balances fluids in her body. Should her lymphatic system become compromised, her body may become more susceptible to infections and swelling.

Your baby's immune system fights harmful microbes when they attack. Her body also can build immunity—thus avoiding the need for a future fight— as it overcomes a particular sickness. Vaccines are another way to help your child build immunity. Yet the safety and efficacy of the vaccines themselves are complicated issues.

Vaccines

Vaccines offer a way for your child to build immunity to disease without actually having to experience the diseases themselves. Scientists developed vaccinations, to fight invading germs by imitating that illness through a weakened form of the bacteria or virus that is injected into the body. When your baby receives a vaccination, her body responds with an increased resistance, or immunity, to that disease. After one or two more injections, her body begins to remember and respond to the pathogen, and this immunizes her from the disease.

In 1796, English physician Edward Jenner infected a boy with matter from an open cowpox sore in the hope of preventing the child from contracting smallpox. The child became ill with cowpox but recovered completely. Later, when he was exposed to smallpox, he did not contract the disease. The first vaccine had been born.

Although vaccines may be somewhat controversial among parents due to the different points of view in philosophy and from the history of past experiences. They have become accepted and common over the past century. Along with improvements in sanitation and food supplies, vaccines have played a major role in the elimination of many serious childhood illnesses. On the other hand, many people feel that vaccines have introduced some very real health risks. Since the health of your child is never guaranteed, the decision of whether to and/or when to immunize your baby is not a simple one. Both vaccines and the diseases they prevent come with risks. Although, serious side effects from vaccines are rare, most of the diseases that vaccines prevent rarely have serious complications. However, that is not always the case.

It is up to you to understand and to weigh the benefits and risks of vaccines and disease, and ultimately to decide whether or not to vaccinate your baby. In this section, I offer information to help you make your decision, as well as strategies to help you follow through on that decision with confidence.

When Emi was born in 1979, there were fewer vaccines for children than there are today. My pediatrician in Japan recommended a later schedule for Emi's vaccines than is recommended in the United States today. After much research, Naoki and I decided not to vaccinate Emi. We made the same decision for Mari several years later. When we made that choice, we took on the responsibility for the consequences of that decision and helped our daughters build their immunity through food and lifestyle. Even though I did all I knew—breast-feeding them for more than a year, providing them with whole foods, and educating myself about the diagnosis and treatment of illnesses with natural remedies—I was still concerned about the risks of not vaccinating. On the other hand, I know that if we had decided to vaccinate Emi and Mari, I would have been just as concerned about those potential risks, as well.

Centers for Disease Control (CDC) Recommendations

As of 2014, the CDC recommended the following 12 vaccines (or series of vaccines) from birth to 18 years to protect children from 16 illnesses:

- Hepatitis B (HepB)
- Rotavirus (RV)
- Diphtheria, tetanus, and acellular pertussis (DTaP)
- Haemophilus influenzae type b (Hib)
- Pneumococcal conjugate (PCV13)
- Inactivated poliovirus (IPV)
- Influenza (IIV, LAIV)
- Measles, mumps, and rubella (MMR)
- Varicella (chicken pox) (VAR)
- Hepatitis A (HepA)
- Human papillomavirus (HPV2, females only; HPV4, males and females)
- Meningococcal (Hib-Men-CY, MenACWY-D, MenACWY-CRM).

When Mari became a parent, after much research and thought, she and her partner chose to vaccinate my grandson, Zo. I understand and respect their decision. As with many other parenting concerns, there are no clear-cut answers, and every situation is a unique case.

Why are many parents hesitant to vaccinate their children? The majority of apprehensions are as follows:

❀ Potential side effects

❀ Number and timing of recommended vaccines

❀ Harmful ingredients used to make vaccines

❀ Long-term consequences on children's health

Vaccines in the United Sates have a strong safety record, with a low incidence of severe side effects. Patients and physicians report severe reactions to the Vaccine Adverse Event Reporting System (VAERS), which is cosponsored by the CDC and the U.S. Food and Drug Administration (FDA). Severe reactions include seizures and autoimmune reactions, among other conditions. Some vaccines are more likely to produce severe reactions than others. For instance, the MMR and DTaP vaccines have a higher incidence of complications than others do.

In *The Vaccine Book: Making the Right Decision for Your Child*, Robert W. Sears, MD describes himself as a pro-vaccine, pro-information doctor. He lists the CDC-recommended vaccines from the safest to the least safe, based on side effects, as follows: Hib, polio, rotavirus, DTaP, pneumococcal conjugate, chicken pox, HepA, HepB, HPV, meningococcal, flu, and MMR. According to Sears, no authenticated numbers exist to verify the actual incidence of severe side effects per doses of vaccine given.

He expresses the odds by integrating facts from the CDC and reports from VAERS:

❀ No vaccine is 100 percent effective or safe.

❀ Approximately 1 in 100,000 doses of vaccine causes a severe reaction.

❀ The chances that a baby will have a severe reaction to a vaccine before she is two years old is approximately 1 in 5,300.

❀ The chances that a child will suffer from a severe case of a vaccine-preventable disease during childhood are 1 in 1,090.

❀ The chances that a child younger than two years old will contract a severe case of a vaccine-preventable disease are about 1 in 300. According to Sears, breast-feeding and avoiding child care centers lower this risk even more.

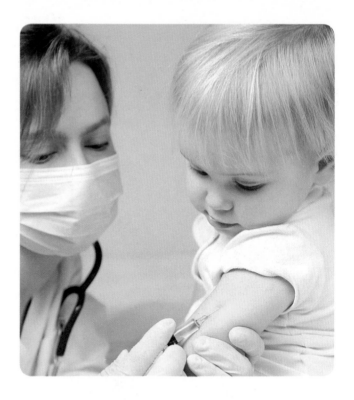

The ingredients used to manufacture vaccines—aluminum, formaldehyde, and other chemicals, as well as animal and human tissue—are also a concern for many parents. On a few occasions, animal and human tissue used to make vaccines have become contaminated with pathogens, which enter the bodies of vaccine recipients and have the potential to cause disease. When this has happened, officials have recalled the vaccines immediately and put in place stronger safety measures to avoid future contamination.

The majority of chemicals used in vaccines are present in trace amounts. Mercury is no longer used in most vaccines. Some flu vaccines still contain mercury, but mercury-free versions are available. Should you choose to give your child a flu shot, ask your health care provider for a mercury-free formula, or use the nasal spray, which is mercury-free.

Aluminum in vaccines continues to be a concern. Overexposure to aluminum can cause kidney damage and neurological impairment. According to Sears, 25 micrograms per liter is the FDA's safe limit for aluminum in injectable solutions for newborns, prema-

ture babies, and patients with impaired kidney function. Vaccines are exempt from this limit, however. The HepB shot recommended for newborns contains 250 micrograms of aluminum, and the combination of HepB shots recommended for two-month-old babies contains 1,225 micrograms for the brands that contain the highest volumes of aluminum. Studies are inconclusive as to whether aluminum in vaccines causes harm. However, Sears suggests that parents ask their child's health care provider to take the following measures:

❀ Use the Hib vaccine that does not contain aluminum.

❀ Use the DTaP vaccine with the lowest amount of aluminum.

❀ Do not give HepB, pneumococcal conjugate, HepA, and HPV vaccines (all of which contain aluminum) at the same time.

❀ Do not give combination vaccines.

The CDC recommends that your child receive 50 vaccines between birth and 18 years of age. Twenty-eight of these vaccines are scheduled to occur in her first two years. This may seem like a large amount of vaccines to process before your baby's immune system is fully developed. If you choose to vaccinate your child, you can work with your health care provider to adjust the CDC schedule and to prioritize the vaccines. This will help satisfy your comfort level, while achieving the immunity you wish for your child. To do this, you need to learn about both the diseases and the available vaccines.

You might also consider the factor of social responsibility when deciding whether to vaccinate your child. Mass vaccination has eradicated smallpox, has reduced polio worldwide by 99 percent, and has significantly decreased the incidence of several severe illnesses. When a large majority of the population is immunized, so-called herd immunity increases, and this protects babies of pregnant women and people whose immune systems are resistant to vaccines. When you choose not to vaccinate your child, you take the risk that she could develop a contagious, preventable disease. If she does, at-risk populations become marginally more susceptible to that disease as well.

Mass vaccination may undermine the common good, however. In recent years, scientists have found that mass immunization may cause strain replacement. The suppression of one or more strains of a pathogen through vaccination can cause other forms of that pathogen to emerge. Scientists are currently researching the relationship between vaccines and chronic illnesses later in life, such as diabetes, eczema, and arthritis.

As a parent, you can protect your child and the greater community when you do your own research and develop a plan for building your child's immunity. To gain a clearer understanding, consider each disease and vaccine individually. The following chart can help with that information.

Chart of Vaccines on Centers for Disease Control (CDC) Schedule for Birth to 3 Years Old

Hepatitis B (HepB)

CDC Recommended Dose and Schedule	3 doses: 1st at birth, 2nd at 1–2 months, 3rd at 6–18 months
Disease Facts	• Virus • Likely to become chronic in infants and school-age children, which can lead to cirrhosis, liver cancer, or liver failure later in life; most adults recover fully • Transmitted by contact with infected blood—thus, through infected razors, toothbrushes, sexual contact with infected person, or infected mother at birth • Per CDC, 38,000 people became infected with hepatitis B in 2009 • Rare for young children, but can have serious consequences
Vaccine Facts	• Effective; incidence of hepatitis B in adolescents and children since 1990 (vaccine was recommended for all children in 1991) has dropped by 95 percent • Some brands contain aluminum • Severe reactions rare, but can include severe allergic reaction • Not recommended for those who are sick or allergic to yeast, or those who have shown a reaction to the vaccine before
Considerations	First dose of three injections is scheduled for day of birth. Because contracting hepatitis B is unlikely for newborns unless the mother has hepatitis B (screened during prenatal care), HepB may be a candidate for postponing. However, because hepatitis B can become chronic in young children, if you choose to vaccinate, you may choose to do it early.

Rotavirus

CDC Recommended Dose and Schedule	Two brands available; one calls for 2 doses, and the other for 3 doses: 1st at 2 months, 2nd at 4 months, 3rd at 6 months (if needed)
Disease Facts	• Virus • Very common • Fever, vomiting, diarrhea • Most cases mild • Severe cases can cause dehydration, which can require hospitalization and can be serious in infants • Can be fatal if severe and left untreated
Vaccine Facts	• Made with animal tissue • Some brands deliver live virus • Per CDC, majority of those vaccinated are protected against severe disease; most will never develop rotavirus • Severe reactions very rare but can include allergic reaction, seizure, Kawasaki disease (autoimmune reaction), and intussusception (intestinal blockage, requiring emergency treatment); CDC estimates the risk of intussusception to be anywhere from 1 in 10,000 to 1 in 100,000 for vaccine recipients
Considerations	Per CDC, before the vaccine, rotavirus was responsible for more than 400,000 doctor visits, 200,000 hospital visits, and 20 to 60 deaths annually. However, almost every nonvaccinated child gets rotavirus at some time, and nearly all recover without professional intervention. Concerns with the vaccine include that it is made with animal tissue and can, in very rare cases, produce intussusception. Babies who are breast-fed and do not attend child care are less likely to contract this disease early, when it is most dangerous.

Diphtheria, tetanus, and pertussis (DTaP)	
CDC Recommended Dose and Schedule	5 doses: 1st at 2 months, 2nd at 4 months, 3rd at 6 months, 4th at 15–18 months, 5th at 4–6 years
Disease Facts	• All three are bacterial • Diphtheria—Throat infection that causes a thick coating on the throat, severe coughing, trouble breathing; most children recover fully, but it is still a serious illness; rarely, it can lead to paralysis, heart failure, and death; 10 percent of cases are fatal • Tetanus—Also known as "lockjaw"; uncommon; develops in deep wounds; affects nerves, can spread to spinal column and brain; can cause tight muscles, leading to inability to swallow and breathe; can be life-threatening; according to CDC, one in five infected with tetanus dies • Pertussis—Also known as "whooping cough"; remains common despite vaccine; produces severe coughing; pneumonia and death can occur; most serious in first six months of life; most children recover; of the few who die, the majority are infants
Vaccine Facts	• Contains aluminum, some brands higher than others • Some brands use animal tissue • Severe but rare side effects can include nonstop crying and severe allergic reaction at injection site; extremely rare side effects may include encephalitis, high fever, and neurological reactions, such as long-term seizures, coma, lowered consciousness, and permanent brain damage • Effective; cases of diphtheria and tetanus have decreased by 99 percent due to the vaccine; cases of pertussis have dropped by 80 percent (the pertussis vaccine is not as effective) • The old version of this vaccine, DTP, was known for causing neurological reactions and some brain injury; the new vaccine, DTaP, has proven much safer; severe side effects are rare
Considerations	Though serious, diphtheria is rare in the United States because of mass vaccination. Most infants are unlikely to suffer a wound that would cause tetanus. However, pertussis outbreaks occur, and the disease is dangerous and life-threatening for infants. There is no vaccine for pertussis alone. Therefore, it is not an option to vaccinate for pertussis early, and then vaccinate for diphtheria and tetanus later. Pertussis poses a real threat during the first six months of life. If you do choose to vaccinate, to enhance safety, consider asking your health care provider for a brand that uses no animal tissue and has the lowest aluminum content.

Haemophilus influenzae type B (Hib)	
CDC Recommended Dose and Schedule	3 or 4 doses, depending on brand: 1st at 2 months; 2nd at 4 months; 3rd at 6 months; if necessary, 4th at 12–15 months
Disease Facts	• Bacterial, lives in the nose and mouth; sickness occurs when spreads to lungs or bloodstream • Symptoms include coughing and sneezing; can turn severe, causing pneumonia, breathing problems, and meningitis, and can lead to death • Severe cases can result in brain damage and loss of hearing • Responds to antibiotics; most cases treatable; however, some extremely rare cases come on so powerfully that treatment does not help • According to CDC, before vaccine, incidence of Hib among young children was 20,000 cases a year, with 3 to 6 percent dying; Hib was the leading cause of meningitis in this age group; Hib is uncommon today
Vaccine Facts	• Very effective; incidence of Hib has been reduced by 99 percent by vaccine • Some brands contain aluminum • Can come in a combination vaccine; also available as a single shot • Side effects are rare and not that serious; most worrisome is a very rare, but severe allergic reaction, occurring in 1 in 1,000,000 doses
Considerations	Hib is a serious disease. Because of mass vaccination, it has become a rare disease in the United States. The vaccine has proven itself to be among the safest. Some brands do contain aluminum, so you may wish to ask for an aluminum-free brand.

Pneumococcal conjugate (PCV13)	
CDC Recommended Dose and Schedule	4 doses: 1st at 2 months, 2nd at 4 months, 3rd at 6 months, and 4th at 12–15 months
Disease Facts	• Common; occurs mostly in infant, toddlers, and the elderly • Caused by bacterium called *Streptococcus pneumoniae* • Can be mild or can lead to pneumonia, blood infections, meningitis, and death • Can be resistant to antibiotics • According to CDC, before vaccine, disease caused 700 cases of meningitis, 13,000 blood infections, 5 million ear infections, and 200 deaths in children under 5 each year
Vaccine Facts	• Vaccine covers only 13 of the more than 90 strains of pneumococcal bacteria • Contains aluminum • According to CDC, about 50 percent of children are drowsy and without appetite after shot; one-third suffers swelling and/or fever, and irritability is frequently reported; severe allergic reactions are rare
Considerations	Some people are concerned that while this vaccine prevents 13 strains of the disease, it makes children more vulnerable to the other 77 of strains and might cause those strains to strengthen. Another consideration is that such a large number of recipients experience side effects. That said, this bacteria is common and the disease it creates can turn serious quickly in a baby. If you do choose to vaccinate, be aware that this vaccine contains aluminum.
Influenza (IIV; LAIV)	
CDC Recommended Dose and Schedule	Annually after 6 months (1st year given twice, each shot one month apart, to boost chances of effectiveness)
Disease Facts	• Virus • According to CDC, thousands of people in the United States die each year from flu; in most people, causes fever/chills, headaches, body aches, sore throat, congestion, and cough • Rare complications include pneumonia and dehydration; very rare complications include inflammation of heart, lungs, brain, and other organs • Can be fatal; most deaths occur in elderly, but young children do die each year; even in mild cases, the illness can be uncomfortable and last up to two weeks • Antiviral drugs can help if given within 48 hours but are only approved for those over a year old
Vaccine Facts	• Not all brands approved for infants; nasal spray contains a live virus—not safe for children under 2 years old • Injection contains killed virus; some brands contain mercury • Should not be given to people allergic to eggs • Should not be given to children who take aspirin regularly, can cause Reye's syndrome • Should not be given to children who wheeze, can trigger an attack • Flu vaccines are not always effective because flu virus is always changing; common side effects include mild flu-like symptoms • Serious side effects are rare, but include febrile seizures; infants under 2 years old at higher risk of seizures, and giving the flu vaccine along with the pneumococcal vaccine further increases risk for febrile seizure • Guillain-Barré syndrome has been associated with the vaccine at a rate of 1 or 2 cases per million people vaccinated, according to the CDC
Considerations	The flu can be serious but usually is not. The vaccine has been shown to be more reactive than most in babies and small children. Should you choose to vaccinate, ask for a mercury-free vaccine, make sure the vaccine is approved for your child's age group, and make sure it is not given with the pneumococcal vaccine.

Inactivated poliovirus (IPV)	
CDC Recommended Dose and Schedule	4 doses: 1st at 2 months, 2nd at 4 months, 3rd at 6–8 months, and a booster at 4–6 years
Disease Facts	• Virus • Most cases mild; becomes serious when enters nervous system; can weaken muscles and paralyze victims, sometimes resulting in death; can also cause meningitis • No known treatments, just supportive care
Vaccine Facts	• Very effective; polio eradicated in the United States • Contains animal tissue • No severe side effects reported, though an allergic reaction is always possible • Old version of vaccine with live virus was documented to have the rare side effect of paralysis; today's polio vaccines have no such side effect
Considerations	Before the vaccine, around 25,000 cases of polio were reported each year in the United States. Today, polio is non-existent in North America, South America, and Europe. However, it is present in other parts of the world, and should an unvaccinated child be exposed to polio, the child would be vulnerable. Also, the vaccine is made with animal tissue. That noted, it has proven to be a safe and effective vaccine. If you are considering creating an alternative vaccination schedule, and your child is unlikely to be in contact with a person from a country where polio exists, this vaccine could be a candidate for postponement.
Measles, mumps, rubella (MMR)	
CDC Recommended Dose and Schedule	2 doses: 1st at 12–15 months, 2nd at 4–6 years. Children who are 1–12 years old can receive MMRV, which adds the varicella, or chicken pox, vaccine to the MMR vaccine
Disease Facts	• Viruses that spread though the air • Measles presents with a fever, rash, cough, congestion, and irritated eyes; most cases in childhood are mild; complications are uncommon but can include ear infection and pneumonia, both of which are treated with antibiotics; very rare but serious complications can include severe pneumonia and encephalopathy; fatality rate is 1 in 1,000; no longer common due to vaccination • Mumps presents with swollen saliva glands, fever, headache, and muscle pain; almost always mild in young children; more potent in adolescents and adults; rare complications, which usually only occur in adolescents or adults, include loss of hearing, meningitis, and swelling of testicles or ovaries, resulting in rare cases of sterility; no longer common due to vaccination • Rubella presents with a rash and mild fever; not dangerous in children; however, if a pregnant woman is exposed to a child with rubella her fetus could experience serious birth defects
Vaccine Facts	• Vaccine contains three live viruses • Made with animal tissue • Extremely effective; has limited measles and mumps to localized outbreaks and has practically eradicated rubella from the United States • Booster may be needed in adolescents • Rare but severe reactions to the vaccine include serious allergic reaction (fewer than 1 in 1 million), deafness, long-term seizures, coma, lowered consciousness, and permanent brain damage; also associated with inflammation of various body parts and organs, autoimmune reactions, testicular pain and swelling, arthritis, and neurological reactions, including encephalitis, encephalopathy, Guillain-Barré syndrome, seizures, and more
Considerations	There is a long list of rare, but severe reactions to the vaccine. However, not giving the MMR vaccine opens the door for the return of these diseases. Should you choose to vaccinate, know that MMR contains three live viruses—this requires your child's immune system to develop antibodies for three diseases at once. Separate vaccines are not available. Should you choose not to vaccinate, educate yourself on the signs of rubella and be mindful that your sick child may pose a threat to a pregnant woman's fetus.

Varicella (VAR)	
CDC Recommended Dose and Schedule	2 doses: 1st 12–15 months; 2nd 4–6 years
Disease Facts	• Virus, spreads through the air; disease was very common before vaccine • Presents with blistering rash, itching, and fever; contagious while rash is present • Most cases occur without issue • Severe complications arise in less than 1 percent of cases and are more likely in people with suppressed immune system; those complications can include staph infection in sores, pneumonia, encephalitis, and, extremely rarely, death • According to CDC, before the vaccine about 11,000 people who contracted chicken pox required hospitalization and about 100 people died each year; CDC does not note how many of these people were immune compromised or adults
Vaccine Facts	• Live virus vaccine; created with animal and human tissues • Protects most people against disease; some people still get it but usually milder version • Reactions include rash, fever, febrile seizure, and rare contagiousness • Severe but rare complications reported include severe brain reactions and low blood count; neurological reactions reported include Guillain-Barré syndrome, facial nerve paralysis, stroke, and encephalitis
Considerations	With vaccination, your child is likely to avoid chicken pox, to avoid infecting a parent who never had the disease, and to avoid infecting someone with a compromised immune system. However, the vaccine contains live virus. If you choose to vaccinate, you might consider getting the shot as a separate varicella vaccine—not as part of the MMRV, which would add a fourth live virus (varicella) to the MMR lineup. If you choose not to vaccinate, you may want to consider exposing your toddler to chicken pox so she gains immunity. If your unvaccinated child has not had chicken pox by late childhood, you may reconsider vaccination before she enters adolescence.
Hepatitis A (HepA)	
CDC Recommended Dose and Schedule	1 dose given between 12 months and 23 months
Disease Facts	• Virus • Common • Spreads easily through contaminated food and drink and through close personal contact (most publicized outbreaks usually linked to contaminated food at a restaurant) • Presents with severe stomach pain, diarrhea, and jaundice; typically mild in small children • Can make teens and adults very sick for up to a month; very serious for people with chronic liver disease; can be life-threatening • Not treatable, but most people make full recovery
Vaccine Facts	• The vaccine is effective; according to the CDC, rates of the disease have fallen steadily since its introduction • Contains aluminum, as well as human and animal tissues • Severe reactions are very rare and include allergic reaction and seizure; seizures are more common (though still extremely rare) the younger the recipient; other rare but reported reactions include Guillain-Barré syndrome, encephalitis, and thrombocytopenia (low platelet count)
Considerations	Hepatitis A can be life-threatening. Mass vaccination could reduce incidence of this disease across the population. However, the disease is unlikely to be contracted by babies and is typically mild when it does infect small children, who are most at risk to a severe reaction to the vaccine. If you do choose to vaccinate, you may consider postponing the vaccine until your baby is past her second birthday. Also, note that the vaccine has aluminum, so you might consider scheduling the vaccine when no other aluminum-containing vaccines are given. If you choose not to vaccinate at all, you may reconsider this vaccine as your child approaches adolescence.

Preparing for Vaccination

Whether you choose to vaccinate on the CDC schedule, to vaccinate on a revised schedule, or to refrain from vaccination completely, you can take several actions to ensure the best possible health for your child. I will discuss the considerations for each choice below.

Choosing to Vaccinate	Choosing Not to Vaccinate

Choosing to Vaccinate

If you choose vaccination, you can reduce the chance of side effects and boost the effectiveness of the vaccines.

Before the vaccination:

- Breast-feed your baby to give her the benefit of the antibodies in breast milk.
- Make sure your baby is healthy, with no fever and no medications in her system.
- If your child has allergies or eczema, delay vaccines until she is symptom-free.
- If your child is on an antibiotic, delay the vaccination for several weeks to give her beneficial bacteria a chance to regenerate.
- Feed your child probiotic foods, which can strengthen her immune system and decrease the likelihood of a reaction. Look for foods containing *Lactobacillus* and bifidobacteria.

At the vaccination:

- Choose single vaccines over combination vaccines when possible.
- Try not to allow too many vaccines containing aluminum at one time.
- If your child is getting a flu shot, make sure it is mercury-free.

After the vaccination:

- Monitor your child for side effects, mild or severe.
- If you see signs of discomfort or illness, call your health care provider.
- If your child develops a fever above 102°F, call your health care provider.
- If your child has a severe reaction to any vaccine in a course, carefully consider discontinuing that course. Reactions are more likely with later doses.

Choosing Not to Vaccinate

If you choose not to vaccinate, then you are taking on the responsibility of keeping your child healthy. It is up to you to build her immunity naturally, to keep her in good health, and to protect others if she contracts a contagious disease. Here are some strategies to help you meet this responsibility:

To keep your child healthy and build immunity:

- Breast-feed your baby for at least two years so that she receives the full benefit of the antibodies in breast milk.
- Provide a diet of whole foods.
- For the first two years, avoid child care, large play groups, and play facilities with large numbers of children.
- Make sure your child is active and gets outside every day.
- Consider exposing your child to contagious diseases that pose little threat to her as a toddler, but can be serious in adulthood, such as chicken pox and mumps.
- Be aware that your child can carry diseases that could harm others. Quarantine her when she is sick. If she could be carrying a disease, keep her away from pregnant women and people with suppressed immune systems.

The bottom line with childhood immunizations is that in the United States, the chances of your child contracting a serous disease or having a serious reaction to a vaccine are small. Even if one of these events happens, your baby will most likely recover from it. On the other hand, both choices—vaccination and refusing vaccination—do involve risk. The best way to approach this decision as a parent is to educate yourself and then choose the course of action that you feel is right for your child, your family, and yourself.

Developing Immunity

You can combat childhood illness defensively through vaccines, medications, and antibiotics. You can also do it by focusing on building your baby's health and immune system naturally right from the start. In her first year of life, your baby's immune system is still developing along with her other systems, and this presents you with the opportunity to help her establish a healthy foundation.

First, you can strengthen your baby's innate immunity by connecting with nature—by providing her with breast milk, whole foods, exercise, a natural environment, fresh air and sunshine, and emotional support, and by living according to nature's principles. Then you can further boost her body's supply of good bacteria by adding fermented foods and probiotic booster to her diet. Her body contains trillions of beneficial bacteria. They live on her skin and in her intestines. They help digest food, produce vitamins, stimulate her immune system, and fight infections. You can find fermented foods and probiotic supplements made especially for infants and toddlers.

You can promote optimal health by educating yourself about natural healing methods and developing your intuition and judgment in making decisions for your baby.

How Your Baby Can Be Well Naturally

Western medicine and East Asian medicine can complement each other to keep your child healthy. Western medicine is miraculous and saves lives. It is very effective for diagnosis and surgery involving high-tech equipment, especially in cases of emergency, trauma, and advanced illness. East Asian medicine takes a holistic approach to preventing and healing illness. Traditional East Asian medicine is the third-oldest form of medicine in the world; it is predated only by medical practices in Egypt and Babylonia. For thousands of years, it has proven to be an effective form of preventive and therapeutic health care.

By employing both East Asian and Western approaches to care, you can take advantage of the best of each. You can use the science of Western medicine and the natural healing of Eastern modalities as both daily prevention and treatment in times of sickness. Below I describe some of the principles of natural healing in East Asian medicine.

A moderate and gradual approach

Natural healing is gentle and noninvasive. Most natural-healing treatment methods are slow, steady, and low risk. Because most of these techniques are mild, you can try one, observe the results, and then try another. You can even safely use multiple treatments at the same time. Perhaps best of all, there are no negative side effects of natural-healing methods, only benefits. Thus, you can safely use natural-healing techniques to increase your child's vitality and energy anytime—even when she is not sick.

Whole and integrated

Natural healing is a holistic approach that treats your whole baby, rather than treating individual parts of her physical body. It views all systems as integrated and working together and considers all aspects of her condition. For instance, if she has an earache, the source of her pain may involve internal systems that you cannot see by looking at her ear. By thinking of her whole system, you can more deeply consider the cause of, relief from, and cure for her earache.

Holistic healing for your baby reflects the following viewpoints:

- ✿ She is not an isolated being. She is influenced by her relationship to her environment—both her physical environment, such as weather and living conditions, and her emotional environment, including levels of stress and nurturing.

- ✿ Her broad physiological landscape, or overall verve and life force, is a significant part of her health. The terrain of her physiological landscape affects her ability to adjust and respond to external forces. If she is sick or injured, the speed of her recovery depends on her overall condition.

- ✿ Repeated patterns tell a story that can be noticed, observed, and questioned. Immediate discomforts, such as an ongoing runny nose or regular temper tantrums, may be signals of another cause to consider in an overall diagnosis.

- ✿ The relationship of different parts is more meaningful than the individual parts alone. Tangible parts add up to make a whole that is intangible; for example, many trees make up a forest. The four vital signs in medicine are: pulse rate, blood pressure, breathing rate, and body temperature. Together they create well-being, which is immeasurable, yet consequential in healing.

- ✿ The discovery and treatment of a sickness's causes may be nonlinear, rather than following the direct cause and effect logic of scientific methods. Fixing a single symptom or place that hurts may have little impact if other factors affect the whole.

- ✿ Healing moves from the inside out and from the roots up. True healing occurs when you strengthen your baby's overall health.

Symptoms are your friends

People often mistake symptoms for illnesses. You may provide temporary relief by extinguishing symptoms, but if you do not address the root cause of a symptom, then long-term healing cannot occur. Aspirin may reduce fever, but it does not address the cause or the purpose of the fever; it merely stops a symptom, and thus may cover up a clue to what is really going on.

While natural-healing techniques can and do relieve individual symptoms, their goal is to find the root of the sickness underlying the symptoms. Symptoms—such as fever, pain, rash, aches, or swelling—are messages that point to a problem; they are signs that something is askew. They are not the problem; they are an expression of the problem. By listening to the messages your child's body is sending through symptoms, you can appreciate their benevolent purposes of healing, bringing balance, and establishing wholeness.

Excess

Every day your baby's body takes in food, liquid, and air in order to produce blood, nerve and other cells, as well as bone and muscle tissue. What her body does not use is eliminated through urination, bowel movements, respiration, and perspiration. If she takes in substances that are low in quality and not useful, her disposal system becomes overwhelmed. Her body becomes unbalanced.

From the East Asian point of view, most sickness in the modern world is caused by too many, rather than too few, nutrients. Excess can cause a disruption in your baby's chi (life force) flow, which appears as a deficiency. When she has too much waste to process through elimination, respiration, and perspiration, she may discharge that waste through a fever and through the openings in her body and skin—manifesting in a runny nose, an earache, coughing, drooling, discharge from her eyes, rashes, or bumps. When she is overloaded and her elimination organs cannot clean her blood, fatty acids accumulate inside her body in the form of hardness, cysts, or mucus deposits in her liver, kidneys, lungs, intestines, and circulatory system.

Because children's bodies are self-balancing, they eliminate excesses naturally and have the ability to heal on their own. For instance, a common cold may be the result of discharging excess from mucus-producing foods. To kill an infection, your baby may develop a fever, which can be cleansing and healing.

Thus, you can contribute to sickness by giving in to your baby or toddler's desire to overindulge. While it can be challenging to say no and to set limits that cause short-term discomfort for both child and parent, a constant answer of yes can end up compromising your baby's health. As your baby grows and begins to make demands, protecting her health may involve helping her to avoid excesses in foods, activities, and stimulation.

External influences

Because of a young baby's inherent weakness, external factors disturb her chi fairly regularly. In an effort to achieve balance during seasonal changes in temperature, her body makes adjustments. In the winter, her body

builds up heat that diminishes in the spring, which may result in a fever. In the summer, her body needs cooling foods, such as fruit, and light cooking to slow down her metabolism. The cool weather of autumn can squeeze out excess liquid in her body through a runny nose or cold. These natural adjustments and discharges cleanse your baby's body. It is healthy and normal for babies and toddlers to have periodic sicknesses that discharge minor excesses and develop and strengthen their immune systems.

The following external influences can influence your baby's health and cause reactions:

❀ Cold can diminish your baby's immune system, resulting in poor blood or chi circulation. This may lead to a cold, cough, other respiratory disorder, stagnation of chi, or weak digestion.

❀ Heat can quickly affect your baby. Babies are naturally hot and yang, with insufficient yin, and heat builds up over time. Excess heat can result in fever or inflammation. When summer begins, excess heat can bring on diarrhea.

❀ Wind causes the quickest injury to your baby's energy system. Symptoms of exposure to wind include chills, fever, and colds. Because babies and children are vulnerable to getting chilled from a breeze, keep your baby's neck covered when it is windy or cool. Damp weather can contribute to excess mucus, which can affect your baby's respiratory system, which in turn may result in swelling or bloating.

❀ Dry air from air-conditioning or central heat can result in dry skin, dryness in your baby's respiratory and digestive systems, and overall dryness in her body.

Disruptions to your baby's rhythms and patterns of energy and emotions can create different kinds of imbalances. Natural healing not only balances and restores harmony to different parts of your baby's physical body, but also revitalizes and rejuvenates her whole system.

Yin and yang for natural healing

Yin and yang create a fundamental concept that can help you characterize your baby's overall condition and move toward a solution to help her maintain her balance.

Children with a yang tendency usually have a large capacity for food and activity and a minimal requirement for rest. They are difficult to ignore, intense in their reactions, comfortable in stimulating environments, enthusiastic, and quick and compulsive in their actions. When they are sick, they suffer severely and recover quickly.

Children with a yin tendency prefer a quiet, calm environment, are choosy about food, and need lots of sleep. They are easy to be with, sensitive, easily startled, and quick to cry. Often these children prefer quiet activities and slower movements, and they may have an interest in artistic pursuits.

If your baby is generally yang, then she may have a tendency to overindulge in yang pursuits, resulting in excessive yang conditions. When she has had too much yang food or has participated in too many yang activities, her cheeks may become red, or she might have a temper tantrum—signs of excess energy. You can help her reduce this energy by providing relaxing activities and by offering foods that are cooling and calming. Emi was my yang baby. In providing her meals, I needed to take care that she did not get too much yang energy from foods such as eggs, fish, and chicken. With Mari, my yin baby, I tried to prevent her from overindulging in yin treats such as ice cream, fruit, and cookies. If your baby has a yin tendency, then exercise and heat-producing foods such as animal proteins can help raise her energy level.

Both yin and yang have strengths and weaknesses. One is not better than the other, but in excess alone or together, they can have negative effects. Extreme yin and yang influences in your baby's environment can cause her condition to swing back and forth like a pendulum. By moderating extremes in the environment, you can help create a smoother flow in her rhythms.

In general, you can establish balance by reducing excessive yin or yang while adding the opposite foods or treatments. If your baby has a fever, which means she is burning off excess yang, you could give her some applesauce to eat and apply a tofu or chlorophyll plaster on her head or back to cool her down.

Another method of creating balance is to reduce both extreme yin and extreme yang moderately, which naturally brings your baby's body toward the middle of the spectrum. Whatever sickness my children had, I gave them simple, balanced food, such as soft brown rice and mild vegetable soup. These neutral foods helped reduce stress on their bodies if they were off balance. You can use this tool as an ongoing daily practice, as well as a treatment for sickness.

Babies grow and develop rapidly, an example of yang energy that can cause rapid-onset fevers and restless sleep. Growing takes energy, and yin and yang unfold in rhythms. Your child may go through cycles of being more yin or more yang. She may have growth spurts that bring surges of yang power, and thus cause her to become stubborn, before experiencing a slower, softer, and more yielding natural growth. Preschool children go through these stages. The terrible twos, terrific threes, fretful fours, and fantastic fives are all examples of the cycles of yin and yang going from stubborn to yielding and back again.

Constitution and condition

When I was pregnant with Emi in Japan, my mother-in-law told me that if I compared the evolution of life to the nine months of my pregnancy, my baby would go through about 10 million years of evolutionary development a day. Her comment made every minute of my prenatal care seem important. The idea was overwhelming, and yet I enjoyed the opportunity to focus attention on taking care of my unborn baby and myself.

Korean and Japanese cultures have rituals for prenatal care called *taegyo* and *tai-kyo*, respectively. This set of rules for fetal education originated from traditional Chinese medical philosophy more than 400 years ago. According to *tai-kyo*, the most important time to build a baby's healthy constitution is during pregnancy; nine months of education inside the womb is considered more important than the ten years after birth.

Tai-kyo suggests that the mother eat quality food, that a mother's physical activity helps build a strong and active baby, and that attitude and environment affect a mother's thoughts and emotions, so she should avoid movies, books, and stories that are violent, loud, or emotionally disturbing. Pregnant woman are also expected to avoid environmental toxins and excessive heat. *Tai-kyo* recommends a clean, orderly, calming environment. Modern *tai-kyo* programs in Korea and Japan encourage pregnant women to talk to their babies, to

Yin-Yang Constitution and Condition

Yang ▲		Yin ▼	
Constitution	**Condition**	**Constitution**	**Condition**
Short	Action oriented: leaps before looking	Tall	Observant: looks before leaping
Round face	Interactive: demanding	Oval face	Content to play alone
Curly hair	Restless, energetic	Straight hair	Calm, relaxed
Bald, red, blond, or black hair	Tough	Brown hair	Sensitive
Energetic	Assertive	Relaxed	Easygoing
Short fingers	Controlling, bossy	Long fingers	Agreeable
Wide bone structure	Self-directed	Narrow bone structure	Reactive to outer direction
Small eyes		Big eyes	
Ears flat to head		Ears stick out from head	
Small mouth		Wide mouth	
Compact body		Soft body	
Rigid		Flexible	
Short hairline		Long hairline	
Physical		Mental	
Moving early		Slower development	
Thick eyebrows		Thin eyebrows	
Tight navel		Open navel	

read stories to them, and to practice yoga. This prenatal education also includes enhancing health and reducing stress by listening to relaxing music, reading classical literature, and appreciating art.

As every pregnancy is different, every baby has a unique set of circumstances that create who she is today and who she will become tomorrow. Constitution, gender, level of daily activity, location, and birth season contribute to your baby's variety of needs, personal tastes, and experiences. The temperament, food cravings, and tastes of a child born in summer are likely to differ from those of a child born in winter. Boys usually have a stronger attraction to physical activity and animal-based foods than girls do. A baby living in Michigan is influenced by cold winters, while a baby living in Southern California is affected by warm weather.

Other factors that affect your baby's constitution include the following:

- Parental and ancestral conditions
- Genetics
- Dates of conception and birth
- Place of birth and growth
- Food that a mother eats during pregnancy and the first year of life
- Family, social, and cultural influences

Your baby's constitution or overall structure is primarily established in utero but is still developing during the rapid growth period of her first year. After that, her basic constitution is established and changes very slowly, if at all. The shape of her nose, her bone structure, and her basic hereditary characteristics are constitutional and mostly unalterable. On the other hand, your baby's condition changes from day to day and is defined by the soft tissues of her body, her daily food intake, her activities, and her attitudes.

Emi was born in June. She has a more yang constitution because I was pregnant during the winter months, when I was eating saltier, cooked foods and animal proteins, such as fish and eggs. Mari, who was born in November, has a more yin constitution because I was pregnant during warmer weather, when I ate more salads, sweets, and cooling foods. Emi was born in Japan, where I had a mentally rigorous work schedule teaching school. Mari was born in North Carolina, where I was more physically active with swimming and walking. Each pregnancy had its own set of circumstances that contributed to each child's unique experience, which influenced who she grew to be.

The chart on the opposite page shows the yin and yang characteristics of both constitutional and conditional features.

Personal responsibility and choice

In natural healing, adults are responsible for their own health. As a parent, you are responsible for your child's health. It may be tempting to give up this responsibility and rely on a health care provider to fix health problems and to make decisions regarding your child. While the support of expert guidance is always beneficial, the ultimate responsibility and decisions about your child's care are yours. By taking ownership of the everyday building of the landscape of your baby's whole self, you assume the responsibility of her well-being.

Essential Skills for Natural Health

ESPECIALLY DURING HER FIRST year, your baby is delicate, and her systems are immature. Many of the common illnesses that she may experience in her first few years are digestive disorders, respiratory problems, and skin conditions. Many of these everyday symptoms or sicknesses will naturally heal as your baby develops and grows. In these cases, medication is not usually helpful or effective; and it may cause other problems.

By providing your baby with regular and consistent care every day, you can help her establish a stabilizing internal balance and immunity. This proactive approach can protect and reduce the invasion of external stresses and help with healing if sickness occurs. Natural healing may move at a slower pace, but it can bring about long-lasting outcomes because it addresses the root causes of sickness.

In addition to providing daily care, you can learn and use simple techniques and remedies to help your child balance minor sicknesses. Serious illnesses may require the expertise of a qualified health care professional. In the following section, I outline the principles of diagnosis in natural healing and provide practical treatments and remedies for common illnesses that your baby may experience.

acute, illnesses tend to develop intensely and go away quickly. Yin, or chronic, illnesses develop gradually, and their symptoms linger. The following chart shows the yin and yang characteristics to look for while trying to understand your child's condition.

Diagnosis

It is easier to apply a solution or treatment when you understand your baby's illness and its cause. Keep in mind that because her condition is always changing, she may need different treatments from day to day. Below are some principles to guide you in determining your baby's condition.

Yin and Yang Diagnosis

If your child's behavior is slow, quiet, and introverted, her condition could be of a more yin nature. If she cannot rest, is irritable and angry, shows aggressive behavior or an overheated condition, or is constipated, she may be experiencing excessive yang influences.

A practitioner of East Asian medicine would first look at your child's overall condition to assess whether she has excess, which is classified as yang, or deficiency, which is classified as yin. A child whose overall condition is more yang needs to relax and disperse her energy. She needs to calm down and slow down. A child whose condition appears to be more yin needs to increase her energy. Her energy flow and strength needs to increase, and her vitality needs to be activated. Yang, or

Yin-Yang Conditions

Yang Conditions	Yin Conditions
Restless	Passive, listless
Unwilling to be held	Constant desire to be held, protected
Aggressive	Disinterested
Excessively energetic	Low energy
Insomnia	Excessive sleep
Hot; throwing off clothing	Cold; needs more clothing
Dark-brown bowel movements	Green stools
Constipation or diarrhea with putrid smell	Diarrhea or loose stools
Colicky and unable to relax, especially at night	Excessive fatigue, tiredness
Irritable, excessively angry, crying	Anxiety; abnormal levels of fear
Fever	Chills
Acute sickness	Chronic sickness
Rapid onset	Gradual onset
Likes to lie outstretched	Likes to lie curled up
Red face	Pale face
Likes cold drinks	Likes hot drinks
Loud voice; talks a lot	Weak voice; dislikes talking
Coarse breathing	Shallow, weak breathing
Scanty, dark urine	Profuse, pale urine
Sweating	Little sweating
Bad breath	Breath not noticeably bad
Big appetite; thirsty	Poor appetite; not thirsty
Red tongue with yellow coating	Pale tongue with white coating
Tantrums and outbursts for no apparent reason	Unable to focus or concentrate

Mother and Baby are One

In East Asian medicine, mother and baby are seen as a unit for a child's first year. The mother's physical and emotional condition affects her baby's health, especially if she is breast-feeding. If she worries or feels depressed, her baby senses it. The principles of *tai-kyo* continue past pregnancy and into her baby's first year. Thus, East Asian medicine practitioners say, "Treat the mother, and you treat the child." In this first year, mothers face many demands. They need care and support. When I had Emi in Japan, my family and community expected me to stay in bed for three weeks to recover from the many hormonal changes of birth and to settle into breast-feeding. Your child's first year is a transition for both you and your baby. When you stay mindful of how you feel, you support your child's condition and remain able to diagnose any imbalances.

Diagnosing with the Senses

When formulating a diagnosis, an East Asian practitioner both analyzes the patient and employs the senses—looking, smelling, touching, and listening. After making sense-based observations, a practitioner does not just focus on individual body parts to come up with a diagnosis. Instead, she synthesizes all the information to gain an overall perspective and draws upon her intuition as well.

When Emi and Mari were small, Naoki and I operated an East-West Center out of our home. Naoki had an acupuncture and consultation practice for natural healing. I taught classes in cooking with whole foods. I also offered boardinghouse-style dinners on Wednesday evenings. For three dollars, people could get a meal, from soup to dessert, with the opportunity to meet others interested in a natural lifestyle. I put

Diagnosing with Your Senses

Parent Action	Body Part	Symptom
Look	Face	Red or pale?
	Eyes	Bright or dull? Look for discharge: clear or thick?
	Mouth	Swollen or contracted? Tongue color? Look for discharge such as drooling: clear or thick?
	Ears	Swollen or red? Pain? Look for discharge: clear or thick?
	Urine and Stool	Color? Is urine clear or opaque? Is stool dark and hard, or green and loose?
	Energy	Strong spirit or tired and sleepy? Quick or slow response?
Smell	Breath, stool and urine, overall body	Five smells: rancid, putrid, fragrant-sweet, burned, rank
Touch	Skin	Hot or cold? Damp or dry? Smooth or rough? Is there a rash, eruption, or coloration? If so, where is it? On which acupuncture meridian does it fall?
	Abdomen	Cold or warm? Tender? Distended?
Listen	Asking or inquiring	Diet? Sleep? Activities? How have these daily activities been recently that would affect her condition?

Mari in my back carrier, and Emi washed vegetables and set the table. Together we served up to 36 people in our house every week. It was a way for me to stay home with my kids, to bring in some income, and to do something that I cared about. We cooked some delicious meals and had fun!

My daughters and I also helped Naoki with his acupuncture clients. Emi and Mari entertained them in our living room, which served as the waiting area. Acupuncture was a part of our daily lives, and we often shared acupoint massages while watching movies or traveling. Naoki used acupoints to treat Emi and Mari when they had various childhood sicknesses. I received the benefit of his acupuncture treatments when I was unbalanced or tired, and I was often the guinea pig when Naoki got together with his colleagues to share and to learn. Because Mari grew up with acupuncture around her every day, it was a natural career path for her, and she now follows in her father's footsteps.

The remedies I describe later in this chapter are ones that we used for our family and clients. These simple treatments include food in general, specific food remedies, homeopathic remedies, Chinese herbs, compresses and other topical treatments, essential oils, acupoint therapy, and Reiki. You may need to buy some special ingredients, but you can keep some necessary items on hand in your cupboard or first-aid kit. For instance, I used to make sure I had apple juice, kuzu, and a Tetra Pack of tofu in case someone got a stomachache or fever.

The remedies are simple and easy to make. You may find it empowering to participate in healing your child's sicknesses. When you are involved in her care through diagnosing, thinking about symptoms and causes, and administering treatments, you get in touch with your child's point of view and develop your intuition about her feelings and needs. Ultimately, the ingredient that she probably needs the most is your tender loving care, which is accessible wherever you are—no special tools required.

Keeping a Health Journal

Recording your pregnancy and your child's health history in a journal provides one document that you can use for tracking her health care. This practice has been used in maternal and child health care programs that are focused on improving prenatal and postnatal care. These agencies have been credited for reducing infant mortality.

After World War II and continuing into the present, the Japanese government has been giving pregnant women a copy of *Boshi Kenko Techo*, or *the Maternal and Child Health Handbook* (MCH).

The MCH has space to record a summary of visits with a health care provider along with child rearing and nutritional information. The parents keep the handbook to share with different providers. You can track your child's health visits by recording them in a small notebook that you use for doctor and dentist visits.

To download a health journal visit growhealthygrowhappy.com

Treatments

Food as Medicine and Remedies

Before birth, your baby does not have to digest food. The transition to digesting food is a healthy baby's biggest challenge after she is born. Her digestive system has to work to its maximum capacity, and it can easily become stressed and overloaded. Therefore, most of her physical imbalances or illnesses are related to indigestion. When your baby is not feeling well, the remedy usually involves regulating and strengthening her digestive system. It is usually helpful to limit her diet to mild foods and give her digestive system a rest.

After you determine whether your child's condition is more yin or more yang, you can adjust her food to help her restore balance. In general, simple, soft, mildly seasoned whole foods that lie near the center of the yin-yang spectrum, such as grains, vegetables, beans, and fruit, can help bring your child back to balance. If her condition becomes excessively yin or yang, you can help her balance by feeding her foods that provide an opposite influence.

With an excessive yin condition, provide plant-based foods that are slightly more yang, such as cooked whole grains, to help her gain energy. Add more yang vegetables, such as roots and winter squash, and cook the foods a little longer for extra heat. At the same time, reduce yin foods, especially fruit, fruit juice, and sugary or processed foods.

If your child has an excessively yang condition, you can help her relax by increasing her intake of vegetables, such as leafy greens, green peas, and zucchini. Serve grains that are soupy in texture, and limit use of salt in the cooking. Add some soft tofu and cooked fruit, too.

In addition to their yin and yang properties, some foods have thermal or probiotic properties, provide specific textures, contain certain specialized nutrients or chemicals, or create or reduce mucus. Foods may also promote an acidic or alkaline condition that helps or interferes with the healing of an illness. Even the cooking methods you use can affect your child's condition. For example, food that is served warm is relaxing, while cold food is chilling to the body.

The following list includes some examples of everyday foods that contain certain medicinal properties that help heal sicknesses:

- Whole grains and flaxseeds provide fiber to help with digestion.

- Radishes, turnips, lemons, and ginger help break up mucus.

- Sea vegetables cleanse your baby's body of toxins and have antimicrobial properties.

- Fermented foods, such as miso and pickled plums, provide probiotics that aids digestion and neutralizes acidity.

- Natural sweeteners, such as brown rice syrup, are relaxing and calming.

- Mushrooms detoxify phlegm and pathogens via antiviral, antibacterial, antifungal, and antimicrobial compounds.

- Chlorophyll-rich foods, such as leafy greens, support the body's ability to produce oxygen. Human pathogens expire in an oxygen-rich environment.

- Brightly colored fruits, such as berries and purple grapes, contain bioflavonoids that help build immunity.

You can use food as medicine by offering simple foods, understanding the yin and yang influences of foods, and providing foods with specific healing properties. (More food-related healing properties are listed with the suggestions for treating each common illness at the end of this chapter.)

The following remedies can help rebalance your baby's condition when she is not feeling well or when she has a cold, a cough, or a digestive upset resulting from excess at a birthday party, exposure at child care, changes in the weather, or imbalances in her activities.

Cereal Grain Milk Remedy

♡ 6 months+

⚱ 7 cups

V Vegetarian

GF Gluten-free

Cereal grain milk is centering, soothing, and nourishing to your baby's digestive tract. This is the first remedy that I use to help restore balance. Soft grains that are cooked to a soupy texture for your baby's first purees keep the fiber of the whole grain, or for a more serious condition, you can squeeze the grain through cheesecloth to take out the fiber.

This special preparation is gentle on the digestive system, can be offered as a first food, and can also be used as a healing food for any kind of illness or imbalance. You can remove the fiber by straining the grain through cheesecloth, thus making a very soothing food for your baby's sensitive digestive system. This porridge can be helpful for an upset stomach or illness at any age. Brown rice syrup can be added for sweetness; for illness, add a few drops of plum vinegar to produce an alkaline balance.

1 cup short-grain brown rice

½ cup sweet brown rice

Water to cover, for soaking

10 ½ cups water, for cooking

1-inch-square piece of kombu seaweed

Pinch of salt (for babies over one year old)

1 tablespoon brown rice syrup or a few drops plum vinegar per serving

Special equipment:

Cheesecloth

Method

1. Cover the grains with water and soak for 8 to 24 hours. If you do not have time to soak them for this time span, soak for at least 1 hour, if possible. Drain.

2. Add the drained rice, cooking water, kombu, and salt to a large pot, and bring to a boil over high heat.

3. Reduce the heat to a simmer and cook for 1 ½ hours. Use a heat diffuser to keep grains from sticking to the bottom of the pot and to prevent burning.

4. When the rice is done, remove the kombu, and let it cool.

5. When the cooked grain is cool enough to handle, form a bag with cheesecloth, and strain the liquid, leaving the rice in the bag.

6. Add either brown rice syrup or plum vinegar before serving.

Variation:

You can substitute millet, whole oats, or barley for the sweet rice. This recipe can be made thicker for older children by adding more grain or less water. The mixture can be refrigerated for up to 4 days; reheat before serving.

Miso Broth Remedy

♡ **7 months+**

🥣 **8 (2-ounce) servings**

V **Vegetarian**

GF **Gluten-free**

Miso soup is made from fermented soybean paste that is added to vegetable broth to make a soup that is alkaline-producing and helps digestion. It calms and settles your baby's stomach and helps build her immunity because it contains beneficial *lactobacillus*, a type of bacteria. Miso helps discharge toxins built up from taking antibiotics, receiving lidocaine at the dentist's office, or getting an X-ray. Be careful if your baby has an overly yang condition, because miso has a high sodium content. See page 472 for the complete recipe.

Apple Kuzu Remedy

♡ 6 months+

⚱ 4 (2-ounce) servings

V Vegetarian

GF Gluten-free

Kuzu was my number-one remedy when my girls were growing up, and it still is now that they are adults. I love it, too—in sickness or in health. Kuzu helps calm and soothe your baby, and it is a powerful remedy for diarrhea, stomachache, acid reflux, colds, cough, fever, and headache. Kuzu helps soothe emotions, eliminates toxins, reduces stress, and diminishes hyperactivity.

Kuzu is a root that comes from a plant similar to kudzu and grows wild along highways in the southern United States. This chalky white substance is native to and usually processed in Japan. Kuzu is alkaline-producing and very soothing to your baby's digestive system. It can be used in daily cooking as a healthy alternative to arrowroot or cornstarch, to thicken sauces, creams, gravies, pies, puddings, or vegetable stir-fries.

Depending on your child's condition and taste, you may choose to use kuzu with brown rice syrup and water, apple juice, or savory ingredients. Emi and Mari usually enjoyed the sweet recipes. Save the savory dish for when your child is over one year old.

2 tablespoons kuzu

½ cup cold water

½ cup apple juice

Method

1. Dissolve the kuzu in the cold water.

2. Place the apple juice in a small pan, and heat over medium heat.

3. Add the dissolved kuzu and water mixture, and stir with a wooden spoon. Continue stirring until the liquid reaches a low simmer and becomes clear.

4. Cool before serving.

Variation

For Brown Rice Syrup Kuzu, substitute ½ cup apple juice for ½ cup water, add 2 tablespoons brown rice syrup, and follow the recipe as directed.

Savory Kuzu Remedy

♡ 12 months+

🥣 4 (2-ounce) servings

V Vegetarian

GF Gluten-free

Kuzu in this slightly salty sauce has a soothing, medicinal effect on your baby's digestive system. It can be used on its own as a remedy for a digestive upset or as a sauce on vegetables or grains.

2 tablespoons kuzu

1 cup water

¼ teaspoon tamari

¼ teaspoon *umeboshi* plum paste

Method

1. Dissolve the kuzu in ½ cup of cold water. Add the tamari and *umeboshi* plum paste, and stir to combine.

2. Place the remaining ½ cup water in a small pan, and heat over medium heat.

3. Add the dissolved kuzu and water mixture, and stir with a wooden spoon. Continue stirring until the liquid reaches a low simmer and becomes clear.

4. Cool before serving.

Pickled Plum Remedies

Japanese plums have medicinal qualities, as well as culinary uses. Pickled plums, plum concentrate, plum vinegar, and tea made with pickled plums and tamari sauce are alkaline-producing and eliminate toxins in your baby's body.

Pickled plums and plum vinegar: My cooking teacher and mentor at Dream Window Kindergarten, Takehara-sensei, used to make her own homemade pickled plums. Mixed with salt and seasoned with a Japanese herb called *shiso*, these plums are useful for digestive upsets, including upset stomach, diarrhea, constipation, and motion sickness. They are very salty, so use small amounts, depending on the age and condition of your child. Pickled plums are traditionally put in the middle of rice balls because the salt helps keep the rice from spoiling. Plum juice is the liquid left over from making pickled plums, and it has the same medicinal properties as the meat of the plum.

Plum concentrate: During the first few weeks of my pregnancy I discovered this remedy, which helped relieve my nausea. Green Japanese plums are slowly cooked down to a dark, thick syrup to make plum concentrate. One day when Emi was a toddler, she was not feeling well and lay listless on the sofa. I gave her some plum concentrate, and within a few hours she was up and about. Plum concentrate is a good basic natural medicine because it is alkaline-producing but does not contain salt, and it has a calming and relaxing effect. Because the taste is very sour, you can mix ¼ teaspoon of concentrate with 1 cup of hot water and 1 tablespoon of honey as a tonic. For 12 months and up.

Plum Tea Remedy

♡ **12 months+**

🥄 **1 cup**

V Vegetarian

GF Gluten-free option

At Dream Window Kindergarten, this tea was given to toddlers for bruises, digestive problems, headaches, and colds. Pickled plum mixed with tea is soothing to aches and pains, as well as to an emotional upset. This drink can help your child restore balance after she enjoys sweets and treats. Because of the sodium content, wait to offer it to your child until she is one year old.

1 cup water

1 teaspoon or 1 tea bag roasted barley or herb tea as a gluten-free option

¼ teaspoon tamari

¼ teaspoon plum paste

Method

1. Boil the water, and steep the tea for 5 to 15 minutes. If you use loose tea, strain the tea.

2. Mix the tamari and plum paste into the tea. Serve.

Alternative Remedies

Homeopathic remedies—Homeopathy is based on the idea that the body can heal itself if it is stimulated with remedies that trigger the body's natural healing system. Homeopathic treatments involve highly diluted substances that treat like with like, which is similar to giving a very mild vaccine. My only personal experience with homeopathic remedies was to use homeopathic tablets when my children were teething. Consult a licensed practitioner for using these remedies for your child.

Bach flower remedies—Bach flower remedies are safe, natural healing methods discovered by Edward Bach, MD in England between 1920 and 1930. The remedies are made from wildflowers, and the primary mixture, Rescue Remedy, was created to help people cope with emergencies and crises. Rescue Remedy is a natural stress reliever that is safe for children. It can help your child deal with everyday fears, worries, self-esteem issues, irritability, anger, shyness, and self-acceptance. Because children have not had many years of emotional imbalances, they respond quickly to Bach flower remedies. The original Bach flower remedies are preserved in brandy, but an alcohol-free mixture is available for children. For babies between 6 and 18 months, put one drop of Rescue Remedy in ½ cup of water, and give the mixture to your child to sip throughout the day. For an older child, you can place one or two drops directly on her tongue. Bach Rescue Cream is helpful for external traumas and conditions, such as blows, rashes, burns, bruises, cuts, sprains, dry skin, and diaper rash. Apply it to the wrist, neck, ankles, or other areas with thin skin. Other Bach remedies are best administered with a trained and qualified practitioner.

Chinese herbs—Chinese herbs are used with the same understanding of energetic balance, including yin and yang, that is used with acupuncture. Certain Chinese herbal formulations can help restore balance to your baby's body systems. Chinese herbal medicine is gentle and effective in treating babies and young

children, and they usually respond and recover quickly. Very strong herbs are not recommended, however. Children require the same formulas as adults, in smaller doses. The easiest way to give your young child Chinese herbs is to administer them in liquid form with a pediatric syringe.

I did not give Chinese herbs to my children when they were small, but Mari uses them regularly with her son, Zo. I recommend consulting a licensed practitioner to get Chinese herbs for your baby or child.

Compresses

Ice packs and tofu and chlorophyll compresses cause blood vessels to contract, so they reduce heat and swelling. Cold packs are used for acute injuries. Ginger compresses and hot water bottles, on the other hand, are warming; they increase circulation by dilating the blood vessels in areas that are constricted or tight. They are used for chronic conditions.

Ice packs—For an injury that occurred within the past 48 hours, an ice pack helps reduce swelling. For a bump, bruise, or sprain, apply an ice or cold pack. Ice should be used after an activity, not before it. Place ice cubes inside a piece of cheesecloth or washcloth, and hold the pack over the painful area. Fun animal packs made with gels can be uplifting for your toddler when she has a minor injury. Keep them in the freezer so you have one ready if your child has a bruise or sprain.

Hara-maki—A *hara-maki* is a band of material worn around the waist as a belly wrap. The first people to use *hara-maki* were Japanese samurai, who wore the bands under their armor. A *hara-maki* helps spread warmth through the body's core and aids digestion.

Tofu compress—This compress brings down a fever and relieves inflammation and swelling with its cooling effects. Tofu plaster can be used on a burn to relieve pain. When my girls were small, I kept a box of tofu in Tetra Packs in my cupboard, in case of an injury or sickness. Wrap a piece of tofu inside a piece of cheesecloth, and press to squeeze out excess water. Place it on your child's head for a fever, or other area of the body, for 15 to 20 minutes.

Chlorophyll compress—Leafy greens take heat out of the body and can be used to bring down a fever or reduce swelling. I usually applied the whole leaf directly to the forehead or injured area. Sometimes I alternated between a tofu and a leafy greens compress. This compress can be convenient to use if you are camping or hiking and have an accident.

Ginger compress or warm water bottle—Ginger is warming to the body when it is taken internally or applied externally. As a compress, it stimulates circulation in areas where there is pain, inflammation, or stiffness. The heat in the compress penetrates into the body and further activates blood circulation. Ginger is also good for congestion in the chest, constipation, and tightness in the muscles or organs. Fresh ginger root has a stronger stimulating effect, but you can substitute powdered ginger, if fresh ginger is not available. You can add ginger juice to sesame oil and massage it into acupuncture points, the chest, or areas of stagnated energy. Pour some ginger juice to bath water for increased circulation all over the body.

Ginger Compress Remedy

♡ 12 months+

🥄 1 compress

I used ginger compress to help Emi and Mari relax or to loosen up blockage from a cold or stagnation in their chest. If you do not have the ingredients, utensils, or time for a ginger compress, a hot water bottle or hot towel has a similar effect. Do not use heat treatments after strenuous activity, and be careful that neither the compress nor the bottle is too hot for your baby. You can use rubber gloves to squeeze out the hot water, if you have sensitive hands. If you do not boil the ginger water, you can save it and reuse it for additional compresses for 2-3 days.

3 cups water

1 tablespoon grated ginger

Special equipment:

Cheesecloth

Method

1. Place the water in a pan, and bring to a boil over medium-high heat.

2. Place the ginger in a piece of cheesecloth, and tie with a rubber band.

3. Place the bag of ginger in the hot water, and steep for 5 minutes.

4. Dip a hand towel in the hot ginger water, and squeeze out the liquid.

5. Place a thin dry towel on the area of the body that needs the compress.

6. Layer with the hot ginger towel and then another dry towel, making sure that it is not too hot.

7. Repeat dipping the towel in the hot ginger tea two or three times when the hot ginger towel cools.

Topical Treatments

Simple, natural treatments with sesame oil, rice or oat bran, calendula, comfrey, clay, and aloe vera can be helpful in treating skin disorders. Arnica is effective on bruises and sprains. Tea tree oil can be used as a disinfectant. If a skin condition persists or a symptom becomes worse, see your health care provider.

Sesame oil—Traditionally used in Japan for daily skin care and for problems such as eczema, diaper rash, and burns, sesame oil has external healing properties for the skin. It works well as a carrier oil for essential oils, and warmed sesame oil can be used for earaches. In addition to the nutrients that sesame oil provides to the skin, it is a healthful source of essential fatty acids. Rub a small amount of sesame oil on the infected area, or pour oil onto a cotton ball to place in your baby's ear if she has an earache.

Rice bran—Used in the same way as oat bran in the West, rice bran is a traditional preventive and natural-healing remedy in Japan. It is good for rashes and other skin issues. Place ¼ cup of rice or oat bran in a piece of cheesecloth and tie it with a rubber band. Dip the bag of bran into your baby's bathwater, and squeeze out the liquid as you wash her skin with the cloth. The milky liquid soothes itching, eczema, scrapes, and burns.

Calendula or comfrey salve—Both of these herbs have skin-healing properties that can treat eczema, diaper rash, cuts, and abrasions. For Emi's and Mari's scrapes and falls, I used "boo-boo goo" made with these herbs, grown by a local producer. You can find calendula or comfrey salve at most natural-food stores.

Eucalyptus chest rub—Eucalyptus menthol breaks up mucus and congestion in your baby's chest. Massage the cream into your baby's chest gently, and cover the treated area with a cotton cloth to protect clothing.

Clay—Bentonite clay, which is composed of volcanic ash, can be used topically for skin problems such as diaper rash, eczema, cuts, burns, and itching. Because it carries a negative charge and is highly porous when mixed with water, bentonite is known for its ability to absorb and remove the positive charge of toxins. At the same time, the clay releases minerals into the body and has an alkaline-producing effect. Apply clay directly to your baby's skin when it is dry, or mix it with water to make a poultice. Wrap a poultice with gauze, and change it every two hours. For a diaper-rash powder, mix the clay with arrowroot flour for a less granular texture. Do not let the clay come into contact with metal, because it will reduce the effectiveness.

Arnica—Used to reduce swelling and the pain of sprains, bruises, and insect bites, arnica can be applied directly to the affected area of the skin as a cream, an ointment, a liniment, a salve, or a tincture. Arnica is usually used topically and should not be used for long periods of time. I keep a tube of arnica cream in my first-aid kit in case of injuries.

Tea tree oil—This oil is used as an antiseptic and a disinfectant. It treats cuts, insect bites, poison-ivy reactions, and other skin problems. It should not be taken by mouth.

Aloe vera—This plant is used as a topical pain reliever, for treatment of psoriasis, eczema, poison ivy, and sunburn. It softens and moisturizes the skin. Aloe vera is known for having special healing capabilities. You can peel back a stem of the plant to get fresh aloe vera or buy aloe vera gel in the natural-food store or drugstore.

Essential Oils

Artificial scents and extreme flavors contain chemicals that can reduce an adult's sensory reaction by numbing the natural sense of smell and taste. Because babies' bodies are sensitive and unpolluted by chemicals, they are very responsive to natural scents. The smell of essential oils can easily relax or stimulate your baby's brain, thus causing psychological and physiological responses.

Essential oils are made from concentrated oils distilled from plants, seeds, bark, leaves, stems, roots, flowers, and fruits. Their characteristics can vary according to growing conditions, such as growing season, fertilizer, geographic location, climate, and altitude. The method of distillation is another factor that determines the quality of the oil. Low-grade oils may smell good, but if they are not naturally processed, they can have a toxic effect rather than a therapeutic one. Pure, therapeutic-grade essential oils are extracted from plants without the use of solvents. They are more effective in natural therapies because they are stronger. A high-quality oil softens the skin and provides nourishing vitamins. Its aroma and vibrational energy pass through your baby's skin as it is absorbed into her body. Her body absorbs small amounts of essential oils into her bloodstream, and the oils affect every cell in her body within 20 minutes. Here are six basic essential oils and their general uses.

Essential Oils		
Essential Oil	**Use**	**Where to Apply**
Chamomile	Relaxes; Anti-inflammatory; Nerve sedative; Neurological disorders; Relaxant for restlessness, hyperactivity, and crying; Digestive discomforts; Respiratory distress; Teething; Skin care; Mild fevers; Colic; All-purpose first aid	Stomach, spine, insides of arms, acupoints, gums, bottom for diaper rash; Place some oil on a tissue, and let your child smell the oil; Use in a diffuser, steamer, or add to bath
Eucalyptus	Clears and opens respiratory system and congestion; Calming and invigorating; Muscle aches; Increases circulation; Antiviral, antifungal, and antibacterial; General immunity; Purifies atmosphere	Lung meridian, acupoints, upper chest and back; Place some oil on a tissue, and let your child smell the oil; Use in a diffuser or steamer
Lavender	Relieves nervous tension, irritability, crying; Sedative for neurological or central nervous system disorders and insomnia; Decongestant for respiratory system; Headaches; Skin care; Antiviral and antibacterial; Boosts immunity; Supports mental clarity; All-purpose first aid	Stomach or digestive meridian, lungs or lung meridian, acupoints, kidney, forehead or back of head, upper chest and back, bottom for diaper rash; Place some oil on a tissue, and let your child smell the oil; Use in a diffuser or steamer, or add to bath
Lemon	Brightens and freshens; Promotes clear thinking; Invigorating, warming, and enhancing; Circulatory, digestive, and respiratory problems; Antiseptic (inactivates bacteria and parasites); Anxiety and hypertension; Immune-system stimulant	Upper chest and back, acupoints; Use as a room freshener or in laundry; Place some oil on a tissue and let your child smell the oil; Use in a diffuser or steamer; Avoid applying to skin that will be exposed to sunlight within 24 hours
Rose	Soothes the soul; Overheating and tension; Lifts mood and atmosphere; Antiseptic, antiviral; Skin conditions	Bladder, liver, or stomach meridians, stomach, acupoints for digestive problems; Use in a diffuser or steamer, or add to bath
Tea tree or melaleuca	Natural antibacterial, antifungal, antibiotic remedy; Immune stimulant; Earaches; Burns; Abscesses; Decongestant; All-purpose first aid	Apply directly to area that needs treatment; Acupoints, ears, upper chest or back; Use in a diffuser or steamer

Essential oils are used in aromatherapy to regenerate and oxygenate the immune system. Because of their concentration, essential oils used for babies and young children need to be diluted with a plant-based carrier oil. Appropriate carrier oils include sesame, olive, almond, apricot, grapeseed, avocado, and jojoba. (If your child is allergic to nuts, then almond oil could cause an allergic reaction.) Follow these dosage guidelines:

❀ Use 1 or 2 drops of essential oil in 2 tablespoons of carrier oil for an infant.

❀ Use 1 or 2 drops of essential oil in 1 tablespoon of carrier oil for 1- to 3-year-old children.

When combining essential oils with a carrier oil, make sure that you shake and mix them well, because some oils are heavy and others are light, with a tendency to separate from the diluting oil. Oil that has not been exposed to high heat or is cold-pressed will stay fresh longer. To keep oil fresh and to prevent rancidity, store it away from heat and light.

You can use essential oils to strengthen and support your baby's internal organs and chi flow by applying them to her meridians and acupoints. To nourish her digestive system, you can apply chamomile to points on her stomach meridian. For respiratory congestion, you can use eucalyptus on her lung meridian.

According to Jean-Claude Lapraz, a French physician and a cofounder of Endobiogenics (an approach to medicine that involves using medicinal plants and essential oils to treat many kinds of sicknesses), people can use essential oils to sedate energy, to stimulate circulation, to break up mucus, to reduce aches and pains, and to build immunity. In addition, essential oils can counteract fungi, parasites, bacteria, and viruses. They have a probiotic effect, promoting beneficial bacteria, while disrupting the life cycles of harmful bacteria and increasing ions that inhibit bacterial growth.

To help an essential oil enter your baby's system quickly, massage her feet with it, or put some into her bathwater. A warm, aromatic bath can relax your baby, increase her circulation, and help expel toxins from her body. Rose, chamomile, and lavender are especially relaxing in a bath before bedtime.

Essential oils destroy odors from mold, animals, and cigarette smoke, so they are useful for freshening and cleaning your home. Use a few drops of lemon, tea tree, or lavender oil to sanitize and freshen your diaper pail, laundry, cleaning products, and drawers.

To freshen the air with essential oils, you can use a simmer pot, a small pot used to combine oils with water and heat them with either a candle or electricity. An aroma lamp is similar to a simmer pot but does not require water. Instead, you place either pure oil or oil mixed with a carrier oil directly on the warming area; heat via electricity or a candle moves the scent into the air. A few drops of diluted essential oil on a burp cloth, doll, or favorite toy can also calm or energize your baby.

Babies and children respond to smaller quantities of essential oils than adults do, and an excessive amount of oil can actually be harmful. More is not better. Your baby's eyes and face are delicate areas, so avoid putting essential oils there. Some essential oils are photosensitive; they should not be applied to your baby's skin and then exposed to sunlight because they can cause a rash or a burn. Be sure to keep essential oils out of the reach of children.

There are many different oils, but if you are new to using them, you may want to keep it simple.

❀ Digestive—chamomile, lavender, lemon

❀ Respiratory—chamomile, eucalyptus, lavender, lemon, tea tree

❀ Skin—chamomile, lavender, lemon, rose, tea tree

❀ Energy—chamomile, lavender, lemon, rose

Guidelines for Preparing Your Baby's Bath with Essential Oils

- For babies three months to one year, one drop is enough for a bath.

- For children one to three years, one or two drops is sufficient.

- Mix the essential oil into whole milk separately before pouring the mixture into the bath, and then stir the bathwater to make sure the oil is completely diluted; otherwise it will float on top of the water. Too strong of a concentration can be irritating to your baby's skin.

Note: Essential oils in bathwater are not recommended for babies under three months old.

Acupoint Massage

East Asian medicine applies the laws and patterns of nature to the treatment of illness, as well as to the process of diagnosis. Just as a plant "knows" how to use nutrients, water, and sunshine to nourish itself and to grow, your baby's body has a natural intelligence. This healing energy is a self-generating, renewable resource that is always in motion. It is life seeking itself.

According to traditional Eastern philosophers, all organic and inorganic substances in the universe are made up of energy called chi. Chi is the vital life force that moves the wind and the planets, creates electricity and magnetism on Earth, and generates movement and breath in your baby's body. If you watch her crawling, you can see the energy moving through her body. She is very sensitive to this flow of chi, which is basic to the survival and health of all living things.

Your baby's chi comes from her constitution along with energy from food and breathing. According to East Asian medicine, your baby's chi starts flowing after she is born. Disharmony can occur if she has chi deficiency—if her chi stagnates or flows in the wrong direction. Maladies such as pain, headache, and stomachache result from chi stagnation.

Three thousand years ago, Chinese Taoists mapped out a network of 12 meridians, or channels, along which chi travels in the body. The aim of traditional East Asian medicine is to enhance and regulate the smooth, balanced flow of chi through the meridians. Twelve of the major internal organs in the human body correspond to the 12 main meridians. If an internal organ is out of balance, the chi of that organ is affected. Imagine that in a system of garden hoses, too much water flows in one area and too little flows in the other. Once the restriction is released, water flows through the whole system more smoothly.

Your baby's meridian network links meridians to each other and connects all her body structures, including her skin, tendons, bones, internal organs, and even cells. In addition, her meridians connect the interior of her body with the exterior, and her upper body with her lower body. The meridians affect all the systems of her body, including her immune, nervous, endocrine, circulatory, digestive, skeletal, muscular, and lymphatic systems. Stimulation of points along her meridians can affect the condition of a specific organ. Likewise, changes in her organs can create changes in her meridians. If the energy of a meridian is obstructed, then the system that it feeds on is weakened, and this weakening will show up in your baby as illness. When there are no blockages, chi flows smoothly and organs work in harmony; your baby's body functions effectively, builds and repairs itself, and avoids disease.

At some points in its journey through your baby's meridians, chi comes to the surface of her body in pools, like amplifiers of energy. These points are called acupoints, and they are used for acupuncture and acupressure. Acupoints are junctures with a higher sensitivity for conducting energy along a meridian. This is why you can treat your baby's stomach by massaging a point on her leg.

Acupoint stimulation helps balance the flow of chi along a meridian as it travels to its respective organ. It also works to strengthen and tonify a weak point and to disperse a stagnant point. The most powerful acupoints are on your baby's extremities, especially in the areas from her elbows to her fingertips and from her knees to the tips of her toes. Yang meridians descend from the back of the arms to the head, down the back, and then to the back of the legs to the toes. Yin meridians ascend from the insides of the legs, up along the front and inside of the body, and along the insides of the arms to the fingertips. In addition to the 12 main meridians, there are 8 extraordinary meridians. Of the extraordinary meridians, only 2 have their own acupoints. Yin and yang meridians are paired: liver-gallbladder, heart-small intestine, spleen-stomach, lung-large intestine, and kidney-urinary bladder.

By paying attention to where a rash, bruise, or other irregularity falls along meridians or acupoints, you can gain insight into both the source of an illness and your child's condition. Extreme foods and medications can block your

Mari and Zo

baby's chi flow and interrupt her inherent potential to heal. Her chi is her own best healer, and it is always available, persistently waiting in her body for a nudge to come forth and awaken her potential to blossom and to flourish. By understanding the meridian system and by learning a few acupoints, you can nourish your child's health with preventive measures such as massage, yoga, and exercise, and you can counteract sickness by stimulating acupoints with massage or essential oils.

Technically, acupuncture is the act of inserting thin needles into acupoints to balance chi flow by dispersing or tonifying energy. In acupoint therapy, hands and fingers stimulate acupoints for the same purpose. Traditional Japanese pediatric acupuncture is called *shonishin*. Practitioners of *shonishin* use special instruments or electrical-stimulation devices that do

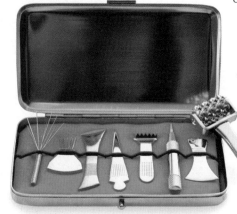

Shonishin (Pediatric Acupuncture) Kit

not pierce a child's skin. However, some practitioners use regular acupuncture needles that pierce the skin of older children.

Because the chi, skin, and muscles of babies and children are sensitive, they respond well and quickly to acupoint stimulation. Babies' bodies are cleaner and more accessible than adults' bodies because they are small and young and have not accumulated a lot of excess. Because frequent stimulation yields better results, East Asian practitioners often instruct parents to massage their children to complement professional treatments.

In general, natural healing is milder and slower to get results than drugs and surgery. Therefore, natural treatments are most effective when they are used regularly over time. Short, repetitive acupoint treatments will have the most impact on your child's condition. This pattern of treatment gives you multiple chances to observe your child's reactions and to make adjustments.

Preparing yourself to treat your child

Babies and children are sensitive to their environment. When you work on your child, you share her energy field and state of mind, so it is helpful for you to remain calm and centered. Here are some guidelines for preparing to perform acupoint massage:

❀ Ensure the room you are using is warm. Use a blanket for cover, if needed.

❀ Make sure your fingernails are cut short and your hands are clean.

❀ Sit quietly for four to five minutes and breathe deeply, with your attention on your breath.

❀ Rub your hands together to warm them while thinking healing, loving, and positive thoughts.

❀ Use touch as a way of connecting with your baby and helping her relax.

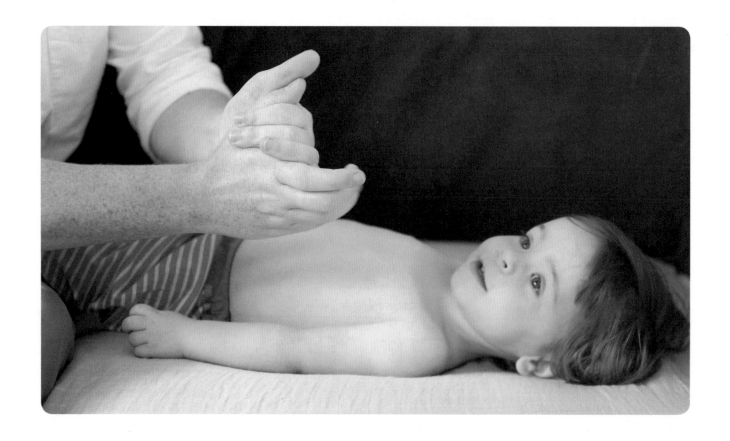

Preparing your child for treatment

A daily massage can provide your child with tactile stimulation, increase her body awareness, soothe her, and strengthen her bond with you. You will most likely use acupoint massage when she is sick or not feeling well, so the atmosphere will differ from that of your daily-care massages. Your baby's state of mind helps determine the effectiveness of the treatment; you can help her relax and open up to acupoint massage by starting with gentle massage. Here are some steps to calm your child so that she feels safe, comfortable, and receptive during treatment:

- Position your child on a sofa, bed, blanket, or mat on the floor, and make sure she is comfortable.

- Make sure she is warm enough (but not hot). Remember, "warm feet, cool head."

- Calm your child with gentle massage strokes on the back of her head, on her forehead, and around the upper sides of her ears.

- Massage down her arms, legs, and back with soothing, gentle strokes from the top to the bottom of her body to help her relax and reorient her energies.

Acupoint massage treatment

Because babies and children are smaller than adults, stimulating specific points is not as important as working in the general area of the points. Your child's body is flexible, and her chi energy is at the surface of the skin, so a light touch is usually enough. The younger your baby, the lighter the touch—an older child can handle more pressure. Watch your child's response to make sure that you are not pressing too hard. Focus on lightly pressing your finger in a circular motion on an acupoint rather than applying strong pressure; your treatment should not be painful for her.

Depending on your child's condition, you can do this two or more times a day. When performing acupoint treatments, it is helpful to know that in East

Steps for At-home Treatment

- Listen to your child's body with your hands and fingers to assess warmth, coldness, tightness, and looseness.

- Generally, make massage strokes in the directions of her meridians. Yang meridians go down, and yin meridians go up.

- Use one, two, or three fingers for massaging a point, depending on the size of the area and the size of your fingers.

- Use a firm but gentle touch.

- For a mild effect, rub the area gently. For a stronger effect, move your fingers in a circular motion.

- Massage each point or area for 30 to 60 seconds.

Asian medicine, the outside of your child's body is considered to be yang, while the inside is considered yin. Her yang outer body is stronger and tougher; it is a protective shield for her yin—the vulnerable inside of her body. The yang meridians are on the back of her body and move downward in the following order: head, back, backs of arms, buttocks, backs of legs, and outsides of legs. The yin meridians for the inside of her body move upward in this order: insides of legs, front of body, and insides of arms. Therefore, for general therapeutic massage, massage her body in the direction of the flow of energy—down her back and up her front. The meridians are based on the position of the arms being raised above her head.

In East Asian massage practice, your baby's *hara* (belly) is the center of her body. Rub her abdomen in a clockwise circle—the same direction as the flow of the intestines. You can assist in moving and unblocking your child's stagnated, weak, or excessive energy through massage. By being in close contact with her and listening to her body, you can develop your understanding and intuition about her condition.

Baby Body Meridians

Large Intestine (LI) Meridian (Yang)

Partner: Lung Meridian

Location: Starts on the index finger and flows up the outer arm, over the shoulder to the outside of the nose.

Association: Metabolizes water and eliminates waste

Points to Use: LI 3, LI 11
Massage up the meridian*

Lung (LU) Meridian (Yin)

Partner: Large Intestine Meridian

Location: Begins at the middle of the body and flows to the top of the chest, then down the inner arm ending at the thumb.

Association: Adminsters respiration of moisture and air

Points to Use: LU 1, LU 5, LU 7, LU 10
Massage down the meridian*

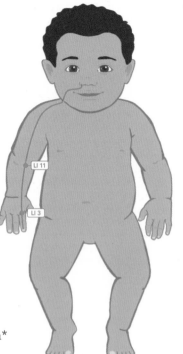

Stomach (ST) Meridian (Yang)

Partner: Spleen Meridian

Location: Begins below the eye and goes up and back down to the bottom of the cheek and then goes down the body through the digestive system ending at the second toe.

Association: Digests food

Points to Use: ST 25, ST 36, ST 40
Massage down the meridian*

Spleen (SP) Meridian (Yin)

Partner: Stomach Meridian

Location: Begins at the big toe and goes up the inside of the leg to the abdomen and chest and then to the side of the body.

Association: Regulates digestion

Points to Use: SP 3, SP 6, SP 9
Massage up the meridian*

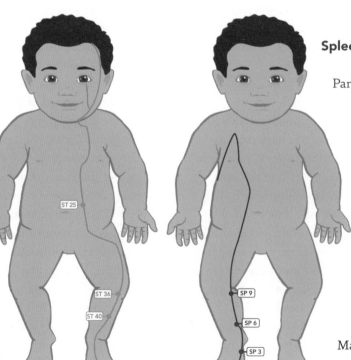

*Meridian flow direction is based on the arms being raised. Meridians are on both right and left sides of the body.

Baby Body Meridians

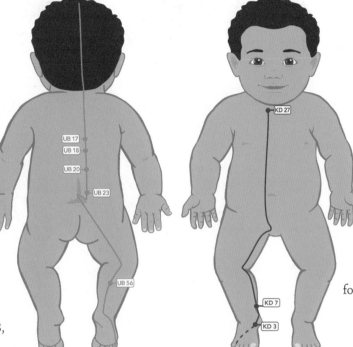

Bladder (UB) Meridian (Yang)

Partner: Kidney Meridian

Location: Starts at the inner corner of the eye and goes over the head, then down the back to the back of the knee, ending at the fifth toe.

Association: Stores wastes before elimination

Points to Use: UB 17, UB 18, UB 20, UB 23, UB 57
Massage down the meridian*

Kidney (KD) Meridian (Yin)

Partner: Bladder Meridian

Location: Begins at the inner tip of the little toe and goes under the foot and up the inner leg and up to the kidneys, then up the abdomen and chest.

Association: Stores chi for growth and development

Points to Use: KD 3, KD 7, KD 27
Massage up the meridian*

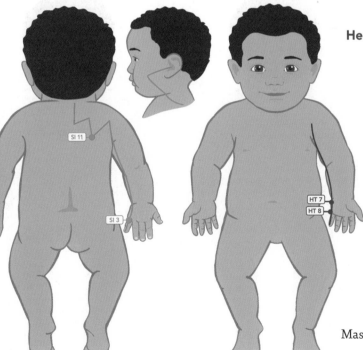

Small Intestine (SI) Meridian (Yang)

Partner: Heart Meridian

Location: Begins at the tip of the little finger and goes up the outer arm and over the shoulder, then over to the face and ear.

Association: Assimilation and movement of food

Points to Use: SI 3, SI 11
Massage up the meridian*

Heart (HT) Meridian (Yin)

Partner: Small Intestine

Location: Begins at the heart and goes to the armpit and down the inner arm ending at the tip of the little finger.

Association: Controls blood flow

Points to Use: HT 7, HT 8
Massage down the meridian*

*Meridian flow direction is based on the arms being raised. Meridians are on both right and left sides of the body.

Baby Body Meridians

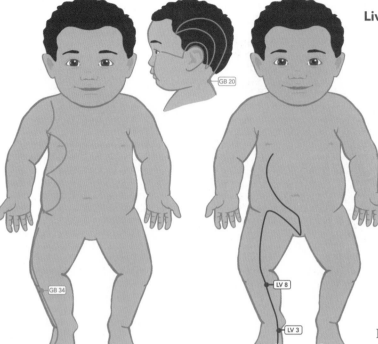

Gallbladder (GB) Meridian (Yang)

Partner: Liver Meridian

Location: Begins at the eye and goes up on the temples and neck, over the shoulder and along the side of the body, to the outer leg and ending at the fourth toe.

Association: Stores and secretes bile

Points to Use: GB 20, GB 34 Massage down the meridian*

Liver (LV) Meridian (Yin)

Partner: Gallbladder Meridian

Location: Begins at the top of the big toe, goes up the inner leg, through the genitalia, over the abdomen, and ends at the center of the ribs.

Association: Regulates emotions and the smooth flow of chi

Points to Use: LV 3, LV 8 Massage up the meridian*

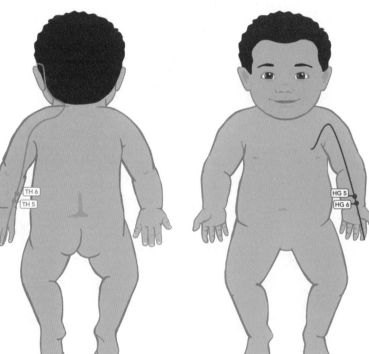

Triple Heater (TH) Meridian (Yang)

Partner: Heart Governor Meridian

Location: Begins at the tip of the fourth finger and goes up the outer arm and over the shoulder , behind the ear and ends at the eyebrow.

Association: Supports digestion, assimilation, and elimination

Points to Use: TH 5, TH 6 Massage up the meridian*

Heart Governor (HG) Meridian (Yin)

Partner: Triple Heater Meridian

Location: Begins in the chest and crosses to the inner arm and down to the tip of the middle finger.

Association: Governs blood circulation and emotions

Points to Use: HG 5, HG 6 Massage down the meridian*

*Meridian flow direction is based on the arms being raised. Meridians are on both right and left sides of the body.

Baby Body Meridians

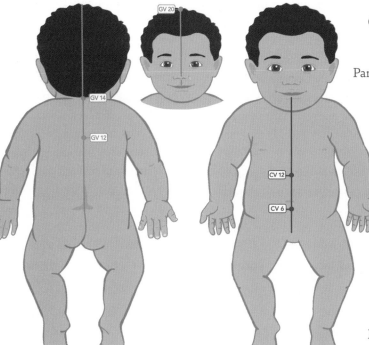

Governing (GV) Meridian (Yang)

Partner: Conception Vessel Meridian

Location: Begins at the tailbone and goes up the spine, over the head, and down the nose, into the upper teeth.

Association: Governs the chi of all the yang meridians

Points to Use: GV 12, GV 14, GV 20
Massage up for problems in the upper body and down for problems in the lower body

Conception Vessel (CV) Merdian (Yin)

Partner: Governing Meridian

Location: Begins at the perineum and goes up the front of the body ending at the bottom of the lips.

Association: Governs the chi of all the yin meridians

Points to Use: CV 6, CV 12
Massage up the meridian*

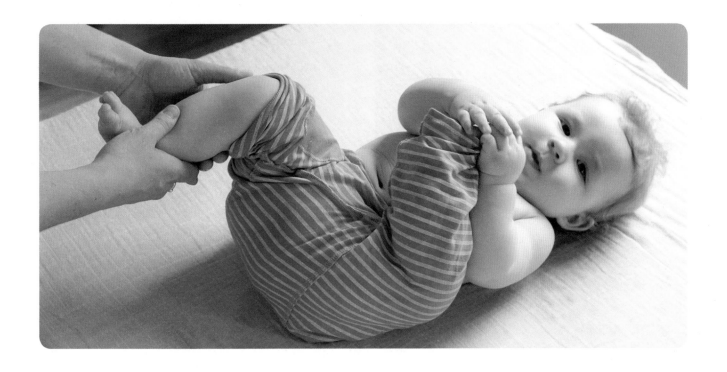

Reiki

Reiki is a way to nourish your child with your touch when she is not feeling well. This technique involves using your palms as conductors of healing energy through massage and touch. People automatically place a hand on their stomach if they have a belly-ache or a hand on their head if they have an accidental bump. This type of touch or light rub, which is an intuitive way of gathering energy to stimulate circulation around an injured or sick area, is the basis of Reiki.

In Japan, Mikao Usui, PhD was the founder of Reiki, a traditional method of healing with the hands that draws on universal energy to support the body's innate healing abilities. Usui taught more than 2,000 people his philosophy, and his students eventually adapted Reiki for the Western world as a support for conventional care.

It was very painful for me when my children were sick. If I could have absorbed their pain into myself, I would have done it. When my daughters were not feeling well, I imagined that my arms worked like a fire hose, with strong energy flowing through them the way water flows through a hose turned on high. I practiced Reiki by placing my palms on their belly, back, chest, head, neck, legs, arms, ears, or throat, depending on the kind of sickness they had or the locations of discomfort. Then I concentrated my energy in a loving and prayerful way. This was something I could do while I waited for their bodies to heal. Breathing exercises helped me get more in sync with their energy while holding my hands on them.

Usui had many techniques for specific illnesses, but his primary concerns were positive intentionality and overall care for his patients. You can easily follow these principles with your child.

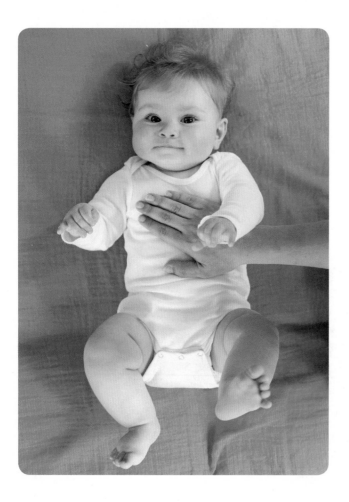

Basic Guidelines to Perform Reiki

1. Meditate, and ask for natural healing power to flow through you.

2. Vigorously rub your palms together to energize your chi.

3. Open up to the energy in your hands, and trust that they will know where to go and what to do.

4. Place your hands on the area of the body targeted for treatment, and listen through your hands.

5. There are no rules about the length of time that you keep your hands in a particular position. Follow your intuition and your hands.

6. You can also do breathing exercises and say a prayer for the health and wholeness of your child.

Natural First-aid Kit

Just as most homes have a conventional first-aid kit, you can create a natural first-aid kit that includes everything you need for emergencies. Place the items in a sturdy box or bag so that you can easily carry the kit when you are on the go. Be prepared for cuts, bee stings, bug bites, motion sickness, burns, food poisoning, poison ingestion, infection, fever, bruises, nosebleeds, choking, cold, flu, and digestive upset.

In addition, make a list of emergency numbers. Keep one copy in the first-aid kit, and post another copy in a location that is in sight and obvious to anyone who cares for your child. Include the phone numbers of your baby's health care provider, the poison control center, and the nearest hospital or medical center.

In addition to being prepared with a first-aid kit and emergency numbers, you may save your child's life by learning how to do CPR and the Heimlich maneuver. Classes in these and other first-aid techniques are often offered at the local YMCA or community health organization.

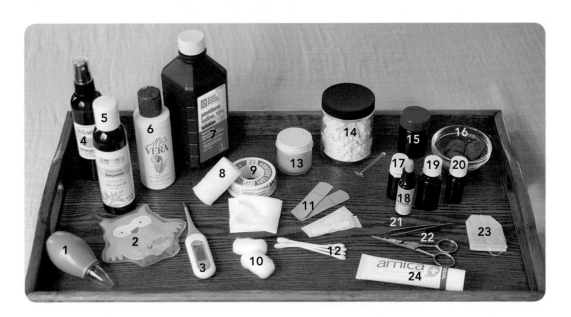

Supplies for Your Natural First-Aid Kit

- ☐ 1. Nasal aspirator
- ☐ 2. Warm and cool packs
- ☐ 3. Thermometer
- ☐ 4. Natural insect repellent
- ☐ 5. Sesame oil
- ☐ 6. Aloe vera
- ☐ 7. Povidone-iodine solution
- ☐ 8. Gauze pads and rolls
- ☐ 9. Adhesive tape
- ☐ 10. Cotton balls
- ☐ 11. Bandages
- ☐ 12. Swabs
- ☐ 13. Calendula or comfrey salve
- ☐ 14. Kuzu
- ☐ 15. *Umeboshi* plum extract
- ☐ 16. *Umeboshi* plums
- ☐ 17. Lavender oil
- ☐ 18. Bach Flower Rescue Remedy
- ☐ 19. Tea tree oil
- ☐ 20. Royal chamomile oil
- ☐ 21. Tweezers
- ☐ 22. Small scissors
- ☐ 23. Chamomile and fennel teas
- ☐ 24. Arnica (for bruises, aches, and pains)

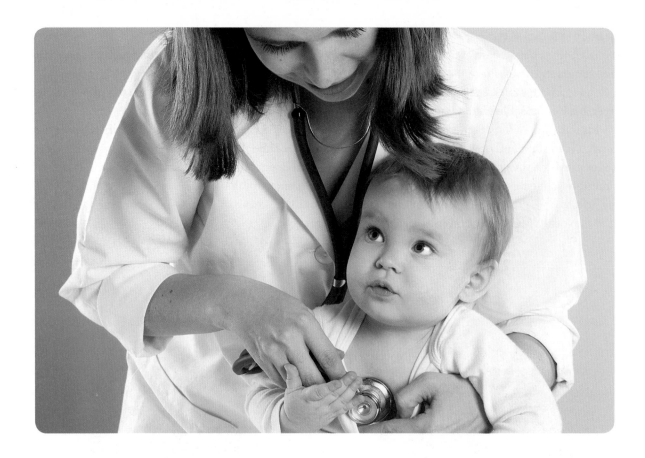

Choosing a Health Care Provider

Your choice of a health care provider has a significant impact on your child. This decision starts with considering your priorities. What are your main concerns regarding your child's health and needs? Are you interested in holistic health or conventional medicine? What kind of relationship would you like to have with your health care provider? Do you seek a partnership in which you are an active participant, or a person who provides authority and direct guidance? It is helpful to educate yourself about health care options and to get clear about the role that you want to play in this aspect of your baby's life.

More specifically, are you looking for a pediatrician who specializes in the care of children, a family-practice doctor who treats your whole family, or an integrative medicine practitioner who combines Western medicine with complementary or alternative treatments that involve the whole person?

As you research options, consider each potential provider's point of view and general philosophy on the following topics:

- Exercise
- Diet
- Integrative or alternative medicine
- Antibiotics
- Immunizations

When you trust that your provider is concerned about your child's health, you are likely to have peace of mind when she is healthy or sick. Considerations for building trust include the provider's level of competence, your relationship and how you communicate, and logistics that meet your needs.

❀ **Competence**—In evaluating your provider's ability to provide quality care for your child, ask about her reputation, degrees, licenses, and certifications. How long has she been practicing, and what kind of experience has she had? How healthy and happy does the health care provider seem?

❀ **Environment**—Is the atmosphere in the provider's office clean and orderly, with sensitivity to your child's needs? Is the staff personable or hurried while communicating? Does the environment feel loving, nourishing, comfortable, and safe for you and your child?

❀ **Communication**—The way that you communicate with your child's provider can make a big difference in your ability to work together for the care of your child. Does the provider collaborate with you as a partner and listen respectfully to your thoughts and concerns? Does she tend to ask for your opinion, or does she tend to give directions? Does she return phone calls? What is her after-hours policy? How does the provider interact with and relate to your child?

❀ **Logistics**—If the provider is popular, she might be especially busy. If the office atmosphere is hurried, however, your child might not get the attention that she needs. What are the office hours? How long does it take to get an appointment? How organized is the office when it comes to returning phone calls and keeping records? What are the costs involved with using this provider, and do they fit with your budget and health care plan? Is the location convenient to your home and workplace?

❀ **Research**—Thorough research educates you and helps you set your priorities. Recommendations and references from other parents and online reviews can help give you an idea of the provider's reputation. Set up an interview with the provider, and talk with the staff to get an understanding of the environment. Keep an eye out for red flags such as staff that seem too busy to help, disorder, and an unhappy environment.

❀ **Your Role**—You can actively participate in your child's health care by educating yourself about her constitution and condition. To support your child's health proactively, you can offer love, care, healthy food, exercise, fresh air, sunshine, and a positive environment every day. When she is sick, you can give her natural remedies and treatments, pay attention to her condition, and make notes to share with her provider. Use a journal to keep track of regular visits to your child's health care provider. By staying confident in your intuition and advocating for your child when necessary, you can play an essential role in her health care. You are the adult consumer in this provider-patient relationship, so be intentional, and speak up about your concerns.

Body Systems and Related Common Childhood Illnesses

As part of your baby's physical development, she will suffer illnesses on occasion. There is nothing more worrisome for a parent than a sick child. However, by educating yourself about a few fundamentals of illness and treatment, you can contribute proactively to your child's healing from the majority of sicknesses that come her way. In addition, when a condition or illness does warrant a visit to the doctor, your efforts at being informed make you a strong advocate for your child. You know what questions to ask, you have ideas and concerns to explore, and you can intelligently weigh your doctor's suggested treatment options.

Even with the best health care provider on your side, as the parent, you will probably be the person to nurse your child though any illnesses that she may encounter. From the perspective of East Asian medicine, sickness is the result of imbalance, and healing means supporting your child's body to bring her condition toward the center of the yin-yang spectrum. The mild, noninvasive techniques of natural healing discussed earlier in this chapter help you support your child and make her comfortable as her body's systems work to restore balance. In addition, your careful observation and attention to her overall condition provide valuable information for your health care provider in case your child's illness requires professional attention.

Your baby's body systems work together to keep her functioning and to help her body convert, use, and store elements that produce blood and other cells, as well as bone and muscle tissue, and then discharge any excesses. Every single second, these systems automatically support her breathing, digestion, and elimination of waste.

As she grew inside the womb, some of these systems were unnecessary. Because your baby received her nourishment through her umbilical cord, she did not need to digest any food. She did not breathe air through her lungs, and the womb protected her from outside pathogens. For the first year of her life, your baby's immune, digestive, and respiratory systems are still developing. Thus, the majority of common illnesses in infancy and early childhood stem from the immaturity of these systems.

Signals That Warrant a Call to Your Health Care Provider

- A fever over 102°F
- Pain
- Severe vomiting or diarrhea
- Stomach cramps
- Blood in urine or stool
- Black stool
- Convulsions or seizures
- Persistent crying
- Lethargy, drowsiness, or unresponsiveness
- Cough with rasping sound
- Difficulty breathing
- Excessive drooling
- Discharge from eyes or ears
- Green mucus from nose
- Swelling around the mouth, lip, face, or eyes
- Paleness
- Rash accompanied by fever
- Purple or red spots on the skin
- Jaundice
- Dehydration; refusal to drink or eat for more than eight hours
- Lack of improvement when ill
- Unexplained or unexpected weight loss
- A feeling or intuition that you should call

Your baby's bodily systems are continually moving toward a harmonious condition by coordinating efforts to maintain a stable internal temperature and environment. Her body regularly adjusts imbalances through temperature changes, thirst urges, hunger urges, metabolism, acid and alkaline balance, and regulation of yin and yang. You can promote your baby's optimal physical health and natural healing intelligence through the daily actions listed earlier in this chapter. These bodily systems are the foundation for her physical health, which is interrelated with her emotional and mental health.

Most disease occurs when a disturbance to this balance causes stress in your baby's body. An understanding of her body's systems can help you support her as she works to regain balance. In this section you will find simple explanations of each body system, accompanied by related common childhood illnesses and conditions.

The body systems with related illnesses listed are:

🌸 Lymphatic and Immune Systems—Fever; Allergies

🌸 Digestive and Urinary Systems—Diarrhea; Constipation; Colic; Stomach upset and vomiting; Hiccups; Teething

🌸 Respiratory System—Croup, cough; Sore throat, strep throat; Cold; Earache and ear infection; Asthma

🌸 Integumentary System—Eczema, cradle cap; Diaper rash; Conjunctivitis (pinkeye)

🌸 Nervous System—Insomnia; Hyperactivity

🌸 Endocrine System—Jaundice

🌸 Muscular and Skeletal Systems

🌸 Circulatory System

🌸 Reproductive System

For each illness, you will find the following information:

• General Information

• Symptoms and Causes

• Suggestions for Care—Food or remedies, topical treatments or compresses, essential oils, acupoints, Reiki, and massage

• Prevention

• Concerns

Refer to the previous sections of this chapter for recipes, preparation methods, and information about how to apply these treatments and remedies.

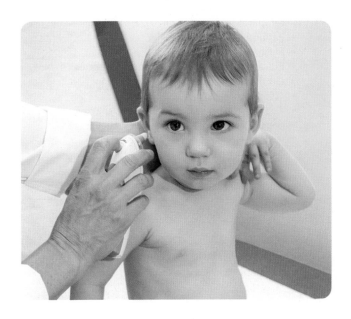

Your Baby's Lymphatic and Immune Systems

Your baby's lymphatic system facilitates her immune response to defend against disease. Her immune system includes her bone marrow, lymphatic, spleen, and liver. Her lymphatic system balances her bodily fluids and provides the mechanisms that filter toxins from her blood, including the spleen. The best ways for you to strengthen your baby's immune system are to continue to breast-feed her, provide whole and fermented foods at the appropriate ages, and avoid refined sugar products.

Common childhood illnesses connected to the lymphatic and immune systems include fever and allergies.

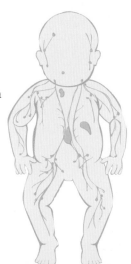

Illness: Fever
System: Immune

A fever is not by itself an illness. It is the body's natural defense to systemic infection caused by bacteria or viruses. In most cases a fever is not dangerous. On the contrary, fever can help your baby fight off infection and help her get rest. Occasional fevers, as well as the viruses and bacteria that cause them, are part of how children build a robust immune system.

Your baby's hypothalamus gland regulates her body's temperature, keeping it around 98.7°F most of the time. With a fever, the hypothalamus turns up the heat, which signals her immune system to act and makes her body less hospitable to pathogens. The measure of a temperature does not correlate to the severity of the disease or stressor. Children routinely run fevers that are higher than those in adults.

In general, fever can be viewed as your child's partner in health. In the past, parents were advised to suppress fever. Now, most health care providers advise parents simply to keep their fevered children comfortable and hydrated and to monitor their temperature.

Fever: Symptoms

- Body temperature above 99°F (normal body temperature ranges from 97°F to 99°F)
- Fatigue, lethargy, irritability
- Flushed face
- Elevated breathing, pulse, and heart rates
- Little to no appetite
- Thirst
- Accompanying symptoms such as sneezing, cough, vomiting, diarrhea, headaches, sore throat, sweating, nasal discharge

Fever: Causes

The causes of fever range from a serious disease to simple overheating. When a fever is present, something else is usually off balance in your child's body. Here are some common causes of fever:

- Bacteria or virus
- A developing chronic condition
- Exhaustion, overexertion, or overstimulation
- Reaction to a vaccination
- Teething
- Dehydration
- Rapid temperature changes in your child's environment, such as seasonal changes
- Any type of body stressor

Fever: Prevention

Fever is a sign that your child's immune system is working. It is not an illness in itself; rather, it alerts you to illness. You can help your child avoid fevers caused by environmental factors by taking care that she does not become overstimulated, stressed, overheated, or exposed to extreme temperature changes.

Fever: Suggestions for Care

When your child has a fever, she needs rest and a calm environment. If possible, keep her at home from school, child care, and other activities. Once her temperature returns to normal, keep her at home for another 24 hours, if possible, to help her regain her strength.

While your child has a fever, encourage her to rest, sleep, and drink plenty of fluids to stay hydrated. Perspiration helps release excess salts and restore balance. In the early stages of a fever, keep her covered, but be careful that she is not wrapped so tightly that she overheats and develops a higher fever. On the other hand, take care that she does not become chilled, which can lead to shivering and thus can increase her fever.

A lukewarm bath can help your child feel better when she has a fever. You can add several cups of chamomile, or other herbal tea, to her bath for a soothing effect. When your child has a fever, do not bathe her in a cold bath or a bath containing rubbing alcohol, which can constrict her blood vessels and make it difficult for her skin to expel excess heat and toxins.

Food and Remedies for Nursing Mother or Baby Older than Six Months

Most children have a low appetite during a fever, so do not worry if your child does not want to eat. Keep her hydrated, and make sure she gets enough nutrients to maintain her strength.

Foods to Emphasize	Foods to Avoid
Water, diluted herbal teas, broths, and rehydrating fluids; simple and easy-to-digest foods such as soft rice porridge and steamed or fresh vegetables and fruits. Other remedies include miso soup, kuzu, and herbal tea, such as chamomile.	Eggs, meat, milk, and sugar.

Essential Oils for Baby	Acupoints for Baby
Lavender, eucalyptus, lemon	Large intestine 11; stomach 36; heart governor 6; gallbladder 20; liver 3; governing vessel 14

Reiki for Baby	Massage for Baby
For two or more minutes, place your hands on the following parts of your child's body: forehead, temples, back of head, back of neck, throat, top of head, stomach, and intestines.	• Massage down the breastbone to her navel. • Massage your baby's upper chest from her breastbone outward. • Massage down the center of her spine and on either side. Pay special attention to her shoulder blades. • Massage your baby's large-intestine channel. Pay special attention to the points on her hand, and work from her shoulder to her fingertip.

Fever: Concerns

Your child's behavior is an indicator of the seriousness of her illness. If she continues to play and to drink fluids, then her body is probably healing by itself. If she is lethargic, even if her fever is mild, then her condition may be more serious. Call for professional medical assistance when your child fits any of these criteria:

• Is under three months old and has a rectal temperature above 100.4°F
• Is three to six months old and has a rectal temperature above 101°F
• Is between six months and two years old and has a rectal temperature above 102.2°F
• Has a fever of 104°F or above at any age

Illness: Allergies
System: Immune

Allergies are reactions of the immune system to a particular substance, such as dust, a plant, an insect bite, or a food. When the body is exposed to that substance, the immune response kicks in and forms antibodies to attack the substance. The antibodies then produce histamines that cause the typical allergic reactions of itchiness, watery eyes, and a runny nose. Most allergies are more bothersome than serious. However, an allergic response can result in anaphylaxis—a drop in blood pressure, extreme swelling, and an inability to breathe. This can be serious if it is not treated immediately.

If you suspect your baby has an allergy, ask your health care provider to recommend an allergist, who can provide a confirmed diagnosis, discuss treatment options, and help you design a plan. Be sure that all the people who care for your baby understand her allergy and know what to do in case of a reaction. When your child is old enough, teach her about her allergy, so she knows how to manage it herself.

Allergies: Symptoms

- Itchy nose and throat
- Congestion, sneezing, runny nose
- Watery eyes
- Difficulty breathing
- Itchy skin
- Swelling or hives
- Itchy mouth and throat
- Throat tightening
- Difficulty breathing
- Nausea, diarrhea, or inflammation in intestines (with food allergies)

Allergies: Causes

The following common allergens cause allergic reactions in many people:
- Foods, such as cow's milk, eggs, peanuts, seafood, shellfish, wheat, gluten, and corn
- Irritants in the air, such as pollen, dust mites, pet dander, and cigarette smoke
- Mold or spores
- Insect bites or stings
- Plants, such as grass, poison ivy, and poison oak
- Wool
- Emotional stress

Allergies: Prevention

The best ways to prevent an allergy are to build your baby's immune system and to avoid the allergen. If your baby is suffering from an airborne allergen, you may consider a high-efficiency particulate absorption (HEPA) air-filtration system for your home or a vacuum cleaner with HEPA filtration. In addition, special coverings for pillows and mattresses can protect against dust mites, feathers, and other irritating particles. If the allergy is seasonal, you can help minimize irritation by keeping your windows and doors closed during peak times. To prevent food allergies, try breast-feeding solely for the first six months. After that, introduce foods one at a time so that you can watch for possible allergens.

Allergies: Suggestions for Care

There is no real cure for allergies, but children often outgrow them. With food and insect bites, it is best to avoid the allergen when possible. For airborne allergens and molds, try to limit exposure. Emotional stress can cause an allergic reaction to worsen.

Food and Remedies for Nursing Mother or Baby Older than Six Months	Topical Treatments
Overall, encourage regular eating habits and foster healthy digestion to keep excess phlegm out of your baby's body and lungs.	• Comfrey salve rubbed into the chest

Foods to Emphasize	Foods to Avoid
Cooked foods at a warm temperature, and foods that promote healthy digestion, such as whole grains (especially rice, which is hypoallergenic), beans, seeds, nuts, cooked vegetables, stewed fruits, and occasional animal protein-rich foods. Encourage your child to drink water (in order to thin her secretions) and to eat flavonoid-rich foods, such as blueberries, blackberries, and purple grapes. Kuzu drinks are alkaline-producing for the blood. Bach's Rescue Remedy is an internal remedy that helps relieve allergies.	Common food allergens (dairy, wheat, gluten, soy, eggs, peanuts, tree nuts, chocolate, seafood, citrus fruits, and processed oils). Even if your baby does not have a reaction to these foods, they can cause low-level inflammation of her airways, and this may lead to greater reactivity and sensitivity. Dairy products also are mucus producing, which can create congestion. Gluten is an allergen irritant, so even if she is not allergic to gluten, eating gluten can inflame other allergies.

Essential Oils for Baby	Acupoints for Baby
Lavender, eucalyptus, lemon	Lung 1, 10 Large Intestine 11 Spleen 3 Gallbladder 20 Liver 3 Governing Vessel 12

Reiki for Baby	Massage for Baby
For two or more minutes, place your hands on the following parts of your child's body: forehead and temples, back and top of head, above and beside nose, back of neck, throat, chest, indentation below sternum, heart, between and below shoulder blades, *hara* (belly), and lower back.	• Gently massage your baby's neck muscles below her ear. • Move down toward her collarbone. • Massage her lung meridian. • Massage her chest downward, using a sweeping direction on her breastbone. • From the center of her chest, push outward toward her armpits and below her rib cage. • Massage the back of your baby's neck along her spine, the tops of her shoulders, and the small of her back.

Allergies: Concerns

While most allergies are merely bothersome, reactions can become serious quickly. Left untreated, some allergic reactions can lead to sinus infections, ear infections, and upper-respiratory infections, so they need to be monitored. Administer an EpiPen or antihistamine pill, if you have one. Put your child on her back with her feet higher than her head. Loosen tight clothes. If she stops breathing, administer CPR until help arrives.

Your Baby's Digestive and Urinary Systems

Your baby's digestive system breaks down food into nutrients so that her body can absorb them and gain the energy to grow and repair itself. The digestive system consists of the gastrointestinal tract (mouth, esophagus, stomach, small intestine, and large intestine, including the rectum and the anus), the liver, the pancreas, and the gallbladder.

Your baby's digestive system is called into action the moment food enters her mouth. Immediately, her salivary glands release enzymes to start digestion, make food more alkaline, and keep her mouth moist. Her tongue tastes and moves the food. As her tongue moves the food to her throat, it also activates her epiglottis, which is the little flap that covers the trachea at the back of her throat, so that food does not go down her windpipe and cause her to choke. Slow eating ensures that the epiglottis has plenty of time to perform its duty. Once your baby has teeth and can chew food, digestion becomes even easier.

Your baby's esophagus is a hollow tube that transports food from her mouth to her stomach. The esophageal valve at the bottom of that tube controls entry into her stomach and prevents food from coming back up her esophagus after it has entered her stomach. This valve is underdeveloped in babies, which is why they often spit up.

Once food reaches your baby's stomach, stomach acid kills bad bacteria and breaks the food down further so it can travel into her small intestine. From there, her liver releases bile that is stored in her gallbladder, and her pancreas releases digestive enzymes into her small intestine to help break food into fats, proteins, and carbohydrates. Nutrients are then absorbed into your baby's bloodstream and moved into her liver. Here, they are filtered and processed before heading back into her bloodstream. Food that is not absorbed passes into her large intestine, where water is absorbed into the blood. The leftover waste is excreted through your baby's rectum and anus.

While in the womb, your baby swallowed amniotic fluid and expelled urine through her urinary system. Because she received her primary nutrients through the umbilical cord, she did not need to use her digestive system. After birth, your baby's sucking reflex signaled her first stool, called meconium, to pass through her large intestine, thus kick-starting her digestive system. Even at this point, however, her digestive system is not fully developed. It takes 6 to 12 months of muscle strengthening before your baby's digestive system can work well.

As a parent, you are probably highly aware of your baby's digestive system, because it regularly requires your attention through her hunger, thirst, and bowel movements. In the first year, due to her sensitive and underdeveloped system, digestive irregularities such as spit-up and upset stomach may be prevalent.

You can help ease many irregularities by breast-feeding your baby exclusively for the first six months. If your breast-fed baby does experience gastronomic distress, it can be helpful to pay attention to the mother's diet and then eliminate foods that cause a reaction in your baby. When she is ready for her first solid foods, include whole grains, vegetables, legumes and seeds, fermented foods, and probiotic booster for easy digestion.

Working to eliminate excesses from your baby's body, her urinary system coordinates with her lungs, skin, and intestines to excrete wastes from blood and to balance her body's fluids, salt, vitamins, and minerals. Your baby's urinary system consists of two kidneys, two ureters, a bladder, and a urethra. Her kidneys are reddish in color, bean shaped, and located in the back of her body, just above her waist. They contain filters that clean her blood, remove acids, and regulate mineral content, which balances pH levels. The kidneys also regulate her blood pressure and make sure that her body tissues receive enough water. Any waste in the kidneys becomes urine.

Your baby's urine moves out of each kidney through a tube called a ureter and travels into her bladder. Her bladder is a hollow, muscular, balloon-shaped organ located in the middle of her pelvis. Urine waits in her bladder until the organ is full and then is released through her urethra and into her diaper. The amount of urine that your baby's body produces depends on hormone levels, the amount of liquid she ingests, and the amount of liquid that her body expels through perspiration.

Because your baby's digestive system is still developing throughout the first year of life, it plays a role in many common childhood illnesses, such as diarrhea, constipation, colic, stomach upset and vomiting, hiccups, and teething. Common illnesses of the urinary system, such as kidney stones and urinary tract infections, are more likely to occur later in life.

Common childhood illnesses connected to the digestive and urinary systems include diarrhea, constipation, colic, stomach upset and vomiting, hiccups, and teething.

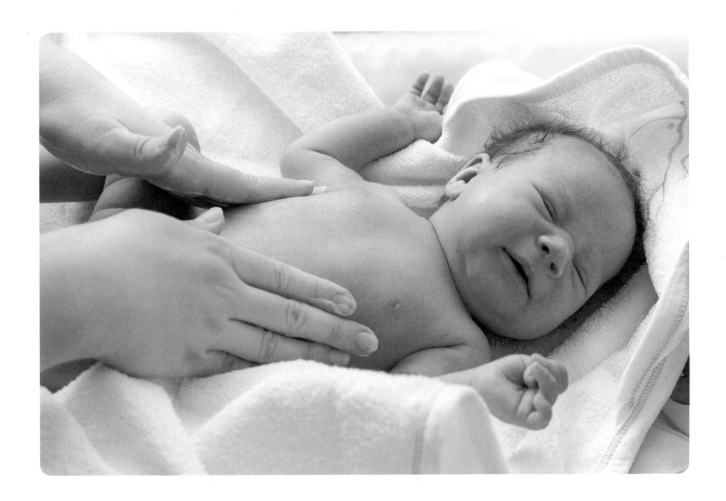

Illness: Diarrhea
System: Digestive

Diarrhea is the passing of loose stools. A common condition for young children, it is caused by various stressors to the body. While most cases are acute and last only a day or two, some cases can become chronic. Chronic diarrhea can be harmful to growing children because it prevents them from absorbing nutrients. The disease's most serious and most common complication is dehydration. With good home care and attention to keeping your baby hydrated, most of her experiences with diarrhea should resolve within 48 hours and should not require a call to your health care provider.

Diarrhea: Symptoms

- Watery, loose stools with decreased consistency
- Greenish color,.mucus, or foul smell in stool
- Passing loose stools more than three times a day
- Abdominal cramps
- Fever or vomiting (only if diarrhea is due to infection)

Diarrhea: Causes

- Sensitive intestines from overeating or from too many acid-producing foods
- Cold, rich, or spicy food
- Transition to solid foods
- Introduction of new or unfamiliar foods
- Food allergy, especially milk-protein allergy (if nursing mother drinks cow's milk, it can cause an allergic reaction)
- Reaction to vaccines or medications, especially antibiotics
- Infection from virus, bacteria, or parasite
- Food poisoning
- Mouthing contaminated toys or objects
- Teething
- Overstimulation, fear, stress, or emotional upset

Diarrhea: Prevention

- If breast-feeding, observe your own diet and how certain foods affect your baby. Consuming alcohol, dairy, gluten, and caffeine can cause a reaction. Boost your baby's immune system with fermented foods, probiotic booster, and foods with zinc, such as roasted pumpkin seeds.
- Avoid citrus, tomatoes, wheat, sugar, soy, eggs, and nuts.
- Be sure all foods she eats are fresh, clean, and safely prepared.
- Wash both her hands and yours before feeding her.
- Wash your hands after diaper changes.
- Introduce foods carefully in order to give your baby's digestive system time to adjust to new foods.
- Be mindful that your baby does not become overstressed.

Diarrhea: Suggestions for Care

Because your baby's intestines are much shorter than those of adults, food moves through them more quickly, and it moves even faster when she has diarrhea. Keep your baby comfortable and hydrated. Keep her bottom clean with warm water and a soft cloth. Be gentle when changing her diaper, because her skin is easily irritated when she has diarrhea.

Food and Remedies for Nursing Mother or Baby Older than Six Months	Topical Treatments
If your child is breast-feeding, continue to nurse her. If she is more than six months old, give her as much additional fluid as possible to prevent dehydration. This may be difficult at first if she has stomach cramps, but as the diarrhea progresses and your baby feels better, it should become easier to get her to drink.	• *Hara-maki* (belly warmer) • Warm ginger compress or warm water bottle

Foods to Emphasize	Foods to Avoid
A simple diet of easily digestible foods, such as grain cream, very mild miso soup, vegetable broth, fermented foods, probiotic booster, toast, small amounts of yogurt, and sea vegetables to replenish minerals. Make sure all food is cooked and served warm, not cold. For the first few meals and until the diarrhea has ceased, keep regular mealtimes without snacks. Other diarrhea remedies include savory or brown rice syrup, kuzu, fennel or chamomile herbal tea, and plum tea.	Frozen or cold foods, refined sugars, raw foods, dairy foods, spices, proteins, fats, fruit, and juice (especially translucent, processed juice).

Essential Oils for Baby	Acupoints for Baby
Chamomile, lavender	Stomach 25, 36 Spleen 3

Reiki for Baby	Massage for Baby
For two or more minutes, place your hands on the following parts of your child's body: abdomen, stomach, and lower back.	• Start by massaging downward, from her upper body to lower body, on the front of your baby. • Massage her abdomen with clockwise movements. • Massage upward on her back from the bottom of her sacrum to the center of her back. • Massage the back of her tailbone and below her tailbone. • Massage all over her body—shoulders, arms, legs, and neck.

Diarrhea: Concerns

Dehydration is the main concern with diarrhea, especially in warmer weather. Call your health care provider if your baby suffers chronic diarrhea.

Illness: Constipation
System: *Digestive*

A baby is constipated when she is uncomfortable due to her inability to pass a stool, and when her stools are hard, dry, and difficult to pass. Usually breast-fed babies have fewer bowel movements overall; an exclusively breast-fed baby may pass a stool only once a week.

Constipation: Symptoms

- Firm, dry, dark, hard stools
- Cramps
- Pain when passing stools
- Swollen or loose intestines, such that muscles cannot move waste

Constipation: Causes

- Lack of adequate fiber in diet
- Dehydration
- Lack of exercise
- Formula that does not agree with your baby's system
- Contracted feces because of excess yang food, such as meat, eggs, cheese, fat, flour products, and refined grains
- Irregular habits—being rushed during regular bathroom times
- Emotional stress, such as pressure to toilet train or arrival of a new baby

Constipation: Prevention

- Breast-feed your baby.
- If breast-feeding, observe your own diet and how certain foods affect your baby. Consuming alcohol, dairy, gluten, and caffeine can cause a reaction.
- Avoid animal foods, such as meat, eggs, and cheese.
- Offer whole grains, vegetables, fruit, and fermented foods.
- Exercise and massage your baby regularly.
- When toilet training, respond to your child's urge to go to the toilet, and try to relax throughout the process.

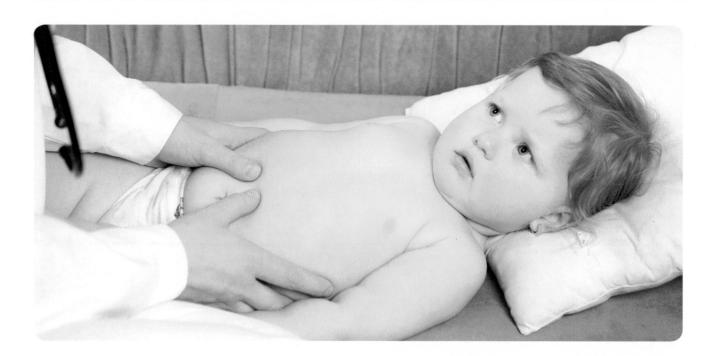

Constipation: Suggestions for Care

Exercise can ease constipation. Move your baby's legs in a bicycle motion. A warm bath can relax her body and get her system moving.

Food and Remedies for Nursing Mother or Baby Older than Six Months	Topical Treatments
Be sure that your child is well-hydrated. If your baby is breast-fed, the nursing mother can drink more liquid. If you use formula, your baby's digestive system may not agree with the brand, so changing formulas may be helpful.	• *Hara-maki* (belly warmer) • Ginger compress or warm water bottle

Foods to Emphasize	Foods to Avoid
Cooked or raw fruits, such as dried fruits, raisins, prunes, apricots, applesauce, and concentrated fruit spread. Add fiber to her diet in the form of whole grains, warm porridge, vegetables (especially green vegetables), and vegetable juices. Add fermented foods and probiotic booster. Other remedies to relieve constipation are ground flaxseed or flaxseed oil added to food and kuzu.	Processed oils, dairy foods, meat, eggs, and sugar.

Essential Oils for Baby	Acupoints for Baby
Chamomile, lavender	Large Intestine 11 Stomach 25, 36

Reiki for Baby	Massage for Baby
For two or more minutes, place your hands on the following parts of your child's body: abdomen and lower back.	• Massage the abdomen clockwise while facing your baby. • Massage the back of your baby's tailbone and lower back. • Massage all over her body (shoulders, arms, legs, and neck) for relaxation.

Constipation: Concerns

The number of stools your baby passes in a week is not as significant as her overall condition and comfort. Observe your baby. Call your health care provider if your baby suffers chronic constipation or has blood or mucus in her stool.

Illness: Colic
System: *Digestive*

When a baby cries for more than three hours a day, she is considered to be suffering with colic. Though nearly 40 percent of babies suffer with this condition, the real cause is unknown. Traditionally, colic has been linked to babies' immature digestive systems. In fact, the word colic comes from the Greek word meaning "intestines." Colic usually begins at around two weeks of age and, for most babies, resolves itself by three or four months of age.

Colic: Symptoms

- Crying for hours at a time over several weeks, usually in the evening
- Gas and bloating
- May pump legs toward abdomen and arch back

Colic: Causes

- Indigestion from foods eaten by the nursing mother—especially cruciferous vegetables, legumes, dairy products, and caffeine—or caused by swallowing air through crying or bottle-feeding
- Allergy to cow's milk, eggs, soy, wheat, and dairy products in general
- Overstimulation or anxiety
- Cold weather
- Reaction to immunizations

Colic: Prevention

- If breast-feeding, observe your own diet and how certain foods affect your baby. Consuming alcohol, dairy, gluten, and caffeine can cause a reaction.
- Reduce digestive-system stress. Do not overfeed or underfeed—watch for signs, such as spitting up or continuing to suck after feeding. If you are bottle-feeding, check the size of the nipple to ensure an even flow.
- Avoid cold and frozen food and drinks.
- Practice acupoint and massage on your baby daily.
- Make time for skin-to-skin and physical contact every day.

Colic: Suggestions for Care

Eliminate extra stress. Keep lights, music, activity, and voices as calm as possible. Give your baby relaxing warm baths and massages. If you are bottle-feeding, hold her bottle upright to prevent her from breathing air as she drinks. Space out your baby's feedings so that her digestive system gets a rest, and she does not get too full. Burp your baby often, and try tummy time to release gas. Most babies like to be held and rocked—try sitting on a yoga ball and holding her while you bounce. Try taking a walk using a baby carrier, a sling, or a wrap. Experiment until you find what works, and use the same techniques consistently. Colic is common, and it does go away eventually.

Food and Remedies for Nursing Mother or Baby Older than Six Months	Topical Treatments
Since colic usually appears when babies are not yet eating solid food, the following food recommendations are for nursing mothers. If your baby is formula-fed, you may experiment with a different brand to see if that relieves her colic.	• *Hara-maki* (belly warmer) • Ginger compress or warm water bottle on abdomen and mid and lower back

Foods to Emphasize	Foods to Avoid
Simple alkaline-producing foods that contain minerals, such as sea vegetables, fermented foods, and probiotic booster. Also, emphasize yogurt or kefir, both of which have enzymes to aid digestion. Eat primarily cooked foods for predigestion benefits. Remedies for a nursing mother include a small amount of *umeboshi* plum or plum vinegar as a condiment or seasoning, kuzu, and fennel or chamomile herbal tea.	Allergy-producing foods, such as soy, dairy (especially cow's milk), and wheat. Stay away from gas-producing foods, such as cruciferous vegetables, beans, tomatoes, garlic, onions, citrus, caffeine, chocolate, cucumbers, peppers, raw berries, bananas, melons, and dairy.

Essential Oils for Baby	Acupoints for Baby
Chamomile, lavender	Stomach 36 Gallbladder 20 Conception Vessel 12

Reiki for Baby	Massage for Baby
For two or more minutes, place your hands on the following parts of your child's body: abdomen and lower back.	• Massage your baby's abdomen clockwise (when you are facing your baby) with light pressure. • Massage the back of the tailbone, lower back, and both sides of the spine. • Calm your baby and her digestive tract with general, light-pressure strokes on her body, head, arms, and legs. • Help your baby do bicycle exercises or the plow yoga pose.

Colic: Concerns

Life with a colicky infant can be extremely challenging. People who care for your child, including you, need to be mindful of their own emotions and frustration level. The most serious concern with colic is that the baby's caregiver may become frustrated by the nonstop crying and physically harm the baby—usually by shaking her. Do not underestimate this danger or believe that it could not happen to you. During these weeks of colic, be sure your baby's primary caregiver has plenty of support and scheduled breaks away. If you leave your colicky baby in the care of others, give them a backup person to call.

Illness: Stomach Upset and Vomiting
System: Digestive

Stomach upset and vomiting are common occurrences during your baby's first few years, while her digestive system is small and still developing. Typical childhood stomach issues create an overall ache and discomfort in the abdominal region and usually improve within one to two days. Sharp pain, or a specific pain in a specific area, can be a sign of a condition that needs immediate attention, such as appendicitis or an intestinal blockage. Vomiting is the body's way of ridding itself of toxins and excesses and restoring health and balance. In general, vomiting is different from spitting up; it has more force behind it, because the food has already been partially digested.

Stomach Upset and Vomiting: Symptoms

- Lack of appetite
- Nausea and vomiting
- Crying and discomfort
- Cramps, tenderness, or stomach pain
- Milk spit-up with a sour odor
- Pale face
- Cold hands and feet
- Accompanying fever, cough, cold, or diarrhea

Stomach Upset and Vomiting: Causes

- Fussy digestive system
- Reflux (common in infants)
- Gas or swallowing air while feeding
- Overeating
- Bacterial, viral, or parasite infection (may be accompanied by fever, cough, cold, and/or diarrhea)
- Overexertion
- Emotional upset or anxiety (emotions can be transferred from nursing mother)
- Formula incompatibility
- Mucus accumulation from animal fats, dairy foods, and refined sugars
- Food poisoning (usually occurs around eight hours after a meal)
- Accidental ingestion of poison
- Food allergies
- Motion sickness
- Urinary tract infection
- Reaction to a vaccine
- Transition to solid foods
- Cold food or environment

Stomach Upset and Vomiting: Prevention

- If breast-feeding, observe your own diet and how certain foods affect your baby. Consuming alcohol, dairy, gluten, and caffeine can cause a reaction.
- Feed your baby in an upright position, burp her more often, and space out feeding times to avoid food stagnation.
- Wash your hands and ensure proper food storage and preparation. These practices should prevent the survival of most pathogens.
- Make mealtimes calm. Once you introduce solid foods, be sure your baby chews her food and eats slowly.
- If your child seems to have stomachaches after eating, try serving simpler foods until her digestive system strengthens. If you suspect her formula is causing upset, change brands. If you suspect a food allergy, eliminate the food from her diet.
- Do not feed your baby or allow her to eat during car rides.
- Keep your baby sitting up after feeding for 15 to 30 minutes.

Stomach Upset and Vomiting: Suggestions for Care

Common stomach upset and vomiting usually heal on their own. You can support your baby by making sure that she remains hydrated, rested, and comfortable. Many children become frightened of vomiting, so it is important that you remain calm and reassuring. An environment with plenty of air and low lights can help with the nausea and general discomfort. While your baby is actively vomiting, do not offer food. Once the vomiting has calmed down (which should be no longer than 12 hours), you can reintroduce fluids one tablespoon at a time; wait for 15 or 20 minutes to see if it stays down, and then offer another tablespoon. Be very careful not to move too quickly with fluids or to overfill your baby's stomach.

Food and Remedies for Nursing Mother or Baby Older than Six Months	Topical Treatments
When your child has gone at least six hours without vomiting, you can reintroduce foods, such as clear broths and simple solids. After 24 hours with no vomiting, your child can return to her regular diet. If your baby is breast-feeding, remember that what the nursing mother eats can be transferred to the baby, so a simple diet can help your baby.	<ul><li>*Hara-maki* (belly warmer)</li><li>Warm ginger compress or warm water bottle over belly and mid back</li><li>Green clay over abdomen or mid back</li></ul>

Foods to Emphasize	Foods to Avoid
Warm foods, such as miso soup and vegetable broth. Once your baby tolerates clear broths and becomes hungry, introduce grain cream. Remedies for stomach upset include chamomile or fennel herbal tea, miso soup, plum extract (concentrated plum) in hot water, *umeboshi* plum, plum vinegar, kuzu, fermented foods, and probiotic booster.	Cold food, dairy products, high-fat and sugary foods, carbonated beverages, and acidic foods.

Essential Oils for Baby	Acupoints for Baby
Chamomile, lavender	Stomach 36 Spleen 3 Heart Governor 5, 6

Reiki for Baby	Massage for Baby
For two or more minutes, place your hands on the following parts of your child's body: abdomen and lower back.	Calm your baby and her digestive tract with general, low-pressure strokes on her body, head, arms, and legs.<ul><li>Rub the abdomen clockwise (when facing your baby).</li><li>Hold your baby facedown on your arm or over your shoulder and gently pat her back.</li></ul>

Stomach Upset and Vomiting: Concerns

The majority of childhood stomach upsets resolve on their own. However, sometimes vomiting or pain in the abdomen can indicate a serious condition. Speak with your health care provider if your baby has had stomach pain or vomiting with a fever for more than 48 hours.

Illness: Hiccups
System: Digestive

Hiccups occur when the diaphragm has a spasm. The spasm causes the body to take in air that quickly stops when the vocal chords snap shut, resulting in the "hic" sound. Your baby has been hiccupping since before she was born and most likely will continue to hiccup throughout her life. More of an annoyance than a health concern, normal hiccups resolve on their own in a few minutes or a few hours. In very rare cases, however, hiccups can last more than 48 hours (persistent) or more than a month (intractable). Both persistent and intractable hiccups can interfere with growth and signal a more serious condition.

Hiccups: Symptoms

- Sudden and abrupt involuntary spasms and contractions of the diaphragm
- The "hic" sound

Hiccups: Causes

- Irritation to the diaphragm
- Eating too much or indigestion
- Eating too fast and swallowing air
- Sudden temperature drop or change in the stomach (cold food in a warm belly or cold drink followed by hot food)
- Raw foods
- Stuck chi in the diaphragm
- Emotional stress or overstimulation

Hiccups: Prevention

- Feed your baby slowly, and burp halfway through feeding and again after feeding.
- If you are bottle-feeding, hold the bottle upright to prevent your baby from swallowing air as she drinks.
- Help your toddler eat slowly and avoid swallowing air.
- Encourage a relaxing atmosphere at mealtime.
- Avoid sudden temperature drops in the air.
- Avoid extreme temperatures in food and drink.
- Avoid stress and overstimulation.

Hiccups: Suggestions for Care

Hiccups are usually harmless and go away on their own within a few minutes, but they can be bothersome. Once your baby has hiccups, it can help to give her something to suck on. If she is more than six months old, you can try giving her small sips of water. For an older toddler, gently hold her ears with light pressure while she drinks water, or have her hold her breath and count to ten.

Topical Treatments

- *Hara-maki* (belly warmer)
- Warm ginger compress or warm water bottle on the upper abdomen (diaphragm area) and below shoulder blades

Foods to Emphasize

Small sips of water for baby and alkaline-producing foods for both mother and baby.

Foods to Avoid

Acid-forming foods, such as caffeine, soy, citrus, wheat, and eggs.

Essential Oils for Baby

Chamomile, lavender

Acupoints for Baby

Stomach 36
Bladder 17
Heart Governor 6
Conception Vessel 12

Reiki for Baby

For two or more minutes, place your hands on the following parts of your child's body: stomach, diaphragm and upper abdomen, back of neck, forehead, and mid back.

Massage for Baby

- Massage the indented area behind her earlobes.
- Massage the area on the back of the middle finger, on the joint closest to the nail.
- Calm your baby and her digestive tract with gentle, low-pressure strokes on her body, head, arms, and legs.
- Rub the abdomen clockwise (when facing the baby).

Hiccups: Concerns

Call your health care provider if your baby has hiccups that last more than a day; interfere with her eating, sleeping, or other regular activities; or result in her crying or screaming.

Illness: Teething
System: Digestive

Even though your baby's first tooth usually comes in at around six months old, teething may begin as early as three or four months. Teething is the process by which your baby's first teeth erupt through her gums. Most babies get their first set of four teeth—two on the bottom, and then two on the top—anywhere between five and nine months old. Typically, four teeth erupt every four months after that. By the time your baby is three years old, she has her whole set of 20 primary teeth. Her permanent teeth will begin to push out the primary teeth between five and seven years of age. Teething can be painful and tough for your baby, and her body may react to it in various ways.

Teething: Symptoms

- Irritability
- Drooling
- Sore, swollen gums
- Biting or gnawing on anything, including her own hand
- Low-grade fever
- Runny nose
- Ear pulling
- Loose stools from time to time
- Coughing (due to excessive saliva)
- Rash around mouth (due to excessive drool)
- Waking in the night
- Crying

Teething: Causes

- Teeth pushing through gums

Teething: Prevention

You can improve your baby's teething experience by providing teethers and other items for chewing, and by feeding her healthy foods. While her body puts energy into bringing in her new teeth, you can help provide nourishment and boost her immune system with fermented foods and probiotic booster.

Teething: Suggestions for Care

When your baby is teething, cold objects to chew on feel awfully good and soothe sore gums. Offer your baby a chilled teething ring made of safe plastic, silicone, natural rubber, or wood; or offer a cold teething biscuit, cool rubber-tipped spoon, or chilled and moistened washcloth.

Food and Remedies for Nursing Mother or Baby Older than Six Months	Topical Treatments
Teething can be upsetting to your baby and can stress her developing digestive system. If she is showing symptoms of teething or you sense that she is irritable, you can use naturally sweet foods to pacify her and to restore her balance. For example, give her a small amount of brown rice syrup on the tip of your finger to suck on.	• Chamomile or fennel herbal tea bags • Frozen washcloth: soak a clean washcloth in chamomile or fennel herbal tea; freeze the washcloth, and then give it to your baby to chew on

Foods to Emphasize	Foods to Avoid
Simple, easily digestible foods given on a regular schedule with breaks of at least two hours between feedings. Bach Rescue Remedy helps calm and relax your baby when she is teething. Kuzu drinks can help her relax and are alkaline-producing for her blood.	Overfeeding, foods that are difficult to digest (such as raw vegetables and whole-grain bread), high-protein foods, and rich foods.

Essential Oils for Baby	Acupoints for Baby
Chamomile, lavender	Lung 1,7 Stomach 36 Liver 3

Reiki for Baby	Massage for Baby
For two or more minutes, place your hands on the following parts of your child's body: stomach and abdomen (to reach the intestines), around the mouth, and above her lips below the center of her nose (use one finger).	• Massage the kidneys, spleen, and heart governor. • Massage the meridians. • Massage and stretch the abdomen to promote digestion and to relieve accumulation. • Massage the feet between the big toe and the second toe. • Massage the hands between the thumb and the pointer finger.

Teething: Concerns

Teething causes many symptoms similar to illness, including irritability, low-grade fever, diarrhea, and extra mucus in the respiratory system. During this time, observe your child to determine whether her symptoms indicate teething or something more serious.

Your Baby's Respiratory System

Your baby's respiratory system supplies her blood with oxygen (inhalation) and expels carbon dioxide waste (exhalation) with every breath.

Your baby's nose, mouth, pharynx, larynx (voice box), trachea (windpipe), bronchi, lungs, and diaphragm coordinate to accomplish respiration. Air enters through her nose and passes through her larynx and trachea to her chest cavity. Here, the trachea splits into two smaller tubes called the bronchi. These tubes lead directly into her lungs, where they divide into many smaller tubes called bronchioles, which are about the thickness of a hair. At the ends of the tubes are hundreds of millions of tiny, spongy sacs called alveoli. Capillaries (blood vessels that enable the transfer of nutrients and waste between blood and tissue) surround the alveoli.

When your baby inhales, her diaphragm—a large muscle beneath the lungs—flattens out, allowing her lungs to fill with air. Once the air is in her lungs, it travels through her bronchi and bronchioles to her alveoli. Her alveoli then transfer oxygen to her red blood cells inside her capillaries. The now-oxygen-rich blood cells travel to her heart, which then disperses her blood in order to oxygenate tissues throughout her body. When oxygen has been delivered and blood is filled with carbon dioxide, the blood travels back to her heart, which then pumps it to her lungs. There, the capillaries deliver carbon dioxide to her alveoli (which actually happens at the same time the alveoli transfer oxygen to the capillaries). Then the entire process happens in reverse, with the diaphragm pushing on the lungs, resulting in the exhalation of carbon dioxide.

Before your baby was born, the placenta did the job of exchanging oxygen and carbon dioxide for her body. She did not use her lungs in utero. In fact, when babies are born, their lungs are still filled with fluid and the alveoli are collapsed, making those first breaths difficult. Immediately after birth, however, your baby begins to breathe regularly, and this starts the use of her respiratory system.

As with her digestive system, your baby's respiration system is developing during her first year, so it is sensitive and can be prone to illness. Even though her body is capable of purifying the air she inhales, the cleaner her external environment, the better for her respiratory process. Dairy products, refined sugar, and fruit juices can be mucus forming and can cause stagnation in your baby's lungs.

Common childhood illnesses connected to the respiratory system include cough, cold, sore throat, earache, and asthma.

Illness: Croup, Cough
System: Respiratory

Coughing is more of a symptom than an illness, in and of itself. When something is obstructing or irritating her airways, her brain signals the muscles in her abdomen to thrust air through her lungs to toss out anything that should not be there. A cough from a cold or other illness can continue after the other symptoms of the illness have passed.

Croup is typically caused by one of several viruses. It infects the upper airways, including the vocal chords, and produces swelling and tightness that result in a cough that sounds more like a bark. It may be accompanied by stridor, a raspy sound made when inhaling. Usually, the cough from croup is worse at night than it is during the day. Crying can make swelling and coughing worse. Croup may last about a week; it usually peaks at three or four days. Most of the time, croup is not serious and resolves on its own. It is contagious, however, and spreads much the same way as the common cold and other respiratory infections do.

Whooping cough, or pertussis, is a common childhood bacterial infection that features a cough. With pertussis, a baby has long coughing spells that end with her gasping for a breath. It is the baby's gasp that makes the "whooping" sound. Though there is a vaccine against this disease, outbreaks still occur. Whooping cough is contagious, more serious than croup, and potentially severe in infants. If you suspect your baby has whooping cough, contact your health care provider.

Croup, Cough: Symptoms

- A cold or other viral or bacterial infection
- Itchy or sore throat
- Fever, chills, or sweating
- Headache or body aches
- Rapid breathing
- Poor appetite
- Swollen upper respiratory passage, including vocal chords
- Sore throat
- Hoarseness
- Seal-like barking cough that is worse at night
- Stridor (raspy sound when inhaling)
- Irritability
- Crying

Croup, Cough: Causes

- A viral or bacterial infection, such as a cold or bronchitis
- Mucus dripping into airways
- Environmental allergies
- Food sensitivities (common foods are dairy products, refined sugars, carbohydrates, excess fruit juices, hydrogenated fats)
- Reflux
- Overproduction of phlegm from the digestive system
- Nutritional deficiencies
- Poor bowel function
- Hot, cold, or windy weather
- Reaction to a vaccine, especially the vaccine for whooping cough or pertussis
- Physical exertion
- Blockage in the throat or choking
- Damp living conditions

Croup, Cough: Prevention

Since coughs are often related to viral and bacterial infections, frequent hand washing and avoidance of people with colds can help prevent coughs. Beyond those precautions, ensure that your baby is breathing the cleanest air possible. Be mindful of keeping the air around her free of pollution, potentially harmful chemicals (such as those used in cleaning and laundry products), strong fragrances, dust, noxious gas, woodstove or cigarette smoke, and other environmental irritants. Also, avoid swings when it is cold outside, and dress your baby appropriately for the weather.

Croup, Cough: Suggestions for Care

With a cough, simply remember RASCL (these methods are good for a cold as well):

Rest: Keep your child at home to rest. As she rests, raise the upper end of her crib or bed to facilitate breathing. Be mindful of your baby's overall condition and energy level. If she is in good spirits, encourage some gentle exercise and activity.

Air: Make sure the air in your home and surrounding your baby is smoke- and allergen-free. If possible, use a cool-mist humidifier (make sure it is clean and free of bacteria) to help thin the mucus and to moisten her respiratory tract. Expose your baby to fresh air, but avoid wind and extreme temperature changes inside and out.

Squirt her nose: Mucus dripping from the nose into the throat causes the majority of coughs in childhood. To clear the nasal passages, use a neti pot or nasal squirt bottle and water containing saline solution, sea salt, or baking soda.

Clap: In a steamy bathroom, with an open palm and with gentle firmness, pat your baby on either side of her back and on her sides ten times, four times a day, to help dislodge mucus.

Laugh: Encourage laughter, playfulness, and fun! The best medicine for a cough is a caregiver's patience and love.

In general, keep your baby as calm as possible. Coughing can become very uncomfortable and can cause your baby to cry. Crying can increase swelling and irritability in her airways, thus making the cough worse. Also remember that coughing is a protective reflex and should not be suppressed by medication unless instructed by a physician. Over-the-counter cough and cold medication should not be given to children under four years of age. These multisymptom medications can make children drowsy and impair their ability to clear phlegm from their airways.

Croup, Cough: Suggestions for Care

Food and Remedies for Nursing Mother or Baby Older than Six Months

Healthy foods can bathe an irritated throat, boost the immune system, and ease discomfort from coughing.

Topical Treatments

- 20 minutes of breathing steamy air from a humidifier or in a bathroom, or breathing an infusion of lavender or chamomile flowers in a bowl of hot water
- Ginger compress or warm water bottle on chest or back
- Bach's Rescue Cream on pulse points, chest, and upper back

Foods to Emphasize

Intake of warm fluids. If your baby is older than a year, offer warm water with lemon and organic, cold-pressed, pasteurized honey, which has antibacterial properties and soothes sore throats. Serve simple, easy-to-digest, warm foods at regular mealtimes. If her cough is dry, offer warm pear sauce. To break down phlegm, soft-cooked vegetables, stewed fruits, bean soup, or soft-cooked whole grains. Fennel or chamomile herbal tea, kuzu, and Bach's Rescue Remedy are remedies to relieve cough or croup.

Foods to Avoid

Solid foods (due to choking danger), cold drinks (especially acidic juices, such as orange juice), bread, raw fruits (including banana), raw vegetables, roasted peanuts, peanut butter, dairy (cow's milk, cheese, and ice cream), sugar, and wheat.

Essential Oils for Baby

Lemon, lavender

Acupoints for Baby

Lung 1, 5, 7
Large Intestine 11
Stomach 36, 40
Spleen 6
Kidney 3, 7

Reiki for Baby

For two or more minutes, place your hands on the following parts of your child's body: front of chest, back (between shoulder blades), sides of chest, lower part of rib cage, and throat.

Massage for Baby

Massage along the lung, spleen, and kidney meridians.

Croup, Cough: Concerns

Most coughs eventually go away on their own. However, a cough may need medical attention or be a symptom of something more serious, such as pneumonia, choking, or epiglottitis (swelling of the epiglottis that closes off the airway). If your child is not improving after several days with a cough, or if she is "whooping," breathing rapidly, or struggling to breathe, see your health care provider.

Illness: Sore Throat, Strep Throat
System: *Respiratory*

The majority of sore throats that babies experience are caused by the irritating phlegm or cough that accompanies allergies, a cold, or another respiratory infection. Thus, most sore throats resolve on their own, as do the accompanying symptoms.

The most common condition that specifically infects the throat is strep throat. Strep is a bacterial infection caused by group A streptococcus, usually present in the fall and winter. It is spread through saliva and nasal secretions. Left untreated, strep can lead to more serious conditions, such as scarlet fever, blood infections, kidney disease, and rheumatic fever. You must see your health care provider to have strep diagnosed, and it can be treated with antibiotics, as well as Chinese herbs and acupuncture.

Sore Throat, Strep Throat: Symptoms

Symptoms of sore throat along with cold, flu, other virus, or allergies can present as follows:
- Throat pain
- Throat redness
- Swollen lymph nodes or tonsils
- Hoarseness
- Body aches
- Runny nose
- Coughing
- Congestion
- Diarrhea

Strep throat may present as follows:
- Throat pain that worsens as day goes on
- Fever
- Abdominal pain (very common)
- Red spots on the palate
- Red patches with white patches (pus) on tonsils and back of throat
- Swollen lymph nodes
- Pain with swallowing
- Low appetite
- Nausea
- Muscle aches and pain; neck pain
- Nasal congestion
- Rash on torso (most common in children more than three years old)

Sore Throat, Strep Throat: Causes

- Common cold, flu, or other virus
- Bacteria, including group A streptococcus
- Allergies
- Dry air

Sore Throat, Strep Throat: Prevention

- Make sure your hands are clean before touching your baby. Teach your child to wash her hands frequently, as well.
- During the cold and flu season, replace toothbrushes monthly. After a bout with strep, replace your child's toothbrush immediately to prevent reinfection.
- Keep play groups small during cold and flu season.
- Keep the air in your home at a good humidity level, and make sure it is pollutant-free (be mindful of wood smoke, chemical smells from cleaning products, and cigarette smoke).
- Outdoors, protect your child's throat from the wind and cold with a scarf.

Sore Throat, Strep Throat: Suggestions for Care

Since most sore throats accompany colds and upper respiratory illnesses and resolve along with the illness, they do not require medical attention. However, they do require attention at home. Keep your baby rested and well-hydrated. In addition to giving her fluids, be sure her room is humid enough. If necessary, use a humidifier to keep the air she breathes moist so that it does not irritate her throat.

If you suspect strep throat, call your health care provider to have a strep test done. Once strep is confirmed, Western practitioners will likely offer treatment with antibiotics. If you prefer an alternative to antibiotics, both Chinese herbs and acupuncture can treat strep throat.

Food and Remedies for Nursing Mother or Baby Older than Six Months	Topical Treatments
Use foods to nourish your baby and to soothe her throat.	• Ginger compress on throat and neck

Foods to Emphasize	Foods to Avoid
Herbal teas and clear broth soups; simple, soft whole grains; cooked vegetables; and stewed fruits. Chamomile herbal tea, kuzu, and mild miso soup are especially effective remedies.	Cold foods, dairy products, fried and greasy foods, sugar, sweets, and refined carbohydrates.

Essential Oils for Baby	Acupoints for Baby
Tea tree, lavender, eucalyptus, lemon	Stomach 36 Spleen 3 Heart Governor 6

Reiki for Baby	Massage for Baby
For two or more minutes, place your hands on the following parts of your child's body: front and back of neck.	Calm your baby with gentle strokes on her back, head, arms, and legs.

Sore Throat, Strep Throat: Concerns

The majority of your child's sore throats will disappear along with the illnesses that caused them. However, on occasion, a sore throat can be a sign of a condition that requires medical attention. Contact your health care provider if your child displays symptoms of strep throat, refuses to drink due to throat pain, has swollen glands that are getting bigger, or has a fever or abdominal pain in addition to her sore throat.

Illness: Cold
System: Respiratory

A cold is a viral infection of the upper respiratory tract that affects the nose, sinuses, throat, and eyes. With most colds, mucus progresses from clear and runny to thick and yellow or green. Your child may become achy, tired, and feverish, and she may lose her appetite. A cold usually heals within a week. A strong immune system is resistant to common viruses, and thus decreases the occurrence of colds.

Cold: Symptoms

- Runny or stuffy nose
- Clear yellow or green mucus
- Wheezing, sneezing, or coughing
- Low-grade fever
- Headache or other body aches
- Watery eyes
- Sinus pain
- Irritability
- Fatigue

Cold: Causes

- Viruses
- Stressed system

Cold: Prevention

- Boost your baby's immune system with fermented foods and probiotic booster.
- Keep your baby home when she has a cold with a fever or has yellow or green secretions.
- Teach your baby to use tissues.

Cold: Suggestions for Care

There is no cure for a cold, but you can treat the symptoms, and most colds usually heal over the course of about a week. You can help by supporting your baby's immune system and by keeping her as comfortable as possible. Keep your child hydrated with water, tea, and broth. In addition, keep her quiet and calm, so her available energy can restore her immune system. Allow her to get up and play if she feels well enough, but keep her at home if possible.

Use a humidifier if the air is dry in your home. If your child does get stuffed up, a nasal aspirator can pull mucus out of her nose if she is too young to blow it. A steamy bathroom can loosen the mucus; you can also gently clap her chest and back with an open palm. To ease breathing as your baby sleeps, put a vaporizer near her. Over-the-counter medications for colds should not be used for children under four years old, and antibiotics are ineffective for viral infections.

Food and Remedies for Nursing Mother or Baby Older than Six Months	Topical Treatments
Keep your baby hydrated, and if she is eating solids, feed her immunity-boosting food when she is hungry. Note that food stagnation can prevent a cold from clearing, so be sure your baby eats slowly and does not overeat.	• Bach's Rescue Cream, rubbed into the chest • Eucalyptus chest rub

Foods to Emphasize	Foods to Avoid
Simple, nourishing food, such as soups, broths, and stews. Serve foods with antibacterial and antiviral properties, such as radishes, ginger, and cooked vegetables. Onions added to broths or foods help break up mucus. Give your child warm food. Kuzu and chamomile herbal tea are remedies that can relieve the symptoms of a cold.	Cold or frozen foods or drinks; spicy foods; mucus-producing foods such as dairy products, refined foods, sugars, and peanuts.

Essential Oils for Baby	Acupoints for Baby
Tea tree, lavender, eucalyptus, lemon	Lung 7 Large Intestine 11 Stomach 36 Triple Heater 5 Gallbladder 20 Conception Vessel 6, 12 Governing Vessel 12

Reiki for Baby	Massage for Baby
For two or more minutes, place your hands on the following parts of your child's body: head, lungs, stomach and intestines, *hara* (belly), and lower back.	• Massage the abdomen to improve digestion. • Massage the front and back of the chest to break up mucus.

Cold: Concerns

Secondary infections, such as earaches, sinus infections, bronchitis, and pneumonia are the major concerns. Pay attention to your child's breathing, body temperature, and overall condition. Call your health care provider whenever you feel it is necessary.

Illness: Earache and Ear Infection
System: Respiratory

Earaches and ear infections are common in babies and toddlers, because their Eustachian tubes can easily become clogged by mucus, and so cultivate infection. These tubes connect your baby's ear to her throat and regulate air pressure in her ear. At birth, her Eustachian tubes are almost horizontal across her cheek, and this positioning can keep mucus from draining and trap bacteria or viruses. As she gets older, her Eustachian tubes begin to tilt downward and drain more easily.

Earache and Ear Infection: Symptoms

- Tugging on ear
- Accompanying upper-respiratory infection with drainage
- Irritability, fussiness
- Wakes up crying
- Fever
- Loss of appetite
- Vertigo
- Drainage from the ear—may be yellow, brown, or bloody
- Temporary hearing loss

Earache and Ear Infection: Causes

- Clogged Eustachian tubes
- Upper-respiratory infection
- Bacterial or viral infection specific to the ear
- Food stagnation, creating excess heat in the belly and rising into internal meridians from intestines to stomach to inner ear
- Reaction to vaccine
- Allergies

Earache and Ear Infection: Prevention

Earaches in babies are often the result of blockage from a cold. If your baby gets a cold, treat it to help her nasal passages clear.

- If you bottle-feed your baby, feed her slowly and make sure she is upright. Allow time for her formula to digest.
- Protect your baby's ear pressure when you travel by plane (especially during takeoff and landing), or change elevations while driving by having her breast-feed or suck on a pacifier or bottle.
- Keep your baby's environment as pollutant-free as possible.
- If your child does require antibiotics, take care to rebuild her immune and digestive systems with fermented foods and probiotic booster.

Earache and Ear Infection: Suggestions for Care

When your baby's ear hurts due to mucus or infection, keep her immune system charged, so it can fight infection, and keep her as comfortable as possible. These methods can help move mucus:

- Keep the air around your baby well humidified.
- Keep the airway passages in her nose clear. Use a nasal aspirator for babies, and have an older child blow her nose. If the mucus is thick, try a neti pot cleanse to get it flowing.
- Gently pull the earlobe of the ear that hurts. Pull downward and outward to help open the Eustachian tubes and the ear.
- When your baby is resting or sleeping, put her on the side with the ear that hurts up toward the open air.
- Do not use eardrops unless instructed by your health care provider.
- In the past, health care providers commonly used antibiotics for earaches. Today, most pediatricians prefer to monitor an earache to see if it turns into an infection that the immune system alone cannot heal before prescribing antibiotics.

Food and Remedies for Nursing Mother or Baby Older than Six Months

With earaches and ear infections, offer foods that boost immunity, and keep your baby hydrated and comfortable.

Foods to Emphasize	Foods to Avoid
Warm foods and a simple diet to keep your baby hydrated and to build digestion and immunity. Frequently breast-feed or bottle-feed your baby. For older children, offer water, broth, herbal tea, fermented foods, and probiotic booster. Chamomile herbal tea can help loosen mucus and relieve an earache. Kuzu drinks help calm your baby and are alkaline-producing for the blood.	Cold foods and beverages, as well as foods that cause allergies or thicken and increase mucus, such as dairy products, wheat, eggs, corn, oranges, and peanut butter. Also stay away from foods that decrease immunity, such as sugar, fruit, and juice.

Essential Oils for Baby	Acupoints for Baby
Put warm sesame oil, lavender oil, or tea tree oil on a cotton ball. Press the cotton ball into the affected ear to ease the pain and to help loosen mucus in the passageway. Ginger compress or warm washcloth over the ear; Bach's Rescue Cream rubbed around the ear and the affected area	Stomach 36 Spleen 3, 9 Kidney 3, 7 Triple Heater 5 Gallbladder 20 Liver 3 Governing Vessel 20

Reiki for Baby	Massage for Baby
For two or more minutes, place your hands on the following parts of your child's body: in front of and behind the ear and at the base of the skull.	Massage your baby's ears by placing the fleshy part of your palm below your thumb onto her ears and rotating. This can help keep her Eustachian tubes open. • Massage the gallbladder and spleen meridians. • Massage the triple heater meridian from her elbow to the back of her hand.

Earache and Ear Infection: Concerns

Earaches are common, and most get better quickly with a little care. Ear infections can recur in some children, however. Be careful to treat an ear infection early, because it can cause the eardrum to rupture if left untreated. Repeated ear infections can cause language-development problems or hearing loss. Contact your health care provider if your baby has swelling, pain, or redness behind her ear or has fluid or blood leaking from her ear.

Illness: Asthma
System: Respiratory

Asthma is an inflammatory respiratory sickness that causes difficulty in breathing. When a child has asthma, irritants can easily inflame her airways. The airways not only begin to narrow and swell, but also to produce mucus, which makes breathing a whole-body labor that further exhausts the child. Asthma is a chronic condition. There is no cure, and if left untreated, it can be life threatening. Asthma also is hereditary. If you or your partner has asthma, your child is more likely to develop it. However, the disease can be managed well.

Asthma: Symptoms

- Chronically inflamed airways
- Wheezing and crackling sounds when breathing
- Tight chest
- Coughing
- Using shoulders and torso to breathe

Asthma: Causes

- Allergies
- Environmental irritants: dust, mold, chemicals, and smoke
- Upper-respiratory infections
- Emotional distress, stress, or excitement
- Changes in weather
- Exercise
- Low energy
- Weak digestion or gastroesophageal reflux

Asthma: Prevention

To prevent an asthma attack, identify, and then avoid the triggers. Keep a journal of your child's attacks. For each attack, record her activity, possible trigger(s), the severity of the attack, and how you reversed it (for example, medications used). Thorough records can help you and your child manage the disease.

To strengthen your child's lungs, encourage her to engage in physical activities that exercise her lungs, such as running, swimming, and singing. Discourage television, video games, and electronic toys that can be overstimulating without physical activity. Encourage good posture with yoga or dance, so that your child's lungs have room to breathe. Support your child to manage her emotions.

Asthma: Suggestions for Care

You and your health care provider can find the triggers for your child's disease and develop a plan. This plan will help lessen the threat of those triggers and to open her airways should another attack occur. Your health care provider will equip you with a peak-flow meter (to help you gauge the severity of an attack at home) and medicines to restore your child's breath. As with allergies, treating asthma at the first sign can reduce the disease's severity.

Ensure that your child gets plenty of rest, and keep the air in her environment humidified. If she is old enough, let her sleep propped up to allow easier breathing. To help prepare your child for future attacks, teach her deep-breathing or relaxation techniques to help her stay calm and to relax her air passages. Panic and crying can cause tension and tightness in the chest. Between attacks, support your child in getting natural treatments to strengthen her body.

Topical Treatments

- Comfrey salve (rubbed into the chest)
- Ginger compress or warm water bottle (against chest or back)

Foods to Emphasize

Help your child form regular eating habits for healthy digestion and hydration through foods (in order to thin mucus). Offer immunity-boosting foods and brightly colored foods high in bioflavonoids, such as berries, purple grapes, and winter squashes. Onion and garlic reduce inflammation. Also, offer plenty of whole grains, fresh vegetables, fruits, and sesame seeds. Bach Flower Rescue Remedy can help calm your baby.

Foods to Avoid

Phlegm-producing foods, such as citrus, cow's milk, cheese, oily foods, peanuts, tree nuts, bananas, sugar, wheat, soy, eggs, shellfish, fish, chocolate, and tomatoes. Also, avoid preservatives such as sulfites, MSG, and food coloring, which can exacerbate asthma.

Essential Oils for Baby

Tea tree, lavender, eucalyptus, lemon

Acupoints for Baby

Lung 5, 7
Stomach 36, 40
Spleen 6
Bladder 17, 18, 20, 23
Kidney 7
Heart Governor 6

Reiki for Baby

For two or more minutes, place your hands on the following parts of your child's body: forehead and temples, back and top of head, lungs, stomach and intestines, heart, *hara* (belly), and lower back (kidney area).

Massage for Baby

- Gently massage the neck muscles below the ear down toward the collarbone.
- Massage the lung meridian.
- Massage the breastbone downward and in a sweeping direction.
- From the center of the chest, push outward toward the armpits and then below the rib cage.
- At the back of the neck, massage along the spine, the tops of the shoulders, and the small of the back, and push apart the shoulder blades.

Asthma: Concerns

Severe asthma requires immediate medical attention. Ask your health care provider to partner with you in managing this chronic condition. Contact your health care provider if your baby struggles to breathe or has a severe asthma attack.

Your Baby's Integumentary System

The skin, hair, and nails make up your baby's integumentary system, her largest organ system. It wraps around her body, holding it together and protecting the internal organs, fluids, and deep tissues.

The skin has three layers: the epidermis (outer), the dermis (middle), and the hypodermis, or subcutaneous fat. Since the epidermis is on the outside, it serves as a protector against environmental threats and infectious organisms.

The dermis is where the skin's blood vessels, nerve endings, and sweat and oil glands reside. The nerve endings send messages about sensations to the nervous system, thus enabling your baby's sense of touch. The dermis also supports thermoregulation—the process of insulating and maintaining body temperature—by opening her blood vessels and sweat glands when they are hot and contracting her blood vessels when they are cold. As her sweat glands push sweat to and through the epidermis, they also rid the body of toxins. Much like the sweat glands, the dermis's oil glands (sebaceous glands) push oil to the skin's surface to keep it both moist and waterproof.

Below the dermis, the hypodermis, or subcutaneous fat layer, is an energy reserve. When you burn calories, this is where they come from. This thick buffer also serves to regulate body temperature.

Your baby's skin, hair, and nails rapidly renew and repair themselves every minute of every day. However, because the skin eliminates body waste, excesses, and imbalances, it can easily manifest rashes, eczema, and sores. To keep your baby's skin healthy and supple, use natural skin products, as well as soaps and detergents that are free of harmful chemicals and artificial fragrances. Avoid exposing her skin to extremes of hot and cold or strong sunshine without protection. Natural fabrics are best for clothes and bedding that are next to your baby's skin.

Common childhood illnesses connected to the integumentary system include eczema, cradle cap, diaper rash, and conjunctivitis.

Illness: Eczema, Cradle Cap
System: Integumentary

Eczema presents as patches of itchy, dry, red skin, sometimes with white or red bumps. Eczema can range from chronically red, irritated, weeping skin to a few patches of dry skin that disappear after a few days. About 10 percent of children in the United States develop some form of eczema during childhood. Chronic eczema can be annoying, but it can usually be treated.

Many babies get cradle cap, a condition that also produces flaky skin. The skin becomes scaly on the top of the head and sometimes around the ears and neck. Experts think that cradle cap is a buildup of extra skin cells and oil. It causes no discomfort and is harmless. Cradle cap usually occurs within the first few months of a baby's life and clears up by 6 to 12 months.

Eczema, Cradle Cap: Symptoms

Symptoms of eczema:
- Itchy and uncomfortable dry, scaly skin
- Tiny white bumps or red patches
- Oozing patches, which may appear where the skin creases around the neck, elbows, wrists, hands, feet, and backs of the knees
- Worsening in winter, when the air is especially dry

Symptoms of cradle cap:
- Scaly, crusty rash on the scalp, especially over the soft spot (fontanel), sometimes on the eyebrows and around the ears and neck

Eczema, Cradle Cap: Causes

Causes of eczema:
- Allergies
- Reaction to vaccine
- Reaction to antibiotics
- Stress and anxiety
- According to East Asian medicine, eczema occurs when there is stagnation that prevents good circulation of the blood to the skin, which can be caused by excess phlegm

Causes of cradle cap:
- Excess skin cells and oil production caused by birth hormones
- Reaction to formula or food

Eczema, Cradle Cap: Prevention

Prevention of eczema:
- Keep the air around your baby moist.
- Keep her out of the wind and cold.
- Anything that touches her skin should be irritant-free. Be mindful of chlorinated pools, soaps, perfumes, and detergents.

To keep her systems running smoothly and to prevent digestive stagnation, burp your baby after feeding, and limit nighttime feedings, if possible.

Prevention of cradle cap:
- Keep your baby's scalp clean and dry.
- Gently but thoroughly brush or comb your baby's hair every day.

Eczema, Cradle Cap: Suggestions for Care

Be gentle with skin prone to eczema. When bathing your baby, use unscented, hypoallergenic soaps and moisturizers and warm water. Avoid bubble baths and hot baths. Use a soft towel to pat your baby dry. Be sure to bathe her after she sweats or plays in dirt or environments where she may have picked up an irritant, such as dust, mold, animal dander, or pollen.

Dress her in loose-fitting, long-sleeved, soft cotton clothing, and use soft cotton bedding. Wash clothes and bedding with scent-free hypoallergenic laundry detergent, and rinse clothes an extra time if needed. Avoid scented products and PABA in sunscreen. Maintain proper humidity in the air surrounding your baby. Do not use steroid creams to treat eczema, because they can exacerbate the condition and push the eczema inward, causing asthma. Unlike eczema, cradle cap usually does not require treatment, but you can oil your baby's head with sesame or olive oil and brush the scalp gently to remove dead skin.

Topical Treatments

- Sesame oil
- Chamomile tea in bath
- Rice bran or oat bran
- Bach's Rescue Cream
- Bentonite clay

Foods to Emphasize

A diet rich in fruits (especially berries), vegetables (especially cooked carrots and leafy greens), and omega-3 fats. Offer fermented foods and probiotic booster.

Foods to Avoid

Foods that trigger allergic reactions and create excess phlegm, such as dairy products from cows, eggs, soy, peanuts and tree nuts, fish and shellfish, chocolate, corn, and wheat. Avoid ice-cold beverages and foods, oranges, bananas, and other damp, phlegm-producing foods. Avoid sugar, food coloring, and artificial flavoring.

Essential Oils for Baby

Tea tree oil, lavender, eucalyptus

For eczema, use these oils in the bath and for massage (combine with a carrier oil).

For cradle cap, massage lavender (combined with a carrier oil) into the scalp and then gently remove dead skin.

Acupoints for Baby

Lung 5
Stomach 25, 36
Spleen 3
Bladder 17, 18, 20, 23
Kidney 7
Liver 3
Gallbladder 20
Governing Vessel 20
Conception Vessel 12
Heart 8

Reiki for Baby

For two or more minutes, place your hands on the following parts of your child's body: abdomen, chest, neck, back, *hara* (belly), and other affected area(s).

Massage for Baby

- Gently massage the neck muscles.
- Massage the back of the neck, the areas along the spine, the tops of the shoulders, and the small of the back.

Eczema, Cradle Cap: Concerns

Neither eczema nor cradle cap is life threatening. However, severe cases of eczema can be painful and irritating, and oozing open wounds can become infected with bacteria. With cradle cap, picking at crusts can lead to bleeding and bacterial infection. Speak with your health care provider if your baby fits any of these criteria:

- Has infected skin from eczema or cradle cap
- Has eczema or cradle cap that seems to be spreading or getting worse
- Has eczema or cradle cap for the first time

Illness: Diaper Rash
System: Integumentary

Diaper rash occurs when your baby's sensitive skin becomes inflamed from a reaction to external irritants. It is not usually dangerous, but problems can occur if it becomes infected. Diaper rash can be very painful for your baby, however, so it is best to address the condition as soon as possible.

Diaper Rash: Symptoms	Diaper Rash: Causes
• Irritated, inflamed skin in diaper area • Red, bumpy rash • Oozing and/or bleeding skin (in severe cases)	• Friction from diapers • Diapers not changed quickly enough after soiling • Bacteria • Yeast • Diarrhea • Ingredients in wipes • Vigorous cleaning • Sensitivity to disposable diapers • Sensitivity to detergent used with cloth diapers • Food allergies

Diaper Rash: Prevention

- Change diapers frequently (at least every two hours) or immediately upon becoming soiled.
- Be sure the diaper area is well-cleaned and dry before putting on a new diaper.
- Use unscented soaps, lotions, and wipes on your baby.

Diaper Rash: Suggestions for Care

If your baby develops diaper rash, be extra careful with her skin. Instead of wiping her bottom, squirt water on it with a bulb syringe and then blot to clean. If you do use wipes, use unscented wipes with calendula. Change her diaper often, let her body air-dry, and make the diaper loose to promote airflow. Once your baby has a rash, apply zinc oxide or calendula diaper cream at each diaper change. If possible, allow your baby to go diaperless for a while each day and get sunlight on her bottom to promote healing.

Food and Remedies for Nursing Mother or Baby Older than Six Months

Pay attention to foods that affect diaper rash.

Topical Treatments

- For a dry, scaly, chapped diaper rash: sesame oil
- For a moist rash: bentonite clay
- For daily care at diaper change: calendula or comfrey salve

Foods to Emphasize

Whole grains, cooked vegetables, fermented foods, and probiotic booster. Drink water, chamomile herbal tea, or miso soup to reduce acidity in your baby's urine.

Foods to Avoid

Sugar, fruit and fruit juices, sweets, citrus, strawberries, tomatoes, dairy, excessive amounts of yeast breads, sugar, and caffeine (through the nursing mother).

Essential Oils for Baby

Lavender, chamomile, rose

Acupoints for Baby

Lung 5
Large Intestine 11
Stomach 25
Spleen 6, 9
Kidney 3
Liver 3, 8
Conception Vessel 12
Bladder 56

Reiki for Baby

For two or more minutes, place your hands on the following parts of your child's body:
hara (belly) and other affected areas.

Diaper Rash: Concerns

Speak with your health care provider if your baby has diaper rash that is inflamed and irritated with signs of infection (redness, swelling, discharge), or if she shows no improvement after one week.

Illness: Conjunctivitis (Pinkeye)
System: Integumentary

When your baby awakens with her eyes crusted with discharge, she probably has pinkeye or conjunctivitis. With pinkeye, the clear membranes inside her eyes become inflamed, red, and irritated. Pinkeye is common and can be contagious.

Conjunctivitis (Pinkeye): Symptoms

- Red eyes that feel gritty and sore
- Yellow or green discharge from the eye
- Eyelids matted with discharge during and after sleep
- Accompanying condition such as a cold, sore throat, or upper-respiratory infection

Conjunctivitis (Pinkeye): Causes

- Bacteria or viruses
- Allergies or irritants
- Blocked tear ducts
- Foreign object in eye
- Excessive heat and dampness
- Imbalance of liver and gallbladder energy

Conjunctivitis (Pinkeye): Prevention

Conjunctivitis that is caused by bacteria or a virus is highly contagious, so be aware of others who have it. If your child has pinkeye, continue to encourage her to wash her hands frequently and to avoid rubbing and touching her eyes. Also, be sure she has her own set of towels and linens at home, and change them after the infection is gone. Keep her home from child care, school, and public swimming pools until the infection clears.

Conjunctivitis (Pinkeye): Suggestions for Care

Conjunctivitis is not usually dangerous, but it needs to be treated. Take the following steps if your child has red eyes with discharge:
- Wash discharge from her eyes with warm or cool water and cotton balls three times per day, wiping from the inside toward the outside of the eye.
- Be sure your child uses separate washcloths and towels from everyone else in the house.
- Do not use over-the-counter eyedrops.

Topical Treatments

- Chamomile tea bags moistened with warm water as an eye compress
- Sesame oil on the eyelids before sleep can make the matted discharge easier to remove in the morning

Foods to Emphasize

Clear fluids and broths, green and yellow vegetables, and fruits (especially berries).

Foods to Avoid

Foods that create heat, such as red meat, garlic, refined sugar, dairy, eggs, spicy foods, and oily foods.

Essential Oils for Baby

Lavender, chamomile, rose

Acupoints for Baby

Stomach 36
Spleen 6
Triple Heater 5
Gallbladder 20, 34
Liver 3

Reiki for Baby

For two or more minutes, place your hands on the following parts of your child's body: over the eyes, between the eyes and the nose, and between the eyes and the temples.

Massage for Baby

- If the cause is a blocked tear duct, gently massage from the inner corner of each eye toward the nose for one minute a few times per day.
- For other causes, gently massage the forehead on and above the eyebrows, stroking outward from the bridge of the nose toward the temples.
- Massage the cheekbones to help cool the eyes and to reduce inflammation.
- Massage the back of the neck at the base of the neck and move across the shoulders. Then gently stroke the back next to the spine down toward the lower back.
- Massage the stomach, kidney, and liver meridians.
- Gently pinch the bridge of the nose between the eyes and vibrate gently for two minutes to expel excess heat from the eyes.

Conjunctivitis (pinkeye): Concerns

Pinkeye usually clears by itself. Speak with your health care provider if your baby has blurred vision or pain in her eye.

Your Baby's Nervous System

Your baby's nervous system controls her body. It comprises her brain, her spinal cord, and her nerves, with billions of neurons (nerve cells). With the brain as the command center, messages from the nerves travel up and down the spinal cord and throughout her body via the neurons to tell the body what to do and how to react. For instance, when the nerves in the skin on your baby's hand feel something sharp, they send a sensory neuron to the brain to report the sensation. The brain interprets the message and sends a motor neuron back to the hand to tell it to move away from the source of pain.

The brain controls unconscious movements and processes, such as breathing, digestion, sensing, heart rate, blood pressure, balance, and coordination. It also controls conscious movement, memory, intelligence, personality, speech, and emotion.

Your baby is born with nearly all the neurons she will ever have. But at birth, the neurons have yet to connect. As she grows and has experiences, her neurons make connections, or synapses, that create pathways in her brain—a process known as learning. With practice, tasks that were once new and called for high levels of concentration (such as tying a shoe) become easier because her brain simply follows the pathways for those tasks. With these pathways in place, her brain is free to create more connections and more pathways—thus building more knowledge.

Your baby's brain and nervous system undergo incredible growth during her first few years. A newborn's brain accounts for about 25 percent of her approximate adult weight. By age three, the brain has grown close to its adult size through stimulation and the building of synapses.

Your baby's kidneys govern her nervous system by regulating the balance of sodium and potassium in her cells. Thus, strong kidney function benefits her nervous system. From that perspective, your baby benefits from gentle and regular stimulation of all her senses, as well as attention to and regulation of sugary foods.

Common childhood illnesses connected to the nervous system include insomnia and hyperactivity.

Illness: Insomnia

System: Nervous

From birth to three years old, children require around 16 hours of sleep per 24-hour cycle, and this sleep generally comes in two-hour intervals. By six months of age, most babies sleep about 12 hours a night, plus four or so hours of daytime napping. As babies continue to mature, nighttime sleeping hours increase and daytime naps become shorter. By three years old, children typically sleep about 14 hours a night and spend two hours a day napping.

When your baby cannot fall asleep, cannot stay asleep (especially if they wake crying in the night), or is drowsy during waking hours, she may have insomnia.

Insomnia: Symptoms

- Trouble falling asleep
- Wakes crying in the night; needs comfort to go back to sleep
- Tired during the day
- Dark circles under eyes

Insomnia: Causes

- Anxiety
- Digestive issues (cold foods, spicy foods)
- Dehydration
- Hunger
- Teething
- Illness
- Antibiotics

Insomnia: Prevention

Create a bedtime routine that may include dinner, a story, a bath, a back rub or massage, rocking, cuddling, singing, or listening to music. Soft noises like white noise can also help your baby relax and fall asleep. Try breathing and relaxation techniques with your baby. Encourage vigorous physical activity early in the day, and take some time in nature. Pay attention to signs such as droopy eyelids, eye rubbing, and irritability. Anticipate when your baby is likely to get tired, and plan around it.

If your child is afraid of the dark, leave on a night-light ,or leave the door open a crack. Encourage your child to talk about any disturbing or frightening events that may have occurred during the day. Avoid scary TV shows or stories before sleep.

Insomnia: Suggestions for Care

Consider foods and environmental factors that may disturb sleep. Make sure your baby's room has an appropriate temperature, comfortably moist air, a low amount of noise, and dim lighting. Also be sure your baby is neither hungry nor overfed before bed and has been well hydrated throughout the day. Dress her for sleep in comfortable, breathable clothing. Overstimulation from watching too much television or other media before bed can contribute to waking at night and nightmares. Antibiotics and immunizations such as HiB or pertussis can cause disrupted sleep as well. Check to see if your baby is teething or suffering from some other ailment or physical discomfort that could cause insomnia.

Food and Remedies for Nursing Mother or Baby Older than Six Months	Topical Treatments
Troubles with digestion can contribute to insomnia.	• Ginger compress on back for relaxation • Warm bath

Foods to Emphasize	Foods to Avoid
Light snacks, such as toast, oatmeal, and crackers, can help your baby sustain her blood sugar throughout the night and keep her sleeping. Chamomile herbal tea is relaxing and can help her sleep.	Stimulants in food and drink, such as caffeine (through the nursing mother), chocolate, and refined sugar. Also steer clear of food additives and other common ingredients in processed food. Avoid foods that are cooling to the digestive system, such as bananas, yogurt, ice cream, and cow's milk, and foods and that are heavy and excessively warming, such as spicy and greasy foods. Be conscious of dyes and synthetic chemicals in processed foods, as they may cause overactivity.

Essential Oils for Baby	Acupoints for Baby
Lavender, chamomile, rose	Stomach 36 Spleen 6 Heart Governor 5, 6 Gallbladder 20 Liver 3 Conception Vessel 6, 12 Governing Vessel 20

Reiki for Baby	Massage for Baby
For two or more minutes, place your hands on the following parts of your child's body: forehead and temples, back of head, top of head, and stomach and intestines.	Give your child a whole-body massage to calm her energy.

Insomnia: Concerns

Insomnia in children can be related to depression, anxiety, chronic ear infection, sleep apnea due to blocked airways, fever, or night terrors. If the insomnia is persistent, consult your health care provider.

Illness: Hyperactivity
System: Nervous

Children who are bursting with energy, are rarely still, and are easily distracted may be described as hyperactive. In infancy and toddlerhood, however, there is no line that differentiates a child who is hyperactive from one who is merely high-spirited. You can help your child regulate her energy level by observing it and by offering ways to increase or decrease it through food, natural remedies, and activities.

Hyperactivity: Symptoms

- Inability to sit sill
- Restlessness while nursing or feeding
- Back arching, muscle tensing, constant wiggling
- Fitful sleep; wakes often; inability to self-soothe

Hyperactivity: Causes

- Unbalanced diet or food allergies
- Lack of sleep
- Genetics or chemical imbalance
- Need for kinesthetic movement

Hyperactivity: Prevention

Proper sleep, healthy food, fresh air, exercise

Hyperactivity: Suggestions for Care

Be sure your baby is getting everything she needs to achieve balance in her body systems—adequate sleep, nourishing food, fresh air, and vigorous daily exercise. Maintain routines and feeding schedules in order to minimize anxiety while regulating blood sugar. With seemingly hyperactive children, daily exercise is especially helpful for expelling extra energy, relaxing, and promoting focus. Discourage television, movies, and video games, which can cause anxiety. Try to keep your home calm and stress-free.

In addition, be sure your child's caregivers and teachers are adequately matched to her temperament. A low-energy caregiver can become exasperated by a high-energy child, thus limiting the child's natural curiosity and hurting her self-image and potential. When she enters preschool, make sure she has learning opportunities that support her learning style.

Once you notice that your baby may have more energy than is typical, begin to keep a diary of her behaviors. If she does need professional intervention, your diary can become helpful in obtaining a proper diagnosis and crafting an effective treatment plan.

Food and Remedies for Nursing Mother or Baby Older than Six Months	Topical Treatments
Food impacts energy. A diet of nutritious, whole foods keeps energy flowing at a steady pace.	• Ginger compress • Warm bath

Foods to Emphasize	Foods to Avoid
A balanced diet that includes cold-water fish such as tuna or salmon, borage oil, flax oil, primrose oil, cod liver oil, and algae.	Sugar, caffeine (through the nursing mother), chocolate, gluten, and casein. Also avoid food additives, especially food coloring, benzoates, nitrates, sulfites, calcium silicates, BHT, BHA, benzoyl peroxide, emulsifiers, thickeners, stabilizers, vegetable gums, food starch, artificial flavorings, preservatives, and monosodium glutamate.

Essential Oils for Baby	Acupoints for Baby
Lavender, chamomile	Stomach 36, 40 Spleen 6 Heart 7 Kidney 3 Heart Governor 6 Gallbladder 34 Liver 3 Conception Vessel 12

Reiki for Baby	Massage for Baby
For two or more minutes, place your hands on the following parts of your child's body: *hara* (belly), lower back, back below the ribs (kidney area), and forehead, temples, and top of head.	Give your child a whole-body massage to calm her energy.

Hyperactivity: Concerns

As your child matures, if you continue to have concerns about hyperactivity, talk to your pediatrician about seeing a professional who specializes in hyperactivity in children. Consider testing for food allergies.

Your Baby's Endocrine System

The endocrine system is a system of glands that secrete hormones to instruct the body's cells about what do to and when to do it. The major glands of the endocrine system are the pituitary, pineal, hypothalamus, parathyroid, thyroid, adrenal, pancreas, ovaries, and testes. When each of these glands secretes a particular hormone, that hormone enters the bloodstream. Together, the glands secrete more than 20 major hormones that are responsible for mood, growth rate, metabolism, sexual function, reproduction, and other body processes. For instance, the pancreas secretes insulin, which allows glucose to enter the body as energy. The thyroid secretes hormones that regulate metabolism, bone growth, and growth in the nervous system. The adrenal glands secrete energy-boosting hormones in times of stress. The pineal gland's hormone, melatonin, regulates sleep and wake cycles. Finally, the ovaries and testes secrete hormones for reproductive functions.

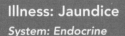

Overseeing all this secretion and keeping the body in balance is the pituitary gland, located in the brain. The pituitary gland produces hormones that control the other glands and tell them when to secrete and when to hold back.

You can help your baby's endocrine system develop and strengthen by feeding her whole foods, especially healthy fats and oils and minerals. Avoid using products or toys that contain endocrine (or hormone) disruptors, such as BPA, PVC, and parabens. Contact with these products can affect your baby's delicate system.

Common childhood illnesses connected to the endocrine system include jaundice.

Illness: Jaundice
System: Endocrine

Jaundice occurs when there is buildup of bilirubin, the waste produced when red blood cells break down. Most newborns experience mild jaundice, with a yellow skin color that usually appears on the face first, and then moves down the torso to the legs. A typical case develops three or four days after birth and disappears within a week or two. Some studies have shown that a slight elevation in bilirubin in infants may actually help their bodies fight off bacterial infections and provide valuable antioxidants to the brain. Jaundice that appears within a day of birth can cause more concern.

Most cases of jaundice resolve on their own, but all cases need to be monitored by a health care provider. Should your health care provider determine that your child's bilirubin level is too high, she will probably be admitted to the hospital for phototherapy. She will be placed in an incubator under a special blue light that breaks down bilirubin. If she has a mild case of jaundice that still requires treatment, she may be sent home with a special blanket and lights that accomplish the same task.

Jaundice: Symptoms	Jaundice: Causes
<ul><li>Dull or bright yellow tinge to skin that starts at the head and travels down the body</li><li>Yellow tinge to the whites of the eyes</li><li>Yellowish mucous membranes and body fluids</li><li>Sleepiness</li><li>Constipation or loose stool</li><li>Reduced appetite and thirst</li></ul>	<ul><li>Buildup of bilirubin</li><li>Premature birth</li><li>Vitamin K shot at birth</li><li>Incompatible blood types between mother and baby</li><li>Diabetes in mother</li><li>Breast milk (very rare; occurs in 1 to 2 percent of cases)</li><li>Mother receiving anesthesia for birth</li><li>Induced labor</li><li>Stressed or difficult birth</li></ul>

Jaundice: Prevention

You can do your own natural light therapy by making sure your baby gets time in the sun every day. Allow her to nap, eat, and play in front of a sunny window. Take her outside for fresh air and sunshine, with as much skin exposed as possible. However, be careful to protect her skin from sunburn, her eyes from bright lights, and her body from overheating.

Jaundice: Suggestions for Care

If you suspect that your baby has jaundice, call your health care provider for an evaluation. Should your child need phototherapy treatment, ask your health care provider to create a schedule for feeding and bonding with you. Jaundice usually occurs within the first few days after birth, which is an important time to establish breast-feeding, if you plan to do so.

Unless your baby has one of the rare cases of breast milk-induced jaundice, increase your breast-feeding schedule. Bilirubin is excreted through the bowel movements, so frequent breast-feeding will help your newborn move her bowels and get rid of the excess bilirubin in her body.

Foods for Nursing Mother

Food impacts energy. A diet of nutritious, whole foods keeps the body's energy flowing at a steady pace.

Foods to Emphasize	Foods to Avoid
Drink warm water with lemon juice. Eat leafy greens, radishes, cooked vegetables, whole grains, apples, pears, and grapefruit	Oily, fatty or sugary foods, and bananas

Essential Oils for Baby	Acupoints for Baby
Lavender, chamomile	Stomach 36 Spleen 6 Gallbladder 34 Liver 3

Reiki for Baby	Massage for Baby
For two or more minutes, place your hands on the following parts of your child's body: • Over the liver below right rib cage • Mid back, toward the right side	Give your child a whole-body massage to calm her energy.

Jaundice: Concerns

Jaundice can develop quickly and can become serious. Check your newborn for a yellowish tint to her skin. In natural light, press lightly on her nose or forehead, and when you pull your finger away, check for a slight yellow tint. Contact your health care provider right away if you think she may have jaundice.

Your Baby's Muscular and Skeletal Systems

Your baby's more than 200 bones and 600 muscles serve to support her, to protect her vital organs, and to allow her to move. When she is born, her bones are very flexible, with growing plates and cartilage. This cartilage is what actually expands and then hardens, or ossifies, into strong bone, allowing her to become taller and bigger. Her bone growth will not be complete until she is about 20 years old. In addition to providing a frame for her skin, your baby's bones store minerals, such as calcium, phosphorus, sodium, and vitamin D, in case her body experiences a shortage.

Ligaments and tendons hold your baby's bones and joints together, and she uses her muscles to move. Through her cerebral motor cortex and cerebellum in her brain, she consciously commands her legs and arms. Her cardiac muscles, which are inside her heart, move involuntarily. Finally, her smooth muscles work involuntarily to move food through her stomach and intestines.

Your baby's skull, rib cage, and vertebrae wrap around and protect her internal organs, and her strong muscles protect her bones. Sea vegetables supply minerals and calcium to help build strong bones, while acidic foods such as sugar and tomatoes can leech calcium from her bones. Regular exercise can help your baby's bones and muscles grow strong and healthy.

Muscular and skeletal issues for babies up to three years old are rare. Therefore, there are no common childhood illnesses to list under this system.

Your Baby's Circulatory System

Your baby's circulatory system moves blood throughout her body, carrying oxygen, nutrients, and gases to her organs and tissues. Before birth, the umbilical cord acts as your baby's circulatory system; it gathers all she needs from her mother's placenta and then removes waste. When the umbilical cord is cut, your baby breathes her first few breaths of air, and that starts her independent circulation. From that moment on, with each heartbeat, her circulatory system carries blood from her heart to the billions of cells in her body.

Your baby's circulatory system depends on three body systems working together: cardiovascular (heart), pulmonary (lungs), and systemic (arteries, veins, and vessels). Her blood circulates through two loops in her body, from her heart to her lungs and back again. Her heart is the key actor, as it sorts and pumps her blood. Good blood flow affects every organ in your baby's body and every aspect of her health. Exercise, stretching, breathing exercises, physical connection through massage, good sleep, fresh air, and wholesome food help keep her circulatory system strong and vibrant.

Circulatory issues for babies up to three years old are rare. Therefore, there are no common childhood illnesses to list under this system.

Your Baby's Reproductive System

Your baby was born with her reproductive systems intact but dormant. This system awakens when her pituitary gland sends a signal to her gonads (ovaries in girls and testes in boys) to release hormones. This typically happens between 9 and 15 years of age, when puberty and reproduction begin.

In girls, the reproductive system consists of the vulva, vagina, uterus, cervix, fallopian tubes, and ovaries. Inside her ovaries are gametes—cells capable of joining other cells to reproduce. In women, gametes are called eggs. In men, they are called sperm. After puberty, a woman's eggs can join with a man's sperm to create a fetus.

At birth, hundreds of thousands of eggs are stored in a girl's ovaries. After she enters puberty, her ovaries release an egg about every 28 days. The egg travels into one of her fallopian tubes, where it is either fertilized by sperm or discharged through menses. In addition to producing eggs and allowing sexual intercourse for fertilization, female reproductive organs harbor and nourish a fetus as it develops.

The male reproductive system consists of his scrotum, testes, spermatic ducts, sex glands, and penis. The system's job is to produce sperm that can fertilize an egg. When a boy is born, the tip of his penis (the glans) is covered with foreskin. People of many religions and cultures perform circumcision by removing this skin. There is no proven medical reason for circumcision.

All babies, male and female, play with their genitalia, which is normal. When your child is old enough to understand, you can let her know that this is normal behavior, but it is best done in private.

Since the reproductive system is not necessary to sustain your child's life and is relatively dormant for her first few years, few common childhood illnesses are associated with it. However, be careful not to expose your baby to materials that might affect her hormones. These can be found in products, foods, or the environment.

CHAPTER 2

Heart and Spirit

HAPPINESS IN LIFE IS an ambition that parents around the world have for their children. What is the meaning of happiness? What does it mean for your child to have a radiant life? And what can you do to help your baby be happy now and grow into a happy adult?

Research on happiness is a growing field. The documentary film *Happy* examines scientific research into the state of happiness based on interviews with people from 14 different cultures. The researchers discovered that people who prioritize intrinsic values, such as relationships with family and friends, and people who have a sense of meaning in their lives, are more likely to be happy than those who focus on extrinsic values, such as money, power, and fame. True happiness does not come from having or doing something. Existential qualities, such as love, unity, truth, beauty, freedom, societal contribution, presence, and peace, are the sources of real fulfillment and satisfaction.

To help foster fulfillment and satisfaction in your child's life, you can start nurturing his emotional development in infancy. By providing him with a strong, healthy connection with at least one person and a space to grow with understanding, acceptance, and unconditional love, you give your child the best opportunity to develop autonomy, competence, and relationships—the elements of a happy life.

When Emi and Mari were babies, their emotions were pure and true. Angry, sad, or happy, they did not hold back. Emotions are present in every moment of your child's life. When he plays with toys, interacts with you, or eats, he is feeling something, and these feelings color his behavior, choices, growth, and development.

When your baby experiences a need or discomfort, he cries. If his needs are not met, he feels angry, afraid, or sad. The emotional support that he receives determines how successfully he acquires the emotional and social skills that he will carry throughout his life. Through brain-imaging technologies, researchers have discovered that the brain responds to emotions. They have begun to understand that emotional intelligence is foundational to learning skills and concepts, and it is necessary for cognitive development. Pediatricians and educators now recognize that a child's emotional development is essential to his overall development. This chapter offers three ways that you can help your child develop emotional intelligence:

❀ Daily Practices—This section discusses the importance of your child's emotional health and provides practical, daily practices that will foster his happiness.

❀ Theories of Emotional Development—The second section includes foundational theories of the process of emotional and social development to help you understand what your child experiences during the stages of infancy and toddlerhood.

❀ Essential Skills for Emotional and Social Intelligence—The third section explains the essential skills needed for positive emotional and social development with recommendations on how to develop them. At the end of this chapter there is information about choosing a child care provider.

As you move through this chapter, keep in mind that your child is unique, with his own personal path, personality, and temperament. You can help him discover and tap into the special qualities that add to his happiness.

Daily Practices

WHEN I WATCH A mother spontaneously nuzzle and kiss her baby's head, I recognize her natural tenderness. I remember the satisfaction that I felt when I held my daughters and breathed in their sweet scent. Humbled by their vulnerability and complete trust in me, I knew that I would do everything I could to provide the best for them. I felt that this love was bigger than my habits and my identity. This love required me to build and expand my point of view so that I could make choices that would give my babies the best chance for a healthy and happy life.

Before I had a baby, I thought love was a special way of feeling, but it was not until my children were born that I truly understood what love means. I realized that a parent's love is somehow fundamentally different from other types of love. I discovered that love was reflected in my aspirations for my children. I wanted my children to be healthy, happy, fulfilled, successful, and satisfied with themselves. Love was also reflected in my everyday actions and choices for my daughters. I understood why parents often care for their children in ways they do not care for themselves. For example, they may pay the extra cost for organic food and healthy products while sacrificing their own needs. Finally, I found that parenthood—and the love it brings—could also be a motivating and transformative force in my own life.

As a parent, you are in a position that impacts your child's emotional health. Your responses to your baby's emotions play a big role in how successfully he learns to use them and to avoid becoming ruled by them. By observing and encouraging his emotional development, you provide him with valuable skills that help him clarify his goals, navigate life's challenges, and find happiness. In this section I will describe practices that you can use every day to support your child's emotional development proactively.

Simple changes to the way you manage everyday activities can influence your baby's emotional health. When you take a moment to become aware of the simple daily processes that matter, you can make choices that inspire your child to grow and to flourish. Overall, the following practices set the foundation for your solid emotional development: remaining mindful, identifying and celebrating your child's positive qualities, acknowledging and accepting your child's feelings, creating a peaceful environment, structuring time consistently and effectively, managing stress, providing healthy food, providing healthy opportunities for movement, having a sense of humor, inventing and participating in rituals. Finally, when you take care of yourself, trust your child, and acknowledge the perfection of imperfection, you allow your child to be his own true self.

adults affect children. Even though I have read the poem many times, I appreciate revisiting these laws of cause and effect as I reflect on my children and on my own upbringing.

Practice Mindfulness

Mindful parenting requires that you be aware of your child, be open to him, and live in the present moment with him. When you are mindful, instead of reacting impulsively to a situation, you observe your thoughts and feelings and then relate to your child with intention and respect.

Your intentional actions and connections with your child begin to shape what he knows about himself and how he relates to the world. No matter which actions you take as a parent, what your child ultimately comprehends and integrates into himself is your intentionality—the thoughts behind your actions.

The practice of mindfulness in parenting helps you make decisions, relieves stress, and creates a stronger connection between you and your child. By practicing mindfulness, you also model mindfulness skills, thus laying the foundation for your child to develop mindfulness in himself. In her book *Sitting Still Like a Frog: Mindfulness Exercises for Kids (and Their Parents)*, Eline Snel, a therapist and the founder of the Academy for Mindful Teaching in the Netherlands, speaks to the many advantages of cultivating mindfulness in children: "By practicing mindful presence and awareness, kids learn to pause for a moment, to catch their breath, and to get a sense of what they need at this moment in time."

Be a Role Model

Your child learns by taking in the world around him and then imitating what he absorbs. He is more likely to copy your behavior, attitudes, and values than to listen to your instruction. Because your child is like a sponge, absorbing and learning from your gestures and actions, the truth of who you are is reflected back to you as he starts expressing himself. The reflection you see is an incredible opportunity for your own personal growth.

Your emotional regulation creates the emotional climate for your child. As in all areas of his life, you are his main role model. Your child absorbs the positive and the negative emotions in his environment, and they affect him, even if they are not directed toward him. He also associates emotions with experiences. For example, if you enthusiastically make cookies together as a fun activity, he will feel the excitement and associate that feeling with making cookies. However, if you feel pressured and hurried while making cookies, he may be apprehensive the next time you start baking. When you manage your own emotions in a way that meets your values and goals, you help your child balance his emotions in the same way.

Positive modeling is far more effective in teaching your child how to regulate his emotions than explanation, criticism, or punishment. I have provided a poem that I first discovered in the office of one of my college professors in 1972. It illustrates how the actions of

Benefits of Promoting Mindfulness

- Reduced stress, increased calm
- More ease in falling asleep
- Better impulse control
- Enhanced critical thinking
- Improved learning due to an openness to the environment and an increased ability to focus

Children Learn What They Live

By Dorothy Law Nolte, PhD

If children live with criticism, they learn to condemn.

If children live with hostility, they learn to fight.

If children live with fear, they learn to be apprehensive.

If children live with pity, they learn to feel sorry for themselves.

If children live with ridicule, they learn to feel shy.

If children live with jealousy, they learn to feel envy.

If children live with shame, they learn to feel guilty.

If children live with encouragement, they learn confidence.

If children live with tolerance, they learn patience.

If children live with praise, they learn appreciation.

If children live with acceptance, they learn to love.

If children live with approval, they learn to like themselves.

If children live with recognition, they learn it is good to have a goal.

If children live with sharing, they learn generosity.

If children live with honesty, they learn truthfulness.

If children live with fairness, they learn justice.

If children live with kindness and consideration, they learn respect.

If children live with security, they learn to have faith in themselves and in those about them.

If children live with friendliness, they learn the world is a nice place in which to live.

Developmentally, an infant or toddler does not have the ability to completely quiet his own mind, to consider a situation, and to act intentionally. However, you can help him cultivate his mindfulness skills as he grows into them naturally. Both you and your baby will begin to reap rewards from simply working toward mindfulness in the following ways.

Connect and Be Present

As is the case with meditation, the act of being present with your child is a form of mindfulness that can start with a few focused minutes a day and grow into longer and more active periods. If you can set aside at least 15 to 30 minutes a day to relax and to be together without interruptions, then you can establish a base of connection. If you are physically present but distracted with electronic devices, preoccupied with worries, or otherwise mentally absent, then your baby may feel dissatisfied and agitated.

You can strengthen your connection during these sessions by making sure all your senses are represented: I see you; I hear you; I smell you; I touch you; I taste you; I move with you. Following are some activities that you can use to be present, attuned, and resonant within your relationship with your baby. They require trust, and they also build trust.

Ways to Connect with Your Baby

- Spend one-on-one time together
- Make eye contact
- Cuddle, and hold him close, using skin-to-skin when possible
- Read to him
- Enjoy bath time
- Go for a walk
- Talk and sing with him
- Dance together to music
- Play and laugh together

"Watch, Wait, and Wonder" is a program used in psychotherapy for babies. Developed by Frank Johnson, PhD, Jerome Dowling, MD, and David Wesner, PhD, child psychiatrists working together at the University of Wisconsin, the program gives children the opportunity to use their innate need for attachment to foster the healing process and the development of a healthy attachment relationship. Even though the program is used for babies with serious emotional problems, it can be very beneficial for addressing smaller problems or for proactively supporting emotional health. Here is how the Watch, Wait, and Wonder method works:

- Start the program as early as four months old, and plan to continue until your child is around four years old.

- Set aside 30 minutes every day.

- Give your full, focused attention to your child by getting on the floor and being present with him.

- Let your child lead the way. Follow his direction as he plays.

This daily time for connection benefits your child in noticeable ways. In general, he will be happier and more enjoyable to be around. He will be more confident and comfortable expressing his creativity and imagination. He will also be more satisfied playing alone, and sibling rivalry will be less of a concern.

Daily time with your baby is a precious gift to you, as well. In his first few years, your baby grows and changes so quickly. As he gets older, you will cherish and appreciate the time you took to connect with your baby and to marvel at his emerging self.

 For more information on "Watch, Wait, and Wonder," visit growhealthygrowhappy.com

Place Attention on Breathing

Awareness of breathing is a gateway to mindfulness. In the practices of yoga and meditation, you can use your breath to connect with your mind, body, and spirit. If you are upset or in pain, deep and deliberate breathing can help you become calm and balanced.

I believe that scientists are only beginning to understand the effects of breath on physical and mental health. In *Breathing: The Master Key to Self Healing*, Andrew Weil, MD, explains that you can use your breath to regulate your nervous system, relieve pain, lower blood pressure, aid digestion, achieve overall better physical health, decrease stress, and improve mental health. No pills. No side effects. Just you, breathing.

Your breath is your connection between your parasympathetic nervous system (which governs normal overall functioning) and your sympathetic nervous system (which governs fight-or-flight mode). When you become panicked or stressed, your nervous system goes into a sympathetic state: your system is flooded with adrenaline, and your heart and breathing rates increase to prepare you to respond to an emergency. By simply focusing on your breath—inhaling and exhaling fully—you can return your body to a parasympathetic state in which you are calm and mindful.

Focused breathing can also help children calm down when they are frustrated or frightened. Alternatively, your toddler can focus on different parts of his body while breathing in order to calm his mind in preparation for sleep. Then, if he needs a boost when he wakes up, he can breathe more vigorously to help increase his energy.

Note that when your infant breathes, he uses his whole torso as his tummy goes up and down. This is called diaphragmatic, or belly breathing because the diaphragm helps the lungs draw air in and push air out. The result is fewer, longer, fuller breaths that fill his body with the oxygen it needs.

As children grow, they tend to shift from diaphragmatic breathing to thoracic breathing. Thoracic breathing involves only your child's upper chest muscles, resulting in quick, shallow breaths that are less nourishing to the body and mind than belly breaths are. Encourage your child to maintain a habit of diaphragmatic breathing, and discourage thoracic breathing. You can do this by watching your child's breathing on occasion to be sure his belly area is moving as he breathes. If it is not, gently direct his attention to his breath and help him to belly breathe again by using some of the exercises listed below. Most people do not trade belly breathing for chest breathing until well into childhood, at around age ten. If you take the time to help your baby establish an intentional habit of belly breathing when he is young, chest breathing may not become an issue for him. In addition, breathing exercises can be a fun activity for both of you.

✿ **Breathing with your baby: body surfing**—Lie down on your back and hold your baby on your chest and belly. As you inhale quietly through your nose, expand your belly and chest. Exhale through your mouth slowly and loudly as your belly contracts and lowers. Allow your baby to experience the rhythm of your breath. While this breathing exercise is geared toward babies, toddlers enjoy it, too.

✿ **Breathing with your toddler: tummy toy**—This technique gives your child awareness that his breath is his own and that he has the power to control it. Let your child lie down on his back, and place a favorite small toy on his tummy. Let him watch the toy go up and down as he breathes. Laugh together in amazement about the motion, and point out that his breath is making his toy go up and down.

✿ **Playing with breath**—Bring your toddler into awareness of his breath and how it affects him with the following playful activities described by Liz Bragdon in her article, "4 Breathing Exercises for Kids to Empower, Calm, and Self-Regulate" at the Move with Me Action Adventures website. Aside from sparking your toddler's imagination, these exercises can help him relax, get calm, ground himself, and become balanced:

Stop and smell the flowers— Pretend to smell a flower by breathing in through his nose and out his mouth.

Snake breath—Take a big belly breath, and then blow it out slowly through closed teeth like a snake.

Bear breath—Pretend to be a hibernating bear. Inhale through his nose to a count of four, hold his breath to a count of two, and exhale through his nose to a count of four.

Bunny breath—Pretend to be a bunny in the garden. Take three short sniffs—as if he is searching for a vegetable in the garden, and then take one long exhale out his nose.

Wherever your child goes in life, his breath is with him. You can help bring about incalculable benefits to his health and well-being by teaching him early in life to use his breath as a tool to regulate his energy and to cultivate a state of awareness.

 For more information on playing with breath visit move-with-me.com

Develop Sensory Awareness

Your child's senses—seeing, smelling, touching, hearing, tasting—bring him directly into the moment. For example, when he smells and tastes a favorite food, the world melts away into that moment. By supporting your child's sensory awareness, you can help him learn to stop the world, stop his thoughts, stop his judgment, and bring himself into the moment and into mindfulness. Here are a few exercises to help your child cultivate sensory awareness. You can practice these exercises yourself when your baby is young and then do them together as your child is able.

> ❀ **Mindful motion**—Pick an action such as walking, picking up a cup, or brushing your teeth. Move very slowly with consciousness and awareness. For instance, as you walk, give your attention to your feet, or as you pick up a cup, notice each tiny motion of your hand and arm.

> ❀ **Mindful eating**—At mealtimes you can guide your child out of his thoughts and into awareness of his senses by pointing out the different tastes and textures of food.

> ❀ **Body scan**—In this exercise, you place awareness on each part of your body in turn. Although babies are too young to do the actual exercise, you can use the body scan to help both of you relax, as your baby will be able to sense your stillness. When he is old enough, you can guide him through the exercise. If your child has trouble falling asleep, the body scan can become a bedtime ritual that he can eventually use by himself. The body scan begins with your feet and moves upward. Start by putting your attention on your toes and staying there for a moment. Next, check in with your toes, and notice how they feel. Then slowly move upward, and check in with your feet, ankles, calves, thighs, hips, back, belly, shoulders, neck, head, arms, and fingers.

Many different practices, such as yoga, can help your child to become aware of his body, his senses, and himself. In general, you can help him stop time by asking him how something tastes or how his feet feel. You can also sit in silence together to bring him into a state of mindfulness.

Practice Meditation

Meditation is a term that covers a wide variety of practices with a wide variety of purposes. The most common forms of meditation bring you into the present moment—and, in doing so, they relieve stress, lower the heart rate, boost brainpower, and enhance well-being. Many forms of meditation are rooted in religion but lend themselves to secular practice, as well. My daily meditation practice is a fairly simple, straightforward practice. If you would like to try it, here is how:

- Find a quiet space at a time when your baby is napping or being cared for by someone else.

- Sit comfortably in a chair with your feet on the floor, your spine aligned, and your arms relaxed. Alternatively, you can sit on a meditation cushion on the floor. If you wish, put your hands together on your belly to help bring your attention inward.

- Close your eyes. Bring your attention inside to your *hara*, or belly (located about two finger widths below your navel and two finger widths inward).

- Breathe slowly and deeply.

- When thoughts come up, notice them and let them go. Redirect your attention to the place inside your belly.

- At first, you can practice meditating for 10 to 15 minutes a day. Then slowly increase to 30 minutes as you feel more comfortable and have more time.

Although your baby is not yet able to meditate, he can absorb the calm energy that you feel through your practice. Meditation balances your emotions and clears your thoughts, thus allowing you to parent less reactively and more mindfully. Meditation is a time for yourself, as well as a gift to your family.

By encouraging connection and presence, bringing attention to your baby's breath, developing his sensory awareness, and practicing meditation, you can pass mindfulness skills to your baby. As Eline Snel writes in the early chapters of *Sitting Still Like a Frog*, "You cannot control the sea. You cannot stop the waves, but you can learn to surf on them. This is the central idea underlying mindfulness practice." Mindfulness pays off in the quality of your daily life and the daily life of your child.

Take a Positive Approach

Metta is a popular form of Buddhist meditation that cultivates loving-kindness. It is an attitude of friendliness that recognizes the best in others with empathy and compassion. It is an expression of love that is without expectations. When you view your child with *metta*, you aspire to imagine his highest potential,

unbounded by limits or restraints. With *metta*, your love for him is unconditional, and you wish the best for him. A positive and helpful approach to your child's development involves being mindful that your actions and words are truly about him, his dreams, and his potential.

Your mental image of your child can become a self-fulfilling prophecy. Your beliefs precede your actions, which in turn reinforce his beliefs and actions. If you think that your child is smart and capable, then you most likely expect him to be intelligent, and do all you can to nourish his mental development, thus making it more likely that he does become a bright, capable child. On the other hand, a negative image of your child can create negative expectations for him. Thoughts and words are very powerful, and they affect not only how you feel about him, but also how he feels about himself.

Children see themselves through the reflection of their parents' eyes. The beliefs that your child develops about himself depend a lot on the feedback that he receives and perceives, especially from parents and other primary caregivers. These messages are a mirror to him because he trusts you and believes what you believe about him. He absorbs your feedback—positive, negative, or neutral—and it helps form his self-image.

Actions speak louder than words, but words still matter, and they should be chosen with awareness. When it comes to reacting positively to your child, Austrian psychiatrist Alfred Adler, MD found that encouragement is a healthier approach than praise. He drew this distinction in the early 20th century, and subsequent studies have supported his conclusions.

According to Adler's theory, the language of praise is judgmental and focuses on a result, while the language of encouragement is inspirational and focuses on a process. Here is an example of praise: "I am proud of you for winning the game." Here is an example of encouragement: "You played hard, and your efforts paid off." Praise can cause children to become motivated by approval alone, thus inhibiting their internal motivation. Encouragement, on the other hand, recognizes the child's own choices and efforts, and thus builds self-evaluation and internal motivation.

When you connect your baby's actions to internal satisfaction instead of tangible rewards, such as stickers, toys, or candy, he develops confidence and learns to associate himself with who he is instead of what he does. Be honest and sincere as you focus on encouraging his process and behavior, rather than merely praising his achievements. Avoid comparing him to other children, either by using him as an example of the better one or by using someone else as an example.

A positive approach also involves recognizing your child for exactly who he is and letting him know that you see him. When you recognize him, you acknowledge that you know him, including his current fears, pleasures, and interests. When you show that you recognize your child, he feels that he is understood, that he is okay, and that the world is right and good.

By remaining as positive as possible, you help your child feel loved, valued, worthy, and confident. Your encouraging words and actions provide the path to his belief in himself.

Acknowledge and Accept Feelings

The ability to regulate emotions helps your child develop awareness, control, and socially acceptable behavior as he grows. Your help begins with acknowledging his emotions and accepting his feelings. When you verbally reframe or summarize his feelings in a way that makes him feel heard, he knows he is accepted and begins to calm himself.

Parents sometimes punish their children for having negative feelings, such as distress, anger, fear, shame, or disgust. These feelings are legitimate, however, and they have a purpose. They are signals that your child may be in trouble and may need help. If you deny these feelings or punish your child for having them, you can suppress these signals in a damaging way.

When your child expresses his feelings, he is giving you an opportunity to understand who he is as an individual. If he feels that it is not okay to express his feelings, he may become stressed, and he may stop trusting his caregivers and his environment.

If you feel uncomfortable when your child expresses emotions, especially negative ones, try looking inward. If you have suppressed feelings that originated in your childhood, or if you are generally uncomfortable with emotional expression, you might find it difficult to allow space for your child to express his feelings of anger, pain, or sadness. Rather, you may unconsciously find ways to prevent your baby from expressing himself. It can be helpful for you to reflect on your past, so you can be sure that you are open to your baby and present to help him learn to feel and regulate his emotions. This is one way in which parenthood is an opportunity to reflect and grow personally.

This type of personal reflection greatly altered my parenting approach. As I was growing up, I was groomed not to express feelings or opinions "forcefully." As a girl and then a young woman, I was taught to keep my feelings and my opinions to myself. When I became a mother, however, I did not teach my daughters to hold back their feelings. Instead, I encouraged them to regulate their expression, so it would be thoughtful. I wanted Emi and Mari to be independent thinkers who were confident enough to speak their minds, yet open to listening to others.

Honest, open communication is a key to your child's healthy emotional development. By listening to him through his words and actions, you will come to understand your baby's true feelings. Then, when you accept his emotions and coach him to manage them, you create an atmosphere of openness and comfort. To help him deal with the intensity of negative emotions, such as fear, anger, jealousy, and sadness, you can encourage your baby to find acceptable outlets to cope with these strong emotions.

The knowledge that you are listening to him and acknowledging how he feels helps your child balance his negative emotions. When you synchronize your feeling state to your baby's and attune and resonate with his rhythms, you can more easily help him balance his emotions. Even if you do not understand the cause of your child's sad or angry feelings, taking time to acknowledge his feelings will help him feel secure. You can hold him, help him with a challenge, or talk to him in a way that shows you understand how he feels. When his negative feelings are directed toward you, you can let him know that all relationships have glitches, and you can re-attune through repair and maintenance.

In *Parenting from the Inside Out*, Daniel J. Siegel, MD and Mary Hartzell, MEd discuss the importance of presence, attunement, resonance, and trust in developing attachment between children and parents. They use the acronym PART to express the progression of these concepts and how they build on one another.

When parents share their child's emotions and reflect or empathize with a similar feeling, the child has a sense of being acknowledged and understood. Siegel explains that attunement and resonance establish connections in the brain that build resiliency.

To make yourself available to attune to your child, take a moment to tune in to yourself during the stresses of the day. As PARTners or PARenTs, relationships benefit from a daily dose of a present moment together with attention focused on responding lovingly and enhancing trust. You do not need elaborate gestures or expensive toys to be PART of someone's life. Instead, you can find creative, playful ways to connect and respond that are unique to you and your relationship with your child.

PART

Presence—A state of being in the moment with respectful attention.

Attunement—A state of harmonious and responsive relationship with a sense of joining.

Resonance—When two people have an alignment of attuned states that create a linking of minds, and each person has memories, thoughts, sensations, and images of the other.

Trust—The belief in or reliance on the care of another.

Create a Peaceful Environment

Each child has a unique level of stimulation that meets his needs, age, and tolerance. Some children are more sensitive or introverted and can easily become overwhelmed with too much stimulation, so they need quiet time alone and a large amount of personal space. On the other hand, extroverted children find it energizing to be surrounded by people and activity. If you pay attention to your child's temperament and personality, you can determine how to adjust his environment to suit his needs. Here are some aspects of your child's emotional environment to think about.

Sound

Do you live in the city, the country, or the suburbs? What kinds of sounds and stimulation does your environment create? Do you keep electronic devices such as a television, radio, or stereo running in the background? Pay attention to how your child responds to noise, and when needed, help him relax through quiet time or soft music.

Visual Surroundings

When you look around, what do you see? Is your living space bright or dark? (This visual context might vary with the season, and you can adjust it with curtains or different kinds of electric lighting.) Are your walls painted in bright or soft colors? Is your space cluttered or spare? Light, color, and distribution of objects affect the feeling of a living space. Studies have shown that chaos or lack of organization in the home affects children's behavior as well as their physical and psychological well-being.

In 2011, the *Journal of Neuroscience* published a study on the impact of too many varied objects in a child's field of view. They found that a cluttered environment can limit his brain's ability to process information and to focus. Mess and clutter can be overwhelming and overstimulating to your child. On the other hand, cleanliness and order create a sense of ease and comfort that allow for physical and mental growth as well as emotional connection.

Touch and Movement

A high degree of tactile stimulation and physical activity is overwhelming for some children and necessary for others. Does your child need more or less roughhousing, rocking, or massage to energize him or to relax him to feel calm and safe?

When you provide an environment that supports your baby's needs and helps him regulate his emotions, you relieve stress on your family, give your child the emotional space to develop, and provide him with a model of how to regulate his emotions on his own someday.

Structure the Day

When your baby is young, it is up to you to help him create an environment that keeps his emotions in balance. Let his temperament and tolerance for stimulation guide you as you schedule his day and yours in a way that keeps him feeling good and prevents emotional meltdowns. For instance, if your baby is introverted, and you attend a birthday party with him, he will probably lose energy from the experience and will need some space at home to regain energy. If your child is extroverted, he may be energized and eager for more activity after the party.

For both Emi and Mari, I tried to keep a schedule that they could count on most days. That structure gave them some security and a sense of calm because they knew what to expect. It also made my life as a working mother easier. I planned phone calls and meetings around naps or times when I knew they would not be hungry or tired.

Regular, reliable activities, such as mealtime, bathtime, and bedtime routines, reflect nature's rhythms. Consistency in these routines profoundly shapes your baby's early learning and gives him a sense of stability, safety, and predictability. When he can depend on regularity in his day, he feels secure and comfortable enough to venture out and explore his world.

The simple familiar activities of the day also teach your child about your family's values, goals, and culture. If your child has a foundation of rhythm and routine, then he can develop self-discipline and grow to be comfortable during transitions.

Manage Stress

Stress is usually caused by a feeling that an external demand or situation is greater than your resources for coping with it. This feeling leads to a sense of being overwhelmed and out of control. In times of stress, the body and mind need extra energy reserves.

As children's experiences become more complex, childhood stress is becoming more common. Many parents want their children's lives to be easy and stress-free, but in the past 20 years, children are experiencing the need to adapt to increasing tensions and pressures in daily life.

Sources of Stress for Your Baby

- Lack of sleep, exercise, or proper nutrition
- Lack of free, unstructured time
- Busy, working parents
- Relationship stress of family members
- Parental feelings of guilt about child care experiences
- Lack of connection to nature
- Overstimulation via media or electronics
- Health issues of self (or family members)
- Peer pressure or social interactions
- Economic stress in family
- Change in parents' marital status
- Birth of siblings
- Death of a family member
- Natural disasters

Young children may not readily show their stress or identify its causes, but they generally experience a negative impact from stress. Stress can release a high level of the hormone cortisol, which can break down neurological connections that affect the brain's ability to learn and process information. If a child experiences prolonged stress without an outlet for release, his healthy development could suffer.

Your child's well-being depends upon a balanced interplay of contraction and expansion, rest and activity. If he spends too long in an inward state, he can become isolated and self-absorbed. On the other hand, if he is distracted in the external world for too long, he may become disconnected from his inner self. As with breathing, he needs a rhythmic ebb and flow of activity to help him maintain balance.

If your child's body is in a state of balanced health, then he can cope with stressors more easily. When he is physically imbalanced, he can become irritated by external influences and begin to hold tension that increases stress, which in turn can release as anger or frustration. Sometimes this release is a relief, and it can create a sense of calm and relaxation.

All stress is not negative. Moderate levels of stress can be motivating and challenging. Stress can prompt your child to take action or to improve himself.

Whatever the situation, some level of stress is inevitable, and stress management is part of creating balance in daily life. Children learn from their role models when coping with stress. Be aware that both your stress level and your response to stress affect your child; he will probably behave like you when facing his own emotional challenges. When stress does occur, you can use it as an opportunity to teach positive stress management through the way you respond to it.

Fresh air, time in nature, and unstructured play are experiences that can calm the nervous system. Massage can be relaxing and can help alleviate stress. Essential oils, such as lavender and chamomile, have a tranquilizing effect that can help your child calm down.

With the responsibilities, demands, and pressures of parenting, it may be easy for you to feel overwhelmed and out of control. In order to create an environment that is nourishing to your child's emotional well-being, it is foundational to take care of yourself, to fulfill your own needs, and to manage your stress level.

Regulate Emotions through Food Choices

The quality of the food your baby eats can affect his brain structure both chemically and physiologically, and it can impact his behavior and feelings. Elizabeth Somer, a registered dietitian and author of the book *Eat Your Way to Happiness*, says that food, mood, energy, and sleep are directly linked. A regular schedule of whole foods helps keep your baby's body fueled and blood sugar levels on an even keel. Whole grains, fresh vegetables, fresh fruits, and protein-rich foods provide the nutrients that support emotional health. Three key food components influence mood in a positive way:

- Complex carbohydrates, found in plant foods, slowly increase insulin levels. The increased insulin signals tryptophan, an essential amino acid, to move into the brain. Tryptophan then prompts the release of serotonin, a neurotransmitter, which is known to have a calming effect while regulating and elevating mood.

- Omega-3 fatty acids, found in flaxseed, walnuts, and fatty fish, such as salmon, can influence behavior and mood, and may protect against depression.

- B vitamins, including B1 (thiamine), B9 (folate), and B12, can improve mood by helping your baby's body produce more serotonin. Whole grains, leafy greens, legumes, fresh fruit, eggs, and shellfish contain these vitamins.

Conversely, other foods can contribute to depression, mood swings, fatigue, and anxiety. For instance, refined sugars and grains can cause blood sugar to spike rapidly and then drop quickly. This fast-releasing energy causes an emotional roller coaster. Too much sodium can cause tension and irritability. Caffeine is a stimulant that can increase anxiety. Some researchers are now finding that gluten may have different effects on mood; it may cause anxiety, irritability, and lack of mental clarity. Casein, a protein component in milk, may have a negative impact on mood. The trans fats found in fast foods cause a heavy and sluggish feeling that is linked to fatigue and depression. Heavy metals, such as lead, mercury, and cadmium, which seep into food during industrial processing, can affect mood in an unfavorable way.

From a yin and yang perspective, a balanced diet supports balance in emotions. Excess amounts of foods with a yang influence, such as salt, meat, cheese, and eggs, can cause impatience, irritability, frustration, stubbornness, and anger. Excess amounts of foods with a yin influence, such as refined sugar, ice cream, chocolate, soft drinks, and large amounts of fruit, can cause confusion, oversensitivity, lack of willpower, and hyperactivity.

If your child's condition is on the extreme end of the yin-yang spectrum, you can guide him toward balance by reducing the yin or yang foods that are causing the excess and by offering foods on the other side of the spectrum, along with activities that move him toward his emotional center.

Yin-Yang Emotional Conditions 🏠

Yang 🔺	Yin 🔻
Bold	Shy
Rigid	Flexible
Tense	Relaxed
Angry	Sad
Assertive	Yielding
Social	Solitary
Arrogant	Humble
Controlling	Cooperative
Confronting Conflict	Avoiding Conflict
Grounded	Absent-minded
Self-centered	Considerate
Narrow-minded	Open-minded
Impatient	Patient
Steady	Insecure
Clear	Confused

Make Time for Movement

Studies have shown that exercise and movement can regulate emotions by altering your baby's brain chemistry. Movement can affect his mood in a way that is similar to antidepressants; in fact, it may be more effective than medication in treating depression. Once your baby is moving on his own, you can provide a safe place for him to crawl, climb, walk, or run every day.

Exercise is a healthy way for your baby to either upregulate or downregulate his emotions. Upregulation of emotions lets out frustrations and excess energy, whereas downregulation of emotions has a relaxing effect. You can help him upregulate by stimulating and increasing his energy through movement, or you can help him downregulate by holding him close and slowing down your breathing and movement.

Cultivate Humor

When Emi and Mari were babies, their laughter was contagious and uplifting, so it does not surprise me that some of today's most popular online videos show babies laughing. I imagine you have experienced the joy of sharing your baby's smiles and laughter.

Interestingly, humor is a quality that your child learns by responding to your feedback; it is not genetic. What your child finds funny partly depends on learning and his stage of development. The sense that something is out of place or different from what is expected is the common thread in most humor. For example, the surprise and suspense of playing peek-aboo or putting a sock on your head tend to make your baby laugh. In order for him to find something funny and to react accordingly, he must reach a developmental stage at which he knows the norm and recognizes that something differs from it.

Stages of Humor Development

Age	Development
Birth–6 weeks	His startles or twitches are reflexes in response to changes in his body. His smile is reflexive, not emotional or social.
6–8 weeks	He now has a responsive smile; that is, he is responding to pleasurable internal sensory experiences. He is not yet smiling as a social response to you.
2–6 months	He displays a social smile. With this smile, he is trying to connect. He is responding to your expressions and repeated actions through imitation. His smile may be accompanied by sounds.
6–9 months	At this stage, he is developing object permanence and stranger anxiety, so he is less likely to smile at someone he does not know. He enjoys playing peekaboo.
9–12 months	He is starting to develop a sense of humor based on things that seem out of place, and he laughs in addition to smiling. He reacts to you and wants to get a reaction from you. Surprises, funny faces, and silly expressions make him laugh.
1–2 years	He starts to find delight in being silly and mischievous. He begins to respond with humor to funny songs and movements, exaggeration, improper use of objects, and behavior that he knows is inappropriate.
2–3 years	His sense of humor is developing around labeling objects and events that are inconsistent with the norm. For example, he finds it funny when you point to your nose and call it your eye. As his language and cognitive abilities develop, he can recognize conceptual incongruity—for example, a dog that says, "Meow."
3 years+	As his language abilities, cognitive abilities, and social skills develop, his preferred humor may change from nonsense words, riddles, and wordplay to slapstick comedy and practical jokes.

Your baby's first smiles are reactions to internal sensations rather than responses to humor. As he grows and learns, he may find different kinds of unexpected experiences funny.

Your baby's cognitive development is interrelated with his sense of humor. Humor is a form of play, and play is how children learn. Imitation, eye contact, smiles, and laughter are key communication tools that help with language development. In part, his vocabulary level and set of life experiences determine his ability to know what to expect in a joke or a funny situation. A good sense of humor can make your child smarter, healthier, and better able to cope with challenges.

When Emi was a toddler and in a bad mood, I used to look at her and lightheartedly say, "Wipe that frown off your face." She would take her hand, smear it across her face, and look back at me with a bright smile. I appreciated her ability to move her emotions from negative to positive with a swipe of her hand.

In addition to being lighthearted and fun on the surface, humor has many deeper benefits at the social, emotional, and cognitive levels. Humor offers a way to connect, to bond, and to share positive emotions with other people, thus facilitating healthy, happy relationships. Babies tend to laugh more with people they know and feel comfortable with. Jokes and laughter can reduce anxiety, relieve stress, and boost your child's mood.

Overall, laughter is a tool that your child can rely on throughout life to help him do the following:

- See things from many perspectives in addition to the most obvious one

- Be spontaneous

- Grasp unconventional ideas or ways of thinking

- See below the surface of things

- Enjoy and participate in the playful aspects of life

- Avoid taking himself too seriously

It is never too early to start developing your child's sense of humor. Most people naturally smile and laugh with babies. However, it is helpful to keep laughing and smiling with your toddler as he goes through different stages of development. Pay attention to aspects of his personality that influence his unique sense of humor. Be spontaneous, playful, and take time as a family to have fun and to be silly with each other.

 For more ideas to develop humor, visit growhealthygrowhappy.com

Establish Rituals, Traditions, and Celebrations

Traditions can provide the glue that brings closeness and unity to a family. They offer your family a source of strength, stability, identity, and faith that can help balance change and uncertainty in a complex world. You can draw on the traditions of the family you grew up in, borrow from your partner's family, and create brand-new traditions that reflect the family you are forming.

Traditions can be simple daily routines, such as eating dinner together or hosting elaborate annual events like decorating a Christmas tree. You can create a sentimental feeling with the familiarity and regularity of baking the same heart-shaped cookies at every Valentine's Day or using a special decoration every Halloween. Customs like these are comforting and grounding for life. Your baby derives a sense of security and satisfied expectations from daily rituals. Later, as a toddler, he can share in the preparation, planning, and excitement of periodic and seasonal traditions.

When Mari and Emi were little, even though we were on a tight budget, we created a simple weekly tradition that was unique to our family. Every Friday, we went together to a local bakery for their breakfast special of English muffins, grits, eggs, and fruit. We even made up a song about it and sang it on the way to the bakery. The Rollin' Pin Bakery is long gone now, and my babies are grown women, but the feelings associated with this and other simple family traditions still connect us as a family.

Mari and Emi wearing *yukatas*

Traditions also provide an anchor during tough times. When he gathers with family and friends on special occasions, your child senses his belonging to something larger than his own small world. You can even provide him with generational and historical continuity by repeating family traditions from your own childhood or that of your parents. This practice helps your child feel safe and held at times when he struggles or feels alone, both now and in the future.

The rituals, customs, and celebrations that you create with your family reflect your priorities and values. Your child will feel connected to these experiences and perhaps pass them along to his children. Here are some suggestions for creating family traditions:

- Reflect on the family rituals and celebrations that you enjoyed as a child. Decide which ones you would like to repeat with your child.

- Blend the cultures of both parents. Whether you come from different cultural backgrounds or grew up in the same community, you each have a unique history of family traditions.

- Take note of your daily or weekly routines. These can include taking walks in the park, singing in the car, sharing stories, playing games, having quiet or meditation time, eating dinner together, reading a book at bedtime, weekly cleaning, making pancakes on Saturday mornings, having pizza-and-movie night, or having get-togethers with relatives. These routine activities become family traditions for your child.

- Post a family calendar marked with events, such as family reunions, vacations, birthdays, holiday celebrations, and neighborhood picnics.

- Make a list of family holidays that reflect your religious or spiritual beliefs and have purpose and meaning for you. In addition, you can always create holidays that are unique to your family or borrow holidays from other cultures.

Take Care of Your Own Emotional Well-being

When Emi was around four months old, we established a routine whereby her Japanese grandmother babysat each week. I used that time to attend a flower-arranging class with friends and then to treat myself at a coffee shop. I felt nurtured from those outings, and they sustained me through the week.

For the first two to three months after a baby is born, the mother's body goes through many physical and emotional changes. At the same time, she is learning to take care of her new baby and restructuring the family with a new member. My Japanese doctor, Dr. Watanabe, recommended that I stay in bed for three weeks to rebuild my strength after Emi was born. While that tradition may seem a bit extreme in today's world, the idea that a new mother needs to rest reflects an often-ignored need for self-care.

Even after you have settled in with your newborn, self-care is an ongoing source of physical and emotional strength. You can think of it as an essential nutrient that restores your energy and makes you a more effective parent. Here are some suggestions for self-care.

Get sleep and rest

Sleep and rest are top priorities, and you may find it challenging to find the time. However, even the recognition that sleep is necessary helps you make decisions about whether to catch up on a magazine or take a nap when the opportunity to rest presents itself.

Eat well

Simple, healthy food gives you the nutrition you need for physical and emotional health. If you are breast-feeding, then you have additional reasons to eat well. Breast-feeding mothers need plenty of fluids, as well as generous amounts of balanced meals.

Get exercise

The endorphins released during and after exercise can relieve stress, energize you, and uplift your attitude. Daily exercise, with or without your baby along, helps you stay healthy and alert. At a time when it is easy to get lost in the details of caring for a new baby in your home, active time outside can remind you of the larger world. Alternatively, you can look for baby-wearing exercise classes in your community. In these classes, you actually wear your infant as you move. You get a workout, and your baby feels your heart rate increase and learns to appreciate movement.

Get support

Babies and young children require a lot of work and create a sharp learning curve, and helpers can ease the adjustment. You can get support from family and friends or from a paid care provider, such as a nanny, an au pair, a babysitter, or a doula.

Set priorities

A positive frame of mind is more important to your baby than an orderly environment. If you are nursing your baby and release your need for the dishes to be done immediately, you relax and your milk flows more easily. Often less is more, and you do not need expensive baby equipment to provide what your child needs for healthy development. To help yourself set priorities, an ongoing question you can ask yourself is, "What are my standards and priorities?"

Get organized

Advance planning increases your efficiency and frees up valuable time. For instance, a weekly menu with a shopping list can reduce your trips to the grocery store. If you schedule self-care "appointments," then you are more likely to take the time to attend to your needs. Organization can help you focus and do less while accomplishing more.

Turn off the inner critic

It is stressful and ultimately meaningless to compare yourself with other parents. Every situation is unique, just as every child is unique. Acceptance and a nonjudgmental attitude make for a happier parent, baby, and family environment.

Trust Your Child

In many ways your baby is helpless and dependent on you, but he also has his own strength, survival instinct, and unique destiny to be honored. Because you know that your actions affect his well-being and that you are responsible for his survival, it may be difficult to trust in your child's own ability, resilience, and will. Babies are born programmed to survive—to breathe, to eat, to explore, to learn, and to thrive. It would require more than a few imperfect parenting moments to take your baby off his instinctive path. Through imperfection, your baby learns flexibility and resilience.

Resilience is the capacity to recover from setbacks, to rise above difficulties, and to move forward with optimism. Children are born with differing capacities for resilience. Emotional balance is similar to buoyancy—the tendency to rise back above the surface after being pushed underwater. Children have natural resilience or buoyancy, but some children need more support than others to overcome challenges, depending on their constitution, condition, temperament, level of experience, and situation.

Your belief and trust in your baby are fundamental to his development of strength and resilience. If he has a deep connection to at least one adult, he can experience unconditional love and security, which allows him to develop the roots that are the foundation for coping with obstacles and building resilience.

Trust Yourself

Parents often question their parenting abilities. When something goes wrong, it can be easy to blame yourself. The amount of information and advice about parenting can be overwhelming, and you may feel pressured to keep up with other parents.

While suggestions for the daily care of your child can be helpful, the best advice comes from listening to your own instincts. Living creatures innately know how to nourish and protect their young. Sea turtles dig in the sand at night to create a haven for their hatching eggs. Birds predigest food for their babies and then teach them to hunt for their own food. This parental know-how comes from instinct.

Parental choice and responsibility in humans are similarly wired. Primal love directs parents to protect and care for their babies, to nourish them and help them thrive. You first feed and protect your newborn, and then you care for his emotional and physical well-being. You nourish his ability to survive, and then you help him become autonomous and independent.

A parent's intuition is a powerful resource. Einstein said that the intuitive mind is a "sacred gift" and the rational mind is a "faithful servant." The intuitive mind can grasp ideas and concepts that are outside of everyday experience, and the rational mind helps

Wabi-sabi Parenting

Wabi-sabi is a Japanese term that describes artistic beauty as something that is imperfect, impermanent, and incomplete—blessed with unique quirks and asymmetrical elegance. This term also applies to the art of parenting. You do not have to be perfect as a parent. *Wabi-sabi* parenting reflects the beauty of perfect imperfection.

to put those ideas into action. Your parental intuition, combined with your intimate knowledge of your child, provides you with a singular insight as to how to parent him and an internal compass you can count on when it comes to making choices about his care.

When a situation overwhelms you, take a moment to step back and to get perspective. Ask yourself, "What really matters?" Through this question, you can connect with your inner self and let your intuition guide you toward the right choice for your child. Your natural instincts guide and empower you in caring for your baby.

Give Them Roots, Give Them Wings

Helping your child develop his character and resilience is similar to helping him develop a healthy immune system through exposure to bacteria or viruses. In both cases, the goal is to build his resistance and strength. If you overprotect him from difficulties and challenges, he may feel secure in the short term but vulnerable and weak in the long term.

Overprotection of your child, especially when accompanied by extreme nervousness about his safety and well-being, can cause tension and anxiety. As your child grows, separation is essential for his healthy development. Your child needs to individuate and to become an independent decision maker with his own purpose and dreams. If you have strong attachments or societal projections regarding your child's future, he may have a difficult time living up to your expectations. Instead, if you empower him with a deep sense of self-worth, he will have the confidence to be himself and to pursue his own way.

Theories of Emotional Development

IN THE FIRST PART of this chapter, you learned about daily practices that you can use to support your baby's emotional growth. In this section, you will learn about the progression of emotional development in babies, as well as the theories, research, and science behind that development. Insight about the "why" behind your baby's development can help you understand her point of view.

Your Baby's Emotional Development

Babies of all cultures smile, frown, and cry with the same facial and vocal expressions. Your baby's first emotions are instinctual responses to internal states or external stimuli. He can feel before he can think. When he is wet or hungry, he feels discomfort and communicates it by crying, groaning, or arching his back. When he is satisfied and content, he expresses his feelings by smiling, making eye contact, and cooing.

As your baby grows, these primary emotions branch off into secondary emotions, and eventually develop into more complex emotions. Your child learns about and develops feelings that vary in intensity, frequency, and duration. His unique rate of development, experiences, physical constitution and condition, hormones, gender, language, culture, temperament, and personality influence his emotions and how he expresses and interprets them.

Your baby's emotions are tied to experiences, memories, and associations that color his lens of perception. His first relationships become the structure upon which he builds other relationships. For example, his experiences with his first caregivers create a filter for his view of reality, his beliefs, and his attitudes, which in turn becomes the foundation of his worldview. He adds experiences, memories, and associations to this worldview throughout his life, but the supportive foundation is established in his first three years.

Knowledge about your baby's emotional developmental stages helps you mindfully provide for his needs and wants. For instance, when you know that it is natural for a nine-month-old to be shy, you can be understanding and compassionate about his behavior when a stranger approaches him. When your two-year-old throws a temper tantrum, you can set boundaries patiently as you realize that he is expressing his independence.

Earlier and faster development is not necessarily better because healthy development builds upon the successful completion of the previous stage. Though each child moves at his own pace, experts agree that children share certain general stages in social-emotional development. The milestones discussed throughout this chapter are flexible guidelines that can vary from child to child. You can use them to enhance your understanding of your baby's emotional and social growth and to become aware of any issues that may warrant outside guidance from a professional.

Primary emotions develop during the time from birth to 3 months. First emotions are categorized as pleasant or unpleasant, positive or negative.

Discomfort

Contentment

Secondary emotions develop during the time from 3 to 7 months. His emotions become more distinct, as he becomes more aware of himself and his environment.

Sadness

Anger

Fear

Surprise

Joy

Complex emotions develop during the time from 18 to 24 months. His emotions become more sophisticated, as he develops his sense of self and relationships with others.

Pride

Eagerness to please

Embarrassment

Guilt

Shame

Milestones in Emotional Development

Birth–3 months	3–6 months	6–12 months
• He has pleasure and annoyance with people or experiences. • At first, his smile is an involuntary neurological activity. Later he develops a social smile that is spontaneous and invites interaction. • He expresses his emotions through behavioral or facial expressions such as crying, cooing, or smiling. • He begins to imitate and engage reciprocally. • He distinguishes his parents from others and recognizes the way one person holds him from another.	• He anticipates the bottle or breast before feeding. • He smiles and laughs when he sees you. • He shows excitement by waving his arms and legs. • He has a distinct cry when hungry and laughs at active stimulation. • He makes high-pitched squeals and sounds such as, "ah," "eh," and "ugh." • He may comfort himself with his thumb or pacifier. • He can be comforted most of the time.	• He insists on doing things by himself. • He pushes away things that he does not want. • He enjoys daily routines. • He responds to his own name. • He enjoys social play and reciprocal exchanges with caregivers. • He reaches for familiar people, and he can be wary of strangers. • He prefers his primary caregiver to others and cries when his caregiver leaves the room. • He may comfort himself by sucking his thumb or pacifier, or holding a special blanket.

12–18 months	18–24 months	24–36 months
• If you hold out your hand, he will put a toy or an object into it. • He greets people with "hi" and gives hugs and kisses to show affection. • He starts to show feelings in a more tangible way by squeezing, holding on, and expressing positive emotions. • He reacts to changes in daily routines. • He may show obstinacy and defiance. • He may express separation anxiety and possessiveness.	• He has a rapidly expanding vocabulary, which helps him to express his feelings. • He responds to "no" and sometimes says it himself. • He plays alongside other children. • He shows enthusiasm. • He does not like to be left alone. • He may experience frustrations and temper tantrums. • He shows self-conscious emotions of shame, embarrassment, guilt, and pride. • He shows sympathy and empathy to other children and reaches out to comfort them.	• He plays independently. • He uses pronouns and follows multistep instructions. • He becomes consciously aware of himself as separate from others. • He imitates the behavior of others. • He gives directions to other children. • He plays games cooperatively with other children. • He enjoys dramatic play and pretends to be familiar role models. • He shows compassion and affection for friends and toys.

Foundations for Attachment

Once my daughter, Emi, was three months old and she could hold her head up by herself, I put her in a baby carrier and covered the two of us in a traditional Japanese "mama coat." We walked to the market or to a friend's house as one unit. I felt her body next to mine; I knew if she was warm or cold, and I was aware of her feelings and needs while I shopped and ran errands.

Baby carriers and mama coats are traditional items that support the Japanese cultural concept of *amae*, a bond of emotional attunement between mother and child. In support of this bond, Emi's pediatrician evaluated Emi and me together, as baby and mother, for her first year. If Emi was sick, he treated me as well as her. In Japanese culture, the mother-baby relationship is the foundation of a child's sense of security and unconditional love. This foundation is the source of self-esteem, motivation, and a feeling of belonging.

When babies enter the world, they are open to love and trust. They lack the ability to distinguish what is nourishing from what is harmful. For the first few months they absorb everything without discrimination and rely exclusively on their caregivers for survival, whether they receive nurturing care or not. Newborn babies are vulnerable and dependent, and they innocently attach to their caregivers for food, warmth, shelter, protection, and love.

Mari and Becky

Attachment is a developmental process that takes place in the first two years of a child's life. It develops through a two-way, mutual relationship between child and parent or caregiver. In this unique relationship, both parties have a profound and ongoing impact on each other throughout the child's development. The relationship helps form the blueprint of how your child perceives his own value, constructs his worldview, and experiences social interactions.

Connection

In the second half of the 20th century, British psychiatrist John Bowlby and Canadian psychologist Mary Ainsworth performed extensive research on bonding and attachment in the mother-child relationship. Central to their theory are the claims that a child needs an emotional bond with at least one primary person in order to feel loved, safe, and secure, and that the nature of that relationship determines the health of the attachment.

Typically, three players play significant roles in your baby's bonding process: his mother, his father, and himself. If one or both parents are unavailable, his primary caretaker and others can share these roles. In the case of a single parent, it may be challenging to satisfy the roles of both parents, but your child needs both. Each brings unique personal traits that create the dynamic and quality of the bonding process.

❀ **The mother's role**—Mothers and babies have a biological connection that starts in the womb and continues during breast-feeding. They share this connection through skin-to-skin contact and the rhythms of movement while holding and caring for their babies. This role provides a warm, secure environment that meets your baby's emotional needs. If the primary caretaker is not the baby's biological mother, the baby can still establish this emotional bond. When a mother consistently responds to her baby's signals with soothing and loving attention, her baby makes a positive connection with her and usually develops a secure attachment.

The father's role—A baby usually develops a primary attachment relationship with his biological mother, but a father or other caregiver who consistently responds to his needs may also become a principal attachment figure. For instance, my mama coat doubled as a papa coat. Naoki often used the coat to keep Emi close to him as he went about his day, thus breaking with traditional gender roles and laying the foundation for a strong father-child attachment. In addition to a secure emotional attachment, your baby needs this father role to help him explore, learn, and discover the world with a sense of adventure.

The baby's role—Your baby also plays a role in the nature of his attachment. Your baby's unique temperament can affect the type of attachment that he develops and the way you relate to him. If you cannot comfort him, you may feel incompetent, and this feeling affects your relationship. Health factors such as colic or premature birth may challenge his early relationship with you.

Secure or Insecure Attachment

In her research, Ainsworth noticed that infants remained aware of their mothers' whereabouts. After exploring for a while, babies returned to their mothers for reassurance. As Ainsworth described this behavior, babies use their mothers as a "secure base." A child's natural instinct for attachment keeps him close to his parent, thus improving his chances of survival.

In the 1970s, Ainsworth studied the effects of attachment on behavior. She observed children between 12 and 18 months of age and determined that the more responsive the caregiver, the more secure the attachment the child formed. She categorized the babies' attachments as secure or insecure.

A secure attachment develops when a baby has a relationship with a caregiver who consistently responds to his needs and is emotionally attuned to him, such that the child has a feeling of connectedness, security, and trust. When a child has a secure attachment, he feels safe to explore and to grow as he faces each stage of development. He may also be more cooperative and more likely to seek help from a caregiver when needed.

An insecure attachment develops when the caregiver is unavailable or does not respond to the baby's needs consistently. Thus, the baby does not have a secure base from which to grow and to explore. When a child has an insecure attachment, he may have difficulty when caregivers leave; he may be bossy and afraid to ask for help. In addition, he may compensate for his insecurity by being overly dependent or independent, overly shy or friendly, or overly concerned about his parents' well-being. Ainsworth further divided insecure attachments into the following three categories:

- ✿ Anxious-avoidant—If a child is rejected repeatedly, then he experiences chronic insecurity and avoids closeness. He then disengages from the attachment system.

- ✿ Anxious-ambivalent—If a parent's availability is inconsistent and he or she is not attuned to the child, then the child may experience intrusiveness, unreliable communication, anxiety, and uncertainty. Here, the child stays close to the parent in the hope of getting a response.

- ✿ Disorganized attachment—This occurs when the caregiver fails to meet the child's needs and engages in bizarre or abusive behavior. In this type of attachment, the parent's behavior is a source of terror that the child is attempting to escape. There is no consistent or predictable pattern that a child can trust, and this affects the child's growing brain and neural integration. As a result, he may have difficulty regulating his emotions, communicating his needs, and integrating cognitive skills.

 For more about attachment cycles visit growhealthygrowhappy.com

Social psychologists Cindy Hazan and Phillip Shaver took Ainsworth's findings a step further. In their study, written up as "Romantic Love Conceptualized as an Attachment Process", they looked at the correlation between a child's early attachment style and his romantic relationships as an adult. According to Hazan and Shaver, securely attached adults usually experience romantic love as enduring. Ambivalently attached adults tend to fall in love often. People who had an avoidant-attachment style describe love as rare and temporary.

Many psychologists believe that babies develop a particular attachment style in their first year of life, and it has a profound effect on their adult relationships. As a parent, you can learn from your own childhood experiences and how they inform your role in your child's attachment process.

The conceptual framework associated with your emotions and behavior influences the decisions that you make as a parent. If you are like many people, you may find it difficult to be completely aware of your conceptual framework, because you probably have learned beliefs that are based on past experiences in your family, cultural, and community. However, you can tease out these beliefs through self-reflection and examination of your past. When you make sense of your history and integrate this understanding into your self-concept, you give yourself the opportunity to choose your behavior, to free yourself from old patterns, and to heal your own attachment style. This process also helps you relate empathically to your child and to support his healthy emotional development.

The Adult Attachment Interview (AAI) is a questionnaire that assesses people's attachment styles. You can learn about your own style by taking this questionnaire.

 Learn about your own style of attachment at growhealthygrowhappy.com

The quality of the parent-infant relationship sets the tone for your child's relationships throughout his life. It is the basis for his emotional and intellectual development as well as his physical health. The Center on the Developing Child at Harvard University, founded and directed by Jack Shonkoff, MD, collects and disseminates information about early childhood development. The center reports a growing body of scientific evidence that shows how early emotional and social experiences affect the body's biological abilities to regulate metabolism, to resist disease, and to foster healthy brain development. In fact, scientists are currently showing that a child's early experiences become part of his body on a molecular level.

Emi and Naoki

The opportunity to attach to a primary caregiver and to form additional early bonds affects your child's life today and in the future. Fortunately, many of the instincts, strategies, skills, and techniques that help a child form a secure attachment come naturally to most parents.

Attachment Cycle

Early on, you and your baby create a rhythm of communication called an attachment cycle. This process is somewhat like dancing with a partner. When you consistently interact and respond to your baby's messages of hunger, thirst, tiredness, messy diapers, and loneliness, you give him the sense that his world is safe and he can depend on you. In the early months, he needs you to help him regulate his emotions until he learns to set his own internal rhythms, which provide a foundation for his emotional development.

Adoptive parents sometimes do not have the instinctual connections of biological parents, so they often study the attachment cycle to help them develop healthy attachments with their children. Whether you are a biological or an adoptive parent, it is helpful to understand this cycle so that you can understand your child better and help him regulate his emotions.

Secure Attachment Can

- Support your baby's immune system
- Give your baby the security he needs to explore and to be curious about the world
- Establish confidence, self-worth, and independence
- Foster high intrinsic motivation and an ability to concentrate and learn
- Enable your baby to form healthy relationships
- Increase your baby's capacity to cope with stress
- Build the foundation for helping your child reach his full potential

First Year Secure Attachment Cycle

The first year, responding to your baby's needs is not complicated. When he needs something, he lets you know, and then it is simple to find a solution to satisfy him.

Baby Needs

Every day your baby has many internal and external stimuli—physical sensations, such as hunger, tiredness, a wet diaper, external sounds, movements, sights, and smells. These sensations and experiences affect his well-being and cause feelings, such as anger, contentment, fear, or discomfort.

Baby Communicates

Your baby responds to his feelings, and then, communicates his needs to you through crying or other cues. He may kick his legs for an invitation to play, or cry because he is hungry or sleepy.

Baby Develops Trust

When you repeatedly and consistently meet your baby's needs, he develops trust over time. If this cycle is broken, and your child does not receive consistent care, then he learns that the world is not a safe place, and that he has to take care of himself. When this cycle is stable, he smiles, his caregiver feels a bond and naturally returns the smile, and the baby feels good about himself.

Caregiver Responds

When you respond to your baby's needs consistently by paying attention to him, picking him up, changing his diaper, and feeding him, this reassures him that you are available. It also acknowledges his needs and reinforces that he matters.

Second Year Secure Attachment Cycle

If a child develops a healthy attachment in his first year, then he is able to move to the next cycle of attachment. He learns to accept limits on his behavior, to control his impulses, to be safe, to engage in reciprocity, and to regulate his emotions. Through this process, he develops his conscience, self-esteem, empathy, socialization, and foundation for logical thinking.

The second-year attachment cycle is a time of negotiation between you and your child, while you continue to provide sensitivity and consistency in response to your child's needs. In the first year, responding to your baby's needs is generally quite simple. When he needs something, he lets you know, and you find a solution to satisfy him. The second year is not as simple and straightforward. This can be a challenging time. At this age, he needs to learn limits. As a parent, it can be difficult to know what to allow and when to set limits.

Child Wants

Your child wants something and expresses a desire for it. He is hungry, thirsty, tired, or bored, and wants to change his situation. He expresses his desire by crying or other cues.

Caregiver Sets Limits

You determine what your child wants and then decide whether or not to provide it. Then you set the parameters of your response, establishing boundaries for your child. For instance, you will get his lunch, but he must sit in his chair to eat. Or you will take him downstairs to his playroom, but he cannot go down the stairs by himself. Or you will help him go to sleep, but he must be in bed. However, if you have restrictions on everything your child does, then he does not have the opportunity to find his own sense of judgment. Being as positive as possible and redirecting him toward a "yes" instead of all "nos" can be helpful. Finding a balance between parameters and freedom is the challenge. If you learn to balance them well, your child will learn to self-regulate and will feel empowered.

Caregiver Responds Approriately

Being consistent and firm, but gentle within reason, teaches your child boundaries and predictability, and gives him a sense of security. When your child receives limitations, he learns predictability and order, which help him to learn behavioral standards.

Child Accepts or Resists

Either your child complies and cooperates, or resists the limits you have established. Setting limits gently and without confrontation helps your child move through the transition from resistance to acceptance.

As you successfully support your baby through these two attachment cycles during his first two years, you encourage him to learn to trust, to engage with you and others, and to manage his emotions. Know that it is natural for occasional breaks in the attachment cycle to occur. As a parent, you cannot satisfy your baby or maintain consistency all the time. However, if you repair the break by returning to a predictable response, then your baby's feeling of security will stabilize once again.

A Baby's Cues

In your baby's first year, it can be challenging to figure out the meaning of his behavior because he probably does not have the language skills to clarify his message. However, by paying attention to your baby's sounds, facial expressions, gaze, and gestures, you can often interpret what he is trying to communicate. Without saying a word, he can tell you what he wants. You may be your baby's first teacher, but your baby can also teach you. All you have to do is observe and listen for cues.

First, notice engagement and closeness cues. Are your baby's eyes open? Is he looking at your face intently? Is he smiling at you? Does he follow your voice and face as you move around the room? Is he making rooting sounds? Is he hungry? Follow his lead. If he is showing interest in a new toy, keep playing. If he points to a safe object, let him touch it.

Also look out for disengagement and need-for-change cues. Does your baby turn or look away? Is he arching his back and pushing away? Does he cry, cough, or frown? Is he yawning or falling asleep? Does he have a glazed-over look in his eyes? Does he need quiet time? Does he need a diaper change? If he turns away or fusses, he may need a break from his current activity, surroundings, or company.

When you respond to your baby's cues, he learns that his actions have an effect on people. Every day is a new adventure in which you and your baby discover more about each other.

Attunement

Attunement is a valuable building block for healthy attachment in your baby's first year. When you and your baby are attuned, you act in harmony. You possess a deep awareness of your baby's feelings and needs, and you know the best ways to respond to those needs. When your baby experiences this support, he feels understood and begins to create a healthy attachment to you.

Attunement begins with sensitivity. By remaining sensitive, you become aligned with your baby's thoughts, feelings, and emotions. Your baby gains a sense of security, which positively affects the development of his nervous system. When he feels attuned to those closest to him, he acquires the self-assurance to reach out and connect with others in the world.

The communication of attunement is largely nonverbal. Signals such as eye contact, gestures, touches, facial expressions, and voice tones are subtle ways of letting your baby know that he is cared for and loved. For instance, the high-pitched voice that parents and caregivers instinctually use when talking with babies creates attunement and is a universal way of relating to babies all over the world. This type of attunement grows not from what is said but rather from how it is said. What appears to be meaningless babble between parent and baby is actually rich, intricate communication. Attunement develops through the reciprocal dialogue, and it creates a state of resonance. When attuned, a mother produces the feel-good hormone oxytocin, and her baby builds positively on his perception of the world.

When you take the time to become attuned and present with your baby, you give him a sense of safety that helps him feel trusting, calm, confident, and ready to learn.

Mirroring

Mirroring is a technique that deepens attunement and reinforces your baby's sense of self. Your baby communicates his feelings to you through facial expressions, body movements, and sounds. When you respond by reflecting back his expressions with empathy and respect, he realizes that he is heard and develops strong self-esteem, self-worth, and self-respect. This type of parental response is called mirroring.

Mirroring occurs subconsciously and consciously. You consciously mirror your child when you copy his gestures, movements, sounds, or expressions. You mirror your baby subconsciously by naturally responding to his cues and being attuned to his needs. Mirroring helps your child feel empowered and gives him a sense of control within his surroundings. It is also a tool for him to bond with caregivers and family members during one-on-one time.

To show the impact of mirroring, Edward Tronick, PhD, conducted an experiment called the Still Face Experiment in 1975. In this experiment, Tronick observed the interaction of a mother and baby when the mother stopped responding to her baby and kept a still (expressionless) face, with no mirroring, for three minutes. In this short amount of time, the baby made repeated attempts to interact via the usual reciprocal pattern. When the mother continued to show no response, the baby withdrew and had physiological reactions such as hiccups, spitting up, and crying.

To watch the Still Face Experiment visit growhealthygrowhappy.com

Tronick's experiment is considered a significant finding in developmental psychology, because it demonstrates the power of caregivers' engagement with their children. A baby can accept a parent or caregiver's absence if he or she is out of sight and unavailable to respond. However, if his parent or caregiver is physically but not emotionally present, the baby is likely to become upset or psychologically impacted.

Seven Tools for Attachment

In addition to attunement and mirroring, other actions encourage a healthy attachment in your child's important first years. Pediatrician William Sears and his wife, Martha, a registered nurse, are leading advocates of the attachment-parenting philosophy. They have popularized this style of parenting through their many books, including *The Baby Book* and *The Attachment Parenting Book: A Commonsense Guide to Understanding and Nurturing Your Baby*. According to the Searses, the attachment-parenting approach is about learning to read and respond to your baby's cues. They believe that both stay-at-home and working parents can build strong attachments with their babies. In their work, the Searses offer seven tools for building a secure attachment. They call these tools the Baby B's. According to the Searses, while most parents will not be able to practice the Baby B's all of the time, the objective is to do what you can to stay connected to your child.

The Seven Baby B's

1. **Birth bonding**—The hours and days immediately after birth are a sensitive time for allowing babies' and mothers' intuitive bonding instincts to develop.

2. **Breast-feeding**—Nursing is an excellent way for a mother to get to know her baby and to build a trusting relationship.

3. **Baby wearing**—Carrying your baby allows you to be very sensitive to his needs and deepens your relationship.

4. **Bed sharing**—Most babies sleep better when they are close to their parents, and nighttime feedings and care are easier when your baby is nearby.

5. **Belief in baby's cries**—When you respond to your baby's cries, you help him develop trust and a sense of security. Babies cry to communicate, not to manipulate.

6. **Balance and boundaries**—Self-care is an important part of your baby's well-being. Trust your instincts in knowing when to say yes, and when to say no to your baby. Set boundaries. Ask for help. Establish balance.

7. **Beware of baby trainers**—You know your baby's needs better than anyone. Trust your intuition rather than outside advice that is pressured and judgmental.

Excerpt from The Attachment Parenting Book : A Commonsense Guide to Understanding and Nurturing Your Baby by William Sears, Md and Martha Sears. © 2001 by William Sears and Martha Sears.

Attachment parenting may be perceived as difficult for working mothers, but the Searses maintain that their approach is primarily focused on encouraging parents and babies to form loving bonds, which research has shown to be beneficial to long-term emotional, cognitive, and physical health. Whether or not you practice all of the Baby B's all of the time, you can help your baby form a healthy attachment by nourishing your relationship with him, however you can and in ways that work for you and your lifestyle.

Overattachment

Psychologists agree that babies need an enduring relationship with a significant and caring adult in order to develop emotionally. However, you may wonder if you will spoil your baby or make him clingy and dependent by giving him too much attention and cuddling. For those first few years of life, probably not.

When a baby has unpleasant sensations, it is important that a caregiver respond to his needs in order for him to develop a sense of security. If his needs are ignored, rejected, or inconsistently met, the baby will probably develop an insecure attachment. This may seem paradoxical, but a secure attachment in infancy leads a child to independence, not dependence. If a child can trust his parents to be there for him, then he will believe that the world is a safe place, and he will have the confidence to play and to explore on his own.

Overcoming Attachment Challenges

While most new parents see the value in a close connection with their baby, the reality is that immediate concerns often override their baby's emotional development. Every family has issues and hurdles that can impede attachment. The following are a few of the more common challenges that parents face today, along with some strategies to overcome them and to ensure that your baby develops a healthy attachment and a strong emotional foundation.

Mothers working outside the home

When I was taking care of Emi in Japan, people on the subway or in the market would offer a soothing and supportive comment: *"Taihen desu, ne?"* ("It is challenging and difficult to be a mother, isn't it?") This comment shows respect for a revered societal position. When they said this to me, I felt acknowledged and encouraged in my role and in my daily efforts.

Although today's fathers are sharing more parental responsibilities than fathers of previous generations did, throughout history and across cultures, the biological and emotional instinct for family care has resided predominantly with women. In many cultures, women carry their babies on their backs, and as the children grow, extended family members help with their care. In the late 20th and early 21st centuries, globalization and other modern trends have caused a shift in the role of women in society. More and more mothers are leaving their children at home or in child care facilities to return to work. According to the U.S. Bureau of Labor Statistics, women made up only 29 percent of the U.S. workforce in 1950. In 2012, women accounted for almost half the workforce, and 57 percent of mothers with infants under the age of one were employed.

If you are a working mother, the combination of working a full day while learning how to care for your new baby, keeping up with other responsibilities, and tending to your relationship with your partner—on very little sleep—can stretch you past your tolerance point. In trying to meet your child's needs and provide him the best opportunities, you may experience internal conflict and guilt because you feel you are not doing enough. It is also emotionally difficult to leave your little one to the care of others, whether they are family members, nannies, or professionals at a child care center.

You can cope with these feelings by first recognizing them as valid. Working parents across the globe share your experiences. Next, recognize that the other option—staying home with your infant—brings its own set of issues. Many stay-at-home mothers experience bouts of loneliness, stress, boredom, exhaustion, and cravings for social and mental stimulation.

Taking care of a baby while working is a challenge no matter what your employment circumstances. Whether or not you return to a paid job, do not be shy about asking for help from your family, friends, and community to ensure that you have the physical and emotional support and social stimulation you need. Parenting can always absorb more of you, and the role of a parent is a balancing act through which you, your partner, and your child are learning and growing together.

Lack of sleep

Babies start off with random sleeping patterns, and it takes time for them to adjust to nighttime sleep and daytime wakefulness. Consequently, most new parents suffer from a lack of sleep, which can affect their emotions and mental clarity. You may find yourself easily irritated or frustrated with your child—and this emotional state does not support a secure attachment.

The obvious solution is to get more sleep. Co-sleeping (allowing your baby to sleep in your bed) is a way for everybody to get more sleep while furthering a healthy attachment, but it may not be a comfortable solution for all parents. Other possibilities include asking for help from a partner, family member, or friend, and hiring a mother's helper, doula, or babysitter.

Postpartum depression

Postpartum depression is a serious illness that involves more than a simple mood fluctuation after your baby is born. It occurs during the first few months after birth and can last for months. Postpartum depression can make you feel anxious, angry, sad, and guilty. These feelings can overshadow the positive aspects of parenting and transform into experiences of regret, disconnection, hopelessness, and lack of motivation and self-esteem. If you have a colicky baby, a poor support system, a history of stress, or a physiological tendency toward depression, you may be at risk for postpartum depression. This illness can also be caused by miscarriage, stillbirth, or changes in hormonal levels.

Postpartum depression not only affects the mother, but also puts a family in potential danger. Prolonged and untreated depression creates a barrier to healthy attachment with your baby. Therefore, it is advisable to seek treatment and support at the first signs of postpartum depression.

A doula is a nonmedically trained professional who aids pregnant women and new mothers through information, physical assistance, and emotional support. Specifically, postpartum doulas are experts at taking care of newborns and helping with household responsibilities such as cleaning and cooking. Doula services are typically not overly expensive, and one week or one month of doula care can be a wonderful baby-shower gift. While postpartum doulas can help with postbirth adjustments, prenatal and birth doulas are just as helpful with the stages prior to and during the birth, and many can help with multiple stages.

For information about doulas visit dona.org/mothers

Some mothers may feel guilty about their negative emotions and too embarrassed to reach out for help. However, postpartum depression is quite common, and there are many resources available for mothers experiencing emotional difficulties. The first steps toward healing are acknowledging your condition and seeking help. It can be difficult to take these steps, but the rewards on the other side are worth while. As many moms who have overcome postpartum depression will tell you, asking for help is a sign of inner strength, as well as care for both yourself and your baby.

Partner differences

In most parenting scenarios, two people bring together different histories, temperaments, values, and personalities. These differences can make it challenging to agree upon and establish a unified parenting method. For instance, one parent may believe in strong discipline, while the other may be more lenient. Differences like this can play out in many areas.

Inconsistent, unpredictable parenting can cause confusion, insecurity, and behavior problems in children. In addition, spousal conflict about parenting methods can undermine your authority with your child. As he gets older, your child may be tempted to take advantage of a situation in which he does not have firm, clear guidelines.

A cohesive plan for caring for your child, setting rules, and communicating consistently empowers both parents to maintain their independent personalities while presenting a unified voice.

Special needs or other developmental challenges

Premature birth or separation due to a medical condition sometimes interrupts the attachment cycle of a baby and his caregivers. Developmental delays and certain physical and mental conditions can affect both your baby's ability to respond and your ability to read your baby's cues. These situations require extra care and attention. Psychologists, psychiatrists, and other experts who work in the field of early intervention with developmental disabilities can support you to form the strongest attachment possible with your child.

How Your Baby Unfolds

One of the main benefits of a healthy attachment is the freedom that it gives your child as he begins to explore the world and to find his unique self.

Essence

Your baby came into the world as a complete and perfect being with a pristine, natural sense of presence that is visible in his attention to the moment and his spontaneous, open, authentic expression. He is uninhibited and unpretentious. Instead of being fixated on the past or the future, his pure awareness is present in the now.

Your baby began life in a symbiotic union. He experiences little distinction between himself and his environment. In this state of awareness, self and other are one. When your five-month-old gives you his innocent, natural smile, you experience the pure delight and spontaneous joy that come from his essential self. He has a unique nature that is fundamental and real.

Often, people do not recognize and mirror essential qualities for simply being; instead, we see them as reflections of actions and accomplishments. Your child is not only developing aspects of his ego that make up his personality; he is also developing essential qualities, including curiosity, joy, strength, love, will, and courage. Because what you reflect back to your baby grows, you can help him develop his essential self by recognizing and acknowledging these qualities. When these qualities are not recognized and reinforced, they still exist, but they fade into the background.

Essence is related to being. In most Western cultures, doing is valued more than being. Since many parents are disconnected from their own essential selves, they neither notice nor encourage the development of their baby's essence. You can help your baby to stay connected to his essence by providing experiences of shared presence with him. Take a few moments every day to play or to simply be together in the moment, without agendas or goals. Also take time to connect to your own essence. This will help you model conscious patterns and ways of being for your baby. Music, meditation, yoga, and breathing practices can help you increase your awareness of your essence. When you recognize your own essential qualities, you support your baby's connection to his essence.

Ego and Identity Development

According to Margaret Mahler, a psychologist and an authority on the ego's early development, as babies grow and interact with caregivers and the world around them, they separate from their pure state of essence to create an ego and an identity of their own. This separation may result from an abrupt experience, or it may occur gradually over time. It is inevitable and necessary, because your baby must differentiate in order to individuate into his autonomous self and to function in society.

Mahler uses the term identity to refer to the earliest awareness of a sense of being. This sense of existence, of "I am," is the first step in the process of the unfolding of individuality. Mahler compares a child's separation-individuation phase to a kind of second birth experience. The child begins to separate from his symbiotic union with reality as his ego, sense of identity, cognitive abilities, and human connections develop. Separation-individuation is a crucial prerequisite for the development and maintenance of a sense of identity.

Mahler identified five steps to the individuation process. Because every child moves at a different pace, the ages can vary and overlap, but children tend to follow this sequence:

1. Symbiosis—From pregnancy to approximately 5 months old, a baby is aware of his mother, but he does not have a sense of individuality; instead, he molds into his mother. He sleeps often, and his attention is directed inward. The baby and the mother are one, and there is a barrier between them and the rest of the world.

2. Differentiation and the development of body image—From 6 or 7 months to around 9 months, the baby is awake for longer periods of time, more alert, and interested in the outside world. He begins to recognize that his body is separate from his mother's by exploring his face, pulling at his hair, and scanning his environment. He uses his mother as a constant point of orientation as he compares various objects to his primary caregiver.

3. Practicing—From around 9 months to about 16 months, as the child develops physical-mobility skills, he begins to explore actively and becomes more distant from his caregiver by crawling, kicking, climbing, standing up, and walking. With his caregiver as an anchor, he ventures out for new experiences and returns for refueling and reassurance. The child actively practices and masters his autonomy skills, but he experiences ambivalence as he pushes and pulls between omnipotence in his independence and separation anxiety in his need for support from his primary caregiver.

4. Rapprochement—Between 15 and 24 months, a toddler has begun walking on his own and is physically moving away from his caregiver. At the same time, he is developing language and cognitive skills. He wants to share his new experiences with his caregiver. He may become tentative and anxious, fearing abandonment in his need for closeness, even as he explores the world.

5. Consolidation of individuality and the development of object constancy—From 2 to 3 years, a toddler now understands that the caregiver is a separate individual. He achieves a stable sense of identity and individuality, while attaining a certain degree of object constancy (knowledge that even if something disappears from his sight, it still exists). This leads to the formation of his superego, which is an internalization of parental demands that provides the child with guiding support. Because the child's ego is not fully developed, parents continue to provide wisdom and responsibility as they assist him in finding his own internal guidance. Deficiency in positive internalization can lead to a sense of insecurity and low self-esteem.

Erikson's Stages of Development

Stage: Infancy (Birth–18 months)	
Basic Conflict	Trust vs. Mistrust
Important Events	Feeding
Outcome	Children develop a sense of trust when caregivers provide reliability, care, and affection. A lack of these leads to mistrust.
Stage: Early Childhood (2–3 years)	
Basic Conflict	Autonomy vs. Shame and Doubt
Important Events	Toilet Training
Outcome	Children need to develop a sense of personal control over physical skills and a sense of independence. Success in these areas leads to feelings of autonomy; failure results in feelings of shame and doubt.

This basic separation-individuation process occurs in a child's first three years. Disruptions in this process can negatively impact his identity later in life. When he experiences a positive process of becoming separate and individuating, however, your child develops a sense of identity, self-confidence, independence, and ability to be his true self.

Mahler's theories (including her conceptions of the id, ego, and superego) were built on the work of her predecessor, Sigmund Freud. Later psychologists built on Mahler's ideas, and theories on personality and identity continue to evolve today.

Erikson's stages of psychosocial development
Developmental psychologist and psychoanalyst Erik Erikson developed theories on the effects of social development on a child's sense of self. Erikson established a life-span model indicating that stages of growth and development continue throughout a person's life. His stages are sequential, and they build upon each other.

The first two of Erikson's eight stages of psychosocial development happen in a child's first three years (see the chart). According to Erikson, one of the most important patterns of association that influences future relationships is learning to trust. The development of trust occurs in a child's first 18 months—Erikson's first stage. His second stage, during age two to three years, involves gaining independence and self-control.

According to Erikson, very young children first perceive their sense of identity in terms of physical characteristics. Gradually, they begin to relate to their moods and preferences. They then identify with personality traits and moral outlooks. As they grow, children learn a great deal about expectations of their behavior through pleasing others and meeting social standards. Because social, emotional, physical, and cognitive development occur simultaneously, all aspects are integrated and interrelated. Additional influences on self-concept include gender identification, relationships with family members, ethnic or religious identification, and connection with a neighborhood, community, culture, and nationality. I will explore all of these influences later in this chapter.

Understanding Individual Differences

Even before outside forces come into play, babies are born ready to respond to the world with their own sensibilities. One child may sit down and cry when he meets an obstacle, while another might push the obstacle away and continue with his previous activity. In addition to a child's genetic background, his temperament, personality, and gender play roles in how he responds to the world. These factors, along with his unique combination of life circumstances, make up his individual self. Some of these factors can easily change through life experience, while others are lasting.

Temperament

A baby's temperament is his individual way of responding to the world. Temperament is the biological, inherent, and innate part of a person's personality. Other parts of personality are influenced by gender, physical constitution and condition, food, activities, circumstances, experiences, and culture.

In addition to the quality of parental care, your baby's inherent temperament affects his attachment style and level of security. For example, temperamentally fearful babies tend toward the anxious-ambivalent attachment style, while fearless children are more likely to have an avoidant-attachment style.

Parents with multiple children readily recognize differences in individual temperaments, even though their children share a genetic pool. Emi was naturally active and outgoing from the beginning. Mari, on the other hand, was born with an innate sensitivity; she held on to her father or me in social situations. Each of my daughters had a unique inborn temperament that affected the way she reacted to situations.

By observing and understanding your child's temperament, you can better understand his perspective and learn how to support him. If your child's temperament matches the demands of his environment, then his development will be supported.

The societal and cultural demands for boys and girls sometimes vary. For example, parents often play more roughly with boys and more quietly with girls, without deference to the individual child's temperament. Similarly, cultural and traditional family expectations might not fit the particular child born into that situation. In addition, a child's interactions with each parent, sibling, and other caregiver create unique dynamics of two temperaments. These dynamics create chemistry that may be positive and complementary or negative and antagonistic.

As a parent, your temperament affects your interaction with your baby, and your baby's style affects your reactions to him. For instance, if you are calm and sedentary, you may find an active, energetic baby more challenging than a baby whose temperament more closely resembles yours. If your child has a temperament that is difficult for you, you can help him (and yourself) by reframing it. Try to view his temperament neutrally, as a part of his basic nature. Then you realize that your job is not to react to his temperament, but rather to purposefully assist him to balance it to his benefit. Effective parenting requires adaptation of your expectations to match the reality of your child's temperament.

Knowledge about your child's temperament can also be useful when choosing a caregiver. Consider the temperament of both the caregiver and your baby as you encourage the highest-quality interaction possible.

One of the oldest and most highly used studies on infant temperament is the New York Longitudinal Study, which Alexander Thomas, MD, and Stella Chess, MD, began in the mid-1950s. Based on interviews of 136 parents of people between two years old and adulthood, Thomas and Chess identified nine temperament traits. In the following chart, I have classified them into yin-yang characteristics.

The value of determining whether your child has a more yin or yang tendency is that you can use that understanding to guide him toward balance. If his nature is more yang (active, outgoing), then he needs activities that satisfy and expel his energy. He also needs quiet time to calm and balance his energy. If your child's nature is on the yin (calm, introverted) side, then he may need encouragement to participate in outdoor or physical activities, as well as patience and consideration of his need to move at a slower pace. Both tendencies have their strengths and weaknesses. The key to supporting your child is to understand and accept his basic nature.

Personality and the Enneagram

While temperament refers to behavioral style, personality describes the "what" or "why" of behavior. The Greek word persona means "mask," implying that personality is a construct that covers and protects a vulnerable essential self. Researchers have crafted several theories on how personalities develop. Most theories share the notion that personality is a psychological construct that can influence or cause certain behaviors, and that personality arises from within the person and remains fairly consistent throughout his life. Personality is the unique pattern of temperament, emotions, interests, and intellectual abilities that develop a child's innate tendencies. Personality is also shaped by social interactions.

One theory of personality that I have found helpful is the Enneagram. The Enneagram symbol can be traced to the works of Pythagoras, and the Sufis used the

Yin-Yang Temperaments			
	Indicator	**Yang**	**Yin**
Activity Level	"Idle speed" or general level of movement and activity	Wiggles and has a difficult time sitting still; enjoys moving from one activity to another; higher energy level	Calm and enjoys sedentary and quiet activities; lower energy level
Distractibility	Degree of concentration when presented with external stimuli	Pays attention and focuses on activities	Easily becomes sidetracked and distracted
Intensity	Energy level of a response that is either positive or negative	Reacts strongly and loudly with a depth of emotion; may be dramatic	Gets quiet when upset; mellow; "goes with the flow"
Regularity	Predictability of biological functions (appetite and sleep)	Is unpredictable in terms of hunger and tiredness	Gets hungry and tired at expected times
Sensory Threshold	Sensitivity to physical stimuli—sounds, touch, tastes, temperature changes	Is not affected negatively by sensory stimulation; eats almost anything	Sensitive; startles easily to sounds; picky eater; artistic
Approach or Withdrawal	Response to a new situation or strangers	Resistant; not shy or afraid; acts before thinking—impulsive	Hesitant; slow to warm up; thinks before acting
Adaptability	Ability to adapt to change	Handles changes quickly and easily and moves from one activity to another without resistance	Resists changes in routines and takes time to become comfortable with new situations
Persistence	Length of time a child continues an activity, and how he overcomes obstacles	Self-reliant; focused; can be stubborn; may react strongly when interrupted	Asks for help; is patient and can wait to get his needs met; easily distracted
Mood	Tendency to react in a positive or negative way	Positive and happy; moves on and does not linger in negative feelings	Focuses on negative view of life; may be serious and analytical

Enneagram in their narrative tradition. In the 1960s, Oscar Ichazo, founder of the Arica School, started recording and using the Enneagram in relationship to the human psyche. His approachable and useful psychological system incorporates traditions and wisdom from mystical Judaism, Christianity, Islam, Taoism, Buddhism, and ancient Greek philosophy.

As a way of explaining motivation and behavior, the Enneagram theory describes nine personality types based on corresponding psychological constructs. According to the theory, a child is born with a dominant type that determines the way he learns to adapt to his environment. Here are some of the theory's basic principles:

❀ One type is not better than another. The numbers assigned to each type have no meaning; they are neutral.

❀ Every type applies to both males and females.

❀ Each type has both positive and negative aspects.

❀ People are the same type for their entire lives.

As a tool for understanding yourself and others, the Enneagram can help you gain insight into your child's personality. It can also help you identify your style of parenting. Today, many psychologists, educators, and business leaders use the Enneagram to help people understand each other and thus improve communication and productivity.

I have enjoyed studying the Enneagram personality theory for more than 20 years. It has served as a valuable tool for understanding myself, my family, my friends, and my business associates. It has been especially helpful to me as a parent because I have used it to understand differences in my children's personalities and to learn how their unique characteristics contribute to their view of the world. It has also helped me to understand my own parenting style. For example, as an Enneatype Seven, I encouraged my children to be independent and adventuresome and to experience life to its fullest. When Emi was born, my father revealed an insight into my parenting style when he said to me, "Now you have someone to play with." While my multiple ideas and activities were stimulating to Emi and Mari, it was probably challenging for them to keep up with me while tuning into their inner selves.

By the time your child is around four to five years of age, you will probably be able to determine his Enneatype because his consciousness will have developed enough to provide a separate sense of self and ways of fitting in to the world. However, even at an earlier age it is possible to identify characteristics that are representative of a type, and it is fun to try. At the very least, the Enneagram can show you that your child is an individual with his own way of viewing the world.

Because the Enneagram is related to a person's motivation, the system can help you understand why your child behaves in a certain way, which in turn helps you to accept him and to offer him compassion. Most often, personality types develop as a defense mechanism—as a way of surviving. Instead of seeing the theory as a way of defining your child, however, use it as way to help him gain freedom through recognition and appreciation of differences among people. This awareness can also lay the groundwork for you to make better parenting decisions as you help your child build on his strengths, recognize and minimize his weaknesses, and develop confidence. The recognition that your child's reactions are often a result of his personality type can also alleviate your concern that you are responsible for everything that he feels and does. You may be worried if he seems overly introverted, dramatic, aggressive, or complacent. When you realize that these responses originate from his personality, you can work with the trait rather than against it. Additionally, when you recognize your own personality-driven tendencies, you can become more intentional in your behavior.

I remember when Emi, an Enneatype One (which is called the Perfectionist), saw some grass growing in the cracks of our driveway and asked to cover them with tape; she wanted to fix what she perceived as imperfect.

When Mari moaned and groaned excessively about minor issues, I thought I must have done something terrible to cause her pain. Later, however, when I realized that she is an Enneatype Four, which is termed both Romantic and Dramatic, I felt relieved to know that complaining was simply a natural way for her to process experiences.

The following Enneagram chart, which includes descriptions and associated motivations for each personality type, is applicable to both children and adults. As you read through the chart, think about these questions: Which type matches your child? What are his strengths and weaknesses? How do you relate to the different parenting styles? As a parent, how can you build on your assets and make improvements to your family relationships?

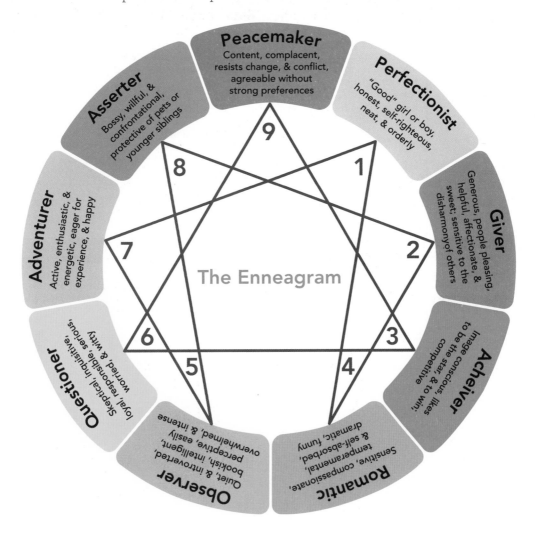

The Enneagram

Peacemaker — Content, complacent, resists change, & conflict, agreeable without strong preferences

Perfectionist — "Good" girl or boy, honest, self-righteous, neat, & orderly

Giver — Generous, people pleasing, helpful, affectionate, & sweet; sensitive to the disharmony of others

Acheiver — Image conscious, likes to be the star, & to win; competitive

Romantic — Sensitive, compassionate, temperamental, & self-absorbed, dramatic, funny

Observer — Quiet, & introverted, bookish, intelligent, perceptive, easily overwhelmed, & intense

Questioner — Skeptical, inquisitive, loyal, responsible, serious, worried, & witty

Adventurer — Active, enthusiastic, & energetic, eager for experience, & happy

Asserter — Bossy, willful, & confrontational, protective of pets or younger siblings

How the Enneagram Can Help

Description	Motivator	Child's Actions	How to Help	This Type as a Parent	How to Enhance Your Parenting
Type 1: Perfectionist					
"Good" girl or boy, honest, self-righteous, neat, and orderly	Wants to get things right and improve	Takes a bath without resistance, follows rules, behaves politely, judges himself; becomes impatient and irritated if things are not done correctly	Avoid nagging; play with him; encourage relaxing activities; acknowledge his efforts to be "good," and also recognize his goodness in just being himself	You are organized, structured, and firm in your discipline; you are reliable and responsible, but often critical of yourself and your child; you want to be the "perfect" parent and do everything correctly	Relax occasionally, and play with your child; know that you are "good enough," and relax your standards of perfection; be aware of being self-righteous; acknowledge your irritation, and try to express it without hurting others; go easy on judging yourself and your child
Type 2: Giver					
Generous, people pleasing, helpful, sweet, and affectionate; sensitive to disharmony in others	Wants to be liked by helping	Considers others and offers help; enjoys taking care of dolls or plush toys; does not like being alone; gets feelings hurt easily; can be manipulative	Take time to relate to him individually; recognize his helping efforts by thanking him; help him get involved in projects; recognize his feelings and encourage him to express his needs	Parenting comes naturally to you, and you encourage your child's individual interests; you enjoy "taking care," and you easily recognize your child's needs; you may not speak up directly about negative issues, resorting to manipulative methods	Acknowledge your child's feelings—both positive and negative; encourage his independence, yet be clear with discipline and boundaries; state your own needs, set limits for yourself, and do something you enjoy every day
Type 3: Achiever					
Image conscious, likes to be the star and to win; competitive	Wants to perform well and succeed	Likes to be well-dressed; has a lot of energy; wants to do many activities; is popular; strives to win and to be the best	Recognize his inner feelings, and encourage him to identify his personal values, likes, and dislikes; help him unwind, relax, and slow down	You are active, energetic, and involved with your child's activities; you schedule and organize your family with positive energy toward accomplishing goals and completing tasks for meeting each child's potential	Slow down, and pay attention: listen to what your child is really saying; take a breath, and practice being present throughout the day, with awareness of "being" over "doing"; avoid comparing yourself to parents and acknowledge your inner worth

How the Enneagram Can Help

Description	Motivator	Child's Actions	How to Help	This Type as a Parent	How to Enhance Your Parenting
Type 4: Romantic					
Sensitive, compassionate, temperamental and self-absorbed, dramatic, and funny	Wants to feel special and unique	Enjoys beauty, art, music, dress-up, and nature; emotional and expressive; can withdraw and isolate; creative, exclusive, and individualist; perceptive; envious, and unfulfilled; may be shy, melancholic, or moody; collects shells, rocks, sticks, or small objects	Soothe hurt feelings; give him space to work through emotions when he wants it; give positive affirmation to help strengthen confidence and inner balance; help him get involved in his own projects and physical activities	You are warm, loving, available, creative, and insightful; you feel connected and recognize the depth of your child's feelings; because of your selfless devotion, it is easy to feel pulled in many directions, forget to keep boundaries, and lose your center; you may have a melancholic longing for other experiences	Provide ordinary experiences for your child so that he does not feel that he has to live up to the standards of being "special" all the time; give him space to have his own feelings and needs; take in and enjoy your child's appreciation of you; set clear boundaries for your child and yourself; take care of logistics and create order
Type 5: Observer					
Quiet and introverted, bookish, intelligent, perceptive, easily over-whelmed, and intense	Wants to understand and know	Likes to be alone with own activities; does not readily participate in groups; does not need lots of attention; self-sufficient; philosophical; shy and withdrawn; notices what is going on around him; may be socially uncomfortable	Be sensitive about invading his space; encourage outdoor and physical activity; support him to stand up for himself and to participate in social situations; take an interest in his world; play spontaneously with him	You are rational and objective in making decisions; you are predictable, nonjudging, and can restrain your emotions in tense situations because you tend to compartmentalize them; it may be challenging for you to express your feelings and respond to immediate needs and demands of your young child	Be spontaneous; express your feelings, instead of just feeling them privately, because your child needs to know that you care; offer praise, recognition, and feedback; trust yourself, and know that you are capable and that there is enough; give yourself alone time and space every day to recharge and process your feelings and intentions
Type 6: Questioner					
Skeptical, inquisitive, loyal, responsible, serious, worried, and witty	Wants security	Can be nervous and worried; looks for danger and takes precautions; may be pessimistic, negative, and paranoid; looks for authority figure and either complies or rebels	Help him trust himself by showing confidence in him; help him feel calm and secure by being steady, consistent, and dependable; provide structure and clear limits; answer questions and encourage independence in small steps	You are loyal, responsible, hardworking, careful, and concerned about your child's welfare; you may be overprotective and worry about every possible danger or scenario that could go wrong; you may be ambivalent about being authoritative; you ask many questions and are analytical and thorough in making decisions for him	Trust that he is capable and resilient; excessive worrying and vigilance can make him uneasy about his own security; take an authoritative role, because he needs the security of your confidence; recognize your tendency to procrastinate and take action, even if you are not absolutely sure of the outcome

How the Enneagram Can Help

Description	Motivator	Child's Actions	How to Help	This Type as a Parent	How to Enhance Your Parenting
Type 7: Adventurer					
Active, enthusiastic, and energetic; eager for experience; happy	Wants fun, variety, and direct experience	Smiles often and is fun-loving; likes to be the center of attention; curious and interested in many activities; easily distracted; has trouble sitting still and concentrating; persistent in getting what he wants; resists limits and rules; tends to be overactive	Help him express his hurt and true feelings; encourage him to relax and slow down; provide different activities to keep him from being bored; support him when trying to stay concentrated and focused, so he can finish projects that he starts; tell him "no" only when necessary	You are optimistic and upbeat with visions, dreams, and plans; your energy can be generous, infectious, and inspiring when it is positive; you enjoy variety, change, and new and interesting experiences, so you may get bored and feel restricted with the routines of parenting; you tend to ignore unpleasant interactions and feelings; you often miss your child's feelings or perspective; you have the tendency to overdo	Listen and respond to your child's cues and needs; reduce your speed to the rate of your child to tune into him; be consistent; simplify everything—meals, activities, and schedules; take time to enjoy the present moment; recognize when you are not being realistic, and ground yourself with physical activity such as gardening, yoga, or running; do something fun for yourself every day
Type 8: Asserter					
Bossy, willful, and confrontational; protective of pets or younger siblings	Wants control and power	Strong, dominant, and energetic; shows anger easily; may be stubborn, pushy, and bossy; takes up a lot of space; likes intensity and looks for ways to match it; not afraid to speak his honest opinion; has a soft, vulnerable side that cares for and protects against injustice	Be direct, honest, and straightforward with him—match him; listen to him, and engage with him; help him settle down with calming activities; recognize his virtues and strengths without trying to minimize him; do not overreact to his anger or temper tantrums	You take action, are a leader, and a good role model for teaching your child to use his "will;" you are passionate about and protective of your family; you are present and a strong, energetic force; you believe in justice and truth and are willing to fight for it; you have a quick temper and express your feelings readily	Relax and play with your child on his level; give him space to take the lead; listen to and empower him to unfold from his own source; reduce your energy to meet the level of your child's; take several deep breaths when you feel excited; recognize your tendency to blame others; take care of yourself, so that you do not burn out
Type 9: Peacemaker					
Content and complacent; resists change and conflict; agreeable without strong preferences	Wants to be content and comfortable	Enjoys sedentary activities; has a mellow, friendly demeanor; moves slowly; is affectionate and likes to be close to you; avoids conflict; gets his feelings hurt easily; cannot make decisions about what he likes; may be stubborn and passive-aggressive	Help him identify what he likes to do by asking him questions; encourage him to speak up and express his opinions; be clear with directions and expectations; support him to be adventuresome and to try new experiences; recognize his accomplishments, and show appreciation	You are warm, understanding, and perceptive with your child's feelings and concerns; you are accepting, flexible, and supportive; you listen well and connect easily, which creates a sense of security for him; your unconditional love is predictable and steady; you avoid anger and conflict, and you may have problems taking authority	Encourage your child to be independent, and recognize your tendency to focus on him; speak clearly and take authority; avoid procrastination by taking action; be spontaneous and playful; recognize your tendency to be stubborn, and let it go; get physical exercise to move your energy; get in touch with your needs and desires, and voice your own opinion

Gender

As parents anticipate the arrival of their new baby, most begin to think about whether they will have a boy or a girl. Many parents have particular feelings, ideas, expectations, and perhaps even preferences when it comes to their baby's gender. Like temperament and personality, gender is a factor that contributes to your child's characteristics. You can help your son or daughter develop their own identity by recognizing gender stereotypes and encouraging a variety of activities.

> *What are little boys made of?*
> *"Snips and snails, and puppy dog tails!"*
> *What are little girls made of?*
> *"Sugar and spice, and everything nice!"*

Scientists agree on the existence of some biological gender differences, including differences in physical strength, weight, certain developmental patterns, and brain structure. In addition, sex hormones influence behavior. However, the reverse is true as well: behavior influences hormone levels. Researchers also have observed gender differences in aptitudes and preferences, but it is less clear whether these differences are biologically determined, culturally determined, or both. Finally, role models and socialized gender stereotypes influence your child's sense of self as a male or a female. By two and a half years old, most children can label their own sex and the sexes of others.

The Difference Between Girls and Boys

Knowledge of gender differences and how they impact a child's development and behavior can be a useful parenting tool. In her article "The Real Difference between Boys and Girls," Anita Sethi reports that experts generally agree that boys tend to:

Boys

- Prefer mechanical motion over human motion
- Prefer looking at clusters (such as the parts of a mobile) to looking at an individual face
- Excel in gross-motor skills: infant boys kick, squirm, and wiggle more than infant girls, even though both genders achieve major motor milestones at about the same time
- Gravitate toward playing in groups
- Engage in pretend heroic play
- Play at a greater distance from adults
- Are more dominant in social situations
- Enjoy participating in and watching active and aggressive play
  - Are more easily agitated and angered and have more difficulty self-soothing
    - Express fear later and less often than girls do, as evidenced by fewer startle reflexes to loud or sudden stimuli as infants
  - Are less likely to heed a parent's facial cue of fear; they disregard the warning and thus enter more dangerous situations
  - Less social expression

Girls

- Imitate movements involving human interaction (e.g., pat-a-cake)
- Prefer looking at an individual face to looking at a group of objects
- Excel in fine-motor skills and activities earlier (e.g., writing neatly, using utensils, manipulating buttons and zippers, and manipulating small toys)
- Gravitate toward playing with one other child
- Engage in pretend social play
- Remain closer to adults while playing
- Are more adept at reading emotional cues
- Have a higher level of empathy
- Develop language skills earlier—both understanding and producing words
- Establish and maintain eye contact earlier and more effectively
- Listen better and are more tuned in to the human voice
- Smile more socially

In her book *Pink Brain, Blue Brain*, Lise Eliot, PhD, acknowledges that boy brains and girl brains are not the same but says it is wrong to assume that all gender differences are hardwired. To show that environmental influences directly affect human biology, Eliot points to recent research on the plasticity (malleability) of the brain and new evidence that experiences can actually cause genes to be turned off or on. These discoveries suggest that it is important to appreciate the ways in which parenting and learning influence your child.

The influences on your child's gender identity development include both natural biological characteristics and learned experiences, such as cultural expectations and societal reinforcement of certain gender-appropriate behaviors. Scientists now emphasize the ways in which biological and social factors interact to produce behavior, so that the classic debate of nature versus nurture is now better understood as nature and nurture. From this perspective, nature and nurture influence each other as they shape a child's development and behavior.

Whether inherited or learned (or both), gender identity affects the development of a child's skills and interests as he grows. Boys and girls are born with biological differences that culture and socialization tend to reinforce and magnify over time. Boys often tend to play actively with balls in large groups, while girls tend to play dress-up quietly in pairs. Some parents become disappointed when they ban toy guns from the playroom, only to observe their boys picking up carrots or crayons to use as guns.

You may see cultural stereotypes as restrictive to your child's process of finding his true self and reaching his full potential. Perhaps you want to encourage your son or daughter to explore all interests despite stereotypes. Although you cannot stop the influence of gender altogether, you can increase your awareness in order to help your child use both biologically based and culturally based traits to the best advantage.

In a 1974 issue of the *Journal of Consulting and Clinical Psychology*, Sandra Bem, PhD, describes a different way of thinking about gender roles. In her article, "The Measurement of Psychological Androgyny," Bem proposes the concept of androgyny: the combination of masculine and feminine characteristics within one person. She suggests that the traits people see as masculine and feminine exist on a continuum within every person. Therefore, people, male or female, may express both assertive and restrained behaviors in different situations without regard for masculine or feminine stereotypes. This idea offers flexibility for children to explore a range of yin and yang feelings, behaviors, interests, and skills. You can encourage your child to develop an adaptable gender identity in the following ways:

- Recognize your own gender stereotypes.

- Recognize cultural pressures to adhere to gender stereotypes.

- Encourage a variety of stereotypically gendered activities.

- Listen to your child's cues and needs.

- Encourage your child to acknowledge unexpected or different feelings.

- Examine child care providers for possible gender biases.

Essential Skills for Emotional and Social Intelligence

THE THEORIES OF EMOTIONAL development unfold in real life as your baby develops and uses certain essential skills that support his emotional growth and determine his level of emotional intelligence. Emotional intelligence includes the ability to read one's own feelings and those of others, the ability to regulate emotions, and the ability to use emotion to motivate oneself and others toward goals. Your child's level of emotional intelligence has a deep impact on the quality of his life, including his abilities to determine his future and to maintain healthy relationships.

As your baby acquires certain essential skills, he gains what he needs to bolster his emotional intelligence. Using these skills, he learns to take control of his emotions, to be confident, and to be his own person when he interacts with others. Further, he expands his social intelligence—specifically his abilities to understand others and to act wisely in human relationships—as he learns to play alone, to play alongside and with others, to share, to empathize, to cooperate, and to respect others.

Self-awareness and relationship building are not only developmental milestones, but also foundational skills for emotional intelligence. Your child will rely on these skills as he reaches out beyond his family and home environment to connect with the natural world, his community and culture at large. As he grows and matures, he will continue to tap in to these essential tools to further his connections and to live the life of his choosing.

Skills That Foster Emotional Intelligence

Since the day he entered the world, your baby has been working on the skills essential to emotional health and intelligence: self-awareness, confidence, self-regulation, intentionality, self-motivation, and judgment. None of these skills exist in a vacuum. They are interrelated and interdependent. Emotional competencies are developed through experience and over a lifetime. Thus, as a parent, you can encourage your child to sharpen these skills through appropriate attention and practice. Building on the secure attachment you enjoy with your baby, you are in the best position to assist him in this process.

Self-awareness

At some point between 15 and 24 months of age, the strong sense of self that you helped your baby establish through attunement and mirroring matures into self-awareness. Your baby is self-aware when he understands that he is separate, physically and mentally, from other people and from the world around him, and they are separate from him. He realizes that he has his own thoughts and his own feelings, that his behaviors have an impact on his environment, and that the same is true for other people. The "Rouge Test", described in a 1972 article in "Developmental Psychobiology," skillfully demonstrated this evolution. Mothers whose babies took the test dabbed their babies' noses with rouge. Each mother then placed her baby in front of a mirror. Younger babies reacted to the rouge as if they were looking at another baby in the mirror. Older babies (some as young as 15 months and nearly all by the age of 24 months) recognized that the rouge was on their own nose; they recognized themselves in the mirror and thus demonstrated self-awareness.

Not surprisingly, the emergence of self-awareness coincides with the emergence of self-aware emotions, such as pride, guilt, embarrassment, and shame. Self-awareness also coincides with developing language. Language that your baby uses to label himself (I, me, mine), to label others (his, yours, hers), and to name his feelings and actions supports his blossoming self-awareness.

Self-awareness is the core skill on which the other essential emotional skills rely. Your baby must be aware of himself in order to be confident, to empathize, and to self-regulate. Here are a few exercises to encourage your baby to develop self-awareness:

- **Name your feelings**—When interacting with your baby, tell him what you are feeling: "When I see you smile, I feel happy and I smile, too."

- **Name his feelings and reflect them back to him**—When he shows an emotion, ask him to name it if he is old enough. Ask, "What are you feeling?" Then acknowledge the emotion he names: "So, you are feeling sad."

- **Name what others are feeling**—When reading a book or watching a movie, talk with your child about how a character is feeling, how those feelings affect the character's actions, and whether the character could have acted differently despite that feeling.

- **Introduce other points of view**—When your child gets into a conflict with a sibling or a friend, encourage him to express how he felt and to imagine how his sibling or friend felt. What was each person feeling and thinking? Why?

- **Give him choices**—Let your baby initiate actions and experience the outcomes. Allow him to choose which toys to play with, which book he wants at bedtime, what to wear, which part of his dinner he will eat first, and so on.

Doing these exercises with your baby will probably increase your self-awareness and emotional intelligence, in addition to his. As with any skill, self-awareness is never "perfect," and it takes consistent practice. Even for adults, it is easy to get caught up in a situation or an emotion and forget to be mindful. You can model an appropriate response in cases like this by taking a deep breath and getting back in touch with your feelings and your situation. Self-awareness helps both you and your baby maintain balance.

Confidence

Hideko Yoshida, the headmaster at Dream Window Kindergarten, used to tell me that it is very important that children learn to do things *jibunde* (for themselves). She felt that parents too frequently interfere with their child's activities, thus interrupting the child's sense of direction and compromising his confidence.

Babies have their own internal sense of purpose. One of the biggest challenges of being a parent is to find a balance between nurturing and letting go, to guide your child to develop confidence through independence and to grow into his own true self. This was one of my main challenges as a parent. It is hard to know when to stop doing certain things for your child and give him the space to figure out how to do them for himself. Sometimes scheduling constraints or mounting frustration on my part tempted me into interrupting my children's process when I could have backed away. Again, here is a place where awareness of yourself and your actions advances your baby's development.

Confidence is a positive attitude toward, perception of, and belief in one's abilities. As with all essential emotional skills and qualities, your child does not inherit confidence; rather, he learns it from his experiences and from the reactions of others. That learning starts in the womb with his mother's wanting him and caring for him. After birth, when you and others respond to his needs, he develops a sense of power and autonomy, and confidence begins to take root.

A confident person is not afraid to try something because he is not afraid of failing. He knows that it is okay to make mistakes and that perfection is impossible. A confident person is comfortable with himself. He knows his strengths and weaknesses, and he does not mind if others know them, too. He meets challenges with optimism and persistence. He can make decisions on his own, and he can take care of himself. Confidence broadens your child's world and opportunities and gives him the foundation to learn, to succeed, and to participate in healthy relationships. Children who lack confidence feel unsure, look for approval, and have difficulty overcoming obstacles.

As a parent, you can encourage your baby's confidence in many different ways. In her book *Young Children's Personal, Social, and Emotional Development*, Marion Dowling, an early childhood education consultant, writes that confidence is linked to three factors that build on each other:

- ✿ **Self-concept**—Becoming aware of oneself

- ✿ **Self-esteem**—Developing a view of oneself (positive or negative)

- ✿ **Self-knowledge**—Getting to know one's strengths and weaknesses

Your baby develops the first factor, self-concept, through the lens of his first relationships. If one or more few loving and significant people recognize your baby's cues and respond to those cues in a way that is attuned to his needs, then his belief in himself strengthens, thus creating confidence in his world and then in himself. As he grows into toddlerhood and his world expands, additional people contribute to the composite picture of his self-concept.

The second factor, self-esteem, forms when your child places a value or judgment on his self-concept. Again, early experiences lay the foundation here. For instance, if the people closest to your baby accept and respect him, he is more likely to see himself as competent and worthwhile, and thus to place a positive value on his self-concept.

Only with outside influence does your baby possess the third factor, self-knowledge. If he has self-insight, it is limited. He looks to the adults around him to gain a sense of his strengths and weaknesses. Therefore, what you as a parent say about those strengths and weaknesses matters, as does the way you respond to your child's successes and failures. As he grows, he becomes more aware of where he excels and where he may need help and support. However,

if he receives an incorrect image about himself in early childhood, he will probably carry it with him as truth until he, someone else, or an experience changes his point of view. For example, if a caregiver or an experience leads him to believe that he is not artistic or smart, then he may hold that assumption until he discovers it is not true.

Sometimes people confuse confidence with extroversion and lack of confidence with introversion. An outgoing child (an extrovert) may appear to be confident because he openly expresses and asserts himself, while a quiet child (an introvert) who prefers privacy and alone time may appear insecure. The truth could very well be the opposite. The extroverted child may be overcompensating for a lack of confidence with his outgoing behavior, while the introverted child may be perfectly confident; he simply enjoys being alone and sees no need to draw attention to himself or to please others. By paying attention, you can distinguish between your child's true level of confidence and your own interpretation of his behavior.

Other Ways to Help Your Child Develop His Confidence

- Provide a safe environment in which he has the freedom to move on his own without your intervention.

- Allow him to make choices whenever possible.

- Model confidence—your child learns by watching you.

- Offer positive encouragement and gratitude instead of blame and criticism.

- Show him that you do not expect perfection. Help him to accept his mistakes and to use them to move forward.

- Allow him to achieve goals on his own, and help him when he proactively asks for your help.

- Encourage him to try new things.

- Let go of an agenda, and accept him as he is.

- Avoid comparing him to others.

- Create small, cozy play areas so that he can feel big.

- Help him assess his accomplishments.

- Treat him with trust and respect.

You might need to show self-restraint when helping your baby to build confidence. It can be tough to watch him try over and over again to force in a puzzle piece that clearly does not fit, or to witness your toddler getting frustrated as he tries to dress himself. However, mistakes and struggles are inevitable bumps on the road to gaining confidence. When you give your child the space to explore and to discover the world on his own without offering solutions to his challenges, he learns that he is capable, that he can persevere on his own, and that he can solve problems. In Japan, people often use the word *ganbatte* to offer encouragement for persistence. They believe that persistence leads to success.

As your child's world expands, it is natural for him to have experiences that hurt his self-image, but they do not necessarily have to cause long-term damage to his confidence. If he learns to repair hurt with your love and support, these life experiences can be a source of strength and wisdom. When you build a loving and fear-free relationship with your child, he feels comfortable enough to show you his vulnerabilities. You have created a space where his confidence and independence can continue to grow and strengthen.

Self-regulation

The essential emotional skill of self-regulation stems from your child's natural ability to maintain homeostasis. As he grows and develops physiologically, your attunement to and support of his needs help him self-regulate at higher levels. Self-regulation involves the ability to control one's bodily functions and impulses and the ability to concentrate. It means controlling urges, weighing consequences, and making informed choices regardless of whether an authority figure is present. Self-regulation is a complex process that emerges slowly.

Over the past three decades, developmental psychologists, neuroscientists, and others have studied self-regulation and its essential role in helping children to thrive and to grow. If your child knows how to calm down when he is upset, he both feels better in the moment and establishes connections in his brain's circuits that help him manage stress. On the other hand, a child with poor self-regulation is likely to act on aggressive impulses, to have difficulty delaying gratification, and to be distractible and unable to focus on tasks. Therefore, he is more likely to have emotional and social problems as he moves out into the world.

Self-regulation is not just about social and emotional skills. It also is related to cognitive behaviors, such as remembering and paying attention. Children who cannot control their emotions at age four are unlikely to be able to follow their teacher's directions at age six. In fact, according to Tools of the Mind, an organization that developed an early childhood curriculum of the same name, kindergarten teachers view a child's ability to self-regulate as a better indicator of school readiness than IQ or entry-level reading or math skills—and an increasing amount of scientific evidence supports these teachers. Self-regulation enables a child to follow classroom rules and, on a cognitive level, to solve problems and to learn.

Your baby requires high-quality regulation and discipline from you in order to develop his own self-regulation and self-discipline. I found disciplining my children to be the most difficult challenge in parenting because I do not enjoy saying no, giving "tough love," or seeing my children experience the pain of not getting what they want. As they grew older, they pressured me with demands based on their desires, and it was hard for me to resist them and to remain confident in my judgment. But when 18-year-old Emi or Mari complained about curfews or driving speed limits, I

 To learn more about Tools of the Mind visit toolsofthemind.org

remembered them as toddlers, persistently demanding a cookie, and wished that I had been more consistent in those early years. If I had set clear boundaries and stuck to them, I would have helped them learn self-regulation; instead, they had to learn it on their own. I have realized that the patterns involved in skills, such as impulse control, delay of gratification, adherence to social rules, and self-regulation, are easier to learn and reinforce through routines, regularity, and consistency at a young age.

Your baby's behaviors are a natural extension of his development. In fact, throughout your child's development and into adolescence, both desirable and undesirable behaviors are often a manifestation of his current developmental stage. Knowledge about what behaviors to expect at different ages can increase your effectiveness at teaching your child to self-regulate.

Writer Kelly Bartlett discusses self-regulation in her article "Natural Discipline for the Early Years" in *Green Child Magazine* (2013). She explains that from birth to age two, it is natural for children to use all of their senses to explore their environment. They touch,

 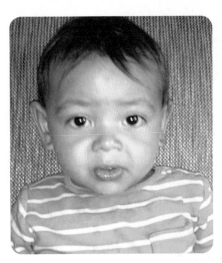 

Faces of my grandson, Zo

pick up, grab, bite, pinch, and throw in order to understand their world. If these behaviors are not controlled, they can cause harm to people and objects. It is helpful to remember that a baby's intention is not malicious; it is simply the result of his instinct to learn. At one year old, your baby's brain is not mature enough to adhere to the word "no." He does not have the neural connections to stop, to remember words, to think through options or consequences, and to decide not to act, no matter how many times you tell him.

At this early age, it makes more sense to work with, not against, your child's natural predisposition to explore and to learn. Bartlett suggests designing a "yes" environment that removes safety threats and allows your baby to explore freely, as much as possible. For example, you might allow your baby to explore the lower drawers in the kitchen or to pull cushions off the couch—activities that are not harmful and are easily adjusted. In addition, you can redirect him from negative to positive activities. When you provide your child with a maximum of freedom and a minimum of "no's," you keep him from feeling constantly restricted. Choices help him feel a sense of control and agency. Humor helps, too.

Most experts agree that you cannot spoil infants or teach them correct behavior. They cannot control their emotions on their own. Although your baby is born with some ability to self-regulate, he needs you to calm and soothe him when he is upset. During his first months of life, as he adjusts to being in the world, he operates on a basic level devoted to feeding, digestion, thermoregulation, and sleep. By tuning in to your baby's emotions at this stage, you instinctively provide the external regulation he needs when he becomes overwhelmed. This responsive relationship helps your baby develop his emerging self-regulatory skills.

Almost abruptly at around three months of age, your baby's learning accelerates. He begins to use some self-calming behaviors more effectively. For example, he brings his hands to his mouth to soothe himself or uses vocalization, facial expressions, and other cues to make a reassuring connection. As weeks pass, your baby adds thumb sucking, rocking, or holding a plush toy to his self-soothing practices.

Another shift in development happens at around eight months and coincides with your baby's newfound independence through locomotion, more intentional communication, and other emerging skills. This stage brings a new set of regulatory demands for caregivers. Your job is no longer about simply helping your baby find comfort. Now you must help him learn to regulate proximity and distance while he deals with conflicting needs for emotional security and increased freedom and exploration. You can help by encouraging him to explore on his own while knowing that you are nearby as a home base when he needs it.

true to his emotions without having tantrums. When you acknowledge and accept his feelings and then mirror them back to him, you show empathy and help him learn to handle his strong emotions. At the same time, you do not have to change your boundaries or give in to his demands.

It may be difficult to believe that your toddler can understand and adhere to limits. If you are consistent in maintaining boundaries and you are clear that they are not negotiable—even if he has a tantrum—then his brain becomes wired to accept the limits, and he learns to manage his emotions. If he does not accomplish this task in early childhood, he will need to rewire himself for self-control when he is older. Self-control helps your child calm his emotions before acting, check his impulses, and postpone gratification. These skills in turn help him listen attentively, learn, and make better choices.

As your baby starts toddling, he moves into the greater world, and the days when you can control his environment are waning. He needs new kinds of limits—beyond simple physical ones—in order to stay safe and to learn self-control so that later in life, when you are not present, he knows how to keep himself safe. For you, the parent, it can be challenging to shift from responding to all of your infant's needs and merely redirecting him, as needed, to setting limits for a toddler, while respecting his need for more freedom.

This shift usually happens when your toddler starts asserting himself and individuating by saying, "no" to you. At two years old, his will is developing, and he strives for autonomy. With increasing mobility and ability to accomplish more activities independently, he gains self-assurance and confidence. Although he regularly adds new capabilities and independence, he does not yet have the ability to make logical choices. So, the task of setting limits and examples, especially regarding health and safety, is still yours.

Your toddler needs to know that it is not necessary to suppress, hide, or feel ashamed of his feelings. At the same time, you can teach him how to express and be

The Marshmallow Experiment

While at Stanford University in the early 1970s, psychologist Walter Mischel, PhD studied the impact of learning self-control on young children through his marshmallow experiment. During the experiment, Mischel placed a single marshmallow in front of a child between four and six years old. He then gave the child the choice of eating that one marshmallow immediately or waiting for approximately 15 minutes to receive another marshmallow. In follow-up studies several years later, researchers found that the children who could delay gratification and wait for the second marshmallow tended to have better life outcomes in education and other measures.

 To watch the Marshmallow Experiment visit growhealthygrowhappy.com

As you step into the limit-setting aspect of parenting, feelings about the way you were disciplined as a child may surface. Just as your child learns from your modeling, you learned from your parents. When you approach discipline with openness and care, rather than that of an inflexible authority figure, you create a climate of trust and support, rather than fear and frustration.

You can use a yin and yang approach to help your child learn to regulate his emotions. By understanding his temperament and noticing when he seems overwhelmed or underwhelmed, you can help your baby increase or decrease his emotional energy and restore balance. For instance, if your child is overexcited, you can actively help him bring his nervous system and energy to a balanced state (downregulate) by redirecting him to a calmer activity. A time-out can help him disengage from an emotional situation, especially if you frame the time-out as time to downregulate (versus time to be punished) and guide him to use this technique for future challenges. When needed, you also can help your child increase his level of excitement (upregulate) by speaking in a more energetic voice, going outside, or playing an active game with him. By helping your child regulate before he is able to do so on his own, you not only provide a model for him, but also demonstrate that self-regulation is possible and pleasurable.

In his blog, *Essential Parenting*, Chris White, MD, a pediatrician and parent educator, describes his own yin and yang approach to discipline. The yin aspects of discipline, he says, speak to unconditional love, nourishment of the parent-child relationship, and acceptance of the child for who he is. These practices create a secure foundation from which your child gains confidence to try new things and to make his own choices. This freedom is balanced by yang aspects of discipline, which are concerned with mentoring your child and setting healthy boundaries for him. He learns from watching you, and when you set firm limits for him, you create an environment that provides security.

Together, yin and yang influences create wholeness in discipline. You can further balance your discipline by making adjustments toward more yin or yang, according to the needs of the situation and your individual child.

In her book *Self-Regulation in Early Childhood: Nature and Nurture*, Martha B. Bronson, EdD, offers the following strategies for helping children self-regulate. Note that each of these strategies can be customized to suit your child, your parenting style, and your family.

- **Observe closely**—Your baby sends cues that tell you when he is hungry, tired, or ready to play.

- **Respond**—By responding, you bring attention to your baby's cues. Be alert to your child's particular needs for regularity, novelty, and interaction.

- **Provide structure and predictability**—Your baby needs consistent caregivers and routines for everyday activities, such as feeding, sleeping, and diapering or toileting.

- **Arrange developmentally appropriate environments**—Low shelves, uncluttered tables, and age-appropriate materials can provide the infrastructure needed for your child to build and challenge his abilities. You can also change and add to the environment as your child's abilities progress.

- **Define age-appropriate limits**—Be direct with your child about your behavioral expectations .

- **Show empathy and caring**—Recognize your child's needs, and treat them as important. When you do this, he feels good about himself and more easily copes with strong emotions.

You will be more patient with both yourself and your child when you recognize your respective temperaments, personalities, and the dynamics between them. If you learn about his developmental process, you can understand his perspective and changing needs. Then, when you combine this understanding with consistency and confidence in your own judgment, you can select strategies that support the development of self-regulation in your child. This process may be difficult, but it is one of the greatest gifts that you can give him.

The World of Spirit

Your baby's budding self-awareness, coupled with his emerging language and physical abilities, creates the fertile soil out of which his spirituality grows. It will be some time before he directly asks, "What is the meaning of life?" By the time he is three years old, however, he will probably assign some meaning to his world.

That common search for meaning can be defined as spirituality. For some people, it is best sought within the defined practices, teachings, and traditions of an organized religion. Others create their own path via a patchwork of philosophies and rituals that resonate for them. Still others may turn away from religion and sacred texts completely and instead search for life's truths, patterns, and connections through nature, science, or logic.

Your child draws on his spirituality to create his sense of morality, his feeling of belonging in the world, and his ability to contend with life's ups, downs, and mysteries. Not surprisingly, many studies have shown that people who are spiritual tend to be happier than people who are not.

Developmental psychologist James Fowler, PhD defined the stages of faith development in his book *Stages of Faith: The Psychology of Human Development and the Quest for Meaning.* Fowler's stages progress from the undifferentiated infant stage to enlightenment, though most human beings remain in a stage that comes well before enlightenment.

As with most aspects of human development, the underpinning for your child's spiritual development forms in his first three years of life. During this prestage, which Fowler calls "undifferentiated faith," your baby is forming his view of how the world works. He will build on this view when he starts to contemplate spiritual questions. If in these first two to three years a loving caregiver meets his needs consistently, he can establish trust and mutuality. He then has a secure foundation from which to look at life's meaning later. If his needs are not met and he does not experience a loving relationship, he does not trust the world to provide for him and does not develop an ability to connect with others. He has then established a negative platform from which to formulate the answers to life's big questions.

As babies move from infancy to toddlerhood, they begin to see themselves as separate entities but are still dependent on what they perceive as a very powerful being: the parent or caregiver. According to Fowler, some researchers hypothesize that human thoughts about God originate in this stage.

At about three years of age, most children move into the stage of language and imagination as their sense of spirituality awakens. In this stage, your child has the language to begin to think and ask "What?" "How?" and "Why?" At this point, he does not separate fantasy and reality, and answers do not need to be logical in order to satisfy him. Fowler cautions that children at this stage are very susceptible to messages and images. He suggests that parents protect young children from violent or terrifying images, stories, or movies.

As your child attains the essential skills that allow him to think beyond himself and to develop spiritually, you can help him create a value system, a moral code, and a supportive spiritual community that will serve him throughout his life.

The following tips can help you help your child confidently enter the world of spirit:

🌸 **Get in touch with your own spirituality**—Take the time to think about your spiritual life, your religion, and your values.

🌸 **Join a supportive community**—Whether it be a church, a community center, or a regular Friday-night dinner group, membership in a community helps your child feel connected.

🌸 **Perform your spiritual practices in front of or with your child**—When you say a rosary, meditate, do yoga, walk in the woods, or get in touch with spirit in some other way, allow your child to participate so that he knows spirituality is a regular and important part of your life.

🌸 **Create traditions and partake in rituals**—From holidays to giving thanks before a meal to birthday celebrations, create family traditions and rituals that stop the clock, make time for reflection, and mark life's milestones and events.

🌸 **Pay attention to your child's stage of spiritual, cognitive, and emotional development**—When you know where your child is in his development, you can respond to spiritual inquiries sensitively. A five-year-old needs a completely different answer to "What happens when you die?" than a two-year-old.

No matter where you are personally on the spiritual spectrum, spirituality—the search for meaning and connectedness—is a natural part of your baby's development. Questions, such as "Who am I?" "Why am I here?" and "What is life?" will come soon enough. For now, from infancy to toddlerhood, while you are his world, you have the opportunity to help him establish a secure foundation from which he can begin to reach out to the world of spirit.

Intentionality, Self-motivation, and Judgment

Intentionality is the ability to act deliberately and consciously with a plan, a goal, or a purpose in mind. Intentionality involves a high level of emotional and mental core competency because only a fairly mature person can consider choices before acting, rather than simply reacting impulsively.

In the first three years of life, your baby will not practice intentionality per se—though he can make decisions and begin to put some thought behind those decisions. By parenting with intentionality, you can use these first three years to prepare your baby to act intentionally when he does develop the skills to do so.

You can begin by showing your baby that you respect his preferences. By taking care of his needs and wants, you honor his first choices and judgments and teach him that his inner judgment is valuable and worthy. You also reinforce his actions and encourage him to express himself.

As your child's world expands, his desire for autonomy and need to strengthen his will also grow. The more practice he has in making simple daily choices now, the easier it will be for him to make more important decisions wisely and confidently later in his life. When you offer him choices, such as which shirt to wear, you give him the chance to develop his analytical and decision-making skills, along with the opportunity to experience his intuition and desires. What are the causes and effects of this choice? What feels right? Over time, he learns to consider a range of factors and viewpoints that contribute to a thoughtful decision.

The process of acting intentionally involves curiosity, reflection, planning, and persistence. By stimulating your child's curiosity, getting him involved with his own projects and responsibilities, sharing control by offering him choices, and helping him reflect on his decisions, you help him develop intentionality.

Hideko Yoshida at Dream Window Kindergarten encouraged me to use the following seven levels of judgment when making a decision. These levels are a set of tools for looking at the aspects of a situation in a holistic way. When your child has a decision to make, consult these seven levels together to explore the decision from a variety of viewpoints. The chart below shows an example of how you could use them when making decisions about food and clothing.

Most people struggle with decision-making for their entire lives. The prospect of making decisions can paralyze them, or they may fearfully follow the crowd and end up living with choices that do not reflect their values or desires. You can help your child create a life of his choosing and increase his chances of happiness by showing confidence in his judgment and teaching him how to make good decisions early in his life.

Seven Levels of Judgment

Level of Judgement	Food	Clothes
Automatic	Eating on a strict schedule	Wearing the same kinds of clothes everyday
Sensory	Enjoying tastes, textures, and visual appeal of food	Choosing clothes with appealing textures, colors, designs, and fashions
Sentimental	Eating mother's cooking has an emotional feeling and memory	Remembering the way that you (caregiver) were dressed and dressing your child the same way; choosing certain outfits for special occasions
Intellectual	Choosing food based on its nutritional components	Choosing clothes based on functions, for example: warmth, breathability, and sun protection
Social	Considering others in food choices; eating grains so that enough food can be produced for the whole world; taking only one piece of the pie to leave some for others	Considering manufacturing practices; choosing clothes based on current trends
Ideological	Using yin and yang as a way to balance diet; eating seasonal and local foods; eating whole foods; considering energy used and environmental impact	Dressing in sync with the seasons, for health and connection to nature; using natural fibers; considering energy used and environmental impact
Supreme	Incorporating all levels of judgment in food choices in a holistic way	Incorporating all levels of judgment in clothing choices in a holistic way

Skills That Foster Social Intelligence

The essential skills that contribute to emotional intelligence are the building blocks for your baby's social development. He is biologically programmed to be social and to develop relationships. The moment he was born, he started interacting with you through touch and hearing. Immediately, he started giving you cues to communicate his needs. Then, as soon as he was developmentally able, he gave you a smile that melted your heart and cemented your devotion to him.

As you learn to read his cues, your baby learns to read yours. He works on forming his first relationship: his relationship with you. He will use the knowledge gained from that first relationship to develop meaningful connections with siblings, extended family members, friends, and others.

Each of these relationships is special, and each has different levels of importance and different influences on your child. His ability to form positive relationships has much to do with the health and quality of his first relationship with you, as well as his mastery of essential skills, such as empathy, compassion, cooperation, and adherence to values.

Following is an overview of social-intelligence skills and their role in your child's life and health.

Empathy and Compassion

"When educating the minds of our youth, we must not forget to educate their hearts." —Dalai Lama

Golden Rule revised: "Do unto others as they would have you do unto them." —David Daniels, MD, professor of psychiatry and behavioral sciences and Enneagram teacher

Empathy is the ability to view other people's situations from their perspective, to place yourself in their shoes, to have a sense of what they are feeling, and to understand why they feel and act the way they do. Empathy is considered one of the most influential components of emotional intelligence. It is the underlying base for relating to others with courtesy and respect, and it is a necessary skill for getting along with others.

Empathy is a precursor to pro-social behavior, defined as actions that benefit another person without an expected reward for oneself. Children who engage in pro-social behavior are more compassionate, generally perform better in academics, make friends more easily, and have higher self-esteem than other children. They also are able to form higher-quality and longer-lasting relationships. These benefits remain with the child throughout adolescence and adulthood. Empathy involves three component skills:

- A sense of self-awareness and the ability to distinguish one's own feelings from the feelings of another

- The acknowledgment and understanding of another person's perspective

- The ability to regulate one's own emotional responses

Although empathy has some biological components, it is developed mostly through experiences. These experiences begin in infancy, when you, his primary caregiver, empathize with him. You show him that you understand him by being responsive, emotionally supportive, and compassionate about his feelings. That attunement creates an attachment, a dependency, and eventually a two-way street of empathy between you and your baby. You are his role model and his first experience with empathy. As he feels your empathy for him, he is likely to mirror this feeling and, eventually, to imitate it when interacting with others.

The fundamentals of empathy are awareness of your emotions and the ability to self-regulate. As your child grows, help him identify and understand his emotions, so that later he can recognize and understand them in others. For example, if he is fussy and refuses a nap, you can explain that he may feel irritable and upset because he is tired. As he matures, your child's experiences, including ups and downs, pains and pleasures, will increase his understanding of other people and further shape his capacity for empathy.

Below are several parenting strategies that you can incorporate into your daily interactions with your child to foster empathy. As he develops, his level of understanding will become more complex.

- Address your child's needs, and help him learn to regulate his emotional responses.

- Respectfully respond to your child's cues with meaningful feelings, thoughts, and intentions.

- Give your child physical affection and pleasant social interactions, which boost oxytocin levels and promote bonding.

- Limit your child's exposure to violent media, which desensitizes children's reaction to others' suffering.

- Model empathy and compassion. Empathic parenting produces empathic children.

- Promote a moral system that depends on intrinsic value systems, rather than rewards or punishments.

- Encourage your child to explore other perspectives by stepping into another person's shoes.

- Promote sharing because it helps a child understand another person's perspective. Ask, "How do you think Max would feel if you shared your new toy with him?"

- As you read books to your child, draw attention to the different characters' points of view. For example, ask, "How do you think he feels now?"

- Help your child discover similarities with people he may perceive as different. Some examples of diversity are people from other races, religions, or socioeconomic backgrounds, or people with physical or mental disabilities.

- Use role reversal as a way to prompt your child's understanding of another's feelings. Ask, "How would you feel if you were in this situation?"

Empathy often leads to compassion—the desire to take action to alleviate another person's pain—although feeling another person's pain is not a prerequisite to a compassionate act. The word compassion comes from the Latin word meaning "cosuffering," and compassion is usually related to suffering. Compassion is a thought ("There are other people in this world"), plus an emotion ("I feel for others, and others feel for me"), plus an action ("I am going to do this to help others").

As with empathy, your child is born with a tendency toward compassion. Starting at a young age, he moves to soothe you, his siblings, and his friends when they are distressed. However, he must hone this natural tendency through experience and through your modeling.

Acceptance and understanding without judgment or criticism are basic to developing compassion. Your child benefits when he witnesses you accepting yourself, as well as others. If you are inwardly or outwardly critical of yourself or others, then your child learns to be critical, too. When you are compassionate and understanding toward yourself and others, he learns to follow suit.

Because Western culture places great emphasis on independence, self-reliance, and self-first thinking, you may have to battle cultural ideals in order to teach your child compassion. In their early years, children need parents and caregivers who consciously nurture their ability to care about others and to act with kindness. When you encourage your child to be empathic and compassionate, you are investing in making the world a better place and helping him to develop meaningful relationships that nurture his happiness.

 To learn more about instilling empathy visit growhealthygrowhappy.com

Cooperation

Cooperation is an extension of empathy and compassion. It is a willingness and ability to work with others toward a common outcome. With the support of others, your child can accomplish goals far beyond what he could do alone. By helping and sharing with others to reach a common objective, he is also likely to gain emotional connection and a sense of meaning.

Before the age of three, children usually play on their own for short periods of time. They can usually play with an older child or an adult for longer periods of time if the other person focuses on what the young child wants. Two children under three years old typically play in parallel, or side by side, using the same or different toys while playing on their own. In parallel play, your toddler may enjoy the company of other children, even though they are not playing together directly. During his third year, your child and his friends may start to play together cooperatively by sharing and by negotiating difficulties without fights.

Although your child may not be able to cooperate fully until around the age of three, he experiences the spirit of cooperation far earlier through his relation-

ship with you. When your baby cries and you respond by feeding him, the two of you engage in a joint effort to satisfy his hunger by means of communication, assessment, and appropriate reaction. Around the age of one, when he discovers a sense of autonomy as he learns to walk, you cooperate with his desire to explore by providing him with a safe environment in which to do so.

By 18 months, children are able to understand their caregiver's wishes and expectations, and they usually can follow simple commands. Your baby can and does cooperate. In fact, most children this age love to help out, and this demonstrates compassion, as well as cooperation.

At this stage, however, your child is also developing a defiant side of his blossoming personality. You may struggle to get your child dressed in the morning as he runs away and refuses to wear certain clothes. Individual differences in temperament and character contribute to the degree to which your child tests his boundaries and exerts his will.

You might find it challenging when your toddler is willful, but seeking his cooperation—not merely his compliance—at these times will pay big dividends in his future and yours. Compliance is the act of doing a task "because you said so." Cooperation, on the other hand, is getting your child to perform the task because he realizes it is in his and everyone's best interest. He wants to be a team player, and his cooperation helps advance the goal.

Cooperation requires your child to have the ability to take another person's perspective, set aside his own needs, and consider the benefits of helping others achieve their goals. This takes a good deal of self-control, a skill that increases in capacity between the ages of one and a half and three years of age. Children who have advanced attention and language skills also exhibit a greater ability to delay gratification, and thus are better able to cooperate.

During his toddler and preschool years, your child becomes more aware of himself as an individual, while simultaneously becoming more attuned to—and affected by—others' feelings. This development repre-

Techniques for Practicing Mindfulness in Parenting

The following parenting techniques can help you to practice mindfulness and can guide you and your child toward positive, harmonious relationships and cooperation.

❀ **Explain the reasoning behind your rules and requests**—Your child will more easily internalize expectations for his conduct, and he will cooperate more readily, if he understands why the rules are in place. Rather than stating the rule as a matter of fact ("You are not allowed to kick the ball in the house"), you can foster a cooperative understanding by further discussing the dangers of the action ("If you kick the ball inside the house, you could break something").

❀ **Clearly state what you would like your child to do, rather than focusing on what you do not want him to do**—Children have a short attention span and a tendency to resist the words "no" and "don't." If you say to your child, "Don't color on the wall," the message he is likely to internalize is "Color on the wall." Rather than using a negative command, you can say, "You may color in your notebook."

❀ **Offer your child choices**—A main goal of childhood is for your child to discover and express independence. When you give your child choices, he has the room to make his own decisions within your boundaries, and power struggles are less likely to happen. An example of offering your child choices as a means of cooperation could be allowing him to choose his outfit from the options you provide: "You can wear either this blue shirt or this gray one."

❀ **Acknowledge your child's wishes**—Validation of your child's feelings is a powerful way to promote mutual understanding and cooperation. If your child refuses to share his toys with his friend, you could say to him, "I know you may be afraid that you will not get your truck back if you share it with Zoe, but she will give it back after she finishes playing with it." You can also redirect children from negative engagement by offering alternatives—for example, "What if you pretend to be the mechanic and Zoe can bring your truck in for a repair?"

❀ **Use positive motivation**—A very young child does not understand the negative consequences of not cooperating. If you are running late, and he refuses to put his shoes on, encourage his cooperation by giving him a positive motive—for example, "Let's get your shoes on so we can listen to your favorite song in the car."

❀ **Distract and redirect**—There will be times when no amount of strategic parenting prevents your child from exerting his will through aggressive behaviors or tantrums. If your child throws a tantrum, you can take advantage of his distractible nature. Try to remove him from the tense environment and re-engage his attention. For instance, ask him if he would like to water the plants outside.

❀ **Engage your child's help**—Your child likes to feel needed. Small, manageable chores give him a sense of belonging. When he completes a chore and receives appropriate encouragement for his efforts, he is likely to internalize the positive feelings of contributing to your family. This provides intrinsic motivation for him to take on helpful roles both within your family and outside of it.

sents a basic internal conflict, as your child experiences the dilemma of managing individual differences for the greater good. If he is unwilling or unable to find a balance between having his own needs met and helping others to meet theirs, his peers may reject him.

A secure attachment nurtures your child's natural tendencies toward cooperation. Trust in you—and, by extension, in the world—gives your child the confidence he needs to engage with others in working toward a common goal. Trust is the safety net that gives him the freedom to be courageous in his acceptance of individual differences and his belief in a common good.

Cooperation begins at home and branches out as your child has more experiences in the wider world. If he feels good about cooperating with his family members, he will continue to be cooperative as he interacts with the world. This will pave the way for meaningful, lasting relationships.

Character and Values

Values are moral principles that guide you in making decisions and setting priorities in life. Your character—a set of consistent qualities in your thoughts and behaviors—is a product of your lived values.

Values vary from culture to culture, from family to family, and from person to person. You may have developed your own set of values over your lifetime, or you may live by values defined by your religion or your family. It is up to you, as a parent, to help your child develop a set of principles that give him a personal compass to guide him soundly through life. Defined values provide him with a sense of rightness and well-being that can be the basis for his spiritual development, as well.

Children as young as two years old start to show morally based behaviors and beliefs. Even before their value systems are fully developed, children's thoughts and actions are based on the values they experience and see others act out.

Before your child was born, you may have wondered about his eye color and whether or not he would inherit your curly hair. You may also have imagined what kind of person he would be. While physical characteristics are inherited, morals, values, and character cannot be passed down until he is in the world. As with so many other aspects of his emotional development, your baby's values begin to form through his observations of and interaction with you.

Reflecting on Your Values

As a parent, it is a good idea to reflect on your own values, to know what they are, and to be conscious of which values you would like your child to embrace.

This process begins by asking yourself:

- ☐ What matters to me in life?

- ☐ What drives me?

- ☐ Which aspects of my personality most fundamentally define who I am?

- ☐ What are the things that I value most—e.g. family, community, hard work, helping others, honesty, personal responsibility, fun, connection to nature, delicious food, etc?

After considering the previous questions, take the following steps:

- ☐ Write down the values that surface in your mind.

- ☐ Prioritize the values on the list you just created.

- ☐ Make a list of values that you want your child to have.

- ☐ Consider whether you currently model the values you prioritized for yourself and the values you would like for your child. Think about ways that you can put these values into action on a daily basis.

When it comes to values and character, actions speak louder than words. Your child learns by closely monitoring your behavior and mirroring what he sees. By living your values, he learns how to live his own. Living within a value system, with integrity in what you do and say, is not necessarily the easiest way to live, but research has shown that values are essential to inner peace and happiness.

To further assist your child in developing good values and a strong character, try the following strategies:

- ☐ Help your child establish a secure attachment.

- ☐ Nurture his self-esteem.

- ☐ Be mindful of your own values and how you model them.

- ☐ Discuss values with your child. Clearly explain to him what values are, which values are important to you, and why you think values are important.

- ☐ Teach and reinforce empathy, compassion, and cooperation.

- ☐ Encourage your child's efforts and feelings, rather than his achievements.

- ☐ Respect your child, and be aware of indirect ways that you influence him.

Developing Relationships

Relationships are central to your baby's emotional, social, and intellectual development. In this section I discuss various types of relationships and provide suggestions for fostering meaningful, fulfilling relationships in your child's life.

Parents

Your baby is dependent on your active support and protection for survival and safety. A close relationship with you is essential for his health and well-being. You are his first and primary relationship and his first teacher. As such, your relationship is central to his emotional development, which lays the foundation for him to achieve and to succeed throughout his life.

Several factors impact the parent-child relationship. While you cannot control all of these factors, you can learn about them and harness them to minimize negative effects and to maximize positive ones.

- ❀ Initial contact—Skin-to-skin contact and early care immediately after birth help you create a special bond with your baby right from the start.

- ❀ Your expectations for your baby—Did you have a preference regarding your baby's gender? Do you have preconceived ideas of how a baby should behave? If you do have expectations for your baby, ask yourself if the fulfillment or lack of fulfillment of these expectations influences how you relate to your baby now.

- ❀ Your goals for your baby—Similarly, your hopes for your baby's future can play a role in your behavior toward him today. Make sure that your behaviors are nonjudgmental and you are not pushing an agenda on him. Ideally, your behaviors encourage security, trust, self-confidence, and a healthy parent-child relationship.

- ❀ Medical concerns—Illness or other physical issues can influence the ways you and your baby relate to each other.

- ❀ Your confidence as a parent—Your feelings about caring for your baby can affect how you relate to him. If this is your first baby, it is normal to be unsure with him. If you are apprehensive, trust that your confidence in caring for him will grow and you will become more relaxed each day.

- ❀ Level and quality of support in your life—A support system of reliable people to help you care for your baby can decrease your level of stress and improve your relationship with your baby. When you take time for yourself, you recharge and become more present for parenting. In addition to providing you with periodic breaks, nonparental adults such as relatives, friends, and paid caregivers can build closer relationships for your baby. By serving as role models, companions, teachers, and guides to your child, they support your efforts as a parent.

- ❀ Financial challenges—Money worries can distract you and keep you from being fully present with and available for your baby. They can also increase the overall level of tension in the household.

- ❀ Your parental relationship history—Until your baby was born, the only parent-child relationship you knew intimately was the one you had with your parents. It is usual for new parents to repeat their experiences in an automatic, habitual way. However, after reflecting on your experiences with your parents and examining this foundational relationship in your life, you can decide to use the good aspects of your parents' techniques while choosing not to repeat techniques that did not work for you as a child. Then you can begin to parent proactively and intentionally.

- ❀ Your relationship with your spouse—Your baby can sense whether your family is supportive of each other and if there is tension or friction between you. This dynamic will color his relationship with both of you.

❀ **Parental absence or presence**—If you are away from your baby for significant periods due to work travel or military deployment, it may be difficult to develop a strong bond, but it is not impossible if you are intentional about it. Regardless, the fact that you are not with your child every day affects your relationship. If, on the other hand, you are the parent at home full-time and interacting with your baby each day while your spouse is absent, your parent-child bond may become tighter than normal. You may consider ways to maintain an open emotional space for the other parent when he or she does return to the family.

❀ **Parenting style**—Your perspective on the task of parenting naturally has a huge impact on how your child relates to you and thus the health and strength of your relationship. The parenting styles listed below refer to the broad overall pattern of relating, rather than a single act. They grew out of the work of Diana Baumrind, PhD, a clinical and developmental psychologist, and her colleagues.

- Authoritarian: Extremely strict and controlling. Stresses obedience with minimal affection.

- Authoritative: Firm with kindness, warmth, and love. Reasons with children and listens to their point of view. Sets limits and relies on natural consequences for learning. Most parents today are authoritative, which tends to be healthiest for both parents and babies.

- Permissive: Indulgent, accepting. Values the child's expression. Does not exert control.

- Neglecting: Uninvolved, unavailable. Demands and responds minimally. Extreme cases involve neglect and rejection.

❀ **Parental roles**—If the traditional parent and child roles are reversed, if a parent is absent, or if the makeup of the family is nontraditional, a child still needs someone to play the mother role and someone to play the father role (or one parent to play both). Traditionally, the mother's role is to support your child's inner perimeter by providing nourishment, love, care, and emotional protection. The other role—traditionally the father's role—is to provide support, protection, guidance, and strength for your child's outer perimeter of development. This role involves providing a presence to make your baby feel that his material and physical needs are taken care of and he is safe and secure. It also encourages him to go out into the world with a sense of adventure.

❀ **Culture**—Customs, traditions, family expectations, religion, race, and ethnic background influence your relationship with your child. You can build the healthiest possible relationship by reflecting on your experiences as a child and being intentional about integrating into your parenting certain parts of your culture.

❀ **Your child's temperament, personality, and behavior**—If your child is compliant and obedient, you naturally respond with a gentler way of communicating. If he is defiant and oppositional, you may react with a firmer style. You influence your child's behavior, and he influences yours. You may think that you are the sole cause of everything your child does, but many aspects of his temperament and personality come from inside him, not you. You are participating in a two-way relationship in which you influence each other.

The interactions of these factors, as well as many others, add dimensions to the unique relationship between you and your child.

Other Family Members

People's definitions of family vary widely and encompass many possibilities. The nuclear family, defined as a husband and wife living with their biological children, may be considered the standard, but it is not necessarily the norm. Family structures take many forms today. Some of the more common alternative structures are the adoptive family, co-custody family, absent-parent family, single-parent family, blended family, extended family, foster family, gay or lesbian family, or multiracial family, transracial adoptive family, and immigrant family.

Whatever the makeup of your family, these are the people who will bond with your child for life and help shape the person he becomes. Family members are more than a group of individuals. They make up an ecosystem—a living, breathing organism with purposes, goals, and individual parts that work together and influence each other. A family is like a toy mobile that hangs above your baby's crib; when you add or subtract an element (or person), all the other elements move around and shift to create a new balance.

Although a child's emotional development begins with his attachment to his parents or primary caregivers, his emotional growth continues within his overall family environment.

A Supportive Family

A supportive family can help your child in the following ways:

- Provide protection, security, supervision, and control

- Promote positive growth and development

- Reassure him that he is valued for his unique identity

- Provide emotional support and comfort

- Allow him to experience secure and meaningful relationships

- Teach him social skills and expand his awareness of others

- Give him a sense of belonging and historical connection

- Enhance his confidence in the world

- Develop his values and character

- Inspire him to pursue his dreams and to make a societal contribution.

Supportive family relationships give your child a secure base from which to grow and develop. Familial connection and support can come from your family, your partner's family, and even your circle of close friends.

Family rituals, routines, and traditions provide rhythm, organization, and predictability in life; give your child a sense of security and belonging; and establish family values. Family mealtimes and other events build your child's sense of connectedness and promote his overall health and well-being. Research shows that children from families who eat meals together are less likely to be obese, to have eating disorders, and to use drugs or alcohol, and they are more likely to succeed in school. Shared meals in a positive atmosphere are opportunities for healthy eating and social interaction.

On the other hand, an unsupportive or abusive family atmosphere can damage a child's emotional well-being. If either you or your partner comes from such a family, it is up to you to protect your child from abusive situations and people, even if they are family members. Your first responsibility is to your child. The demands of grandparents, extended family members, and close family friends are secondary.

Your child's relationships with family members have a profound impact on how he grows, how he views his place in the world, and his happiness in general. To build family connections for your child, take the time to nurture these relationships and to model their importance in his life by sharing family history, having regular get-togethers, and engaging in caring actions with family members every day.

Siblings

Relationships with brothers and sisters are typically the longest relationships that people have in their lives; they continue long after their parents pass on and last for more years than relationships with spouses do. Sibling relationships are usually close and familiar. Brothers and sisters share living space, clothes, food, and toys, and they may spend many hours together each day.

Various types of sibling relationships—sister-sister, brother-brother, and brother-sister—are associated with different interactions, qualities, and dynamics. Other types of sibling relationships include adopted, step-, and half siblings. The energy and reactions between any two siblings have qualities of their own. The combination of temperaments, personalities, and other characteristics shapes the way siblings relate to each other.

For most people, sibling relationships are filled with contradictions. Brothers and sisters may feel warm and loving, yet resistant and competitive toward each other. The success with which siblings work through these contradictions and continue to build their relationships into adulthood can affect self-image, future relationships, and happiness throughout their lives.

Brothers and sisters can play many social roles for each other. Depending on the situation, a sibling may play the role of a parent substitute, a playmate, a friend, a companion, or all of these. Sometimes children relate to their siblings through imitation and take on similar traits. Other times they relate by differentiating—striving to express an individual identity. Siblings who are the same sex or close in age are more likely to try to be different. When there are both boys and girls in

Dott, Mari, and Emi

a family, children can become more familiar and more comfortable with the opposite sex, and this familiarity may be helpful in future relationships.

Your relationships with your children and your relationship with your spouse impact how your children feel about themselves and how they relate to each other. Siblings tend to have the same attachment status, especially if they have a similar relationship with their primary parent. If there is stress or discord in a family, siblings may compensate by bonding together for support, or they may isolate or look outside the family for comfort.

The birth of a new baby in the family can be exciting and challenging for a young child. He may not fully understand what it means to expect a younger brother or sister. After his new sibling arrives, he experiences new circumstances because of the care needed for the new baby. To ease this transition and to start off the sibling relationship as positively as possible, you can involve your child in the pregnancy, the birth, and the care of his new brother or sister.

I was deliberate in preparing Emi for the arrival of her sister. In the months leading up to Mari's birth, we talked about it often. One evening, toward the end of my pregnancy with Mari, I went in to Emi's room to check on her before I went to bed. She had fallen asleep with a ball under her nightgown, in clear imitation of my figure at that time.

When Mari was born, Emi was at her birth, and she cut the cord. We gave Emi a baby carrier for her dolls, similar to the carrier I was using with Mari, so we could care for our babies together. Yet even with preparation and inclusion, the reality of having to share my attention was still disruptive for Emi, as it usually is for firstborns. Even if your firstborn shows love for his new sibling, he may not be happy with this little intruder at all times.

A child's birth order plays a part in his identity and in the way that he operates in the world. A first-born child tends to be assertive and responsible. He conforms to standards and is a high achiever because his parents have a special bond with him and set high expectations. A middle child may be more relaxed, independent,

Emi

and popular because he faces less pressure from his parents. However, he also may feel that he gets overlooked in the family. The youngest or later-born child usually enjoys a lot of individual attention. He may strive to express his individuality by rebelling or being different.

Because of the intimacy of sibling relationships, conflict is inevitable, and young children may fight several times an hour. On average, children ages two to four engage in an argument every 6.3 minutes. This means that for every hour, parents can expect 9.5 fights. The majority of these fights involve property—specifically, who had what first and who touched something that did not belong to them. Even though fighting can be stressful to parents, children can make developmental strides within this safe relationship. They learn to deal with conflict, to share, and to work through relationship issues with their brothers and sisters. They can later transfer these skills to other relationships in their personal, professional, and romantic lives.

An only child misses out on having siblings to teach him to negotiate conflict and to share his belongings. He does have some advantages, however. An only child gets the chance to learn and to develop affectionate relationships through extra attention, resources, and expectations from his parents, without being interrupted by the needs of another child. In addition, if the parents of an only child make an effort to provide regular interaction with children of family members or friends, then the child has ample opportunities to learn to be empathic, to share, and to get along with others.

Your attention is your child's most important resource. Thus, if you have two or more children, it is natural for them to compete for your attention. If your temperament is more compatible with one child, your other child may feel that you favor his sibling over him. He may feel jealous or rejected, and this can affect his self-esteem. Sibling rivalry is more common when two children are the same sex and close in age. Children have an innate sense of right and wrong, and when siblings are close in age, the differences and perceived injustices in their lives are more pronounced.

If you consider each child's needs and find a way to spend one-on-one time with each child, you can ease sibling rivalry. In addition, you can encourage a positive sibling relationship by avoiding comparisons and favoritism while acknowledging each child's strengths, weaknesses, and needs. You can help your children build their self-esteem and their sibling relationships by planning fun family activities that involve everyone, encouraging teamwork, and celebrating each family member's individuality.

Throughout life, brothers and sisters offer each other connections to the past, the present, and the future. As they grow older, siblings reinforce one another's identities. As they share memories, they can make sense of their lives, who they are, and where they come from.

Friends

Friendship is a mutual relationship in which two people agree that they have an affinity for each other. Early childhood friendships are the stepping-stones to a healthy, socially competent life. To make friends, your child must integrate his thoughts, feelings, and behaviors in a way that enables him to get along with others. Friendship also requires the ability to balance intimacy and autonomy. These social skills are not present at birth. Rather, he acquires them through experiences and through his first relationships with parents and other family members.

Below are the general steps of friendship development, along with the ages at which you can expect your child to take those steps. Remember that every child is different, and yours will gain social skills and make friends at his own pace.

The ability to make and to keep at least one close friend is essential to your child's well-being. As his coach, you can help your child develop social skills and form friendships:

❁ Respond to your baby's needs so he develops trust.

❁ Provide opportunities for him to play with others.

❁ Make sure that he is rested, fed, and dry at playtime.

❁ Provide a safe and age-appropriate play area.

❁ Match social expectations to your child's developmental stages.

❁ Observe and be sensitive to his social interactions.

❁ Pay attention to children to make sure that they are getting along, and intervene if necessary.

Milestones in Forming Friendships

3–6 months	6–12 months	12–18 months
As early as two months old, your baby may become interested in another baby. Even though he primarily sees the world through his own needs, he has a magnetic attraction to other babies, both in real life and in pictures. He may stare at or get excited when he sees another baby, or he may cry when he hears another baby cry—a physiological reflex called distressed compassion, whereby he interprets another baby's cry as his own distress.	At this age, your baby is more alert and aware, and he may respond socially by smiling, cooing, or laughing at another baby or at himself in the mirror. He may also try to get the attention of another baby. At around nine months, he interacts with other babies or children by imitating and responding to their facial expressions, gestures, or sounds.	As your child gains mobility and language skills, he becomes interested in the world around him, particularly as it relates to him. He enjoys the company of other children and may reach out to interact with another child, although he lacks the skills to engage in true, interactive social play. He may imitate another child and play simple games with him, such as peekaboo.

18–24 months		24–36 months
Your child can interact with other children for a longer period of time and in a more complex way. He experiences reciprocity as he takes turns in handing over a toy and then taking it back. Even though he may be cooperative at times, he is primarily focused on getting his own needs met and may be impulsive and impatient in the face of conflict.		By now your child's language and cognitive skills bring out more complexity in his ability to interact with peers through communication, cooperation, problem solving, and imagination for pretend play. Your child can participate in games and play complementary roles in interactions.

Factors that Influence Friendship Building

Both internal developmental skills and external factors contribute to your child's social competence and ability to form lasting friendships. Social, cultural, spiritual, economic, and political factors are part of the landscape as your child learns about people and how to relate to them. Some of these factors are not within your control, while others are. It is worth being aware of all of them, however, and shaping them to your child's advantage when possible.

Internal Factors	
Attachment style	If your child has a secure attachment and feels connected to a parent or caregiver, then he is more likely to engage with other children and to develop social skills.
Self-regulation	Your child's ability to control and manage his emotions contributes to his relationships with peers.
Temperament	Your child's temperament influences his patterns in developing relationships. For instance, if he is shy and inhibited, he may need more space and time to relate to another child. If he is aggressive, he may need to develop empathy for others.
Cognitive and language abilities	Your child's abilities to imagine how others think and feel, to understand what others say, and to communicate his own thoughts influence his social competence.
Learning style	Your child perceives, acts on, and processes social information in his own way, in his own learning mode.

External Factors	
Setting	In what settings does your child spend time and form ideas and behaviors—at home, at his grandparents' house, at his play group or child care center, or in the homes of friends and family members? Are these settings conducive to forming friendships? If making friends is a challenge for your child, you can invite playmates to your house, where he is in familiar, safe surroundings. An outdoor setting in a natural environment can also be conducive to relationship building.
Parenting style and support	Friendship does not always happen on its own. You can support your child in making friends by providing social opportunities for him. You can also observe his social development and coach him if needed. Try modeling social skills and showing him that you can feel comfortable in social situations. He will pick up on your cues and react accordingly. Are you giving him social support in a warm, responsive, and nourishing way or a controlling, demanding, and punishing way?
Peers	Close proximity of children of similar age and interests provides opportunity for friendship. When children play together frequently, they gain a sense of familiarity and close relationships develop naturally.

Culture and Community

As your child's inner foundation becomes established, and he learns to relate to others, he also reaches out to understand and connect to his environment. He looks to his culture and community at large, to find a sense of belonging and to discover more about who he is.

Culture is the pattern of behavior and way of life of a social group. It includes values, beliefs, traditions, kinship and economic systems, assumptions, child rearing practices, and many more aspects of life. Culture is learned, shared, and ever-changing. Most people participate in both a larger mainstream culture and smaller cultural groups. Some people think of themselves as having no culture, but everyone has an individual and unique way of being part of a culture. Just as a fish does not know that he is in water until he is out of water, you may take your culture for granted.

When I moved to Japan from Mississippi, I experienced culture shock as I noticed the differences in lifestyle practices. I did not think that I had an accent, and I did not realize the extent of my cultural habits, until I had the opportunity to compare my values, beliefs, and behaviors with those of another culture. While in Japan, I made a list of some of the Japanese cultural practices that were opposite to my own:

❀ Driving on the left side of the road

❀ Writing from top to bottom and right to left

❀ Addressing a person with the family name before the personal name

❀ Addressing a letter with the name of the country first and the person's name last

❀ Addressing God as "She" (I grew up calling God "He")

The experience of being in another culture and recognizing differences, both extreme and moderate, helped me understand my own way of life and culture.

Our Japanese family

It also gave me the framework to question what I had always known and to make informed, proactive choices about my beliefs and how I wanted to live.

Culture influences a child's development through expectations of goals and aspirations; values related to gender roles; religious or spiritual values; and ideas about sleeping, feeding, and playing. These factors shape his cognitive, linguistic, and social-emotional development.

Harvard anthropologist Robert LeVine, PhD suggests that parents from all cultures have a common set of goals for their children, and that these goals build on each other:

1. Physical survival and health

2. Development of the capacity for economic self-maintenance

3. Development of the behavioral capacities for maximizing other cultural values—morality, prestige, wealth, religious piety, intellectual achievement, personal satisfaction, and self-realization

Much of the research on culture has come from European and American scholars who believe that the ideas and findings from their own communities can be applied to people everywhere. In the 19th and early 20th centuries, anthropologists had a basic assumption that social evolution progresses in a linear path from primitive to civilized, and that "Western" schooling and culture would support any civilization. Such ethnocentrism prejudged other cultures as inferior and denied the importance of deeper understanding. For example, these scholars did not consider that literacy might not be as important to a child in West Africa as understanding weather and other patterns in nature. Because different cultural circumstances give rise to different needs, it is invalid to suppose that all cultures should share a single desirable set of criteria for a child's success in life.

When I was in Japan, I experienced the dramatic cultural difference between individualism (which predominates in European and North American societies) and interdependence (which prevails in Asian, African, and Latin American societies). Individualistic societies are concerned with individual achievement and self-fulfillment, while interdependent cultures encourage their children to focus on responsibilities to others and the value of collective goals.

At Dream Window Kindergarten, the idea of *wagamama*, or self-centeredness, was highly discouraged. Children were encouraged to consider the group's needs over their individual desires. In contrast, in the United States, through my experiences in teaching and my involvement with my daughters' education, I found that individualism and competitiveness played more prominent roles in school than encouraging students to make a contribution to a collective group. I believe there are strengths and weaknesses to both approaches. Both sets of values helped their respective cultures progress in their own way. My opinion today, as we become a more global community, is that an integrated and satisfying life includes both individual and collective achievement.

During the past 150 years, with industrialization and the systemization of education and medical services in the United States, the cultural concept of age has become a measure of development and a way of sorting people. In the past, students progressed in their education as

they learned, regardless of their age. For generations, however, our education system has been very age conscious: students of the same age expected to be at the same level in their studies, without regard to their unique abilities and sensibilities.

The separation of home and workplace in American culture also brought the segregation of children into child-focused settings. In many cultures, however, young children learn to be autonomous and responsible beginning in infancy. As part of a young child's daily play and work, he helps with younger siblings, works in a garden, goes to the market, or completes other tasks. Different cultures have different assumptions for children's capabilities and skills, and these expectations can influence a child's ability. In her book *Bringing Up Bébé*, Pamela Druckerman, who is American, tells her story of raising her children in France. She points out that the French expect their children to eat certain foods and to act a certain way, and these expectations influence their capabilities and behavior.

In comparing two cultures, it is impossible to reduce the differences to a single variable. People in different cultures may move toward the same purpose with different means. Other times they may use similar means to accomplish different goals. In Mei-Ling Hopgood's book, *How Eskimos Keep Their Babies Warm: And Other Adventures in Parenting*, she describes the special ways that parents in 11 different cultures traditionally take care of their children. Hopgood acknowledges that globalization has changed the ways that people in many cultures feed, sleep, teach, and play with their children; many people have left behind their customary ways and means. She says that looking at parenthood through the eyes of parents in different cultures has opened her mind and changed some of her beliefs and practices. Hopgood believes that, despite cultural differences, most societies share the desire to raise children who can thrive in the reality in which they live. She concludes that parenting is an evolving process and that there is more than one way to be a good parent in the world.

You can understand your own cultural heritage by observing the perspectives of other cultural communities without a value judgment and with an open mind.

This does not necessarily mean that all ways are acceptable to you or that you have to give up your own ways. However, examination of different circumstances can open up possibilities that do not exclude each other. Like individuals, cultural communities change. Variations in cultures are a resource to draw from and to use when building new ways of understanding human development. My experience of parenting in Japan inspired me to observe and to question my own cultural history and habits, and to use that understanding to parent intentionally.

Here are some ways that you can support your child's awareness of his cultural experience:

- Bring awareness to the beliefs and values of each parent's family of origin, and talk about how they come together to create your family culture. Discuss common ground, as well as differences.

- Make a list of some of your nuclear family's cultural behaviors.

- Observe and talk about cultural habits in a group in which you participate, such as a church, extended family, neighborhood, parent's group, or play group.

- Travel to different cultures with your child. If you live in a city, you may only need to go around the corner to find a different culture. If you live in a rural area, you may need to travel farther to experience a different culture.

- Discuss with your child what customs from other cultures you would like to borrow and incorporate into your family's culture.

Awareness of his own culture, in the context of understanding other cultures, opens your child's mind to different areas of life and increases empathy and other social competencies. This awareness also helps him realize that there are many ways to look at issues, to solve problems, and to be in the world.

Exceptional Situations

As you take a closer look at your own culture, you start to see its influences on your expectations for your child. You probably wonder how your baby's life will unfold, and you may have specific hopes and dreams for his future. Often, the child of your dreams may not be your child in reality. Your child is his own unique person unfolding in his own way; he is not an extension of you. This realization requires some parents to reconfigure their expectations—for instance, when the child they dreamed they would coach in Little League becomes passionate about music instead.

For parents of exceptional children, the life path that their child has been handed can demand a complete new set of expectations, in addition to causing parents to rethink what they need to do to nurture their child and to ensure he has the emotional tools to live a healthy and full life. Exceptional children can be defined as children with a trait, a characteristic, or health status that is seen as outside the norm for your family or community.

After interviewing more than 300 families with exceptional children for his book *Far from the Tree: Parents, Children, and the Search for Identity*, author and lecturer Andrew Solomon separated people's traits or identities into two categories: vertical and horizontal. In his book, he writes that vertical identities are shared traits, both genetic and cultural, within a family and a community. Ethnicity, language, and religion are vertical identities. Horizontal identities, on the other hand, are particular to the child and usually come as a surprise to his parents.

Examples of Solomon's horizontal identities include being a prodigy in some area of life, having Down syndrome or autism, being sight or hearing impaired, or suffering from a physical or mental illness. A child with a dominant horizontal identity can be considered an exceptional child. Vertical identities tend to strengthen a child's bond to his family and to enhance healthy attachments, thus promoting a positive self-image. When parents do not accept children who have horizontal identities, the children often develop an insecure attachment and a poor self-image. On the

My great-niece, Claire

other hand, when parents accept, love, and support their exceptional children, their children can develop a positive self-image and reach their full potential.

Coming to full acceptance and support of a child with a horizontal identity may take some work. Here are some guidelines:

- ❁ Recognize your feelings—You likely had an expectation of how your child was going to be, and the reality is different. While your child's exceptional trait may bring unforeseen treasures, it will require you to adjust the life you had planned. That expected life deserves to be acknowledged, processed, and set free, so that you can move into acceptance and parent your child fully.

- ❁ Accept your child fully—It may be difficult for you to accept your child's horizontal identity. Some parents feel guilty about the fact that their child has to struggle with a difference; others feel their child's difference reflects badly on their parenting. These feelings can manifest as a rejection of the child himself. Especially in his first three years of life, your child looks to you to reflect his value, and your unconditional love and acceptance give him self-acceptance. Try working with a counselor to acknowledge and process your feelings so that you can fully accept your child.

❀ Cultivate mindfulness—Mindfulness practices, such as yoga and meditation, can reduce stressful feelings, reveal situations for what they really are, help you parent with clarity and intention, and help you choose your actions intentionally from a place of rationality and balance.

❀ Participate in a community—Membership in a supportive community of families dealing with the same challenges you are facing can relieve stress and bring great insight into the journey you are on. You, your child, and your entire family get the opportunity to feel "typical" within such a community. You can also gain knowledge; learn practical tips for common challenges; glimpse what the future may hold; and share your feelings, joys, and frustrations with people who have a similar experience.

❀ Accepting your child as he is—Accepting your child's horizontal identity does not necessarily mean "normalizing" him. Should a deaf child be given cochlear implants? Should a child with dwarfism go through bone-lengthening surgeries? Solomon cautions parents that taking an exceptional child to specialist after specialist to "fix" him may send the message that he is not good enough as he is. Reflecting on your own motivations, ask yourself whether the outcome that a particular intervention promises will relieve your child's suffering and improve his life, or merely comfort you by moving your child closer to a social norm. The nurturing of an exceptional child is a balancing act of helping him discover—and become—the best that he can be.

❀ Be mindful of yourself and your family—Tending to an exceptional child can consume all of your attention and energy. This is not healthy for your child, his siblings, your partner, and you. By making your exceptional child part of your family rather than the centerpiece, you promote everyone's sense of belonging and well-being.

When you nurture the emotional health of an exceptional child and love him unconditionally, he learns to love himself. You can support him by making your family a safe space where he can find acceptance and draw strength. When you set an example of openness to life's diversity, he can learn to accept himself and appreciate differences in others.

I believe that every child has some form of horizontal identity that is not exactly what his parents expected. Because every child is unique, every child is exceptional. When you recognize, accept, and love the similarities and differences in your child as his true self, you give him the nourishment that he needs to grow and flourish.

Welcome to Holland

By Emily Perl Kingsley

I am often asked to describe the experience of raising a child with a disability, to try to help people who have not shared that unique experience to understand it, to imagine how it would feel. It's like this…

When you're going to have a baby, it's like planning a fabulous vacation trip—to Italy. You buy a bunch of guidebooks and make your wonderful plans. The Coliseum. The Michelangelo's David. The gondolas are in Venice. You may learn some handy phrases in Italian. It's all very exciting.

After months of eager anticipation, the day finally arrives. You pack your bags and off you go. Several hours later, the plane lands. The flight attendant comes in and says, "Welcome to Holland."

"Holland?!?" you say. "What do you mean Holland?? I signed up for Italy! I'm supposed to be in Italy. All my life I've dreamed of going to Italy."

But there's been a change in the flight plan. They've landed in Holland and there you must stay.

The important thing is that they haven't taken you to a horrible, disgusting, filthy place, full of pestilence, famine, and disease. It's just a different place.

So you must go out and buy new guidebooks. And you must learn a whole new language. And you will meet a whole new group of people you would never have met.

It's just a different place. It's slower-paced than Italy, less flashy than Italy. But after you've been there for a while and you catch your breath, you look around…and you begin to notice that Holland has windmills…and Holland has tulips. Holland even has Rembrandts.

But everyone you know is busy coming and going from Italy…and they're all bragging about what a wonderful time they had there. And for the rest of your life, you will say, "Yes, that's where I was supposed to go. That's what I had planned."

And the pain of that will never, ever, ever, ever go away…because the loss of that dream is a very, very significant loss.

But if you spend your life mourning the fact that you didn't get to Italy, you may never be free to enjoy the very special, the very lovely things…about Holland.

Choosing a Child Care Provider

It takes special thought to choose child care for your baby. When your child begins care outside your home, he enters a whole new world and leaves behind your small, intimate world. If you need to go back to work, it may be difficult to leave your baby with someone else. I have seen some women cry at their desks for their first week back at work because they miss their babies. It is a natural instinct to want to take care of your baby full-time, but that option is unrealistic for many parents today.

To make the best decision for you and your baby, start by sorting through your priorities. For his first year especially, the establishment of a strong attachment is foundational to his development on all levels—physical, emotional, and mental. If you cannot be with him every day all day long, he can thrive if one other person cares for and responds to him in a loving way.

With that in mind, what are your main concerns for your child care needs? Are you looking for individual care, family child care (programs operated in the caregiver's home), or a child care center? Factors to consider include the quality of care, the safety and energy levels of the environment, and the kind of relationship you expect with the care provider. How much time do you need for your baby's care? Cost and location are also factors. As you determine your needs and priorities, you can research options and figure out the role you want to play.

❀ Quality of care—Research suggests that the main priority for your baby's care for his first year is for him to have regular, loving interaction with a stable individual. The best way to ensure this is to use one caregiver, such as a grandparent, other family member, nanny, or babysitter. If this is not possible in your home setting, ask about one-to-one responsiveness in a child care center. What is the ratio of children to caregivers? How long has the child care provider been in business? After checking to be sure that the provider is reputable, licensed, and

certified, observe him or her in action, and assess whether he or she is loving, kind, and caring.

❀ Environment—Is the child care atmosphere clean, safe, orderly, and welcoming? Do the babies have space and support to move and to explore? Do you see toys or utensils made of unsafe materials or ingredients? Do caregivers wash their hands after every diaper change and before preparing food? Are naps on a fixed schedule, or are they adaptable to your baby's needs? Is the environment calm or frenzied? What are the facility's plans for handling emergencies? Are the caregivers and children healthy and happy?

❀ Communication—Observe the interaction of the caregiver(s) with the other babies. Do they hold and caress the babies? Do they respond to babies' needs when they are hungry or have a wet diaper? Do they talk directly to the babies? What kind of training does the staff have? What is the turnover? Will one person give your baby consistent, responsive, care and attention? What kind of relationship will you have with the caregiver and the administration? Does the staff communicate with you about your baby's activities, health, and concerns? Do you feel that you can work together in partnership with mutual respect and trust in the care of your baby?

❀ Logistics—Certain practicalities are significant factors to consider when choosing a caregiver for your baby. What are the provider's policies on breast-feeding, cloth diapers, and food? Does the caregiver have the availability to meet your schedule? Is the time flexible for holidays? Is the provider open to parents dropping in for a visit? Is there a waiting list for admission? Will the provider meet your standards of food preparation and nutrition? Is there a written contract or agreement? Is the cost acceptable? Is the location convenient? What are the snow day policies?

❀ Research—The process of educating yourself about the various child care options in your area can help you get a clearer idea of your priorities. Check references and recommendations from peers, and read online reviews. Make an on-site visit, and interview the individual caretaker or the administrators and staff. Look for general red flags, such as a hurried and messy environment or an unhappy atmosphere.

❀ Your role—You can actively participate in your child's care by paying attention to your child and by noticing the environment when you drop him off and pick him up every day. Be aware of any changes that you may sense in your child. Ask questions about your child's day. Keep track of any illnesses or other concerns, and communicate them with the provider. Make sure that you provide all the items necessary for your baby, such as a change of clothes, diapers, food, sunscreen, a hat, and any remedies or medications. When you are involved in your child's care, you can be confident in your intuition and advocate for him when he needs you. You are the consumer in this relationship, so be intentional and speak up about your concerns.

CHAPTER 3
Discovery and Learning

PARENTS NATURALLY HAVE HIGH hopes of brilliance and success for their children. Many of today's companies play on these hopes by claiming that their books and programs will make your child a genius, a super baby, or a little Einstein. You may want your child to be advanced for her age, but it can actually be unhealthy for your baby to rush through her development or to skip stages entirely. As a parent, how do you determine and measure your child's brainpower and potential for achievement? What can you do to build on your child's intelligence in a healthy, encouraging way?

You can guide your child to discover and to nurture her unique combination of intelligences. By encouraging her to develop the curiosity to explore, the ability to solve problems, and the persistence to overcome challenges, you can help her to build on her strengths, to create her own knowledge, and to express herself by contributing to the world in her distinctive way.

First, take a step back and consider the basics. Your child needs healthy food, clothes, warmth, and a safe environment. When you understand how her physical health and emotions are interrelated with her cognitive development, you can create an environment filled with experiences and opportunities that help your child flourish. By meeting her physical and emotional needs, you free her to explore the world, to learn, and to find her passion, purpose, and potential.

Like health and happiness, success is not a static condition. Your child's internal conditions and outside circumstances are continually changing. Therefore, success can be defined generally as a strong, stable, resilient, positive life force. The specifics of where this life force takes your child are up to her.

This chapter offers foundational information that you can use as you support your child in learning and in developing her intelligence. It is divided into three sections:

🌸 **Daily Practices**—This section provides basic information about your child's cognitive development and suggests ways that you can help foster this development every day.

🌸 **Theories of Mental Development**—The second section delves into the science and theories behind brain development and function, foundations for learning, and types of learning.

🌸 **Essential Skills for Whole Learning**—The final section explores essential skills for helping your baby learn, including seven pathways that you can use to understand and support the learning process. The end of the section is a guide to the process of choosing a preschool.

As you move through this chapter, be mindful that your child has her own way of building her view of the world. Since birth, she has been developing her own gifts and skills. Your definition of your child's success may be different from hers. Ultimately, your responsibility as her parent is to help her uncover her unique brilliance as she grows.

Daily Practices

AS SOON AS MY babies were born, my natural inclination was to place them on my stomach. From there, they demonstrated their innate ability to root in order to find milk. They instinctively knew what to do to survive. As they nursed and I held them in my arms, they demonstrated that they needed me to care for them and to guide them.

By design, your baby was born to learn. Her instincts, her genes, and her physical constitution work together to move her into the world. Intrinsically, she observes, explores, mimics, and eventually reasons in an effort to make sense of all she encounters. Also by design, your baby is born to you, her first guide in this life. The experiences and the examples you provide are fundamental to her mental development and her ability to learn.

In the first three years of your baby's life, she makes extraordinary leaps in her physical and emotional growth and capabilities, and she makes remarkable leaps in her intellectual growth and competencies, as well. The depth and extent of her intellectual growth depend on the quality and range of experiences she encounters.

As a parent or primary caregiver, you provide the nutrition, emotional stability, safe environment, and stimulation that influence your baby's brain and intellect as she develops. Despite the essential role you play in helping her to discover her unique potential, you cannot alter your baby or mold her to fit to your expectations. Your baby is her own being, with her own intrinsic learning processes and abilities. You can best help her achieve her full potential by listening to her and letting her blossoming intelligence guide you. By doing so, while her knowledge grows, you engage in a reciprocal dance.

If you push your child to learn faster when she is young, you will not give her an advantage. In fact, rushed development can cause your child to miss key building blocks that protect against future learning deficits. Your baby has her own path and timing for growing and learning. You are a guide and a source of encouragement along that path, rather than a creator of the path itself.

Your baby's brain will grow and develop more rapidly from conception to her second birthday than at any other time in her life. In her first two years, her brain lays the foundational connections to acquire future knowledge and build skills. Fortunately, parents naturally take many of the actions that encourage a baby's intellectual growth and help her establish patterns for learning. By following the suggestions in this section, you can provide your child with the inner and outer resources she needs to build strong neural connections for lifelong learning.

Feed Your Baby's Brain through Food Choices

Your baby's brain is an organ that requires a steady stream of nutrients in order to grow and to function. Since her brain goes through such rapid growth and development between conception and age two, healthy nutrition during this time has a lifelong positive impact on your baby's cognitive abilities.

For structural strength and healthy development, your baby's brain needs energy from protein, carbohydrates, fats, micronutrients, and good hydration. Many studies have shown that breast milk is the best brain food available, and that children who were breast-fed tend to have higher IQ scores and to perform better in school. According to scientists, breast milk contains the right combination of nutrients, growth factors, and hormones. Although formula has yet to duplicate this exact combination, if breast-feeding is not possible, you can still promote healthy brain development.

Whether you are pregnant, nursing, formula-feeding, or serving your baby solids, healthy foods for your baby's optimal brain development include:

- ❁ Complex carbohydrates for balanced blood sugar levels: whole grains, including brown rice, oats, millet, and quinoa

- ❁ Proteins to aid with your baby's brain growth: legumes, seeds, nuts, and lean fish

- ❁ Essential fats to form myelin, which enables neuron transmission in your baby's brain: ground flaxseed, fish, seeds and nuts (if not allergic), and avocado

- ❁ Vitamins and minerals for building her brain: fresh vegetables (especially leafy greens and sea vegetables), fruits, and whole grains

- ❁ Iodine and salt for metabolism and intellectual development: sea vegetables and sea salt

- ❁ Fermented foods and probiotic booster for a healthy gut: pickles, miso, fermented drinks, and yogurt

Antinutrients are foods that can inhibit your child's healthy brain development. For instance, refined sugars, hydrogenated fats, chemical food additives, and highly processed foods rob your child's brain of nutrients. Many food additives and food colorings are neurotoxins. Finally, genetically modified foods, foods containing growth hormones, and antibiotics in animal foods can have negative effects on your child's mental health.

People sometimes refer to the digestive system as a second brain because the central nervous system and the gastrointestinal system are intimately connected through pathways of nerves. These systems have a two-way communication path. The brain affects the stomach by releasing stomach juices in response to hunger or by causing an upset stomach in response to anxiety. The intestines send alert signals to the brain if there is a problem, even before the body can feel the symptoms. The gut lining is the core of the body's immune system. If the body is deficient in nutrients or the digestive system is not working properly, mental health disturbances, such as depression and anxiety can occur.

Recharge with Sleep

The Millennium Cohort Study demonstrated the relationship between sleep and brain development in children. Researchers found that children who slept less than ten hours a night before age three were more likely to exhibit ADHD and problems with spatial awareness, language, and reading than were children who got more sleep. The authors concluded that the first three years of life are a particularly sensitive time when it comes to sleep and its relationship to brain development.

Sleep is essential to promote your child's curiosity and openness to learning. Lack of sleep can disrupt her natural body rhythms and make her irritable and distracted. Solid, regular sleep recharges her entire body, including her brain, thus increasing her memory capacity and ability to learn. During sleep, your baby's body also releases growth hormones. You can make sure that your baby's brain is ready for learning by following a regular bedtime and nap schedule. As your baby grows, the world becomes more fascinating, and going to sleep can become difficult for her. A regular routine can help her get the rest she needs.

Stimulate Your Baby's Senses

Your baby learns by using all her senses. She touches everything. She puts things in her mouth and near her nose so that she can taste and smell them. She shakes objects, responds to noises, and looks at everything in sight.

According to Swiss developmental psychologist Jean Piaget's theory of cognitive development, the first stage of cognition is the sensorimotor stage. For her first two years, your baby gathers information about the world through her reflexes, movements, and senses. Her nervous system then transmits the information to her brain, which sorts and uses the information as it creates connections between neurons. As those connections multiply, your baby's neural network builds, and her knowledge increases.

Piaget's stages build on each other sequentially. By providing an environment that encourages your baby to use her senses, you can help her build a foundation for language and cognitive development. You can enhance sensory stimulation through the following everyday routines:

- **Eat together**—Eating uses all of your baby's senses. Food tastes, colors, smells, and textures—even the sounds of chewing—stimulate her brain.

- **Talk about senses**—Converse about senses with your child. Observe how a vegetable or flower feels, smells, tastes, sounds, or looks. If she does not yet have words to express her thoughts, she can still take in yours.

- **Create a touch zone**—Make a box of safe objects that have different textures, shapes, and surfaces. Talk about how different textures feel: "Feel the smooth wooden block. Touch the soft pillow."

- **Take a walk**—Encourage your child to touch the grass, examine a leaf, and put her fingers in the sand or mud. Talk about how these objects and materials look, feel, smell, and sound.

- **Take a bath**—What does the water feel like when it drips on your child's arm? Is it warm or cool? How does the soap smell?

- **Cook together**—More than any other sense, smell has a direct line to your baby's brain, especially her memory. Shop, cook, and bake with your baby. Talk about the scents in the market and in your kitchen.

In her book *Smart Start: Building Brain Power in the Early Years*, Pam Schiller suggests using your baby's sense of smell to boost learning. The scents of peppermint, lemon, cinnamon, and rosemary have all been shown to increase alertness. Be aware that the scents of synthetic chemicals and strong perfumes can be distracting and disruptive to your baby's system.

Create Pathways through Movement

Activity and physical movement join with your baby's senses to form a key pathway to learning. The physical movements of picking up and putting down objects, pushing things over, rolling and sitting up, crawling, pulling up, and walking offer opportunities for exploration and discovery. They also activate your baby's brain.

In his book *Spark: The Revolutionary New Science of Exercise and the Brain*, John J. Ratey, MD, explains, "The neurons in the brain connect to one another through 'leaves' on treelike branches, and exercise causes those branches to grow and bloom with new buds, thus enhancing brain function at a fundamental level." Physical activity increases key proteins that your baby's brain needs in order to grow. In addition to enabling your baby to gather knowledge through movement, physical activity enhances cognitive ability and growth of brain cells. It also reduces stress by keeping cortisol and other stress-related hormones in check. When your child moves, her body pumps more blood to her brain, and the blood provides oxygen that nourishes her brain tissue. Many studies show that the positive cognitive effects of physical activity occur throughout life. This evidence gives parents even greater incentive to make physical activity routine for their babies.

One connection between physical movement and brain development is your baby's progression toward bilateral coordination, or crossing her midline. She has achieved bilateral coordination when both sides of her brain and body work in tandem, and she takes actions that cross from one side of her body to the other (for instance, she reaches across her body to grasp a toy or uses her right hand to touch her left knee). This type of brain-body coordination is essential to reading, writing, playing sports, dancing, and performing many everyday activities. It begins to appear prominently in your child's movements at about three or four years of age.

Here are a few methods you can use to get your baby moving in ways that increase knowledge, promote brain health and growth, and develop bilateral coordination:

- **Play with your baby**—Take at least 10 minutes every day to play with your baby, through tummy time, yoga, massage, swimming, and developmental exercises. Your baby feels most secure when she is on the floor and you meet her at her level.

- **Give her space**—Be sure your baby has a safe open area, both inside and outside, to move her body—to roll, crawl, or walk freely.

- **Practice crossing the midline**—Move a toy across the room so that your baby's eyes can follow it. As she begins to make more physical movements, offer activities that cross her midline. For example, play pat-a-cake, or practice windmills together—spread your arms and alternate touching the opposite side of your body with each hand.

- **Provide toys that encourage movement**—Give your baby balls, blocks, push toys, and pull toys.

- **Promote fine-motor connections**—Give her small objects to hold. Encourage her to turn pages when you read. Give her toys with tools, zippers, buttons, and other objects to manipulate. Give her objects to pick up off the floor. Drawing with crayons or chalk stimulates her brain on many levels.

- **Model daily exercise**—Take time for your own workout. Show your baby that you make your physical fitness a priority, too.

- **Be an active family**—Hike, bike, swim, or ski. These activities nourish your child's brain and build healthy habits for life.

Provide a Positive Emotional Environment

Stress influences physical and emotional health and can interfere with your baby's learning process. Too much stress, or stress that is too severe, can inhibit her immune system, short- and long-term memory, thinking, and creativity. In his book *How the Brain Learns*, education neuroscience consultant David A. Sousa, MD explains that positive emotions increase endorphins in the blood. These endorphins produce a feeling of euphoria and fuel the frontal lobes, the parts of the brain where thinking occurs. Therefore, positive emotions put your baby in the right frame of mind to think and to learn. In contrast, negative emotions release cortisol, a hormone that produces anxiety, pulls activity away from the frontal lobes, and initiates the more reflexive fight-or-flight sections of the brain. When your baby is in a negative emotional environment, her brain focuses on the threat, and she is not available to learn.

Positive emotions can also help your child learn and retain information. Humor and laughter help her relax, reduce stress, and make her more receptive to learning. When you express excitement and curiosity, your child will probably feel and emulate these emotions. If you pay attention to what she instinctively enjoys, you can help her discover her passions. For instance, if she loves being outside, give her opportunities to play in the park or in a sandbox. If she gets excited about animals, take her to a petting zoo. Tap into her passions to help her get in touch with what inspires her.

To create a positive emotional climate in which your child can learn, consider the following:

- ❀ **Form a secure attachment**—A secure attachment between you and your baby gives her confidence to explore and promotes learning.

- ❀ **Be mindful of your frame of mind**—Your approach to a situation affects your child's feelings, which in turn influence her ability to learn. Be aware of your feelings and the impact that they can have on your child. If you feel tense, she may pick up the tension and be inhibited by it.

- ❀ **Encourage and reward**—Praise your child for her efforts in learning, and reward her with your attention and interest. If she examines a leaf and shares her discovery with you, chooses a book she would like you to read, or sings you a song, then respond to her with authentic delight and curiosity.

- ❀ **Be aware of people**—The people in your baby's environment—including friends, family members, and regular caregivers—affect her feelings, which affect her openness to learning. Positive, engaged people help her feel more positive and open, and negative people can inhibit her.

- ❀ **Create a positive environment**—A pleasant, clean, uncluttered home environment is conducive to learning. Keep noise to a minimum. Fill your space with natural or soft light when possible. Create areas where your baby is free to move and to touch objects and surroundings. When choosing a child care provider, pay special attention to the look, smell, and feel of the environment.

Interact with Your Baby

Before your baby speaks with actual words, she communicates to you with cries, smiles, and other signals. You foster her abilities to focus and to learn by actively paying attention to her sounds, body language, and other cues, and then responding to her.

In a 2003 study, Patricia Kuhl, PhD of the Institute for Learning and Brain Sciences at the University of Washington demonstrated the importance of social interaction to a baby's developing language skills. Kuhl exposed American babies to native Mandarin speakers who read them books in Mandarin. At the end of the experiment, the babies showed that they recognized and responded to core sounds for both American English (their native tongue) and Mandarin. When the researchers exposed another group of American babies to Mandarin through audiotape or videotape, the babies did not recognize any core Mandarin sounds.

This and other research shows that social interaction is key to learning for babies. As your baby's first teacher, your engagement and interaction with her are essential to her learning process. Frequent distractions from mobile devices can be distressing to her. For healthy, encouraging interaction with your baby, try these steps:

- **Pause**—When you hear or see that your baby is making an effort to communicate via sounds or words, pause and pay attention.

- **Reframe**—Repeat and reflect back what you heard her say, whether or not she used words: "Your diaper needs changing," "You are hungry," or "You like that song on the radio."

- **Respond**—Change her diaper, feed her, or tell her you like the song, too. When your response shows that you understand her signal, she can experience the satisfaction of the communication process.

Talk and Read to Your Baby

The amount of time you spend talking to your baby before she is three years old can influence her language capabilities, her IQ, and her future academic success. Researchers Betty Hart, PhD and Todd R. Risley, PhD of the University of Kansas found that the more words babies hear, the more successful they are in school. In their groundbreaking study, which they wrote up in their 1995 book *Meaningful Differences in the Everyday Experience of Young American Children*, Hart and Risley recorded 42 families talking to their babies over a three-year period. They then followed the children's academic progress until they reached nine or ten years of age and found that the number of words a child heard as an infant and toddler had a significant impact on later learning.

Your baby's brain will never be more open or receptive to language than it is between birth and seven years of age. In a TED Talk about her 2003 study, Patricia Kuhl explained that in the first few months of life, a baby's brain hears all sounds equally. By the time babies are eight to ten months old, they begin to discriminate and recognize the core sounds of the languages to which they have been most exposed. This period is a good opportunity for your child to become bilingual. Between your baby's first and second birthdays, her vocabulary has the potential to quadruple.

By talking to your baby and introducing her to as many sounds and words as possible in these first few years, you can provide her a foundation of neural pathways that will result in a rich vocabulary, a mastery of grammar and syntax, and a wealth of complex thoughts. Here are some ways to accomplish these goals:

- **Narrate the day**—As you go about your day with your baby, provide a narrative: "Look, the floor is dirty. Let's clean it up," "It is time to feed the cat," and "I love to be outside with you."

- **Repeat**—Your child learns from the reinforcement of repetition. She likes to hear words and phrases over and over—probably beyond the point where you are tired of them.

- **Label things for her**—Provide names for people and things: "I am using a broom to sweep the floor," and "Look at the tree, the bird, and the pond."

- **Read to her**—Reading is both an educational and a bonding experience. Starting from before birth, you can read to your baby and give her the opportunity to hear words. The act of reading a book together connects reading with positive emotions, which helps motivate her to read in later years.

- **Sing and play music**—Putting words to music is not only a fun way to build your baby's vocabulary, but also a way to build memory and to enhance word meaning through tone and mood, further expanding her communication skills.

- **Avoid TV and electronics**—As Kuhl's research shows, babies do not learn language by listening to audio or video recordings. When learning language, they respond best to person-to-person interaction.

- **Talk to her**—You are the most fascinating person to your baby. She loves your voice and your face, and she loves being close to you. Hold your baby and give her your full attention with eye contact as you talk to her. She is open to learning through connection and interaction within your relationship.

Encourage Active Experience

Your baby learns through active participation. The more she experiences, the more neural connections her brain makes, and the greater her capacity for learning becomes. Keeping in mind the value of lived experience, you can turn simple daily occurrences into fruitful educational opportunities. For instance, you can stimulate her senses and her brain while playing in the dirt at the park, smelling herbs while shopping, or tasting a lemon while you are cooking. If you are involved in shared experiences with her, then she will be more present in her learning.

You can incorporate learning experiences with your child into your daily routine as you do your own projects. As you clean, cook, or work, invite your child to engage in your activities. By encouraging her to interact with her environment, you give her the confidence to be curious, to investigate what interests her, and to seek new experiences and learning opportunities. Pay attention to dangerous situations, and set limits so that she can be safe in her explorations.

Here are a few ways to make it easy for your baby to discover new things and to interact with her environment:

- **Take your baby with you**—You can expand her world by opening your world to her. Put her in a baby carrier, or keep her close by as you go about your day—doing chores, running errands, and meeting with people. By your side, she can see and experience all aspects of life.

- **Let your baby lead**—As you go about your day, encourage her to touch, to feel, and to investigate. You can support her curiosity by talking to her and describing her experiences.

- **Make home an interactive environment**—Create safe spaces in your home where she can explore and make her own discoveries—for example, in a cabinet, closet, or drawer.

- **Visit interactive environments**—Children's zoos, discovery centers, and children's museums are designed to be interactive for babies and toddlers. Through their exhibits, your baby can use her senses to engage in new experiences and to take in new information.

- **Show curiosity**—Model a curious mind for your child. Ask questions, and wonder out loud. She can then observe you as you discover answers to your inquiries.

Shared experiences with your child are a delightful aspect of parenting, because these experiences help restore your own childhood freshness and openness to discovery. Mundane objects and daily chores become new and exciting again, seen from your baby's eyes. By encouraging her to reach out and interact with the world, you nurture her cognitive development and set a pattern for future learning.

Stretch and Challenge

While following your baby's lead is fundamental to her cognitive growth, stretching and challenging her mind can enhance her development and help her use her cognitive abilities to their full potential at every stage.

One stimulating way to excite, engage, and challenge your baby is to introduce her to something new. When your baby experiences novelty, her brain is activated, dopamine (the "feel-good" hormone) flows, and she begins to process the new information. Her brain works to fit her new knowledge into a pattern that meshes with what she already knows, thus allowing her to integrate her recent learning. When you introduce new experiences, objects, and ideas that stretch and challenge your child just beyond the limits of her cognitive abilities, you help her learn at the next level up, relative to her current abilities.

In their book *Tools of the Mind: The Vygotskian Approach to Early Childhood Education*, Elena Bodrova, PhD and Deborah J. Leong, PhD explain that some physiologists think that children can learn only up to their current level of developmental maturity. However, early-20th-century Russian psychologist Lev Vygotsky believed that brain development and learning work together and support each other. Therefore, exposing your child to information and learning experiences just beyond her developmental stage helps her attain the next level of cognitive development. In Vygotskian terms, this period is called the "zone of proximal development", and the approach to learning is called "scaffolding." With scaffolding, you provide supported learning for an emerging skill and then slowly pull away those supports as your child becomes independent in exercising this skill.

By teaching to the zone of proximal development, you continually provide novelty and keep your child reaching toward the next challenge. While this strategy may cause some struggle, it can also establish patterns of fearlessness, persistence, and a sense of accomplishment when learning. In many East Asian cultures, struggle is accepted as part of the progress of learning and accomplishment. Often the most successful person is not the most intelligent one, but the person who is not afraid to try, to work hard, and to head toward the unknown. You can support your child in attaining new knowledge and skills just beyond her reach by staying one step ahead of her learning.

Here are some tips for stretching and challenging your child:

❀ Know where she is developmentally—When you are aware of your baby's current level of cognitive development, as well as the skills that are likely to emerge next, you can provide activities that support the next stage.

❀ Make novelty a regular occurrence—Your child needs some degree of routine, yet novelty inspires her to keep her mind active and challenged. Providing novelty can be as simple as varying your regular habits. Rotate her toys. Take her to places she has never seen. Go on a picnic, or simply take a bento to your backyard instead of serving it inside. Play a new song, or introduce a new game.

❀ Encourage imaginative play—According to Bodrova and Leong, children use self-directed play to try on mature thinking, which builds their neural pathways and aids in cognitive development. As they play house, doctor, mother, store, and school, they develop rules, follow those rules, and behave as the adults they are playing. Imaginative play can stretch your child to learn beyond her current level of development.

❀ Offer choices—When you encourage your baby to choose what to eat, what shirt to wear, or what toy to play with (within safe limits), you give her the opportunity to learn to weigh options, to make choices, and to experience the consequences of those choices. The opportunity to practice decision-making builds her sense of control, personal responsibility, and confidence.

A note of caution: As you use these techniques to stretch and challenge your child, be careful not to push her too much. Provide a support of scaffolding, and then slowly withdraw it as your child reaches her next level. Brain development is a series of stages that build upon each other, and each stage is significant. Rushing the process or skipping developmental stages can result in weaknesses in her cognitive functioning. If you push your child to learn something before she is ready, she may begin to fear failure, and her natural curiosity may be squelched. Each child is unique and develops at her own pace; be aware of your child's emotional and developmental needs as you stretch and challenge her.

Moderate Media

Many kinds of media compete for children's attention today—television, movies, smartphones, tablets, computers, MP3 players, and video games. Multiple media presented at the same time can force your child to split her attention. This means her brain shifts its attention back and forth, even though it can focus on only one medium at a time. Children are sensitive to sensory stimulation and can become overwhelmed easily. Overstimulation can negatively impact their development.

Even if parents monitor and control electronic media and use only the most educational programs, apps, and games, any form of sitting in front of a screen is passive learning. Physical movement in response to sensory input best supports your child's learning and healthy development. The moving images that children watch on television and other media are often dramatized, violent, and reactive. They are unlikely to offer a calm presence as an image for your child to remember.

Language presented in electronic media often involves slang, negative messages, and sarcasm. As Patricia Kuhl concluded in her 2003 study, babies learn language optimally through interaction with live speakers, rather than from television or audio recordings. They learn to communicate by actively listening and participating in conversations in a reciprocal way.

When your child watches screens, her brain interprets what she sees as real occurrences. If she sees violence, her nervous system responds as if she is having the experience that she is watching. These responses distract her energy from learning, creativity, and imagination.

In her book *Superbaby: 12 Ways to Give Your Child a Head Start In the First 3 Years*, Jenn Berman, PhD provides evidence that watching television leads to poor sleep habits, poor eyesight, lower grades in school, a decrease in creativity, and an increase in aggression and violence. The American Academy of Pediatrics recommends that children under the age of two years watch no television at all. As children get older and become more skilled with language and attention span, educational videos without commercials can be instructional, especially if you and your child watch them together and discuss what you see and learn.

Time spent in imaginative play, interacting with family members and friends, drawing, dancing, singing, and exploring on her own does more to stimulate your child's brain and to foster her cognitive development than television, videos, or computer games.

To give your baby's brain a rich environment in which it can grow and develop to its full potential, consider the following:

❀ Engage with your child in conversation, and provide opportunities for creative activities with her.

❀ Avoid screen time before your child is two years old.

❀ Monitor media, and choose to use media purposefully.

❀ If you do choose to let your child watch television, watch it with her and engage her in discussion afterward. Limit her viewing to educational, commercial-free shows and videos.

❀ Let your baby's caregivers know your screen-time policies, so that your child experiences consistency.

❀ Be aware of how much you use technology in front of your child. You are a role model in this area as in all others.

Appreciate the Arts

Your baby expresses herself without inhibitions, and she naturally enjoys listening to music, singing, dancing, acting, storytelling, and painting. Artistic expression exercises her brain across sectors and increases her cognitive functioning.

According to David A. Sousa, MD in his book *How the Brain Learns*, neuroscientists think that the creation of art involves the collaboration of different areas of the brain. In order to create, your child must intentionally think, focus, solve problems, and initiate. These artistic functions build her brain and create and strengthen multiple neural pathways. You can support your baby's cognitive development by encouraging her to participate in the arts.

Because producing art is a universal human experience, your baby instinctively generates art. You can help her to stimulate her brain and establish the pathways that allow her various brain networks to work together by encouraging creativity in the following ways:

❀ **Sing to your baby**—Introduce music by singing, whether or not you can carry a tune. Your singing focuses her attention and creates a positive environment—both building blocks for learning.

❀ **Play music for your baby**—Play a wide variety of music. If you or your friends play musical instruments, play and sing for your child. Take your child to age-appropriate concerts and live music events.

❀ **Make sounds together**—According to psychologist Diana Deutsch, PhD, scientific evidence shows a link between music and language development. Exposure to music, both vocal and instrumental, helps your baby become attuned to the subtler meanings in a person's tone and builds her neural network in preparation for becoming an effective communicator.

❀ **Dance with your baby**—Before your baby can move on her own, play music or sing and move rhythmically with her. As she learns to stand on her own, she can feel the music in her body and bounce by herself.

❀ **Provide materials for creativity**—Offer items that encourage creativity and art, such as drawing materials (paper, crayons, chalk, markers), simple musical instruments that make sounds and rhythms (pots, pans, spoons, drums, bells, maracas, xylophones), books, and dolls or plush toys.

❀ **Expose your child to art**—Display paintings or prints in your home. Take your child to age-appropriate plays and art museums. Make art a part of her daily life.

❀ **Create together**—In addition to supporting your child to be self-directed in her creativity, collaborate with her on occasion. Let her direct you in play. Be the audience when she has a story to tell. Display her art prominently in your home.

❀ **Follow your own artistic pursuits**—Express yourself through poetry, painting, music, theater, or other artistic passions. By being an artist yourself, you show your child that you appreciate the value of the arts.

When Emi was a toddler, we decorated Easter eggs as a family. I noticed that she was concerned about being messy as she decorated her eggs. While I appreciated that she did not spill the dye and was careful to be clean, I became concerned that her sense of creativity was restricted. I got some finger paints and encouraged her to dig her fingers in and enjoy the mess. For children, much of the creative experience comes from feeling free to know that it is okay to be messy—within some limits.

Get Outside and Explore

The outdoors offers novelty and opportunities for exploration and discovery that cannot be duplicated even in the richest indoor environments. Through sensory stimulation and a multitude of materials, nature feeds your baby's brain with experience and keeps her alert and focused as scenes and surroundings change. Nature gives her a world of fresh elements to examine. Simply digging in the dirt with a stick or listening to a bird sing can be fascinating for your baby and stimulating for her brain. A routine of spending a portion of each day outside benefits your child's brain development in multiple ways.

Being in nature is a way of getting in touch with the world. Nature is physical and tangible, yet it is also mysterious, inspirational, and full of abstract beauty. In nature your child can connect with herself by experiencing her senses, and she can find freedom, fantasy, and creativity. Outdoors, she can find peace, harmony, and a sense of relationship in nature's order and patterns.

Robin Moore, a professor of landscape architecture at North Carolina State University and an international authority on the design of children's play and learning environments, leads the university's Natural Learning Initiative, whose purpose is to ensure that every child has access to a natural learning environment every day. Moore says that being in nature involves direct experience of the senses as opposed to the secondary, one-way experience of electronic media. Young children live and learn through their senses, and nature provides sensory-stimulating experiences. Children can experience and learn from nature directly through their senses by touching sand, rocks, and water; smelling flowers and herbs; looking at a beautiful butterfly, rock, or sunset; listening to the rain, wind, or crunch of autumn leaves; smelling the ocean or the forest; and tasting wild blueberries.

In nature, children can make new discoveries. They can spot a ladybug, a tadpole, or a bird's nest. Outside your child can pretend to fly like a bird, to swim like a fish, and to use her imagination without judgment or restrictions.

The rhythms and patterns in nature can feed your child's soul and spirit. Let her hear the sound of waves in the ocean, feel the nourishing warmth of the sun, or witness the birth of a kitten. Nature can surround her with its support and calm her confusion, stress, and tension. Time spent in nature with your family can establish connections and improve the quality of your relationships.

In my family, walks in the woods, days at the beach, camping trips, and outdoor picnics brought us together. On outdoor excursions, Emi and Mari were free to get dirty and to explore, and we had time to enjoy each other as a family. Because we were on a tight budget in those early years, our family getaways consisted mostly of camping. Being out in the woods together gave us the quiet and the space to strengthen our connections to ourselves, to each other, and to the natural world.

Richard Louv, author of *Last Child in the Woods: Saving Our Children from Nature-Deficit Disorder*, says that the child in nature is an endangered species, yet the health of children and the health of the earth are inseparable. He believes direct exposure to nature is essential for a child's healthy physical and emotional development;

further, nature is healing for a child. In nature, a child is relieved of the pressures of society, and she can find the freedom and the space to examine both her inner world and the world around her.

According to Robin Moore, because children learn through their senses, through discovery and free play, and through autonomous interaction with their environment, the multisensory experiences in nature help build the cognitive constructs necessary for sustained intellectual development. They also stimulate imagination. Time spent in nature nourishes a sense of flow and presence through being while doing.

You can support your child's connection to nature by helping her develop her naturalist intelligence. You can also share this experience with her by getting in touch with your own connection to nature. Your enthusiasm and sense of discovery can be contagious and inspirational to your child.

Activities to Promote Interest in Nature

- Read or tell nature stories that stimulate the imagination.

- Help her detach from electronics and get outside.

- Take a discovery walk in your backyard or in a park. See what you find.

- If you have outdoor space, set up a sandbox, swing set, or tree house.

- Collect sticks, rocks, and shells, and arrange them in your child's room.

- Get a pet. Pets teach children about the needs and rhythms of animals.

- Grow a plant in a pot or in your yard.

- Go on a hike, or go camping.

- Go on an excursion to a local nature center, zoo, or aquarium.

Seek Balance in Activity

Watching your child as she gains cognitive skills is like watching a butterfly emerge from a chrysalis. You cannot see what is going on inside her brain, yet periodically, as suddenly as a new wing appearing, words and thoughts that she has been incubating tumble out all at once. She naturally finds her own equilibrium by adjusting her needs to fit the situation. However, sometimes she needs your support and guidance to challenge her to grow, to help her build resilience, and to help her find balance.

Since the day your baby was born, you have watched her grow and learn. You know how her brain gathers and absorbs information. You know if she quietly observes before practicing a new skill, or if she jumps in and persists until she masters a task. You know if she is naturally a bold explorer or if she needs encouragement to step out of her comfort zone. By watching her every day, you also know what she can do and what she has yet to master.

If you are familiar with your child's learning style and current skill level, you can determine when your intervention is beneficial and when it disrupts her process. If you know your child's skill level, you can step in with guidance and help her stretch herself with a slightly more difficult task. Once she has a basic understanding of the task, then you can step back and allow her to become competent on her own.

As your baby's guide, you are in charge of setting limits and creating boundaries for her. You must answer the age-old questions of "How much is enough?" "How long can she stay up past her bedtime?" "How many cookies are too many?" Children naturally push their limits, and they need you to help them learn to moderate their desires and activities. Sometimes it can be challenging to know when your child is on the edge and needs to return to balance.

You probably know intuitively what your child needs in order to achieve and maintain balance. By being attuned to her yin and yang characteristics, you can offer yin- or yang-influencing activities to help her restore balance. If she is quiet and shy, then perhaps she needs to play in the sand to ground her and to energize her. If she is energetic and active, she may need time in nature or mellow music to calm her down. The chart below lists some characteristics to help you determine if your child is in a more yin or yang state. These characteristics could be relevant to her current condition, or they could relate to her general personality. The second part of the chart lists environments and activities to help her restore balance. If your child has more yang characteristics, she may need more yin activities or environments to help her settle down. If she has more yin characteristics you may encourage her to be more active with yang activities and create a more stimulating environment.

Yin-Yang Influences 🏠

Yang 🔺	Yin 🔻
Characteristics	
Active	Passive
Loud	Quiet
Energetic	Sensitive
Concentrated and focused, involved	Relaxed with open mind, playful
Competitive	Cooperative
Quick reaction	Slow reaction
Activities	
Stimulate the nervous system	Relax the nervous system
Movement	Sit or lay still
Run, jump	Swim, yoga
Participate in math and science	Participate in music and art
Dig in the earth or sand	Play with water in bath
Environment	
Pressured, tense	Comfortable and secure
Bright lights	Low lights
Loud music	Soft music
Warm, sunny weather	Cool, rainy or snowy weather

For your child to become competent, she needs your support as she learns to think for herself and find her own answers. Your challenge is to find balance between coaching and letting go. When your child follows her own initiative, tries to put a round peg in several square holes, and then finds the round hole through her own testing, she participates in active learning. When you direct her to the right hole, she participates in passive learning. How do you know when to offer guidance (passive learning)? When do you allow her to learn through her own initiative (active learning)?

Active learning makes a deeper impression on your child and fosters independence because she finds the solution through her own resourcefulness. However, sometimes safety or the level of difficulty dictates that passive learning is necessary before active learning can take place. For example, the acts of swimming and tying shoes first require the support of a parent or other guide. After your child learns the basic skills involved in these activities, she can become an active learner. Every child and every situation moves at a different rate and has its own balance point.

Theories of Mental Development

THE FIRST SECTION OF this chapter provides simple daily actions that you can take to support your baby's cognitive development. This next section takes you deeper, showing how your baby's brain develops, foundational cognitive skills that she needs to learn, and a range of theories about ways that she can learn. An understanding of her developmental process can help you guide her to discover her potential.

While your baby's intelligence can increase throughout life, the cognitive development that takes place between birth and three years of age is foundational. Because learning builds upon learning, the knowledge that your baby gains between birth and her third birthday underlies her self-image, motivation, and view of the world throughout her life.

Your Baby's Mental Development

In her first few years, your baby progresses from reactivity to intentionality—from instinct to thought, from reactive expression to language, and from reflexive movement to deliberate grasping and walking. Her ability to reach her cognitive potential depends on both the knowledge she gathers from her experiences and her ability to use that knowledge, which is influenced by her confidence and belief in herself.

Physically, your baby's brain grows to 60 percent of its adult size by age one, reaches 80 percent by age two, and is nearly at adult size by age five (though it will not reach full physiological maturity until she is in her twenties). She was born with almost all the neurons she will ever have, although those neurons have few connections between them. Before she was born, she acquired some knowledge by making neural connections through her senses of touch and taste in the womb. Then, beginning at birth, new neural connections have increasingly given her knowledge that helps her adapt and thrive in her environment. The more opportunities she has to gather information, the more connections she makes, and the more knowledge she obtains.

In the beginning, your child makes neural connections through sensory experiences. As her connections multiply, they form networks that build on previously gathered information and coordinate her thoughts. Repeated experiences strengthen her connections and create neural pathways that allow her to perform routine tasks quickly. For instance, picking up a cracker and eating it may be a challenge when she is first learning. Through repetition, however, she establishes a neural network for picking things up and putting them in her mouth. Now she can pick up a cracker and eat it without thinking.

To support her in using the knowledge that she takes in, your child needs both a large quantity of experiences, as well as high-quality experiences. As your baby builds neural networks, she also prunes unused neurons. This pruning process unclutters her thinking and keeps her brain from overloading. Due to pruning, rare or one-time experiences fall away and routine experiences become primary to her thought processes. As long as she is learning from positive experiences, the combination of forming neural networks and pruning unneeded neurons keeps her brain functioning well. However, if her early experiences are negative, frustrating, or limiting, the same combination can stunt her intellectual growth.

Plasticity is the ability of your baby's brain to change in form and function as a result of input from the environment. During early development, her brain has the most plasticity, meaning it is both the most vulnerable to harm and the most capable of recovery. While the mind is malleable and capable of new learning at every age, unlearning takes more effort than learning does—especially when ideas or habits are formed at a young age. Think about false viewpoints or aspects of your self-image that you learned in childhood. Even if you know they are not true today, you may still be vulnerable to them. Positive and negative early experiences can play a significant role in forming your child's perspective, for better or for worse.

Your child draws confidence from the sense of security that comes from a healthy attachment. For her to thrive intellectually, to believe in herself, to succeed, and to reach her full potential, she needs your love, your attention, and a stable environment.

Milestones of Mental Development

You can observe and measure concrete changes in your child's physical development, and her emotional expression has landmarks that you can quantify fairly easily. Changes in cognitive development, however, are more qualitative than quantitative. Even after your child learns to talk, you may wonder what is going on in her mind and how she processes information.

A basic understanding of stages and milestones in your child's cognitive development can help you support her current skills and prepare her for her next stage. Keeping in mind that each child moves at her own rate, these markers can also be useful in helping you determine whether your child is on track developmentally and alerting you to any signs that you may wish to discuss with your health care provider.

Here are some of the general developmental stages in your child's cognitive growth.

Milestones in Cognitive Growth

Birth–3 months	3–6 months	6–12 months
• She pays attention to things that interest her • She focuses on toys, pictures, and engages with people • She anticipates everyday routines • She is stimulated by a new toy and bored by an old one • She recognizes the difference between new and familiar	• She touches and feels different textures • She reaches for and grasps things • She drops objects on purpose to see your reaction	• She plays with toys and household items • She investigates • She looks at objects and people in her environment • She listens to instructions

12–18 months	18–24 months	24–36 months
• She begins to use objects or utensils properly • She makes "yes" and "no" gestures • She can sort shapes and blocks • She wants to do everything herself	• She categorizes and sorts objects by colors and shapes • She has her own interests • She starts to understand time concepts • She asserts herself in accomplishing tasks, but may be frustrated if she is not successful	• She can draw a circle • She enjoys simple puzzles • She shows an interest in counting • She can say her name

Earlier and faster mental development is not necessarily better. Each stage builds on the last, and in order to attain certain cognitive skills your child's brain needs time to mature physically. Monitor your child for indications of delayed development, seek guidance if needed, provide love and security, and trust her brain to develop at its own pace.

Foundations for Learning

Your child starts learning before she is born. As she grows, she encounters certain windows of time to acquire knowledge. Awareness of how her brain works can help you understand what is going on inside her head and how it is the foundation for her to learn. You can help cultivate her intelligence by supporting the building blocks that she needs to learn.

Optimal Learning Opportunities

Throughout your child's growth and development, she will reach certain sensitive periods for learning—times when her brain is especially receptive to mastering certain skills or absorbing an area of knowledge. Different windows open at different times after birth, and nearly all openings for optimal learning periods close by puberty. During puberty, the brain begins to set its most useful connections and to discard or prune the rest.

Even though the adult brain maintains plasticity and can still learn a skill and incorporate new knowledge, learning a new skill becomes more difficult after puberty because a foundational neural network for that skill was not established in childhood. When you know that your child is in an optimal learning period, you can provide experiences that promote her learning in that specific area.

Below I have listed your baby's optimal learning periods, categorized by type of skill. Keep in mind that these windows are only guidelines, and that the brain is forgiving. Overall, however, it takes more effort to learn outside of an optimal period of opportunity. Most children follow a typical path of development, but every child is different. For example, stress or illness may cause a child to miss a learning opportunity, but this can usually be made up later. Observing your child and her interests is the best way for you to determine her learning opportunity windows.

Language

This period extends from birth to approximately five to seven years of age, and the window closes around ten to twelve years old. From birth through age three, your baby learns to sort sounds, to assign meaning to cadence and pitch, to recognize words, to use words, to recognize and establish patterns of grammar and syntax, and to express herself in sentences. The best ways to support your child during this learning window are to talk and read to her reciprocally.

Emotional control

This period lasts from 2 to 30 months. Your baby cannot be open to learning if she is in an unstable emotional condition. In his book *How the Brain Learns*, David A. Sousa, MD explains that between 2 months and 30 months the brain's limbic system and frontal lobes compete to meet your child's needs. The limbic system, which manages emotions, is more developed at this age, so it is more likely to succeed in moderating two-year-old temper tantrums. Before three years old, the window for learning to use rational thought is open. If your child misses that opening, her brain may form neural networks that use only emotions to meet her objectives. These networks will be tough to modify later in life.

Motor development

This period lasts from prebirth to eight years old. The window opens in utero as your baby stretches, punches, and kicks. As she develops over the next three years, she builds neural networks that take her from an infant who cannot control her limbs, to a toddler who can walk, run, feed herself, and much more. Opportunities for movement build neural networks for physical competence. Sousa points out that even though your child can always learn new skills, most concert virtuosos, Olympic medalists, and professional players of individual sports begin to practice their skills by the age of eight.

Problem solving

This period extends from birth to six years old. According to Sousa, researchers have found that babies have a rudimentary sense of numbers and that young children recognize quantity and the relational aspects of numbers. You can encourage these mathematical skills by providing your child with experiences that show relationships, such as bigger and smaller, and more and fewer. In addition, you can count with your child, and sort objects by shape and color.

Your Baby's Brain

The components of your baby's brain work together and act like a control panel for her nervous system. In her first few years, her brain makes connections faster than at any other time in her life. By understanding how her brain processes information, you can support your baby in this significant period of cognitive growth and development.

Your baby's brain has three sections:

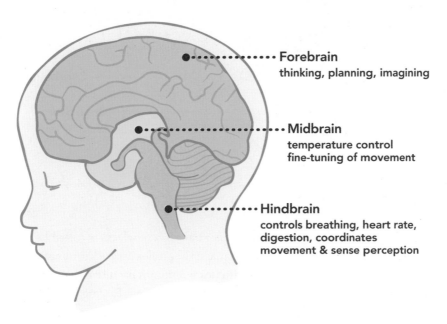

Forebrain
thinking, planning, imagining

Midbrain
temperature control
fine-tuning of movement

Hindbrain
controls breathing, heart rate,
digestion, coordinates
movement & sense perception

- **Hindbrain**—At the back of your baby's head, the hindbrain connects her spinal cord to the rest of her brain. Evolutionarily speaking, it is the oldest part of the brain. It controls many automatic functions, such as heart rate, blood pressure, digestion, and breathing. It includes the cerebellum, the pons, and the medulla.

- **Midbrain**—Your baby's midbrain controls many functions—including temperature control, visual and auditory systems, and fine-tuning of movement—and coordinates sensory information with her body movements.

- **Forebrain**—Your baby's forebrain has many wide-ranging functions. It consists of the cerebrum, which is divided into hemispheres. One hemisphere includes her cerebral cortex, subcortical structures, and corpus callosum. The other hemisphere includes her thalamus and hypothalamus. In her forebrain, more complicated motor skills and sophisticated cognitive functions, such as thinking, planning, and imagining, take place. Language, memory, speaking, and voluntary movements are rooted in her forebrain.

When your baby is born, no part of her brain is fully developed. Her midbrain and hindbrain are mature enough to maintain basic body functions, and they have sufficient untapped potential for future development. Her forebrain is ready for sensations and experiences to give rise to thoughts and actions. Much of your baby's brain development in her first few years is focused on refining her midbrain and hindbrain functions, developing her forebrain, and coordinating all sections of her brain.

Exterior Brain

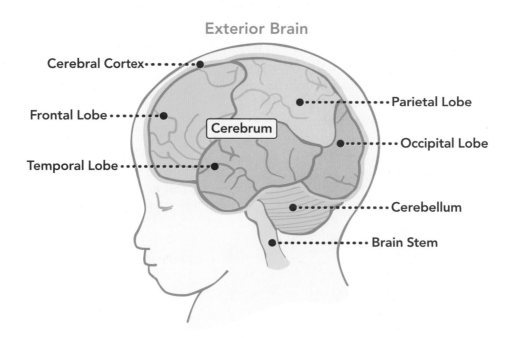

Cerebral Cortex

Frontal Lobe

Temporal Lobe

Cerebrum

Parietal Lobe

Occipital Lobe

Cerebellum

Brain Stem

Exterior brain

Located behind her brain stem and below her cerebrum, your baby's cerebellum is called her "little brain" because it looks like a small cerebrum. At birth, her cerebellum manages her reflexive and automatic functions, and as she grows and begins to move purposefully, it also coordinates her voluntary movements, such as walking. The cerebellum is also responsible for her balance, posture, and sense of timing. During your baby's first year of life, her cerebellum triples in size. While her cerebellum is responsible for only about 10 percent of your baby's brain mass, it contains half of her neurons.

Just above her cerebellum, your baby's cerebrum is the largest part of her brain. The surface of her cerebrum is her cerebral cortex. It consists of folded ripples called "gyri," which add surface area and thus increase your baby's gray matter and the quantity of information that she can process. Your baby's cerebrum is the most complex part of her brain. It is divided into four lobes. Although various areas of the brain may be described as "matching" a particular function, the brain operates through interplay and integration among areas. The four lobes of the cerebrum are as follows:

- Frontal lobe—Your baby's frontal lobe is the last area of her brain to mature fully, and it continues to develop into early adulthood. This lobe is associated with movement and motor skills, such as walking, dancing, and playing an instrument or sport. It is also used in problem solving, exercising judgment, decision-making, concentration, goal-directed behavior, and self-motivation. The majority of your baby's language production takes place in this lobe.

- Parietal lobe—Her parietal lobe processes sensory input, such as touch, recognition, and spatial orientation, as well as some speech and visual perception.

- Temporal lobe—Your baby's temporal lobe is responsible for hearing, language comprehension, language organization and sequence, sense of timing, and musical awareness. It is the location of high-level visual processing, such as face recognition. It also contains the hippocampus, which holds long-term memory.

- Occipital lobe—The occipital lobe is the main area of visual processing. It makes reading possible. It is also thought to be where dreams are produced.

Interior Brain

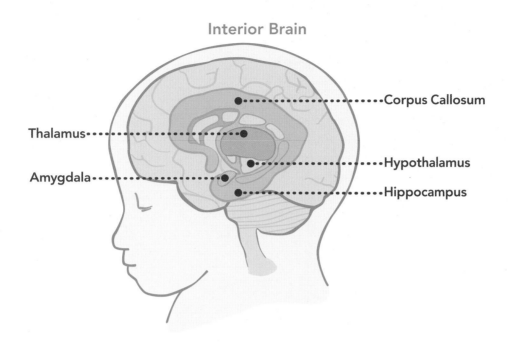

Interior brain

The interior parts of your baby's brain include her brain stem and limbic system. In addition to coordinating communication between her brain and her spinal cord, her brain stem is a structure that connects the brain and the body. It coordinates motor control signals that are sent from the cerebrum, and affects your child's ability to sleep, swallow, and maintain a sense of balance.

Your baby's limbic system, known as the "emotional brain," is located above her brain stem and tucked into her cerebrum. Her limbic system consists of the following components:

- Thalamus—Your baby's thalamus transmits motor and sensory signals to her cerebral cortex. It is responsible for consciousness and alertness.

- Hypothalamus—The main responsibility of her hypothalamus is to maintain homeostasis, which is a state of balanced body systems. It does this by producing hormones that regulate temperature, hunger, thirst, circadian rhythm, mood, reproduction, and growth, and by deciding when glands will release those hormones. The hypothalamus also balances emotional response. If your child senses a threat, her hypothalamus releases cortisol and other hormones that prepare her body to protect itself. Once the threat passes, her hypothalamus restores homeostasis.

- Hippocampus—This area aids with spatial navigation and also controls short- and long-term memory. The hippocampus acts as the brain's librarian, filing memories in the proper place and then retrieving them when needed.

- Amygdala—In charge of processing emotions and emotional reactions, the amygdala also decides when a threat is present and sends out an alert. It also determines when an event becomes a long- or short-term memory and coordinates the autonomic and endocrine responses.

Right and left brain 🏠

Your baby's brain can be divided into many parts that perform different tasks, but all of these parts work together. Another way of looking at her brain structure is by differentiating it into right and left hemispheres. The right hemisphere deals with information using more yin processes, such as imagination, spontaneity, sensitivity, and intuition. Her left side is more yang, using analysis, facts, and logic. Her right brain controls the left side of her body by gathering information from images and detecting visual patterns. Her left brain controls the right side of her body as it takes in literal interpretation of words, governs sequences, and perceives visual details.

Even though each hemisphere may have its special functions, your child needs both sides of her brain to work together for optimal results in her thought processes. Her corpus callosum is a wide bundle of neural fibers that connects the hemispheres of her brain in order to share information. At birth, your baby's corpus callosum exists, but it is undeveloped. At this early age, your baby's corpus callosum grows to bridge her two hemispheres and to conduct information between them. It can also shut down to inhibit this communication when exclusive focus on a specialized function is necessary.

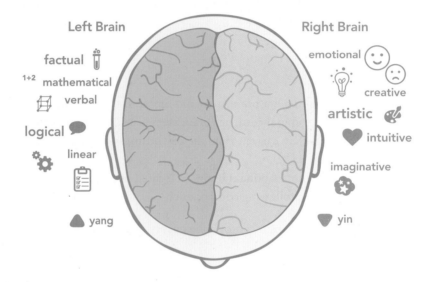

The left hemisphere of the brain specializes in these functions:

- Logic and analysis
- Noticing details and differences
- Control of small muscles
- Spoken language and reading
- Thoughts and processing external information
- Recognizing words and numbers
- Reading
- Arithmetic and calculations
- Conscious motivation

The right hemisphere typically manages the following brain functions:

- Big-picture thinking
- Abstract thought
- Control of large muscles
- Emotions and internal emotional processing
- Interpretation of nonverbal communication, such as gestures, body language, and tone
- Understanding of information, creating context, seeing patterns
- Special visual recognition, such as faces and specific places
- Relational mathematics
- Unconscious motivation

The hemispheres of the brain do not grow at the same rate. In fact, your baby's left brain is undeveloped at birth. According to a 1997 study by pediatric neurologist Catherine Chiron MD, PhD, director of research at the French Institute of Health and Medical Research, children are more right-brain dominant during their first three years. From your child's right-brain perspective, her world of imagination, fantasy, and make-believe lead, until her left brain begins to develop and she can incorporate more advanced language and logic. Young children are naturally inspired to imagine and to play as they learn, unless they are interrupted or do not have the opportunity to explore from their own initiative.

When I compare the brain dominance of my daughters, I would say that Emi tends to be more left-brained (yang) while Mari leans toward the right-brained (yin) side. After Emi attended a birthday party as a toddler, she remembered the details of the clothes that everyone at the party had worn. Meanwhile, Mari has always excelled at art and abstract thought. However, even though both daughters have overall tendencies, both sides of their brains work together, and through many experiences, they have learned to use their whole brains.

Whole brain

Traditional schools and other learning environments often emphasize left-brain skills while neglecting right-brain skills. To many educators, reading, writing, and mathematics seem more important than aesthetic sense, spontaneous expression, and creativity. However, the hemispheres of your baby's brain do not work in isolation; both sides are necessary for her brain to function optimally. They work together in a complementary way as a system that collaborates, balances, and integrates to enable whole thinking.

In *The Whole-Brain Child: 12 Revolutionary Strategies to Nurture Your Child's Developing Mind*, Daniel J. Siegel, MD and Tina Payne Bryson, PhD explain that when a child's brain is integrated, she has harmonious flow between extremes. Her brain has right and left hemispheres with opposite tendencies. As with the dual extremes of yin and yang, movements toward the center of the spectrum help her achieve a state of equilibrium. By combining the raw emotions of her right brain with the logic of her left brain, she maintains balance, avoids the extremes of chaos and rigidity, and learns to handle her emotions positively. For example, if your child has more opportunities to use her right brain, her left brain can balance and function holistically.

All parts of your baby's brain work together to make a whole that is greater than the sum of its parts. Siegel and Bryson say that when the hemispheres of your child's brain cooperate, they are horizontally integrated. Likewise, when the higher parts of her brain work together with the lower parts of her brain, her brain is vertically integrated. The lower parts of your child's brain—collectively called her "reptilian brain"—are instinctual, impulsive, and concerned with survival. Her reptilian brain governs her reactive lower mental functions. Her cerebrum, or "mammalian brain," is the higher part of her brain, and it is the center for intellectual ideas, planning, thinking, and reflecting. Her mammalian brain manages higher mental functions that are deliberate, such as pausing before acting, considering consequences, and thinking of others' feelings. According to Siegel and Bryson, the brain works best when the upstairs and downstairs are vertically integrated—and you as a parent can help your child build a staircase between the two floors.

In your child's first three years, you can help her build whole-brain neural pathways in the following ways:

❀ **Acknowledge her emotions**—When your baby is overwhelmed with emotion, acknowledge her feelings: "It must have been frustrating when your friend took your toy." Encourage her to feel her emotions, to notice her reactions, and to respect her instincts. After she calms down, she will be more able to use her rational processes.

❀ **Tell stories**—After your child is calm, help her create a story about an emotional situation. Stories can help her understand her feelings, find solutions, and learn intellectually. According to Siegel and Bryson, children start telling stories even when they are barely verbal. Let her tell as much of her story as possible, and then you can fill in the missing words. Stories help her integrate different parts of her brain, achieve balance, and make sense of her world: "My friend took my toy. The toy belonged to me, but he wanted to play with it, so he took it. Maybe if I asked him to give it back, he would give it to me. Or maybe we could play with the toy together."

❀ **Give her a reason**—Explain your behavior to your child. When you ask something of her, give her the reason behind it. "I know that you may not want to put on your coat, but it will keep you warm so you can play outside," or "Waiting in this checkout line is tiresome, but we need groceries to cook dinner."

❀ **Let her make decisions**—Give your child the opportunity to make decisions as often as possible. For instance, she can choose what to wear, which vegetables to have for lunch, which toy to play with, and so on. When she is old enough to understand, ask her to explain the reasoning behind her decisions. The process of making simple choices gives her the neural networks and confidence to think through more difficult issues as she grows.

❀ **Explain her brain**—Siegel and Bryson suggest that when your child is old enough, you talk to her about the various parts of her brain, how her brain works, and how she can control it.

❀ **Connect with the right, and redirect with the left**—When your child is upset, she will not understand logic until you first respond to her emotional needs. When you become attuned to your child and understand how she feels, you can connect with her and acknowledge her feelings by using touch, empathic facial expressions, a nurturing tone of voice, and nonjudgmental listening. Connect your right brain to her right brain. Then you can connect left to left and redirect her to understand what you want to say logically. This allows your child to use both sides of her brain in an integrated way.

As Siegel and Bryson say, "An integrated brain is capable of doing much more than its individual parts could accomplish alone." By understanding how your child's brain works and where she is developmentally, you can coach her from an early age to use all of her brainpower by communicating between hemispheres.

Building Blocks of Learning

Your child's survival is dependent on her ability to learn. She is born with a basic core set of knowledge, as well as the capacity for memory and focus, intelligence, and the motivation to gather information. While these characteristics are innate in your baby, she needs to exercise and strengthen them to build her foundation for learning.

Core knowledge

Research shows that rather than being a blank slate, a newborn begins life with a fundamental understanding of the world. Elizabeth Spelke, PhD, a cognitive psychologist and a leading researcher in the field of infant and toddler cognition, divided this instinctive knowledge into four "core cognitive capacities": object sense, number sense, spatial sense, and language sense.

Researchers continue to develop new theories about how babies learn and what they know. Some scholars think that babies are born with more than four core cognitive capacities; they might add a social sense, for example. Overall, however, scientists have established that learning is essential to human survival, and nature provides your baby with basic competencies that she needs to thrive. As her parent, you can trust in your baby's inborn knowledge as you support her in learning.

Before she is six months old, your newborn has a basic understanding of the following:

- **Object sense**—She understands that objects are whole and cannot pass through other solid objects; she knows that objects are permanent even when they are not visible.

- **Number sense**—She can estimate quantities; she knows when an object has been added to a small group and when an object has been taken away; she can recognize a number of sounds, such as the number of drum beats or dog barks.

- **Spatial sense**—She can orient in space using angles and distance between objects; she uses geometric cues to navigate.

- **Language sense**—She can recognize familiar sounds, cadences, and tones of language; she sorts sounds, make sounds, and assigns meanings to sounds.

Memory

Memory is necessary for your baby to learn. Her memory started working before she was born by storing sounds, tastes, and smells in the womb. Every experience she has activates neurons in her brain and links them with other neurons, so that they fire at the same time. This process constantly changes the makeup of her brain.

Your baby associates present experiences with ones that she had in the past; memories of her past experiences influence her present thoughts and feelings. For instance, if you and your baby enjoy dancing together to a favorite song, when she gets older and hears the same song, she may feel happy without knowing why. In addition, her present emotional state can influence how she remembers a past experience. For example, if her older brother shares his toys today, she may forget that he grabbed a toy from her yesterday.

Your child uses two types of memory: explicit and implicit. Explicit memory is a conscious recollection of a specific experience in the past. When your child remembers the time that she dug in the garden at her grandmother's house, she has an explicit memory of that event.

Implicit memory is based on automatic perceptions, emotions, bodily sensations, and behaviors that are embedded in her brain. Your child uses implicit memory when she rolls over, sits up, walks, or tosses a ball without thinking about it. Habits, or conditioned responses from repeated experiences, cause her to form expectations. For example, when she retrieves a previous memory that is related to her current experience, she anticipates what will happen next based on that memory.

Implicit memory is a generalized, ingrained type of memory. It requires no explanation as to why something happened because it does not relate to recall a specific event. Implicit memories can be both positive and negative. The feeling of love and safety in your home is an example of a positive implicit memory that your child may carry into adulthood. However, if she hears you say that she is sweet but not too smart, she may view these impressions as truth and then conclude that she is not smart without understanding why. This is an example of a negative implicit memory. Your child uses only implicit memory until she is about 18 months old.

You can help your child integrate her memories by reframing her implicit memories as explicit ones through storytelling. When you talk to your child about the specifics of each day's events, you help her put her feelings and thoughts into perspective before they become implicit memories.

Memory helps your baby make sense of her world, recognize patterns, and create expectations for the future. With use, her memory gets stronger, fuller, and more supportive as she makes connections and learns.

Focus

Focus is a process that uses multiple senses and parts of the brain to direct attention toward something specific. The ability to focus is essential to learning. Your baby must block out unnecessary stimuli, tune in to the task of absorbing information, process that information, and use the information to solve problems. In the beginning, your baby naturally pays attention to familiar things in her world, such as your voice or facial expression. When she can focus her attention on one thing and ignore others, she learns to control her impulses and delay her reaction.

Infancy and toddlerhood are times to explore the world and to openly take in and respond to various stimuli. Young babies do possess the ability to focus, however, and they use this ability to achieve their goals and to learn about the world in their own way.

In Pathways to Competence: Encouraging Healthy Social and Emotional Development in Young Children, Sarah Landy, PhD and Joy Osofsky, PhD explain that babies pay attention to what interests them. They can focus when they want or need to.

Your child's ability to focus will continue to improve well into adulthood. While she is young, however, you can make it easier for her to exercise focus in the following ways:

- Provide a calm environment with stimulating experiences.
- Encourage her to choose her interests.
- Relate to her directly—talk, read, and play.
- Be patient when she is engrossed in an activity.
- Follow her lead when playing with her.
- Allow extra time for her to dress herself when using zippers, buckles, or snaps.

Stages of Focus

- In her first few months, your baby can stare at your face contentedly, become absorbed in kicking at a mobile, or be persistent in her cries when she is hungry. Between three and six months, her hand gestures and eye motions begin to work together in joint focus.

- At six months and throughout her first year, your baby's ability to focus grows. She can work diligently to pull herself to sit, stand, and walk. She can focus on an object and move to get it.

- At two years old, your baby can become engrossed in play or in exploring an object. Her attention span is now about seven minutes.

- At three years old, she can follow simple directions and complete a task. She can sit through a short play, a story, or a movie.

Intelligence

In his book *Brain Rules for Baby*, John Medina, PhD reminds readers that the brain's primary purpose is to support the body's survival. Your baby's brain regulates her body systems and helps her navigate the world to find safety, food, and shelter and to build relationships. To assist her in survival, the brain needs to store and use knowledge. Medina calls these two survival functions memory and improvisation. Together they create intelligence.

Traditionally, scientists viewed a person's level of intelligence as a fixed property that affected performance in logic, mathematics, and language. In 1905, French psychologist Alfred Binet developed the first quantifiable IQ test that measured intelligence in those three areas. His assessment of people's minds was based on their ability to answer items on written tests. In 1983, with the publication of *Frames of Mind: The Theory of Multiple Intelligences*, Howard Gardner, PhD greatly expanded on the definition of intelligence. Through his research, he found that people could use a variety of aptitudes, talents, and abilities—or intelligences—to learn, to use skills, to create products, and to solve prob-

lems. Originally, Gardner identified seven intelligences. Later he added an eighth intelligence (naturalist) and a half intelligence (existential). Gardner explains that he made the existential intelligence only half an intelligence because he could not identify the regions of the brain responsible for it, and he was concerned that it could be misunderstood as a connection to religious belief. Following are Gardner's eight and one half intelligences:

1. Musical-rhythmic intelligence—The ability to use music and rhythm to identify, think about, and create patterns

2. Bodily-kinesthetic intelligence—The ability to use the whole body to express thoughts and to move smoothly to perform tasks, such as athletics, acting, and dancing

3. Logical-mathematical intelligence—The ability to use underlying numerical systems and patterns and to take a logical approach to a problem

4. Linguistic intelligence—The ability to use language to express an idea or to solve a problem; an aptitude with words

5. Spatial intelligence—The ability to see an actual space and then reproduce it accurately in your mind; an ability to build, engineer, and navigate

6. Interpersonal intelligence—The ability to connect with other people and to understand their needs

7. Intrapersonal intelligence—The ability to know yourself and to develop a clear idea of your own abilities and limitations

8. Naturalist intelligence—A sensitivity and attraction to the natural world

8.5. Existential intelligence—A drive to ask and explore the big questions in life: Why do human beings exist? What happens when we die? Is there a God?

Provide Natural Motivation

You can help your child sustain her natural motivation and love for learning in the following ways:

- Praise her efforts rather than her success. For example, say, "You worked hard painting your picture," instead of "You painted a beautiful picture." Your words of praise for her process help her learn to put forth effort, not to concentrate only on the goal.

- Pay attention to what inspires, interests, and excites her.

- Provide a motivating, inspirational environment. An environment that invites learning has good light, low noise, natural materials, and clean spaces for working.

- Model your own intrinsic motivation for learning. Your enthusiasm for learning is contagious and shows your child that learning is fun and enjoyable.

While some scientists claim that Gardner's categories are not types of intelligences but merely areas of talent, many educators have found Gardner's distinctions useful in identifying how particular students think and how it is best to teach them. Gardner is opposed to labeling people with one type of intelligence. He says that everyone has a unique blend of intelligences, though one type is perhaps more pronounced.

Your baby's eagerness to engage her world lets you know that she is an intelligent being. Although she is born with innate intelligences, how she develops them largely depends on your nurturing support and her environment. As a parent, you can use the concept of multiple intelligences to identify your child's innate abilities and approaches to learning. For example, maybe she learns best by listening to or making music (musical-rhythmic intelligence), by acting something out (bodily-kinesthetic intelligence), or by seeing a concept reflected in nature (naturalist intelligence).

In your baby's early years, an awareness of her unique blend of intelligences can help you support her natural interests and learning process. As she heads off to school, this awareness can help you advocate for her and guide her education.

Motivation

Your baby needs motivation in order to learn. Motivation to learn can be an intrinsic and natural desire, or it can be an extrinsic drive, such as the desire to be number one in the class, to make a parent proud, or to get a degree. Your baby is intrinsically motivated to learn; she does not need prompting, direction, or bribery to explore and experience her surroundings. She naturally perseveres and enjoys making discoveries for the pure delight and pleasure of explanation and understanding. In addition to solving problems, she may seek novel challenges.

Motivation can come from inspiration, the drive to know, and the eventual satisfaction of expressing ideas or finding solutions. It can also arise from a need or deficiency. According to Maslow's theory of human motivation, people are motivated by physiological needs, safety, love, self-esteem, and self-actualization. These motives are hierarchical. When one need is satisfied to a certain degree, the next level of need emerges. Maslow says that the human desire to know and to understand may satisfy needs of basic safety, as well as expressions of self-actualization.

Motivation is the motor for learning. When you encourage your baby without pressure to enjoy acquiring knowledge for its own reward, she will be inspired to be self-directed and intentional as she learns, rather than focused on gold stars and other extrinsic goals.

Readiness to learn

Nature's gifts to your baby form a basic foundation for learning that includes core knowledge, the ability to remember and to focus, multiple intelligences, and a natural curiosity that motivates her.

As her parent, you have the opportunity to nurture her with safety, love, and an environment where her learning can thrive. Because her experiences help structure her brain, your support during her first three years greatly impacts her readiness to learn. Here are some suggestions for keeping her ready to learn:

🌸 Take care of your baby's emotional needs. A healthy attachment between your baby and you gives her the security and confidence to explore new experiences, to focus her attention, and to build the resilience that is necessary for her to succeed in the face of challenge.

🌸 Know your child. Consider her temperament, personality, yin-yang constitution and condition, intelligence, strengths, and preferences. Pay attention to her zone of development, so that you can stimulate and challenge her to learn and grow.

🌸 Acknowledge her fears and frustrations so that you can help her to overcome obstacles in learning. Encourage her to recognize past negative experiences that affect her feelings as she learns. Give her space to learn and grow without unnecessary limits or restrictions.

🌸 Accept and appreciate your child's unique gifts, and nourish her to develop her own passions. Be mindful not to pressure her, and allow her to lead the way in her interests at her own learning pace.

Trust that your child is in the right place at the right time on her path. Believe in her and in her abilities, and support her with challenges that she faces. Your child was born with her own unique set of gifts, and with your support they can unfold naturally.

How Your Baby Learns

Until the 1980s, psychologists believed that a newborn's mind was a blank slate, or tabula rasa, that gained knowledge by passively receiving impressions from the environment. Newborns may appear to be passive and unknowing because they are limited in their expression—they are dependent, they need help to fulfill their needs, they sleep a lot, they do not move much, and they cannot talk. However, psychologists now believe that young children are competent, active participants in their own learning.

Your baby is born with a natural drive to learn on her own. With persistent, instinctual curiosity and optimism, she seeks to understand the world around her. Her motivation comes from the enjoyment of discovering something new by simply engaging with the world.

Humans need care from their parents for a long time. Therefore, it is natural for children to want their parents to take care of them, and it is equally natural for parents to want to take care of their children. Due to this supportive biological relationship, your baby was able to enter the world in an immature state. Her brain can develop slowly, and she can take full advantage of its ability to learn in many different ways.

There are multiple theories on how babies and children learn, and scientists are still conducting new research to gain a deeper understanding of the learning process. Whatever the method of learning, however, most psychologists and educators agree that babies learn best in two ways: (1) by interacting with people through relationships, and (2) by actively participating in direct experiences.

Your baby makes sense of her world by engaging with you and other trusted loved ones. You are her first teacher and role model. She watches and imitates you. The reciprocal dance between you builds a foundation for her to learn. She needs this emotional security and stability in her relationships with herself and others in order to focus, to learn, and to develop confidence in her ability to succeed.

Active, enriching experiences that require your baby to use her whole body and mind are essential to her brain development and learning. Children learn by doing—by directly engaging in their experiences. Your

baby is learning in some form at every moment. As she grows and matures, her brain and capacity to learn grow with her. Often, parents feel pressure to promote early learning with intricate toys that are meant to put children ahead of the learning curve and to support brain development. However, your baby does not need complicated, expensive toys to provide stimulation and experience. Simple, inexpensive household items—such as pots and pans, a cardboard box, or a paper-towel roll—can provide the basics to help your baby learn. In addition, she can enjoy rich sensory experiences by spending time in nature, modeling your actions during daily routines, engaging in unstructured play, and doing age-appropriate activities to stimulate her brain development. She needs you or other caretakers to interact with her and guide her along the way.

Russian psychologist Lev Vygotsky divided mental processes into lower and higher functions. Lower mental functions, which are based on biological maturation, consist of reactions to external stimuli. Humans, as well as other animals have lower mental functions. For instance, if a dog hears an unexpected loud noise, he instinctually reacts by startling. Your baby has the same visceral reaction to an unexpected loud sound. The methods of learning that involve lower mental functions may begin before birth or soon afterward and continue throughout your child's life.

Only humans possess the higher mental functions of complex language, inquiry, and reflection, mental processes that are developed through learning. They are self-initiated and deliberate. For example, when your child is around two years old, she becomes more intentional in solving problems, such as how to get a cookie by herself. She deliberately moves the stool next to the counter, climbs onto the stool, opens the cookie jar, and gets the cookie.

Your baby's first learning experiences involve lower mental functions—through her senses and movements, through reinforcement of environmental stimuli, and through memory from repetition. Her methods of learning begin to include deliberate thought processes as she develops her higher mental functions, such as sign and symbol use, focused attention, deliberate memorization, and logical thinking.

These methods of learning are blocks that build upon each other. Through her senses and movements, a baby perceives the environment around her. She can feel the difference between a silky blanket and a terry-cloth towel. She sees your face, recognizes the sound of your voice, and integrates these different stimuli. Her movements and activities send messages to her brain and result in cognitive development. As she grows, her understanding develops from pure perception to imitation, and eventually she responds to positive and negative reinforcements of her behavior. She learns through trial and error: if she drops her spoon, it will fall on the floor. She then begins to adapt her behavior to fit different contexts, such as child care versus home environments. Your child also learns when she memorizes information. These methods of learning call upon her lower mental functions.

As your baby's brain develops, she uses her higher mental functions. Her thinking becomes more structured, she becomes deliberate in her learning, and she uses a newfound capacity for reflection and understanding. As she learns to attach sense and meaning to information that she has memorized, she develops

concepts on her own. Then she learns to transfer previous learning experiences and concepts to other situations. From her culture she learns how to think and what to think, and these lessons influence her language development. As she develops her language skills, she learns to communicate through listening, observing, and creating body language, and by speaking, drawing, reading, and writing. Through play, a valuable and important part of learning, she learns on many levels and develops the confidence to explore and learn on her own. The curiosity it takes to discover her unique gifts at her own pace is instinctual to her. With your support, she can realize her potential to be her highest self.

Following are some of the learning methods that I have experienced as a mother and grandmother, as a teacher of children, and as a leader of adults. Understanding the possibilities of discovery and human potential is a fascinating, lifelong study for my children and me.

Sensory Integration

As your baby spontaneously explores and discovers her world, she relies on her sensory receptors and motor activities to gain information from her environment. She takes in information through her senses in her own distinctive way and learns by responding physically, emotionally, and cognitively. Rather than interpreting her senses in isolation, she integrates and organizes the input in her mind. For example, when she eats carrot puree, she simultaneously sees the bright orange color, smells the freshness, tastes the sweetness, feels the texture, and hears your voice as you feed her.

Your baby also has unconscious sensations, called somatosensations, which come from within her body. Three kinds of somatosensation are as follows:

❀ **Tactile**—Your baby has receptors embedded in her skin, which is her largest sensory organ. Her skin protects her body and senses temperature, texture, irritation, affectionate touches, playful touches, and unpleasant sensations.

❀ **Vestibular system**—Attached to your baby's ear canal is her vestibular system. It helps regulate her balance and equilibrium, her level of attention, her muscle tone and coordination, and her emotional state.

❀ **Proprioception**—This internal body awareness helps your baby know where her body parts are when she is not looking at them. Proprioception assists her in identifying individual parts and how they relate to her whole body as she moves through space.

Given these different levels of sensory input, children learn in different ways. One model for learning recognizes visual, auditory, and kinesthetic, or tactile, learning as different sensory strengths: Visual learning associates information with images.

Auditory learning is a preference for learning through listening. Tactile or kinesthetic, learning involves physical activity and doing.

As she grows, your child's preferred learning style may change. An understanding of which style your child prefers helps you communicate with her and help her learn.

A particular sound or touch can evoke different responses from your baby, depending on her situation. If she is rested and fed, music may make her laugh, but if she is tired and hungry, the same song could irritate her. Three attributes of sensory input are intensity, duration, and location:

❀ **Intensity**—When you give her a massage, does she prefer light or heavy pressure?

❀ **Duration**—How long can she sit still and relax?

❀ **Location**—Does she like her back or feet to be rubbed?

These different attributes can vary according to her condition or situation. You can provide a rich environment of experiences to enhance your baby's perception, while being sensitive to the intensity, duration, and location of stimulation that satisfies her needs.

Your baby's focus moves from her own body to the outside world as she grows. First, she focuses on hunger, sleep, and comfort. Then, as her vision develops, she can see outside herself. At this stage, she thinks through her actions. You can support her learning by using physical movement together with music, nursery rhymes, poems, and songs.

Sensory integration lays the groundwork that influences your baby's physical health, emotional growth, and intelligence. It is a foundational type of learning that combines with other methods.

Imitation

Your baby learns indirectly by observing your actions and then mimicking them. At a very young age, she imitates your facial expressions and gestures, and she learns language by copying the words that she hears. These imitations can become lifelong behaviors.

Because she experiences her world with an open and fresh approach, your child does not know how to discern positive and negative actions. Everything that you do in her presence can easily make a lasting impression on her, even after long intervals of absence of the behavior. She may store an image in her memory and then retrieve it when she is in a similar role or situation. For example, as a parent, you may unexpectedly say or do things the way that your mother or father did. Your child most readily does as you do, not as you say. She is always observing you and remembering what she sees and hears.

Parents also unconsciously and unintentionally imitate their babies, which can create a reciprocal game of rapport and mutual imitation that comes naturally. When your baby smiles at you and you smile back, she smiles again. You clap your hands, she claps hers, and then you clap yours again.

Your child also learns from the interaction of her peers and other caretakers. Imitative learning tends to increase when your baby is in a positive, nurturing, familiar environment, when she has received rewards for imitating in the past, and when she is in the presence of an admired authority figure. When your child watches violent behavior, memories of the violent images can influence her to have aggressive thoughts, feelings, and behaviors.

Rahima Baldwin Dancy, author of *You Are Your Child's First Teacher: Encouraging Your Child's Natural Development from Birth to Age Six*, writes about a Waldorf style of understanding child development from birth to three years: "Every action, every sight, sound, or other sense impression, every emotion from those around the child is taken in and absorbed right in the child's inner being. Even when not obviously imitated or reproduced in the child's actions, these impressions become indelibly etched in the child's nervous system and can affect the

development of the whole organism. Young children do not have the buffers and filters that adults have to block out impressions. Indeed, all that babies can do to stop the flow of impressions is to go to sleep" (*Mothering Magazine* 1987). Teachers at Waldorf preschools, which are based on Rudolf Steiner's philosophy of education, try to act in ways that are both worthy of imitation and instructive. Waldorf teachers model behavior and speech that they wish to teach.

Learning through observation is subtle but powerful. Because this method of learning is primarily reactive, it involves lower mental functions. However, when a child decides to go against her role model, she may be either reactive or intentional. If she rejects her parent's behavior and reacts by doing the opposite without thought, then she is using a lower mental function. If she dislikes her parent's behavior and intentionally chooses an alternative, then she is using a higher mental function.

Reinforcement

When your baby cries, your natural response is to offer her some milk, to check her diaper, or to see if she is in pain. If she has a need or receives some kind of uncomfortable external stimulation, she cries. From your consistent response, she learns that when she cries, you will respond to her needs. If you do not respond to her needs, over time, she will stop crying as a way to get your help. Repetition strengthens and reinforces connections in your child's brain. At the same time, connections that she does not use are eventually eliminated. Reinforcement is a way of learning that uses lower mental functions, because it is based on reactivity.

Your baby learns physical actions, movements, and emotional and mental behaviors from repeated feedback. When she receives a reward, such as praise or a treat, she learns to do something. A negative reinforcement, on the other hand, reduces the likelihood that she will repeat the action:

* **Reward**—If your child has a blankie that she uses to comfort herself, and repeated cuddling relaxes her, then she learns to ask for her blankie when she needs to calm down. In this case, she is learning to get pleasure through the reinforcing comfort of her blankie.

* **Negative feedback**—If she touches the stove when it is hot several times, then she soon learns that it does not feel good to her, so she stops putting her hand on the hot stove through the reinforcement of pain.

Your baby stores repeated experiences in her memory. When you read her the same book over and over, she learns and remembers the story. The duration and persistence of stimulation also affect your child's response and learning. If she practices riding her tricycle every day, then she remembers how to ride through repetition. Repetition can bring new levels of understanding because it is not goal-directed, so new discoveries can appear unexpectedly.

Another aspect of learning through reinforcement is association. If you cuddle your child while you are reading to her, then she may associate reading with a warm feeling of being held. I used to read books to Emi and Mari at bedtime in place of nursing them. This warm and cozy time together before going to sleep had an association similar to the closeness of breast-feeding.

When your baby learns through reinforcement, you can see a visible change in her behavior. If she wants a cookie, and you ask her to say "Please" before giving her the cookie, then she is showing you an observable behavior that she has learned.

Learning from repetition can become a conditioned response—that is, an action that your baby does without thinking. When she first learns to eat with a spoon, she focuses her attention on the spoon and the food as she repeats the movement of scooping food into her mouth. After she learns this skill, she can eat with a spoon easily and automatically. Learning through repetition and reinforcement gives your baby physical, emotional, and mental skills and habits that help her function.

Habits that your baby learns may stay with her for life. Food, hygiene, communication, and relationship habits can become automatic and central to her identity. Your child may outgrow the need for certain learned habits, or they may become detrimental over time. Fortunately, she can unlearn or relearn a habit when she receives a different stimulation and response. Your child learns from your actions, words, and ideas until she has an experience that provides the possibility of a different identity.

Adaptation to the Environment

Adaptation is the evolutionary process in which organisms adjust to their environment. When your baby has an experience, she learns by taking in information through her senses in a distinct way and attempts to adapt to her environment. Based on experience and learning, she spontaneously adjusts her behavior. She naturally revises, reshapes, and restructures new knowledge to meet her needs in her environment.

Your baby has a long learning period before maturation to help her adapt to her own environment. She adapts by assimilating and accommodating information to help her survive, and she also adapts to develop resilience and creativity to help her flourish and maximize her potential. Jean Piaget, a Swiss psychologist who developed a theory of children's cognitive development, coined the terms assimilation and accommodation.

Together, he said, these two processes make up adaptation through equilibration:

- Assimilation is the way your child takes in new information and integrates it with her existing knowledge. For instance, she knows how to suck on her mother's breast, and she uses that knowledge to suck the same way when she is given a bottle or a pacifier.

- Accommodation happens when your child takes in new information and adjusts her existing knowledge based on a new way of thinking. If she is given an object and learns to use it in a different way, or if she learns that it should not be sucked, then she changes her thinking. She accommodates her behavior and learns something new.

- Equilibration occurs when your child finds a balance between assimilation and accommodation. When she maintains balance between applying her previous knowledge and changing her behavior to accommodate new knowledge, she can move to her next stage of development. At first she is satisfied with her state of knowledge, but then she becomes dissatisfied as she takes in new knowledge and becomes aware of the weaknesses of her current knowledge. When she blends the old knowledge with the new knowledge, she becomes satisfied with her new mode of thinking and comes to a state of equilibrium.

Because of the nervous system's plasticity, human nature is flexible. Your baby can adapt to a wide variety of environments. Due to this adaptive capability of restructuring and reorganizing, her nervous system has unlimited potential for change and growth. To foster your baby's adaptability and resilience as she develops and learns, you can provide an enriched environment with space to explore and to move safely, high-quality food and water, fresh air, and social interactions. Resilience helps your child overcome difficulties, push her limits, and learn from her mistakes.

Due to her plasticity, your child can develop new approaches and remain open to creation and discovery. In the same way that her brain responds to external stimulation, it can respond to its own response. By questioning her own thoughts and actions and trying to improve, she develops an attitude of innovation and imagination. Creativity can often come from the need to adapt, as the saying goes: "Necessity is the mother of invention." In this case, adaptation moves from reactive to deliberate.

Your child's brain adapts to both positive and negative situations. When she is flexible, cooperative, and accommodating, she can move through the world with ease, because she ends up receiving less resistance from her environment. On the other hand, when your child adapts and complies so much that she foregoes her own will, needs, and passions, she may limit her potential. You can help her find balance between being overly adaptive and overly assertive.

Adaptation is a form of learning that can be reactive or deliberate. Your baby is adaptive when she assimilates and accommodates, which involves lower mental functions. When she adapts by intentionally improving, innovating, and creating, however, she is using her higher mental functions.

Memorization

Memorization is another way that your child learns. Her brain's capacity to hold information is unlimited. She has about 100 billion neurons, each of which has thousands of dendrites. When her brain stores information, it develops new neural pathways and strengthens existing pathways.

Your baby takes in information, stores it, relates the information to existing ideas, and then retrieves it when she needs it. She may learn information in isolated pieces that are kept in different areas of her brain. For instance, she stores the information about the shape, color, smell, and taste of an apple in different parts of her brain. When these areas of her brain are activated, they simultaneously bring together the experiences and thoughts that comprise her existing knowledge about an apple. Repeated firing of the neurons of the associated group increases the chances that they will fire together. When your baby experiences all the attributes of an apple many times, she develops an overall concept of an apple.

As she develops a concept of the apple, she attaches sense and meaning to the apple. That is, she comprehends and understands logically what the apple is, and she files that meaning away. Now she is likely to identify a photo of an apple in a book or to point out an apple in the grocery store. As she connects the apple to significant past experiences, she attaches additional meaning to the apple. For instance, if you are on a picnic in the countryside and your child picks up an apple under a tree and tastes its sweetness, then later she relates an apple to this meaningful past experience. When she understands sense, she can answer the question "What?" When she understands meaning, she can answer the question "Why?" When information has both sense and meaning, the information becomes easier for your child to remember.

Through repetition and reprocessing, your child learns to assign sense and meaning to information. She needs time for this reprocessing in order to retain the information and, ultimately, to learn. When you provide feedback or acknowledge her process, you reinforce and strengthen her learning.

When your child is first learning something through memorization—for example, when using flash cards or singing a song—she may repeat information without being aware of its meaning. Rote memorization can be valuable for certain situations, such as learning the alphabet or counting to 10. However, when the information is filed away in her brain in this way, it must be retrieved through a sequence. Rote learning does not necessarily help her understand information or use it in different situations.

The next step—reviewing and making sense of the information by connecting it to previous knowledge and assigning value and meaning—helps your child understand and use the information in different situations. When she learns the meaning of the words of the lullaby that you sing at bedtime, and when you sing the lullaby every night, then she associates the meaning of the song with going to sleep. She may sing the same lullaby to her doll as she rocks the doll to sleep. In this way, she is acquiring knowledge, using it in various settings, and shifting from the reactive storing of information to deliberate memory.

Rote memorization requires a transfer of information from someone who knows to someone who does not know. It is an approach of instruction, training, and pedagogy that deemphasizes the active role of your child as learner; it emphasizes quantity of information over quality of knowledge. Memorization is a reactive form of learning that uses lower mental functions. When your child attaches sense, meaning, and connections to previous knowledge, she starts using higher mental functions to process memorized information.

Concept Development

As your child begins to actively learn information and assign meaning to it, she can develop her own knowledge by building new ideas and concepts that are based on her current knowledge and past experiences. She can learn more profoundly from her own experience, rather than from listening to a teacher.

Your child's brain gathers information through her senses and then compares it to information that already exists in her brain. She studies similarities and differences to recognize patterns, and then she applies sense and meaning to them. When she transfers factual information to usable knowledge, she can learn with a greater understanding. Then she builds new knowledge based on meaningful patterns, as well as information that she already knows and believes to be true.

Your child develops concepts by organizing information into categories that change chaos to order in her mind. To do this, she needs to learn how to master something in depth. Only then can she understand how a process develops. When she understands information in multiple areas, then she can develop context. From there, she can transfer and organize information from one area to another. Finally, she can use the information to understand logical reasoning, to take action to solve problems, to create something, or to question and improve a situation or behavior. Her brain talks to her brain.

To organize information in a conceptual framework, it helps for your child to "chunk" information into familiar patterns or to use tools to help her remember by creating meaning. She actively looks for patterns in her environment, tests hypotheses, and seeks explanations.

When your child develops a knowledge base and learns to categorize information, she creates clusters, applies significance to those clusters, and links them to prior knowledge so that she can remember and use them in building and developing concepts. As she begins to recognize categories and structures, she can put them together to intentionally create strategies for her own learning. She learns what it means to learn and to organize her learning by planning, observing successes and failures, and correcting mistakes. With a broad range of

Patterns

Patterns are a way to create order from chaos. You can find patterns in nature, such as the Fibonacci sequence (1, 2, 3, 5, 8, 13, and so on), which exists in pineapples, seashells, sunflowers, art, architecture, music, language, thoughts, and behavior.

strategies, she has more flexibility to solve problems in different circumstances. Even though her experiences are limited and her foundation of knowledge may be incomplete, your child has the ability to reason and to solve problems.

This kind of learning involves independently finding and using information rather than memorizing it. Through concept development, your child discovers principles for herself and constructs knowledge by solving realistic problems. Concept development requires more time than memorizing does because it requires more processing, reprocessing, and rethinking. Concept development builds on the other methods of learning and uses higher mental functions, such as being deliberate, solving problems, and thinking strategically.

Transfer of Knowledge

Learning by transfer of knowledge involves activating previously learned background knowledge and applying it to a new situation. When your child uses her knowledge in new ways to solve different challenges, she learns to think creatively, to solve problems, and to use other higher mental processes. The ability to transfer knowledge to a wide variety of situations is central to your child's success in life. Various factors can influence her ability to transfer knowledge.

Past learning can impact new learning negatively or positively.

Impact of Past Learning

Negative Impact

• Past learning is based on rote memorization without significance or meaning

• Past learning has not been repeated enough to be well established

• Past learning has been learned in only one context

• A skill has been learned that interferes with learning the new skill

Positive Impact

• Past learning is based on sense and meaning

• Past learning has been mastered

• Past learning has been learned in multiple contexts

• Many connections and associations are made between past and new learning

• Similar skills tend to transfer from past learning to new learning

• There is an overlap from past learning to new learning

There are two kinds of knowledge transfer: transferring past learning to a present situation and transferring present learning to a future situation. Your child's past learning influences her new learning. When she learns to transfer previously learned information to her everyday life, she can solve problems in practical and meaningful ways. Knowledge transfer involves higher mental functions based on intentional thought processes.

Social Interaction

According to Vygotsky, learning is based on cultural adaptations that are passed through generations. He believed that children are shaped through the tools, language, and actions of their culture, and that their cognitive growth originates in social experiences. Even though babies may learn through the same process all over the world, the substance of what they learn is influenced by their culture.

Culture affects your baby's cognitive development through its influence on her interactions with people and objects, and through tools, symbols, music, art, and language. Values and beliefs vary from culture to culture, and what a child is taught depends on the roles she is expected to play in that society. Children come to understand their function as they learn to handle tasks and problems that their caregivers consider important. Their thinking is influenced more by day-to-day activities than it is by educational settings. Competent adults in their environment teach them both information and problem-solving strategies—how to think and what to think.

Consider the differences between the intellectual tools of children who grow up in hunter-gatherer, agrarian, industrial, and technological societies. In Figi, a small child may learn how to help her father weave reeds to build a basket for fishing; a child in Ghana may learn to tailor clothing or keep a shop in her home; while a child in Turkey may do household chores with his parents.

The process of learning from cultural influences involves social awareness, which requires your child to use higher mental and psychological processes. It also involves the use of language, which itself is highly affected by culture.

Language

Your child has an innate capacity for language, and her brain grows as that capacity develops. Spoken and written language separates humans from other animals. It helps your child communicate her needs, think about and process information, and use her imagination to generate new ideas. Your baby starts learning language as soon as she is born. She listens and takes in what is being said around her, and she understands what she hears before she can talk.

Children in all cultures learn to speak in a similar progression and timetable. Also, in every culture, some children speak more words sooner, while others speak fewer words later. Without formal instruction, your child learns to talk in an organic manner. The brain has an innate mechanism that allows children to learn complex language skills early in life without direct instruction. Noam Chomsky, PhD, an American linguist, says that babies have universal grammar, which is an understanding of the basic properties that apply to all human languages. Children have developmentally sensitive periods after which the opportunity to master language can be missed. Therefore, learning a foreign language is easiest during early childhood. Hideko Yoshida of Dream Window Kindergarten told me that the muscles for speaking a language develop by three years old, and after that age, it is difficult to change those muscles' movements and to learn new sounds.

Your child's first few years are a unique period for language and literacy learning. With your help, your baby first learns to babble, to say single words, to speak in phrases, and to speak in complex sentences. On average, at 18 months old, toddlers learn about 10 words per month, and by two years old, most children can say at least 50 to 100 words. This rate accelerates, and by the time they are six years old, most children have a vocabulary of over 10,000 words. In this short time, your child learns to understand and create sound patterns; to recognize the meanings of many words; and to structure words grammatically through verb tenses, singular and plural noun constructions, and other distinctions. In addition, she learns to put these pieces together to communicate.

For her first two years, your child does not need language in order to solve problems, because her thoughts are associated with sensorimotor movements and object manipulation, rather than with using concepts or words. Between two and three years old, your child's thinking and speech merge when she starts using words to think. At this time, thinking and talking occur simultaneously. As she speaks out loud to herself, her thoughts and understanding get clearer. She also speaks out loud to communicate to others.

Your baby's first experience of expressing language is speaking. Then she learns to think, to draw, to write, and to read. She learns to talk to herself privately, and she learns that she can use it to help regulate her behavior. In the beginning, her private speech is audible yet self-directed. As she matures, she learns to talk to herself silently in an inner dialogue that may be a condensed version of what she would say out loud. This inner conversation becomes an automatic way of thinking with words—for example, "I will put this puzzle piece in here." When she begins to think with words, language becomes a part of her learning process, as well as a skill in itself.

Drawing is a prerequisite to writing because it helps your child confer meaning, label an object, and remember information. When she draws, she is learning the purpose of writing. At first her scribbles are kinesthetic, and as she attaches meaning to those scribbles, her drawing becomes a tool of communication and expression.

One of my favorite activities to do with young children is to make a book with several blank pieces of paper stapled together. The child says a phrase or a sentence, and I write what she says on a blank page. She then draws or scribbles a picture underneath the phrase or sentence. Finally, I read aloud the words that she originally spoke.

When your child tells you a story and you write it down, her words and ideas become more explicit. The process of writing down thoughts forces her to make her ideas more sequential and clear, because only one idea at a time can be written. When she speaks out loud, it is easy to forget her words, but when they are written, you can read them back to her again and again. She can take on the role as "reader," even if she cannot actually read the letters or words.

Throughout her language development, social interaction and the emotional quality of communication influence your child's ability to associate meaning and understanding. You can help her to feel comfortable and safe in expressing herself by responding to her through positive facial expressions, eye contact, and the tone of your voice. Reciprocal conversations with your baby start when she interacts with smiles and coos at three to four months old. Later on, you help your child build her vocabulary and thought processes by engaging her in quality conversations with focused attention on listening, storytelling, singing songs, asking questions, and reading.

Learning through language starts early as a receptive process through hearing, listening, and remembering, and by understanding sounds and learning how to make them playfully. These activities use your child's lower mental functions. As she deliberately imitates sounds and attaches meaning to them thoughtfully and intentionally, she uses her higher mental functions.

Play

Play is an essential part of your child's learning, brain development, and health. All stages of your baby's physical, emotional, and mental development integrate through play. When she is in the sensorimotor developmental stage, she explores with her senses as she touches, watches, listens, moves, imitates, and practices through play. Outdoor play gives her a connection to nature, where she can further explore her senses and develop her naturalist intelligence. She learns to share, to negotiate, and to cooperate by playing with adults and other children.

As she reaches about three years old, your child uses her imagination to try out adult roles in creative play, she learns to concentrate, and she naturally develops her intellect and logical thinking through trial and error while playing. Through pretend play, she can overcome fears by trying out new competencies that lead to confidence and resilience. Your child plays for the simple joy and sake of it. When she plays, she is fully and passionately involved in the present moment.

If children are pushed to learn too much information or to master technical toys before they have a chance to develop their imagination, they have to leave their magical world early and are deprived of the fantasy-filled and creative processes of play. When I was teaching at Dream Window Kindergarten, the classes were divided among three-, four-, and five-year-old children. *Asobi* (play) was their main purpose at the kindergarten, as they engaged in art, music, drama, drawing, storytelling, problem solving, and outdoor activity.

The Lemelson Center at the Smithsonian's National Museum of American History, in partnership with the Science Museum of Minnesota, hosted an exhibit called "Invention at Play," which explored the similarities between children's play and the inventive processes used by inventors and scientists . The exhibit emphasized the following aspects of play:

- **Make-believe**—Pretending helps both children and scientists navigate between the real and imaginary worlds while learning the differences between them. Imagination encourages original thinking, flexibility, adaptability, empathy, and the ability to generate multiple solutions to a problem. Pretend play encourages people to think visually and spatially and to capture and express ideas.

- **Problem solving**—The process of changing or manipulating patterns can generate new ideas. Playing with puzzles and games helps people recognize and understand categories and associations. This helps them to find new patterns and to break out of old ones in order to solve problems.

- **Exploration**—Experimenting with materials and pushing limits encourage people to find multiple ways of creating results.

- **Collaboration**—Social play teaches people how to share, to communicate, and to collaborate. Discussing ideas with others can enhance creative abilities and provide options when solving problems.

Through play, inventors develop persistence, curiosity, imagination, communication, and problem solving—all of which are essential items in their tool kit. As part of the exhibit, the Lemelson Center posed an important question: if the quality and quantity of play are changing so that children have less time for unstructured play, how will that influence future inventions?

In a hurried and pressured lifestyle, free play may get lost. Unstructured play provides the opportunity for your child to engage in curiosity and wonder. Through self-driven play, she actively participates in initiating and organizing her own play activities. This allows her to move at her own pace, to develop her ability to make decisions, and to discover her own interests and passions. When you join her in child-driven play, you have the opportunity to see the world from her perspective, which helps you to understand her needs better and to communicate with her more effectively.

Indoors, her imagination can flourish with pretend play and creative projects, while outdoor play means fresh air, sunshine, exercise, reflection, and conversation. The relaxed nature of unstructured play provides a balance to the tension of structures and routines. Your role, as a parent, is to provide a safe environment that is rich in resources, while encouraging your child's opportunity for natural learning.

Play engages all kinds of learning and involves both lower and higher mental functions. I named my company "i play." because play is fundamental to children's healthy growth and development. I believe that when children play, they find their natural state of essence, a state of presence in which doing and being merge.

Passion, Purpose, and Potential

Your child is unique in her strengths, weaknesses, aptitudes that inspire her, and gifts that she has to contribute to the world. She has unique talents that satisfy her and help her find meaning and purpose in her life. The most exciting method of learning incorporates all methods and involves helping your child find her own sense of purpose that helps her maximize her potential in the world. Purpose is an intention to achieve something or to be someone who makes a difference in the world in a way that is meaningful to you. A sense of purpose is essential to happiness. It can also give your child the energy and strength to overcome obstacles.

When you help your child tap into her passions and develop her gifts and talents, you help her find her natural motivation to learn. When she connects to her essence, she gets knowledge simply from being. She can probably find this internal motivating energy by engaging in something that she can do well—often something that contributes to others, as well. As American theologian, Frederick Beuchner, author of *Wishful Thinking: A Seeker's ABC*, says, "The place God calls you to is the place where your deep gladness and the world's deep hunger meet."

What does your child do well? What does she love? What lights her up and sparks her natural curiosity? Does she get excited about nature, music, or playing with puzzles? While recognizing and supporting her weaknesses, you can also reinforce her natural abilities to help her find her unique intelligences and pursue her dreams.

Mihaly Csikszentmihalyi, PhD, author of *Flow: The Psychology of Optimal Experience*, developed a theory of optimal experience based on the concept of flow—"the state in which people are so involved in an activity that nothing else seems to matter; the experience is so enjoyable that people will do it even at a great cost, for the sheer sake of doing it." You know when your child is in a state of flow when she becomes so absorbed and engaged in what she is doing that she is unaware of anything else.

You can support your child in being self-directed as she finds her purpose, will, and passion. You can help spark her curiosity by exposing her to a range of experiences—books, music, art supplies, outdoor excursions, and simple toys that inspire imagination. When you build a close relationship with your child that shows you believe in her, she will be confident and open to your support and influence. Pay attention to her special interests and talents, and take notice of activities that she dislikes or abandons. Encourage and challenge her to develop her skills (such as building with blocks or telling stories), and acknowledge her character traits (such as courage, kindness, and a good sense of humor). When she is involved in choosing her interests, she will be more motivated and persistent in developing her passion and potential. The process of learning through finding purpose, passion, and potential uses your child's highest mental functions.

Essential Skills for Whole Learning

WHILE SHE IS YOUNG and dependent, you are responsible for keeping your baby safe, fed, sheltered, and loved. It is also up to you to give her opportunities to develop her mind. You can create an environment for her to learn and grow by integrating the daily practices that support her mental health in the first section of this chapter. She gains the nourishment she needs to think and learn through healthy foods, sleep, experiences that stimulate her brain, and her secure attachment to you.

You can put this chapter's information about brain development, foundations for learning, and learning methods into practice by fostering the essential skills for whole learning. You provide support for her to learn when you recognize your role as her teacher or guide. The conditions, toys, and materials that surround her as she learns also contribute to her learning process.

As your baby demonstrates particular interests and abilities, her learning patterns and pathways take shape and act as natural motivators. Listed here are pathways that you can use to help support your child's whole learning process. Understanding these pathways and preferences can help you and her future caregivers and teachers to encourage her throughout her education. Your baby's ability to learn and to become competent is key to creating a full and meaningful life and developing her potential.

Support for Learning

As a parent, you play an important role in helping your child develop the essential skills of learning. You are her model and teacher, and you create and choose the environment in which she learns. In her first years, you present her with experiences that enhance her mental tools for learning. Finally, you provide her with resources and materials to expand her knowledge, encourage her imagination, challenge her brain, and prompt her to take her thought processes to the next developmental level.

Parents and Teachers

Learning is often described as the process of an expert or teacher imparting knowledge to a student. However, real and effective learning occurs best through social interaction—an active exchange between individuals. As her parent, you help form your baby's first relationship. Through exchange and imitation, she learns how to navigate the world. Later, as she develops relationships and interacts with friends, caregivers, and teachers, she learns from them as well.

It may be helpful to think of yourself as your baby's guide rather than as her teacher. When you follow your baby's interests to determine her daily activities and encourage her by asking questions, you can help her develop her enthusiasm for learning. In *Pathways to Competence*, Sarah Landy states, "Effective learning takes place when caregivers build on children's natural curiosity and interest and their inborn passion for learning and discovery." While your child is young, learning occurs best through play. Formal curricula or forced programming in the first years of life can disrupt a child's natural development and hinder more complex learning later on.

Children are self-motivated and self-directed to know and to learn. They need freedom and space to explore and to discover, but they also need structure and support from an adult. Your child needs balance between autonomy to discover on her own and direction and support from you to keep her on track while adapting to her changing needs. You can provide structure by

helping her make connections between new situations and familiar ones. You support your baby's learning by understanding where she is developmentally, meeting her there, and then introducing the experiences she needs to take her to the next developmental level—what Vygotsky called the zone of proximal development.

As your child's guide, your observation of her developmental stage and interests, your engagement in her work, and your feedback are key to her continued progress. If you enthusiastically share her interest and curiosity, your delight encourages her to continue to explore and to learn more. According to Sousa in *How the Brain Learns*, "When students get prompt, specific, and corrective feedback on the results of their thinking, they are more likely to continue processing, making corrections and persist until successful completion." In other words, if you respond to your child's intellectual development, she will learn more effectively and enthusiastically.

Learning is a reciprocal process; your child is your teacher, as well. As you share learning experiences, her brain processes information in its own unique way. When you see her point of view, you can learn something new, too.

Conditions

Before Emi was born, while I was living in Japan, I watched a mother change her baby's diaper one day. As she changed the diaper, I was deeply impressed by her approach. Every move she made considered her baby's point of view. She used cloth diapers because she said they felt good next to her baby's skin, and she folded the diaper so that there were no rough spots to rub against her baby's bottom. She was thinking of how her baby's bottom felt. Even when using cloth diapers, I had always prioritized quickness, sometimes leaving my baby's bottom with a rumpled diaper. I have remembered this incident many times in my parenting and also in developing products for my business.

Optimal conditions that support your child's learning begin with thinking from her point of view. How does she feel internally and externally? What environmental conditions help her learn best? The quality of your child's learning environment influences her learning experiences. She will likely thrive in surroundings that are orderly, clean, and considerate of her unique needs. Does she learn best with background noise or in peace and quiet? Does she respond best to bright or low-intensity light? Is she happier in a warm temperature or a cool one?

What are your child's preferences for her body? Does she learn best when sitting, lying down, or moving? Does she do better on an empty or a full stomach? How does she respond to sleep or lack thereof? Does she learn best early in the morning or later in the day? How does she react to stress? What is her current developmental stage?

When you pay attention to your baby's needs and provide her with optimal conditions that meet her needs both inside and out, you help her create a smooth path to take in experiences and to process them. You can create optimal internal learning conditions by making sure your baby is:

- ❁ **Healthy**—When your child is sick, her attention and energy become focused on bringing her body back into balance, not on learning. Take care that she is well nourished with healthy foods, movement and exercise, fresh air, stimulation through touch, daily hygiene, and care for her wellness.

- ❁ **Secure**—If your baby is anxious or stressed, her energy and thoughts become directed toward getting her needs met rather than exploring the world around her. If she feels secure, she will be comfortable enough to direct her attention outward. Through freedom and exploration, she gains experience that cultivates her self-esteem and self-regulation and prompts her to continue learning as her knowledge base expands.

- ❁ **Well-rested**—Research shows that sleep is a basic component of processing memory—and thus a key foundation for learning. According to Sousa in *How The Brain Learns*, "Encoding information into long-term memory sites occurs during sleep, during REM (rapid eye movement). During sleep, your baby's brain reviews and stores experiences of the day into her memory."

You can create optimal external conditions for learning by making sure your baby's environment includes the following:

🌸 **Calm and positive energy**—Distractions and distress interrupt your baby's learning process. An environment that is messy, filled with tension, or unusually loud will probably affect her learning negatively. In a calm and positive environment, your baby's mind is free to focus.

🌸 **Rhythm and balance**—A day filled with routines and a regular tempo helps your child feel secure. An optimal daily rhythm includes a balance and flow of focused time for thinking, outdoor time for movement and fresh air, and quiet time for resting.

🌸 **Play space**—As your child goes through different developmental stages, her needs change. A comfortable space that is safe, orderly, and suited to her needs encourages her exploration and participation. You can set up a corner of a room with a rug, cushions, a small table and chairs, toy bins, and shelves. She may enjoy space for a workbench, an art area, a kitchen, costumes, or dolls. Here she can store her toys, draw, build, and host imaginary events. You can help her maintain order by setting up shelves and baskets with photographic labels for storing toys and supplies. A roll-out mat can help define her play space.

🌸 **Novel experiences**—Variety stimulates your child's brain. Try serving her different vegetables, such as parsnips or brussels sprouts, or check out different books from the library. New experiences keep her brain active.

🌸 **Experiences that offer participation**—Your child learns best by actively participating and engaging in experiences, rather than passively viewing media. In addition to playing with her, you can involve her with your day-to-day activities, such as cooking, cleaning, shopping, and gardening.

🌸 **Unstructured time**—Albert Einstein said, "Imagination is more important than knowledge. For knowledge is limited to all we know and understand, while imagination embraces the entire world, and all there ever will be to know and understand." Babies and toddlers are fascinated and creative when they have free time to explore on their own. When your child has regular unstructured time, she can dream and discover her own imagination.

You can create optimal learning conditions for your child by cultivating your awareness and turning daily activities into learning opportunities—for instance, measuring ingredients for cooking, sorting laundry by color, and counting the stepping-stones to the mailbox. Hugs, humor, and encouragement add warm feelings and fond memories to your child's everyday learning opportunities.

Gender Balance

Be mindful of gender differences. In her book *Pink Brain, Blue Brain*, neuroscientist Lise Eliot, PhD, states that there are slight differences between a newborn girl's brain and a newborn boy's brain. However, because experiences form the brain's architecture, the differences between an adult woman's brain and a man's brain are much greater. Eliot reports, "Studies of gifted teenagers confirm that intelligence and academic excellence are associated more with cross-gender abilities and less with stereotypical gender roles."

Your baby's brain is most malleable and open to experience in her first few years, as its architecture is being built. Talk, listen, and read to your toddler boy. Physically challenge your baby girl to learn to throw a ball, to build with blocks, and to put together puzzles. The goal is not to erase gender differences completely but to make sure that you give both boys and girls the opportunity to develop a wide range of tools and skills for learning.

Tools

In addition to your guidance and positive internal and external conditions, your baby needs tools to assist her learning. Some of those tools are internal, and some are external. You can engage your child in activities to help her develop these internal mental tools. In addition, external tools, such as simple toys and other items for play, support, encourage, and enrich your child's learning and mental development.

In *Tools of the Mind*, authors Bodrova and Leong write that through his research, Vygotsky concluded that "similar to the way physical tools extend a person's physical abilities by acting as extensions of the body, mental tools expand mental capabilities by acting as extensions of the mind." When your baby is born, she uses lower mental functions that are instinctive and reactive. As she matures, she uses her higher mental functions to act deliberately. The ability to act thoughtfully and purposely requires tools of the mind, such as deliberate memory, focus, logic, symbolic thinking, and language. With these tools, your child can read, write, consider the past, plan for the future, strategize, cooperate, and think abstractly and creatively. By honing these tools, she can take information processing and problem solving into new realms.

Your baby's mental tools are further enhanced and developed through play and enriching activities. As the tools of her mind expand her mental capabilities, the tools of play—toys—expand the effectiveness of her play.

In selecting toys for your child, consider the following:

- **Safety**—With small children, take care that toys do not present a choking hazard. In general, if a toy can fit through a toilet-paper roll, it is too small for a child under the age of three. Be aware of small buttons, magnets, and breakable items. Remove strings, ribbons, or cords over 12 inches long from a baby's environment. Avoid screen toys for children under two years old and battery-operated toys for children under eight. Supervise your child when she is playing on a riding toy, and make sure that she is wearing a helmet.

- **Natural materials**—Toys that are made of natural and nontoxic materials have less risk of containing harmful substances such as lead, PVC, and BPA. When possible, choose toys made of safe plastics, bioplastics, silicone, stainless steel, organic cotton, wool, or wood. Avoid added finishes such as formaldehyde.

- **Simplicity and open-endedness**—Less is more when it comes to toys. Learning is an active process, and toys that are open-ended and simple in form engage your child's imagination. Toys that can be used for a variety of purposes include boxes, blocks, building sets, and stacking cups. Toys that inspire imaginary role-playing are push toys, tool belts, kitchen sets, playhouses, and costumes. Screen toys, computer games, and television do not challenge your child's imagination.

- **Familiarity**—Boxes that toys come in often interest children more than the toy does. Household items such as funnels, sifters, wooden spoons, metal bowls, pots and pans, water hoses, garden tools, pieces of cloth, cornmeal, homemade play dough, and beans in a snack cup can provide hours of play, fun, and mental stimulation.

- **Size- and age-appropriateness**—Tools and toys that match your child's developmental stage and age are easier for her to use. Some examples are gardening tools (shovel, rake, watering can), kitchen tools (bowls, spoons, table, chairs, play stove, play refrigerator), and home tools (hammer, brushes, brooms).

- **Versatility for different stages**—Some toys grow with your child through many developmental levels. Simple, open-ended toys tend to interest and stimulate your child at different ages. For instance, a two-year-old may be interested in knocking over a pile of blocks, while a four-year-old uses the same blocks to build a tower. At each age, the blocks meet your child at her current developmental level and help her begin working on her next level.

You can teach your child everyday life skills by encouraging her to take care of toys, to keep them neat and orderly, and to clean up after playing. To keep her from getting bored and tired of her toys, you can periodically rotate them. For fun, arrange her toys in order or set a stage or activity to stimulate her play experiences.

The following considerations, activities, and toys help your child learn:

Sensory—Give her a variety of textures to touch: soft and cuddly, crinkly, firm but not hard, and so on. For visual stimulation, look for harmonious and appealing colors and designs. For auditory stimulation, seek the soft sounds of bells and rattles rather than loud and overstimulating electronic noises. For her sense of smell, choose natural instead of artificial scents. To stimulate taste, look for safe materials that will not repel her when she puts them in her mouth.

Movement—Create a safe space that has boundaries, and then allow your baby to move freely; do not restrict or limit her natural movements with bouncers, rockers, or walkers. Riding toys, play gyms, and balls inspire active movement; yoga, swimming, running, crawling, dancing, and jumping encourage gross-motor coordination and spatial awareness; drawing, playing musical instruments, origami, puzzles, buttons, zippers, and eating with utensils build fine-motor skills.

Interactive—Tell stories with plush toys or puppets. Mirrors and photo albums prompt interaction with herself and others. Games and songs encourage social interaction.

Communication—Talk, read, and sing to your child. Books, art, interactive games, and conversation encourage language development. Speak to her or play music in a second language.

Cognitive—Give your child problems to solve. Stacking and sorting toys, puzzles, and board games engage your child and stimulate her memory, ability to focus, concept development, logic and reasoning, mathematical ability, and other mental functions.

Creative—Inspire your child's imagination. Art supplies (crayons, chalk, markers, paper, glue, and clay), musical instruments, music recordings, dress-up clothes, and costumes give her the opportunity to express her imagination.

Naturalist—Explore a sense of natural wonder with your child. Sticks, shells, rocks, leaves, grass, pinecones, sand, water, flowers, and garden vegetables are some of nature's toys that stimulate her senses and imagination.

As a parent, you can nurture your child's natural development by taking a role as her teacher and guide, creating an environment with optimal learning conditions, providing her with internal and external tools, and encouraging stimulating activities that help her realize her full potential.

 To learn more about child safety visit growhealthygrowhappy.com

Pathways of Whole Learning

Your baby starts life with an innate curiosity that serves as a primary force for her to explore the world, to seek new experiences, and to learn. As your child is exposed to different experiences, her brain makes neural connections and forms pathways of learning. Repetition of experiences reinforces these developing pathways so that they become stronger and wired together, and thus create a foundation for her lifelong learning.

As her parent, you can observe your child's natural stages of development while providing varied and stimulating experiences that support her as she matures. In addition, you can enhance your child's learning through personal contact and connection just by being present with her.

As a way of understanding your child's natural learning patterns, and to guide her in all aspects of learning, I have identified seven basic pathways for whole learning that provide your baby with seven different kinds of learning experiences. When you intentionally offer stimulation and experiences in all seven pathways, you give her the opportunity to develop in a whole, balanced, and integrated way.

Even though she may have strengths in certain pathways, your child benefits most by using all seven. Creating these experiences does not have to be complicated, expensive, or time-consuming. When you are aware of the pathways, you can use them as tools in the course of your daily activities. To reinforce your baby's sensory pathway, simply take a moment to point out the smell of the bread at the bakery, the taste of an apple, or the color of flowers. To stimulate her movement pathway, wiggle her toes while holding her in your lap, or make sure that she has some time to move her body every day.

The pathways are easy to categorize, to remember, and to use. The basic building blocks are physical, emotional, and mental development. Your baby develops physically through her sensory and movement skills. She develops emotionally by interacting with herself and others and by expressing herself through communication. Mentally, she learns by developing her cognitive and creative skills. Exploring nature integrates all three of the building blocks—physical, emotional, and mental—to develop your whole child. Your baby learns naturally in the course of biological maturation, but she needs your love and guidance to intentionally provide experiences for her to maximize her learning potential.

Pathways of Whole Learning

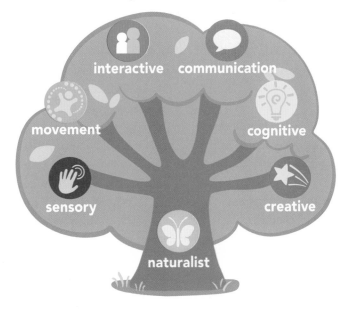

The pathways are not isolated or distinct. They overlap; they are interdependent; they work together and complement each other. For example, your baby's sensory and motor skills are integrated; they develop simultaneously while reinforcing each other. When your baby sees a toy on the floor and picks it up with her hand, she uses hand-eye coordination—a combination of visual and movement skills.

Through her stages of development, you will notice that your baby focuses on specific areas at different ages. For example, in her first year she concentrates on sensory and motor development. During her second year, her language and cognitive skills grow at a faster rate. In her third year, she develops more sophisticated creative skills and refines her existing skills in other areas. Throughout her first three years she develops increasingly higher levels of social skills. She also uses the naturalist pathway during these years, integrated with all the other six pathways.

Your child's development follows a biological course that is chronological and sequential: she naturally rolls over, crawls, and walks in predictable stages. However, even though her natural process of development may be similar to that of all babies, she also has her own individual progression that follows a wavy line with ups and downs. She may have one area of development that seems to lag, while another area accelerates. Then she may hit an explosion of unexpected growth in the pathway that seemed to be developing more slowly. When you accept your child's unique self and recognize her level of development, you can be less concerned about stages of slow growth, and you can support her optimal learning potential by helping her grow to her next level.

Your baby may have unique gifts with a tendency to have a preference to use certain paths. You can help her by recognizing and nurturing those gifts and by using her preferred learning pathways. You can provide experiences for other ways of learning to help her balance and integrate other paths. For example, she may excel at cognitive skills, such as problem solving and building with blocks. By offering large building blocks and bigger toys, you give her the chance to play in ways that she enjoys while developing her motor

and sensory skills. My grandson, Zo, is very physical. By capitalizing on his enthusiasm for movement, Mari, his mother, guides him to learn through the other pathways. For instance, she gives him chances to interact with his friends through physical play in order to help him develop his social skills.

To study the qualities of a home environment that support young children's learning, Robert Bradley and Bettye Caldwell developed the Home Observation for Measurement of the Environment (HOME) inventory. The results of their study showed that children whose home environments were rated as conducive to mental development scored higher on achievement and school-readiness tests. In their study, they evaluated homes according to the criteria of providing developmental toys and a variety of stimuli, encouraging language development through books and games, showing warmth and affection, maintaining an orderly environment, and avoiding violence. This study affirms for me that a variety of experiences, combined with the support of a loving caretaker, can optimize a child's learning.

Development of all the pathways strengthens your baby's foundation and broadens her potential for learning. As you become familiar with these pathways, you can get creative and discover your own ways of incorporating them into your baby's daily routine.

Sensory Pathway

Learning through her senses is a foundational part of all ways that your baby learns. She receives stimulation from the environment through her sensory systems. These systems start developing through stimulation when she is in utero. Sensory information reaches your baby through tactile interactions, visual stimulation, auditory experiences, her sense of smell, and exploration of taste and touch with her mouth.

As a parent, you can help your baby develop her sensory pathways by exposing her to a variety of experiences that use her senses. Smell the pungency of herbs, try the sour taste of yogurt, feel the roughness of a piece of wood, listen to a bird chirp, or gaze at the blue sky. As she learns, she may develop a preference for different sensory learning styles—for example, tactile and kinesthetic, visual, or auditory.

Touch

One of your baby's earliest senses is touch. As an embryo, she can sense touch with her nose, lips, and the surface of her skin. Through development, she may remember different early tactile sensations—the comfort of her mother's kiss or the tickle of her father's beard.

As your baby grows, her tactile skills increase. She develops her sensitivity to temperature. To protect and defend herself from too much stimulation, she may withdraw from touch that feels overbearing to her. Her sense of touch is also tied in with her visual and kinesthetic development. If she touches an object and looks at it, or if she touches an object and moves an area of her body at the same time, her pathways coordinate the different stimuli.

You can help your baby develop her sensory pathway of touch by offering her multiple repetitive experiences. Be aware of her clothing and how its textures feel next to her skin. Baby wearing, skin-to-skin contact, massage, bath time, soft plush toys, and blankets are tools for tactile stimulation. Give her chances to play with mud, dirt, and sand in places where she can be free to explore different sensations and textures. Offer her food with different textures. As she develops this pathway, she will build an expectation of tactile sensations from her past experiences.

Vision

Vision is the most complex sensory system and the least mature one at birth. Your baby's eyes, her ability to move her head and body, and her brain work together to coordinate her ability to see. When she is born, her vision is blurry and unfocused. In her first year, she continues to develop color perception, visual acuity, the ability to focus and distinguish patterns, depth perception, binocular vision, and the ability to watch and follow movement.

You can help your baby develop her sensory pathway of vision by providing a variety of things for her to look at. As a newborn, she particularly enjoys and responds to faces—especially your face when you talk to her with expression and movement. In her early months, she responds to mobiles, hanging items for her to grasp, and objects in motion. Offer toys in bright colors and pictures or photos in her crib or on the wall of her nursery. You can help her recognize different visual images by changing her environment: take a walk to the park or a ride in the car.

Hearing

In addition to developing her senses of touch and vision, your baby develops her ability to hear while she is in the womb. By the time she is one year old, she can hear, remember, discriminate, and respond to different sounds at the same level as an adult. Her sense of hearing is sensitive to loud noises, which may startle her. She alerts and responds when you speak to her in a high-pitched voice, she finds low-pitched voices soothing and often calms to these.

You can help your baby develop her auditory sensory pathway by being sensitive to the level of sound with which she is comfortable. Offer her sounds that are appealing and stimulating without being too loud or overstimulating. Talk, sing, and read to your baby. Shake rattles and play musical instruments, and play your favorite songs while dancing and bouncing her to the music. Point out different sounds in her environment, repeat the sounds, and invite her to repeat them.

Smell

Your baby's sense of smell is linked most directly to her brain. The molecular structure of different substances makes up a scent or smell. The smell stimulates your baby's smell receptors, which send signals to her brain. Her olfactory system then brings up memories that activate her brain. Just as the smell of the ocean may bring up past beach experiences for you, your baby remembers her past feelings of comfort when she nurses and smells your milk and your skin. In studies where a baby was presented with five different cloths infused with the milk of five different mothers, the baby recognized her own mother's scent.

Your baby's sense of smell is there to protect her. Unpleasant smells, like the scent of a skunk or raw sewage, repel her. Likewise, the smells of smoke, gas, rotten eggs, or spoiled fish can protect her by stimulating her to avoid them.

You can help your baby develop her sensory pathway of smell by being aware of the scents in her environment and providing appealing ones—fresh flowers, essential oils, cooking aromas, and scents in nature. Chemical perfumes and artificial fragrances are made by putting molecules together to reproduce smells; they do not elicit a natural sensation. Artificial synthetic smells can be harmful to your baby's sensitive nose, so it is most effective to use natural scents in her environment to evoke her sense of smell.

Taste

Before she is born, your baby starts developing her sense of taste, which may affect her food preferences later. If you are breast-feeding, she can taste the foods you eat through your milk, and she can taste the difference between your milk and formula. Even though taste and smell are separate senses with their own receptor organs, these two sensory systems are connected. Taste tells her whether a food is sweet, salty, sour, bitter, pungent, or umami (savory). Smells influence your baby's perception of taste.

Your baby also explores her senses of taste and smell through her sense of touch as she feels different textures and temperature of foods and other objects that she puts in her mouth. You can help your baby develop her sensory pathway of taste by offering her a variety of foods with different tastes. Her taste receptors send messages to her brain to stimulate and develop this pathway, and she learns from a broad experience of tastes.

Movement Pathway

Movement is closely interrelated with your baby's sensory development. In fact, movement has been called the sixth sense. Before she could move, she was dependent on adults for her location, but with the possibility of movement, she can purposefully impact her environment. For instance, once she can move, she can come closer to you, which increases her sense of security and promotes interaction for learning. Your baby's movement is also related to her cognitive processes. Body movements send messages that stimulate her brain, and when she has ideas, she connects them to her body by putting them into motion. She experiments by testing cause and effect when she drops something on the floor for you to pick up over and over again.

As she learns to crawl and walk, she gains the mobility to exercise her curiosity, to explore, and to learn. Movement is also related to her other ways of learning: when she rolls a ball to you in the backyard, she may use her sensory, interactive, communication, naturalist, cognitive, and creative pathways, in addition to her motor pathway.

Motor memories create a foundation for other skills by making strong pathways through repetition. Your child can then generalize these skills and transfer them in order to learn other skills. You can help her to build her gross-motor skills, fine-motor skills, and spatial awareness in her body by encouraging her to engage in fun physical activities.

Gross motor

Gross-motor control refers to your baby's ability to move her large muscles purposefully and proficiently with whole body movement. Examples of gross-motor skills include rolling over, crawling, sitting, standing, walking, running, jumping, skipping, and riding a tricycle or bicycle. She develops control of the larger muscles in her body from head to toe, starting with her head and moving to her torso, legs, and feet. Aligned posture, strength, balance, and a sense of weight bearing give your baby control of her large muscles. Gross-motor and fine-motor skills develop together, and one type influences the other. Related to movement is your baby's vestibular system, which is responsible for balance via her inner ear. Her vestibular system is vital for her posture and her sense of position in space and motion.

You can help your baby develop her movement pathway of gross-motor skills by being an active role model and encouraging her to move. You can help her stimulate her vestibular system to develop her balance by rocking, swinging, and swaying together. For other kinds of gross-motor development, get down on the floor with your baby and let her lead the way during tummy time. Give her massages, practice yoga or movement exercises, and create a safe space for her to explore on her own. Give her a bat to hit a ball on the ground so that she can feel an extension of herself through action. Take her on excursions to the pool, to the park, and to the woods.

Fine motor

Fine-motor skills involve coordinating small muscle movements of your baby's fingers, hands, wrists, toes, feet, tongue and other interior mouth structures, lips,

and facial features. She develops this type of dexterity by picking up small objects with her thumb and pointer finger, holding a spoon or other utensil, drawing with a crayon, putting a puzzle together, doing origami, using scissors, or playing a musical instrument. She develops her fine-motor skills in coordination with her gross-motor skills.

You can help your baby develop her sensory pathway of fine-motor skills by massaging her fingers, toes, hands, and feet. Give her finger food, and show her how to feed herself. She can learn from moving small pieces of cereal from one cup to another. Let her hold the book at story time, provide her art supplies to use, help her draw, show her how to play a xylophone, and teach her to use chopsticks.

Spatial awareness

Spatial awareness is your baby's ability to recognize where she is in space and to understand the relationships of the locations of different objects to herself or to each other. When she first develops her sensory and motor skills, she may interpret the world as a set of sensations that accompany actions. As she develops object permanence, she begins to understand that an object is a separate entity that does not disappear when it is not in her sight. Awareness of herself as separate from others is an essential part of your baby's spatial development.

When your baby learns to sit up and she has a clearer view of her surroundings, her spatial awareness changes dramatically. Crawling and walking also give her a different perspective and an ability to integrate different scenes in her environment.

Your baby's vision is directly related to her sense of spatial awareness. Before she develops depth perception, she is not afraid of a vertical drop. However, once she can crawl and begins to connect her own actions to visual events, she learns to recognize the danger of a vertical drop. When she can move voluntarily, she can understand how the locations of objects change as she moves.

Proprioception is your baby's ability to sense movement and to know where her body is in space without looking at it. A physical feeling of deep pressure can help her focus and calm down if she is overstimulated or excited. To help your baby be still, press your hand on her back or belly firmly. For her first few months, swaddling provides pressure that helps her settle down and sleep; at any age, you can give her a massage or hold her close. When your baby is a toddler, a big bear hug can help her calm down and relax.

Your baby learns motor skills by moving on her own and by watching and imitating you. You can help her develop her sensory pathway of spatial awareness in the following ways:

- Make a defined play space for her. This will give her a sense of place.
- Give her a box to crawl into and steps or a ladder to crawl on to help her develop balance and body awareness.
- Make connections between her eyes and movements by playing games that help her with hand-eye coordination and foot-eye connection. For example, have her make the motions of pat-a-cake with her hands or feet.
- Point out the direction, distance, and location of objects to help her recognize where they are in her environment and how they are related to her and to each other.
- Give her directions to move different parts of her body or to pick up objects.

Interactive Pathway

One of the primary ways that your baby learns is through interaction with herself and with others. As her sense of self emerges, she learns intrapersonal skills and develops her emotional intelligence. She becomes aware of herself, acquires confidence, learns to regulate her emotions and to be intentional, and connects with the spiritual world. She develops her social intelligence by learning to get along with others through interpersonal skills such as empathy, compassion, and cooperation, and by developing strong character and values. These intra- and interpersonal skills are another foundation for your child's social development.

Your baby's relationships with her parents, caretakers, and family members in her first few years create her attachment style. This is the foundation of her abilities to know herself and to work with others. These abilities prepare her to listen, to learn, and to focus in order to optimize her potential. You can help your baby develop her interactive pathway by exposing her to experiences that stimulate her self-understanding and her understanding of others, as well as experiences that help her learn to integrate her personal growth and her relationships with others.

Self

The pathway for your child to develop her sense of self requires understanding and supporting herself. When your baby becomes aware that she has a separate body and mind that is distinct from those of others, she begins to recognize that she is a unique individual. As she further develops her understanding of object permanence, she begins to recognize herself, which helps her form her self-identity. She begins to identify with her body and with her actions when they produce an effect. She is also aware of her gender. As she gets older, she can learn to discriminate her emotions as a way to direct her behavior and to develop her autonomy. These discoveries lay the foundation for her self-esteem, confidence, spirit, and will, as she learns to reflect and to act intentionally. This pathway of self-understanding needs the support of observant parents who can affirm her self-discoveries.

You can help your child develop a sense of herself by giving her a chance to see her reflection in a mirror, talking to her directly so that she sees your face and your smile, calling her name, pointing to her, and showing her photos of herself. Encourage her to become aware of her body by massaging and exploring her fingers, toes, eyes, ears, nose, and other areas. Be attentive to your baby by responding to her needs and actions and by acknowledging her accomplishments. Set limits that are clear, consistent, and fair. Let your child do things for herself and complete simple chores so that she feels valuable and competent.

Others

The pathway to interact with others requires understanding and working with others. Your child learns through relationships with parents, caretakers, siblings, family members, and friends. In her first few months, she can distinguish between different faces and voices. When she is around other people, she watches and imitates their actions as she learns to interact with others. Because she does not have a clear boundary between herself and the outside world, she sees everyone as an extension of herself.

For her first two to three years, your child may not understand how to share, compromise, or negotiate with other children. However, she can still learn social skills by regularly interacting with others. In order to interact successfully, your child must be able to understand her own emotions and to express them appropriately. She also needs to know how to read and respond to social cues. You can help your child develop her sense of others by arranging times and a variety of experiences for interaction. In her early months, she does not have a clear boundary between herself and the outside world. She sees everything as an extension of herself. Later, she can distinguish between different faces and voices. When she is around other children or adults, she watches and imitates their actions as she learns how to interact with others.

When you set up play dates with other children, prepare activities that can be played side by side in a way that promotes peace and discourages conflict. Use dolls and puppets to role-play feelings and interactions. Reflect your child's feelings back to her, and discuss her emotions. Model the act of showing respect and compassion for others. Offer opportunities for your child to be in diverse contexts so that she will learn and appreciate the perspectives of other races and cultures.

Communication Pathway

Your baby's communication skills develop rapidly during her first few years of life. Her language skills progress as she learns the nuances of body language, listening, and talking. Her abilities to draw, to write, and to read are also emerging at this time. During her first three years, your child is able to learn another language as a native speaker with more ease than if she studies that language in school later on.

Your baby learns from her environment and culture by imitating and repeating your words. One theory of language development proposes that the human brain is innately wired to learn a universal language. Your child is naturally ready to learn language quickly and without instruction on rules and grammar. When you stimulate your baby's natural instincts, you can support her in optimizing her language development.

All languages have representations and symbols that young children identify, remember, and categorize. When your baby organizes and categorizes these images in her mind, she lays the groundwork for language, as well as for other aspects of cognitive development. For example, playing with toys and puzzles that involve sorting and stacking helps her develop building blocks for thinking and communication.

Language has a powerful influence on your child's development in many areas. The ability to communicate influences her interactive and imaginative skills; language affects her cognitive processes and gives her opportunities for many types of success; and her sense of self, identity, culture, and place in the world are linked to her ability to communicate.

You can help your child develop her communication skills by recognizing her developmental stages and being aware that she is developing language skills starting at birth. Communicate with your baby by being present, listening, reading, and responding to her cries and other cues. Communication is a two-way street; reciprocity is a critical part of the process.

Body language

Before your child has words, her main way of relating with you is nonverbal communication through her body. She makes facial expressions and eye movements, wrinkles her nose, covers her eyes, turns away, kicks, pulls her legs up, and arches her back. Your baby uses body language to tell you that she is tired, bored, or interested in interacting and playing. She also reads, interprets, and responds to your gestures, movements, and body language.

Your child's body language consists of building blocks for the representations and symbols she will use to communicate through spoken language later on. In the beginning, her gestures are reflexes that she does not control. For example, she initially grasps an object as a reflex to something touching her palm. Then over her first year, she develops the ability to consciously override the automatic reflexes to achieve more purposeful actions. She learns to intentionally grasp an object, to hold it, or she may choose not to grasp it just because it touched her palm.

You can support your child in developing her body language as a tool by paying attention and then responding to the needs that she expresses in a timely period through her movements and gestures. Your responses let her know that you understand and value her and what she is telling you. Pay attention and listen to what she is communicating. Before she has words, your baby can communicate to you with simple signs, such as waving good-bye, shaking her head for "no," or nodding for "yes." Body language may provide clues to your child's physical and emotional feelings, as well as her state of mind. Just as you can read your baby's body language, you can also communicate your feelings with her through your body language.

Listening

Your baby starts learning language long before she begins to talk. She learns words by listening to the tone and inflection of your voice, by experiencing repetition, and by associating objects and experiences with words. Listening is a receptive form of communication through which your baby can learn about feelings even though she does not know the words and meanings behind it.

By listening to language, your baby acquires linguistic knowledge and structure without formal teaching. Like a sponge, she takes in the words that you say, and eventually she starts to mimic the sounds that she hears and the movements that she sees your mouth and tongue make. When learning language, she prefers to hear your voice rather than a recorded one.

You can help your child develop her listening skills by engaging with her in conversation, telling her stories, singing to her, and reading to her. You may feel silly talking to a one-month-old baby about what you are doing, what you are serving for dinner, or where you are going. However, when you give her your attention and communicate with her, you recognize her and show her respect. When you give her opportunities to listen, you help her to understand the rhythm of speech, to build her vocabulary, and develop the language skills that will enable her to talk to you.

Talking

Talking is an active form of communication because it involves expressing and vocalizing sounds. In her first three years, your baby starts with simple sounds. Then the sounds get more complex as her oral structure develops. The first sounds your baby makes are vowel sounds, and then she learns sounds with consonants, such as "papa," "mama," "baba," and "dada." Her speech develops in the following order: crying, cooing, vocal experimentation, babbling, saying single words, repeating your words, saying two-word sentences and phrases, and saying three- and four-word sentences.

Verbal skills are recognized as important components of intelligence. As your baby learns to talk, her language skills and cognitive functions build upon each other. In your baby's first 18 months, she instinctively absorbs the sounds around her and learns the rules of language. You can help your child develop her speaking skills by providing her with a language-rich environment. You can reinforce her confidence to talk and express herself by being present, paying attention, and listening to her. Everyday talk helps her build her vocabulary. Repeat her words as a way of acknowledging her. Finally, consider her current level of language development and then offer stimulation to move her to the next.

Writing and reading

Drawing, which helps your child connect words with images, is the foundation for writing and reading. At first, your child may draw as a kinesthetic activity without relating her drawing to concepts. Later, she learns to make a mark that relates to something, and then she makes associations with patterns and symbols on paper. If she puts dots on a circle for eyes to make a face, or draws petals to make a flower, then she is connecting symbols and concepts. Puzzles and shape sorters help her learn the shapes on which letters are based—for example, triangles, circles, and squares. At some point she will understand that the symbols connect with words and that writing and reading are forms of communication.

Reading and writing open the world of literacy for your child, and this discovery can shape and transform her life. Literacy is key to learning, communication, quality of life, career and financial success, and the ability to function and contribute to society. Literacy enables your baby to process information, to create concepts, and to develop her imagination.

You can help your child learn writing and reading skills by talking, singing, reading, writing, storytelling, drawing, and playing games with her. Materials for drawing and writing include crayons, markers, sidewalk chalk, pencils, and finger paint. Matching shapes, colors, and logos can help your child recognize letters. Model the enjoyment of reading by establishing a time when she looks at her books while you read to yourself. Take your child to story time at the library, and get her a library card of her own. Above all, make reading and writing fun and relaxing activities that you enjoy together.

Bilingual

Healthy babies are born with the potential to hear and speak any language. Children who consistently hear the different sounds of two languages during this time develop the neural pathways to speak more easily as a native speaker in both languages. If a child hears certain sounds regularly, then her neurons are strengthened for recognizing and using those sounds. If she does not hear those sounds regularly, those neurons will be pruned, or discarded. Your baby's brain is shaped by what it hears; she learns by repeated exposure. The optimal learning time for formal language education is from 6 to 10 years old. After she is 10 years old, learning a second language requires significantly more effort.

Learning two or more languages can provide lifelong benefits to your child. It can enhance her memory, creativity, flexibility, and ability to focus. It also improves literacy skills by giving her a greater understanding of words, better reading skills, and more avenues for abstract thinking. Bilingualism can help form a bridge between cultures and offers social advantages as well. Even a small amount of exposure to a second language can provide cognitive and academic benefits.

You can help your child become bilingual or incorporate another language into her daily life by providing her with experiences that expose her to another language. If you speak a second language, talking to her in that language is the best way for her to learn it. Give her the same experiences that help her learn any language—for example, reading books, telling stories, and singing songs. When you add movement, emotion, and music to words, your child can easily assimilate, associate, and remember new words. Engage with your child and explore together to discover experiences that support learning a new language. Travel to the country of the second language to immerse her in the culture of the language and to promote experiential learning. Eating at a nearby restaurant and pronouncing the names of foods such as sushi, crepes, tacos, or pad thai will help your child make connections between words and objects.

Cognitive Pathway

Your baby's mental activities include learning, remembering, and using knowledge. Interactions and experiences stimulate her brain's wiring to develop pathways that allow areas of her brain to communicate with each other. Your baby's cognitive pathway overlaps with her six other pathways of learning. When she moves her arms, tastes a banana, smiles at you, listens to your voice, watches a butterfly, or bounces to music, she makes connections in her brain and learns through these activities. Her cognitive pathway includes curiosity, memory, and problem solving.

Cognitive skills enable your baby to understand the world and to function purposefully in it. She starts with lower mental functions that are reflexive and reactive. As she matures, she becomes deliberate through her higher mental functions. Her cognitive development in her early years has a positive correlation to her level of success later in life.

You can help your child develop use of her cognitive pathway by creating an environment that stimulates her intellect. Talk to her, play games that encourage thinking, ask her questions, and get involved with ideas together.

Curiosity

Curiosity is an internal desire to learn through exploring, discovering, and figuring out how the world works. From birth, your baby is interested in understanding new things. The more learning opportunities she has, the more her curiosity grows. The joy of discovery reinforces her desire to learn and to know more.

When you encourage your child's curiosity, you build her self-esteem and her confidence in the learning process. On the other hand, when your child receives negative reinforcement for her curiosity, her desire to learn can diminish. If you express disapproval or impose unnecessary limits, she may withdraw and feel too uncomfortable to reach out and discover. A fearful environment can make her anxious about trying new experiences.

When you get down on your child's level and share in the discovery of nature by involving her while cooking, doing art projects, or taking outdoor adventure walks, you model interest in the world. You can help her develop her pathway of curiosity by providing an environment that has novel and interesting opportunities for discovery. Rotate her toys, the pictures on her wall, and her books. Provide toys that are not electronic and evoke open-ended experiences with dramatic play, art, and nature. Follow her lead, and encourage interests that she initiates. Make sure that she has some unstructured playtime so that she can follow her imagination.

Memory

Memory is the ability to recall and recognize experiences and objects. Your child's memory gives her a record of her unique history and helps her link her past experiences to potential future actions. Without memory, she could not develop a sense of meaning in life.

Memory is foundational to all learning. Your baby needs memory to develop concepts, to understand cause-effect relationships, to learn language, and to solve problems. With memory, your child can learn from her mistakes and adapt her behavior for future experiences.

You can help your child develop her pathway for remembering by being fully present with her in your experiences and by pointing out events, objects, or situations with attention and focus so that she becomes aware of what is happening and can remember it later. Repetition and meaning help your child develop her memory. For instance, when you repeatedly talk about the sounds that animals make, they stick in her mind. When she has a strong feeling that is related to an experience, she can remember it easily.

Problem solving

Problem solving begins when your baby is hungry or needs her diaper changed and she cries until someone takes care of her need. She learns about logic and problem solving through cause and effect and through trial and error. Without memory, she will forget the relationship between causes and effects. To solve a problem, it is necessary to identify the goal, the current condition, and the gap in between. For instance, if your child wants to get a cookie out of the jar, she may have obstacles to overcome. If the cookie jar is on the counter and out of her reach, she may move a chair to stand on and thus reach the cookie jar. If your child only encounters routine experiences, her brain repeats habits and patterns. On the other hand, when she is presented with problems to solve, her brain has the opportunity to learn something new. In addition, problem solving is basic to learning logic and mathematical skills.

If you overindulge your baby and she does not have the chance to struggle and to figure out solutions on her own, she will not learn how to think for herself. When your child has the opportunity to try, fail, and try again, she learns to be persistent and to solve problems. These skills, in turn, enable her to adapt, to focus, and to be successful and confident.

You can help your child develop her pathway of problem solving by taking time to let her do things for herself—to get at a toy that is out of reach, to feed herself, and to walk on her own. Provide challenges, and ask her opinions about how to face them. Respect your child's intelligence when you talk to her. Give her responsibility, get involved with her projects, and let her lead the way. When you are teaching her to do something, explain the steps in a simple order that she can understand. Model problem-solving skills, and be creative in finding solutions by thinking out of the box. Give your child toys that help her connect shapes and patterns, organize her thoughts, and think conceptually.

Creative Pathway

For your child's first two years, she learns primarily through her senses and her motor development. Then her imagination starts to develop. Creative play precedes and is foundational to the process of abstract thinking. Opportunities to explore stories, fantasy, pretend play, art with her hands, and music help her build this foundation. Creativity and innovation are based on the ability to see new and original relationships between concepts or objects that already exist. Qualities that support creativity include the ability to be aware of the needs in a situation, flexibility, and willingness to take risks or to do something new. The process of creativity yields a product or result that evokes emotions. Innovation is not just about artistic design; it exists in many other domains, such as problem solving, social studies, math, and science. As your child starts to develop her imagination and creativity, she uses her higher mental functions and discovers her personal passion and purpose.

The creative pathway overlaps and is integrated with the other pathways because open exploration and play are the basis for creative problem solving and lifelong learning. The flow of creativity fosters flexibility, calmness, and confidence in learning and accomplishing goals. On the other hand, tension, fear, anxiety, and stress undermine creativity.

You can support development of your child's creative pathway by providing open space, open-ended toys and materials, and unstructured time for her to play. Offer her opportunities to use new materials and ideas to construct new knowledge and skills.

Imagination and art

Imagination and art are both expressions of reinvention; they are creative activities that combine new ideas or concepts. For a child, putting a silly hat and sunglasses on a dog or making a puppet with her finger expresses imagination and art. For the purpose of the

pathways, I have categorized imagination and art into using hands and eyes for artistic expression, fantasy or pretend play, and storytelling.

Through artistic expression, your child learns about herself in order to dream, to imagine, and to form her relationship with the world. She learns about all the pathways and can develop as a whole person through art—fine-motor skills, spatial awareness, problem-solving skills, interaction with others and herself, and connection to nature. Art can help your child develop both sides of her brain for whole-brain integration. It also helps her develop confidence, self-discipline, and emotional and social intelligence.

You can help your child develop her pathway for imagination and art by encouraging spontaneity and creative play and by providing a space for unstructured activities. Some craft activities are designed to make a certain product with specific materials and instructions, but art activities are open-ended, without a specific goal or result. To help your child engage her emotions and feelings, say, "Tell me about your picture" instead of "What is that?" Encourage her freedom to make mistakes so that she does not feel that there is a right or wrong way, or that she has to be perfect.

For artistic expression using her hands and eyes, your child can explore a variety of colors, forms, and textures with various art forms—crayons, watercolors, finger paints, clay, pencils, markers, and paper. With

fantasy and pretend play, she can use her imagination and simple props, such as scarves, hats, glasses, and costumes. For another type of pretend play, she can reverse roles with you or her doll. Storytelling offers opportunities to develop linguistic and imaginative skills. When you tell stories, include fairy tales, nursery rhymes, songs, and spontaneous stories that you or your child creates. Storytelling is enjoyable in many contexts—for example, at bedtime or while riding in the car.

Music

Music involves organizing sounds in combinations to create rhythm, melody, and harmony. Rhythm is a natural part of daily activities, movements, and language. Through the ages, people have used music for social purposes, rituals, worship, emotional expression, coordination of movement, and community entertainment.

Listening to sounds is part of your baby's language development. Just as music has notes, rhythm, and melody, language has words, clauses, and sentences. Songs help make it easy for your child to remember sounds, words, and meanings. Music overlaps with all academic curricula and helps develop all seven pathways—sensory through listening to sounds, movement through dance, interaction through playing or singing together, language through setting language to melodies, cognitive through learning to play instruments, and naturalist through feeling the rhythms and listening to the sounds in nature.

Music can lift your child's mood by increasing endorphin levels and promoting a sense of safety and well-being. It can help her brain by slowing down and equalizing her brain waves, strengthening her memory and learning skills, and enhancing her sensitivity to symbols and images. Music can have a balancing effect on your child's body by regulating her pulse rate and blood pressure, increasing her stamina and endurance, and boosting her immune function.

You can help your child develop her music pathway by singing or playing together, dancing, taking her to performances, and providing instruments for her to play. Play a variety of kinds of music for her to experience. Pay attention to her sensitivity to and connection to music, and ensure that it is not too loud for her sensitive ears.

Sarah and Emi

Naturalist Pathway

This pathway, which involves learning through nature, integrates all of the other pathways for whole learning. In developing this pathway, I was inspired by Howard Gardner's concept of naturalist intelligence. My naturalist pathway taps in to my principles of nature's intelligence. Your child has a natural curiosity and sensitivity to nature that motivates her to connect with the natural world. She likes to play in sand and water and to explore animals, bugs, and plants.

According to research, children who regularly play outdoors are happier, healthier, and stronger. Being in nature can help your child develop respect for herself and others, enhance her creativity, lower her stress levels, provide vitamin D, and support her immune system. A calm state of mind supports her readiness and ability to learn.

Through exposure to the natural world, you can encourage your child's naturalist tendencies.

You can bring the outdoors indoors by collecting and displaying rocks, building a terrarium or aquarium, reading books about nature, and growing indoor plants. You can enhance the world of nature in your child's life through small excursions to a park, to your backyard, to a nature center, or to a botanical garden. Bigger excursions may include trips to the beach, picnics, hikes, and camping trips.

Pathways of Whole Learning | Birth–3 months

Pathway	Developmental Stage	How to Nurture	Appropriate Toys
🤚 Sensory			
Taste	Taste buds are sensitive; likes a sweet taste but turns away from sour or bitter taste; uses mouth and tongue to explore	Offer soft objects that are too big to swallow so she can explore with her mouth	Textures to put in mouth: flexible materials such as silicone or rubber; fabric with textures such as terry cloth or flannel
Smell	Smells fragrances around her; turns toward pleasant smells and away from unpleasant ones; can recognize own mother's breast milk vs. milk of other mothers; recognizes scents of caregivers from soap, shampoo, or aftershave	Put a few drops of diluted essential oils on an object in the nursery, a blanket, or a toy; place fresh flowers in her room; let her smell food cooking; use natural scents in skin care products; use familiar smells of caregivers for comfort	Blankie with sachet; essential-oil sachets or sprays for nursery
Auditory	Jumps at loud, sudden sounds and gets used to routine sounds in her environment; responds to a high-pitched voice; finds soft music or lullabies soothing	Talk to her in both a low voice and a high-pitched one; sing songs; move around as you talk so that she can follow you; shake a rattle and move it around to different places so that she can follow it	Toys with sounds, such as rattles, musical sounds, bells, or squeaky toys
Visual	Vision is nearsighted and changes from blurry to focused; at first can only see black, white, and gray; first color is red, and then by 3 months can see a full spectrum; watches objects that are 6–12 inches away and can follow a 180-degree arch; develops distance vision from 9 inches to 8 feet; likes to look at faces; perceptual vision is stronger than central vision	Move a brightly colored object horizontally while her eyes follow; show her a plush toy or puppet with a distinct face, such as a teddy bear; hang a mobile over her crib in high-contrast colors	Mobiles and other objects with bright colors; toys that dangle; black-and-white toys; add red, then green, then other colors
Tactile	Enjoys being held, kissed, and given any skin-to-skin contact; can feel different textures and temperatures; displays sucking or rooting reflex when hungry or being touched; begins to develop proprioception, or body awareness	Hold, kiss, cuddle, and rock her; massage her body after a bath or her feet while feeding; make a sound when you touch different parts of her body; be consistent in the way you hold her; swaddle her for calm and comfort	Variety of textures; soft, lightweight objects; rattles help relate a noise made by a movement of a body part to that body part
🌀 Movement			
Gross Motor	Stretches out limbs, waves arms and legs, kicks, turns head to side; swipes at and reaches for objects; shows early signs of eye-hand coordination; can hold head up while sitting; while on stomach, can lift head 45–90 degrees; brings hands together	Place her on her tummy on your chest; yoga; swimming (with assistance) in tub; body movement and exercises; hold a dangling object for her to swipe	Mobile; hanging objects; balls; tummy-time toys that build abdominal and neck strength
Fine Motor	Grasps small objects (toys, clothes, your finger) with her fingers; opens hands from fist; grasps first reflexively and then with control	Offer your finger, a toy, or small pieces of ribbon or string for her to grasp	Thin, cylindrical objects to hold
Spatial Awareness	Spatial perception improves; starts to understand the difference between above and below	Hang mobiles and use a baby gym to encourage her to track objects; make eye contact with her; facilitate swatting, reaching, and touching opportunities	Mobiles and other hanging toys, such as baby gyms
👤 Interactive			
Self	Watches and studies her hands; looks at herself in the mirror	Place her hand on her face or tummy and say, "Hand"; hold her in front of the mirror and talk to her	Wrist and ankle rattles; toys with mirrors; large photos of baby faces
Others	Responds to your words and smiles by smiling back; enjoys social interactions; starts to show excitement; actively watches her environment from stroller or carrier	Make eye contact; interact with her directly or using a puppet or toy; smile at her, and respond when she smiles back; play peekaboo; stick out your tongue and see if she imitates you; imitate the noises she makes	Puppets; toys with faces; stuffed animals with high-contrast facial features

Pathway	Developmental Stage	How to Nurture	Appropriate Toys
🗨 **Communication**			
Listen	When you talk to her, she hears and recognizes your voice and turns her head toward your voice; she becomes relaxed in response to noises in your home and may withdraw in response to noises outside	Talk in a gentle voice; make an "O" with your mouth; sing songs with actions like "Itsy Bitsy Spider"; speak to her before she sees you	Puppets, plush toys, toys with sounds, music; small squeeze toys that make noise
Speak	Makes cooing and gurgling sounds; begins to make vowel sounds regularly; cries to express needs; when she wants to talk, she giggles, babbles, or smiles; when she is tired, she fusses, spits, or whines	Respond to her cries by meeting her needs; respond to her coos by making sounds back; imitate head bobbles, smiles, and other expressions and movements	Puppets or plush toys as a means of communication
Read and Write	Takes in sounds and rhythms of books being read to her	Read out loud to her from baby books or from books, newspapers, and other materials that you read	Soft books with different textures and sounds
Body and Sign Language	Makes eye contact; communicates with whole body; when she is ready to play, her face brightens, her eyes widen, and her hands open; when she is tired, she breaks eye contact, stiffens her body, and pulls away	Make eye contact; respond to her with physical actions such as swinging, rocking, jiggling, bouncing; begin one or two simple signs, such as "eat"; wave bye-bye to her	Wrist and foot rattles; interactive bibs and clothes with fun designs
Second Language	Hears and absorbs the sounds and intonations of a second language	Keep talking to her; repeat a word while demonstrating it; read books in the second language; talk to her in the second language every day; play music in the second language; use puppets and plush toys to communicate	Books, music, puppets, plush toys
💡 **Cognitive**			
Curiosity	Watches and follows movements or objects with her eyes; shows an active interest in a person or toy	Play games with her: alternate between surprised and happy faces; wiggle an object in front of her face and then take it away	Puppets, plush toys, mirrors
Memory	Remembers your face and specific objects; remembers the smell of mother's breast milk; movement helps develop memory	Play peekaboo with your face and other objects; make things disappear and reappear; do stretching and other movement exercises when changing her diaper	Small blanket
Problem Solving	Recognizes that she will be fed soon when she sees the breast or bottle; learns that if she hits a hanging object with her hands, it moves; cries when hungry, tired, overstimulated, wet, hot, or cold	Respond to her cues by taking care of her needs (feed, change, swaddle, help get her hands to her mouth); shake a rattle and then give it to her to shake; hold out a toy for her to reach and then give it to her	Rattles and other noise-making toys; plush toys; textured toys
⭐ **Creative**			
Art & Imagination	Begins to distinguish color and form; likes round shapes; responds to organized patterns and symmetry	Hang objects above her head, such as a shiny spoon and colorful objects such as toys, scarves, or clothes	Toys with vivid colors, symmetry, and organized patterns
Music	Enjoys listening to music, rhythms, and sounds; learns the music she hears	Sing nursery rhymes, songs, and lullabies to her; play music repeatedly so that she becomes familiar with it, and occasionally introduce a new piece of music	Music with calming sounds such as the ocean, waterfalls, or birds
🌳 **Naturalist**			
Naturalist	Listens to sounds of birds and other animals; observes leaves falling; smells flowers and other fragrances in nature; enjoys space, air, sunshine, sounds, time outdoors	Place a bird feeder outside the window for her to watch; put her in a carrier or stroller and go on a walk in a park or a hike; put a blanket under a tree and look up at the leaves with her	Toys and books featuring animals, sea life, bugs, vegetables, and flowers

Pathways of Whole Learning | 3–6 months

Pathway	Developmental Stage	How to Nurture	Appropriate Toys
Sensory			
Taste	Puts everything in her mouth, which is full of touch receptors; chews with gums; likes sweet tastes; teeth are preparing to break through	Offer chewy and cool materials to put in her mouth for teething and exploration; start solid foods as her front teeth break through; offer her a teether to chew; massage her gums with a toothbrush	Teethers; chewy necklaces for parents to wear; silicone toothbrush if teeth start to emerge
Smell	Recognizes familiar smells, such as breast milk and your skin care products; recognizes other household smells	Dip cotton balls in different fragrances such as vanilla, lemon juice, and peppermint, and wave them in front of her nose	Fabric toys with sachets for applying essential oils
Auditory	Shows improvement in processing and distinguishing sounds; recognizes her name	Vary the tone of your voice—gentle, lively, laughing; shake objects that make a sound to get her attention; shake rattles with different sounds; make animal, car, train, and other sounds	Rattles, musical instruments, bells
Visual	Depth perception starts developing; vision can be as good as 20/20; central vision is more developed	Move a flashlight around a dark room and let her follow the light; hang colorful pictures within her view, and move or change them every few days; make a photo album of familiar people and objects	Toys with bright colors, colorful pictures, and movements; flashlights; pinwheels; objects that move, such as balls and cars, for practice tracking visually
Tactile	Discovers different textures such as hard and soft, rough and smooth; holds and scratches clothes; enjoys water in the bath	Stroke her with different objects—a piece of silk, a feather, a cotton ball; massage, acupoints, touching, cuddling; say nursery rhymes, such as "This Little Piggy"; pour water over her with a cup in the bath; roll a soft ball across her tummy or back; let her play with pieces of food on a place mat	Toys with different textures; bath pouring toys and sponges
Movement			
Gross Motor	Sits supported with a pillow; rolls over; further develops hand-eye coordination; moves head from side to side while on her back; while on tummy, lifts her head up and begins to straighten arms, pushing chest off floor; gets on hands and knees; develops muscle control; grabs feet with hands and puts feet in her mouth; can stand when holding on to someone; kicks in the bathtub	Place her on a blanket and pull the side of the blanket to gently roll her over; place a bucket in the bathtub, fill it with water, put her in the water, hold under her arms, and let her kick; place a toy on the floor, just out of reach, and give her a boost from behind to stretch and get the toy; give her knee rides while chanting nursery rhymes; do yoga and movement exercises; encourage cross-lateral movement; name her body parts	Blanket, balls; yoga mat or play mat for floor play
Fine Motor	Grabs a toy, waves it around, and moves it back and forth from hand to hand; rakes with her whole hand to pick up small objects with thumb and fingers; can move blocks; does not have a dominant hand yet	Give her toys and objects that are thin enough to wrap her fingers around, such as a spoon, string, noodles, dry cereal, or small pieces of vegetable; give her a plastic cup with a small amount of water in it; put a toy on a blanket and encourage her to move it toward her	Rattles or balls with thin parts that she can hold with her hands; fabric blocks
Spatial Awareness	Reaches for toys and faces; begins to connect seeing with doing; coordinates eye and head rotations; can orient herself toward an object of her attention	Hold safe objects directly in front of her and move them slowly left to right, up and down, and allow her to reach for and touch them; place her on her stomach and encourage her to stretch, roll, scoot, squirm, and wiggle toward her toys; play pat-a-cake	Safe toys that she can touch; toys to drop into a container
Interactive			
Self	Recognizes herself in the mirror and smiles and coos in response	Put colorful socks on her hands and feet; put an unbreakable mirror within her view for her to look at on her own (this can be helpful at the changing table)	Colorful socks, gloves, and hats; unbreakable mirror; wrist rattles
Others	Acts differently toward strangers versus familiar people; recognizes a friendly or angry tone of voice	Play hide-and-seek and other interactive games; use puppets and plush toys to interact; let her explore other babies	Puppets, plush toys; books with simple baby faces

Pathway	Developmental Stage	How to Nurture	Appropriate Toys
🗨 Communication			
Listen	Turns her head in response to a loud noise; looks in the direction of your voice when you call her name	Talk to her in a conversational tone; tell her stories and sing songs; use a puppet to talk to her	Puppets, plush toys, toys with sounds, music videos; books read over and over
Speak	Makes high-pitched squeals and growling sounds; repeats sounds back to you; makes sounds with combined consonants, such as "ba ba ba," "da da da," "ga ga ga," and "ka ka ka"; laughs and smiles; facial expressions and body language are more complex	Imitate the sounds that she makes, and let her touch your mouth when you speak; wave bye-bye; make simple gestures or baby signs	Puppets or plush toys as a means of communication
Read and Write	Enjoys stories told and books read to her while sitting in your lap	Hold her on your lap and read magazines and picture books to her, explaining what is in the pictures; read poetry to her; let her watch you draw on paper with crayons	Soft fabric books with textures, interactive board books, or flash cards; paper with different colors and textures to crumple
Body and Sign Language	Expresses feelings and needs through body movements and facial expressions (sad or happy); mimics your facial gestures	Respond to her expressions with your body language and facial expressions; use a couple of simple baby signs	Wrist and foot rattles; interactive bibs and clothes with fun designs
Second Language	Listens to and takes in the sounds of a second language; recognizes familiar phrases that are repeated; assimilates phonetic sounds	Keep talking to her; repeat a word while demonstrating it; read books in the second language; talk to your baby in the second language every day; play music in the second language; use puppets and plush toys to communicate	Books, music, puppets, plush toys
💡 Cognitive			
Curiosity	Looks for a dropped object; interested in hands, feet, and other body parts	Put cups or boats in bathtub and float or sink them; pour water on her head or back; blow bubbles for her; crank a popping toy such as a jack-in-the-box; hide and uncover objects with a blanket	Plastic cups or boats; jack-in-the-box; avoid technical toys and instead offer simple, natural ones
Memory	Remembers toys and other familiar objects; remembers her name; exercise helps develop memory	Reverse peekaboo: cover her head with a small blanket and uncover while saying, "Surprise!"; do the same with toys or other objects; provide simple daily routines so she can anticipate what comes next	Small blanket, small toys to remember; infant-size photo album or photos of familiar faces
Problem Solving	Reaches for a toy in front of her; shows intentionality; uses hand to push away something she does not want; knows how to get your attention or a specific response through gestures; objects if you take a toy away; moves a toy behind or through something and makes it continue out the other side	Show her how to shake noisemakers such as rattles and squeaky toys; hold a ball above her when she is lying down so that she can swat it with her hands and kick it with her feet; put a noisemaker under a blanket, behind her, or behind you, and then make the sound and let her try to find the toy; cover your face with a scarf for her to remove	Rattles, squeaky toys, soft blocks to knock over; toys that pull apart easily
🎨 Creative			
Art & Imagination	Is drawn to colors, patterns, and shapes of different objects; enjoys more complex designs and distinguishes between colors; enjoys brightly colored pictures	Finger paint with food puree on a plate; show her brightly colored fabrics or pictures when you go to a new place; make her footprints with nontoxic paint; large, removable wall-art stickers	Flash cards or books with bright pictures; nontoxic paint
Music	Enjoys rhythm and repetition of sounds from shaking toys or musical instruments; likes to hear favorite songs over and over	Shake a jar with beans, a maraca, a rattle toy, or a bell; show her how to shake it; add movement to music: swinging, bouncing, dancing	Rattles, musical instruments, or other toys with noise; music boxes; wrist and foot bells
🌳 Naturalist			
Naturalist	Shows interest in plants, animals, and the outdoors	Make animal sounds with puppets or plush animals; take her outside to explore in the grass, sand, dirt, rain, snow, and wind	Toys and books about animals, bugs, sea life, and plants; bubbles

Pathway	Developmental Stage	How to Nurture	Appropriate Toys

Pathways of Whole Learning | 6–12 months

🖐 Sensory

Pathway	Developmental Stage	How to Nurture	Appropriate Toys
Taste	Puts everything in her mouth; with foods, moves from eating creamy purees to lumpy and chunky textures; chews and bites objects; teeth erupt, starting with central incisors (front upper and lower teeth) and then lateral incisors (side upper and middle teeth); feeds herself finger foods and drinks from a cup with your help	Offer a variety of tastes and textures with foods and safe objects for exploring with her mouth; gently use a soft, small-bristle toothbrush; offer cold teethers and frozen pieces of food in a protective bag for chewing; offer hard pieces of bread or teething biscuits	Teethers; toys that are safe to put in her mouth with different textures for exploration; silicone finger toothbrush or safety toothbrush
Smell	Sensitive to smells or fragrances inside or outside; remembers familiar smells	Offer opportunities to experience a variety of natural scents such as foods, the outdoors, and people; point out smells of flowers, fruit, vegetables, animals, and other natural scents; point out smells associated with daily routines, such as cooking items, hand soap, shampoo, and baby wipes; point out unappealing smells such as rotten food or burning toast	Fabric toys with sachets for applying essential oils
Auditory	Turns her head when she hears a sound and can find the source of a sound; recognizes sounds that are part of daily routine, such as common household sounds and environmental sounds	Give her toys with sounds such as rattles, keys, objects she can shake, bells, squeaky toys, and musical instruments; turn off other sounds so that it is quiet and point out a bird singing or a clock ticking; talk to her through a tube	Rattles, musical instruments; jars or cans with beans; squeaky toys; pots and pans; animal or pet sounds
Visual	Vision is improving and pictorial depth perception has developed; she can see the world more realistically	Point out objects and their shapes; hang colorful pictures and banners within her view, and move or change them every few days for stimulation; blow bubbles; find simple objects in picture books and distant objects like airplanes, squirrels, etc.	Toys with bright colors, colorful pictures, and movements; flashlights; pinwheels; bubbles; toys that roll or move on tracks
Tactile	Feels different sizes, shapes, and textures with her hands; likes the feeling of water poured on her; distinguishes hot and cold; likes to help hold a book and turn the pages	Water play (in bathtub or sink): pour, squeeze, and drip; put objects with different textures in a box and let her explore; point out objects with different temperatures and describe them to her; massage, touch, and cuddle with her	Bath toys; toys that expose her to a variety of textures; sand or bean trays; hidden toys; homemade play dough

🌀 Movement

Pathway	Developmental Stage	How to Nurture	Appropriate Toys
Gross Motor	Sits up independently; leans on hands while sitting; lunges forward unsupported; scoots on hands and knees, and then cross-crawls; climbs furniture and crawls up stairs; pulls herself up to standing; stands independently; walks with assistance; rolls a ball; grasps feet and tries to put them in her mouth	Make an obstacle course for her to maneuver, with pillows and blankets for her crawl around, planting toys and snacks as incentives; roll a ball back and forth; do yoga and movement exercises; encourage cross-lateral movements by offering something that she has to reach across her body to get	Push toys, balls, play mat; hanging objects or mobiles; pull toys with strings
Fine Motor	Picks up small objects with thumb and forefinger; can feed herself with fingers; easily transfers objects from one hand to the other; can pick up a toy with only one hand and hold it in the center of her hand; points and pokes with fingers; shows hand dominance; drops toys and stacks blocks	Play "drop and dump" with a bucket and small objects; stack soft blocks; bang pots and pans; help her pick up small objects (beware of choking hazards); play with floating objects in the bathtub; do not try to influence hand dominance; encourage finger-feeding and early utensil play	Clackers; soft blocks; bath toys; large beads on a string; toys stuck together with hooks and loops
Spatial Awareness	Becomes aware of vertical space and fears heights; can reach for a toy behind her without seeing it; sees objects as separate and detached; is able to see and reach with accuracy	Play hide-and-seek with toys to help her realize that objects do not disappear just because she cannot see them; hide objects and allow her to uncover them; point out things in the distance; allow her to look in a mirror	Soft toys that can be dropped; toys she can grasp; soft books; containers that open and close easily

👶 Interactive

Pathway	Developmental Stage	How to Nurture	Appropriate Toys
Self	Smiles and coos at self in the mirror and pats reflection; clasps hands; plays alone for long periods; pokes at different parts of her body; looks at photo of herself; feeds herself a cracker	Stand in front of the mirror and have a conversation with her; point out body parts and repeat their names; ask her to locate body parts; play "This Little Piggy"	Safe mirror; clothes with colorful patterns and designs such as animals or vehicles; make gloves from brightly colored socks by cutting out fingers; photos of familiar people and objects
Others	Responds to her name; pulls on jewelry or objects in your shirt pocket; develops fear of strangers and separation; is very alert to people; offers toys to others; likes to be near a familiar adult; shows humor and teases; notices the feelings of others; starts to test limits	Play peekaboo; point out your facial features or body parts and ask her to locate them; make your voice go up and down; be funny; set limits; ask questions; provide commentary about the day; explore each other	Puppets or plush toys for interaction

Pathway	Developmental Stage	How to Nurture	Appropriate Toys
🗨 Communication			
Listen	Understands meanings of words such as no, go, eat, up, down; understands simple phrases or commands with gestures	Play pat-a-cake and other games; say nursery rhymes; talk to her as you go about the day, and explain what you are doing; give simple directions for her to follow; say, "Thank you" to her	Puppets, plush toys, toys with sounds, music videos
Speak	Knows how to attract your attention; uses two-syllable words ("ma-ma," "da-da") and attaches meaning to them; imitates sounds, such as a cough; uses tuneful babble; if you repeat a sound she makes, she will repeat it back to you	Repeat the sounds that she says back to her; put a puppet on her hand or finger; use simple gestures to indicate objects and actions	Puppets or plush toys as a means of communication
Read and Write	Likes stories with sounds that relate to the pictures (animals, babies, objects)	Read to her every day, and cuddle so that reading is a bonding time; help her turn the pages; make a simple photo album with photos of her	Soft, fabric books with texture, interactive board books, flash cards
Body and Sign Language	Uses arms and gestures to ask to be lifted; waves "bye-bye"; understands and makes gestures; can follow simple instructions	Look at her upside down; dance and encourage her to move with the music	Wrist and foot rattles; interactive bibs and clothes with fun designs
Second Language	Listens to and takes in the sounds of a second language; recognizes familiar phrases that are repeated; assimilates phonetic sounds	Keep talking to her; repeat a word while demonstrating it; read books in the second language; Talk to your baby in the second language every day; play music in the second language; use puppets and plush toys to communicate	Books, music, puppets, plush toys
💡 Cognitive			
Curiosity	Curious about other babies; pokes and reaches for jewelry or eyeglasses on adults; crawling gives her the mobility to explore the room; very curious, but may be shy to venture out	Make a space with boundaries so that she can crawl independently; cover her toys in paper and put them in a bag for her to unwrap; make a tunnel with a sheet and two chairs for her to crawl under	Measuring spoons and cups, plastic containers, wooden spoons, pots and pans with lids; avoid technical toys and instead offer simple, natural ones
Memory	Strengthens sense of object constancy (knowledge that an object still exists when it is out of sight); remembers more specific things, such as where her toys are; imitates actions; remembers places, situations, and recent events; remembers words and associates them with pictures; remembers the past and anticipates the future; exercise helps memory	Play peekaboo; play "follow me" by asking her to do what you do: "Wash your face," "Comb your hair," "Wipe the chair with a sponge"; play hide-and-seek; read her favorite book repeatedly and pause for anticipation of the next page; name songs and do gestures along with songs	Flash cards, books, toys to hide, small blanket; use daily routines—e.g. "Where's your cup?"
Problem Solving	Recognizes how smaller containers fit inside larger ones; understands "in" and "out"; can focus attention; shows greater interest in details. Understands that putting on a bib means it is time to eat, and putting on a coat means it is time to go outside; understands that words relate to people and objects; recognizes patterns of cause and effect; likes to drop objects to notice the result; likes to bang objects and explore sounds	Play "find the toy" with a squeaky toy; pull a piece of cloth back and forth with her; play hide-and-seek; make jokes involving the unexpected (e.g., try to put on her shoe or drink out of her sippy cup). Give her objects to put in a container, put a lid on it, shake it, pour the items out, and repeat; sing when she kicks, and stop when she stops; roll a small ball back and forth; establish daily routines for simple tasks such as hand washing or diaper changing	Simple sorting toys (e.g., shape-sorting toys), balls, stacking cups, blocks, noisemakers
🕊 Creative			
Art & Imagination	Begins to develop images and remember them; enjoys experiencing and exploring different colors, textures, and materials	Set up a sandbox made of flour or cornmeal on her high-chair tray; give her pieces of paper to tear; pull a scarf through a plastic tube; finger paint	Books with bright pictures; non-toxic paints; sidewalk chalk
Music	Enjoys songs and action rhymes; bangs a toy on the floor or table or against another toy; likes rhythm	Bounce or dance to music with her; play different kinds of music: marches, rock and roll, lullabies, symphonies, children's songs, and jazz; repeat a favorite piece so that she becomes familiar with it; help her clap along with music	Simple musical instruments; noisemakers; music
🌳 Naturalist			
Naturalist	Interested in animals, birds, and bugs; enjoys time outside in nature	Take a walk outside; pick up sticks, rocks, and leaves and start collections of natural objects	Toys and books about animals, bugs, sea life, and plants; magnifying glasses

Pathways of Whole Learning | 12–18 months

Pathway	Developmental Stage	How to Nurture	Appropriate Toys
Sensory			
Taste	Mouthing of objects decreases; may become picky with eating; digestive system is more developed and can manage a larger variety of foods; first molars and canines start to appear	Wean her from a bottle to prevent tooth decay; move from sippy to straw or cup for jaw and speech development; offer foods with new flavors and textures; offer a molar teether for chewing on back gums; brush her teeth; give her hard pieces of bread or teething biscuits; play imitation games of mouth and tongue movement	Molar teether; child's vibrating toothbrush; blow toys (whistles, flutes)
Smell	Responds to different scents; learning is affected by different smells; chemical smells can block learning	Provide essential oils that enhance learning (peppermint, basil, lemon, rosemary) or promote relaxation (lavender, chamomile); point out different smells in nature, cooking, and your home environment	Essential oils on blankie or plush toys
Auditory	Learns the meaning of nonspeech sounds; fascinated by the sounds different objects make; may begin to cover ears to sounds she dislikes; starts to show preference in music	Clap along to songs to emphasize rhythm; play different types of music; point out new sounds such as water falling from the faucet or a key entering a lock	Squeak toys, rattles, measuring spoons, and other items with unexpected sounds; xylophones, bells, tambourines, and other instruments
Visual	Continues to develop eye-hand-body coordination, eye teeming , and depth perception; points to pictures or objects; starts to scan to find objects in pictures	Ask her to find an object among many to encourage scanning; point out distant things like birds or airplanes	Toys with bright colors, colorful pictures, and movements; flashlights; pinwheels; bubbles; books with smaller pictures; cereals or raisins in small snack containers
Tactile	Learns the use of touch to direct others; improved bowel and bladder control; shows discomfort with a soiled diaper; wants to do things herself with her hands; washes her hands, puts lids on, unwraps packages	Go barefoot to feel the floor; massage, stimulate acupoints, touch, and cuddle her; give her objects or toys that she can manipulate with her hands (blocks, sorting toys, art supplies); have her help you put groceries in the cart and pull clothes out of the washer	Blocks; stuffed animals for cuddling; sorting toys; leaves, flowers, sticks, rocks; sand play
Movement			
Gross Motor	Takes steps with assistance; walks alone; stands up on the floor by herself; bends over and looks through her legs; squats to pick up an object; backs up; walks backward and sideways; climbs onto furniture; tries to climb out of crib; rides on four-wheel toys; throws ball; can climb stairs with help; develops an awareness of heights	Provide opportunities for movement of joints and muscles and balancing: crawling, kicking, running, jumping, dancing, walking, swimming, splashing; provide outside play for throwing, swinging, climbing play equipment, and hanging on bars; do yoga and movement exercises; encourage cross-lateral movements by placing objects such that she has to reach across her body	Push carts, push and pull toys; use socks with nonskid soles; ride toys; balls to pick up and throw; kiddy pool
Fine Motor	Picks up crumbs or small objects with tips of fingers and thumb; helps turn pages of a book; pushes, pulls, or carries a toy; stacks small toys or blocks (1-inch size); marks with a crayon; starts to feed herself with a spoon; opens drawers; manipulates toothbrush or telephone; holds regular cup	Do not try to influence hand dominance; give her a sponge or washcloth and ask her to squeeze it; stack cartons or blocks	Rubber hammers; toys that nest, stack, or thread; shape sorters; books with pictures to open; pegboards
Spatial Awareness	Mentions objects or people who are not present; imitates actions and sounds; can differentiate between her own reflection and that of another baby	Give her personal space; encourage siblings and others to respect her space by not putting their faces very close to hers; use tables and chairs or large boxes to make mazes and tunnels; point out things at a distance—higher and lower	Baby-safe mirrors; mazes and tunnels; peekaboo toys; cereals in containers; books
Interactive			
Self	Cooperates in dressing and undressing (e.g., lifts her feet to get out of pants); responds to her name; knows the names of body parts and points to them on request	Play peekaboo; chase her; make eye contact; call her by name; communicate positive emotions to enhance learning and to help her to be alert, attentive, and responsive; teach relaxation techniques (deep breathing, stretching); make and play audio/video recordings of her; show her photos of herself; allow choices in clothes to wear	Dress-up items; dolls for mirroring body parts; soft mirrors
Others	Imitates daily life; responds to suggestions more readily than commands; hugs plush toys or dolls; rolls a ball to you; starts to understand taking turns; will push or pull others to initiate game playing; develops the desire to be the center of attention; expresses preferences for specific people and toys	Be physically present and pay attention to her cues; sing to create a positive environment; make jokes and create surprises; tell stories or look at photos with emotional messages; ask her questions and make observant comments; promote interaction with relatives, friends, poses, siblings	Dolls for mirroring affection; soft books with family photos; toys that promote parallel play

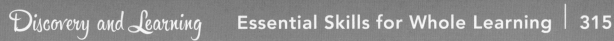

Pathway	Developmental Stage	How to Nurture	Appropriate Toys
💬 Communication			
Listen	Recognizes names and points to familiar people; laughs; understands verbal requests and greetings; absorbs the things you say; you can communicate with less baby talk and more normal conversation; receptive understanding is ahead of expressive language	Talk to her about what you are doing; speak slowly and simply; give her simple directions; point out sounds outdoors; attend story time at the library	Reading aloud; toys with sounds; nursery rhymes
Speak	Comes to you when she needs help; repeats a two-word sentence that you say; is learning to say more words; chatters; vocabulary is growing; words become whole words; speaks with more syllables; communicates ideas; is developing intonation and rhythm in speech	Engage her when she talks—have a conversation; encourage her to use two words together to make a sentence or phrase ("more juice"); ask her questions; ask her to repeat what she said; discourage older siblings from speaking for her	Puppets or plush toys as a means of communication; construction toys (ask her to tell what she is building)
Read and Write	Points to and pats pictures in a book; has mental images of objects	Find times to "read" different materials (not just baby books) during the day, including restaurant menus and signs at the grocery store; point at the words as you read them aloud	Soft books with different textures, interactive board books, flash cards; soft photo album
Body and Sign Language	Gets attention by pulling on your hand or clothes; points at something to show she wants it; uses a combination of gestures, facial expressions, and vocalizations to communicate	Get down to her level to communicate; describe what she is asking for or pointing to; mirror her gestures to acknowledge her communication; demonstrate new, useful gestures	Puppets or plush toys as a means of communication; dancing; pictures of different faces and expressions
Second Language	Has an innate ability to differentiate between the first and second languages, so she can handle the introduction of new words in both languages simultaneously	Talk to her in the second language every day; repeat vocabulary words; read books and play music in second language; use puppets and plush toys to communicate; play games with words from second language	Books, music CDs, puppets, plush toys, videos
💡 Cognitive			
Curiosity	Does not tire of repetition; enjoys games and exploration (holding, stacking, playing with toys); likes learning animal sounds; interested in how things work	Place toys and objects in a treasure basket for exploration; play hide-and-seek; ask her to make animal sounds; show her how things fit together and work	Avoid technical toys and instead offer simple, natural ones; large magnifying address; terrarium, aquarium
Memory	Has long-lasting memories of conscious events; can remember words or phrases and associate people with experiences; mimics animal sounds; can remember people and objects when they are out of sight; memory is related to emotion; recognizes objects and their use; can identify objects that are identical	Exercise helps memory; help her relate to new experiences or items by pointing out similar ones that are familiar; ask her questions to stimulate her memory; play hide-and-seek; play "Simon says"; encourage anticipation of the next event in a routine or a familiar book	Matching toys; books
Problem Solving	Begins to understand size and how things fit together; sorts and stacks blocks; turns knobs and presses buttons; matches shapes; attention is in present (future is a dim concept); attention span is 2–3 minutes; looks for hidden objects; uses a trial-and-error problem-solving technique; begins to shake head for "No"; needs and expects routines and rituals; recognizes that her behavior influences your actions; may become frustrated with solving problems	Chase her; offer choices; be patient and let her do things herself, noticing her threshold of needing help (Ask, "Do you need help?"); show and discuss how things work	Stacking blocks; graduated rings and cups; shape and sorting toys; jack-in-the-box, balloons, bubbles, vehicles, music boxes; backpacks with pockets or zippers; containers with different types of lids
🖌 Creative			
Art & Imagination	Enjoys making a mess with food, water, and play dough; pretends; scribbles with a pen, pencil, or crayons; bright colors help develop the brain's wiring for recognizing color	Walk like different animals (bear, dog, cat, bunny, etc.); dance with her; take her to puppet shows; attend story time at the library	Books with shapes and real-life pictures; nontoxic paints and brushes; art materials like sidewalk chalk; movable wall stickers; fabrics with patterns
Music	Enjoys listening to music of all kinds and dancing individually or together to the music; likes to make rhythms with toys or instruments	Sing songs and makes movements that she can copy, or urge her to move on her own; play various kinds of music (classical, rock and roll, jazz, children's songs)	Drums, bells, xylophones, small pianos, music CDs
🌿 Naturalist			
Naturalist	Enjoys exploring nature with newfound physicality (walks on sand, picks up rocks and sticks, rolls in grass)	Take a walk outside and allow her to lead you to what interests her; talk about what you are seeing and where you are going; encourage her to touch natural objects	Toys and books about animals, bugs, sea life, and plants; magnifying glasses; flashlights

Pathways of Whole Learning | 18–24 months

Pathway	Developmental Stage	How to Nurture	Appropriate Toys
Sensory			
Taste	Second molars appear; interested in new tastes (spices and herbs)	Provide sport-top bottles and regular cups to encourage healthy dental development and mature mouth development ; offer molar teethers for comfort; take her on her first trip to the dentist	Molar teether; toddler utensils; vibrating toothbrush; bubbles; flutes and whistles
Smell	Responds negatively and positively to different scents; begins to develop preferences	Match words to scents while out on a walk; allow her to smell and taste during meal preparation, and describe the flavors so she can begin to associate foods with smells and tastes; point out different scents	Flowers, herbs, and fruits for exposure to new and interesting scents and tastes
Auditory	Likes to imitate sounds, including phrases from songs and speech	Listen to the environment together and ask her what she hears (wind chimes, people talking, crickets at night, etc.)	Musical instruments; recording devices; CDs with simple songs
Visual	Looks at an object when you point at it; points to interesting objects; has good tracking skills; judges distances more accurately	Ask her to point to a specific object; refer to objects as close or far; place visually engaging objects at different heights; play hide-and-seek with objects; attend child-friendly exhibits at zoos, nature centers, museums, etc.	Visually appealing books; colorful mobiles and artwork; push and pull toys
Tactile	Using hands and fingers stimulates muscles and brain and makes connections; the sense of touch helps to ground abstract ideas to concrete experiences	Massage, stimulate acupoints, touch, and cuddle with her; play games involving use of hands; play with puzzles, Legos, and other toys that involve putting objects together with your hands	Modeling clay; finger paints; plush toys for cuddling; sound boxes; sensory trays
Movement			
Gross Motor	Steady on feet; can kick a ball and catch with arms; throws a ball overhead ; can walk up or down stairs without alternating feet; jumps; looks down to dodge; pedals a tricycle; may climb out of crib; likes swinging in the park	Engage in outside play (throw a ball) and floor play (somersaults and stretching); do yoga and movement exercises; encourage cross-lateral movements; make a mountain out of pillows to crawl over; put a piece of tape on the floor and let her walk on the tape; stack blocks; have her carry groceries and do other household chores	Push and pull toys; ride toys, wagons, wheelbarrows, garden implements
Fine Motor	Can rotate forearm and turn doorknobs; likes to squeeze objects; uses eating utensils; folds paper; can do a simple puzzle	In warm weather or in the bathtub, set up a place for water play with eyedroppers and sponges; have her drop an object into a container that has a small opening (e.g., piggy bank) so that she is required to aim	Place mats for drawing; containers with a variety of lids to open; dolls with clothing
Spatial Awareness	Has a sense of self as separate from others; shows definite signs of self-recognition; understands more about how things go together and where items belong	Ask her about toys or people she cannot see; turn toys upside down, see if she notices, and then encourage her to put them back the right way	Simple puzzles with big pieces; graduated boxes, stacking cups
Interactive			
Self	Can take off clothes; seats herself at the table; knows her own name; self-centered; has temper tantrums; attempts to control herself; can feel shame and guilt; experiments with independence; sometimes lacks confidence; gazes at people or objects; notices physical differences between herself and others	Acknowledge her emotions her (happiness, anger, sadness); tickle and kiss her; provide words to express her feelings; allow simple choices between preferred foods, clothes, or activities; share meals as a family; have regular cuddle time	Toddler cutlery and toothbrush (for independence); mirrors; toys for pretend scenarios
Others	Tells needs, but does not converse; runs away; resents punishments, especially when she does not understand the reason; responds to familiar adults and may be shy with strangers; holds an adult's hand while walking; engages in solitary or parallel play; likes to be near you in group situations; does not cooperate or share; may pinch, bite, have tantrums, or scream	Be physically present and pay attention to her cues; express your emotions openly and honestly; ask questions and make observant comments; comfort her when she is feeling unsettled; prepare her for upcoming social encounters and events; begin modeling the concepts of sharing, taking turns, and noticing the feelings of others; play hide-and-seek	Interactive toys during play dates; shared "presents" with siblings; audio children's books

Pathway	Developmental Stage	How to Nurture	Appropriate Toys
Communication			
Listen	Responds to humor or distraction; has a vocabulary of approximately 300 words; enjoys repetition and nonsense rhymes	When going out, talk about sights and sounds on the way; make jokes with silly words	Books and nursery rhymes read aloud; toys with sounds; hand puppets used by adult
Speak	Says 20–50 words; uses some adverbs, adjectives, and prepositions; asks for objects by name; creates singsong phrases of 2–3 words; talks to a doll or plush toy; answers questions	Encourage her to verbalize her thinking; pause and wait for responses to questions; give her a phone to say "Hello" to a caller; attend sing-alongs	Puppets or plush toys as a means of communication; books; pretend play sets
Read and Write	Likes to touch and look at books; identifies and locates pictures in a book; turns pages one at a time; can enjoy quiet time with books; asks you to read the same book over and over again	Read stories every night; talk about pictures in books; introduce new words; use letter-learning apps	Fabric books with different textures, interactive board books, or flash cards; soft photo album; crayons for writing
Body and Sign Language	Sees and reaches out at the same time; reads facial expressions; uses more complex gestures	Slow down your movements so she can mimic you; model good behavior and appropriate gestures; dance together	Puppets or plush toys as a means of communication; play kitchens and dolls for mimicry
Second Language	Can mimic sounds	Talk to your baby in the second language every day; repeat vocabulary words; read books and play music in second language; use puppets and plush toys to communicate; play games with words from second language	Books, music CDs, puppets, plush toys, videos
Cognitive			
Curiosity	Intrigued by water; likes humor games; explores objects by dropping, shaking, banging, and throwing them; likes small challenges; the brain responds to new or novel experiences by releasing adrenalin, causing an increase in brain activity and alertness	Create a play bag to take on excursions, and change out the toys periodically; do something out of the regular routine occasionally (e.g., wear funny clothes, a hat, or sunglasses to get attention); change the furniture around; rotate toys, car seats , and meals to keep her alert; go on outdoor exploring expeditions; attend events at a nature center	Avoid technical toys and instead offer simple, natural ones; fish bowls; binoculars; nature videos; collection boxes for special finds in nature
Memory	Knows names and words for things, people, actions, and situations; imitates clapping and other actions accurately; recognizes favorite toys; stressful situations interfere with brain function and slow down the processing of information	Give her objects that she can use to imitate real-life situations (old telephone, cup, unbreakable containers); engage in relaxation techniques (yoga, deep breathing, lullabies, rocking), keep down noise levels at times of stress; ask, "Where is the . . .?"	Favorite songs she can remember and sing; books; play kitchen; organizing containers for toys and clothes
Problem Solving	Likes to experiment to elicit reactions; enjoys objects that bounce, make noise, light up, or change colors; puts objects in and out of containers; likes to rearrange furniture; helps around the house; assembles and disassembles things; does not distinguish between play and reality; understands two-part requests; shows preferences and expresses opinions; figures out what might happen before acting	Provide safe objects or toys that can be pulled apart and put back together; look in a mirror together and copy each other; ask for help with projects and then thank her; be patient and give her time to remember; let her play with dustpans, brooms, unbreakable dishes, pots, and pans; play with puzzles and sorting toys to help develop concentration; offer choices; promote independence in dressing	Toy vehicles on ramps and tracks; flashlights; pinwheels; bubbles; dolls and animals wearing clothes; puzzles; boxes; objects she can open (backpack, seat belt)
Creative			
Art & Imagination	Can copy a circle or make a line drawing; has a vivid imagination; enjoys dramatic play, building things, digging in sand	Give her pictures to paste on paper; use bright colors in daily use (clothes, eating utensils, play mats, toys); give her costumes or old clothes for playing dress-up	Art supplies; simple wood toys for imaginative play (doll houses, kitchen sets); brightly colored items for daily use; dress-up items
Music	Can clap in rhythm; likes to listen to music and imitate the sounds; dances to music; hums and sings; identifies some instruments; pretends to use an instrument	Provide streamers or scarves to move with music; play with simple or homemade musical instruments (maracas, cymbals, sticks, drums, pie pans with spoons, tambourines, chopsticks); take her to live music festivals or performances	Drums, bells, xylophones, small pianos, music CDs
Naturalist			
Naturalist	Enjoys textural aspects of the natural world, such as playing with mud, sand, rocks, and water; likes to organize "souvenirs" from nature	Go on a nature walk; collect rocks, leaves, and sticks; sort them; and put them in bags or other containers	Sand toys; funnels; water toys; collection displays; pressed flower or leaf books

Pathways of Whole Learning | 24–36 months

Pathway	Developmental Stage	How to Nurture	Appropriate Toys
Sensory			
Taste	Has a full set of 20 teeth by 3 years; curious about different tastes such as herbs and spices	Encourage good hygiene by establishing a tooth-brushing routine; offer regular cups for drinking; share your meals and create a ritual of dining together as a family; offer adult food like whole apples	Vibrating toothbrush; mouth instruments; balloons to blow up
Smell	Has established likes and dislikes, as well as scent preferences; can distinguish foods from smell alone	Provide words for scents she likes and dislikes, ("A flower smells sweet," "The trash smells rotten"); play a scent identification game by hiding a favorite scent, such as lavender or popcorn, in a sock or small bag and asking her to identify it by smell	Essential oils on blankie or plush toys
Auditory	Likes to hear repetition of favorite songs and books; follow 2- or 3-part spoken directions	Read her favorite books and sing her favorite songs; play games with verbal instructions like "Simon says"; ask her to identify animal sounds; attend sing-alongs	Rhyming books
Visual	Shows continued development and refinement of depth perception and eye-hand-body coordination	Read books that allow her to "see" the story in her mind; stack blocks and roll balls back and forth for depth perception; color and draw with her for coordination; have her first eye exam so the doctor can look for any vision impairments	Kaleidoscope; binoculars; magnifying glass; small "seek and find" picture books
Tactile	More sensitive to textures and touching; may fuss about the feeling of clothing (such as socks) and may remove it; may be fearful of new tactile experiences, such as wet sand or sticky food	Massage, stimulate acupoints, touch, and cuddle with her; play games involving the use of her hands; play with puzzles, Legos, and other toys that involve putting objects together with her hands	Puzzles; Legos; linking toys; plush toys for cuddling; gardening tools; clay
Movement			
Gross Motor	Jumps with two feet in the air; walks on tiptoes; develops bladder control	Encourage cross-lateral movements; play games with balls; dance together	Balls; riding toys; jungle gyms and climbing gyms; swing sets
Fine Motor	Holds pencil correctly in writing position; imitates strokes; builds more complicated towers with blocks and simple bridges	Provide tweezers, clothespins, and chopsticks for picking up items; have her pick up pom-poms with her toes; fold paper together; ask her to put on her own shoes and boots	Origami paper; dress-up dolls; dollhouse play; rocks for stacking
Spatial Awareness	Aware of surroundings and notices things to the right and left of her; intent on possessing objects around her and will grab them without hesitation	Ask her to put her toy "on the table" or "under the chair"; drop a bite-size snack into a clear bottle and encourage her to turn it upside down to get the snack; encourage her to use a small step stool to reach things above her	Simple obstacle courses for a push or pull toy; necklaces and bracelets to take on and off
Interactive			
Self	Likes feeding and dressing herself; wants to please adults; embraces independence and can separate from parents in familiar settings	Show her how to do basic daily activities such as putting trash in the trash can, wiping the table with a sponge, sweeping with a small broom, soaping herself in the bath, and cleaning up her toys; give positive reinforcement following tasks	Varied toys for play dates and group activities
Others	Resists being forced; may not share willingly; engages in parallel play	Ask her questions and make observations; set up play dates; coach and model social behaviors in public settings	Games or toys that require sharing and interaction with others; varied toys for play dates

Pathway	Developmental Stage	How to Nurture	Appropriate Toys
Communication			
Listen	Vocabulary has increased to about 1,000 words; listens on the telephone	Make noise with 3 different objects, hide them, make noise with one of them, and ask her to guess which one it is; whisper to her; have phone calls with family members (real or imaginary)	Toys with sounds; books read aloud
Speak	Says 75 to 300 words; cares less about the answers to questions she asks than about keeping the conversation going; uses longer sentences with 3 or more words; actually comprehends more than 75% of what she is saying	Encourage her to verbalize her thoughts; play with puppets to develop communication skills; socialize with peers; ask about her day; ask her to tell you her preferences; discuss the day's events; call grandparents and friends	Puppets; books; varied toys for play dates; phones
Read and Write	Likes to look at the signs in stores or restaurants; can identify logos and symbols for familiar things	Ask her to find something in a picture in a book; go to the library and read books together—share the task of turning pages and pointing to pictures	Interactive board books, flash cards; crayons or markers for writing
Body and Sign Language	Exaggerates gestures; more variety in facial expressions	Add words to your movements and gestures; encourage her to use her words along with her body language; model calm, appropriate gestures; dance together	Puppets or plush toys as a means of communication; play kitchen and dolls for mimicry
Second Language	Can determine which language is the "most important" and instinctively develops a primary language	Talk to your baby in the second language every day; repeat vocabulary words; read books and play music in her second language; use puppets and plush toys to communicate; play games with words from second language; hire a bilingual babysitter; have play dates with children who speak the second language	Books, recorded music, puppets, plush toys, videos
Cognitive			
Curiosity	Intrigued by water; likes humor games; explores objects by dropping, shaking, banging, and throwing them; likes small challenges; brain responds to new or novel experiences by releasing adrenalin, causing an increase in brain activity and alertness	Create a play bag for excursions, and change out the toys periodically; do something outside of your regular routine occasionally: wear funny clothes, a hat, or sunglasses to get her attention; change the furniture around; rotate toys and meals to keep her alert	Avoid technical toys and instead offer simple, natural ones; explorer gear for nature walks; toys with gears
Memory	Information sticks in her memory when it has context and is relevant; remembers events from 6–12 months earlier	Exercise helps memory: repeat or practice skills such as rolling a ball or playing a game; explain why you want her to do or not do something so that it has meaning; explain how something is similar to a familiar object or situation so that she can relate to it	Memory cards; games; simple puzzles; books; photos of past events to discuss
Problem Solving	Realizes there are alternatives or choices; hesitates when she cannot make a choice or decision; wants to know how things work; problem solving fuels self-confidence	Offer simple choices and alternatives during daily activities such as getting dressed, eating meals, and playing with toys; read books with alternative narrative choices; play hide-and-seek; create opportunities for success at problem solving to develop self-esteem; create challenges for her; play a matching game: hold up an object and ask her to find a similar or identical one	Blocks; stacking cups; coloring materials; simple puzzles; musical instruments; natural events such as sticks moving down a river or waterfalls; puzzle boxes; tangled string; sticks for reaching objects
Creative			
Art & Imagination	Enjoys dramatic play and dressing up; imagination is flourishing; has difficulty distinguishing fantasy and reality; enjoys pretending to be an animal; can see patterns in designs such as circles, squares, triangles, lines, and dots	Use puppets for role-playing; give her a bucket of water and a brush to paint objects outside on a warm day; make a dress-up box with scarves, masks, old clothes, and costumes	Play kitchen; puppets; dress-up items; books with imaginative themes; dollhouse; gardening tools
Music	Begins to play musical instruments more accurately; music can have a stronger emotional effect, such as soothing or energizing; enjoys live music performances	Roll a ball to music; put on rhythmic music and point to different body part to move with music; practice dancing or playing musical instruments to develop her skills	Real musical instruments; recorded music; sing-along and dance-along songs
Naturalist			
Naturalist	Loves to be outdoors; enjoys playing in water; asks a lot of "Why?" questions about things in nature	Experiment with science and nature by planting a fast-growing bean or pea plant; watch a chick hatch or a butterfly emerge from a chrysalis; go strawberry or blueberry picking; go shopping at a farmer's market; visit an aquarium	Outdoor toys like jungle gyms; water toys

Choosing a Preschool

Choosing your child's preschool may require more considerations than you realize. The philosophy behind a learning environment can have a significant impact on your child's cognitive development. Programs vary in style and philosophy: some offer an academic curriculum that emphasizes discipline, while others provide play-based activities centered on a child's social development, needs, and initiatives.

A growing body of research supports the value of play over highly structured learning programs for young children. The philosophy of Dream Window Kindergarten was based on play as the foundation for learning for children from three to five years old. I observed and participated in the children's abundant learning experiences, which were integrated through participation in physical activity, exploration of nature, music, art, and interaction with teachers and other students. As you develop your priorities in choosing your child's first formal learning experience, keep in mind that your child learns primarily through social interactions and enriching experiences.

Children can thrive and learn even in a structured environment, as long as they have opportunities for interactions and experiences. As you research preschools or other early-childhood programs, consider the quality of the program, the environment, the communication that you and your child will have with the school, and the practicalities of cost and location. As you analyze your needs and priorities, you can research options and determine the role you want to play in your child's early education.

A Memo from Child to Parents

- Don't spoil me. I know quite well that I ought not to have all I ask for. I'm only testing you.
- Don't be afraid to be firm with me. I prefer it. It makes me feel secure.
- Don't let me form bad habits. I have to rely on you to detect them in an early stage.
- Don't make me feel smaller than I am. It only makes me behave stupidly "big."
- Don't correct me in front of people, if you can help it. I'll take much more notice if you talk quietly with me in private.
- Don't make me feel that my mistakes are sins. It upsets my sense of values.
- Don't protect me from consequences. I need to learn the painful way sometimes.
- Don't be too upset when I say, "I hate you." Sometimes it isn't you I hate but your power over me.
- Don't take too much notice of my ailments. Sometimes they get me attention I don't need.
- Don't nag. If you do, I shall have to protect myself by being deaf.
- Don't forget that I cannot explain myself as well as I should like. That's why I am not always accurate.
- Don't put me off when I ask questions. If you do you'll find that I stop asking and seek my information elsewhere.
- Don't be inconsistent. That completely confuses me and makes me lose faith in you.
- Don't tell me my fears are silly. They are terribly real, and you can do much to reassure me if you try to understand.
- Don't ever suggest that you are perfect or infallible. It gives me too great a shock when I discover that you're neither.
- Don't ever think that it is beneath your dignity to apologize to me. An honest apology makes me surprisingly warm toward you.
- Don't forget that I love experimenting. I couldn't get along without it, so please put up with it.
- Don't forget how quickly I am growing up. It must be difficult for you to keep pace with me, but please try to.
- Don't forget that I don't thrive without lots of love and understanding, but I don't need to tell you that, do I?

Excerpt from How to Live with Your Children: A Guide For Parents Using A Positive Approach To Child Behavior by Don H. Fontenelle, PhD.
For more information on other books by Dr. Fontenelle contact him at 504-834-6411, 517 N. Causeway Blvd., Metairie, LA 70001.

❀ Quality of the program—Preschool activities and learning experiences emerge from the philosophy of the program. Do the children have opportunities for creative, imaginative play? Are music, art, movement, and nature parts of the curriculum? Do the children go outside every day? Is their movement restricted? What kind of food does the school serve for snack or lunch? How many children are in the program, and what is the ratio of children to teachers? Is the school reputable, licensed, and certified?

❀ Environment—Is the atmosphere clean, safe, orderly, pleasing, and welcoming? Does the school have books and opportunities for story time? Are there simple toys made of safe materials available for building, sorting, and stacking? Is there child-sized equipment for pretend play, such as kitchen items and tools? Are there mixed ages in the program? Are the teachers warm, loving, healthy, and happy?

❀ Communication—Is the curriculum designed in a way that considers what the children already know so that teachers can offer stimulating experiences that stretch the children to grow beyond their current knowledge? Do the communication pathways with the teachers allow for flexibility so that the curriculum develops along with the students? Is there a reciprocal relationship between teachers and students that is responsive and has give and take? Do the teachers express love for the children? What is the background of the teachers? What kind of relationship will you have with teachers and the administration? Do teachers and staff members openly and professionally communicate with you about your concerns and your child's concerns? Do you feel that you can work in partnership with mutual respect and trust in the education of your child?

❀ Logistics—By considering practicalities while choosing a preschool for your child, you can narrow the options more quickly. Is there a waiting list? What is the cost? Where is it located? Who are the other children who attend? Is the student body diverse? Does your child know the other children? Are the other children available for friendship outside of preschool hours? Can you carpool? Are the school's food standards in alignment with or supportive of yours? Is there an open-door policy so that you can visit your child for lunch or participate occasionally? What are the school's snow-day policies?

❀ Research—By educating yourself about your child's cognitive needs and researching the various options when choosing a preschool, you can gain a clearer idea of your priorities. Ask for references and recommendations from peers, and check online reviews. Make an on-site visit, and interview the administrators and staff. Look for general red flags, such as a hurried and messy environment or an unhappy atmosphere.

❀ Your role—You can actively participate in your child's education by communicating your needs with the preschool's staff and administration. Get involved with the school by participating in and attending children's events or by donating art supplies or extra food. Pay attention to your child, and notice the environment when you drop her off and pick her up every day. Observe the situation, and be aware of any changes. Ask your child specific questions about her day. Keep track of any illnesses or other concerns, and communicate them with the school. Make sure that you provide all the items necessary for your child, such as a change of clothes, food, sunscreen and sun hats, and any remedies or medications. By being involved in your child's education, you can be confident in your intuition and advocate for her when she needs you. You are the consumer in this relationship, so be intentional and speak up about your concerns.

Whole Food

Whole Food

A PIECE OF BROCCOLI is more than its nutritional components. Where did it come from? How did it grow? How is it cut, cooked, and served? All of these factors contribute to the energy in food and the effect that it has on your baby. Food that is broken and processed has a fragmented energy with compromised nutrition. Whole food is simply one ingredient—the food itself. When you offer your baby food that is whole, you offer him energy that is not splintered and split. You offer him completeness and integration. He absorbs the energy in the food that he eats, and it permeates the cells in his body. He takes in the life force of food and he becomes what he eats.

Because food plays such a significant role in your baby's development, I have devoted a large part of this book to it. The food that your baby eats nourishes his body to grow, affects his emotions, and gives his brain the nutrients it needs to develop, think, and learn.

Part 2, "Whole Food" gives you everything you need to know about feeding your baby from the time that he is breast-fed until he is three years old. It contains material about your baby's needs as he begins to eat solid foods, food preparation, basic food information, menu planning, eating out with your baby and holidays.

❀ Chapter 4—"Baby Food Basics" includes information about whole, digestible, fresh, local, traditional, organic, and plant-based foods. I discuss acid and alkaline, genetically modified foods, and the yin and yang of foods. The last part of the chapter outlines the nutrients that your baby's body needs for healthy development.

❀ Chapter 5—"Garden to Table" takes you through the process of food preparation, including the steps of gardening, planning, setting up your pantry and kitchen, menu planning, and shopping. This chapter also includes information about energy in food, hygiene, washing and cutting vegetables, cooking methods, and stocking your pantry. The chapter also contains ideas on when to introduce your baby to solid foods and information about feeding concerns.

❀ Chapter 6—"Food Groups" covers eight different groups of food: Breast Milk, Grains, Vegetables, Protein-rich Foods, Fruits, Fermented Foods, Seasonings, and Beverages. Each section discusses special considerations and influences, different types of food in that category, yin-yang characteristics, preparation methods, and methods for feeding the food to your baby. Recipes are also included for each food group.

❀ Chapter 7—"Menu Plans" has detailed suggestions of menu plans for six stages of development: 6–8 months, 7–9 months, 9–12 months, 12–18 months, 18–24 months, and 24–36 months.

❀ Chapter 8—"At Home in the World" offers ideas on how to deal with situations that are out of the ordinary, such as travel and holidays. Recipes for travel and family meals are included.

CHAPTER **4**

Baby Food Basics

I BELIEVE THAT EATING WITH nature as a guide can create a positive, proactive foundation for a life of radiant health. Growing up, I ate many processed foods, including meat, dairy, sugar, and foods that had artificial coloring and chemicals. At age 23, I felt sluggish and overweight, and I lacked mental clarity and optimism for my life. At that point, I turned my personal health around by switching to a diet of whole, plant-based foods—grains, vegetables, legumes, and fruits, with little to no animal products— while I learned to use the principles of yin and yang. I am thankful to have discovered these principles of nature, which have served as a tool for creating health and vitality for myself and my family. They have helped restore health during times that we had imbalances and illness.

This chapter offers the foundational basics to help you in choosing foods for your baby. It includes the benefits of homemade baby food, information about foods that are easy to digest, and foods that are plant-based, traditional, locally grown, organic, and free of genetically modified organisms. Next, the chapter offers different foods that are acid- or alkaline-forming in your child's body, and how you can help him maintain a healthy pH balance. After that, you can find how to use the principle of yin and yang in using foods to help your baby find balance in his overall condition.

Food for Your Baby

"Let food be thy medicine and medicine be thy food."
–Hippocrates.

Not only is food medicine, it is a way of bringing your family and community together. It is a means of passing down tradition, and a way to have a savored experience. If you choose to breast-feed, food also serves as one of the first opportunities you have to connect with your baby, and to nourish him through your own dietary choices. Today's culture places a lot of emphasis on the importance of getting the right amounts of macronutrients (proteins, carbohydrates, and fats) and micronutrients (vitamins and minerals). While these aspects of your baby's diet are a critical part of his development, they cannot substitute for his sensory experience, his enjoyment of food, and eating in harmony with his environment. Food nourishes your baby's body and soul far beyond ensuring proper quantities of nutrients. His first home-cooked meals can provide balanced nutrition, as well as pleasure and vitality.

Your shopping decisions and cooking methods shape your baby's tastes and dietary habits. Choosing his food is an opportunity to give him a healthy start and influence his tastes for the rest of his life. As you contemplate options of new foods to introduce to your baby's plate, consider ingredients and their source, as well as preparation methods, to maximize his growth and development.

A common and familiar option that many parents choose is packaged baby food. This is a convenient choice when life is too busy to cook at home, or when traveling. Some brands of packaged food come in jars or pouches and use quality organic vegetables with single ingredients, and they do not include artificial flavors, thickeners, preservatives, or additives. However, many packaged baby foods are inferior in their digestibility, nutritional value, and taste. Many brands mix fruits with grains or vegetables to make them sweet and appealing, which can lead to digestive problems for your baby. Most prepackaged baby food tastes bland because it has been heated at a high temperature for sterilization. Although this process is necessary for safety, it destroys flavor, essential nutrients, and key enzymes. Often, instant grain cereals are stripped of their naturally occurring micronutrients through processing. Manufacturers then try to compensate by adding these stripped nutrients back into their foods. These fortified grains may provide as many micronutrients as unprocessed grains; however, the fortified vitamins and minerals are not as easily absorbed as those from natural, whole grains cooked at home. While whole, uncracked grains can last centuries without spoiling, instant cereals require preservatives to ensure freshness. Packaged baby food has usually been grown and harvested in an industrial setting, processed in a factory, and then transported and stored in a way that compromises its freshness and vitality.

Another option is to make your baby's food at home with whole food staples and fresh, locally grown, organic produce.

The Benefits of Homemade Baby Food

The best nutrition

You can offer a wider variety of grains, vegetables, legumes, and fruits to your baby than those found in packaged baby foods, thus providing a broader range of key nutrients. Whole, organic, and seasonal foods grown locally provide more nutrition than processed and refined foods.

Safe ingredients

When you cook food at home, you can be confident about what is and is not in the food because you selected the ingredients and prepared them yourself. You know that there are no thickeners, sugar, dyes, or chemicals in the meals that you have cooked in your own kitchen, and you have no reason to worry about food safety.

Simple, single-ingredient foods

Your baby's sensitive taste buds appreciate simple foods without mixtures and seasonings found in packaged baby food. By introducing foods one at a time, you can help your baby distinguish each new flavor and check for allergies. Discerning allergies becomes more complicated if you are serving packaged baby food that mixes multiple ingredients.

The best taste

Whole, uncracked grains and beans, fresh vegetables and fruits, and natural seasonings are more delicious and satisfying than canned or frozen foods. Take a bite of the food that you feed your baby and see for yourself. In addition, offering a variety of natural tastes stimulates your baby's brain development.

Custom-made baby food

Your baby's taste buds are new and inexperienced. As he experiments with new flavors and develops his own tastes, you will get to know what your baby loves. Making your own baby food lets you mix and match flavors to give your baby just what he wants.

Save money

The convenience of packaged baby food comes at a price. With just a little effort, you can save money while giving your baby higher quality food.

Easy to make

Homemade baby food can be easy to make using simple cooking methods and recipes based on fresh, whole foods. When you become familiar with techniques and ingredients, you will not need recipes and you can feel confident in preparing healthy, nutritious meals for your baby. You will not need special cooking equipment to prepare the food, either.

Organization yields convenience

With planning and organization, you can efficiently fit food preparation into your busy schedule. You can make batches of food, store multiple servings in your refrigerator or freezer, and then dish out small portions over several weeks. Menu planning makes shopping and cooking more efficient and economical as well.

Decrease your carbon footprint

While some jars and tubs used in packaged baby foods can be recycled, pouches end up in the landfill. Throwaway packaging is not necessary when cooking with whole foods. They can be transported without refrigeration, and locally grown produce requires little transportation. Whole foods cause less strain on the environment than the production and transportation of packaged baby foods.

Strengthen the family bond

Breaking bread together as a family is a chance to connect with one another. When you cook for your baby, you can enjoy the same food by preparing extra food, and by adding seasonings separately for other family members. Sharing the same food creates connection and supports harmony within the family.

Whole Foods

A whole food is one that has not been altered by processing, refining, or adding chemicals. It has only one ingredient—itself. A fresh carrot, an apple, or a grain of rice in its natural state is a whole food. It has all of the original vitamins and minerals, plant chemicals (known as phytochemicals), and fiber still intact. A diet of whole foods provides everything your baby's body needs and offers satisfaction at a deep, physiological level. Eating processed foods can result in a fragmented feeling—a sense of disconnection or deficiency when his body craves missing nutrients. The partial satisfaction derived from eating processed and refined foods often leads to overeating to satisfy cravings.

Processed foods are often canned, packaged, or frozen, including many boxed cereals, crackers, chips, cookies, candies, sodas, and meats. Reading the labels of packaged foods helps develop your food consciousness. Look for foods on the label that you recognize,

and if you cannot pronounce an ingredient, it is a good indicator that it is not a whole food.

In the 1950s, processed foods started becoming popular for convenience. Fast food burgers and fries, ready-made lunches, microwavable dinners and cakes in a box have evolved with the support of extensive processing, packaging, and shipping to save time. Whether purchased in a grocery store, restaurant, or fast food establishment, processed foods are often heavily laden with high levels of salt, sugar, and artificial colors, flavors, sweeteners, and preservatives to increase their shelf life. Added chemicals can strain your baby's digestive system, liver, and kidneys, because his body does not know which artificial ingredients to dump, and which to store, nor how to do so.

It is estimated that the average American annually consumes approximately nine pounds of chemical additives from processed foods. Although tasty at first, artificially processed foods often include calories without much nutritional value. Flavor enhancers such as monosodium glutamate (MSG) cause the taste buds to swell, increasing their sensitivity to flavors. Chemicals and flavor enhancers like MSG can confuse your baby's taste buds by introducing more extreme flavors too early in his development. You can help your baby establish sensitivity with his palate by starting with the simple sweet and savory tastes found naturally in whole foods.

American health agencies, such as the U.S. Department of Agriculture (USDA) and the Department of Health and Human Services, are now promoting whole foods. These foods provide the nutrients that help build a strong immune system, while maintaining health and avoiding illness. Whole foods keep insulin levels low, which helps to keep your child's weight in a healthy range. Low in saturated fats, whole foods offer plenty of healthy fats like omega-3 fatty acids, which promote brain development and immunity. They are also high in fiber, which supports healthy digestion and elimination. Whole grains contain B vitamins, which promote deep and restful sleep, something all parents want for their children (and for themselves). In considering all of these preventive health care advantages, the extra time you spend in food preparation can ultimately save on medical bills and illness-related stress.

In addition to their health benefits, whole foods are less expensive than processed convenience foods. Although whole foods require more planning and preparation time, simple recipes and techniques can get your family into a rhythm of cooking and eating easy, nutritious, and satisfying meals.

Foods for Healthy Digestion

Digestion is one of the biggest challenges in your baby's first year, because his digestive system is inherently weak and still developing, according to Bob Flaws, a well-renowned practitioner of East Asian medicine. Even if you offer the most nutritious food, if the food itself cannot be digested, then those nutrients offer no real value. Here are a few points to consider as you introduce new foods to your baby.

Guiding Principles for Your Baby's Digestion

Start with simple, whole, plant-based foods, like whole grains, beans, and vegetables.

Animal foods, such as fish and red meats, are more difficult to digest than plant-based foods; they are recommended after your child's first year.

Soaking grains and beans before cooking predigests them.

Cooking food thoroughly makes less work for your baby's digestive system.

Pureeing or mashing foods helps with assimilation, because your baby cannot chew. Start with a soupy texture, and as your baby grows, you can adjust the thickness of the puree to fit his needs.

Serve food warm or at your baby's body temperature, so that his body does not have to expend energy to heat up his food as it digests. Chilled, frozen, iced, or cold foods add stress to his digestive system.

Serve one food at a time in the beginning to check for a reaction. After you have checked each food individually, you can combine different grains or add a complement of beans or vegetables.

Combining fruits with grains, vegetables, or proteins can cause gas in your baby's stomach, which may be painful and disruptive to his digestive system. Serve fruit at least 30 minutes after eating other foods.

Raw fruit and juices can chill and weaken his digestive system and lead to respiratory illnesses. Bob Flaws recommends cooking fruit for babies to help predigest it, and offering moderate amounts of raw fruits for your baby's first year until his digestive system is stronger.

Fermented foods and probiotic boosters promote healthy digestion and help build good bacteria in your baby's stomach.

Fresh, Local, and Seasonal Foods

Produce at your grocery store has traveled an average of 1,500 miles through trucks, planes, and refrigerated warehouses to get to your shopping cart. This transportation process can take up to two weeks and is referred to as "food miles." Some conventional growers pick vegetables and fruits early, use chemical gases to ripen the produce, and use preservatives to keep produce looking fresh. Some growers use genetically modified organisms (GMO) seeds engineered to give produce a uniform appearance and long shelf life. Since foods grown from GMO seeds have a longer shelf life, they can withstand more food miles. However, the long-term health and ecological effects are unknown.

Recently, chefs, nutritionists, authors, and other "foodies" have been advocating for dietary practices that are in line with the values of a balanced body and ecosystem by eating local, seasonal foods. The "locavore" movement is based on eating foods, especially perishable items like vegetables, fruits, and animal products that are grown or raised within 100 miles of one's home. Recently, the U.S. Department of Agriculture (USDA) created a new definition of a local region, which is within "400 miles of where the food was grown or produced, or within the same state where it is sold." In addition to reducing food miles, sustainably grown local produce is often more delicious and nutritious than industrially grown conventional produce.

Eating seasonal foods helps your baby's body acclimate to changes in the weather. On hot summer days, it is natural to crave foods that help his body stay cool and balanced—noodles, salads, and steamed vegetables are light and cool. During the winter months, hearty soups and stews taste good and provide warmth from the inside out.

When you buy local, seasonal produce for your child, you offer him flavor and nutrition in foods that balance and harmonize with his body and the ecosystem while minimizing your family's "food miles."

Tried-and-True Traditional Foods

Before the development of modern refrigeration and transportation, traditional cultures had limited means of food preservation. These cultures used only locally grown, seasonal foods, prepared in traditional ways. The Mediterranean region is known for its healthy traditional diet with a focus on whole grains, seasonal vegetables and fruits, beans, and locally caught fish. Asian cultures eat rice as their principal grain; Native American and Latin cultures eat corn as their main dish; many African cultures eat yams as a staple; and European cultures use wheat, barley, millet, and oats as traditional staples.

Most traditional cultures usually have active lifestyles and eat balanced meals made with natural ingredients in modest portions. Traditional food rituals often reflect cultural heritage and family history when meals are shared at the dinner table. What are some dishes that have been passed down in your family? You can develop your own family customs and traditions with certain foods that have meaning for you. Saturday morning pancakes or pasta night, special holiday dishes, summer barbecues, or religious ceremonies that involve food can become traditions when you repeat them time after time.

Organic Foods

In the United States, the USDA regulates the standards for organic foods. Organic crops are grown without synthetic pesticides or artificial fertilizers, and are not genetically modified. Animals raised on organic farms eat organically grown feed without supplemental growth hormones or antibiotics and are given access to more spacious living and grazing accommodations than conventional farm animals.

In general, organic farms operate by the principles of biodiversity and sustainability. These principles include responsible land use practices such as crop rotation, natural fertilizers, and composting, as well as the use of natural fertilizers and pest control methods. According to North America's Organic Trade Association, organic farming reduces pollution in groundwater, aids plant growth, creates richer soil, and reduces soil erosion. Organic or pesticide-free farming methods also reduce the contamination of rivers, streams, oceans, and drinking water.

Becoming certified organic is an expensive process, and many small farmers operate under organic principles and methodologies without the certification. Reading about the companies you buy from or introducing yourself at farmers' markets can help you make conscientious purchases. When you are eating local, organically grown vegetables, you can easily appreciate the difference in quality and taste. Purchasing organic food, you can have confidence in the food you are providing for your baby.

Prioritizing purchases

Babies and children are more vulnerable to toxins while their immune system is still building strength. Some experts maintain that the levels of toxins in conventionally grown foods are safe enough for most healthy adults, but they acknowledge that low-level pesticide exposure can be toxic for children and pregnant women. If you serve animal foods to your child, keep in mind that animals raised by conventional methods may contain hormones, antibiotics, and other chemicals. Most plant-based foods are water soluble and do not hold these chemicals in the same way that animal foods can retain these toxins. Choosing organic is a higher priority for animal foods.

Although organic food is more expensive, good health can be less expensive in the long run. Buying organic produce in season and freezing them for the off-season can actually save money. If a complete organic shopping list is cost prohibitive for your budget, you can prioritize your purchases. For example, eggs, dairy, chicken, and meat are on my organic priority list, because of the added hormones and antibiotics.

Look for the USDA certified organic seal to verify that your purchases are organic. You can also ask the farmer directly about his practices when shopping at a local farmers' market. Some foods are safer to eat than others when grown by conventional methods. The Environmental Working Group (EWG), a nonprofit organization that promotes policies to support global and individual health, published a list called the "Clean 15" and the "Dirty Dozen." This list shows which conventionally grown produce is safer or more dangerous to consume based on pesticide contamination levels.

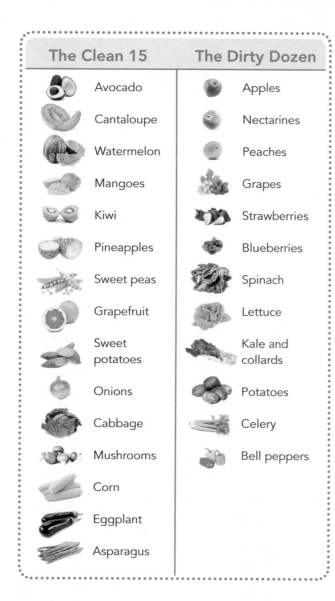

The Clean 15	The Dirty Dozen
Avocado	Apples
Cantaloupe	Nectarines
Watermelon	Peaches
Mangoes	Grapes
Kiwi	Strawberries
Pineapples	Blueberries
Sweet peas	Spinach
Grapefruit	Lettuce
Sweet potatoes	Kale and collards
Onions	Potatoes
Cabbage	Celery
Mushrooms	Bell peppers
Corn	
Eggplant	
Asparagus	

Genetically Modified Foods

Genetically modified organisms are plants or animals created through the gene-splicing techniques of biotechnology, or genetic engineering. This technology merges DNA from different species, creating combinations of plant, animal, bacterial, and viral genes that do not occur in nature or in traditional crossbreeding. Most GMO crops are engineered to withstand industrial herbicide and insecticide applications and to produce larger, more beautiful harvests with longer shelf lives. However, these vegetables and fruits lack the robust flavor of their GMO-free counterparts

According to the Non-GMO Project, a nonprofit committed to informing consumers and building sources of non-GMO products, a growing body of evidence connects GMOs with health problems, environmental damage, and violation of both farmers' and consumers' rights. Health risks include allergies, organ damage, and hormone disruption. Most developed nations do not consider GMOs to be safe, and nearly 50 countries around the world, including Australia, Japan, and all of the countries in the European Union, have restrictions and bans on the production and sale of GMO foods. In the United States, the government has approved GMO foods based on studies conducted by the same corporations that created them along with profit from their sales.

 For more about genetically modified foods visit nongmoproject.org

The Clean 15

The Clean 15 vegetables and fruits do not have high levels of pesticide and other chemical contamination. Health advocate, Andrew Weil, MD, suggests that when purchasing vegetables and fruits, the Clean 15 are safe to eat, even if not organic.

The Dirty Dozen

The Dirty Dozen list includes foods that are most heavily sprayed, and therefore contain the most dangerous levels of pesticide residues. Nutritionists and other health authorities recommend buying organically grown vegetables and fruits from the Dirty Dozen list.

Plant-based Foods

Traditionally, people in Asia have predominantly eaten rice and vegetables with small amounts of animal foods that do not include dairy. *The China Study* (Ben Bella Books, 2005), based on research done by T. Colin Campbell, PhD, of Cornell University, followed 6,500 Chinese people in 65 counties throughout China, tracking their diets and disease patterns over 20 years. He found that those who ate mainly whole, unprocessed plant foods had the lowest rates of all the major diseases, including obesity, diabetes, heart disease, and cancer. Conversely, those whose diets included substantial amounts of animal-based foods, such as meat and dairy, were far more likely to suffer from the major illnesses that are more common in the West.

In a 2011 interview with the *New York Times*, Campbell recommended a plant-based diet as a result of his studies. He said, "The effect [that a plant-based diet] produces is broad for treatment and prevention of a wide variety of ailments, from cancer to heart disease and diabetes." Campbell's study suggests that whole foods can prevent and reverse many serious illnesses. His book has sold more than 500,000 copies, making it one of America's best-selling books about nutrition.

My family has primarily eaten a plant-based diet and enjoyed animal foods in moderation, while using the tools of yin and yang to create balance with them. Hideko Yoshida from Muso Yochien (Dream Window Kindergarten) used to advise me that when I ate fish or other animal foods, if I ate less rice and more fresh vegetables and fruits, I could ensure balance. She also suggested that animal foods be eaten more often in the cold winter months instead of in the summer because of their warming effects on the body.

All foods have an energetic force, as well as a nutritional profile. Plant-based foods create a calmer, quieter, and more peaceful energy than animal foods

do, which activate movement and assertiveness. If you observe your child when he eats plant-based foods or animal-based foods, you can get a sense of how the energy in what he eats affects him, and whether he needs more or less based on his condition.

Acid and Alkaline

Illness thrives in acidic environments, so a slightly more alkaline environment is a healthy state for your baby. Your baby's body has a buffer system to maintain the balance of acid and alkaline. Because of this buffer system, the food he eats does not have a direct and immediate effect on the actual pH balance in his blood. However, eating alkaline-forming foods creates an alkaline environment, and eating acid-forming foods generates an acidic environment in your baby's body.

Most land and sea vegetables, and foods that are high in vitamins and minerals have an alkaline-forming effect on your baby's body; most animal foods that are high in protein and fat, along with highly processed carbohydrates have an acid-forming effect. Whole grains and dried beans have a slightly acid-forming effect on your child's body, but soaking or sprouting converts them to become more alkaline-forming. The sprouting process releases enzymes and other phytochemicals, which makes them slightly alkaline-producing. Offering a variety of whole grains provides options for an alkaline-producing effect. You can be confident that whole and natural foods are generally more alkaline-producing, while refined foods are more acid-producing.

Your child's body maintains its balanced (homeostatic) condition and naturally keeps the pH of his body fluids in a slightly alkaline range. When the net acid- and alkaline-forming effects of his diet match the slightly alkaline pH of his blood, it is much easier for his body to stay in balance than if he eats foods that are extremely acid- or alkaline-forming.

To assist his body in maintaining this condition, you can make whole grains and fresh vegetables the center of your child's diet. In general, foods toward the center of the yin-yang spectrum are more alkaline-forming, and foods on the extreme ends of the spectrum are more acid-forming.

It is difficult to provide a reliable list of acid- and alkaline-forming foods, because some foods such as fruits can be acid- or alkaline-forming, depending on the situation. Several factors that influence the acid- or alkaline-forming effect on your baby's body when eating fruits are: the condition of his body at the time, and the ripeness, quality (organically or conventionally grown), and preparation method of the fruit. The amount eaten and combination with other foods also play a role in how eating fruit can affect your baby's body. If he eats a balanced diet with moderate amounts of fruit, then eating fruit can be alkaline-producing to his body fluids.

The following lists indicate which common foods have an alkaline-forming effect on your child's condition, and which ones result in acid formation when they are digested and assimilated into his body.

Aside from choosing a balance of acid- and alkaline-producing foods, you can also help your child maintain his natural alkaline condition by adjusting his environment. Because lifestyle factors such as stress and pollution can create acidic reactions in his body, make sure that he gets outdoors, is around oxygen-producing plants, and has free time away from electrical devices, such as televisions and computer screens. This will help your child maintain his slightly alkaline state.

Balance: The Yin and Yang of Foods

Typically, the term *balanced diet* describes a meal plan that offers a calculation of macronutrients and micronutrients. Assessing food with the ancient concept of yin and yang is another way to balance food as living energy. Because yin-yang energy is present in every substance, the food your baby eats has yin and yang properties that affect his balance, which influences his physical and mental growth and development, and how he feels along the way.

The yin-yang spectrum of foods compares a range of foods and how they are relative to each other in terms of yin and yang. Extremes are on the ends of the spectrum. Eating extreme foods on one side of the spectrum creates an attraction to an extreme food on the other side. For example, salty chips pair well with a cool drink, and animal foods balance sugar. Imagine a pendulum swinging back and forth from extreme yang foods to extreme yin foods. You can slow that pendulum to a more moderate swing by giving your baby foods that are toward the center of the spectrum—primarily grains and vegetables. Eating balanced foods is less stressful on your child's body because it does not overcompensate for extremes.

Grains, beans, sea vegetables, and vegetables are in the center range of the yin-yang spectrum of foods. Eating these foods on a daily basis helps create a steady, even, and balanced diet. Eating foods outside of the center creates a wider swing in the pendulum—yang

Acidity and Alkalinity of Food Groups

	Alkaline	Neutral	Acid
Whole Grains			●
Refined Grains			●
Vegetables	●		
Sea Vegetables	●		
Dried Beans		●	
Fish			●
Eggs		●	
Dairy Products		●	
Poultry			●
Red Meat			●
Fruits	●		
Fermented Pickles (made with sea salt)	●		
Vegetable Oils		●	
Sea Salt	●		
Refined Salt			●
Refined Sugar			●
Artificial Sweeteners			●
Drugs and Medications			●

Please note that this list of acid- and alkaline-forming foods is not comprehensive.

Adapted from *Acid Alkaline Companion* by Carl Ferré and used by permission of George Ohsawa Macrobiotic Foundation. Learn more at OhsawaMacrobiotics.com.

animal foods stimulate the taste for yin sweets, which then creates an attraction for yang foods again. Yin and yang flows back and forth and are not static. One element is relative to another: vegetables are more yin compared to grains, but more yang compared to fruits.

Because children are inherently yang and are growing, they generally need more yin food to expand and develop. Listed in the chart are balanced foods toward the middle for daily use, foods on a wider spectrum for occasional use, and extreme foods to avoid.

You can use the knowledge of yin and yang to influence your baby's condition and help him return to balance when he gets out of balance. For instance, if your child has an overly yin condition, such as lethargy, whininess, or diarrhea, reducing yin foods, such as fruit, juice, or sugar, can help him come back toward the center. Feeding him more cooked whole grains and yang vegetables, such as root vegetables, can also help him become more centered.

If your child shows signs of an excessively yang condition, such as hyperactivity, irritability, or constipation, you can reduce salt and animal food in his diet for a relaxing effect. Feeding him more yin vegetables, such as leafy green vegetables and fruits, can help him return to the center. Other factors, such as changing seasons, food preparations, and cooking methods also play a part in determining the yin-yang balance of food.

The concept of yin and yang does not mean that one is good and the other is bad. There are no specific rules for using the principles of yin and yang. You can experiment and try different foods to observe their effect. If you listen to your child's preferences while considering these principles, then you can follow his lead and discover how the pendulum goes back and forth. You can moderate the swing of his pendulum by offering him higher quality foods that are nearer the center of the spectrum to satisfy him. For example, if he craves ice cream, then offer him fruit; if he craves salty chips, offer him foods that have less sodium, such as tamari or miso. He craves what he needs and you can be the moderator to help him maintain a centered balance.

Trial and observation, with these principles in mind, will help you develop your own intuition of how it works. Knowledge and understanding of this principle of attraction can help you be a guide for your child. These recommendations are based on my experiences using these principles for myself, as a parent, and as a grandmother. The Food Groups chapter includes more yin-yang charts with examples to help you guide your baby toward balance.

Yin-Yang Spectrum of Foods

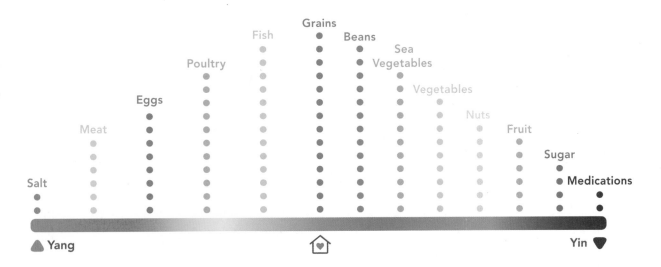

Indicators of Yin and Yang

Indicators	Yang ▲	Yin ▼
Growing Season	Winter	Summer
Growing Climate	Temperate	Tropical
Growing Conditions	Wild	Cultivated or farm-raised
Growing Time	Longer	Shorter
Direction of Growth	Downward	Upward
Perishable	Less	More
Size	Small	Large
Shape	Round	Thin
Texture	Firm	Soft
Color	Red	Purple
Moisture Content	Low	High
Sugar Content	Low	High
Sodium Content	High	Low
Mineral Content	High	Low
Fat Content	Low	High
Element	Animal	Plant
Preparation Method	Cooked	Raw
Process	Natural	Chemical
Amount of Yin Food	Less	More
Amount of Yang Food	More	Less

Yin and yang are always changing and are not static or concrete, so a food is not specifically yin or yang. Various influences contribute to the individual energy of each food. Above are some factors that determine the yin-yang of foods to help you find balance for your child.

What Your Baby's Body Needs

A nutrient is a substance that provides energy for your baby's body to grow and develop, repair or heal tissue when needed, and sustain his body's functions. A healthy diet for your baby includes both macronutrients and micronutrients, along with water and enzymes. Macronutrients are the major food categories that his body needs for energy, including carbohydrates, proteins, fats and oils, water, and certain minerals. If your baby's body were a car, macronutrients would be the fuel that powers its daily operation. Micronutrients are smaller doses of vitamins, minerals, and other chemicals that are just as important for long-term maintenance. In the car analogy, these micronutrients and enzymes are the radiator fluid, coolant, engine oil, and other fluids that do not get checked as often but are critical to your car's long-term functioning.

Carbohydrates

Carbohydrates are macronutrients that include a significant amount of fiber, which is essential for brain and bowel function and for supplying basic energy. There are two types of carbohydrates: simple carbohydrates, such as glucose and fructose, and complex carbohydrates. Carbohydrates have gotten a negative reputation because simple carbohydrates are found in many refined foods with processed flour and sugar, such as white breads and pastas. However, complex carbohydrates, such as those found in whole grains, vegetables, fruits, and breast milk, are both healthy and essential. Simple carbohydrates create spikes and dips in blood sugar, whereas complex carbohydrates provide steady, prolonged energy.

Protein

Protein, another macronutrient, is the primary external source of amino acids for your baby's body. Although his body can produce some amino acids on its own, others must be obtained through food. Amino acids are often called "building blocks" because they are essential for building muscles, skin, tissue, and hair. Breast milk provides complete protein for your baby during the first six months of his life. Whole plant-based foods that contain protein include grains, beans, nuts, seeds, and vegetables. If you choose an animal-based diet, dairy products, eggs, fish, and meat will also provide high levels of protein.

Fats and Oils

Fats and oils, another category of macronutrients, are essential to the development of your baby's brain, nervous system, and eyes, and are vital for proper functioning of his immune system, blood, blood vessels, adrenal glands, and other organs. They are a good source of energy and also help maintain healthy hair, skin, and nails. "Good fats" are found in coconut, sesame, and olive oils, nuts, seeds, fish, avocados, flaxseeds, and breast milk. Meat and dairy products, such as cheese, are high in saturated fats, which can clog cell membranes and raise cholesterol levels, and they are not necessary for a healthy diet.

Water

Water is essential for all your baby's body functions and is the solvent in which chemical reactions take place. Water regulates body temperature, digestion, and metabolic functions. Water is taken in through drinking, eating fresh vegetables and fruits, and bathing.

Vitamins

Vitamins are natural organic compounds that are plentiful in plant-based foods like vegetables, grains, beans, and fruit. They contribute to the absorption of the macronutrient proteins, fats, and carbohydrates. A wide variety of vitamins is necessary for healthy growth and development. If you are strictly vegetarian or vegan, you may consider supplements of vitamins D and B12.

Minerals

Your baby's body needs macronutrient minerals including iron, calcium, phosphorous, potassium, sulfur, sodium, chloride, and magnesium. These minerals are essential for building bones and for vital body functions. Most minerals are ample in a well-balanced diet of grains, vegetables, sea vegetables, nuts, seeds, dried fruits, fresh fruits, and miso, as well as optional foods such as dairy, kefir, yogurt, and eggs.

Minerals regulate your baby's hormones and nervous system, and they are necessary for the development of his bones, teeth, and muscles.

Enzymes

Enzymes regulate chemical activities and are necessary for the digestion of carbohydrates, proteins, and fats. Enzymes can be found in fermented and raw foods. Cooking at high temperatures and microwaving can destroy enzymes.

Your baby's nutritional needs are very high in his first year of life, because he is growing so much and so quickly. He needs quality food that includes these essential nutrients for his healthy physical, emotional, and mental development.

Supplements

Micronutrients are necessary for your baby's energy and balance. Whole food sources of vitamins and minerals are more bioavailable and come in more appropriate doses than micronutrients found in supplements and fortified foods. In the case of vitamins and minerals, bioavailability refers to the proportion of the micronutrient that is able to be absorbed and digested by the body, relative to the total amount of the nutrient present. Natural preparation methods, such as soaking, sprouting, fermenting, and cooking can increase the bioavailability of vitamins and minerals in foods. Supplements and fortified foods have been processed to contain a high concentration of vitamins and minerals, and this high concentration can overwork your baby's organs. Although supplements and fortified foods have higher levels of vitamins and minerals, they are often not as bioavailable as those in breast milk and whole food sources and can end up in your baby's waste. Ferrous sulfate, an iron supplement added to many formulas, is difficult to absorb and can cause indigestion and constipation. Check with your health care provider to see if it is necessary to give your baby supplements or fortified foods.

Primary Vitamins and Their Functions

 Vitamin A is a fat-soluble vitamin, important for support of your baby's immune system and for his eyesight, and to help increase his body's resistance to infections.

Found in: orange vegetables and fruits, leafy greens, and sea vegetables.

 Vitamin B1 is essential for the metabolism of carbohydrates, for energy production, healthy skin, and support of your baby's nervous system.

Found in: whole grains, legumes, nuts, and seeds.

 Vitamin B2 is important for energy production, supports your baby's nervous and immune systems, and is necessary for tissue repair and healthy eyes.

Found in: whole grains, legumes, nuts, seeds, sea vegetables, and eggs.

 Vitamin B3 is important for energy production, metabolism of carbohydrates, fats, and proteins, and support of your baby's immune system.

Found in: whole grains, legumes, and seeds.

 Vitamin B5 is a main component in creating and processing fats and energy, utilizes carbohydrates, proteins, fats by bonding with sulphur molecules to create Coenzyme A.

Found in: meat, vegetables, cereal grains, legumes, eggs, and milk.

 Vitamin B6 is the most studied of the B vitamins and found to keep skin healthy by reducing inflammation. Breaks down sugar and carbohydrates, especially glycogen. Produces "amines" which help your baby's nervous systems transmit signals.

Found in: fish, meat, vegetables, nuts, and bananas.

 Vitamin B7 is essential for the metabolism of carbohydrates, fats and proteins. The most common B7-related symptom in infants is known as cradle cap, a scaly skin rash that can occur on the scalp of newborns.

Found in: nuts, avocado, vegetables, eggs, and cow's milk.

 Vitamin B9 is part of the vitamin B complex. B9 works closely with vitamin B12 in the synthesis of protein, as well as production of genetic materials, and it is a key player in the development of your baby's red blood cells.

Found in: whole grains, legumes, nuts, yellow and orange vegetables, leafy greens, berries, and sea vegetables.

 Vitamin B12 is necessary for the production of red blood cells and folate metabolism.

Found in: yogurt, brewer's yeast, eggs, sea vegetables, fish, and cow's milk.

 Vitamin C is an antioxidant, supports the immune system, and is vital in helping your baby's body cope with stress.

Found in: leafy greens, avocados, berries, melons, and sea vegetables.

 Vitamin D plays a major role in calcium absorption and mineralization of bones. It is the only vitamin that can be manufactured in your baby's body. Breast-fed infants absorb it very well and can make adequate amounts with moderate exposure to sunlight.

Found in: sunshine (10-15 minutes per day over 1 year old), cow's milk, soy milk, fish, eggs, and sea vegetables.

 Vitamin E is a fat-soluble vitamin and powerful antioxidant. It protects your baby's body from harmful toxins and carcinogens, including mercury, lead, benzene, nitrates, cigarette smoke, and pollution.

Found in: almonds, avocados, oats, and sea vegetables.

 Vitamin K is necessary in the production of an essential substance in blood clotting. Vitamin K is made by intestinal bacterial.

Found in: greens and sea vegetables.

Primary Minerals and Their Functions

 Calcium Calcium is one of the most abundant minerals in your baby's body, 99% of it is stored in bones and teeth, and it is important in maintaining bone density and strength.

Found in: leafy greens, sea vegetables, nuts, seeds, tofu, and legumes.

 Chromium Chromium is very important in glucose metabolism and regulations, insulin production, and the manufacture of proteins.

Found in: whole grains, green vegetables, fruits, and sea vegetables.

 Copper Copper is important in helping your baby's body use iron to make hemoglobin, and is necessary for taste sensitivity. It is an essential component for bone, cartilage, connective tissue, and skin.

Found in: whole grains, legumes, nuts, seeds, leafy greens, and berries.

 Iron Iron is a mineral needed by every cell in your baby's body, and essential for growth and development. Healthy, full-term babies are born with an adequate amount of iron for 3 to 6 months (provided the mother consumed enough iron during pregnancy), after which these stores begin to decrease.

Found in: whole grains, legumes, nuts, seeds, berries, dried fruit, molasses, and sea vegetables.

 Fluoride Fluoride is essential for your baby's tooth development. Fluoride supplementation is not recommended for newborns because too much can be toxic.

Found in: whole grains, vegetables, and fruits.

 Iodine Iodine is necessary for proper function of your baby's thyroid gland.

Found in: sea vegetables, fish, and eggs.

 Magnesium Magnesium is necessary for healthy bones and teeth. Vital in helping muscles relax.

Found in: grains, legumes, nuts, seeds, leafy greens, berries, dried fruit, molasses, and sea vegetables.

 Manganese Manganese plays a role in carbohydrate, fat, and protein metabolism, and the proper functioning of your baby's nerves. It is important for various enzyme systems.

Found in: whole grains, legumes, nuts, and seeds.

 Molybdenum Molybdenum helps regulate proper pH levels, is involved in carbohydrate metabolism, and is a component of tooth enamel.

Found in: whole grains, legumes, nuts, and seeds.

 Phosphorus Phosphorus is important for strengthening your baby's bones and teeth, and for energy metabolism, and is a component of tooth enamel.

Found in: whole grains, legumes, nuts, seeds, yogurt, and sea vegetables.

 Potassium Potassium supports your baby's cardiovascular system and is necessary for proper fluid balance in his cells, muscle contraction, and nervous system.

Found in: whole grains, legumes, nuts, seeds, leafy greens, orange vegetables, sea vegetables, melons, berries, and avocados.

 Selenium Selenium supports your baby's cardiovascular system and is necessary for proper fluid balance in his cells, muscle contraction, and nervous system.

Found in: whole grains, legumes, nuts, seeds, leafy greens, orange vegetables, sea vegetables, melons, berries, and avocados.

 Sodium chloride Sodium Chloride is an electrolyte necessary for making hydrochloric acid in your baby's stomach. It must be in balance with potassium for his proper cardiovascular health.

Found in: leafy greens, sea salt, eggs, fish, dried fruit, and sea vegetables.

 Zinc Zinc supports your baby's immune system, blood-sugar balance, and taste and smell.

Found in: nuts, seeds, and sea vegetables.

CHAPTER 5

Garden to Table

WHEN MARI WAS A toddler, I loved gardening with her by my side, digging in the dirt. As she sifted through the dirt and pulled out worms, she called out, "Worm, Mama, worm!" I can still hear that sweet, enthusiastic voice in my head. Growing plants can give you a strong connection to, and appreciation of, where food comes from and how it grows. If you have space in your yard, growing vegetables can help your child feel a connection between food and the earth. Growing herbs in pots is another way to participate in the growing process. Many herbs, such as thyme, rosemary, and sage, survive winters and last year after year. Other herbs, such as basil and parsley, need a fresh start every spring. A sweet potato plant or an avocado plant grows quickly, and bean sprouts are easy and practical to grow in your own kitchen. Because they transform from seeds into sprouts within a few days, bean sprouts provide an easy example for your toddler to see how plants grow.

When you grow plants yourself, it is easy to understand the meaning of organic. The idea of putting chemical fertilizer in your soil, or spraying your homegrown garden vegetables with pesticides, seems more real than the disconnection you may have when buying produce at the grocery store. When you have had a real gardening experience, the thought of giving your baby vegetables to eat that are grown with chemical fertilizers or pesticides seems irrational. Growing your own close to home becomes a reality check of what organically grown means.

Many schools are experimenting with gardens for kids to participate in a hands-on gardening experience. Children love watching vegetables grow, and their curiosity for eating fresh vegetables can grow along with the experience. Some communities also have shared neighborhood gardens where you can grow something together with your child.

When your child experiences the process of growing food and eating it herself, she can apply that understanding to other foods and their sources. Where did it grow? How did it grow? How was it processed? How was it transported? These are questions that help your child connect to nature through food. Getting in touch with the source of food is the first step in the process of bringing it to the table for your little one. The next steps in this chapter include: organizing, planning, shopping, energy in food, hygiene, food preparation, cooking methods, stocking up, timesaving tips, introducing solid foods, feeding concerns, food journal, and stages of eating.

Organization and Planning

Cooking food for your baby can be simple and easily incorporated into your schedule with some planning and organization. Getting the basic tools, setting up your pantry and refrigerator, and making a menu plan and shopping list will help integrate simple cooking into your daily routine. With prior planning, you can coordinate your baby's food with your family meals together and save time, energy, and money.

Most ordinary kitchen equipment made from safe materials is all you need, with the exception of small storage containers to store individual servings for future use. I do not recommend cooking foods in plastic cookers, pouring hot food into plastic containers, and microwaving food in plastic dishes, because the heat melts the plastic and releases chemicals, which can leach into your food. If you use plastic containers and equipment, it is very important to be sure that the plastic is food-safe and that any contact is made after the food has cooled. Stainless steel, glass, ceramic (lead-free), and cast iron are the safest materials for equipment and containers to use in cooking food for your baby. Avoid aluminum and nonstick coatings such as Teflon®.

The recipes included throughout the book are simple methods based on principles of balance, so they are easy to use with a variety of grains, vegetables, beans, and fruits. When you become familiar with the ingredients and cooking methods, recipes will not be necessary, and you will be able to cook your baby's food quickly and easily.

To cook efficiently, make a space for your main tools and utensils with easy access. Each motion takes energy, especially when carrying your baby. If you have to move an object that is in the way, or spend time looking for a utensil, it can slow you down and take more physical and mental energy. Therefore, the most frequently used items deserve the best location for easy access in your kitchen. Clearing out unnecessary items or equipment that is used infrequently leaves space for the things that you need most often.

My kitchen in Japan

"My kitchen in Japan was so tiny that I could stand in the middle and touch everything in the room. The top of the refrigerator provided storage space, and I set up shelves for books and utensils on the walls. The hot water heater was a small, "on-demand" style, and because baking is not a regular part of Japanese cooking, our kitchen did not come with an oven. However, Naoki found a small gas oven that someone discarded, which was big enough to make 12 cookies at a time. I had to organize my time, as well as the space in my kitchen, to take care of all my baby's daily needs and to cook nutritious food for my family."

Setting Up Your Pantry

The ingredients that you need for preparing whole, organic meals at home for your baby are: some basic dried foods, bottled or canned goods, and fresh vegetables and fruits. Basic staples, or foods that keep for several months without spoiling, include: grains, beans, sea vegetables, and seasonings. In addition, some convenience foods, such as packaged baby food, canned beans, teething biscuits, and quick-cooking cereals are handy to have for those just-in-case times. When your baby starts eating solids, set aside a cabinet or some shelving for these staples. Fresh foods can go in the refrigerator, in a hanging basket, or on the countertop. Once you organize your kitchen, with basic equipment and ingredients, you will find that cooking your baby's first foods is surprisingly easy.

Storage containers

Many attractive and efficient storage containers are available today. Look for ceramic, stainless, or glass, containers with an airtight seal to keep grains, beans, and other staples fresh and free of bugs. Storing grains, flours, and beans in plastic bags can increase the risk of grain moths, because the moths can bore small holes through the bags and lay their larvae inside. Glass jars are economical containers that are available at grocery, hardware, and kitchen stores, and they come in sets of 12 per size. A case of 12 jars may seem like a lot, but you may be surprised at the various ways you can use them. In addition to storing dry goods, they are convenient for storing prepared foods, such as soups, purees, and beverages. They also have measurement markings on the side that can be helpful for measuring and mixing ingredients. Glass jars are a practical way to keep your staples organized.

Glass Jar Sizes

- **2 quarts** (64 ounces or 8 cups)

- **1 quart** (32 ounces or 4 cups)

- **1 pint** (16 ounces or 2 cups)

- **½ pint** (8 ounces or 1 cup)

- **Small** (4 ounces or ½ cup)

Buy a package of labels at an office-supply or craft store and write the date of purchase on these labels and put it on the jar.

Pots, Pans, and Cooking Utensils

Lightweight pots and pans made of stainless steel are efficient for quick-cooking methods, such as sautéing, boiling, and steaming. Heavier ones made of cast iron, enameled cast iron, or enameled stainless steel work well for slower cooking methods, such as soups and stews. Aluminum pans and nonstick cookware are not recommended. I recommend glass over plastic for storing food, but if you do use plastic in your kitchen, make sure that is food-safe and that food is cooled to room temperature before storing it in the plastic. This prevents chemicals from the plastic from leaching into your baby's food. Bamboo, wood, clay, and ceramic (lead-free) are all-natural materials for cooking utensils. Silicone is man-made, but it is made from silica and not from petroleum, so it is considered a safe cooking material. The following tools and utensils are the main items that you need for basic cooking and to make the recipes in this book.

Storage jars: Several sizes are convenient for storing foods in the pantry or refrigerator.

Vegetable brush: A natural-bristled brush will not bruise vegetables the way a plastic one does. A traditional Japanese brush made from stiff palm fibers, cleans produce well without damaging it.

Vegetable peeler: Used for peeling vegetables and fruits that are too fibrous for baby to eat, such as potatoes or apples, and it is also convenient if produce was not grown organically.

Wooden or bamboo cutting board: Wood or bamboo cutting boards are best for cutting plant-based foods, such as vegetables and fruits. When cutting animal food such as fish or poultry, I do not cut on the same cutting board that I use for vegetables and fruits. Wipe clean regularly and keep dry in between uses to prevent bacteria growth.

Vegetable knife: For cutting consistency, a vegetable knife is one of the most important kitchen tools for me. A sharp, rectangular-shaped knife made of carbon or stainless steel cuts precisely and evenly.

Paring knife: Helpful for cutting off rough spots, stems, or leaves of produce.

Scissors: Used for opening packages that are vacuum packed, or boxes and bags. Also convenient for cutting stems, herbs, flowers, or your toddler's foods.

Strainer: Used for washing grains or beans, and for straining foods.

Colander: Used for washing produce, and for draining pasta, cooked vegetables, and fruits.

Prep bowls: Small bowls for organizing cut pieces of vegetables, fruits, grains, sauces, or seasonings.

Measuring cups: A basic set made of stainless steel for measuring ingredients.

Measuring spoons: A basic set made of stainless steel for measuring ingredients.

Wooden spoons: Used for stirring while cooking or preparing baked dishes.

Spatula: Used for scraping puree from the side of the blender, or for preparing baked dishes.

Steamer: Used for steaming vegetables and for warming previously prepared food that has been frozen or refrigerated. Stainless steel is recommended.

Saucepans: Two to three pans made of stainless steel in various sizes are convenient for cooking grains, vegetables, beans, fruits, soups, and beverages. Glass lids are helpful for monitoring cooking.

Skillet: A small skillet made of stainless steel or cast iron can be used for sautéing with water or oil; also convenient for cooking fish or tempeh dishes.

Baking dish: A small dish made of ceramic, Pyrex, cast iron, or enameled cast iron is convenient for cooking individual dishes for your child. It is used for roasting vegetables, fish and poultry, or baking casseroles. A larger casserole dish can be used for batch cooking or for cooking for the whole family.

Heat diffuser: Used to keep food from burning or sticking to the bottom of the pan.

Blender or food processor: Essential for first purees when the consistency needs to be very smooth, creamy, and soupy; convenient for making batches of food for storing. A blender or food processor made with a glass bowl or jar is recommended for pureeing hot food.

Baby food mill: A food mill that mashes food into puree, and separates the fiber. It is easy to use, especially when preparing fresh food daily. You can serve food directly from the mill bowl at the table. If it is made of plastic, wait until food cools before putting it into the food mill.

Grinding bowl: A bowl made of clay with grooves in it and a wooden pestle that is very convenient for grinding or mashing baby food puree, seeds or nuts, and sauces.

Seed grinder: Used for grinding toasted seeds for a condiment for porridge or vegetables.

Rolling pin: Used for rolling dough for pies, cookies, or teething biscuits.

Cookie sheet: Used for baking cookies or teething biscuits.

Cheesecloth: Used for straining grain, milk, or nut milks. Also used for ginger or tofu compress.

Unbleached parchment paper: Used in baking to keep the food from sticking, such as roasted vegetables or baked flour products.

Timer: Used for measuring cooking time of grains, vegetables, fruits, beans, soups, and baked dishes.

Food cubes: Individual serving-sized cubes for storing puree. The smaller size (2 ounces) is useful for the first few months of feeding grains, and then for side dishes. A few of the larger size of cubes (4 ounces) are helpful as your baby grows, especially as she eats more grains.

Labels and marking pens: Used to mark the ingredients and date on food for storage.

Dry ingredients

Whole grains, pasta, beans, sea vegetables, nuts, and seeds can be purchased in bulk or in their own box or bag. These dry ingredients are easily stored in airtight glass jars. Staple ingredients should be stored away from light, especially from direct sunlight, and they do not usually need refrigeration. Ideally, whole grains should be stored at temperatures that do not exceed 80°F for a long period of time, so I often store them in the refrigerator in the summertime. Grains that are cracked, such as rice cereal, rolled oats, and flours, also can begin to oxidize in warm weather; therefore, refrigeration keeps them fresher and protects them from pests. Pantry pest traps are a safe way to control these moths.

Bottled, canned, and packaged items

Seasonings, such as tamari, plum vinegar, and oil, do not usually need to be refrigerated, so these items can be stored in a cabinet or on a countertop. Most seasonings last longer when kept away from light and heat. Oil is susceptible to turning rancid, so look for dark green or brown glass containers, to protect it from exposure to light. If tamari is unpasteurized, store it in the refrigerator after opening. Miso paste that is not pasteurized should be stored in the refrigerator. You can store plum vinegar, rice syrup, and maple syrup on the countertop or shelf for a few months after opening, and then store it in the refrigerator for longer periods of time. Salt and *umeboshi* plums are the least perishable, and they do not need refrigeration.

Vegetables and fruits

Vegetables and fruits are more nutritious and delicious the closer to home and the fresher they are from your garden or from a local tailgate, or farmers' market. When warehouse stores transport fresh and frozen food from across the country and from other countries, produce loses its vitality as the food miles add up.

The longer food is stored, the more of its life force it loses. Less perishable vegetables and fruits keep longer, so you can buy them in larger quantities, and then purchase the more perishable foods more frequently. This way you can have fresh food available that is tasty and healthy.

Storing Fresh Vegetables and Fruits

Vegetable or Fruit	Location	Air	Humidity	Notes
Lettuces, greens, herbs	Refrigerate	Airtight container	Moisture	Remove bands or twists.
Broccoli, brussels sprouts, cabbages	Refrigerate	Breathable or open container	Moisture	Cabbage can be left unrefrigerated for a few days.
Cucumbers, zucchini, yellow squashes, green beans, peas, sugar snap peas	Refrigerate	Breathable or open container	Moisture	Squash and cucumbers can be left unrefrigerated for a few days.
Carrots, beets, turnips, parsnips	Refrigerate	Breathable or open container	Moisture	Cut off greens or tops to keep fresh longer.
Sweet potatoes, onions, winter squashes, potatoes	Cool, dark place	Breathable or open container	Dry	Do not refrigerate.
Tomatoes	Countertop	Breathable or open container	Dry	Do not refrigerate.
Berries: strawberries, blueberries, raspberries	Refrigerate	Breathable or open container	Moisture	Fragile—do not stack.
Melons: cantaloupes, honeydews, watermelons	Countertop	Open container	Dry	Refrigerate after cutting.
Temperate tree fruits: apples, pears, plums, peaches, nectarines, apricots, cherries	Countertop	Open container	Dry	Refrigerate after cutting.
Tropical fruits: citruses, avocados, bananas	Countertop	Open container	Dry	Refrigerate after cutting.
Grapes	Countertop	Open container	Dry	Refrigerate after cutting.
Dried fruit	Cool, dark place	Airtight container	Dry	Refrigerate after cutting.

Meal and Menu Planning

After you have introduced your baby to a few tastings of single-grain and single-vegetable meals, and you have observed her for possible allergic reactions, you can try combining ingredients and offer several foods at a time. Present a variety within each food group: grains, vegetables, protein-rich foods, fruits, fermented foods, seasonings that include fats, salt, sweeteners, and herbs or spices, and beverages. The season, weather, and location of where you live can play a part in choosing warming or cooling foods, and cooking methods can add variety to the nature of the food you cook. You can use different colors, tastes, textures, and cooking methods in a simple, intuitive way to create a balanced menu plan. Consider balance for the whole day or week, not just for one meal. Planning a menu for the week saves time and money so that you stay focused when shopping. Planning helps you to buy only what you need, and to remember necessary ingredients so that you do not have to make a return trip to the store.

Make meal and menu plans that are appropriate for your baby's age and stage—first creamy, then crispy, and finally crunchy. When she is capable of eating all three textures, she will still enjoy and benefit from eating a variety of these textures.

The Five Tastes in East Asian Medicine

Use different colors and tastes to make sure you are getting a variety of different foods.

Sweet is the first taste for your baby, especially a natural sweetness from breast milk and whole foods; it tonifies and balances your baby's body. Examples of naturally sweet whole foods are: grains, such as rice, millet, and quinoa; starchy vegetables, such as sweet potatoes, carrots, and green peas; legumes, such as adzuki beans, chickpeas, and kidney beans; ripe fruits, such as apples, pears, cherries, and bananas; and for a more concentrated sweetness, rice syrup, maple syrup, and honey (after the first year).

Sour is the second taste for your baby to enjoy, and it manages fluids in her body. Examples of sour tastes are grapes, melons, pickles, plum vinegar, and brown rice vinegar.

Salty flavoring can be added after your baby's first year; it focuses her body for physical energy and mental concentration. Examples of a salty taste come from salt, tamari, miso, and *umeboshi*.

Bitter is usually not a popular taste for children during their first two years. According to East Asian medicine, bitter sedates and hardens the body. Examples of a bitter taste are in lettuce, asparagus, and chocolate.

Pungent is a taste that may be appealing to your child, usually after one year. A spicy and astringent taste expels pathogens from her body. Examples of pungent are fennel, chives, basil, ginger, scallions, mustard, curry, and garlic.

Five Colors in East Asian Medicine	
Yellow and Orange	Millet, squash, carrots, sweet potatoes, pumpkins, cantaloupe
Black, Blue, or Purple	Nori, wakame, kombu, black beans, blueberries, blackberries
Red	Strawberries, raspberries, tomatoes
Green	Peas, green beans, broccoli, kale, collards, zucchini, avocado
White	Rice, quinoa, sesame seeds, tofu, onions, cauliflower, potatoes

Your baby's tastes may change in response to previous foods that she has eaten, as her condition changes, and when she is in different climates, seasons, or weather. If she has a lot of sweet treats, then her taste for a milder sweetness in vegetables will diminish, and she may also have an attraction to salty foods to return to balance after eating sweets. If she is feeling weak or tired on a cloudy, winter day, then her taste for sweets may diminish, and she may be attracted to salty or animal foods. If she is feeling energetic on a hot, sunny day, then she may be attracted to ice cream or fresh fruit. You can observe and respond to her needs as her tastes change.

In 1908, the Japanese researcher, Kikunae Ikeda, PhD, found that the substance, glutamates, contained in seaweed sauce imparts another taste called umami. This concept came from a broth made with kombu sea vegetable, which is used as a base in Japanese cooking, similar to the way chicken stock is used in Western

cooking. Umami has depth and is more complex than taste alone. It means a rich, delicious, soulful, and savory flavor that comes from the synergy of amino acids triggered in food pairings.

When foods rich in L-glutamates are combined with certain other foods, together they produce a higher, incomparable taste intensity that is more than the sum of its parts. You can find umami taste in tamari (soy sauce), miso, Parmesan cheese, black olives, mushrooms, olive oil, celery, and other foods. Breast milk contains the same umami that is found in kombu broth.

Monosodium glutamate (MSG) is a chemical method of creating a glutamate taste in low-quality and inexpensive foods. It does not contain the salts that create the natural umami taste.

Another factor to consider in planning food for health and comfort are the thermal properties of food. Different foods can warm up or cool off your baby's body:

❋ Foods that are on the cool color spectrum (blue, green, and purple) tend to be cooling, while the warm tones (red, orange, and yellow) are warming. A lemon is more warming than a lime.

❋ Quick-growing foods, like cucumbers and zucchini, tend to be more cooling, while foods that take longer to grow are more warming, such as onions, turnips, and carrots.

❋ Tropical foods balance your baby's body when she is in the hot sun by offering cooling properties, while foods grown in a temperate zone tend to be more warming. Oranges grown in Florida are more warming than apples grown in Vermont.

❋ The amount of water in a food influences its thermal properties. Dried foods and denser foods, such as raisins, are more warming than juicy grapes.

When you purchase foods that are grown locally, you will naturally choose foods that are in season and will help your baby find balance. Generally, foods that cool her body grow in the summer, and foods that are warming grow in the autumn. Notice that giving her avocados and bananas can cool her body, which may be comfortable in the summer, but chilling in the winter.

Observe your child and see what she seems to crave, enjoy, and select from her plate. Consider factors such as colors, smells, textures, and tastes as you plan her meals and menus, but it does not have to be complicated. You can develop your intuition and flexibility, while encouraging your child to experience a range of foods. If you include the basic food groups, and think about a variety of colors and textures, you can easily make healthy food for your baby that includes the nutrients she needs.

Shopping

I loved my daily living experiences in Japan, especially shopping at the open-air markets. Around the corner from our tiny apartment was an *ichiba*, or market, with the various vendors in a row that a Japanese housewife needs for her daily shopping. I put Emi in her stroller every week and went shopping in our neighborhood. At that time, I managed our finances without credit cards or checking accounts, so all of my transactions were done in cash. Before shopping, I budgeted and planned, because I had no wiggle room when using cash. I went to small shops for produce, tofu, fish, flowers, and beer. To save time, I shopped weekly and had the *yaoya-san*, or produce shopkeeper, deliver my fresh vegetables and fruits to our family's apartment. She was surprised at my method, because Japanese women usually shopped daily for produce to get the freshest vegetables and fruits for cooking. However, she just nodded and said, "*Hai.*" I imagined that she was thinking, "Why does this *gaijin* (foreigner) eat vegetables that are a week old, instead of shopping daily for fresh produce?" At this busy time of my life, the trade-off was worthwhile.

Family farms are not as plentiful as they once were in the United States, but over the past decade, there has been a notable increase and interest in local tailgate or farmers' markets. Fresh, local food tastes better and has more nutrients and vitality than produce from large-scale growers. A local market usually has a friendly ambiance, with a chance to interact with the farmers who grew the food. If you take your baby shopping, you can introduce her to the sights and smells of fresh produce, baked goods, and plants. As she gets older, she can help choose vegetables and fruits and interact with the vendors.

Another convenient option for local, seasonal food is to purchase a Community Supported Agriculture (CSA) share. This usually means that you pay the farmer in advance, like a subscription, and each week you pick up a box of fresh produce at the farm or a market. Participating in a CSA can be an efficient way to buy seasonal and local produce, if your time is limited. Getting to know your local farmers, bakers, and others in your community who are committed to high-quality food can increase your gratitude for food, and you can experience a closer connection to its source. Buying locally keeps money in your community, supports farmers, and continues family traditions. You may also find a sense of community amongst like-minded people.

Natural products stores and most grocery chains now offer options for healthy eating. They usually have organic produce and sometimes carry locally grown produce. Encouraged by the FDA, they are now labeling produce with the state and country in which it was grown. In addition to giving you information about food miles, it is interesting to know where vegetables and fruits were grown and to consider their growing conditions.

Although it requires extra time to measure and bag food yourself, buying dried foods in bulk saves money. If you are shopping for the whole family, the volume of ingredients may make it worth your extra time and energy. However, prepackaged staples are convenient, and sometimes they can be the most reasonable option if you are buying ingredients just for your baby's food and need only a small amount.

By shopping the perimeter of the grocery store, you can easily find the fresh ingredients, while the interior aisles have the packaged and processed items. Shopping early in the morning or late at night, when there are fewer shoppers, can be more efficient. If you eat before you shop, unnecessary extras will be less likely to appear in your cart. Allow time to read labels, so you can be sure to get the best-quality foods without additives. Also, it is fun to leave some room in the budget for surprise impulse buys, such as seasonal vegetables or fruits, a fresh catch of fish, or a new brand of natural snacks.

A principle in organization that works for me for running my business, as well as running my kitchen, is to think in terms of categories. The food groups in this book can be used for planning menus and shopping lists. The chapter on foods groups lists them in order of priority: Grains, Vegetables, Protein-Rich Foods, Fruits, Fermented Foods, Seasonings, and Beverages. If you check your cupboard and refrigerator for existing food, and make your shopping list in these groupings, then your list will be in sync with the aisles of the grocery store. With a menu plan and shopping list, you can provide a variety of balanced foods, and also reduce waste and save money, so that you know which ingredients you need, rather than from just shopping impulsively.

Shopping List

Grains

- [ ] Brown rice
- [ ] Sweet brown rice
- [ ] Millet
- [ ] Quinoa
- [ ] Barley
- [ ] Amaranth
- [ ] Buckwheat
- [ ] Corn
- [ ] Oat flakes
- [ ] Pasta
- [ ] Polenta
- [ ] Grits
- [ ] Couscous
- [ ] Dry cereal
- [ ] Snacks

Vegetables

- [ ] Acorn squash
- [ ] Butternut squash
- [ ] Japanese pumpkin
- [ ] Green beans
- [ ] Sugar snap peas
- [ ] Green peas
- [ ] Yellow squash
- [ ] Zucchini
- [ ] Sweet potatoes
- [ ] Carrots
- [ ] Parsnips
- [ ] Onions
- [ ] Asparagus
- [ ] Beets
- [ ] Rutabaga
- [ ] Cauliflower
- [ ] Chinese cabbage
- [ ] Bok choy
- [ ] Brussels sprouts
- [ ] Cabbage
- [ ] Collards
- [ ] Kale
- [ ] Turnip greens
- [ ] Watercress
- [ ] Celery
- [ ] Cucumber
- [ ] Lettuce
- [ ] Mushrooms
- [ ] Potatoes
- [ ] Okra
- [ ] Spinach
- [ ] Peppers
- [ ] Tomatoes
- [ ] Eggplant
- [ ] Nori
- [ ] Wakame
- [ ] Kombu
- [ ] Agar-agar

Protein-rich Foods

- [ ] Sesame seeds
- [ ] Tahini
- [ ] Tofu
- [ ] Tempeh
- [ ] Adzuki beans
- [ ] Black beans
- [ ] White beans
- [ ] Kidney beans
- [ ] Chickpeas
- [ ] Lentils
- [ ] Pumpkin seeds
- [ ] Sunflower seeds
- [ ] Chestnuts
- [ ] Almond butter
- [ ] Almonds
- [ ] Peanut butter
- [ ] Fish
- [ ] Cheese
- [ ] Eggs
- [ ] Poultry

Fermented Foods

- [ ] Miso
- [ ] Plum vinegar
- [ ] Tamari
- [ ] Yogurt
- [ ] Dairy kefir

Remedies

- [ ] Kuzu
- [ ] *Umeboshi*

Fruits

- [ ] Apples
- [ ] Apricots
- [ ] Peaches
- [ ] Pears
- [ ] Plums
- [ ] Cherries
- [ ] Blueberries
- [ ] Cranberries
- [ ] Grapes
- [ ] Blackberries
- [ ] Raspberries
- [ ] Strawberries
- [ ] Cantaloupes
- [ ] Honey dew
- [ ] Watermelon
- [ ] Pomegranates
- [ ] Kiwi
- [ ] Avocados
- [ ] Bananas
- [ ] Mangoes
- [ ] Papayas
- [ ] Lemons
- [ ] Limes
- [ ] Nectarines
- [ ] Oranges
- [ ] Pineapple
- [ ] Tangerines

Dried Fruits

- [ ] Apples
- [ ] Apricots
- [ ] Currants
- [ ] Peaches
- [ ] Pears
- [ ] Prunes
- [ ] Raisins

Seasonings

- [ ] Sea salt
- [ ] Brown rice Syrup
- [ ] *Amazake*
- [ ] Maple syrup
- [ ] Honey
- [ ] Sesame oil
- [ ] Olive oil
- [ ] Flaxseed oil
- [ ] Coconut oil
- [ ] Almond oil
- [ ] Safflower
- [ ] Sunflower oil
- [ ] Butter
- [ ] Fennel
- [ ] Bay
- [ ] Basil
- [ ] Dill
- [ ] Thyme
- [ ] Mint
- [ ] Cilantro
- [ ] Parsley
- [ ] Cinnamon
- [ ] Curry
- [ ] Garlic
- [ ] Ginger

Baking

- [ ] Vanilla
- [ ] Baking powder
- [ ] Arrowroot flour
- [ ] Whole wheat flour
- [ ] Brown rice flour
- [ ] Pastry flour
- [ ] Unbleached white flour
- [ ] Oat flour
- [ ] Frozen pie crust

Condiments

- [ ] Jam
- [ ] Mayonnaise (no refined oils)
- [ ] Ketchup/catsup (without sugar)
- [ ] Mustard (natural)

Beverages

- [ ] Water
- [ ] Barley tea
- [ ] Herb tea
- [ ] Rice milk
- [ ] Coconut water
- [ ] Vegetable juice
- [ ] Fruit juice

To download shopping lists, visit growhealthygrowhappy.com

Energy in Food

All foods have an energy force, as well as their nutritional composition. This life force is the same chi that your baby's body carries along her meridians or channels. Living foods are those that have energy and the potential to create life: dried grains and seeds can sprout with added water, some root vegetables sprout and can be planted to grow new plants, and fermented foods are made up of living organisms. Animal and processed foods have less life force energy.

Your physical and emotional state can influence the vibration of your baby's food, as you cook, in either a positive or negative way. Your feelings of anger and irritation, or love and joy goes into her food and then transfers to her.

While living in Ashiya, Japan, Naoki took care of Emi early one morning while I went to a small tofu shop to watch their manufacturing process. Taniwaki-san, the owner of the shop, stirred the steaming pots of soy curds and whey, while he said prayers to bless his tofu. I imagined that those blessings transferred into good energy for his customers. When you are cooking for your baby, you can intentionally think good and loving thoughts, so that the positive vibrations go into her food. Even if cooking is not really your thing, you can try to enjoy the opportunity to be creative, while nourishing, giving, and eating together with your family. Cooking is creating life.

A Positive Environment for Good Energy in Cooking

A quiet, calm environment without the TV on makes cooking a relaxing experience.

A neat, orderly kitchen makes it easy to find utensils and ingredients, reducing stress.

Simple meals take less time and energy, whereas complicated meals can add stress.

Slowing down helps you focus on the food.

Cooking recipes that you are enthusiastic about makes it more fun and interesting.

Food Preparation

Good hygiene is essential for healthy food preparation. Keeping a clean kitchen and work area, taking care to wash your hands with plant-based soap before cooking, and storing food properly can prevent foodborne illnesses. Animal foods need more care and are more of a concern than plant-based foods in terms of dangerous bacteria. Antibacterial soaps kill the good bacteria, as well as the bad, and are not recommended. Chemical cleaners can also be a concern for your baby's health. Make sure dishes are completely rinsed of soap and dried before storing or using. Sponges need to be changed regularly or washed in the dishwasher. If you have a dishwasher, the high temperature sterilizes dishes and utensils. Otherwise, you can use hot water for washing dishes.

Before cooking, start by reviewing the recipes, then get out the utensils, storage containers, and necessary ingredients. See what kind of food preparation needs to be done first or can be done in advance.

Wash and Soak Grains and Beans

Depending on your schedule, you can wash and soak dried foods up to 24–48 hours. Soaking whole grains and beans causes them to sprout, becoming more digestible and making the nutrients more bioavailable. Soaking also creates a slight fermentation or enzyme activity that aids in your baby's digestion. You can buy dried grains that have been previously soaked and then dried again, and they have a shorter cooking time. A small amount of pickle juice, kefir, or whey from yogurt can be added to give an extra probiotic boost. Drain the soaking water and use fresh water for cooking. Soaking and cooking grains is not difficult, but it takes prior planning. Once you have the routine down, it can be the easiest part of cooking your baby's food.

Wash and Prep Produce

Scrub fresh vegetables and fruits with a natural-bristle brush, instead of using one with plastic bristles, which can bruise the food. Clean off tough or rough spots and leave on the peel of organic vegetables or fruits if it is not too tough; for example: carrots, parsnips, yellow squash, zucchini, and cucumbers. Peel hard and fibrous skins, such as sweet potatoes, beets, turnips, winter squashes, pumpkins, apples, pears, avocados, bananas, and cantaloupes. Take off fibrous parts of the vegetable, such as the strings on beans and peas, and the hard stalks on broccoli, cauliflower, bok choy, kale, and other greens. Cap strawberries, and take off the stems and seeds of grapes, berries, cherries, and other fruits.

Cut Vegetables and Fruits

The way food is cut affects its energy, taste, and balance. Thinly sliced slivers, matchsticks, or large chunks all have a different chi. I prefer the term "cutting" to "chopping." Cutting at a consistent size in either single or mixed ingredients helps the pieces cook evenly together. For puree, small- to medium-sized chunks cook quickly; finger foods can be cut into pea-sized pieces at first, and then longer sticks as your baby's eating skills develop. Toddlers can enjoy mouth-sized bites of simple, fun shapes such as stars or flowers.

Cooking Methods

The method of cooking you use to make your baby's meals adds energy that affects the appearance, taste, and feeling of the food. Cooking changes the flavor, consistency, temperature, and chemistry of food, and is essential for proper digestion. Cooking is the transformation of food. Using fire to transform food has contributed to the evolution of human development.

Michael Pollan, author and expert on food, claims that cooking connects plants, animals, the soil, farmers, history, and culture, as well as relationships with family and friends. In his book, *Cooked*, he argues, "Taking back control of cooking may be the single most important step anyone can take to help make the American food system healthier and more sustainable. Reclaiming cooking as an act of enjoyment and self-reliance, learning to perform the magic of these everyday transformations, opens the door to a more nourishing life."

Cooking transforms and predigests food, and although it may destroy some nutrients, it makes the remaining nutrients easier to assimilate, which results in a higher net absorption of nutrients. Cooking does some of the work of digestion before food enters your baby's body, which is a benefit to her underdeveloped digestive system. Different methods of food preparation have profoundly different effects on the nutritional value, energy, balance, and digestibility of food.

Learning a variety of cooking methods can help you adapt to your baby's changing needs and tastes. During the first few months of cooking for her, you need very simple cooking methods. Her first foods need to be moist, soft, and light for digestibility. To achieve this, you can boil, water sauté, steam, and make soups. As she gets older, she will crave more variety, so you can add more complex ingredients and cooking methods that include oil, dry heat, and pressure.

Boil

During your baby's first few months of eating, I prefer to boil grains, beans, and vegetables because it is the easiest method for pureeing. Before cooking, soak grains and beans, then boil and puree. As she grows, the same cooking method can be used with less water and without the puree step. For these recipes, the water used in cooking is pureed with the grains or beans to retain nutrients. For vegetables and fruits, boiling retains the fat-soluble nutrients, and loses some of the water-soluble nutrients. Boiling ensures that vegetables and fruits are completely cooked and are moist enough to puree. You need liquid to make the puree a smooth consistency, so it is convenient to boil with water, and then mix together in a blender or food mill. Bring the vegetable or fruit to a boil, reduce the temperature to a low simmer, and cook until soft, adding more water as needed. Leftover water from boiling or steaming can be a nutritious drink, stock for soup, or can be added to the puree for a smooth consistency.

Steam

Steaming is a lighter form of cooking that preserves flavor and nutrients. It is refreshing in warm weather, balances heavier foods, and is uplifting and relaxing. Steaming can be used for making purees, but when steaming, be sure that the food is thoroughly cooked for digestibility. When your baby can chew well, steaming can be a convenient method for quick meals or bentos. Food stored in glass cubes can be heated in a steamer before serving. Stainless steel steamers are easy and practical to insert into your cooking pot. Once your child is old enough to need seasoning, a sprinkle of salt, tamari, or plum vinegar can be added to vegetables while they are cooking or still hot.

Soup

Soup is delicious for a first course to start digestive juices flowing, or it can be served alone as a meal by itself. Vegetable broth and vegetable soup puree allow your baby to drink nutrients as a beverage before she can use a spoon. You can make soups with boiled or sautéed vegetables, beans, grains, and sea vegetables. Wakame flakes and kombu have natural glutamates and they add a satisfying taste to soup, while providing valuable minerals. At six months, a very small amount of miso or tamari can be used to flavor soup. Add them at the end of cooking to preserve the healthy living bacteria and enzymes. Puree the soup when all the vegetables are completely cooked.

Bake

Baking brings out a rich and delicious sweet flavor in vegetables. For sweet potatoes you may bake them whole, and for winter squash you can simply cut them in half and scoop out the seeds. You can cut different vegetables into chunks, such as carrots, onions, zucchini, and beets. Preheat your oven to 350° to 400°. Oil the baking pan, drizzle on sesame or olive oil, and add herbs for flavor. Add a few tablespoons of water to avoid drying out. To keep the vegetables moist, cover with a casserole lid or foil to create a tenderizing, steaming effect. This method of cooking is especially warming in the winter.

Water sauté

Water sauté is an efficient and healthy cooking method, because it retains nutrients and flavor in the vegetables. Put a small amount of water into a saucepan and bring to a boil. If using salt, add a small pinch to the water, and then add vegetables or fruits. Cover with a lid and cook until tender, adding water as needed. This is a quick-cooking method, which requires attention to avoid burning. You can either puree the vegetables or use this cooking method, without pureeing, when your baby is old enough to chew her food and she can appreciate the added flavor.

Oil sauté

Sautéing vegetables is a cooking method that adds both richness and nutrition to satisfy your baby's needs. Especially for a plant-based diet, quality fats are important for health and satisfaction. This method is used more often for cooking whole vegetable pieces when your child can chew foods. Add ½ teaspoon of oil to the pan. Stir in vegetables and enough water to cover the vegetables. Add salt or seasoning, if using. Cover with a lid and cook until vegetables are tender and there is very little water left in the pan.

Pressure-cook

A pressure cooker is a sealed pot that cooks food quickly using the pressure from the internal steam of boiling water. Because beans take a long time to cook, pressure-cooking is a method to speed up the process, if you are in a hurry. Grains and vegetables can also be cooked in a pressure cooker.

Raw

Fresh foods have beneficial enzymes that are lost when heated, and they can provide balance to heavy foods, or in hot weather. Some fresh fruits can be mashed and served raw when your baby is eating puree, such as avocados, bananas, and melons. Once you are confident that your child can chew well, raw vegetables, such as carrot sticks and cucumber slices are healthy snack options. Until your child is experienced with eating raw vegetables and fruits, be sure to serve her very small pieces to avoid a choking hazard.

Pickle

Even though heat is not used in pickling vegetables, time, pressure, and salt offer a food preparation that helps predigest the food. Fermented foods and pickles provide good bacteria to help build immunity and aid digestion. In the beginning stages of eating, you can puree pickles or give your child the juice from pickles. After she can chew, you can serve her pickles in small pieces. Be conscious of the sodium content in pickles and adjust to meet your child's age and needs.

Pop

Rice cakes, popcorn, and puffed grains are a convenient snack. However, because they are cooked under intense, high heat, they can be dry and hard to digest. Your toddler can enjoy rice cakes and puffed grains for a treat. When she can chew well enough to eat popcorn here is a tasty recipe that Naoki taught me: put oil (coconut, olive, or sesame) and popcorn kernels in a pot at room temperature, and heat while stirring constantly. When the kernels start popping, put on the lid, and shake the pan, back and forth, over the heat. When the popping stops, add seasoning, such as brewer's yeast, tamari, or plum vinegar.

Deep-fry

Deep-frying is a cooking method that uses oil with extreme heat. After your child is eating a variety of foods, and her digestive system is working well, deep-fried foods can be a delicious treat. Tempura vegetables made with a batter, white or sweet potato French fries, and fried croquettes are fun for special occasions. The oil should not be saved and reused because it oxidizes and goes rancid between uses.

Grill or broil

Using high, dry heat, fish or vegetables can be broiled or grilled to add variety to cooking methods. Since food that is broiled or grilled is usually tougher and drier, as well as more difficult to digest, I recommend giving your child foods cooked with this method after she is two years old, and can chew well.

Thermal properties of cooking methods ⌂

Food itself has inherent energetic properties that cool or warm your baby's body. In addition to the intuitive idea that frozen foods are cooling, and hot cooked foods are warming, different cooking methods can also have cooling or warming effects. The same food will have different thermal properties when prepared in different ways. Ice cream cools your baby's body, while drinking warm milk warms her. Listed below are ways that cooking methods can influence your baby's body.

The elements in food preparation and cooking have an influence on food. Yang-producing elements include salt, pressure, fire, and time. Yin-producing elements include water, oil, and air. Sprinkle salt on cucumbers and watch the contraction of the cucumber as the water squeezes out. Pressure on cabbage causes the liquid to release. Cooking methods such as deep-frying, popping grains, pressure-cooking, grilling, baking, and broiling all use high or dry heat, and have a more yang influence, which results in food that is firm and dry.

Longer cooking times, like when making a slow-cooked stew, exert a more yang influence effect on food. Sautéing, boiling, and steaming use liquid, which softens food and creates a yin effect. Using oil in salad

dressing or in cooking adds a yin influence and is more digestible when combined with salt. Raw food is usually more yin than cooked food, because it does not have the heat of fire. Cooking methods are not only yin or only yang because you may combine a yang element and a yin element, such as heat and oil for deep-frying.

The source of heat also has an effect on the energy in food. Direct fire, on a woodstove or campfire, is the method of cooking that offers the most yang influence. Gas stoves have a balanced and natural heat source for daily cooking, because the flame is similar to fire, and it is responsive to heat adjustment. Cooking with electricity gives less heat to food than cooking with actual fire. Using an electric stove or electrical appliances may have a tendency to dry food out, so you may need to add extra water while cooking.

Microwaves can cause "hot spots" that can cause burns. Cooking in plastic containers or packaging in a microwave can melt the plastic and release toxins into the food. There are also dangers of radiation leakage, so make sure your child is not near a microwave when it is in use, and see that the door hinges seal properly. The following are basic methods for cooking healthy and delicious foods for your baby or child.

Influence of Cooking Methods	
Raw	Very cooling
Steamed	Cooling to neutral
Water sauté	Neutral
Boiled	Neutral
Pickled	Neutral to warming
Oil sautéed	Mildly warming
Soup	Warming
Baked	Warming
Pressure-cooked	Warming
Popped	Warming
Grilled or broiled	Very warming
Deep-fried	Very heating

Stocking Up

With menu planning, a shopping list, and basic cooking utensils, the process of making homemade baby food can be easy and efficient. If both parents are working, it is probably easier to take a few hours once a week to prepare food. For the first two to three days, you can store food in the refrigerator, and you can put food for the rest of the week in the freezer. Another option is to make smaller batches two or three times a week, store them in the refrigerator, and use as needed. As your baby moves to lumpier purees, and then you can also make a batch of grains and beans for several days, and then make fresh vegetables every day, and puree them at the table with a food mill or grinding bowl. Cooking baby food can be integrated with family meals by sharing pureed soups, breakfast porridge, noodles, and steamed or baked vegetables.

Freezing foods into serving-sized portions is easy and convenient. As she grows, your baby's serving size will increase from 1 or 2 ounces, and then to 3 or 4 ounces, depending on the food. If you freeze food in ice cube trays or muffin tins, then you can put the frozen cubes in larger storage containers or freezer bags. Food cubes specifically designed for storing baby food are convenient, and they come in different sizes and materials. You can heat glass cubes directly in a steamer or double boiler, and then serve without transferring dishes. When using plastic cubes, to avoid the plastic releasing toxins into the puree, wait for the puree to cool before pouring it into the cubes for storage, and remove from cubes to reheat food. While glass cubes can be more versatile, plastic cubes are less expensive and it is convenient to have plenty of cubes for storing food. When storing food in the freezer, leave enough space for the serving to expand during freezing. Make sure the seal is airtight to prevent freezer burn, which dries out the food and reduces flavor and nutrients. Also, be sure the food has cooled before placing it in the freezer, because putting warm food in the freezer can change its temperature.

Label the bags or cubes with the name of the puree and the date of freezing. Color-coding can also be helpful for storing grains, vegetables, proteins, and fruits. If you use cubes and color-code them, you can arrange a balanced meal on one tray ahead of time. In one month, your baby will need a thicker consistency, so it is not efficient to make too much of the same food ahead of time. Good inventory practices are first in, first out (FIFO) to give your baby the freshest food first.

Shelf Life

In the refrigerator, cooked grains and beans keep for three to four days, and vegetables and fruits keep for two to three days. Additional care is needed for fish and poultry, which will keep for at least one to two days in the refrigerator after they are cooked. Plant-based foods such as grains, beans, vegetables, and fruits will last for up to three months in the freezer. You can keep fish and poultry in the freezer for one to two months. Tofu does not freeze well. Raw foods such as avocados, bananas, melons, and cucumbers change quality, color, and flavor when frozen, so they are best eaten fresh.

The refrigerator temperature should be between 35° and 38°F. Freezer temperature should be 10° to 0°F.

Thawing Frozen Food

If you have time to plan ahead, take servings out of the freezer and put them in the refrigerator for 4 to 24 hours before using. Otherwise, you can run warm water over the container or soak it for 15 to 20 minutes, and then transfer the frozen puree to a small pan and heat it until thawed. You can thaw food that has been frozen in a glass cube on the stovetop, directly in a steamer basket or double boiler. Do not thaw food at room temperature, because the bacteria can grow on the outside, while the inside is still frozen. Always stir food that has been previously frozen well, and check its temperature before serving to your baby. Make sure food is completely thawed before serving because small pieces of frozen food can present a choking hazard. After food has been frozen and thawed, do not refreeze it.

When your baby eats food, her saliva goes onto the spoon, and when the spoon is placed back into the serving bowl or container, her saliva starts digesting the food in the bowl. Therefore, once food has been used for a serving, the leftovers should be discarded. Also, do not reheat the same food more than once.

Time-saving Tips

If you have a friend who has a baby of the same age, sharing cooking can be convenient and fun. At hurried or stressful times, frozen or canned vegetables or beans can be quick options. Oatmeal flakes and quinoa cook more quickly than rice or millet, and gluten-free pasta is a convenient grain option, too. Pressure-cooking is a speedy way to cook beans, grains, and vegetables occasionally.

In one cooking session, you can make fresh food for serving immediately, food for storing in the refrigerator for the next few days, and food for freezing for future use—all at the same time. Planning ahead helps you to remember to buy the necessary ingredients for a recipe; to soak grains, beans, or dried fruit; and to have food ready when your child is ready to eat.

Introducing Solid Foods

When your baby is ready to start solid foods, you can set up an area for feeding her, taking the atmosphere for presenting and serving food into consideration. These factors create a pleasant, balancing atmosphere in which your baby can learn to appreciate food and have a healthy appetite.

Signs Your Baby Is Ready to Eat Solid Food

When your baby sits without assistance, holds her head up with confidence, and grasps small objects and brings them to her mouth, she may be ready to eat solid foods. At this point, she will probably have roughly doubled her birth weight, and will either nurse or take a bottle more frequently, because she is hungrier and less satisfied with breast milk or formula. Her nursing patterns may increase to eight to ten times a day, with shorter intervals of time between feedings. If your baby is formula-feeding, she may drink more than 32 ounces of milk a day, and her sleep cycles may also be shorter due to hunger. Other signs to look for are more subtle: she watches you eat and shows an interest in table food, she makes chewing motions with her mouth, and she reaches out to grab your food as you eat. Depending on appetite, some babies are more eager for first foods than others, so this phase may be an easy time, or it may require extra patience. Cutting teeth is also a significant sign that she is ready to start solid foods.

The American Academy of Pediatrics recommends that babies start eating solid foods at around six months, because breast milk supplies the best nutrients until then. Around the age of six months, your baby's body starts producing the enzyme amylase, which shows that her digestive system is maturing and how she can now digest new "solid" foods. Her nervous system development helps her recognize a spoon in her mouth, and helps her coordinate swallowing; she knows whether she is full or hungry; her sucking pattern has developed to the point that her tongue can make a thrusting motion that will allow her to push food out of her mouth to protect her from choking; and her taste buds have also developed.

Every baby is an individual with unique needs that include her original constitution and condition, her size, sex, the climate and location where she lives, and various situations that contribute to making her who she is. Therefore, the time to eat only solid foods can vary from child to child. If there are reasons that you feel strongly that your baby is ready to eat earlier than six months, then at least wait until she is four months old to start solids. If your child's digestion is not mature enough to digest food, she will have some signs of indigestion such as colic, gas, constipation, or loose stools. According to Jay L. Hoecker, MD, of the Mayo Clinic, starting solid foods early (before four months) may increase her chances of obesity. The following charts, ages, and stages are guidelines, and can be adjusted to meet your baby's individual needs. Keep in touch with your health care provider as your baby goes through the transition of eating solid food, so that you can customize a program that fits her individual needs.

Extrusion reflex

For her first few months, your baby has a normal response to push her tongue outward when it is touched or depressed. This is part of sucking and is called the extrusion reflex. While she has the extrusion reflex, she cannot take food from a spoon, because she cannot pass food to the back of her mouth for swallowing. At around four to six months, the extrusion reflex will be gone and she can eat solids, without pushing the food away. Breast-feeding or drinking from a bottle uses a sucking motion, but eating solid food requires learning new skills, such as swallowing.

Gag reflex

At about eight months, your baby can make chewing movements so that she can accept lumpier foods that have more texture. As she begins to eat thicker foods, she may naturally "gag" if food catches at the back of her throat, if she eats too much food that is too thick or lumpy, or if she eats too fast. The reflex happens when her throat or back of her mouth is stimulated, and it helps prevent choking. Do not leave her alone while she is eating food, in case she chokes. As she gets older,

eating only smooth purees can make it difficult for her to learn to chew, which is a downside of many packaged baby foods that come in only one consistency. Introducing lumpy textures at this age helps your baby learn the chewing process, which is part of her teeth and jaw development.

The Feeding Area

Making a consistent area for feeding your baby while at home helps her know when to expect food. When your baby is feeding herself, it is typically a messy time, so easy-to-clean surfaces come in handy. Set her chair on a floor surface that wipes up easily, if possible. If your feeding area is carpeted or not soil-proof, use a mat that has a waterproof covering. For tile or linoleum floors, sweeping is probably easier than shaking out a piece of plastic. Arrange the high chair near a table or countertop, so that you can place the food out of your baby's reach and organize the equipment so that it is available and ready when she is hungry. When weather and space allow, you can take the high chair outside for easy cleaning.

Presentation and Atmosphere

Eating good food is a wonderful part of life in which your baby can enjoy flavors, take in nourishment, gain energy, and participate in a shared experience with you. The visual appeal of food and ambience can have a calming effect that also stimulates her appetite. It may seem far-fetched to think of "slow food" when feeding your six-month-old baby, but perhaps some of the principles of the Slow Food movement can be applied to your child's dining experience.

Slow Food is an idea, a way of living, and a way of eating. It is part of a global, grassroots movement with thousands of members in more than 150 countries, and it links the pleasure of food with a commitment to community and the environment.

 To learn more about Slow Food visit slowfoodusa.org

Food Presentation Tips

- Eat at least one seated family meal together a day without distractions of TV, electronics, etc.

- Gather all the necessary equipment before feeding your baby, to avoid interruptions.

- Express appreciation for the food.

- Give attention to the visual appeal of the meal, with dishes, food arrangement and color, and flowers.

- Create a relaxed, unrushed atmosphere with conversation and sharing.

- Encourage your child firmly with patience to taste different foods, but do not pressure, force, or bribe your child.

- Chew your food well and encourage your child to do so as well.

- Enjoy!

A study at Cornell University showed that presentation of food, including a variety of colors, shapes, and ingredients, influences children's eating choices. Your baby will learn your attitude about food, and while she is young she will develop her lifelong relationship with food. If you choose to make your baby's food at home with whole grains, fresh vegetables, beans, and fruits, then you are exercising a commitment to a healthy and quality eating experience for your baby because of the extra effort and attention you are devoting to it. Below are some tips for developing healthy feelings about food.

Itadakimasu *(Gratitude)*

Itadakimasu (i-ta-da-ki-ma-su) is a concise thank-you blessing in Japanese that includes all the forces that have contributed to bringing the food to the table—the earth, rain, sunshine, farmer, truck driver, vendor, storekeeper, and cook; the plants and animals that gave their life for the meal; and the support of Mother Nature. Literally, it means, "I humbly receive." Appreciation for and recognition of the awe and source of life is something wonderful to cultivate in your child.

Mari and Emi giving thanks

Consistency of Food

Although termed "solid," first foods need to be closer to the liquid consistency of breast milk or formula for digestion to occur. Single whole-grain purees (short-grain brown rice and millet are the most digestible) with a soupy consistency are easily digested first foods. Adding breast milk or formula to first foods gives your baby a familiar taste and consistency to help make her transition easier.

Your baby's needs for texture and consistency change as she develops and grows. She explores the world with her mouth, so you can offer a range of textures once she has developed her ability to swallow. Three transitional stages of learning to eat coincide with different consistency needs. These three basic stages and textures of food are: creamy and smooth (6 to 12 months), crunchy and crispy (12 to 18 months), and chewy (18 months to 2 years+).

Creamy and smooth (6 to 12 months): The first transition is from liquid food, whether breast milk or formula, to cooked foods. A blender is essential to get a smooth, liquid puree that is soupy for your baby's first few months of eating. During this first stage, she can experiment with new tastes and consistencies such as soft foods with smooth and creamy textures, and gradually shift to a thicker puree that uses less water in cooking, and then to foods that are dense with a lumpy texture. A food mill or grinding bowl is sufficient for this thicker consistency. By the time she is one year old, she can learn how to swallow foods and eat for nutrition. As she begins to feed herself, she can enjoy finger foods that she can pick up—soft pieces of steamed or boiled vegetables, chunks of tofu, noodles, and soft raw foods, such as avocados and bananas, that become smooth as she gums and swallows them. Her digestive system is still underdeveloped, so it is necessary to introduce foods slowly and watch for reactions.

Crunchy and crispy (12 to 18 months): The second transition is learning to eat foods that require chewing, such as lightly steamed vegetables, dry cereals, breads, muffins, and crackers. She can eat larger pieces of finger foods and small portions of some adult foods. After her first birthday, her digestive system is more developed and she can gradually try many foods that were previously avoided. As you introduce new foods, observe her reactions to make sure she is not allergic. At this age, she can feed herself and participate in family meals. As her teeth come in, you can serve crispy pea-size chunks or sticks of vegetables and fruits that are lightly cooked or raw, baked vegetables, and flour products, such as bread, crackers, cookies, and puffed grains.

Chewy (18 months to 2 years+): The third transition is eating food that is similar to adult food, and at this stage she can add chewy textures. At 18 months old, she probably has most of her baby teeth, and she can chew most things, although she still may need help with some foods cut into small pieces, such as fish or poultry, rice crispy treats, whole nuts, and dried fruits. By now, your toddler probably has developed her personal tastes and preferences. At this stage, it is easy to integrate cooking for your toddler with that of the rest of the family. Use mild seasonings while cooking, and then family members can add condiments at the table.

Temperature of Food

Bob Flaws, the traditional Chinese doctor and author of *A Handbook of TCM Pediatrics*, says that for digestion to take place in your baby's stomach the temperature needs to be 100°F, which is near her body temperature. He says that digestion is a process that needs warm chi, or energy, and that cold, chilled, or frozen foods can weaken the digestive system, because it has to work harder to warm up the foods so that the nutrients can be assimilated.

You can heat food that has been frozen to kill bacteria or pathogens and to make it warm. Then it needs to cool to body temperature before serving. Eating cold food by itself or mixed with warm food can be upsetting to your baby's digestive system. Warming food in a stainless steel, silicone, or glass heat-resistant steamer over a pan of hot water is an easy and safe way to prepare food that has been refrigerated or frozen. Test the food after stirring to make sure the temperature is about 100°F before serving.

Introduce One Food at a Time

When you introduce solids, it is easier for your baby's digestive system if foods are simple and separate for the first two to three months. You can start with the following order of solid foods: 1) grains, 2) vegetables, 3) protein-rich foods, and 4) fruits. This order also helps your baby develop a palate with a wide range of natural tastes by starting with the savory taste of vegetables before the sweetness of fruits. Introduce foods one at a time, without mixing foods, until you have tried each and are sure that your baby does not have an allergic reaction. At first your baby may eat only a small amount of food, and then she will gradually increase solid food over breast milk or formula. You can introduce new foods every three to five days.

Your child may need to try each food several times to get used to the taste and texture, and she may resist certain foods and combinations. If you offer a food, and she repetitively turns it down, then maybe she does not need that food at that time. She will eat if she is hungry, so it is not necessary to force her. You can try again in a few days or weeks, and see her reaction. Regular persistence in periodically trying nutritious foods gives her the opportunity to develop a variety of tastes, provides nutritional options, and helps her maintain balance.

Your baby's tastes can change daily, affecting her food preferences. Because food tastes can vary as her physical condition changes, what she does not like today could be different in a month. About 70 percent of a child's basic food preferences are developed before the age of two.

During the first few weeks of eating cooked foods, check your baby's diaper for her response to new foods. As she eats more solid food, her stools naturally change. If you notice that your baby is not gaining weight or still seems hungry after eating, check with your health care provider for possible causes.

I have photos of myself feeding Emi and Mari with a determined look on my face while spooning puree in their mouths. I also remember moving my tongue in a motion across my lips as if to wipe or lick the food and swallow it for them. At busy times, it may be challenging to relax and listen to your baby's needs, but the best intention is to start your child on the path toward solid foods, and then guide her to discover her own tastes, as well as her feelings of hunger and fullness.

Baby's First Meal

Like a mama bird, partially chewing food yourself, and then offering the chewed food to your baby is an age-old tradition in many cultures. This may or may not be appealing to you as a way to puree food for your baby.

In the beginning stages of eating, you can use a long spoon to feed the puree directly from the feeding cubes, a small bowl, or a divided plate. At first you need to hold the container of food out of reach from your baby, because if she gets her fingers in the puree, she will make a mess since she does not know how to feed herself yet. As she begins to eat finger foods, you can put a few pieces of food directly onto the high chair tray or a waterproof place mat. When she can use utensils and dishes, unbreakable ones are best for safety, and she can enjoy dishes with fun designs on them.

Your Baby's First Meal

- You can start by nursing or giving your baby a bottle for a few minutes, so that she is relaxed but still hungry, and her digestive juices are activated.

- Wash your hands, and sit her in her high chair or in your lap.

- Put a small taste of food on the tip of your finger, and let her suck on your finger.

- She may use her tongue to push food back out, which is a natural reflex. It may take a few times for her to learn to swallow.

- If the food comes right back out repeatedly, then she is not ready yet, and you can try again a few days later. If she swallows easily, you can try feeding her with a spoon.

How Much to Eat

During her first few months, your baby will need to breast-feed or take a bottle often because her stomach is small, and it cannot hold much food. As her stomach gets bigger, she can eat more at a time, so she will not need to eat as often. When she is first eating solid foods, the amount she eats from day to day may vary. Eating is a new experience for your baby, and her body is learning how to digest unfamiliar foods. She will also have growth spurts during which she may eat more at certain times. Setting up regular feedings gives your baby's body a break between meals, because too frequent meals can result in overfeeding. Your child will eat when she is hungry, and she needs periods between meals for healthy digestion. When your baby is able to feed herself, an occasional snack during the day between meals is normal. However, offering food irregularly throughout the day as solutions to emotional upsets, and developing a habit of "grazing," does not give your baby's digestive system a rest. All-day snacking can interfere with a good appetite at mealtimes and can contribute to problematic eating habits throughout her lifetime.

Overeating can also numb out your baby's body signals that tell her whether she is truly hungry or satisfied. These body signals are the cues that help her learn to self-regulate her own balance and develop healthy eating habits that will prevent obesity. In most Western cultures, children generally have more illnesses from excess and overeating than from being underfed.

Establishing a Routine

Once your baby starts solids, you will probably already have some regular routines established: bedtime, waking up, naps, nursing, etc. Getting into a routine with eating solids will happen gradually as you replace some of your nursing with meals of solid foods. You can start with one meal, then gradually work up to three meals a day and a snack. Meals scheduled around at the same time can be reassuring and can help create a sense of security and order. At around nine months, you can shift from demand feedings to a more regular schedule. Having meals at consistent, scheduled times will help your baby's body adjust to a routine.

Some parents worry that they will be tied to the home in order to keep a schedule. Occasional schedule changes may have consequences, and your baby may become irritable when you travel or when meals do not happen as expected, so it may take a day or so to get completely back on track. I like the idea of developing a disciplined routine with the ability to be flexible when needed.

Feeding Concerns

The highest risk for choking is before one year old. Here are precautions that you can take to prevent choking:

- Keep your child in sight while she is eating, because if she chokes she will need immediate assistance.
- Feed your baby while she is sitting at the table, and do not allow her to eat while moving or walking.
- Encourage your child to chew or "gum" food slowly.
- Always have your health care provider's number on hand in case of emergency, and keep poison control's number on hand as well.

Checking for Allergies

Allergies are unusual with whole grains, vegetables, and most fruits, but keeping a food journal and noting how much you feed your baby each type of food will help your observations. Pay attention to your baby's responses to different foods, including her stools. With each food, look for an allergic reaction. Around 2 to 8 percent of children under three develop allergies. Some signs of allergies include a rash on the face, runny nose, sneezing, watery eyes, congestion, shortness of breath, difficulty swallowing, diaper rash, diarrhea, stomach pain, or crankiness after eating a certain food. Some children are allergic to wheat and corn, so those grains are not recommended during the first few months of introducing solid food.

Up to 95 percent of all allergies are caused by cow's milk, eggs, fish, nuts, soy, wheat, and corn. You can avoid allergies by waiting until after the age of one to introduce these foods and after three years old for peanuts. Often, minor symptoms like a runny nose may be a response to a change in the weather or a natural adjustment, and there is no need for concern. Sometimes other stress factors, food combinations, or a delicate digestive system are causes for symptoms, rather than a true food allergy. A major symptom, such as shortness of breath, is more serious and needs immediate attention. If you notice a possible allergy, eliminate that food from your baby's diet and avoid it for a while. As long as the reaction is not severe, you may offer the food again after a few weeks or a few months, while being alert to signs of an allergy. If a sibling has a food allergy, pay close attention to how your younger child responds, too.

Foods to Avoid for the First Year

- Wheat or gluten products
- Corn and corn products
- Juice (especially unpasteurized)
- Citrus and other acidic fruits
- Raw sprouts
- Fat-free foods
- Peanut butter
- Whole nuts or seeds
- Cow's milk
- Eggs
- Raw fish
- Shellfish
- High-mercury fish
- Deli meats
- Processed or fried foods
- Honey
- Sugar
- Artificial sweeteners
- Chocolate
- Sodas
- Marshmallows
- Chewing gum and hard candy
- Ice cubes

 To download a food journal visit growhealthygrowhappy.com

CHAPTER 6
Food Groups

NATURE'S FIRST HUMAN FOOD is breast milk, if possible. Breast milk offers all the nutrients your baby needs for his first year. As he starts eating solid foods, a wide variety of whole foods can give him the nutrients he needs for a foundation of optimal growth and development for his first three years. This chapter is a resource of eight different food groups with information on how they influence your baby, considerations about each food group, types of foods in each group, their yin–yang characteristics, how foods grow, and a chart with information about when and how to introduce each food group to your baby, along with recipes.

The following food pyramid shows the eight food groups that are included in the next chapter. They are listed in the order that I recommend to introduce them to your baby: breast milk, grains, vegetables, proteins, fruits, fermented foods, seasonings that include fats, salt, sweeteners, herbs and spices, and beverages.

A Guide to the Recipes

When cooking dishes that I know, I rarely use cookbooks and prefer to just cook with a little of this and that, according to my inspiration and the situation. However, if I am cooking a special new dish with unfamiliar ingredients, or cooking for a specific purpose, then I appreciate the details and instructions of a recipe.

Cooking your baby's first foods is very simple, intuitive, and commonsense, even though there is a lot to think about—your baby's physical condition and needs, and how different foods affect your child.

My goal is to offer you cooking principles and general methods that can be used for a variety of foods. Instead of dividing the recipes according to age, these are incorporated into their food groups, with adjustments by age and developmental stage. Your seven-month-old who later becomes 12 months old can enjoy quinoa cooked with a different ratio of water to grain at each stage. The consistency of sweet potato that your child needs changes from smooth to lumpy to chunky as he grows. The basic principles in these recipes provide the foundation necessary to cook for your child's first three years and older. I have tried to make the instructions simple, clear, usable, and adjustable.

There are variations for substitutions of ingredients, and additions of flavors to adapt to his individual tastes and for variety. When you use the same methods of soaking and cooking grains, for example, then the process takes on a rhythm that is easy and familiar so that you do not need a recipe, and you can create your own variations and adjustments to meet the specific needs of your child. If you use quality, local, and fresh ingredients, you can create delicious and satisfying meals for your baby with simple cooking that is easy and fun.

fermented foods and probiotics

quality, natural fats and seasonings

simple beverages

plant-based proteins

fresh, organic fruits

fresh, organic vegetables and sea vegetables

whole grains

Breast Milk

Breast Milk

NURSING MY BABIES WAS one of the most fulfilling experiences of my life. I remember the satisfying feeling of my milk "letting down," while my hungry little one vigorously drank from my breast. I could forget the dirty dishes in the sink because I knew my main priority was to relax, make milk, feed my baby, and feel a love that I had not previously experienced.

At birth, your baby is very vulnerable and dependent on you, because he does not have protection from the elements; he cannot walk, crawl, or eat solid food. Mother's milk is the ideal liquid to meet his complex physical and emotional needs.

The decision to breast-feed or formula-feed is a significant one and must be made conscientiously. If you choose to breast-feed, it is easy to change to formula-feeding, but if you start with formula, it is very difficult to stimulate your body to return to breast-feeding. Going back and forth between the two in the beginning can be confusing for your baby, because he learns different sucking styles for the nipple and the bottle. If you and your baby are healthy and able, you will both derive the most benefit from feeding him the milk from your body. However, if breast-feeding is not an option for you, there are healthy alternatives.

The Power of Breast Milk

Exclusive breast-feeding is defined by the American Academy of Pediatrics as "an infant's consumption of human milk with no supplementation of any type (no water, no juice, no nonhuman milk, and no foods) except for vitamins or minerals, if recommended by a doctor, and medications, if necessary." The Academy, along with the American College of Obstetricians and Gynecologists, American Academy of Family Physicians, Academy of Breast-feeding Medicine, World Health Organization, and United Nations Children's Fund, recommend that mothers breast-feed their babies for six months as their exclusive form of nourishment. In addition, health experts suggest that mothers continue breast-feeding as a primary food source after introducing solid foods and other liquids to their babies. Breast-feeding should continue as an important part of your baby's diet until he is at least one year old. In Sweden, it is considered unethical to feed infants anything but human milk. To support this belief, a woman is given time off from work for 16 months to nurse her baby, and there are banks of human milk available for those who cannot nurse.

Becky, Emi, and baby Mari

Mothers produce a unique kind of milk that meets all the nutritional requirements of a newborn baby. Every mammal species is biologically equipped to make milk for babies that support survival in a particular environment for specific developmental needs. For example, mother seals produce milk high in fat because their pups need a plentiful amount of body fat to survive in cold water. For human babies, mental development is key to evolutionary success, so human milk provides nutrients for babies' rapid brain growth.

In a fascinating example of evolution and physiological intelligence, the composition of breast milk changes to correspond with a growing baby's needs. The first milk a mother produces is colostrum, which is especially rich in immunity-building cells and antibodies to protect against infections in vulnerable areas such as the nose, throat, ears, lungs, and digestive tract. Colostrum is low in fat, rich in sugars and proteins, and easy for a newborn baby to digest. It is a natural laxative that helps pass your baby's first stools. Colostrum also helps eliminate bilirubin, which can cause jaundice.

Colostrum is only produced during the first couple of days after giving birth. Milk then changes to transitional milk, which is yellowish in color and contains more lactose, a specific kind of milk sugar that converts easily into energy. Transitional milk is followed by mature milk several days later, which may be bluish in color.

Mature milk undergoes changes during any single nursing session. At the beginning, you produce foremilk, which has a watery, free-flowing consistency that encourages your baby to start nursing. By the end of the session, the breast produces hindmilk, which is a more filling and satisfying milk that is three times richer in fat and higher in protein than foremilk. The proteins, fats, carbohydrates, hormones, vitamins, and minerals in mother's milk are uniquely proportioned to promote the growth and development of a human infant. As long as your baby is nursing for a full cycle (which is about 15 to 20 minutes), there is no need to wonder if your baby is getting enough nutrients.

Carbohydrates

Breast milk contains lactose, the carbohydrate that provides energy for a growing baby. It also breaks down into lactic acid, helping to protect him from harmful bacteria.

Proteins

Milk proteins fall into two categories, curds and whey. The curd portion—the casein protein—appears as white clots, and the liquid is the whey. Human milk has more whey than curd, and the curds are softer and digested more efficiently than the curds in cow's milk. Comparatively, cow's milk is mostly casein protein, which forms a rubbery, hard-to-digest curd in a human baby's stomach. Calves double their birth weight in less than fifty days because they need to grow quickly and walk on their own to forage and eat. To accommodate this growth rate, cow's milk is significantly higher in protein compared to breast milk. Humans do not need the high concentration of protein in cow's milk. Breast milk is naturally equipped with healthy protein levels and all of the key amino acids, such as taurine, which plays a critical role in the development of your baby's brain and eyes.

Fats

More than 50 percent of the calories in breast milk come from fat, and much of it contains the cholesterol and saturated fatty acids, or omega-3 fatty acids, necessary for growth and healthy brain development. In addition, breast milk fats contain enzymes that help break down nutrients for absorption. Most fats in breast milk exist in hindmilk, and complete nursing sessions produce more fat-rich hindmilk. Therefore, going through a full cycle in one session when pumping creates whole milk with both foremilk and hindmilk, which includes all the nutrients for healthy development.

Vitamins and Minerals

Although mother's milk and infant formula may contain the same vitamins and minerals, the micronutrients found in breast milk are more bioavailable than those found in formula. For example, formula has higher levels of calcium, phosphorus, and iron than natural breast milk. However, the bioavailability of these important minerals in breast milk enables your baby to absorb them in just the right dosages. Your baby absorbs 50 to 75 percent of the iron contained in breast milk, while with fortified formula, he absorbs as little as 4 percent of the iron. Manufacturers increase vitamins and minerals to make up for the low bioavailability of these nutrients in formula, making it hard on your baby's immature intestines and other organs to absorb and dispose of the excess nutrients. Some of that excess—especially iron—can upset the normal balance of his gut and interfere with the growth of healthy bacteria. This can result in constipation and hard, strong-smelling stools.

Hormones

Breast milk contains hormones that shape brain development and behavior. Researchers have found that the breasts extract hormones from the blood, concentrate them into milk, and generate hormones. A cow's hormones offer specific nutrients that may align with human babies' developmental needs in some ways, but cannot provide the necessary hormones that a mother's milk can. Some of the hormones found in human breast milk are listed below.

- Melatonin helps regulate your baby's circadian rhythms, including his appetite.

- Oxytocin promotes the experience of a loving bond between mother and child, and helps your baby relax and let go of anxiety.

- Thyroid hormones protect against symptoms of congenital hypothyroidism.

- Bradykinin helps your baby recognize pain.

- Endorphins protect against pain and elevate mood.

- Insulin-like growth factors promotes brain and nervous system development, and healthy skin.

Advantages of Breast Milk

There is no question about the dietary benefits of breast-feeding, but the advantages go beyond nutrition.

Advantages for Your Baby

❀ *Bonding*

After birth, nursing keeps you and your baby biologically connected. Nursing provides emotional comfort, and it is the ultimate form of bonding between mother and child through skin-to-skin contact.

❀ *On-demand feeding*

Breast milk is sanitary, and it is always the right consistency and temperature for your baby. There are no bottles to carry and sterilize, and no worries about toxins leaching from baby bottles.

❀ *Easy digestion*

Because mother's milk is easy to absorb, your baby's digestive system does not have to work overtime to break down food, as it does with formula. This can mean less gas, softer stools, and a more comfortable baby.

❀ *Immunity boost*

Your breast milk protects your baby from environmental threats like viruses, bacteria, and fungi. Your immune system recognizes an illness-causing agent and produces a specific immune defense against that particular threat, which then transfers to your baby during nursing. This process is fast-acting. Within a couple of hours of being exposed, the proteins in your milk combine to form protective antibodies to send your baby what he needs for protection against the illness. These antibodies are anti-inflammatory, which means they fight the swelling, fever, and pain associated with infections.

Advantages for Mothers

❀ *Physical benefits*

There are also physical benefits to nursing. Breast-feeding causes the uterus to contract, which reduces the blood flow after birth and begins the process of post-labor healing. It suppresses ovulation and menstruation, acting as somewhat of a natural birth control. However, nursing is not a dependable form of birth control because ovulation can start any time and fertilization can occur. As your baby reaches five or six months old, nursing can help return mothers to their pre-pregnancy weight by burning an additional 500 calories per day.

❀ *Health benefits*

A study published in the May 2009 issue of the *Journal Obstetrics and Gynecology* found that mothers who breast-feed have significantly lower rates of certain cancers, including breast, endometrium, and ovarian cancer. Nursing mothers were also shown to have lower rates of osteoporosis. Mothers who breast-fed for one year had lower rates of heart disease, diabetes, and high cholesterol.

❀ *Convenience*

Breast-feeding gives mothers the convenience of traveling or feeding at night without the additional task of planning and organizing bottles and formula. You can feed your baby at any time or place without having to worry about how to prepare something for him to eat.

❀ *Saves money*

Breast-feeding is free food for your baby. According to *Consumer Reports*, the cost of formula-feeding is about $2,000 in the first year. Breast-feeding will cost you about $150 to $350 if you purchase a breast pump. Plus, breast-fed babies have higher levels of antibodies and get sick less, which translates into fewer medical expenses and fewer work absences for parents.

Weaning

Beginning to walk, emerging teeth, and eating solid food for nutrition are all signs that breast milk or formula is no longer necessary for your baby's basic nutritional needs. She may still enjoy the comfort of nursing or a bottle before bedtime, but as she gains more stability in her eating, the choice to continue with breast- or bottle-feeding is a personal one. Most breast-feeding advocates recommend gradual, child-led weaning because stopping abruptly can be difficult for both you and your baby. The American Academy of Pediatrics issued a policy statement in 2005 that recommends breast-feeding exclusively for the first six months, then gradually introducing solid foods while continuing to breast-feed for at least six months until 12 months of age, and after that for as long as mother and baby both want. The World Health Organization recommends breast-feeding for at least two years.

I breast-fed Emi for 18 months, and she gradually led the way to weaning. When Mari was 14 months old, we made a trip to Japan, and she got sick and stopped breast-feeding abruptly. Perhaps the intensity of the long-distance travel, or the change in my food prompted her to quit. It was a challenge for me, because I had to get a hand breast pump to relieve the pressure. She did continue to breast-feed after the trip, but not at the same rate as before, and then gradually weaned herself.

Weaning foods consist of:

- Staples (complex carbohydrate) such as grains, roots, or tubers

- Energy-rich foods (fats, oils, sugars)

- Protein-rich foods (legumes, animal products, meat, eggs)

- Vitamin- and mineral-rich foods (fruits and vegetables)

- These complementary foods should be low cost and prepared locally.

Immunity Booster

Nursing boosts your baby's immune system. The sugars in breast milk also act as prebiotics, meaning they promote the growth of friendly bacteria known as probiotics. Among these health-promoting bacteria is *Lactobacillus bifidus*, which protects against the growth of harmful bacteria like *Staphylococcus aureus*, which can cause infections of the throat, sinuses, lungs, and skin. Probiotics break down food particles into nutrients that can be absorbed by the small intestine to create a healthy and balanced environment. They also give off oxygen to make the intestinal environment more alkaline, which is helpful because acidic conditions in the intestines can contribute to a variety of illnesses. According to a study published in the *American Journal of Clinical Nutrition*, breast milk has been shown to protect against inflammatory conditions, including bowel disorders such as colitis and Crohn's disease.

Studies published in the *Journal of Pediatrics*, *American Journal of Clinical Nutrition*, and *British Medical Journal*, among others, show that breast-fed babies have one-fourth the rates of serious respiratory and intestinal diseases and one-tenth the risk of being hospitalized for life-threatening bacterial infections compared to formula-fed babies. According to a 1997 report by the American Academy of Pediatrics, human milk may also protect against sudden infant death syndrome (SIDS), insulin-dependent diabetes mellitus, lymphoma, and other chronic digestive diseases. Additionally, studies have shown that breast milk provides significant lifelong protection against allergies, juvenile rheumatoid arthritis, celiac disease, pneumonia, meningitis, and certain cancers. Breast-fed babies also have significantly lower incidences of childhood obesity than children raised on infant formula. They have better vision, stronger facial muscles, and better dental alignment due to suckling.

Alternatives to Breast Milk

For many reasons, breast-feeding may not be an option for you and your baby. If that is the case, you will need a formula or breast milk substitute. Formula has been fortified to emulate breast milk with different ingredients—milk or soy, vegetable oils, corn or brown rice syrup, added vitamins and minerals, and possible chemicals. Most formulas are low in saturated fats, and most soy formulas do not have cholesterol at all. Some organic formulas contain higher quality ingredients, and they avoid ingredients that are treated with hormones or pesticides in their production and processing.

Infant formula comes in three preparation methods: ready-to-feed, concentrate, and powder. Ready-to-feed is prepackaged in liquid form, is ready to use without adding water, and is the most expensive option. Concentrated formula comes in liquid form in a can, requires mixing with water, and is less expensive than ready-to-feed formula. The least expensive and most widely used formula is powdered, which is reconstituted by adding water. If you choose a concentrated or a powdered formula that requires additional water, the quality of the water you use affects the formula.

There are primarily three types of infant formula: cow's milk, soy milk, and hydrolyzed milk. They vary in terms of the proteins and sugars contained in them. A fourth type, goat's milk, is also discussed below.

Cow's Milk Formula

Purified cow's milk formula is the most popular type of formula, and it is prepared with supplemental fats, vitamins, and minerals. The proteins are processed to imitate human breast milk because regular cow's milk is too difficult for a baby to digest until after about one year of age. The primary proteins in cow's milk formula are casein, or curds, and whey, with casein being the principal compound. Cow's milk contains approximately ten times more casein than human milk. There are two types of cow's milk formula: first-stage formula that is designed to meet the nutritional and digestive needs for your baby's first year; and second-stage formula for older babies, which contains less fat and calories.

Some cow's milk formulas have added omega-3 and -6 fatty acid supplements of DHA (docosahexaenoic acid) and ARA (arachidonic acid) that are present in breast milk and aid in the development of your baby's nervous system, brain, and eyes. Lactose, which is present in breast milk and cow's milk formula, provides energy, promotes calcium absorption in the stomach, and stimulates the growth of healthy bacteria in the intestines. Most babies tolerate lactose, but some may be allergic to it. If your baby is allergic, he may have symptoms of abdominal cramping, bloating, or gas about 30 minutes to two hours after eating dairy. In this case, you may consider switching to a different type of lactose-free formula.

Soy Milk Formula

Soy milk formula is an alternative to breast milk or cow's milk formula, and may be an option if your baby is lactose intolerant. However, this option requires sensitive trial and error, because many infants who experience allergic reactions to cow's milk formulas cannot accept most soy formulas either. According to East Asian medicine theory, soybeans can be chilling to the body and disruptive to the digestive system. For babies who cannot process soy milk formula, a third choice, hydrolyzed formula, may be the ideal solution.

Hydrolyzed Formulas

Hydrolyzed formula contains cow's milk proteins that have been reduced, or hydrolyzed, into their component parts: amino acids, for easier digestion. Words that describe hydrolyzed formulas are partially hydrolyzed, extensively hydrolyzed, predigested, partially broken down, or extensively broken down. This formula is more expensive than other alternatives because of the extra processing required. It is also not as sweet as the other options, so babies may not immediately accept it after having tried the other kinds.

Goat's Milk Formula

The composition of goat's milk compared to cow's milk has more fat, less lactose, and protein with softer curds. Theoretically, these differences add up to a less allergenic and more digestible milk. Like cow's milk formula, goat's milk is not an adequate formula for babies under one year old, but it can be used occasionally instead of cow's milk as a beverage for children over one year.

Breast Milk for Your Baby

The best time to start breast-feeding is immediately after your baby is born. A doula, a midwife, a lactation consultant, an experienced family member, or another support person can help you get started and assist your baby in latching on. Keeping your baby with you after birth (referred to as "rooming in") rather than sending him to the hospital nursery will ensure that you are present the moment he is ready to eat.

In spite of all of the positive aspects of breast-feeding, it is not uncommon for new mothers to feel awkward and anxious while nursing. If you are surrounded by friends or relatives who are not supportive, then breast-feeding may be challenging for you. You may experience pain when you first start nursing, with cracked nipples, engorgement, mastitis, or clogged ducts. Perhaps you have a low milk supply and are worried about your ability to nurse. In taking on this new and important role, it is helpful to find a supportive community. Seek guidance from those who can offer advice and comfort for first-time nursing mothers to help you work through these issues.

The environment in which you breast-feed your baby may affect the experience for both of you.

A chaotic and noisy setting with overly bright lighting could make it difficult for you and your baby to relax. Calmness in the surrounding space helps your milk flow, and your baby can absorb your nourishment more easily. You may have anxiety about nursing in public, and it may not always be easy to find a private location, such as a department store dressing room or an unoccupied space in a friend's house. You can be discreet with a blanket over your shoulder or by wearing a loose blouse that can be opened from the waist. If you get tension in your upper back, shoulders, and neck, make time to stretch to help your posture and ease the tension.

A hospital or birthing center usually has resources, such as a lactation consultant, who can assist you with nursing and follow up with you in the first weeks; a lactation consultant can also connect you to other new or experienced mothers for support. The La Leche League (llli.org) is an excellent resource for breast-feeding support and they can refer you to a chapter in your area. I hosted La Leche League meetings at my house when I was nursing my children, which was a good chance for me to learn about the importance of breast-feeding, any complications, and possible solutions. This was also a way to meet other mothers and connect through your experiences. The International Childbirth Education Association (icea.org) is another good resource.

Breast-feeding operates on the law of supply and demand: the more you nurse, the more milk you produce. Your body and your baby's body are in sync: when your breasts are full usually coincides with when your baby is hungry, and the cycle starts again for each meal. The biological communication between mother and baby is one of nature's miraculous intelligences.

Developing a rhythm and structure in feeding your baby allows for complete cycles so that he gets all of the nutrients from both foremilk and hindmilk. Nursing can be an emotional comfort for your baby's occasional bumps on the head or upsets, but regular snacking can overstimulate his digestive system. According to Bob Flaws, practitioner of East Asian Medicine and author of *A Handbook of TCM Pediatrics*, irregular feeding cycles can result in overfeeding and congestion in the spleen, which obstructs the stomach and intestines. Flaws says that overfeeding and food stagnation can cause colic, earaches, coughs, colds, and childhood obesity. He asserts that feeding regulation diminishes these conditions, and can change the trajectory of a child's health

from infancy. If my babies were significantly upset, I had a hard time resisting a soothing nursing session just to stay on our regular feeding schedule. However, I did develop a routine and rhythm with a flexible schedule to give their digestive system a rest in between nursing cycles. In this way, I found that feeding was much more satisfying for me because my breasts had a chance to replenish. It also seemed better for my children because they were actually hungry when it was time to nurse and could get a full amount of foremilk and hindmilk in one session. I found that a schedule was better than grazing or snacking, and this helped my babies develop a rhythm that continued into their solid food habits. Establishing routine and rhythm in your life can also help keep structure and order in your baby's routine.

Bottle-feeding Breast Milk

If you need to go back to work while still nursing, or find that you need to be away from your baby during feeding time, you can pump your breast milk and store it in the refrigerator or freezer for his meals in your absence. The more you pump, the more milk you produce, and you can store large quantities of breast milk in the refrigerator for three to five days or in the freezer for three to six months. Remember to return the milk to a warm temperature before feeding your baby. Finding a private place to pump at work may be a challenge, so check with your human resources department to find out how your workplace can accommodate your pumping needs before returning to work.

Bottle-feeding with expressed breast milk or formula allows fathers, siblings, grandparents, and other caregivers to participate in feeding. Holding your baby close and making eye contact while feeding gives him a sense of security and comfort and allows for special moments of bonding. Your baby's head should be elevated and supported while bottle-feeding to prevent too much air or milk from entering his mouth, which can cause gas and discomfort. Inserting the entire nipple into his mouth helps prevent air from entering as well.

Breast-feeding Tips

- Learn about the practicalities of breast-feeding.

- Get support from your local La Leche League (llli.org) and other breast-feeding mothers.

- Room in to keep in touch with your baby's needs.

- Create a calm environment.

- Use pillows and a stool for support and comfort.

- Eat foods that make nutritious milk.

- Drink plenty of liquids.

- Feed on demand to develop your milk supply.

Breast-feeding Diet Recommendations

Daily During Breast-feeding	Occasionally During Breast-feeding	Avoid During Breast-feeding
Whole grains	Baked foods	Nicotine
Vegetables	Nightshade vegetables	Large amounts of alcohol
Sea vegetables	Tropical fruit	High-dosage vitamins
Legumes	Poultry (organic if possible)	Artificial sweeteners
Nuts and seeds	Yogurt	Caffeine
Temperate fruit	Kefir	Dairy products
Warm herbal tea	Goat cheese	Soft drinks
Water		Drugs (recreational and pharmaceutical)
Natural desserts		Sugary foods
Eat 500 additional calories		Salty snacks
Sleep and rest		Dieting

Eating for Your Baby

As with pregnancy, the food you eat has a direct effect on your baby when you are breast-feeding. He will double in size in his first six months and again by the time he is three years old, so the diet you choose for yourself during the first year of your baby's life will have a direct and significant impact on his growth and development. Your liver filters toxins up to a certain point, but the quality of the food you eat is ultimately passed along to your baby. The foods to curb during breast-feeding are the ones that most doctors tell you to limit or monitor closely in your day-to-day life. Fried or salty foods can make your baby irritable, overheated, and constipated. Alcohol and excessive sugary, fatty foods, or spicy foods can cause symptoms such as diarrhea and hypersensitivity. Common allergens for babies are cow's milk and dairy products, corn, soy, wheat, peanuts, and other nuts, which you may note by hives, swelling, gastrointestinal problems, or eczema. If they are not cooked thoroughly, cruciferous vegetables, such as cabbage, bok choy, and broccoli, can cause digestion issues and discomfort for your baby in his first few months. Beans can cause gas, but you can add kombu, a dried sea vegetable, while cooking to make them more easily digestible.

The food you eat can also affect the taste of your breast milk. "The fact that the flavor of foods is passed to breast milk is known," said Nicolas Stettler, assistant professor of pediatrics and epidemiology at the Children's Hospital of Philadelphia. He believes that there is a link between a mother's breast milk and the child's future eating habits, that a child's exposure to a variety of tastes affects his willingness to eat different foods. So eating a variety of nutritious foods while breast-feeding will encourage your child to do the same when he moves on to solids.

Integrating a diet of fresh and healthy food, such as mildly seasoned soups, moist grains, beans, vegetables (especially leafy greens and sweet, starchy vegetables), and some fish (which has essential fatty acids) will help produce abundant, rich breast milk, provide core nutrients to your baby, and help you get back into your pre-pregnancy jeans. Finally, as difficult as it may be with a newborn, it is important to get enough physical and emotional rest in addition to a healthy diet to produce abundant and nutritious milk.

Breast Milk Booster Recipes

When I was breast-feeding my babies, I especially enjoyed eating simple and delicious food, because I had such a big appetite. Nursing Emi and Mari during their first year required me to eat more calories on a daily basis than "eating for two" during pregnancy. Nutritious whole foods, cooked with plenty of liquid for a soft, moist consistency, helped produce nourishing breast milk. Whole grains offer essential nutrients, leafy greens and sea vegetables provide calcium and other minerals, protein-rich foods, healthy fats, fermented foods, and beverages give nourishment that you need for replenishment and that your baby needs for growth and development.

Hearty Miso Soup

♡ Nursing mothers and busy fathers

🥄 5 or 6 adult servings

A Animal protein

GF Gluten-free

A traditional soup made in Japan after childbirth is *koikoku*, or carp soup, which is made with fresh fish and lots of vegetables to help the uterus contract and to make breast milk flow. The following nourishing and restorative soup is a Western version that is both centering and satisfying for nursing mothers, and also provides a great source of calcium, protein, and omega-3 fatty acids found in fish oil.

1 tablespoon sesame, olive, or coconut oil

1 cup onion, cut into ¼-inch pieces

¾ cup celery, cut into ¼-inch pieces

½ cup shiitake mushrooms, cut into ½-inch pieces

1½ cups carrots, cut into ½-inch pieces

1½ cups yellow squash, cut into ½-inch pieces

½ teaspoon sea salt

6 cups water

1 teaspoon wakame flakes, or 1-inch square kombu sea vegetable, soaked in ¼ cup water for 5 minutes, and drained

1 bay leaf

½ pound salmon, skinned and boned, cut into 1-inch pieces

4 tablespoons white miso

Method

1. Pour oil into pan, and add one vegetable at a time, stirring slowly.

2. Add sea salt and sauté over medium heat for 5 to 10 minutes.

3. Add water, sea vegetable, and bay leaf.

4. Bring to a boil, turn down to medium heat and cook for 20 minutes, or until vegetables are tender.

5. Add fish to soup, and cook for 4 to 5 minutes, or until done.

6. Mix miso with 2 tablespoons water in a small dish until it has a smooth consistency.

7. Add miso and serve.

8. To retain the *Lactobacillus* in miso, do not boil soup after miso has been added.

Variations

• Cook fish in a separate pan and serve as an option.

• Substitute any other fatty fish.

Steamed Kale

♡ Nursing mothers
and busy fathers

🥄 2 adult servings

V Vegetarian

GF Gluten-free

Leafy greens, rich in vitamin A, chlorophyll, and calcium, are an excellent food for nursing mothers. Magnesium is also present in kale, and the calcium is more easily absorbed than calcium in dairy products. Because kale is a cruciferous vegetable, make sure that it is cooked thoroughly to avoid gas and reduced iodine levels. Kale grows in very cold weather and is also abundant in local farmers' markets during spring and fall.

2 cups kale, cut into ½-inch pieces

½ cup water

⅛ teaspoon sea salt

Method

1. Place kale and water into a skillet.

2. Bring to a boil and add sea salt.

3. Cook for 5 to 10 minutes, or until tender. Kale should retain a bright green color.

4. If liquid remains, drink separately, or add to soup or beans for extra flavor and nutrition.

Variation

In addition to the traditional curly variety, kale is now available in several different types. Substitute collards, mustard greens, or turnip greens, or use a mix of greens.

Mochi for Nursing Mothers

♡ 2 years+

🥄 10 (2-ounce) patties

V Vegetarian

GF Gluten-free

Traditionally in Japan, *mochi* is used for special occasions, and is also known for encouraging the flow of breast milk and for restoring strength and stamina. Whole-grain *mochi* is rich and nutritious for both mom and baby.

Sweet rice is called "glutinous rice" because it is sticky, but it does not contain gluten that is found in wheat. It is used to make *mochi* because it has a sticky consistency when pounded. *Mochi* is made without salt, so the grains break down and stick together.

Mochi has a chewy texture, so it is important to wait until your child has teeth, and he can chew well, before offering *mochi*. Also, make sure *mochi* is cut into small pieces before serving it to your young child.

2 cups sweet brown rice

Water to cover for soaking

2 ½ cups water for cooking

Arrowroot or sweet rice
    flour for dusting

Planning Ahead

Cover sweet rice with water and soak for 8 to 24 hours. If you do not have time to soak for the longer time span, soak for at least 1 hour, if possible.

Method

Preparing rice

1. Strain soaking water, place rice and cooking water into pot, and bring to a boil over high heat.

2. Reduce heat and cook for 45 minutes to 1 hour, until all water is absorbed.

3. Use a heat diffuser to keep grains from sticking to the bottom of the pot, and to prevent burning.

4. Allow the rice to cool slightly.

Note: Do not use salt when cooking rice, because salt keeps the grains separate and firm. The lack of salt makes it easy to break down the grains.

Pounding mochi

1. Transfer to a large bowl.

2. Using a potato masher or mallet, pound rice and break grains until sticky. Form into balls that are about ¼ cup in size, and dust with arrowroot flour until lightly coated.

3. Air-dry for 2 to 4 hours before refrigerating. *Mochi* can be put into a toaster until it puffs up like a marshmallow, and eaten with nori seaweed and soy sauce, or it can be put into soup so that it becomes soft like a dumpling.

Mochitsuki

Mochitsuki (making *mochi*) is traditionally a time of fellowship and socializing in Japan that involves cheering and enthusiasm. The *mochi* is pounded with a big wooden mallet in a stone bowl until the rice is smooth and shiny and there are no individual grains left. Eating *mochi* is thought to bring good luck.

Hideko Yoshida

Saburo Yoshida

Grains

WHEN I FIRST WENT to Japan and took cooking classes in Tokyo, I lived with the Tokutsu family. On hot summer nights, we gathered in their small *tatami* (straw mat) room and watched *beisu boru* (baseball) on the *terubi* (television). Just like *beisu boru*, rice was a significant aspect of my Japanese life. To the Tokutsus, eating white rice was a sign of status and wealth, while eating brown rice signified a lower position in Japanese society. My love for the latter truly perplexed them. They were befuddled as to why a modern American girl would eat brown rice, so they nicknamed me *genmai-san*—"brown rice girl."

The Japanese word for rice, *gohan*, also means "meal." Rice is the principal food for breakfast, lunch, and dinner, and a Japanese meal is not complete without it. All the other dishes, such as vegetables, fish, or meat, are considered secondary to the heart of the meal: rice. Today, white rice is popular in Japan, but for many centuries, brown rice was the staple.

Grains have been the central food of most cultures for thousands of years. Rice and millet have historically served as the primary grains in Asia, as have teff and millet in Africa. Barley, oats, wheat, and rye are traditional in Europe, and corn reigns in Mesoamerica. From an evolutionary standpoint, grains are the most advanced plant food, with the fruit and the seed of the plant being one and the same. Some biologists believe that the evolution of plants and animals are synchronized and that humans evolved alongside cereal grains. Sustained across cultures and time, grains are one of the most essential components of the human diet.

The Power of Grains

Many nutritional and health experts encourage a return to grain-centered diets for both human and environmental health. Grains are more economical and require less energy to grow, process, package, and transport than meat and dairy products. For example, to produce one pound of industrially processed meat, a single beef cow has to eat about three pounds of grain. One pound of that cow equates to three or four adult servings, while one pound of cooked grains provides seven servings.

Alan Greene, MD, pediatrician and clinical professor at Stanford University School of Medicine, developed his White Out program to replace the old idea that white rice cereal should be your baby's first or main food. He says that feeding your baby white rice cereal is much like feeding him a spoonful of sugar, and that it is a form of junk food. Greene supports parents in making homemade baby food using whole and organic ingredients for optimal health.

In this chapter, the term whole grain refers to the nutritious, original state of grains that have never been cracked or broken. Brown rice and quinoa are examples of whole grains, while flour, pasta, and bread are processed grains. Conventional baby food instant cereal, and even organic rice cereal are made of processed and cracked grains. Foods made with cracked grain, such as pasta, bread, cookies, crackers, oatmeal are delicious and healthy foods to offer your baby occasionally. However, feeding him whole grains as his central food provides him an opportunity for optimal health.

Why Give Your Baby Whole Grains?

❀ **Whole grains are living foods:** If you planted a handful of brown rice in good soil under the right conditions, it would grow into rice plants that would sprout, send down roots, grow a stalk, mature, flower, and produce more seeds. Once the grain is cracked or ground into flour, it is still nutritious, but it has lost some of its life force and ability to regenerate. In addition, the cracked grain has begun the oxidation process.

❀ **Nutrition:** Whole grains contain all of the major nutrient groups needed for your child's healthy development—complex carbohydrates, amino acids, protein, fats, vitamins, minerals, and fiber. Phosphorus in whole grains is a component of nucleic acids, the building blocks of the genetic code. Whole grains are a good source of thiamine, believed to support mental health.

Grain Structure

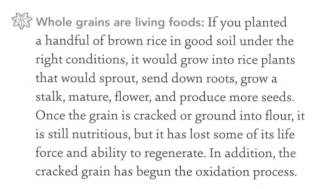

Endosperm is the kernel of the grain which accounts for 80% of the total size of the plant and its sweetness.

Bran is the outermost layer of the grain which contains protein, fat, fiber, vitamins, and minerals.

Germ is the reproductive component of the grain. It contains high levels of niacin, thiamin, iron, and zinc, along with vitamin A, B, and E, protein, and fat.

As soon as a grain is ground, oxidation begins and the oil in the grain begins to degrade, eventually turning rancid. Processing grain, which entails removal of the bran and the germ, reduces the grain's most nutrient-rich components, including more than half of vitamins B1, B2, B3, and E, as well as folic acid, calcium, phosphorus, zinc, copper, iron, and fiber.

Processing strips all of these essential nutrients away, leaving only the endosperm. While this part has far fewer vitamins and minerals than the whole grain, it contains a greater amount of protein and complex carbohydrates than the bran or the germ, as nature originally intended. The full nutritional value of the grain is only available when all three of its parts are intact. White and wheat flours and white rice are processed grains that offer only fractions of their maximum nutritional potential.

Health: Whole grains offer hormone-balancing phytoestrogen compounds and protective anti-oxidants that lower cholesterol. The B-complex vitamins support your baby's blood production, nervous system function, and immune system. Minerals support the health of your baby's bones, muscles, and brain.

 Steady energy: As a complex carbohydrate, whole grains help sustain your baby's hormone, insulin, and pancreatic secretions and equalize pH and sugar levels in his blood. Whole grains help your baby sleep, which helps your nervous system, too. Additionally, as a centering and harmonizing food toward the middle of the Yin–Yang spectrum, whole grains provide an overall balance in your baby's body.

 Good for digestion: Many of your baby's discomforts and simple illnesses are related to digestion, colic or gas, diarrhea, constipation, and upset stomach. In East Asian medicine, these ailments are caused by stagnation, mucus, or congestion. Uncracked whole grains offer a natural remedy that is warming, easy to digest, and nourishing to his stomach. They also offer a source of fiber, which helps promote bowel regularity.

Grain Considerations

When choosing grains, consider whether they are organic and where they are grown. You can buy some grains that have been sprouted. Soaking or sprouting grains improves digestion and neutralizes phytates, which normally inhibit mineral absorption. This increases the bioavailability of the nutrients—namely iron and zinc. In addition, you may look for signs and symptoms of gluten intolerance in your baby as a reaction to grains that contain gluten.

Gluten Intolerance

Gluten is a protein found in wheat, rye, barley, and spelt, that can be difficult for some children to digest. Gluten acts as a binding agent and can attract a variety of allergens, making it difficult for your baby's body to flush them out. Celiac disease is a genetic disorder associated with a gluten allergy. It is relatively rare, but if a child's parent is celiac positive, then there is a chance that he could also be celiac positive.

Some parents of autistic children report improvements in speech and behavior when following a gluten-free dietary regimen. Research by Harumi Jyonouchi, MD, an associate professor at the New Jersey Medical School in the Department of Pediatrics, shows that 91 percent of people on the autism spectrum who were put on a strict gluten-free, casein-free, sodium-free (GFCFSF) diet showed improvement. Some reported that their child experienced fewer digestive problems, greater mental clarity, and improved speech after starting a GFCF diet. Although this research is anecdotal, the indications are worth considering.

When my children were little, I did not know about the possible negative effects of gluten. If I had a baby today, I would introduce gluten around 12 to 18 months and watch for any sensitivity or reaction. Fortunately, due to increased awareness of gluten intolerance, gluten-free foods are now easier to find.

Signs and Symptoms of Gluten Intolerance

- Abdominal distress, chronic diarrhea, gas, bloating, and nausea
- Fatigue
- Headaches
- Joint pain
- ADHD/ADD
- Delayed growth
- Seizures
- Acid reflux

Types of Grains

Whole-grain brown rice, soft cooked to a semi-liquid consistency, is an ideal first food for your baby. In addition to its dietary benefits, the consistency of soft rice is similar to that of milk, is naturally sweet and easy to digest, and rarely related to food allergies. Consequently, it serves as a transitional food from breast milk. Examples of unprocessed whole grains to cook for your baby include short grain brown rice, sweet rice, and millet. Occasionally, your baby or toddler can also enjoy cracked grains such as rolled oats, noodles, couscous, and treats made from wheat flour if he shows no signs of gluten sensitivity. Moreover, eating whole grains as first foods helps your baby develop a strong foundation for tastes and flavors that will last a lifetime.

Brown Rice

There are more than 7,000 varieties of rice found around the world. Whole-grain rice is called "brown" due to its golden-brown hue. Brown rice is a body-building food for your baby's bones, muscles, hair, and teeth.

White rice is brown rice that has been milled to remove the outer bran. Brown rice is more nutritious than white processed rice, with higher levels of fiber, fatty acids, vitamins B and E, thiamin, riboflavin, niacin, iron, and potassium. Rice contains no gluten and is one of the easiest grains to digest. Hideko Yoshida, my mentor at the Dream Window Kindergarten in Kyoto, Japan, said that for simple daily food, brown rice is best because it offers everything the body needs on its own. Eaten together with a legume, rice makes a complete protein. Easily accessible in most groceries and natural stores, brown rice comes in three sizes: short, medium, and long grain. Short grain is soft and starchy, and has a creamy consistency when cooked for puree, so it is used most often for children.

In November 2012, Consumer Reports published a report regarding inorganic arsenic in rice. Arsenic is a carcinogen that can end up in soil and water from animal feed, fertilizers, and poultry waste. There are pollutants in today's environment and it is impossible to avoid these contaminants completely. Soaking or sprouting grains helps minimize these contaminants. Choosing organic and whole-grain rice along with a variety of other whole grains can provide your baby a healthy start. You can also help your baby build a strong immunity that can eliminate waste toxins by eating other whole and fermented foods.

Sweet Brown Rice

Sweet brown rice is sticky, and as indicated by its name, is sweeter than short or long grain rice. For Japanese New Year's celebrations and other special occasions, sweet rice is pounded into *mochi* with a big mallet. I especially like to mix sweet rice with millet for porridge or with regular brown rice for making rice balls.

Sweet brown rice is beneficial for nursing mothers because its protein and fat content boost breast milk production. When I was nursing Emi in Japan, each week we ordered homemade *mochi* made with different ingredients. Mugwort *mochi* contains a wild green plant with lots of chlorophyll that turns the *mochi* green and adds extra cleansing phytonutrients for mother and baby. Other variations contain black beans or sesame seeds for protein. Toasted in the toaster or in a skillet, *mochi* puffs up like marshmallows; dropped into soup, it gets soft like dumplings.

Millet

You may think of birdseed when you think of millet, but this golden, gluten-free grain is healthy for humans, too, and is dinner for about one-third of the world's population from Africa to China. Millet is alkaline-producing, is high in minerals, and serves as a complete protein. East Asian medicine claims that millet soothes morning sickness and helps prevent miscarriage. Millet is soothing to the stomach, so it is ideal in times of digestive distress.

Many varieties of millet are grown for human consumption around the world, the most common of which is pearl millet. After soaking millet for a couple of hours, it cooks in 20 to 30 minutes and absorbs more water than rice does, so the ratio of water to grain is higher for millet than for rice. This healthy grain has a creamy texture that is easily digested and combines well with other grains, beans, and vegetables.

Quinoa

The Incans called quinoa (pronounced "keen-wa") "the Mother Grain," and believed its consumption could lead to a long life. Quinoa is an excellent grain because it is gluten-free and packed with protein. It also contains a higher percentage of calcium than milk; is a good source of phosphorus, iron, vitamin E, and B vitamins; and is easy to digest. Quinoa adds texture to soups, stews, and porridges and cooks quickly—only 20 to 25 minutes in boiling water. Quinoa is often prepared together with other grains for babies and children due to its strong taste.

Oats

The fat content in oats is the highest of all the grains, so along with the satisfying taste, oats are valuable for warmth and stamina. They are among the most nutritious of cereals, containing high levels of protein, fat, and fiber. Oats grow best in northern climates and have been an essential food since ancient times in Ireland, Scotland, northern Europe, and Russia.

Instant oats, or quick oats, have been precooked in water, dried, and rolled very thin, a process that reduces their nutritional value and flavor. They can be cooked in 3 to 5 minutes.

Rolled oats are made by pressing whole oats between two rollers. For babies and toddlers, rolled oats have a smooth texture and are convenient for occasional use to make a breakfast porridge or for baking.

These oats take 15 to 20 minutes to cook, but have more nutrition and flavor than instant oats.

Steel-cut oats are oat groats (hulled grains) made by cutting whole oats into two or three pieces. They require 20 to 30 minutes to cook, and are more flavorful than rolled oats, with a nutty and chewy texture. Whole oat groats retain the beneficial bran and germ of the oat and they store well. Whole oats take as long to cook as brown rice does—around 50 to 60 minutes.

Barley

Barley was a primary grain in Europe before wheat and rye became more popular. Barley is high in essential minerals like selenium and tryptophan. It contains gluten, so you may prefer to wait until your child is over one year old with a stronger digestive system before introducing this grain. It is most commonly available in the pearled form, which requires removing the bran. Pearled barley and barley flakes cook to a soft consistency and can be added to stews and soups. Barley flour can be used in muffins or cookies.

Amaranth

Similar to quinoa and fellow native to the Americas, amaranth is botanically classified as a grass instead of a grain. The color of amaranth  ranges from golden yellow to deep red to black. Its protein content is almost double that of rice and corn, and it is also high in the amino acid lysine, which aids the body with growth and regeneration. Cooking a small amount of amaranth with other grains adds a rich depth of flavor, and it takes 20 to 25 minutes to cook.

Wheat

Due to bread's popularity around the world, wheat has become the most widely distributed grain. Wheat is classified as either hard or soft:  hard wheat has more protein, and soft wheat has higher levels of carbohydrates. Soft wheat is good for pastries, cookies, and crackers, or it can be mixed with hard wheat for bread. The gluten in wheat can cause allergic reactions, which may be difficult for your baby's digestive system. To avoid potential allergies or digestive concerns, I suggest to wait until your child is one year old before introducing him to whole wheat.

Wheat bran and wheat germ are nutritious components of wheat. Wheat bran comes from the outer layers of the wheat kernel, is high in fiber and protein, and is effective for helping reduce blood cholesterol. Wheat germ contains the embryo of the wheat kernel and most of the vitamins and minerals found in the grain.

Cracked wheat can be cooked as a cereal grain or used as *bulgur*—a popular staple of Middle Eastern and Mediterranean diets. *Bulgur* is a form of whole wheat that has been cleaned, steamed or dried, and then ground into grains. *Bulgur* is most often made from durum wheat and is a good source of protein, iron, magnesium, and B vitamins. Fine *bulgur* can be eaten as a cereal and used in desserts; coarsely ground *bulgur* is delicious in salads and casseroles. *Bulgur* is precooked and is ready to eat

after 10 minutes of steaming or boiling, and offers an easy, nutritious substitute for pasta. However, because it is a cracked rather than a whole grain, I recommend using *bulgur* occasionally.

Buckwheat

Because buckwheat grows more like a bush than a slender grass, it is not classified as a true grain, but nutritionally it aligns  with other grains. The largest consumer of buckwheat is Asia, with its production and consumption of soba noodles, and Europe integrates buckwheat into its dietary traditions as well.

Russians are especially fond of this grain (called *kasha*) because of its warming properties. Whole-grain buckwheat is very nutritious, containing key essential amino acids and high levels of lysine, which helps synthesize protein. Also rich in B vitamins and minerals, it is a good source of choline, a compound in the vitamin B complex that plays an important role in metabolism, blood pressure, and cholesterol regulation.

You can cook buckwheat in its whole-grain form and serve it as a soft porridge like rice; boil buckwheat soba noodles for a delicious and satisfying meal or snack; or make a hearty breakfast of buckwheat pancakes from the flour. However, as a very heavy and hearty grain, it tastes better when mixed with a lighter grain, such as oat flour (which is gluten-free) or unbleached whole wheat flour. Offer it to your child occasionally, and you can balance its flavor by cooking it with white potatoes as *kasha* or serving it as pancakes with sweet maple syrup. Soba noodles can be served warm in winter or cool in summer, and they are a Japanese celebration food for New Year's Eve to provide strength and health.

Corn, Polenta, and Corn Grits

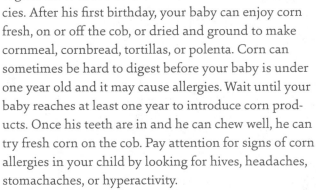

Due to low levels of niacin, which is an essential B vitamin, corn is healthiest when combined with a variety of other wholesome grains, beans, and vegetables to avoid deficiencies. After his first birthday, your baby can enjoy corn fresh, on or off the cob, or dried and ground to make cornmeal, cornbread, tortillas, or polenta. Corn can sometimes be hard to digest before your baby is under one year old and it may cause allergies. Wait until your baby reaches at least one year to introduce corn products. Once his teeth are in and he can chew well, he can try fresh corn on the cob. Pay attention for signs of corn allergies in your child by looking for hives, headaches, stomachaches, or hyperactivity.

Corn is everywhere

In many cases, high-fructose corn syrup is used in children's foods such as cereals, spaghetti sauces, and even canned soups. Michael Pollan, expert in the health and food industry and author of *The Omnivore's Dilemma*, says that corn is the primary ingredient in today's food: it is used as a sweetener, fed to animals raised for meat, and used as an additive in fast and processed foods. Pollan explains that due to agricultural policy and subsidies, an overabundance of industrially produced cheap corn is an incentive for food scientists to use the excess in other food products. These by-products offer no

nutritional value for your baby, and generally come from corn crops that have been genetically modified. Read the labels on processed foods to make sure there are no corn by-product ingredients before your child is one year old.

Corn Considerations

Common corn-based products that could cause health concerns

- Baking powder and cornstarch
- Caramel color (may contain corn syrup)
- Confectioners' sugar
- Corn syrup
- Dextrin and dextrose
- Fructose
- Maize
- Maltodextrins
- Sorbitol and mannitol
- Vanilla extract (may contain corn syrup)
- High-fructose corn syrup

Common foods containing high-fructose corn syrup

- Ketchup
- Pancake syrup
- Sodas
- Flavored or sweetened yogurt
- Breads
- Frozen pizzas
- Canned soups
- Salad dressing
- Applesauce and canned fruits
- Cereals
- Cereal bars

High-fructose corn syrup is linked to

- Obesity
- Compromised learning ability and memory
- High blood pressure
- High levels of mercury

How Grains Grow

Understanding how grains grow helps you appreciate where your food comes from and how it affects you. It can also help you and your child connect to nature.

Amaranth

Amaranth has been cultivated for more than 8,000 years by the Aztecs. It is a tall, broadleaf plant, with thick stems that grow 2 to 8 feet tall. It produces large seed heads that grow in a variety of shades of maroon, green, or gold. The tiny, round, cream-colored seeds are 1 millimeter in diameter. The yield is approximately 1 to 2 ounces of seed per plant.

Corn

Corn originated nearly 6,000 years ago in Mexico. Domesticated plants grow up to 8 feet tall with a leafy stalk, which is thick and segmented like a bamboo stalk. The plants produce ears, which contain the grain kernels. One plant produces two or three ears of corn.

Oats

Oats were first grown around 4,000 years ago. Cultivated oats are native to northern Central Asia, and are grown in temperate zones with cooler climates. The plant grows 2 to 5 feet tall when it is mature. The plant has a central stem with side branches that rise in whorls with spikelets that have flowers and edible seed heads. There are from 20 to 150 spikelets on one plant, and each spikelet produces one or two seeds, so one plant can make from 20 to 300 grains.

Quinoa

Quinoa is around 4,000 years old and is native to the Andes Mountain range in South America. Quinoa thrives in extreme conditions, such as high altitudes, thin cold air, hot sun, radiation, drought, frost, and poor soil. Quinoa is not truly a grain, but it is used as one. The plant grows from 4 to 6 feet high and has many angular branches with large clusters at the end of a stalk, which are multicolored in pink, red, brown, and ivory. Each stem holds about an ounce of grain.

Rice

Rice originated from 8,200 to 13,500 years ago in China. It is a grass plant with a root base and long, slender leaves. Rice is usually grown in fields with water to control weeds, and it can grow from 2 to 6 feet tall. One mature rice plant can yield more than 3,000 grains.

Wheat

Wheat originated more than 10,000 years ago, and the common ancestor of wheat, einkorn, was first cultivated in what is now known as Iraq. It needs a cool, moist growing season followed by warm, dry weather for ripening. Wheat has an average height of about 4 feet, and a stalk of wheat can have up to 200 grains.

The Yin and Yang of Grains 🏠

On the Yin–Yang spectrum of foods, grains are balanced toward the center for daily eating. The degrees of difference between one grain and another are relatively subtle in terms of yin and yang. Some determinants are the fat and moisture content, the shape, size, and color.

Starting on the yin side, corn has more liquid and is closer to being a vegetable. Oats are large and are higher in fats, which have a more yin influence. Quinoa is naturally more yin because of its higher protein content, and is soft when cooked. Rice is near the center of the spectrum; sweet rice has a yin influence because it is softer and naturally glutinous. People who live in hot climates, such as India, favor long grain rice, because it is cooling to the body with a more yin influence. Short grain rice has a more yang influence, and therefore more energizing and warming in fall and winter. Wheat is dry and warming to the body because it is grown in cooler climates. Next are amaranth and millet, which are small and round. Buckwheat has the most yang influence because it is grown in a cold climate, and it is very warming to the body.

Listed in the chart are balanced grains, toward the center for daily use and foods on a wider spectrum for occasional use.

Grain Preparation

In kitchens across different cultures, and for generations, families crack, dry, mash, and boil grains to suit their recipes and palates. Whole grains are easier to digest when they are soaked before cooking. Here are a few forms of preparation as you experiment with cooking grains for your baby.

Puree

The first method of food preparation for your baby is a thick pureed soup that is blended in a blender or food mill. As your baby transitions from breast milk or formula to solid foods, you can adjust the consistency of his puree with his chewing ability by going from a thin and milky mixture to a thick and lumpy one. Cook his first foods well so that he can easily digest and assimilate them. Cooking starts the digestion process so that your baby's stomach does not have to do all of the work.

Chewing Grains

After your child has his teeth and he is able to chew, you can reduce the amount of water when cooking grains and serve them in their whole, rather than pureed, form. You can cook grains individually, or mix them with other grains, or cook them with beans and vegetables.

Yin-Yang Spectrum of Grains

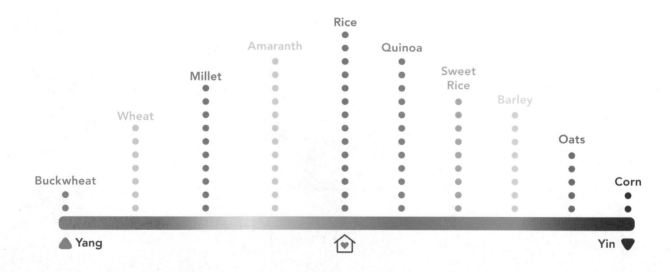

Mari making pancakes while camping

Baked Flour Snacks

Stone-ground flour is more nutritious, because stone mills retain the flavor and integrity of the grains better than high-speed steel rollers in commercial production. The best flours for baking include whole wheat all-purpose flour, whole wheat pastry flour, brown rice flour, oat flour, and unbleached white flour. Recipes are included in this book to bake teething biscuits, pancakes, muffins, cookies, cakes, and pies.

Pasta

Pasta is a happy food, and most cultures around the world enjoy noodle dishes of some sort. My family enjoys noodles of all kinds, eaten by themselves with a sprinkling of seasonings or combined with vegetables in lasagna, spaghetti, ramen, or pasta salad. For babies, noodles are a fun finger food and easy to digest because they are soft and wet, which helps them break down more easily than other cracked grain products, such as dry crackers or bread. When your baby is sitting up in his high chair and eating finger foods, you can introduce him to small noodles or pasta. A first noodle could be a small, gluten-free macaroni that will not cause a choking hazard. For the next stage of eating noodles, you can break or cut long spaghetti into 2-inch strips before cooking so that the pieces are manageable for her to eat. Steamed dumplings are a moist, easily digestible form of pasta that is cooked with liquid rather than baked. Couscous is another pasta with similar benefits of simple preparation and easy digestion.

There are two basic ways of making dried pasta: the roll-and-cut method and the extrusion method. The roll-and-cut method is used for smaller, local operations, homemade pasta, and handmade Japanese pasta. An extruder mixes, kneads, and pushes the dough through a plate with pasta shapes, which then get dried. Most commercial pasta makers use this method.

Traditional soft Italian pasta is usually made with eggs and does not contain salt, but now you can find many whole-grain brands that are eggless. Japanese pasta is not made with eggs and does contain salt. Various combinations of wheat, quinoa, corn, rice, buckwheat, and sesame flours (along with dried vegetable powders) provide an array of colors, tastes, and shapes for pasta.

Italian pastas, such as spaghetti, linguini, lasagna, rotini, macaroni, shells, and alphabets, can be eaten in sauces, salads, casseroles, and soups. The most popular Japanese pastas are udon, soba, somen, ramen, and glass or cellophane noodles. You can serve these with a garnished soup broth, as a salad, or stir-fried. Simple noodles with or without a sauce are delicious and fun for toddlers. Babies and toddlers often prefer pasta completely plain or with a simple tasty flavoring such as a few drops of sesame or olive oil and tamari or plum vinegar.

The cooking time of this pasta is usually three to 15 minutes, which is quicker than cooking a pot of whole grains. You can check the package for an estimated cooking time, but test a noodle to see whether it is cooked firm without being hard before draining the pot. Along with the cooking method, the freshness of the flour and the quality of the grain affect the taste of the pasta.

Cereals and Snacks

Dried and puffed cereals, crackers, and rice cakes are convenient snacks for babies and toddlers. There are gluten-free options available, such as oat circles or puffed rice, and they can be easily dispensed in snack cups. Be aware that these cereals are baked or puffed under extreme heat, which makes them dry and hard and can cause constipation. However, the dried cereals are a healthy and convenient alternative for snacking or on the go. Homemade puffed cereals make a delicious crispy candy for toddlers and other family members.

Grains for Your Baby

When Emi and Mari were ready for solid food, I started with brown rice made without salt. I cooked a pot of soft rice porridge every few days and stored it in the refrigerator. At mealtimes, I heated a small portion of porridge and put it through a blender or food mill before serving. Preparing whole grains for your baby takes more time than preparing instant cereal, but it is well worth the effort. It requires planning ahead to soak the grains for eight to 24 hours, and then cooking takes 45 minutes to an hour. However, one batch can last for several days, or it can be pureed and frozen in individual servings. It is quite easy once you understand the process and get a routine going.

In Japan, a soft rice called *kayu* is the traditional first food for babies. You can add some breast milk or formula to the grain porridge to ease the transition. Traditionally, Japanese mothers chewed the rice themselves, and then fed it to their little one, like a mama bird does for her babies. The mother's saliva provided the first step in digestion and made the grain more alkaline, which helped boost her baby's immune system. You may choose to skip this step and use a food mill instead.

Usually your baby will show interest in trying food at around the age of six months by reaching for your food. If his first teeth are coming in, that is another indication that he is ready to eat. Good nutrition depends on how well his body absorbs what it takes in, so his first foods need to be soft and moist for easy digestion. Brown rice cooked with a ratio of one part rice and seven parts water, and then pureed, has a liquid consistency that is similar to breast milk and a taste that is naturally sweet.

Soaking grains before cooking makes the nutrients more digestible and enhances their natural flavor. For your baby's first few meals, you may consider squeezing the rice through cheesecloth to take out the bran. If the porridge is too thick for him, add more water. You can reduce the ratio of water to grain to make the porridge thicker as your baby grows.

Once your baby is accustomed to brown rice, introduce him to other non-gluten whole grains such as millet, quinoa, amaranth, or rolled oats. Mix half and half millet and sweet rice, or combine brown rice with another grain for a variety of tastes and nutrition. Another quality combination is 70 percent rice, 20 percent millet, and 10 percent quinoa. East Asian medicine suggests that millet is a good first grain, because it strengthens the digestive system and is alkaline-producing.

Grains can be cooked as a single ingredient, or with vegetables and legumes. Sesame seeds, sunflower seeds, or pumpkin seeds can be boiled with the grain to add protein.

When your baby is seven months old and beginning to get teeth, gnawing on dry toasted bread and teething biscuits of gluten-free flour can be satisfying for him. At nine to 12 months, you can introduce gluten-free pasta and add seasonings such as nori flakes or a few drops of tamari, plum vinegar, or rice syrup for flavor. After 12 months, your toddler can also enjoy noodles, couscous, and treats made from wheat, corn, or barley flour. At 18 to 24 months, when his teeth are in and he can chew well, he can eat grains in their whole form with the rest of the family.

Helping your baby develop a taste for whole grains as a core component of his diet will set his foundation for creating a sensitive palate and a strong digestive system. The following chart gives an overview of which grains to start feeding when and how frequently. Add probiotic booster to puree for digestive support.

When to Introduce Grains

	Grains	Age Range	Frequency
	Brown rice short, medium, long grain	6 to 8 months	Daily
	Sweet brown rice	6 to 8 months	Daily
	Quinoa	6 to 8 months	Daily
	Millet	6 to 8 months	Daily
	Oats gluten-free	6 to 8 months	Daily
	Amaranth	7 to 9 months	Daily
	Teething biscuits gluten-free	7 to 9 months	Occasionally
	Bread gluten-free	7 to 9 months	Occasionally
	Pasta gluten-free	9 to 12 months	Occasionally
	Barley	12 to 18 months	Occasionally
	Wheat couscous, bread, pasta, dry cereals, muffins, crackers, dumplings, toast sticks	12 to 18 months	Occasionally
	Polenta and corn grits	12 to 18 months	Occasionally
	Udon, spaghetti	12 to 18 months	Occasionally
	Corn	12 to 24 months	Occasionally
	Buckwheat noodles or flour	18 to 24 months	Occasionally

Occasionally: 2–3 times a week

Daily Grains

♥ **6 months+**

🥄 **6 to 8 (2-ounce) servings or 3 to 4 (4-ounce) rice balls**

V **Vegetarian**

GF **Gluten-free**

Age	Water-to-grain ratio	Water	Grain
6–8 months	7 : 1	2 1/3 cups	1/3 cup
8–10 months	6 : 1	2 cups	1/3 cup
10–12 months	5 : 1	1 2/3 cups	1/3 cup
12–18 months	4 : 1	1 1/3 cup	1/3 cup
18–24 months	3 : 1	1 cup	1/3 cup
24–36 months	2 : 1	2/3 cup	1/3 cup

As your child gets older, she can eat a thicker consistency. Generally, the ratios of grain to water are the following, but they can be adjusted to meet your child's needs.

The transition from breast milk to solids is a big step for your baby, and whole-grain brown rice is a balanced and complete food that he can easily digest. Millet, sweet rice, and quinoa are also very nutritious, whether cooked alone or in combinations. In the beginning, add breast milk or formula to porridge before serving for a more liquid consistency, and because it is familiar to your baby. This helps him make the transition to solid foods. Mix in probiotic booster and ground flaxseeds before serving, if desired.

1/3 cup short-grain brown rice

Water to cover for soaking

2 1/3 cups water for cooking for 6 months (adjust water-to-grain ratio as baby grows)

1/8 teaspoon sea salt for 12 months+

Grain Cooking Times	
60 minutes	Sweet rice Brown rice Whole oats
40 minutes	Millet Corn grits
20 minutes	Quinoa Amaranth

These are suggested cooking times for easy digestion. They can cook longer if there is enough water to avoid scorching. Cooking time may vary according to the weather, your stove, and soaking time.

Planning Ahead

Cover grains with water and soak for 8 to 24 hours. If you do not have time to soak for the longer time span, soak for at least 1 hour, if possible.

Method

1. Strain soaking water, add rice and cooking water to pot. Bring to a boil.

2. Reduce heat and cook soaked grain for 1 hour, until all water is absorbed.

3. Use a heat diffuser to keep grains from sticking to the bottom of the pot, and to prevent burning.

4. Puree in a blender, food processor, food mill, hand grinder, or a grinding bowl.

5. Adjust consistency to meet your baby's needs, by adding more water, breast milk, or formula.

6. Modify grain-to-water ratios as your baby gets older for a thicker consistency.

Grain Superfood

♡ 12 months+

🥄 6 to 8 (2-ounce)
servings or
3 to 4 (4-ounce)
servings

V Vegetarian

GF Gluten-free

3 tablespoons short-grain brown rice

2 tablespoons millet

1 teaspoon quinoa

½ teaspoon sesame seeds

2 ⅓ cups water for cooking for
6 months (adjust water-to-grain
ratio as baby grows)

1-inch square kombu sea vegetable
or 1 teaspoon wakame flakes

⅛ teaspoon sea salt for 12 months+

Options:

Short-grain brown rice
and millet

Millet and sweet rice

Millet and quinoa

Planning Ahead
Cover grains with water and soak for 8 to 24 hours. If you do not have time to soak for the longer time span, soak for at least 1 hour, if possible.

Method
Follow the same directions for cooking Daily Grains, adding sea vegetables to grains while cooking.

Variations

- Cook single or combinations of grains—brown rice, sweet brown rice, millet, quinoa, or oats.

- Combine grains with vegetables when making puree.

- Add ¼ teaspoon sesame, sunflower, or pumpkin seeds to grain before soaking. Cook seeds with grains and puree together.

- Add ¼ sheet nori sea vegetable to grain in blender to puree, or sprinkle small pieces on top of grain dish, making sure that nori is moist, so that it is easy to swallow.

- Mix in ¼ teaspoon of sesame, olive, flaxseed, or coconut oil when serving.

- Mix in a few drops of plum vinegar when serving.

- Mix in ¼ teaspoon of rice syrup or tahini when serving.

- Sprinkle ground toasted seeds on top of grain when serving 9 months+.

Teething Biscuits

♡ 10 months+

⚗ 24 rectangle or 12 round biscuits

V Vegetarian

GF Gluten-free

Most commercial teething biscuits are made with wheat and sugar, but you can make your own whole-grain teething biscuits with grains that are gluten- and sugar-free. The best texture is hard, dry, and stiff. Keep an eye on your baby when he is eating teething biscuits to prevent choking hazards. These will stay fresh for 1 to 2 weeks, and you can double the recipe and freeze some biscuits for later.

1 ¼ cups oat flour

1 cup brown rice flour or quick-cooking oat flakes

⅛ teaspoon sea salt

¼ teaspoon baking powder

⅓ cup applesauce

2 tablespoons sesame oil

¼ cup brown rice syrup

Method

1. Preheat oven to 325°F. Oil cookie sheet.

2. Mix dry ingredients together in a bowl.

3. In a separate bowl, mix together oil, brown rice syrup, and applesauce.

4. Add the wet to the dry ingredients and stir to combine.

5. The mixture should be moist, but stiff enough to form a ball. Dust with oat flour. Use your hands to roll the dough ¼ inch thick.

6. Use a knife to cut the dough into approximately 1 x 3-inch rectangles.

7. Place biscuits on cookie sheet, leaving space between biscuits.

8. Bake for 40 minutes. Turn over while baking. Turn off the oven, leaving the biscuits in the oven for 1 hour.

9. Transfer biscuits to a plate and let cool.

10. Store in an uncovered container for 24 hours to let them harden. Freeze for extra relief in teething.

Variation

• Substitute yogurt, mashed banana, or vegetable puree for the applesauce.

Pasta

♡ 9 months+

🍽 8 (2-ounce) servings

V Vegetarian

GF Gluten-free

Pasta is not a whole food because the grain is partially refined, or "cracked." However, it is easier to digest than bread, crackers, cookies, and other baked flour products that are dry and hard, because it is soft and moist. Pasta is a quick food to cook and a fun finger food for your baby, especially short pasta shapes or cut pieces of long noodles. Introduce gluten-free pasta before 12 months to avoid gluten allergens. Wheat pasta can be offered after your child is one year old, and buckwheat noodles after two years old. Watch for signs of allergens, especially if you have gluten intolerance in your family.

1 cup whole-grain pasta (shells, elbow macaroni, linguini, spaghetti, or udon) gluten-free before 12 months

6 cups water

1 teaspoon sesame, olive, or coconut oil

⅛ teaspoon sea salt

Dressing (optional):

1 tablespoon lemon or orange juice

2 tablespoons sesame, olive, flaxseed, or coconut oil

Plum vinegar:
½ teaspoon for 9–12 months,
1 teaspoon for 12 months+

Method

1. If using long noodles, break into smaller pieces before cooking for younger children.

2. Bring water to a boil in pot.

3. Add oil and sea salt to water.

4. Add pasta to boiling water and cook until tender, according to package directions.

5. Drain and rinse with cold water.

6. Mix dressing ingredients and pour over pasta before serving.

Variations

- Add sautéed vegetables.

- Add ¼ teaspoon minced fresh or dried herbs while cooking, such as fennel, bay, basil, thyme, dill, cilantro, or parsley.

- Add thin strips of nori sea vegetable, making sure nori is moist so that it is easy to swallow.

- Add cubes of cooked tofu or pieces of poached fish.

- Pour miso or tamari soup over noodles for a warm dish (for toddlers who can feed themselves).

Pancakes

♡ 9 months+

🥄 16 (3-inch) pancakes

V Vegetarian

GF Gluten-free

Pancakes are a fun breakfast that can become a Saturday or Sunday morning tradition. This basic recipe can be a first finger food, cut up into small pieces or strips. As your baby learns to eat with utensils, you can offer toppings that are sweet or savory. Leftover pancakes travel well and can be a snack for later. Use cookie cutters to make different shapes and decorate with pieces of fruit and nuts.

1 ½ cups brown rice or oat flour

½ cup arrowroot flour

2 teaspoons baking soda

¼ teaspoon sea salt

2 eggs

¾ cup water

2 tablespoons sesame oil for mixing

1 tablespoon brown rice syrup

1 teaspoon vanilla

1 tablespoon sesame oil for cooking

Method

1. Sift flours together with salt and baking soda in a bowl.

2. In a separate bowl, mix together eggs, water, oil, brown rice syrup, and vanilla.

3. Add the dry to the wet ingredients and stir to combine. Mix until thoroughly moistened, with lumps remaining. Do not over mix.

4. The batter should be thin enough to pour, and thick enough to spread to ¼ inch thick.

5. Heat skillet or griddle to 375°F or medium heat if you do not have a thermostat.

6. Pour ¼ cup of batter onto griddle or skillet and cook until the tops are full of bubbles and the edges are dry.

7. Turn the pancake over and cook the opposite side until it browns.

8. Serve with brown rice syrup, maple syrup, jam, or fruit sauce on top.

Variations

•   Add 1 cup of fresh fruit to the batter—blueberries, bananas, raspberries, peaches, or apples.

•   Add 1 cup of sauteed vegetables to the batter—onions, mushrooms, carrots, green peas, or yellow squash.

Fritters

♡ 12 months+

🥄 16 (2-inch) fritters

V Vegetarian

GF Gluten-free

You can clean out your refrigerator by using leftover grains, vegetables, and beans to make these pan-fried fritters. Use this basic recipe as a guide to combine your available ingredients. The amount of moisture in different foods can vary, so add water as necessary. Pop them in the toaster later for a snack. Little fingers can eat independently with fritters as a finger food. They are also convenient for packing in bentos for travel or school lunches.

1 cup (approximately) vegetables, peeled and cut into ½-inch pieces

1 cup arrowroot flour

½ teaspoon sea salt

1 egg

3 tablespoons water

2 cups cooked brown rice, oatmeal, millet, or other grain

⅓ cup black beans

½ cup cornmeal

1 tablespoon sesame oil for cooking

Water, as needed

Method

1. Put vegetable in a pan and cover with water, cooking until tender.

2. Sift flour together with salt in a bowl.

3. In a separate bowl, stir egg. Add 3 tablespoons water to eggs.

4. Add the dry ingredients to the eggs and water and stir to combine.

5. Add grain, vegetables, and beans to mixture and stir. The batter should be thick enough to roll into balls. Add water, if necessary.

6. Use a small bowl of water to moisten hands. Scoop about ¼ cup of batter and form into a small ball.

7. Put corn meal in a small bowl. Dust fritter in corn meal.

8. Heat skillet to medium heat. Cook fritters in skillet for 5 minutes.

9. Turn fritters over and cover skillet, reduce heat and cook for 10 to 15 minutes.

10. Serve warm and store extras in the refrigerator in an airtight container.

Variations

• Substitute different grains, vegetables, and beans.

• Substitute small pieces of fish, tempeh, or tofu for beans.

Vegetables

WHEN EMI AND MARI were little, I remember strategizing how to get them to eat more vegetables. They naturally liked sweet and starchy vegetables, such as sweet potatoes, Japanese pumpkin, and peas, but getting them to eat leafy greens required creativity on my part. I discovered that they loved the creamy texture of pureed soups, dips, and sauces. I often made a gravy of blended vegetables and poured it over rice or noodles. Pureed vegetables offer your baby the ideal progression into solid food after grains, and they are a way to incorporate hearty and savory nutrition into the diets of toddlers and older children, too.

"Eat your vegetables" is a frequently repeated mantra at dinner tables everywhere, and for good reason. According to the 2005 Dietary Guidelines Advisory Committee Report, consumption of the fiber, vitamins, minerals, and phytochemicals found in vegetables is linked to lower risk of major chronic illnesses, such as type 2 diabetes and cardiovascular disease. Sea vegetables offer the richest source of minerals in the plant kingdom, and are considered superfoods for growing babies and children—foods noted for their nutrient density and benefits to overall well-being. Feeding your baby a variety of vegetables from land and sea enhances his development and stimulates his brain with different tastes. More specifically, fresh, organic vegetables cooked at home have a vitality and nutritional density that canned, packaged, and frozen foods cannot match.

After feeding your baby soft, whole grains as a first solid food, you can introduce him to land and sea vegetables. Starting with grains, and then vegetables, helps develop your baby's palate for savory flavors and appreciation for a variety of vegetables offering a broad range of nutrients. Introduce vegetables before fruits so that the extra sweetness of fruits does not overwhelm his natural desire for the milder sweetness of vegetables.

The Power of Land Vegetables

In most traditional cultures, vegetables are an essential food, served together with whole grains and legumes. An important source of fiber, fat, and antioxidants, vegetables are also high in vitamins and minerals, including vitamins A, all the B vitamins, C, and K, potassium, phosphorus, magnesium, calcium, selenium, iron, manganese, copper, and zinc. Vegetables provide generous nutritional value, especially relative to how low they are in calories compared to other food groups.

A veggie-packed diet promotes overall well-being. Vegetables have phytonutrients that are powerful in preventing diseases. Most nutritionists recommend that children eat at least three to five servings of vegetables a day, and that two- to three-year-olds eat one cup of vegetables a day. Vegetables' high concentration of fiber aids digestion and helps prevent stagnation and disease. Their alkaline-producing properties also neutralize acidity in your baby's body.

Healthy Choices for Life

The American Diabetes Association advocates eating high quantities of non-starchy vegetables, such as carrots, broccoli, and green beans in order to protect against diabetes. Helping your baby appreciate vegetables can increase his chances of making healthy eating choices later in life, leading to a lower chance of diabetes and other diseases. Vitamin A in vegetables, for instance, can benefit your baby's vision.

The Harvard-based *Nurses' Health Study and Health Professionals Follow-Up Study* did the largest and longest study to date on the benefits of vegetables. For 14 years, they followed the health and dietary habits of 110,000 men and women. Those who averaged eight or more servings of vegetables and fruits a day were 30 percent less likely to have a heart attack or stroke, and the higher the daily average intake of vegetables and fruits, the lower the chances of developing cardiovascular disease. Dark leafy green vegetables, such as arugula, bok choy, broccoli, brussels sprouts, cabbage, collard greens, kale, mustard greens, romaine lettuce, and turnip greens, appeared to have the most positive health impacts.

Most chronic diseases generate from an excess of macronutrients and a deficiency of micronutrients. Particularly during your baby's developmental stages, he needs to receive both macronutrients, as well as micronutrients from a variety of whole grains and vegetables. A helpful guideline for providing these micronutrients is to "eat the rainbow"—to integrate colors across the spectrum from deep-green broccoli to bright-orange carrots, and from purple beets to golden grains. There is no white in a rainbow—white foods are often refined or processed, and typically high on the glycemic index. Offering a variety of colorful veggies will ensure that your baby establishes a strong foundation for a healthy heart, digestive system, and long-term vitality.

Land Vegetable Considerations

When choosing vegetables, consider where they are grown, whether they are in season, whether they are organic, and which plant families they come from.

Locally Grown, Organic Vegetables

Conventionally grown vegetables are often treated with chemical fertilizers, fungicides, and pesticides, and chemical companies make genetic modifications to vegetable and fruit seeds to standardize their appearances and last longer during transportation. Synthetic chemical preservatives, such as petroleum-based waxes and coloring agents, are often added after growing to increase visual appeal and shelf life.

Buying local, naturally grown produce offers a multitude of benefits. Even if vegetables are not organic, locally grown vegetables are fresher and more flavorful. Feeding your baby locally grown produce also means connecting him to the seasons with foods that warm his body in winter and cool it in the summer. In addition to these health and environmental perks, shopping at farmers' markets strengthens your local economy.

Emi and Mari helping in the garden

Vitamins in Vegetables

Important Vitamins Are Contained in Specific Vegetables

 Vitamin A — Asparagus, avocado, broccoli, carrot, bell pepper, kale, peas, sweet potato

 Vitamin B1 *Thiamine* — Avocado, peas

 Vitamin B2 *Riboflavin* — Avocado, peas

 Vitamin B3 *Niacin* — Artichoke, asparagus, avocado, broccoli, carrot, corn, kale, lima beans, mushrooms, peas, potato, sweet potato

 Vitamin B5 — Avocado, broccoli, carrot, corn, lima beans, mushrooms, potato, sweet potato

 Vitamin B6 — Avocado, broccoli, carrot, corn, lima beans, mushrooms, potato, sweet potato

 Vitamin B9 *Folic acid* — Asparagus, avocado, bell pepper, broccoli, corn, kale, lima beans, onion, peas, potato, sweet potato

 Vitamin B12 — Kelp, nori

 Vitamin C *Absorbic acid* — Kelp, nori

 Vitamin D — Mushrooms

 Vitamin E — Bell peppers, broccoli, brussels sprouts, carrot, chard, collard greens, turnip greens

 Vitamin K — Bell peppers, broccoli, brussels sprouts, carrot, chard, collard greens, turnip greens

Cruciferous Vegetables

Cruciferous vegetables have an abundance of fiber, vitamins, and minerals. This group, however, contains goitrogens that may affect hormone production in the thyroid gland if eaten raw, so it is important to cook cruciferous vegetables for your baby. Cruciferous vegetables can be difficult for your baby to digest at early stages, so wait until seven to nine months to introduce them as a solid food. Make sure they are well cooked, and monitor your baby for possible digestive upsets. For a nursing mother, eating raw cruciferous vegetables can reduce the iodine levels in her breast milk. Cook thoroughly by steaming, boiling, sautéing, or preparing a soup.

Nightshades

Potatoes, tomatoes, bell peppers, hot peppers, and eggplants belong to the *Solanaceae* plant family, known as nightshades. Nightshades contain solanine, a low-level toxin adapted to keep predators away from the plants by causing diarrhea, vomiting, hallucinations, and headaches. I recommend waiting until your child is over one year old to introduce nightshades, and observe his condition for a reaction.

Nightshade vegetables are grown mostly in a hot climate and provide a cooling effect on the body. If you want to balance the yin and yang within a meal

comprised of nightshades, you might consider a yang cooking method with high heat, such as grilling or deep-frying, or using yang ingredients, such as salt or miso. The combination of tomatoes cooked with a little bit of miso produces a perfect match and a delicious, hearty pasta sauce.

Oxalic Acid

Spinach, Swiss chard, parsley, and rhubarb all contain oxalic acid, which hinders calcium absorption.

Nitrates

You may hear that it is unsafe to feed your baby home-cooked food made with vegetables that are high in nitrates. However, the chances that your baby will get nitrate poisoning from homemade baby food is very unlikely. Avoid feeding your baby vegetables that are high in nitrates (spinach, beets, green beans, squash, and carrots) before three months of age. By six months, your baby's stomach has developed the acids needed to fight the bacteria that help nitrate conversion.

Nitrates can be due to groundwater contamination near a commercial agriculture site from chemical fertilizers or can be added as a preservative in packaged foods. Nearly all vegetables contain a natural level of nitrates that vary according to growing conditions and the soil's nitrate levels. Organic vegetables have a naturally lower risk of exposure because they are not grown in soil treated with chemical fertilizers.

If you live in an agricultural region, do not use use well water for mixing formula. For concerns about nitrates in water, speak with your health care provider, and have your water tested. Reverse osmosis and distillation water filters can remove nitrates from well water.

Fungi

Fungi are separate from plants, animals, or bacteria—they grow in soil and on dead matter, plants, animals, or other fungi. Despite their anti-cancer properties, raw mushrooms contain carcinogenic compounds that get destroyed in the cooking process, so mushrooms need to be cooked before eating. You can introduce cooked mushrooms to your child between 12 and 18 months of age. Cooked mushrooms break down toxins and mucus, and they are a natural flavor enhancer.

The Yin and Yang of Land Vegetables

Vegetables are near the center of the food spectrum for daily use. Nightshades, such as potatoes, bell peppers, hot peppers, and eggplants have more of a yin influence because they grow in a hot climate, they require a lot of water while growing, and they are soft and perishable. Because fungi grow quickly and are soft, they have a more yin influence. White mushrooms grow in a dark, damp climate and are more yin than shiitake mushrooms which grow on wood bark. Cremini and Portobello (large cremini) mushrooms are in between white and shiitake mushrooms. Upward-growing plants, such as kale and collards, are more perishable. Round vegetables, such as cabbage and squashes, are usually not as firm, and have more of a yin influence than root vegetables, but are firmer and have more of a yang influence than upward vegetables. Root vegetables, such as carrots, sweet potatoes, turnips, and onions are firm and usually grow in cooler temperatures. With the exception of agar, all sea vegetables have a high concentration of iron, sodium, and other minerals, in comparison to most land vegetables. Where and how a sea vegetable grows in the ocean has a subtle influence on its yin-yang qualities, but nori, wakame, and kombu are all relatively close to each other.

Listed in the chart are balanced foods toward the center for daily use and foods on a wider spectrum for occasional use.

Yin-Yang Spectrum of Vegetables

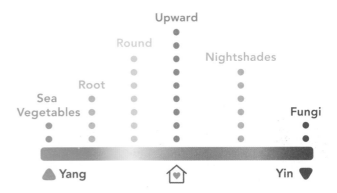

How Land Vegetables Grow

Understanding how land vegetables grow offers insight into their nutritional benefits, as well as a way to connect with nature and food. There are three simple ways to categorize land vegetables based on their growth: on-the-ground or round, below-the-ground or downward, and upward. Each category of vegetable contributes a different energy to your baby's body, and offering all three helps create balance. In addition to choosing from different categories, choosing seasonal vegetables in a variety of colors provides a range of tastes and nutrients.

On-the-ground Vegetables

On-the-ground vegetable plants grow low to the earth or directly on it, and often contain seeds within their vegetables. For example, if your baby is feeling off balance, on-the-ground vegetables can help bring him back toward equilibrium. Squash of all types—summer squash and winter squashes, such as acorn, butternut, and buttercup—as well as cucumbers, beans, and zucchini—are included in this category. With their natural sweetness and harmonizing properties, on-the-ground vegetables make excellent first vegetables for babies.

Upward-growing vegetables

Upward-growing vegetables have leaves, stalks or stems, flowers, and buds. These include leafy greens, such as kale, collards, broccoli, salad greens, celery, and watercress, as well as peas and beans. Their green chlorophyll rebuilds and replaces red blood cells, and their calcium and alkaline minerals help neutralize your baby's stomach acid.

Below-the-ground vegetables

Below-the-ground vegetables are roots, such as carrots and beets; tubers, such as sweet potatoes and potatoes; and bulbs, such as garlic and onions. Consider the energy necessary for root vegetables like carrots, parsnips, and turnips to grow downward and penetrate the soil. Root vegetables provide strength for your baby. These vegetables enhance his digestive functions because of their substantial amounts of fiber. You can leave the skins on unless they are exceptionally tough. The skins also contain the majority of the vegetable's vitamins and minerals. Offer your baby cooked sweet potatoes, carrots, parsnips, onions, turnips, rutabagas, and beets; save white potatoes for occasional use because they are nightshades, and they are high in potassium and glucose.

The Power of Sea Vegetables

While living in Japan, I enjoyed going to the market and browsing the vats of various sea vegetables to explore their many colors, textures, and aromas. The Japanese value this nutrient-dense food, grading it in much the same way the U.S. Department of Agriculture grades beef. In per capita sea vegetable consumption, Japan consumes the most, but sea vegetables are not exclusive to Japanese cuisine. New England and California have large-scale sea vegetable operations, and coastal residents across the globe incorporate these greens into hors d'oeuvres, baby food, and main courses. Much more than their slimy stereotype, sea vegetables are commonly found in skin care products and as thickening agents in other products like ice cream, shampoo, and toothpaste.

Sea vegetables brim with essential vitamins, minerals, antioxidants, and phytochemicals, and they contain both soluble and insoluble fiber, as well as easily digestible proteins and healthy fats. Unlike any land vegetable, sea vegetables provide all of the 56 minerals neces-sary, including calcium, iodine, iron, magnesium, and sodium, and also trace minerals like copper, manganese, phosphorus, potassium, selenium, and zinc.

Nori is an excellent source of dietary fiber, plant-based protein, and omega-3 fatty acids. It has more vitamin A than carrots; generous amounts of B and K vitamins; calcium, iodine, iron, and potassium; and trace elements that can strengthen your baby's nervous system. Kombu is high in dietary fiber, calcium, iodine, iron, magnesium, potassium, vitamins A, B, and C, and trace minerals. It helps tenderize beans and other protein-rich foods, which aids in digestion. Kombu has 150 times the amount of iodine and eight times more magnesium than leafy vegetables. Agar is a mineral-rich and alkaline-producing, naturally calorie-free thickening agent that can be used to make sauces and puddings.

Sea vegetables can be especially valuable during your child's first three years, when his body and brain are developing rapidly. They balance acidity in his body, and their minerals strengthen his muscles, nerves, hair, skin, and nails. Because sea vegetables are so nutritious, I tried to include them as much as possible in cooking for my family. I found it easy to incorporate nori, wakame flakes, kombu, and agar into dishes for Emi and Mari when they were young. Even though these ingredients were not part of my mother or grandmother's recipes, I substituted kombu for ham hock in my black-eyed peas for flavoring. I found that cooking beans with kombu helped make the proteins and fats more digestible for improved nutrient absorption. Emi and Mari's favorite sea vegetable was nori, which they enjoyed munching on as a snack. Our cat, Dandelion, loved to eat nori, and he learned to beg for his daily ration when he heard the package being opened. When buying sea vegetables, look for natural and dye-free products rather than those with added food coloring or bleach. With a little imagination, you can integrate these healthy gifts from the sea into your daily cooking and gain many health benefits for your child.

The Yin and Yang of Sea Vegetables 🏠

With the exception of agar, all sea vegetables have a high concentration of bioavailable plant-based calcium, iodine, and iron, along with other minerals, in comparison to most land vegetables. Where and how a sea vegetable grows in the ocean has a subtle influence on its yin and yang qualities, but nori, wakame, and kombu are all relatively close to each other in their merits.

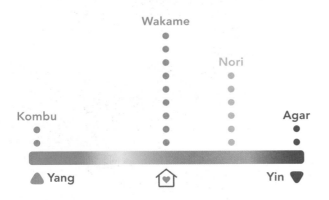

Yin-Yang Spectrum
of Sea Vegetables

How Sea Vegetables Grow

Most sea vegetables are salt-water tolerant, land-dependent plants that grow at the connection point between land and sea. They need to be attached to something so they can receive sufficient sunlight to grow.

Types of Sea Vegetables

Nori

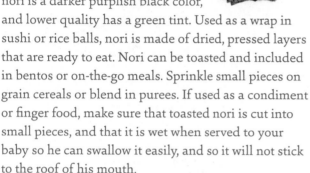

Nori is the paper-thin black wrapping on sushi rolls. It is hand-harvested, washed, chopped, and spread on bamboo mats to dry into paper-thin layers. Higher quality nori is a darker purplish black color, and lower quality has a green tint. Used as a wrap in sushi or rice balls, nori is made of dried, pressed layers that are ready to eat. Nori can be toasted and included in bentos or on-the-go meals. Sprinkle small pieces on grain cereals or blend in purees. If used as a condiment or finger food, make sure that toasted nori is cut into small pieces, and that it is wet when served to your baby so he can swallow it easily, and so it will not stick to the roof of his mouth.

Wakame

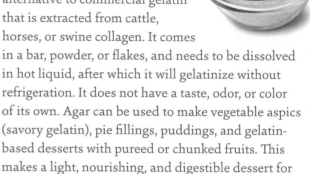

Wakame is an olive-green-colored sea vegetable, and when it is wet, it has the slimy texture that you find when you come across seaweed in the ocean. You can cut wakame flakes into small pieces for cooking to curtail the vegetable's naturally slippery texture. Your baby will enjoy wakame cooked in soups or combined with other vegetables as a side dish. You can also toss the flakes on salads for older children.

Kombu

Kombu is a gray, dried sea vegetable that either needs to be soaked or added to a liquid, and then cooked. It has natural glutamates, or umami, which enhance flavor while adding minerals. Kombu can be used as a seasoning for soup stock, grains, beans, and root or ground vegetables. Cooking grains and beans with a small piece of kombu aids in their digestion and reduces cooking time. You can cut kombu into one-inch strips and add it to almost any dish. Be sure to remove the kombu before serving, or cut it into tiny pieces to mix in with other ingredients. Powdered kombu is also available, which can be used in cooking instead of salt.

Agar

Agar (also called agar-agar) is a vegetarian gelatin that offers an alternative to commercial gelatin that is extracted from cattle, horses, or swine collagen. It comes in a bar, powder, or flakes, and needs to be dissolved in hot liquid, after which it will gelatinize without refrigeration. It does not have a taste, odor, or color of its own. Agar can be used to make vegetable aspics (savory gelatin), pie fillings, puddings, and gelatin-based desserts with pureed or chunked fruits. This makes a light, nourishing, and digestible dessert for your baby or toddler. Serve cool in warm weather and at room temperature in other seasons.

Vegetable Preparation

Cooking vegetables for your baby may seem like a lot of work, but it can be quite easy with a few basic tools. Keep it simple by cooking vegetables separately in the beginning, and then mixing them as your baby's tastes develop. Wash, cut, and cook the vegetables. Adjust the consistency to match his chewing ability.

Puree

Your baby can digest his first foods most easily as a soft puree that has a smooth consistency; this puree also offers a sensory satisfaction for older children and adults. Start with a thin, watery mixture, and then add less water and mash to a thicker consistency as he gets older. You can use a blender, food mill, or a grinding bowl to make puree for your little one. Purees are delicious in soups, dips, and sauces for toddlers and other family members.

Finger Foods

Finger foods are more for learning how to eat than for providing nutrition. Start with small, pea-sized pieces, and as he learns to pick them up and chew with his gums, he can eat larger pieces of steamed cut vegetables, such as carrot sticks or broccoli florets. Make sure that they are well-cooked, and keep an eye on your baby when he is eating finger foods.

Chewing Vegetables

When he has all of his teeth, your baby can eat vegetables in larger cooked pieces. Cut vegetables into pieces before or after cooking. When he has more control and choking is less of a hazard he can enjoy crunchy, raw vegetables, as well.

Vegetables for Your Baby

Your baby will probably be ready to start eating vegetables between six and eight months. Start with sweet, starchy vegetables, such as winter squash, carrots, and green peas. When first introducing vegetables to your baby, prepare them as broth, blended soups, and simple purees. Before your baby has any teeth, water sauté, steam, or roast the vegetables until they are soft, then puree them. A blender purees a smoother consistency for high-fiber vegetables. A blender, food mill, or a

grinding bowl works well for starchy vegetables that are easy to mash into a more lumpy consistency as your baby gets older and needs a transitional texture. At around seven to nine months, offer cruciferous vegetables that are well-cooked, such as broccoli, bok choy, and others. At around nine months old, once he has learned to gum his food and pick up pieces of food, water sauté or steam the vegetables until soft, and then cut them into pea-sized pieces for finger foods.

Cooking vegetables offers predigestion for your baby so that his digestive system does not have to work as hard to assimilate the nutrients. Raw vegetables should be avoided until your child can chew very well, at around 18 months old, because small pieces can become a choking hazard. At that time, nightshade vegetables can offer variety occasionally. If your baby does not eat a lot of vegetables at first, just keep re-introducing them over time, and be patient as his palate adapts to the new flavors. To check for allergies and observe his reaction to different foods, try the same vegetable for three days in a row before introducing another. His tastes can change rapidly, so a vegetable that he spits out today could be what he wants next week. Children tend to like a smooth consistency, so pureed soups, sauces, and dips are creative options to get toddlers to enjoy vegetables.

The following chart gives an overview of which vegetables to introduce and when. The chart also includes how frequently to serve these vegetables.

When to Introduce Vegetables		
Vegetables	Age Range	Frequency
Acorn squash	6 to 8 months	Daily
Butternut squash	6 to 8 months	Daily
Carrots	6 to 8 months	Daily
Green beans	6 to 8 months	Daily
Green peas	6 to 8 months	Daily
Japanese pumpkin	6 to 8 months	Daily
Nori	6 to 8 months	Daily
Parsnips	6 to 8 months	Daily
Sweet potatoes	6 to 8 months	Daily
Sugar snap peas	6 to 8 months	Daily
Yellow squash	6 to 8 months	Daily
Zucchini	6 to 8 months	Daily
Bok choy	7 to 9 months	Daily
Broccoli	7 to 9 months	Daily
Brussels sprouts	7 to 9 months	Daily
Cabbage	7 to 9 months	Daily
Cauliflower	7 to 9 months	Daily
Celery	7 to 9 months	Daily
Chinese cabbage	7 to 9 months	Daily
Collard greens	7 to 9 months	Daily

Occasionally: 2–3 times a week

Vegetables		Age Range	Frequency
	Kale	7 to 9 months	Daily
	Kombu	7 to 9 months	Occasionally
	Onions	7 to 9 months	Daily
	Purple cabbage	7 to 9 months	Daily
	Turnip greens	7 to 9 months	Daily
	Wakame flakes	7 to 9 months	Daily
	Watercress	7 to 9 months	Daily
	Beets	9 to 12 months	Daily
	Nori pieces	9 to 12 months	Daily
	Rutabaga	9 to 12 months	Daily
	Asparagus	12 to 18 months	Daily
	Potatoes	12 to 18 months	Occasionally
	Mushrooms	12 to 18 months	Occasionally
	Cucumber (raw)	18 to 24 months	Daily
	Lettuce (raw)	18 to 24 months	Daily
	Okra	18 to 24 months	Occasionally
	Spinach	18 to 24 months	Occasionally
	Sweet peppers	18 to 24 months	Occasionally
	Tomatoes	18 to 24 months	Occasionally
	Eggplant	all ages	Occasionally

Occasionally: 2–3 times a week

Everyday Puree

♡ 6 months+

🥣 4 (2-ounce) servings

V Vegetarian

GF Gluten-free

Puree is a basic, simple preparation for your baby's first daily foods. Cooking methods for stove-top purees are boiling, water sautéing, and steaming. For all the methods, be sure to use the cooking water in the puree to retain the nutrients from the vegetables, or serve as a beverage in a cup. Start with a soupy texture, and gradually adjust to a thicker, lumpy texture, as your child's chewing skills develop. You can also multiply the amount you prepare and store extra in the refrigerator for the next two or three days or in the freezer for later. Use stainless steel or glass pots for cooking. Mix in probiotic booster before serving, if desired.

2 cups vegetables, peeled and cut into 1-inch pieces

Options:

Butternut squash, green beans, yellow squash, sugar snap peas, zucchini, broccoli, brussels sprouts, carrots, sweet potatoes, kale

Method

1. Place vegetables in a pan and add water to cover. Place lid on pan.

2. Cook over medium heat for 10 to 20 minutes, or until vegetables are tender.

3. Add more water if necessary—if water on the bottom of the pan dries up.

4. Use a heat diffuser to prevent burning.

5. Drain cooking water off, and save for later use. The cooking water is rich in nutrients and can be used in purees, soups, or grains.

6. Puree in a blender, food processor, food mill, hand grinder, or a grinding bowl.

Variations

- Add a 1-inch square piece of kombu sea vegetable or ¼ teaspoon wakame flakes when cooking. Remove kombu before pureeing.

- Cook combinations of vegetables when your baby has tested several vegetables.

- Add ¼ teaspoon minced fresh or dried herbs while cooking, such as fennel, bay, basil, thyme, dill, cilantro, or parsley.

- Combine vegetables with grains when making puree.

- Nori sea vegetable is high in iron, calcium, iodine, and other minerals. Add nori sea vegetable in blender to purees, or sprinkle small strips on top of a vegetable dish, making sure the nori is moist, so that it is easy to swallow.

- Mix in ¼ teaspoon of sesame, olive, flaxseed, or coconut oil when serving.

- Sprinkle ground flaxseeds on top of vegetable puree when serving 6 months+.

- Mix in a few drops of plum vinegar when serving 7 months+.

- Sprinkle ground toasted seeds on top of vegetable puree when serving 9 months+.

- Add ½ teaspoon sesame, sunflower, or pumpkin seeds while cooking, and puree together.

- Add tahini to purees for a protein boost and to give a cream consistency to fibrous vegetables.

- You can use a variety of vegetables including, butternut squash, green beans, yellow squash, sugar snap peas, zucchini, broccoli, carrots, sweet potatoes, and kale.

Veggie Cream Soup

♡ 6 months+

🥄 8 (2-ounce) servings

V Vegetarian

GF Gluten-free

In this recipe, the entire soup is pureed for a delicious flavor and creamy texture. You can experiment with vegetable combinations, but I recommend limiting the number of vegetables to two or three different ones. For color, do not mix yellow or orange vegetables with green ones.

2 cups water

2 cups mixed vegetables, peeled and cut into 1-inch pieces

1-inch square kombu sea vegetable or ¼ teaspoon wakame flakes (For kombu, remove before pureeing)

½ to 1 teaspoon sesame, olive, or coconut oil

⅛ teaspoon sea salt for 9–12 months, ¼ teaspoon for 12 months+

Options:

Onion, carrot, and cauliflower

Onion, string beans, and broccoli

Onion, cauliflower, and fennel

Summer squash, carrot, and onion

Winter squash, carrot, and onion

Peas, bok choy, and onion

Method

1. Bring water to a boil in a pot over high heat. Add vegetables, kombu, and salt, if using.

2. Reduce heat and simmer for 10 to 25 minutes, or until vegetables are tender.

3. Use a heat diffuser to prevent burning.

4. Remove kombu. Add oil.

5. Puree in blender or food processor.

6. Serve with a spoon in a reusable pouch, sippy cup, or straw cup.

Variations

- Add cooked leftover pureed grain, such as millet, quinoa, or rice, to soup.

- Add ¼ teaspoon minced fresh or dried herbs while cooking, such as fennel, bay, basil, thyme, dill, cilantro, or parsley.

- Add miso or tamari for a rich creamy soup. Use ½ teaspoon for 7 to 12 months, 1 teaspoon for 12 to 18 months, 2 teaspoons for 18 months+.

- Sprinkle small pieces of nori as a garnish, making sure that the nori is moist, so that it is easy to swallow.

- Make into kanten gelatin: In a separate pot, heat 1 cup water with 1 ½ tablespoons agar flakes. Bring to a boil and simmer until the flakes are dissolved. Mix with vegetable soup puree and put into containers for individual servings.

Baked Vegetable Puree

♡ 9 months+

🥄 8 (2-ounce) servings

V Vegetarian

GF Gluten-free

Baking brings out the delicious sweetness in vegetables, and it is a very easy method of cooking. As your baby gets older and can eat a thicker consistency, the puree can be easily mashed or ground with a grinding bowl, so getting out the blender is not necessary. This is also an easy recipe to coordinate with family meals. Many vegetables are easy to cook whole, or cut into large chunks. It is not necessary to peel them first, because the peel comes off easily when cooked.

4 cups vegetables, single or in combination, peeled and cut into 2-inch pieces

2 teaspoons sesame, olive, or coconut oil

2 to 3 tablespoons water

¼ teaspoon minced fresh or dried herbs, such as fennel, bay, basil, thyme, dill, or parsley

⅛ teaspoon sea salt for 9–12 months, ¼ teaspoon sea salt for 12 months+

Options:

Beets, winter squash, yellow squash, zucchini, carrots, parsnips, onions, sweet potatoes, Japanese pumpkin

Method

1. Preheat oven to 400°F.

2. Spread vegetables in casserole dish.

3. Mix in oil, water, herbs, and sea salt (if using).

4. Cover with aluminum foil or casserole lid.

5. Bake for 45 minutes to 1 hour, until vegetables are soft and tender.

6. When cool enough to handle, mash vegetables with a pestle in a grinding bowl, or with a fork in a bowl.

7. Vegetables shrink to approximately half the amount of raw vegetables when cooked.

Finger Food Veggies

♡ 6 months+

🥄 4 to 6 servings

V Vegetarian

GF Gluten-free

When your baby starts to grasp and scoop objects, offering finger foods supports his development, as well as his nutrition. He likes to feed himself, even though it can be very messy. Before he can chew well, he can "gum" small pea-size pieces, and then move on to larger chunks. Make sure that they are cooked well to avoid choking. Veggie pieces can be eaten alone or dipped into hummus and other bean purees. Place pieces of vegetables directly on the high chair tray or place mat. Veggie pieces can be steamed, boiled, sautéed in oil, or sautéed in water as a side dish for older children or adults.

2 cups mixed vegetables, peeled and cut into ⅛- to ¼-inch cubes or 2- to 3-inch sticks, depending on child's age

½ cup water

⅛ teaspoon sea salt for 12 months+

Options:

Carrots, summer squash, broccoli, cauliflower, pumpkin, zucchini, sweet potato, green beans, sugar snap peas, green beans

Method

1. Put vegetables, water, and salt (if using) into pot.

2. Steam, boil, or water sauté with enough water to prevent burning, but not too much to waste nutrients. Save left over water for a beverage or to add to dishes when cooking.

3. Use a heat diffuser to prevent burning.

4. Steam just until tender, but still a bright color.

5. Steamed veggie pieces can be stored in the refrigerator for 2 or 3 days, or in the freezer for later use.

Veggie Butter

♡ 9 months+

🥄 12-ounces

V Vegetarian

GF Gluten-free

This slow-cooking method creates a concentrated, rich, and delicious taste that brings out the sweetness of the vegetables. The protein in tahini provides both taste and nutrition; use as a spread on bread or crackers.

½ teaspoon sesame, olive, or olive oil

3 cups vegetables, peeled and cut into ½-inch pieces

¾ cup water

1 tablespoon tahini

⅛ teaspoon sea salt for 12 months+

Options:

Yellow squash, butternut squash, onion, carrots, cauliflower, broccoli, parsnips.

Method

1. Heat oil in skillet, and sauté vegetables for 5 minutes.

2. Add water and salt (if using), and bring to a boil.

3. Reduce heat and cook over low heat for 30 minutes, or until vegetables are tender.

4. Use a heat diffuser to prevent burning.

5. Add more water while cooking, if necessary.

6. Remove from heat and let vegetables cool.

7. After the vegetables cool, add tahini and puree until smooth, adding more water, if necessary, when blending.

Protein-rich Foods

WHEN EMI STARTED EATING solid foods, I carefully chose each meal to ensure that she would get whole and natural foods, avoiding any harmful ingredients. For her first year, I made extra sure that she ate a completely plant-based diet. One day, she was playing outside my family's apartment in Ashiya, Japan, and a well-intentioned neighbor gave her a bright red hot dog. I was afraid that my pure and perfect baby had been contaminated by the chemicals and dyes from this unfamiliar and highly processed protein-rich food, but Emi survived with no side effects. Protein is necessary for human growth and development, and it is an essential nutrient for your baby. My neighbor's gift to Emi came from a caring desire to give her a tasty snack with these building blocks.

Along with carbohydrates and fats, protein is one of the three macronutrients of your baby's daily food. Protein is essential to biological processes, including growth, metabolism, digestion, brain development, bone strength, tissue growth, the maintenance and repair of cells, and the transportation of nutrients and oxygen in his blood. Unlike fats and carbohydrates, your baby's body does not store protein, so it has no reserve from which to draw when a new supply of protein is required. Without enough regular protein, your baby's growth and mental development can be compromised. This chapter highlights information about a variety of protein-rich foods and their nutritional benefits and concerns.

Protein-rich Food Considerations

Many traditional cultures are built on diets of whole grains, legumes, and land and sea vegetables. While every child has different needs, there is plenty of history and evidence to suggest that a vegetarian diet can provide growth, strength, and vitality without the need for animal-based nutrition. In New York and San Francisco, an organization called the Monday Campaigns has implemented "Meatless Mondays" that engages food service sites, restaurants, and even public schools to be vegetarian for one day of the week. As long as you make sure that your child has a regular balance of carbohydrates, proteins, fats, vitamins, and minerals, he can grow strong and healthy on a vegetarian or a vegan diet.

Animal protein may provide concentrated protein that supports growth. However, because of the concern for proteins as body builders, animal-based foods are often eaten in excess. This excess may be stored as fat because the body cannot store extra protein. In addition, animal proteins often contain higher levels of saturated fats than plant-based proteins.

Within the wide range of animal and plant-based protein-rich foods, you can find your own choices of foods for healthy growth and development that match your lifestyle. Whether you are a strict vegan or if you enjoy fish, poultry, or red meat regularly, you can create a healthy diet for your child by considering the quality and quantity of foods in making balance.

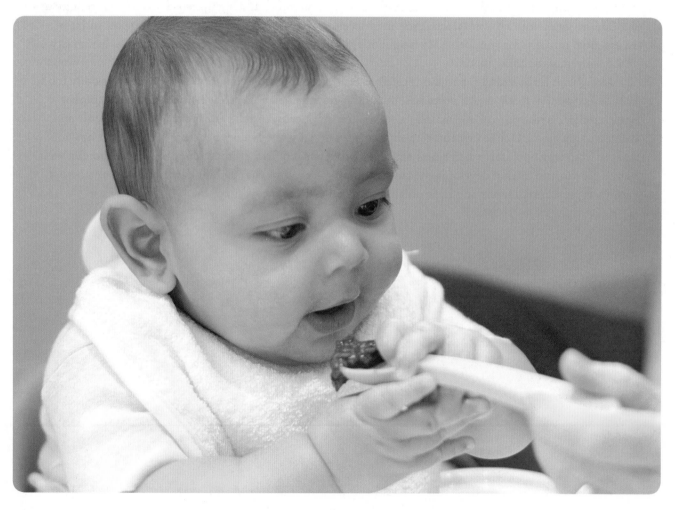

Zo's first adzuki beans

Types of Plant-based Protein-rich Foods

Plant-based protein-rich foods come from three basic groups: legumes, soy-based products (soybeans are a common type of legume high in protein), and nuts and seeds. These protein-rich foods offer savory nutrition for your baby and are the basis for recipes from all across the world. They can be simply and creatively integrated into your baby's first foods.

Legumes

Legumes are plants that include beans, peas, and lentils. They are among the most versatile, affordable, and nutritious foods available, which is why they are a staple in cuisines around the world. Despite their beneficial fats, legumes are cholesterol-free; in fact, their soluble fiber helps lower cholesterol and the risk of heart disease. They are high in folic acid, potassium, iron, and magnesium. Folic acid is essential for brain function, mental and emotional health, and fetal growth and development. Beans are also rich in copper, iron, magnesium, calcium, zinc, and selenium.

Supermarkets and natural food stores usually stock a wide variety of dried and canned legumes. Dried beans, especially those that have been sprouted, are more nutritious with less sodium and preservatives than packaged legumes. Canned beans are a more convenient option, and there are a few organic brands that have no added sodium or preservatives and are cooked with kombu sea vegetables for improved digestibility. Even with the awareness of the chemical, BPA, many cans for food processing are still lined with this chemical, so check for brands with BPA-free cans. Cooking dried beans takes time, but they are more delicious than canned beans. You can prepare them in bulk and freeze them for later meals or use a pressure cooker to shorten the cooking time. To help your baby digest legumes, buy sprouted beans, soak them for 8 to 24 hours, and add a small piece of kombu sea vegetable while cooking.

Soy-based Products

A protein-rich legume, the soybean often serves as an alternative to meat and dairy. Soy products that use the whole bean, such as miso and tempeh, and that are fermented with salt, are more nutritious than unfermented soy. Like raw cruciferous vegetables, unfermented soy contains goitrogens that can inhibit thyroid function; its phytic acid blocks the absorption of important minerals like copper, zinc, and iron. Soy introduces phytoestrogens into the body, which some believe are linked to the disruption of the endocrine system. Soy comes in a variety of forms that can easily be a part of your child's diet, in moderation.

Tofu

Tofu is a staple food in Asia that is easy to prepare and serve as a first protein for your baby. Tofu is soft and creamy and easy for him to eat. Because it is a processed, unfermented form of soy, cook tofu thoroughly so that your baby can digest it. Offer him small amounts occasionally.

Miso

Miso is a highly concentrated source of protein with 17 amino acids and trace nutrients. It can reduce cholesterol in the blood and aid digestion. This fermented form of soy offers two grams of protein per tablespoon.

Tempeh

Tempeh is a cake of pressed, hulled, cooked soybeans mixed with a vegetable culture and fermented. With a high protein content and a nutty texture, it has very little flavor and easily absorbs any added seasoning. Steaming tempeh opens it up before sautéing, which allows flavor absorption and ensures that the tempeh gets fully cooked. Tempeh's unique fermentation process makes it a good source of probiotics. Low in saturated fats and high in dietary fiber, it contains generous amounts of B vitamins, iron, calcium, and lecithin.

Nuts and Seeds

Nuts and seeds are a source of plant-based protein for your baby that provide the highest level of essential fatty acids of all unprocessed foods. As with vegetables and fruits, seeds and nuts vary with the seasonal climate. Cashews, Brazil nuts, and macadamia nuts grow in warmer climates and are higher in fats. Sesame seeds, sunflower seeds, pumpkin seeds, chestnuts, and almonds grow in colder climates and have a moderate amount of healthy fats that are easier for your baby to digest. The American Academy of Pediatrics warns against feeding peanuts or peanut butter to children under the age of three. Observe your baby for potential allergic reactions, especially if your family has a history of nut allergies.

Nuts are one of the best sources of vitamin E, which is essential for nerve development. They also boost immunity with their high levels of antioxidants, and their omega-3 fats can help prevent heart disease and diabetes. Before your child can chew well, he can drink nut milk or eat nut butter, or you can cook nuts with grains, and then puree them together. When he can chew well, whole nuts or nut pieces can provide him a nutritious snack or condiment. Toasting nuts in an oven or skillet or boiling them in water first is easier on your baby's digestive system than eating them raw. Nuts and seeds can become rancid and lose their nutrients once they are hulled or shelled. Taste them to verify their freshness before feeding them to your child. If you grind extra nuts or seeds for later use, storing them in the freezer protects them from becoming rancid.

Almonds

Almonds contain more nutrients than any other nut. They are full of vitamin E, calcium, niacin, iron, phosphorous, zinc, selenium, copper, and magnesium. Like the others, they can be toasted and ground to incorporate into other purees; they also are processed into a nutrient-dense nut butter, as well as almond milk. As with many juices, the milk form is a concentrated food that contains the nut's sugars, but has stripped away the nutritious fibers and vitamins that are in the whole nut.

Chestnuts

Chestnuts are high in carbohydrates and low in fat, and they are the most easily digested nut. They have been used medicinally for colic and for digestive disorders. Fresh, dried, or packaged, they can be boiled and mashed to make a naturally healthy pudding puree.

Sesame seeds

Sesame seeds add a delicious taste to dishes, and they are ground and blended with oil to make tahini. Mixing tahini or ground sesame seeds into vegetable purees can add a creamy texture and subtle flavor, as well as healthy proteins and fats. Sesame seeds are a good source of vitamin B1, calcium, copper, iron, magnesium, manganese, phosphorus, zinc, and beneficial dietary lignans, which can help lower both cholesterol and blood pressure. Roast, grind, and sprinkle them on porridge, or cook the raw seeds together with a grain, and then blend them into a puree after cooking.

Sunflower seeds

Sunflower seeds are packed with insoluble fiber and easily digestible proteins, fats, vitamin E, minerals, and phytochemicals. They can enrich any meal, from sprinkling ground seeds on your child's cereal to offering them as a protein-rich snack after he is two to three years old. Brimming with cholesterol-lowering phytosterols, sunflower seeds are also high in choline, which supports memory and cognitive functions. Roast, grind, and sprinkle them on porridge, or cook the raw seeds together with grain, and then puree them after cooking.

Pumpkin seeds

Pumpkin seeds, which provide nine grams of protein per ounce, are also an excellent source of calcium, iron, phosphorus, zinc, omega-3 fatty acids, and vitamins A and B. Roast, grind, and sprinkle them on porridge, or cook the seeds together with the grain, and then puree after cooking.

Flaxseeds

Flaxseeds are one of the richest sources of alpha-linolenic acid (ALA) omega-3 fatty acids, which help strengthen your baby's immunity, encourage healthy brain development, and maintain good cardiovascular health. Grind flaxseeds in a blender and add them to his porridge for a boost of protein and essential fatty acids; they are also a digestive aid.

Chia Seeds

Chia seeds are another rich source of dietary fiber, protein, alpha-linolenic acid (ALA) omega-3 fatty acids, and minerals, such as calcium, manganese, and phosphorus. These tiny seeds develop a thin, gelatinous coating around them after soaking in liquid, making them have a caviar-like texture. Chia seeds are considered a superfood because they aid hydration.

Types of Animal-based Protein-rich Foods

Because your baby's main source of protein for his first year comes from breast milk or formula, animal foods are not necessary as a source of protein during this time. Animal-based proteins are more concentrated than plant-based proteins and are more difficult to digest, so I recommend waiting until your baby's first birthday to introduce them. If you do choose to offer animal foods to your child, you can make choices, regarding quality and nutritional value, to provide him with the healthiest options.

Milk and Dairy Products

Emi and Mari did not have milk or dairy products as a daily food, but they occasionally enjoyed yogurt, cheese, and ice cream. They loved that creamy taste and that blissful feeling. Dairy products are a popular source of protein, but they have many health risks as well. The American Academy of Pediatrics warns against replacing breast milk with dairy products for babies under the age of one. Early milk consumption can cause colic, iron deficiency, and other food allergies. Milk proteins, sugar, fat, and saturated fat in dairy products may produce mucus, which can contribute to earaches, sinus, lung, and digestive problems. Dairy consumption has also been correlated with the development of chronic diseases, such as obesity and heart disease.

Lactose is a natural sugar found in milk and other dairy products. Lactase, an enzyme produced by cells lining the small intestine, breaks down lactose into compounds that can be absorbed into the bloodstream. Lactose intolerance occurs when the body does not produce enough lactase enzymes, which prevents the breakdown of lactose and leads to various gastrointestinal problems.

Some children are born without the ability to produce lactase. More commonly, children can develop lactose intolerance after about two years of age as their body decreases its production of lactase enzymes. When children have fewer or a complete lack of lactase enzymes, dairy foods can cause nausea, cramping, diarrhea, bloating, and gas. The symptoms usually occur between 30 minutes to two hours after eating or drinking dairy. Cheese offers protein, but it is high in saturated fat and cholesterol.

Probiotic dairy

Probiotic dairy products include yogurt and kefir, which contain live bacteria that promote healthy digestion. The lactose in the milk is broken down with culturing, making these dairy products easier to digest. If you opt for probiotic yogurt, be sure to choose one that has active or live cultures. Some yogurts are pasteurized, which kills the probiotics. Flavored yogurts tend to have high concentrations of sugar, so be sure to check the label before purchasing for your child.

The yin and yang of dairy

Determinants for the yin and yang of dairy foods include liquid, fat, and salt content. Milk is liquid and has more of a yin influence. Hard, dry, and salty cheeses that have been aged have more of a yang influences, so they are on the opposite side from milk. Butter has more fat, so it is more yin than yogurt, which is more liquid, and therefore more yin than soft cheese. Listed in the chart are balanced foods toward the center for daily use and foods on a wider spectrum for occasional use.

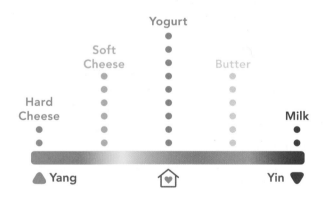

Yin-Yang Spectrum of Dairy

Fish

If you choose to offer animal foods to your child, small amounts of cooked fish can be a healthy protein option after your child is one year old. Fish is low in fat and high in protein, and some fish contain omega-3 fatty acids, a type of unsaturated fatty acid that reduces inflammation throughout the body, decreases triglycerides (compounds associated with hardening of the arteries), lowers blood pressure, reduces blood clotting, and boosts immunity. Omega-3 fatty acids have also been associated with mental clarity and the improvement in learning ability, which is why fish is often called "brain food." One of the most important omega oils is docosahexaenoic acid (DHA), which is essential for brain and eye tissue development for infants in utero, as well as after they are born. Omega-3 fatty acids are significant for your baby's development before and after birth. Compared to saltwater fish, most freshwater fish have lower levels of omega-3 fatty acids, though some varieties of freshwater trout have relatively high levels. Fish with the most omega-3 acids are fatty saltwater fish, such as salmon, sardines, and smelt. As a flavorful, and relatively economical fish, salmon is a healthy option for children.

Risks and benefits of fish consumption

Saltwater fish have higher levels of mercury exposure than their freshwater counterparts. Oceans' mercury levels have risen in the past half century due to industrialization. Once mercury enters a waterway, certain bacteria absorb the mercury and convert it into methyl mercury. This transition is particularly significant for humans, who absorb methyl mercury easily and are especially vulnerable to its effects.

Mercury works its way up the food chain as large fish consume smaller, contaminated fish. Instead of dissolving or breaking down, mercury accumulates at increasing levels. Predatory fish, such as large tuna, swordfish, shark, and mackerel have the highest mercury concentrations, while white fish have the lowest. Exposure to mercury can be particularly hazardous for pregnant women, infants, and small children.

In 2006, Harvard School of Public Health researchers conducted a comprehensive analysis of fish and health. They studied the major health effects of omega-3 fatty acids and health risks of mercury, poly-chlorinated biphenyls (PCBs), and dioxins in adults, infants, and young children. The results showed that eating a modest amount of fish per week reduced the risk of death from coronary heart disease by 36 percent. The study found that to balance the benefits of fish consumption with the risk of mercury intake, women of childbearing age, pregnant women, nursing mothers, and young children should eat up to two servings of fish per week and avoid four species of fish: tilefish, king mackerel, shark, and swordfish. These findings are in accordance with recommendations from the U.S. Food and Drug Administration and the Environmental Protection Agency.

Farm-raised vs. wild-caught fish

Most farmed fish are fattened with ground fishmeal and fish oils that are high in polychlorinated biphenyls (PCBs). PCBs are chemicals used in various industrial and mechanical applications, such as paints, sealants, and coolants. As a result, salmon farming operations produce inexpensive fish with higher fat content and concentrated levels of PCBs. According to data from the U.S. Department of Agriculture (USDA), farmed salmon contains 52 percent more fat than wild salmon. Wild Alaskan salmon are naturally leaner and they eat Pacific Ocean fish that have lower concentrations of pollutants.

Salmon farming has made salmon the third most popular fish in America. However, an Environmental Working Group analysis of government data also found that farmed salmon are likely to be the most PCB-contaminated protein source in the current U.S. food supply. PCB production was banned in the United States in the late 1970s and is among the chemical contaminants slated for global phase-out under the United Nations treaty on organic pollutants.

The yin and yang of fish

Some determinants for the Yin–Yang influences of fish are their activity level, their fat content, their diet, and the habitat in which they grow.

Relatively, fish are more yang than vegetable foods, so the nature of their influence is more yang, but different fish have variations of yin and yang. Fish that are more active have a more yang influence while less mobile shellfish, like crabs and shrimp, are higher in fat and therefore have more of a yin influence. Herbivorous fish have more of a yin influence, and carnivorous fish have more of a yang influence. Fresh water near the shoreline is a more yin habitat, and salty water in the deep ocean is more yang. Fish that swim in the salty ocean, such as swordfish and tuna, have more of a yang influence than freshwater fish, like trout, which have more of a yin influence. Listed in the chart are balanced foods toward the center for daily use and foods on a wider spectrum for occasional use.

Yin-Yang Spectrum of Fish

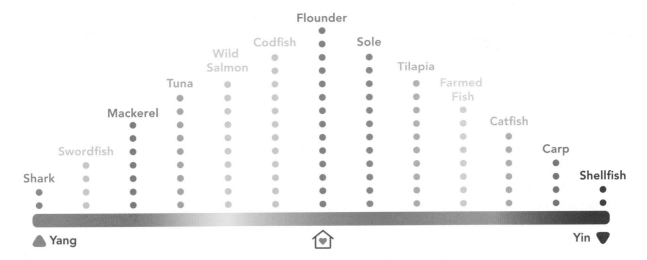

Chicken

If you choose to include meat in your child's diet, poultry has advantages over beef. For example, skinless chicken provides protein along with a variety of B vitamins, selenium, phosphorus, and multiple essential amino acids, and has significantly lower levels of cholesterol and fat than red meat.

Organic, pasture-raised chicken is produced more sustainably, and the chickens live in more humane and sanitary conditions than those on industrial farms. Conventionally raised chickens are packed into cramped cages in warehouses without access to natural sunlight or fresh earth. These birds have their beaks removed to prevent pecking at one another to create space, and flocks are injected with a series of preventive antibiotics to counteract diseases caused by their living environment.

Buying organic meat from local, sustainable farmers helps protect your food from being contaminated with antibiotics, chemicals, and diseases

commonly found in industrial farming. Apart from the organic label, you can look for one of the humane certifications on chicken packages. Humane certifications ensure that the animal was raised in cruelty-free and more sustainable living conditions. If you give your child poultry, make sure that the chicken or turkey is served in tiny pieces and that all bones and skin have been removed.

Eggs

Eggs are compact and concentrated; the whites are high in protein and the yolks are high in fat. Eggs provide numerous vitamins, including vitamin A, B4 (choline), B7 (biotin), B9 (folic acid), B12, and minerals, such as iodine, iron, phosphorus, potassium, selenium, and zinc. They also contain high levels of sodium. Eggs are one of the most common causes of food allergies, and they occur most frequently in babies under 12 months old. Many children tend to be allergic to egg whites because of the high protein content, so most pediatric resources recommend for children to wait until one year old to eat egg whites.

In most cases, children outgrow these allergies by the time they are five years old. An occasional egg can give your child a host of vitamins that are not as easily available in plant-based foods. As a life force, eggs are a very powerful food, because they hold the potential of a chicken. As with chicken, purchasing eggs requires careful attention to labels. The following are a few classifications of some of the options.

Mari and Emi

Every summer Emi and Mari made a trip to visit their grandparents in Mississippi. A highlight of their trip included enjoying fried chicken with mashed potatoes and gravy at the Round Table Restaurant—southern fare served with a lazy Susan in the middle of a big round table. Spinning the food around was half the fun, and the other half was digging in to the tasty, greasy chicken legs.

Organic eggs come from chickens that are fed organic feed, which is free of animal by-products, synthetic fertilizers, pesticides, and other chemical additives. There are no genetically modified foods in the organic feed of egg-producing chickens, and these birds only receive antibiotics in cases of infection. In purchasing organic eggs, you know that they were raised in humane conditions and that they do not have antibiotics or chemicals.

"Free range" as defined by the USDA, signifies that chickens have access to some open space, but it does not regulate the amount of space or time that they have outside. Free range does not mean access to pasture, so most of these chickens are raised on dirt, concrete, or gravel floors.

"Cage-free" means the egg-laying hens are not kept in cages. Often these chickens are crammed into a space without a cage and with limited access to the outside, so cage-free is no guarantee that the animals are treated humanely either.

Organic chicken and eggs offer the highest standards, and even though they cost more, they are the only option that I trusted for feeding my children. Since nonorganic animal foods may contain antibiotics and

growth hormones, the difference between organic and nonorganic is more significant for animal foods than for plant-based foods.

Meat

According to the American Dietetic Association, beef is one of the highest food sources of protein, A and B vitamins, and zinc. It offers generous amounts of omega-3 fatty acids and iron that are easily absorbed into the bloodstream. However, its nutrients come at a cost not found in many plant-based proteins. Compared with grains or beans, beef takes longer to digest and is higher in saturated fats than plant-based proteins. In excessive amounts, meat has been linked to heart disease, obesity, and colon cancer.

Ninety-nine percent of all meat consumed in the United States is raised on large-scale industrial farms. These cows are artificially inseminated and fed genetically modified grain. Additionally, with their close living conditions and demand for rapid growth, they are fed antibiotics and synthetic hormones, like recombinant bovine growth hormone (rBGH). The residue from these hormones is stored in the animal's fat, which ends up in the meat eaten by consumers. Raising conventional beef cattle also requires a great deal of natural resources. For each pound of beef produced, nearly 2,500 gallons of water is used; around three pounds of grain feed is required to create one pound of edible beef.

Organically raised cows do not receive antibiotics or genetically modified growth hormones; they eat organic feed with organically produced grain that is milled in certified facilities. This does not mean that they are raised on pastures with fresh grass, however. Cows' natural diet is comprised of grasses; their stomachs are not equipped to process corn, which is a staple of industrial cattle feed. Even if beef is not certified organic, "grass fed" denotes a natural, healthier lifestyle for cattle, resulting in richer, more nutrient-dense meats. Only about 1 percent of animals in the United States are still raised on family farms. Meat from small family farms is more likely to be grass-fed and treated more humanely than animals on a factory farm.

Yin-Yang Spectrum of Meats

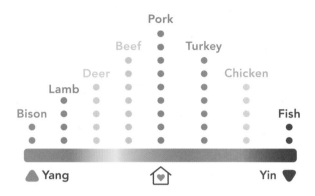

The yin and yang of meats 🏠

The yin to yang spectrum of the animal kingdom follows a line of evolution from fish to mammals. After fish which have scales and gills, live underwater, and lay eggs, came birds, which have feathers and two legs, live on land, and lay eggs. Mammals have red blood and produce meat with the most yang influence. The more active the mammal, the more concentrated the yang energy. Fish has less of a yang influence compared to poultry and red meat.

If you plan to give your baby animal foods, fish is more balanced for daily or weekly eating, and chicken and turkey can be a treat for special occasions. Beef and pork have extreme yang influences, especially for your baby's first year. Listed in the chart above are balanced foods toward the center for daily or weekly use, foods on a wider spectrum for occasional use, and extreme foods to avoid.

Protein-rich Foods for Your Baby

Given babies' rapid growth in the first two years, they need a significantly more protein-dense diet than adults do. In his first year, your baby needs one gram of protein per pound of body weight. When he is 12 to 15 months, that amount decreases to ½ gram of protein per pound of body weight.

For your baby's first 12 months, breast milk or formula is his main source of protein, but you can start incorporating some soft protein-rich foods after six months. Cooked tofu at six to eight months is easy to digest as a first protein-rich food. Dried beans that are cooked and pureed, including lentils, chickpeas, and adzuki beans, along with cooked and ground seeds, such as sesame, sunflower, and pumpkin, can be introduced at seven to eight months. At nine months, offer some yogurt or kefir that is made from whole milk. Tempeh can be offered at one year, and if you plan on giving him animal foods, you can introduce fish, eggs, and cheese at this time. At 18 months when he can chew well, chicken or turkey may be an option for your baby. At 24 months, if you are confident that he does not have a nut allergy, you can offer peanuts and peanut butter.

When introducing protein-rich foods, offer one type of protein at a time, because mixing proteins in the same meal can cause digestive problems. Over time, you can find combinations of protein-rich foods, grains, and vegetables that fulfill your child's nutritional needs and satisfy his palate.

The chart on the following page gives an overview of which proteins to introduce and when. The chart also includes how frequently to serve these proteins and which ones to avoid.

When to Introduce Protein-rich Foods

	Proteins	Age Range	Frequency
	Sesame seeds • ground	6 to 8 months	Daily
	Tahini	6 to 8 months	Daily
	Tofu	6 to 8 months	Occasionally
	Adzuki beans	7 to 9 months	Daily
	Black beans	7 to 9 months	Daily
	Chestnuts	7 to 9 months	Daily
	Chickpeas	7 to 9 months	Daily
	Flaxseeds • ground	7 to 9 months	Daily
	Lentils	7 to 9 months	Daily
	Pumpkin seeds • ground	7 to 9 months	Daily
	Sunflower seeds • ground	7 to 9 months	Daily
	White beans	7 to 9 months	Daily
	Yogurt and dairy kefir • organic	9 to 12 months	Occasionally
	Almond butter • ground	12 to 18 months	Daily
	Eggs • organic • optional	12 to 18 months	Occasionally
	Fish • wild-caught • optional	12 to 18 months	Occasionally
	Tempeh	12 to 18 months	Occasionally
	Cheese • organic • optional	12 to 18 months	Occasionally
	Almonds	18 to 24 months	Occasionally
	Poultry • organic • optional	18 to 24 months	Occasionally
	Beef and pork • organic • optional	18 to 24 months	Occasionally
	Peanut butter • nonhydrogenated	24 to 36 months	Occasionally
	Peanuts	24 to 36 months	Occasionally
	Farm-raised fish	all ages	Avoid
	Nonorganic animal food	all ages	Avoid

Occasionally: 2–3 times a week

Silken Tofu with Kuzu

♡ 6 months+

🥄 4 (2-ounce) servings

V Vegetarian

GF Gluten-free

Silken tofu has a creamy, pudding-like texture, and is an easily digested first protein-rich food for your baby. Because kuzu is alkaline-forming, it provides a health benefit, and it is smooth and gelatinous. Kombu sea vegetable adds minerals, and tamari balances the tofu, making it more digestible. For easy digestion, make sure tofu is cooked before serving to your baby.

1-inch square kombu sea vegetable

½ cup water

½ block silken tofu, cut into 1-inch cubes

1 teaspoon gluten-free tamari for 6–12 months, 2 teaspoons for 12 months+

1 tablespoon kuzu

1 tablespoon water for dissolving kuzu

Method

1. Soak kombu for 5 to 10 minutes in a pan with the ½ cup water.

2. Add tofu cubes and tamari.

3. Bring to a boil, and reduce to a low simmer, cooking for 10 minutes.

4. While tofu is cooking, dissolve kuzu in 1 tablespoon water in a separate bowl or a grinding bowl. Use a pestle or fork to dissolve thoroughly. Kuzu must be dissolved in cool or room temperature water before adding to hot food or liquid.

5. Add kuzu liquid into simmering tofu, and stir until it turns transparent.

6. Remove kombu, let cool, and serve.

Variation

• Substitute arrowroot flour for kuzu as a thickener.

Toasted Seeds and Nuts

♡ 7 months+

🥣 8 to 16 ounces toasted nuts or seeds

V Vegetarian

GF Gluten-free

Seeds and nuts are protein-rich complements to grains or vegetables, as well as condiments and snack foods. Soak them with grains before cooking or cook them together with vegetables, and then puree. After your child is one year old, you can toast, grind, and sprinkle them on grains or vegetables as a condiment. When your child is old enough to eat whole nuts and seeds, you can mix them with dried fruit and dry cereals for convenient healthy snacking at home or on the go. The oil in seeds and nuts is more digestible when cooked than when eaten raw.

1 cup seeds or nuts

Water for soaking seeds

Options:

Sesame seeds, sunflower seeds, pumpkin seeds, flaxseeds, and almonds

Method

1. Preheat oven to 250°F.

2. In a bowl, cover seeds with water and soak for 30 minutes.

3. Rinse and strain.

4. Spread seeds or nuts onto cookie sheet or casserole dish.

5. Place in oven and cook for 20 minutes. Stir and cook for another 20 minutes. Stir again, and continue roasting for 10 to 15 minutes, or until seeds are completely cooked.

6. Let cool, then store in an airtight container.

7. Grind seeds with a hand grinder or a grinding bowl to sprinkle on grains or vegetables, or eat whole as a snack.

Variations

- Add ½ teaspoon of sesame, sunflower, flax, or pumpkin seeds to grains while soaking, and then cook together. Puree thoroughly, until there is a creamy consistency.

- Add tahini to purees for a protein boost and to give a creamy consistency to fibrous vegetables.

- Seeds and nuts can be toasted in a heavy skillet on the stove top. Heat skillet to a medium temperature, add seeds, and stir until done.

Bean Puree and Whole Beans

♡ 9 months+

🥄 4 (2-ounce) servings

V Vegetarian

GF Gluten-free

Beans provide plant-based amino acids and are rich in nutrients. At nine months, your baby can eat pureed beans while the rest of the family enjoys them as a dip, with pieces of steamed or raw veggies, chips, or crackers, and as a spread on bread for sandwiches. As he gets older, he can share these dishes, too.

Cooking beans with kombu sea vegetable softens the protein and makes it more digestible, in addition to providing minerals. My Japanese friend told me that the foam that bubbles up when cooking beans has a gas, called *aku* in Japanese. She said that it is important to skim off the foam when it bubbles up for better digestion and health.

Bean purees are convenient for bentos and snacks for travel. Soak dried beans overnight, or use high-quality unsalted, canned beans for convenience. Toddlers usually like the creamy consistency, so it is an easy way to get them to eat beans and vegetables. When your baby can chew, you can use the same recipe to make beans and vegetables without pureeing them.

Adzuki:

¼ cup dried adzuki beans

1 ½ cups water for puree,
    ¾ for toddler

1-inch square kombu sea vegetable

1 cup butternut squash, peeled and
    cut into ½-inch pieces

1 teaspoon sesame, olive,
    or coconut oil

⅛ teaspoon sea salt for 9–12 months,
    ¼ teaspoon for 12 months+

Lentils:

¼ cup dried lentils

1 ½ cups water for puree,
    ¾ for toddler

1-inch square kombu sea vegetable

1 cup carrots, cut into
    ½-inch pieces

1 teaspoon sesame, olive,
    or sesame oil

⅛ teaspoon sea salt for 9–12 months,
    ¼ teaspoon for 12 months+

Chickpeas:

¼ cup dried chickpeas

1 ½ cups water for puree,
    ¾ for toddler

1-inch square kombu sea vegetable

½ cup onion, peeled and cut into
    ½-inch pieces

1 teaspoon sesame, olive,
    or coconut oil

⅛ teaspoon sea salt for 9–12 months,
    ¼ teaspoon for 12 months+

Planning Ahead
For each of these versions, cover the legumes with water and soak overnight.

Method
1. Combine the remaining ingredients in a pan, bring to a boil—skim off foam, reduce heat to simmer, and cover with a lid.

2. Cook for 45 minutes to 1 hour, or until beans and vegetables are tender. Add salt (if using), and cook for 5 more minutes. Beans will not get tender if salt is added at the beginning of cooking. For whole cooked beans, cook until water is absorbed.

3. Use a heat diffuser to prevent burning.

4. Remove kombu.

5. For puree, blend in a food processor, food mill, or food grinder. If necessary, add water to puree. For finger foods and toddler foods, serve whole beans.

Variations
• For a quick version, substitute one 15-ounce can of precooked, unsalted beans, add vegetables and seasoning, and cook for 10 minutes, or until vegetables are tender, and puree.

• For puree, add tahini in puree at the end, for extra-creamy consistency and protein.

• Add ¼ teaspoon minced fresh or dried herbs while cooking, such as fennel, bay, basil, thyme, dill, cilantro, or parsley.

• Add miso or tamari for probiotics—¼ teaspoon for 9–12 months, ½ teaspoon for 12 months+.

Tempeh

♡ 9 months+

🥄 6 (2-ounce) servings

V Vegetarian

GF Gluten-free

Tempeh is a traditional Indonesian food that is made with fermented soybeans, and has probiotic properties. It is packaged in "cakes" that are 4 x 8 x 1 inch, and can be found in the refrigerated section of the natural food store or supermarket. Although tempeh has its own distinctive taste, it needs seasoning from other ingredients, such as tamari, vegetables, and herbs, to make it an appetizing dish. Cooking for at least 20 minutes over low heat is essential for digestion, because it is a soybean product. Since tempeh is a fermented food, it can be a source of probiotics.

For ages nine to 12 months this recipe can be pureed, or small pieces can be given for a finger food. This recipe can be adapted for the family by taking out a portion for your baby or toddler, and then adding more tamari seasoning.

2 cups carrots, cut into ¼-inch pieces

1 tablespoon sesame, olive, or coconut oil

One 8-ounce package tempeh, cut into ¼-inch cubes

¼ teaspoon minced fresh or dried thyme

1-inch square kombu sea vegetable, soaked in 1 cup water

½ teaspoon gluten-free tamari for 9–12 months, 1 teaspoons for 12–18 months, 2 teaspoons for 18–24 months

Method

1. In a skillet over medium heat, sauté carrots in oil for 5 minutes.

2. Add tempeh, and continue to sauté for another 5 minutes.

3. Add thyme, kombu, water, and tamari.

4. Cover with a lid, and simmer for 20 minutes over low heat.

5. Use a heat diffuser to prevent burning.

Variations

•   Add or substitute other vegetables, such as onions, celery, bell peppers, or mushrooms.

•   Add ¼ teaspoon garlic to sautéed vegetables for 12 months+.

•   Slice tempeh into 4 x 4 x ½-inch cakes and substitute onions for carrots to make sandwiches or veggie burgers. Makes 8 pieces.

•   Substitute thyme for other herbs, such as fennel, bay, basil, dill, cilantro, or parsley.

Poached Fish

♡ 12 months+

🥄 4 (2-ounce) servings

A Animal protein

GF Gluten-free

If you plan to give your child animal food, this dish is a simple and nutritious protein-rich food for a starter. The recipe has a mild taste, and is easy to make. It can be adjusted for your family with condiments or a separate sauce. Multiply the amount of fish as needed. Wild-caught fish is more nutritional.

½ cup fish, cut into ½-inch pieces

¼ cup water

1 teaspoon lemon juice

⅛ teaspoon sea salt

¼ teaspoon minced fresh or dried herbs, such as fennel, bay, basil, thyme, dill, cilantro, or parsley

Options:

Cod, scrod, halibut, haddock, flounder, salmon, red snapper

Method

1. Rinse fish in cold water and take off skin and bones.

2. Bring water, lemon juice, sea salt, and herbs to a boil in pot over high heat.

3. Reduce heat to a low simmer and add fish.

4. Use a heat diffuser to prevent burning.

5. Cook 5 minutes, or until fish is soft. Do not overcook.

6. Serve small bites of plain fish or combine with vegetable or grain.

 To learn about seafood sustainability, visit seafoodwatch.org

Fruits

WHILE LIVING IN JAPAN, I took natural foods cooking classes in Tokyo. One day, the teacher announced that the menu included *ichigo sarada*, or strawberry salad. It was a hot summer day and the idea of fresh, juicy fruits sounded delicious to me. However, once the cooking was completed, I was disappointed to discover that each person's dish only included one half of a strawberry. I savored that sweet piece of strawberry, as a special treat. Portions of fruits are small and fresh fruits are considered a special delicacy in Japan, due to cost and availability. Later, I laughed about that cooking class when I was in my third trimester of pregnancy with Emi, and I treated myself to a basket of fresh strawberries every day from the local market. Their juicy sweetness was delicious and they were cooling to the heat I felt in my body from being pregnant.

Fruits are sweet, cooling, refreshing, and relaxing. The properties of fruits can be medicinal for your baby, balancing his compact, yang nature. Fruits are low in fat and high in fiber, vitamins, and minerals. They are packed with essential nutrients, phytochemicals, and antioxidants, with a high water content. The natural, sweet taste of fruits can also provide a source of healthy pleasure and enjoyment for your baby. Eaten in a balanced proportion, fruits provide sweet, natural goodness to your baby's diet.

However, when fruits take a central place on your baby's plate, or if they are mixed with other foods as a major portion of his food intake, they can cause digestive disturbances and imbalances. As a primary first food, fruits do not have the nutritional value of grains and vegetables to support your baby's development. If he eats too many fruits, the sugars can be addictive and can weaken your baby's digestive system, according to Bob Flaws, a well-respected teacher of East Asian medicine and author of *A Handbook of TCM Pediatrics*. To aid digestion and avoid disturbance in your baby's stomach, serve him fruits separately (at least 30 minutes after a meal), not mixed with other foods, and offer him moderate portions compared with grains and vegetables. The weather, climate, and preparation methods also make a difference in the effects of different fruits on his body—fresh fruit is refreshing on a hot summer day, and the warmth of baked apples in winter helps bring your baby's body into balance. As a grandmother, I delight in watching my grandson, Zo's enthusiasm as he relishes chunks of watermelon for dessert.

The Power of Fruits

Low in calories and fat, whole fruits provide natural sugars that can satisfy your baby's innate taste for sweetness. Fruits are high in dietary fiber, vitamins, minerals, enzymes, phytochemicals, and antioxidants. They are also easy to digest, and their sugar can offer quick energy. Antioxidant values are high in fruit, which helps clean out free radicals in your baby's bloodstream and strengthen his immune system. The fruits that are highest in antioxidants have distinctive, bright colors, such as blueberries, raspberries, cherries, and grapes.

Although fruits can cause digestive problems when eaten together with foods that digest at a different rate, such as grains, proteins, and vegetables, they can aid digestion when they are eaten separately. They provide soluble fiber, which soaks up water as it passes through your baby's digestive system. Insoluble fiber provides bulk to the digestive system to relieve and prevent constipation by triggering regular bowel movements. Sour fruits, such as lemons, limes, and grapefruits, stimulate and cleanse the liver of bile formation, which allows your baby's body to break down and digest

protein and fat. I recommend waiting until your baby is one year old to introduce citrus; observe his reaction when you do as he may get a mild rash or indigestion.

High concentrations of natural sugars in fruits can create a noticeable difference in your baby's daily health. Excess fruits can create a green color in his bowel movements, which means that his stool is on the yin side of the spectrum. On the other hand, cooked or fresh fruits can help him relax when he is tense, or ease constipation.

Fruit Considerations

When choosing fruits, consider whether they are organic, where they are grown, whether they are in season, and how they are ripened.

Organic Fruits

The most popular fruits in the United States, such as oranges, apples, and bananas, are often heavily sprayed with chemical fertilizers and pesticides. Chemicals may not be inside the fruits, but the growth and quality can be affected. Large, shiny fruits are not always the most delicious or nutritious, and they may have been genetically altered to give them the most visual appeal. Whenever possible, buy organic fruits for your baby, especially ones with exposed skin. The "Clean 15" and the "Dirty Dozen" can help you prioritize your organic shopping budget.

Seasonal and Local Fruits

The most nutritious fruits you can offer your baby are the ones that are in season where you live. Vitamins and phytochemicals are at their peak vitality and energy when fruits are fresh. Buying local fruits ensures they were not picked green weeks ago, and then shipped to a store. Fresh local fruits are more balanced to meet your baby's daily needs and also have the most flavor.

Naturally Ripened Fruits

Some fruits, such as bananas and avocados, sweeten after they are harvested, so you can purchase them when they are firm and slightly green, and then they can ripen at home. The starches in most other fruits do not become sweeter after they are picked, because they do not continue to ripen. If you do buy unripe fruits, let them ripen at room temperature before serving them.

Top Ten Fiber-rich Fruits

Fruit	Serving	Calories	Fiber per 100 calories
Raspberries	1 cup	60	8 g
Blackberries	1 cup	74	7.6 g
Strawberries	1 cup	45	3.4g
Prunes	½ cup cooked	113	7 g
Papaya	1 medium	118	5.5 g
Orange	1 medium	50	3 g
Apple	1 medium	81	3.7 g
Pear	1 medium	98	4 g
Figs	5 dried	237	8.5 g
Avocado	half	150	4 g

(Source: askdrsears.com)

Types of Fruits

Temperate

Temperate fruits grow on deciduous trees, vines, bushes, and on the ground. Temperate zones usually have equally long winters and summers. The north temperate zone extends from the Tropic of Cancer at about 23.5 degrees north latitude to the Arctic Circle at about 66.5 degrees north latitude. The south temperate zone extends from the Tropic of Capricorn at about 23.5 degrees south latitude to the Antarctic Circle at about 66.5 degrees south latitude. Tropical fruits, such as bananas and avocados, cannot withstand a light frost. Subtropical fruits need warm or mild temperatures, but they can survive a light frost. The most common subtropical fruits are oranges, grapefruits, lemons, and limes.

Spring and Summer

| Apricot | Blackberry | Cantaloupe | Cherry | Honeydew melon | Peach | Plum | Raspberry | Strawberry | Watermelon |

Fall and Winter

| Apple | Blueberry | Cranberry | Grapes | Kiwi | Nectarine | Pear | Pomegranate |

Tropical

Tropical fruits usually have a thick skin that is not edible, because they help retain water in a hot climate and protect the fruits from predators like monkeys and birds with sharp beaks. Coconuts, avocados, and bananas have a thicker skin than apples and pears. Temperate fruits tend to be firm and juicy with a high sugar content, and flesh that supports seed growth.

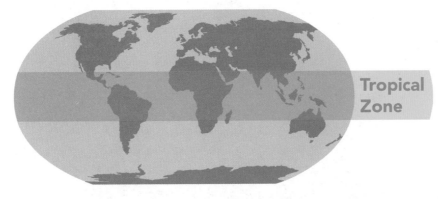

Tropical Zone

| Avocados | Bananas | Lemons | Limes | Mangos | Oranges | Papaya | Pineapples | Tangerines |

How Fruits Grow

Discovering how fruits grow can help you understand more about the food your baby eats, where it comes from, and how it affects him. This can also help you and your child connect to nature. When he eats fruits, he absorbs energy from its source. Fruits grow on vines (grapes), on bushes (blueberries), on the ground (strawberries), and on trees (apples).

Fruiting vines that grow upward
Grapes, blackberries, raspberries, and kiwis

Fruiting bushes
Blueberries, cranberries, blackberries, and raspberries

Fruiting trees
Pears, apples, apricots, cherries, peaches, nectarines, plums, pomegranates. Tropical: bananas, lemons, limes, tangerines, oranges, pineapple, avocados, mangos, and papaya

Fruits that grow along the ground
Strawberries, cantaloupes, watermelons, and honeydew melons

The Yin and Yang of Fruits

Fruits generally have more of a yin influence than vegetables and grains because they are usually sweeter. Many fruits have various Yin–Yang factors, so it can be complex to clearly define Yin–Yang characteristics. For example, apples grow on a tree, so even though they grow upward (yin influence), they are small and firm (yang influence) because they grow in a cool climate. Apples are more yang than sweet, juicy watermelons that grow in hot weather.

Some indicators of Yin–Yang influences in fruit include moisture content, growing climate and season, and direction of growth. Size, color, and shape are also factors. Because of the variations of these factors, the easiest way to determine the Yin–Yang characteristics of fruit is by the amount of sugar they have on the glycemic index.

Compare a small, yang apple that is harvested in autumn to a larger watermelon that is juicy, sweet, yin, and grown in summer. Tropical fruits, such as bananas and pineapples are on the yin side of the spectrum, because they grow in a warm climate, and since they are cooling, they tend to create balance with hot weather.

Most temperate fruits have a lower sugar content—apples, pears, plums, peaches, cherries, berries, and sour tropical citrus fruits. Medium levels of glycemic impact are sweet tropical fruits such as bananas,

Indicators of Fruit Yin and Yang

Indicator	Yang ▲	Yin ▼
Size	Big	Small
Harvesting season	Spring Summer	Autumn Winter
Liquid	More juicy	Less juicy
Sugar content	More sweet	Less sweet

mangos, papayas, pineapple, and others are grapes, cantaloupes, and apricots. Watermelon and dates are highest in sugar content, although since the sugars in dates are much more concentrated than those in watermelon, dates have a much higher glycemic load. The ripeness of the fruit can also determine the level of sugar content.

Cooking method and food preparation affect the yin-yang influence of fruits—dried or cooked fruit has more of a yang influence than fresh fruit served cold. Listed in the chart are balanced foods toward the center for daily use and foods on a wider spectrum for occasional use.

Yin-Yang Spectrum of Fruits

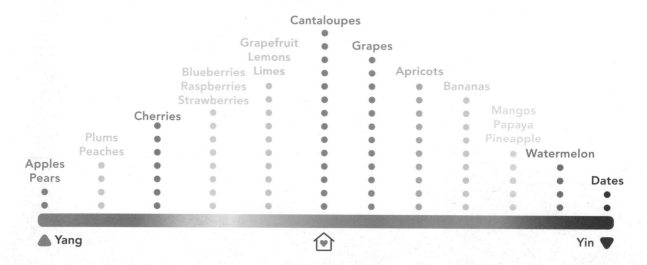

Fruit Preparation

There are many ways to prepare fruits, and each method has its own benefits to your baby's health.

Cooked Fruit Puree

Cooking fruits brings out their sweetness and reduces liquid. Cooking also changes the cooling properties of the fruits, which helps your baby predigest them. Apple and pear sauce or baked fruits are easy to make, and you can store them for several days in the refrigerator, or freeze batches for later use. Kuzu is a highly alkaline-producing food and also has a calming effect on babies. Cooking fresh fruits in apple juice or water with kuzu can be used as a soothing dish during an illness, and it is also a healthy, easy, and delicious filling for pies or cake frosting.

Fresh Fruits

Fresh fruits are a delicious and refreshing treat or dessert, especially on a warm summer day. They can have a cooling effect on your baby's body, which helps balance hot weather. Raw fruits can relax, calm, or cool your baby.

Fruit Gelo

When Emi and Mari reached around eight months old, I made them delicious fruit gelos made from vegetarian gelatin, or agar. Diluted fruit juices, pureed or fresh fruits, combined with agar make a tasty dessert with a delicate texture. You can adjust the recipe to accommodate the age of your child, and other family members can also enjoy this healthy, natural gelatin.

Dried Fruits

Raisins, currants, and dried apricots and cherries are fresh fruits that have been dehydrated. The drying process removes the liquid and makes the fruits sweeter and more yang than their fresh counterparts. Because of their concentrated sweetness, you can boil dried fruits in water and use that water as a sweetener in other dishes. Dried fruits that are cooked can be served as a puree or spread on bread and crackers.

Often, conventional dried fruits are treated with sulfur dioxide, which is a preservative and makes the color lighter; some people are sensitive to this ingredient and may develop allergic reactions to it. Sometimes fruits are blanched before drying, which reduces their flavor and nutrition. Organic dried fruits are unsulfured and have a darker color. They do not last as long as fruits containing preservatives, but you can freeze them for a longer shelf life.

Jams and Spreads

The summer that I was pregnant with Mari, I got the idea in my head to make 52 pint jars of jam, one for every week of the year. On several early mornings, Emi and I went with buckets and sunhats for an excursion to our local strawberry, blueberry, and raspberry fields. We ate and picked our berries, and then returned home and industriously cooked and canned the fruits. After Mari was born, we did not eat a jar of jam per week, but we did enjoy delicious homemade jam for several years. You never know what projects the progesterone of pregnancy will initiate!

Jam is made of whole fruits, including seeds and skins. Blueberries, strawberries, blackberries, raspberries, peaches, and apricots make delicious jam and can be combined with sweeteners such as rice syrup, maple syrup, or honey, and pectin, arrowroot, or kuzu as a thickener. Most packaged all-fruit spreads and apple or pear butter are made by slow cooking pureed fruits over low heat without using additional sweetener. Jams and spreads are a healthy way to satisfy your toddler's sweet tooth, and they are convenient for nut butter and jelly sandwiches.

Fruit Juices

Juicing fruits extracts fiber and nutrients, and concentrates its sweetness and cooling properties. Diluting fruit juices with water as a drink for your child diffuses the impact of the concentrated sweetness, providing a refreshing drink and a sweetener for desserts. As a daily beverage, however, too much fruit juice can cause problems for your child, such as diarrhea, childhood obesity, and early tooth decay.

Combining Fruits with Other Foods

Certain foods combine well together, while others do not. Carbohydrates, proteins, and fats take longer to digest than fruits do, because fruits take less time to break down. Mixing fruits with other foods such as grains, vegetables, or beans that take longer to digest can create gas in your baby's digestive system. They can cause indigestion, cramps, and belching. Most vegetables require different enzymes than fruits require for digestion, so combining vegetables and fruits disturbs the effectiveness of the enzymes and interferes with your baby's ability to absorb nutrients.

If sweetener is needed for grains, beans, or vegetables, brown rice syrup is more digestible because it comes from a grain source. Apples are an exception because they have

a neutral effect and can mix with vegetables or grains without causing digestive problems. Cooking fruits makes them more digestible, so they may be combined with grains in some desserts such as rice pudding.

Fruits for Your Baby

When your baby is seven to nine months old, offer him cooked fruits served separately from other foods that are easy for him to digest. Apples, apricots, berries, peaches, pears, plums, and dried fruits, cooked and served at room temperature, are naturally sweet. When your baby is nine to 12 months old, you can continue with these same cooked fruits, and add soft, fresh seasonal fruits that can be mashed, such as berries, melons, grapes, avocados, papayas, mangoes, and bananas. At 12 months, he can eat small fruits such as blueberries, cherries, and blackberries and cut pieces of fresh fruits that are hard, such as apples, apricots, pears, and citrus fruits. At 18 months, when he can chew well, he can eat dried fruits that require chewing, such as raisins and prunes. For best digestion, wait 30 minutes after eating grains, vegetables, and beans to offer fruits as a dessert or snack. The following chart gives an overview of which fruits to start feeding and when. The chart also includes how frequently to feed these fruits. At all of these stages, take special care to cut small, round fruits in half, and remove pits from all stone fruits, so these do not become a choking hazard.

Emi eating strawberries

When to Introduce Fruits			
Fruits	Cooked	Raw	Frequency
Apples • organic • fresh or dried	7 to 9 months	18 to 24 months	Daily
Apricots • fresh or dried	7 to 9 months	18 to 24 months	Daily
Blackberries	7 to 9 months	18 to 24 months	Daily
Bananas	7 to 9 months	9 to 12 months	Occasionally
Blueberries	7 to 9 months	18 to 24 months	Daily
Cherries • take out seeds	7 to 9 months	18 to 24 months	Daily
Currants • fresh or dried	7 to 9 months	18 to 24 months	Daily
Nectarines • organic	7 to 9 months	18 to 24 months	Daily
Peaches • organic • fresh or dried	7 to 9 months	18 to 24 months	Daily
Pears • fresh or dried	7 to 9 months	18 to 24 months	Daily
Plums	7 to 9 months	18 to 24 months	Daily
Prunes • fresh or dried	7 to 9 months	18 to 24 months	Daily
Raisins • fresh or dried	7 to 9 months	18 to 24 months	Daily
Raspberries	7 to 9 months	18 to 24 months	Daily
Strawberries • organic	7 to 9 months	18 to 24 months	Daily
Avocados		9 to 12 months	Occasionally
Cantaloupes		9 to 12 months	Daily
Grapes • organic • remove seeds		9 to 12 months	Daily
Honeydew melon		9 to 12 months	Daily
Kiwis		9 to 12 months	Daily
Mangos		9 to 12 months	Daily
Papayas		9 to 12 months	Daily
Watermelon		9 to 12 months	Daily
Limes, lemons		18 to 24 months	Occasionally
Oranges		18 to 24 months	Occasionally
Pineapples		18 to 24 months	Occasionally
Tangerines		18 to 24 months	Occasionally
Pomegranates		24 to 36 months	Occasionally

Occasionally: 2–3 times a week

* small fruit choking hazards; citrus seeds; beware pits, skins

Fruit Sauce

♡ 7 months+

🥄 8 (2 ounce) servings

V Vegetarian

GF Gluten-free

Applesauce is a traditional first fruit for your baby and toddler; and other family members can enjoy it, too. Substitute or add other fruits for a variety of cooked fruit sauces. Apples are a neutral fruit, which make a base that mixes well with other fruits for creating combinations.

5 cups fruit, peeled, cored, and cut into 1-inch pieces (leave on soft peels of organic fruits)

½ cup water

⅛ teaspoon sea salt for 12 months+

Options:

Pears, peaches, plums, blueberries, blackberries, strawberries, raspberries, cherries, bananas (alone or in combination)

Method

1. Put fruit, water, and sea salt (if using) in a pan over medium-low heat.

2. Cook for 20 minutes, or until soft.

3. Puree the mixture in a blender, food processor, hand grinder, food mill, or a grinding bowl.

Variation

Place cut fruit, water, and salt (if using) in a ceramic or glass dish, and bake at 350°F for 30 minutes.

Fruit Kuzu

♡ 7 months+

🥄 8 (2 ounce) servings

V Vegetarian

GF Gluten-free

Cooking fruit with kuzu makes a gelatinous, pudding-like consistency that can be served alone as a gelatin, used as a filling in a pie, or spread on a cake for icing. The alkaline-forming effect of kuzu is a healthy plus in any dish, and it can create a calming effect on your baby. Adjust the fruit for your baby's age.

2 cups fruit, peeled, cored, and cut into ½-inch pieces (leave on soft peels of organic fruits)

½ cup water or unsweetened apple juice

⅛ teaspoon sea salt for 9 months+

2 tablespoons kuzu

¼ cup water for dissolving kuzu

Options for fruit:

Apples, pears, peaches, plums, bananas, strawberries, blueberries, raspberries

Options for juice:

Pear or grape

Method

1. Put fruit, water, and sea salt (if using) into a pan.

2. Bring to a boil, reduce heat, and simmer until fruit is tender. Use a heat diffuser to prevent burning.

3. If your baby is eating purees, transfer the fruit to a blender or a grinding bowl and puree to the consistency that fits his stage of eating, and then transfer back to the cooking pot.

4. Dissolve kuzu in water in a separate bowl or a grinding bowl. Use a pestle or fork to dissolve thoroughly. Kuzu must be dissolved in cool or room temperature water before adding to hot food or liquid.

5. Add kuzu liquid into simmering fruit, stirring until it turns transparent.

Variations

• Mix fruits for delicious combinations.

• Substitute arrowroot flour for kuzu as a thickener.

• For a sweeter taste, and for a special dessert, add 1 tablespoon brown rice syrup or maple syrup.

• For a sweet dessert, substitute apple juice for water for 12 months+.

• For pie filling, double recipe and add ⅓ cup maple syrup.

• For cake icing, double recipe and add ⅓ cup maple syrup.

Dried Fruit Puree

♡ **7 months+**

🥄 **7-8 (2 ounce) servings**

V **Vegetarian**

GF **Gluten-free**

Dried fruit puree is an alternative to fresh fruit, especially because it can be stored and used when needed. The process of drying fruit concentrates the sweetness so it can also be used as a spread on bread or crackers. Make sure that the fruit you buy is not dried with sulfur. Apples have a mild taste and are not as sweet as raisins, so they are a good base for mixing with other fruits.

⅔ **cup unsulfured dried apples**

⅓ **cup unsulfured apricots, prunes, or raisins**

1 ½ cups boiling water for soaking

⅛ **teaspoon sea salt for 9 months+**

½ to 1 cup water for cooking and blending

Options:

Dried apricots, peaches, pears

Method

1. Put fruit and sea salt (if using) into pan, and pour boiling water to cover.

2. Soak for 15 minutes. Remove the rehydrated fruit.

3. Cut soaked fruit into ½-inch pieces. Return to pot with soaking water.

4. Bring fruit and water to a boil.

5. Add more water, if necessary—if water on the bottom of the pan dries up.

6. Lower heat, and simmer for 30 minutes, or until fruit is soft.

7. Use a heat diffuser to prevent burning.

8. Puree in a blender, food processor, food mill, hand grinder, or a grinding bowl.

Stewed Fruit

♡ 9 months+

🥣 8 (2 ounce) servings

V Vegetarian

GF Gluten-free

This is a very simple recipe that is easy to make with most fruits. Cooking fruit is warming to the body in cool weather and is more balanced for daily eating than raw fruit. Cooking fruits, such as bananas, brings out its natural sweetness. Small chunks or pieces of lightly cooked fruits are convenient for finger foods and on-the-go snacks. Adjust the fruit for the age of your baby.

2 cups fruit, peeled, cored, and cut into ½-inch pieces

¼ cup water

⅛ teaspoon sea salt for 9 months+

Options:

Apples, pears, peaches, plums, bananas, strawberries, blueberries, raspberries

Method
1. Put fruit, water, and sea salt (if using) into a pan.

2. Bring to a boil, reduce heat, and simmer until fruit is tender, about 20 to 30 minutes.

3. Use a heat diffuser to prevent burning.

Fruit Gelo

♡ 7 months+

🥄 12 (2 ounce) servings

V Vegetarian

GF Gluten-free

Kanten is a basic, light, and refreshing dessert made from the sea vegetable agar, which is a natural, vegetarian gelatin. It has a delicate texture, and is refreshing when served slightly cool, after a heavy meal, or in warm weather. Agar comes in dried flakes that are dissolved in liquid to make gelatin.

4 cups unsweetened
  fruit juice

3 tablespoons agar flakes

2 cups fresh fruit, peeled, trimmed,
  cored, and cut into ½-inch pieces
  (optional)

⅛ teaspoon sea salt for 9 months+

Options:

Strawberries, blueberries,
raspberries, blackberries,
peaches, apricots, apples,
plums, pears, bananas

Method

1. Put juice, agar flakes, and sea salt (if using) into a pan.

2. Bring to a boil, reduce heat, and simmer for 10 minutes, or until agar is dissolved.

3. Reduce heat to low, add fruit, if desired, and simmer until fruit is softened, about 5 minutes, depending on the fruit.

4. Use a heat diffuser to prevent burning.

5. Pour mixture into individual dishes, into one large casserole dish (cut into squares once set), or into food cubes. Cool in refrigerator until mixture is jelled.

Variations

• Use half water and half fruit juice.

• Add fruit after pouring juice and agar mixture into dishes.

• Substitute carrot juice for fruit juice.

• Substitute vegetable broth for fruit juice and substitute vegetable pieces for fruit pieces.

Fresh Fruits

♡ 9 months+

🥄 5 or 6 servings

V Vegetarian

GF Gluten-free

Fresh fruit is sweet and delicious when it is ripe and in season, and all the more so when it is grown in your local area. Avocados, bananas, strawberries, cantaloupe, watermelon, and honeydew can be mashed and eaten raw on a daily basis. Occasionally, you can offer other tropical fruits, such as papayas, mangos, and kiwi in warmer weather. At 12 months, blackberries, raspberries, and blueberries are perfect small bites for your baby when he is fascinated by learning how to pick up food. After his first birthday, citrus fruits, such as oranges, tangerines, and pineapple make a fun occasional snack, if his overall health is good.

Cut into bite-size pieces when he can chew, so there is no choking danger. Apples, pears, peaches, plums, apricots, and nectarines, are convenient for snacks or bentos. Be sure to take out the seeds of cherries and grapes for his first two years.

Fermented Foods

WHEN I WAS PREGNANT with Emi in Japan, I received a gift certificate for *ichi-man en*, 10,000 yen, or about $100, to the Isetan department store from the mother of one of my kindergarten students. You could spend the whole day exploring the seven floors of Isetan, visiting the restaurants and museums, shopping for the latest fashions, home goods, and traditional Japanese kimonos and crafts, and discovering every type of gourmet Japanese food imaginable in the basement. As I wandered around, I found a stall that had naturally fermented pickles, where I spent my entire gift certificate on pickles and their friendly flora. During both of my pregnancies, I often craved the sour, salty, and soulful taste of those probiotic-rich pickles, which nourished my pregnancy cravings.

After Emi was born at Dr. Watanabe's small, home clinic, the first meal I ate was a bowl of miso soup. Miso is a paste made from fermented soybeans, *koji* (a yeast starter that can be inoculated into rice, barley, or wheat), salt, and rice or barley. Miso is often used as a soup base, and is helpful for nursing mothers to produce breast milk. As I drank the salty broth, I felt the rich, *Lactobacillus* enzymes go through my digestive system. Mari was born three years later at my home, with Dr. Jeff Tait, my husband Naoki, my mother, a friend, and Emi there to cut Mari's umbilical cord. After her birth, everyone attending celebrated with birthday cake and Champagne, but I wanted miso soup.

Around the world, people have used fermentation as a method of food preservation, and also as an aid to digestion. Germans and Koreans ferment cabbage into sauerkraut and kimchi; Japanese turn soybeans into miso; French make cheese; Greeks prepare yogurt; Africans make fermented porridge from millet; and Indians enjoy chutneys.

In the past fifty years, however, many traditional fermented foods have disappeared because of pasteurization, and most of today's pickles and sauerkraut are made with vinegar instead of the traditional method of lacto-fermentation that uses *Lactobacillus* and lactic acid. Most breads and pastas are made with commercial baker's yeast instead of natural leavenings, such as sourdough yeast. The majority of processed foods have been pasteurized to keep them bacteria-free. Pasteurization kills potentially harmful bacteria in foods, but it can also destroy healthful nutrients and the beneficial bacteria in foods.

Fermentation, on the other hand, encourages the beneficial bacteria to grow as they break down carbohydrates, proteins, and fats and convert sugars into acids or alcohol. Fermented foods are a form of probiotics, meaning "for life," and are often called "friendly flora." Thus, incorporating traditionally fermented foods, which are a type of probiotics, into your child's diet at an early age is a way to build his immunity and long-term health. These friendly flora are beneficial for digestive health and are helpful in overtaking potentially harmful bacteria and viruses.

Beneficial Bacteria

In the womb, your baby has no bacteria in his gut, and at birth as he goes through the birth canal, he takes in bacteria from his mother and starts to develop his own personal colony of gut flora that is unique to him. The birth canal is a microbe-rich environment that coats him as he is born and begins the process of developing his intestinal flora. If he is born through Caesarean section, his bacteria is mostly colonized from his mother's skin instead of her vagina, which has a higher concentration of *Lactobacillus*, a kind of bacteria that aids in the digestion of milk. Babies born through Caesarean section and who cannot breast-feed may need additional probiotic boosters to help establish their gut flora.

Approximately 10 to 30 percent of pregnant women carry Group B strep (GBS), which is a kind of bacteria that colonizes in her vagina or intestinal tract. While GBS is generally harmless in healthy adults, it may pass to the baby during labor and birth. The standard care for GBS is to receive antibiotics during labor to protect the baby. Like any antibiotic, this flushes out the good, as well as the bad bacteria, so a mother in this situation can benefit from replenishing her healthy bacteria with probiotics and fermented foods, such as miso soup or yogurt, after labor.

Breast milk, especially colostrum, is your baby's first probiotic food, and it has a wealth of beneficial bacteria that helps him begin to establish his individual bacteria. Aside from breast milk, using fermented foods and probiotics can help your baby develop healthy bacteria in his digestive system, which supports his digestion and absorption of nutrients and helps build his immunity.

There are more than 100 trillion beneficial bacteria that live in the intestines, in the mouth, and on the skin. These bacteria have a symbiotic relationship because they have evolved in response to one another and are dependent on each other. Bacteria break down food and protect the walls of the digestive tract by establishing a foundation of flora to defend against viruses, fungi, pathogens, and toxins. They stimulate cell growth, repress the growth of harmful microorganisms, and help the immune system fight disease. In return, they benefit from the stable environment inside the digestive system. Bacteria colonize on

the skin, where they provide protection against more dangerous microbes in exchange for nutrients from the surface of the skin. Bacteria need food to live in an environment without oxygen, and humans need probiotic bacteria to stimulate their immune system and help keep harmful bacteria under control.

The Hygiene Hypothesis

In the past hundred years of Western culture, the "germ theory" has developed and dominated Western medical practice. It comes from the belief that bacteria found outside the body attacks when the immune system is weak and causes disease in the body. Because of this fear of external bacteria, or germs, it is common to try to eradicate bacteria from the environment with antibacterial soap and cleaning products.

Antibiotics are also used for fighting bacteria, and they can be extremely helpful in combating life-threatening bacterial disease. However, overuse of antibiotics leads to drug-resistant germs and increased risks and side effects. Antibiotic resistance is one of the world's most pressing public health threats. Many health and science professionals call this phenomena the hygiene hypothesis, linking the increase in autoimmune diseases, irritable bowel syndrome and inflammatory bowel disease, asthma, and other illnesses to the lack of natural exposure to the diverse world of microorganisms found in soil and water. Deprived of contact with microorganisms, due to the use of antibacterial and antimicrobial cleaners, and antibiotics, the natural balance has been disturbed.

The Power of Fermented Foods

Because Western society is very conscientious about the danger of germs and bacteria, there is a tendency to rely heavily upon antibacterial soaps, antibiotics, food pasteurization, and other forms of cleansing. These products and practices tend to kill the good bacteria along with the bad, but you can boost your baby's immunity through nutrition, and with the consumption of probiotic-rich foods.

Your baby is first introduced to beneficial bacteria and probiotics through the birth canal and breast milk. These are powerful sources that naturally help build his initial immunity against disease and infection. However, if he was been born via a Caesarean section or is not breast-fed, then fermented foods and probiotic booster can help build his immunity. They can also protect your baby from infection, support healing from illness, empower him to heal diseases, aid in digesting his food, and help remove toxins from his body.

Build Immunity

The live cultures found in fermented foods increase the disease-fighting antibodies in your baby's immune system; they line the small intestine to ward off harmful pathogens. Some fermented foods create antioxidants that fight against free radicals in his body, and they aid in the absorption of beneficial nutrients that build immunity. In *The Art of Fermentation*, author Sandor Katz says that probiotics have been linked to treating and preventing diseases of the digestive tract and reducing the incidence and duration of upper respiratory symptoms. Given the proven beneficial effects of probiotics on the immune system and in fighting off infections, researchers are currently studying the effects of probiotics on these health issues common to children, including digestive and respiratory health, colic, and eczema.

Support Healing

Beneficial bacteria are primary agents that support the natural propensity of your baby's body to heal itself and regulate its many functions. By replenishing his gut's healthy microflora, probiotics foster an environment that wards off invasive pathogens, like parasites, fungi, and diarrhea-causing bacteria; and they strengthen his gut to resist the effects of exposure to bacteria-contaminated food. Fermented foods and probiotics can strengthen a system that has been weakened by antibiotics, stress, processed foods, and refined sugars. Probiotics, from either powder or fermented food sources, can also help prevent or relieve diarrhea that can come from taking antibiotics, by restoring the balance of healthy flora in the gut.

The bacteria provided by probiotics can help treat symptoms of gluten intolerance, irritable bowel syndrome, and diarrhea associated with antibiotics, yeast infections, and asthma. Eating fermented foods can also reduce cravings for sweets. Donna Gates, author of *The Body Ecology Diet*, says that the healthy microflora in fermented foods feed on prebiotics, or sugars, which thereby can reduce the negative effects of sugar on the body.

Aid Digestion

Fermentation is an active process of breaking down and metabolizing organic compounds by active enzymes, such as yeast or bacteria. Friendly bacteria that aid fermentation help to predigest food, breaking down some of the compounds that are more difficult to digest. This is why people who are lactose intolerant can eat fermented dairy foods—because the lactose has been transformed, or cultured, into a more digestible food. Fermented cheeses, yogurt, and kefir all have live cultures that break down the lactose in milk. Similarly, fermentation breaks down phytic acid, which binds to certain minerals in grains, making them harder to absorb. For example, by eating sauerkraut with brown rice, you can increase the bioavailability of calcium, iron, magnesium, and zinc that might not otherwise be absorbed. Although soybeans are a source of protein, they can be hard to digest. Fermentation and production of foods like miso and tempeh facilitate their digestibility. Finally, fermented foods replenish the gut with beneficial bacteria and acids that continue to strengthen the digestive system.

What Are Prebiotics?

Prebiotics are nutrients that contain a non-digestible food ingredient that stimulates the growth and activity of probiotics. When bacteria reach the large intestine, prebiotics stimulate the growth of beneficial bacteria. Unlike probiotics, prebiotics target the microorganisms already present within the ecosystem, acting as "food" for the target microbes.

Prebiotics occur naturally in breast milk, whole grains, asparagus, artichokes, leeks, garlic, onions, legumes, and fruits. Prebiotic compounds are added to many foods, including yogurts, cereals, breads, nutritional supplement bars, drinks, water, and some infant formula.

The international scientific community, including organizations, such as the Food and Agriculture Organization of the World Health Organization and the International Life Sciences Institute, continue to research prebiotics, and their use as food ingredients or supplements is gaining momentum.

 For more about prebiotics visit growhealthygrowhappy.com

Fermented Food Considerations

The physical conditions that microbes live in can make a difference in their growth and survival. Consider these factors when making your own fermented foods or buying packaged yogurt, pickles, or probiotic boosters.

Temperature

Temperature affects the survival of probiotics. High heat of 113° to 131°F in shipping, storage, or pasteurization can kill the bacteria. Low temperatures or freeze-drying during processing and storage help keep probiotic organisms stable, because colder temperatures hold less moisture and keep the organisms in an inert state. Refrigeration inhibits the growth of organisms in fermented foods and probiotics, and exposure to warmth and moisture activates the organisms. Thawing and refreezing can damage cell membranes and be detrimental to probiotic survival, but once frozen, yogurt and other fermented foods can survive frozen for a long shelf life.

Detoxification

The fermentation process also removes toxins from food and acts as an antioxidant, detecting and destroying "free radicals," which are the precursors to cancer cells. Fermented foods that contain healthy bacteria, such as *Lactobacillus*, compete with diarrhea-related bacteria, including *Salmonella* and *E.-coli*.

Although probiotics and fermented foods have many benefits, they should not be considered a "cure-all" for every illness. Probiotics' infection-fighting effects are temporary because they do not build up in your child's gastrointestinal system. "Once you stop taking any probiotic, whether it is in food or medicinal form, it disappears from the GI tract and the microflora levels return to what they were," says Frank R. Greer, MD, professor of pediatrics at the University of Wisconsin, Madison, and a coauthor of the American Academy of Pediatrics' (AAP) report on probiotics. Therefore, making fermented foods an ongoing part of your child's daily diet helps him build and maintain his immunity.

Water

Water and temperature interact and affect the survival level of the probiotic bacteria. As temperature increases, the impact of moisture is magnified. The higher the moisture levels and water activity, the lower the survival of probiotics. If the product is dried, the bacteria viability can be maintained for 12 months or more in unrefrigerated storage. Chlorine in water can kill the bacteria, so use filtered, boiled, or spring water in processing fermented foods.

Oxygen

Oxygen can be detrimental to the survival and growth of most probiotic bacteria. Fermentation occurs best without oxygen, so that beneficial organisms can establish a strong colony. If oxygen is present, the fermentation process will be interrupted and ruined. Some fermentation methods use an airlock to create a water barrier; others use modified-atmosphere packaging. When making pickles, covering the vegetables or fruits with brine helps reduce the contact of the pickle with oxygen to prevent spoilage.

Bacteria, Yeasts, and Molds

There are three types of organisms that can start the fermentation process: bacteria, yeasts, and molds.

Bacteria are single-celled microorganisms with a cell wall, but no nucleus. They consume starches and sugars in food. They serve as the basis for both fermentation and infectious diseases. They can live in almost any type of environment—in soil, acidic hot springs, radioactive waste, seawater, deep in Earth's crust, in the stratosphere, and in the bodies of other organisms. There are both beneficial and harmful bacteria in the human body.

Yeasts are single-celled fungi, which reproduce asexually by budding or dividing. Yeasts are in nature—in the air, soil, and in the intestinal tract of warm-blooded mammals. Like bacteria, yeasts can have beneficial and harmful effects in foods and in the body. Mushrooms and sourdough starter are beneficial fungi; thrush, a yeast infection of the mouth and throat, are harmful fungi.

Molds are multicelled fungi, and they grow in moist environments by multiplying spores. The spores of molds can be on many surfaces and will grow with the appropriate moisture content, nutrients, and temperature. Certain molds can have toxic effects when inhaled or ingested. Beneficial molds are used in food production and make enzymes that break down starches and make them more absorbable.

pH Level

All bacteria require a certain pH level to survive, which can vary widely according to the bacteria, says Trudy Wassenaar of Argonne National Laboratory. Extreme changes in the pH balance of the local environment

for bacteria tend to kill the bacteria. Bacteria cannot abide in extreme pH environments. They have a hard time growing in highly acidic fruits or very alkaline vegetables. Meats have a neutral pH and are more likely to develop illness-causing bacteria, so they need more restrictions in food preparation requirements. Raising the pH level may kill certain bacteria, but new bacteria may grow in a new pH environment. Whey, lemon juice, and vinegar are easy ways to increase acidity.

Nonreactive Materials

In preparing fermented foods, acids are produced during the process that can react with the material that they contact. Reactive materials include: aluminum, brass, copper, iron, zinc, and some plastics. Nonreactive materials include: aluminum, enamelled cast iron or steel, food-grade plastic, glass, nylon, and stainless steel. If using plastic, make sure that it is BPA-free, and that it does not break down easily.

Salt

Putting salt on vegetables or fruit, draws out the moisture from the food and creates a natural brine that begins the development of the *Lactobacillus* bacteria while curbing the growth of harmful bacteria. This works as a natural preservative and contributes flavor. You can also submerge the food in a brine made of saltwater that is nonchlorinated. Sometimes you may need a combination of dry-salting and brining if the food does not have enough moisture to make enough brine to cover the food.

Fermentation Methods

Fermented foods are the opposite of most commercially processed foods because fermentation increases a food's natural nutrient and enzyme content, whereas most commercially processed foods strip the nutrients from the whole food. As they transform the food, the microbial cultures found in fermented foods increase the nutritional value by creating B vitamins, including thiamin, riboflavin, niacin, biotin, and folic acid, as well as vitamin K. Miso is an example of soybeans that are transformed through fermentation. In the fermentation process the miso increases protein content and its digestibility so that it is easy for your baby's body to absorb.

The fermentation process also preserves food by making it resistant to microbial spoilage and the development of toxins. Kefir and yogurt last longer than milk does; sauerkraut and pickles will stay fresh for months. It makes sense to turn summer vegetables into pickles to store for the winter. Fermentation can occur naturally from bacteria, yeasts, and molds in the environment, or by introducing a starter to a food. Both forms of fermentation take one of two forms: alcohol or lactic acid fermentation. In both cases, the environment becomes too acidic for harmful bacteria to thrive.

Alcohol

Alcohol fermentation converts grains or fruits into alcoholic beverages, such as beer, wine, and *sake* (Japanese rice wine). Yeasts convert the sugars–glucose, fructose, or sucrose–into alcohol anaerobically, or without oxygen. Acetic acid fermentation occurs when alcohol is exposed to oxygen. In acetic acid fermentation, bacteria convert starchy, sugary, or alcoholic substances into acetic acid. Apple cider, balsamic, rice, and red wine vinegars are examples.

Lactic Acid

Lactic acid fermentation is the process of fermenting foods in which yeasts and bacteria convert sugars and starches into lactic acid. This is a more nutritious method of food fermentation than the other two methods. Lactic acid is not derived from milk, as the name might suggest, but is formed from the breakdown of glucose and is present in every form of organized life. Lactic acid comes from *Lactobacilli* bacterial organisms that produce this acid. Lactic acid improves digestion, blood circulation, and the function of the pancreas. Three ways of taking lactic acid into the system are through lacto-fermented foods, probiotic booster, and a topical application on the skin.

Types of Fermented Foods

There are many different ways to give your child probiotics, ranging from fermented foods, such as pickles and miso, to probiotic booster. Making your own fermented foods is easy and inexpensive, and you do not need expensive equipment or supplies. Homemade fermented dishes have a distinctive tangy flavor. The more types of fermented foods you introduce to your child, the greater diversity of flora he will develop, which offers him diverse health benefits. The combination of both eating fermented foods and using probiotic booster is most effective in creating a healthy gut.

When making or purchasing fermented foods, keep in mind that their true value lies in their live cultures. Avoid the word "pasteurized" which means the food was heated to the point at which microorganisms die (115°F). Many brands of yogurt now say "contains live cultures," and have high probiotic value. You can either purchase fermented foods that are unpasteurized, or make them yourself. In his book, *The Art of Fermentation*, author Sandor Katz debunks the myth that botulism poisoning comes from homemade pickles. *C.botulinum* spores persist when canning techniques (home or industrial) have not heated the foods to a high enough heat, for a long enough time to destroy them. Fermenting live cultures does not harbor botulism. Following are different types of fermented foods and probiotics that you can offer your baby, as well as their preparation methods.

Sprouted Grains and Beans

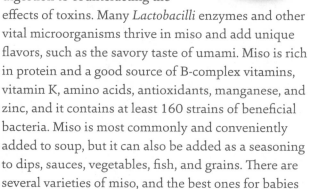

Whole grains and beans contain phytic acid, a compound that can block the absorption of calcium, iron, magnesium, zinc, and other minerals, which can result in mineral deficiency. Soaking or sprouting grains and beans before cooking is a mild fermentation process that neutralizes phytic acid, breaks down complex sugars, and increases the mineral absorption rate of the grain. You can soak oats, rice, millet, quinoa, and barley in water for 8 to 24 hours prior to cooking. This process ferments the grain, makes it easier to digest, and allows its full range of nutrients to come through. Soaking grains and beans for a longer time can make them sprout, which further decreases phytic acid and produces vitamin C.

Sweet Potato Mash

Sweet potato mash is made from a baked sweet potato that is slightly fermented with a small amount of yogurt or kefir for 48 hours. Sweet potato mash is a low-salt fermented first food that is easy and delicious for your baby to eat.

Miso

Miso has a number of health benefits, ranging from aiding digestion to counteracting the effects of toxins. Many *Lactobacilli* enzymes and other vital microorganisms thrive in miso and add unique flavors, such as the savory taste of umami. Miso is rich in protein and a good source of B-complex vitamins, vitamin K, amino acids, antioxidants, manganese, and zinc, and it contains at least 160 strains of beneficial bacteria. Miso is most commonly and conveniently added to soup, but it can also be added as a seasoning to dips, sauces, vegetables, fish, and grains. There are several varieties of miso, and the best ones for babies are low in sodium and usually fermented for one year or less, such as sweet white miso.

Plum Vinegar

Plum vinegar is the brine created through the fermentation of pickled *umeboshi* plums. It adds a healthy seasoning to soft rice, pasta, steamed vegetables, and salads. Plum vinegar is not a true vinegar, because it contains salt, and it has a unique flavor that is fruity, salty, and sour. This plum juice helps neutralize an acidic condition, and it has many of the medicinal properties of the pickled plum, in a more diluted form. Because it is salty, use it sparingly when you give it to your baby or toddler. I discovered plum vinegar when I was pregnant, and the alkaline-producing effect and sour taste helped settle my morning sickness nausea. To this day, I enjoy the taste of plum vinegar.

Tamari and Soy Sauce

These salty, sweet, and slightly tart fermented seasonings are made from soybeans, salt, and water. Making tamari also includes the liquid that rises to the surface during the production of miso. Traditionally made soy sauce is brewed for more than a year, and is different than the soy sauce that is chemically brewed in a 24-hour process. Soy sauce is made with a wheat *koji* (yeast) as a starter, and tamari is made without wheat, and is therefore generally free of gluten. Amino acids are released from the breakdown of proteins, imparting an umami flavor. Unpasteurized soy sauce retains the living enzymes and *Lactobacillus* that offer a probiotic benefit. Tamari and soy sauce impart a savory flavor in soups, vegetables, beans, and other protein-rich foods.

Pickles

You can ferment pickles with a small amount of sea salt, or by adding wakame and kombu sea vegetables. Fermenting with salt or with the sodium in sea vegetables can kill harmful bacteria and help grow beneficial bacteria. Starter cultures such as whey, kefir, and kefir grains can be added to speed up the fermentation process. Many vegetables make delicious pickles: beans, carrots, cabbage, cauliflower, cucumbers, greens, onions, and squash. Fruits, such as apples, berries, pears, and dried fruits create sweeter pickles for your baby or toddler. Using vinegar is not recommended, because it can weaken or kill the beneficial bacteria in naturally fermented pickles. If you buy pickles instead of making them, look for pickles that are naturally fermented without sugar or vinegar.

Water Kefir

Water kefir is made from *tibicos* (water kefir grains), a culture of bacteria or yeast that can be used as a starter and combined with sweetener, dried fruit, citrus fruit, and filtered water to make a beverage. Kefir grains feed off the sugar to produce lactic acid, alcohol, and gas, which slightly carbonates the drink. Each culture creates a unique set of microbes and provides a probiotic drink that is dairy-free. Chlorine in tap water or sulfites in dried fruit will inhibit the fermentation. Your first batch of kefir grains cannot be made like a sourdough bread starter; you will need to purchase them online, from a natural foods store, or get them from a friend's existing kefir culture. Kefir grains can also be used as a starter for pickles.

Yogurt, Dairy Kefir, and Whey

Yogurt, a traditional food from southeastern Europe, Turkey, and the Middle East, is the most popular fermented food in the world. In the past, it was most often eaten as a savory dish. Today in the United States, it is usually sweetened with fruits or sugar. Yogurt is made from live *Lactobacillus* cultures added to milk to start the production of lactic acid and fermentation. Look for yogurt brands that are made from organic whole milk, do not contain sugar, are unpasteurized, and contain "live, active cultures." Take note of the expiration date, because the probiotic potency can diminish with time.

Dairy kefir is a beverage from Eastern Europe that can be made from any type of milk: cow, goat, rice, almond, coconut, or soy. It starts with "grains," or colonies of bacteria and yeasts, that are added to the milk, starting a live culture that begins fermentation. While it does create mucus, the mucus coats the digestive tract and protects the beneficial bacteria on the way down to the intestines, where they then colonize. Kefir has the consistency of liquid yogurt and a taste that is slightly sour. There are many varieties available with added flavor, but they usually have sugar. You can add natural flavor, such as cooked blueberry, strawberry, or raspberry, along with rice syrup. Look for organic unsweetened whole milk kefir, if possible.

Usually, those who are lactose intolerant can drink kefir because the beneficial microorganisms in the kefir culture consume most of the lactose, or milk sugar. If you decide to include cultured dairy in your child's diet, I recommend using products made with whole milk. Children up to three years old can benefit from the nutritional value of whole milk, and the *Lactobacillus* will aid in the digestion. Introduce the beverage gradually, and observe how your child's body reacts.

Whey is the thin liquid that separates from the solids in milk, yogurt, or kefir. If you hang yogurt or kefir in cheesecloth over a bowl, the liquid that drips out is whey. The curds of yogurt or kefir may separate easily when left at room temperature for a few hours, and you can easily pour off the whey. This is rich in vital bacterial cultures, and it can be used as a starter or to speed up the process of fermenting foods, such as pickles and sweet potato mash. You can also add whey to the liquid used in soaking whole grains before cooking them.

Umeboshi Plums

Umeboshi plums are made by fermenting apricot-like plums with sea salt and red *shiso* (beefsteak or Perilla) leaves. These plums are traditionally considered to be a digestive aid because they increase the production of digestive enzymes in the body and reduce excessive stomach acid. They strengthen the body's resistance to coughs, flu, colds, fevers, and sore throats due to their potent antibacterial properties, and they also can act as a natural antibiotic. *Umeboshi* are good for many ailments, because they help neutralize acidity in the body. The red *shiso* leaves are rich in vitamins E and K, iron, and zinc. They are added as a natural preservative and to give a pink color to foods. Because of the salt content, *umeboshi* plums can help preserve the rice inside rice balls. You can add small amounts of the pickled plums in rice balls for toddlers, or use them medicinally in

remedies. They are very salty and should be used sparingly, after your child is one year old. You may want to soak the pickled plums before using to remove some of the salt.

Tempeh

Tempeh is a traditional Indonesian food that is made by pounding, cooking, and then fermenting soybeans with an active culture. Tempeh that is sold in vacuum-sealed packaging is usually pasteurized to kill harmful bacteria, but it also kills beneficial bacteria. Fresh or fresh-frozen tempeh has usually not been pasteurized. Tempeh is an easily assimilated protein-rich food, an energy-building food, and a great source of B vitamins, magnesium, copper, iron, omega-3 fatty acids, and monounsaturated fats. Tempeh produces a natural antibiotic that supports immune system functions. It is healthier and more versatile than tofu, and it can be cooked in a variety of ways. Vegetarian burgers, kabobs, and sandwiches made from tempeh are a fun way to introduce children to fermented foods. Tempeh does not have a strong taste of its own, so it needs marinating or added seasoning, such as soy sauce or miso, to give it a flavor. Make sure tempeh is cooked at a low heat for at least 20 minutes, to cook the soybeans thoroughly, and to soften and moisten it for easy chewing and digestion. Steaming can open up the outer layer, which easily absorbs seasonings.

Sourdough

Sourdough is the way that bread was traditionally made, before baker's yeast was widely available. Sourdough is a natural process that combines wild yeast and *Lactobacilli* to partially digest the grains and make the bread rise. Commercial baking yeast ferments sugars present in the flour and gives off carbon dioxide and ethanol, which causes the dough to rise. Baker's yeast cannot survive in an acidic environment, but sourdough can. Sourdough bread is made with a starter by mixing flour and water together and allowing it to ferment. You must feed the starter every day with flour and water, and then you can refrigerate it for several months. You can use the starter for making pancakes or for baking breads, muffins, scones, and other baked goods.

Cheeses

Cheeses can be made from a variety of fermentation processes. Soft-ripened cheeses such as cottage cheese, farmer's cheese, and crème fraîche are examples of fermented cheeses made with bacteria as part of the fermentation process. Unpasteurized versions of these soft cheeses keep their living probiotic microbes. The longer a cheese is aged, the fewer bacteria remain alive. The exception is aged cheese made from raw or unpasteurized milk, which typically keeps probiotic bacteria alive for longer.

Probiotic Booster

Probiotic booster for children and infants is available in capsule, powdered, and liquid form. Because probiotics are considered food supplements, they are not regulated by the U.S. Food and Drug Administration (FDA). However, the FDA has released a short list of guidelines for manufacturers. Probiotic booster can cause gas at the beginning of treatment, until the body achieves balance with the new bacteria, but otherwise, it has almost no side effects.

When purchasing probiotics for your baby, check the labels for the benefits, when to use, the bacterial strain, the colony forming units (CFUs, a measure of the viable cells that can grow inside the body), proper storage conditions, and serving size. Make sure the booster is nondairy, gluten-free, wheat-free, corn-free, soy-free, and non-GMO. Also check to see that it is acid and bile resistant, so that the microbes can survive when they pass through the stomach. Probiotic booster should be stored in a cool place and in an opaque jar or container. Refrigeration will extend the life and potency of the microbes. Contact the product manufacturer for advice and dosage instructions, if you have questions, and communicate with your health care provider about your baby's diet.

Questions about Probiotics

Q: Are there harmful effects of probiotics?

A: The American Academy of Pediatrics says that healthy, full-term babies do not appear to have ill effects from high doses of probiotics. However, you may need to stop the dosage during acute illness.

Q: How do probiotics help my child when he takes an antibiotic?

A: Antibiotics kill the "good bacteria," as well as the "bad bacteria." Giving probiotic booster to your child after he takes an antibiotic can help replenish his healthy microbes. If possible, give probiotics at different times and in between doses of antibiotics to give the bacteria in probiotics a chance to survive. Continue the use of probiotics for at least one to four weeks after the cessation of antibiotic administration.

Q: Which are the best strains of probiotics for my child to take?

A: *Lactobacillus* and *Bifidobacterium* strains aid in maintaining healthy intestinal flora. It is best to have at least two strains.

Q: At what age can my child take probiotics?

A: If you are breast-feeding, your milk has natural probiotics right from the start, which you can increase by eating fermented foods and by taking probiotic booster yourself. For your baby's first year, he is developing his individual colony of bacteria that is unique to him, and after one year old, his flora can only be changed temporarily. You can support the development of your child's basic colony for his first year and the maintenance of it thereafter. At around six months, when he is starting to eat solid foods, you can add probiotic booster to his puree to help build his immunity and to prevent sickness. Before six months old, if he did not pass through the birth canal, or if he is taking formula, you may consider a formula that has added probiotics.

Q: How much probiotic booster should I give my child?

A: You can give your child 5 billion CFUs every day from six months to three years of age.

Probiotic Snacks and Drinks

Many probiotic snacks and drinks are now available in the form of granola bars, chocolate, pizza, kombucha, and water kefir. Often these items have refined sugar, so check the labels for ingredients before giving them to your child.

Vinegars

Vinegar is produced when a sugar-containing liquid ferments through the acetic acid bacteria fermentation method where alcohol (ethanol) is exposed to oxygen. Traditionally, local sweet liquids were made into vinegar—grapes into balsamic vinegar, apples into apple cider vinegar, and rice into rice vinegar. Unlike modern vinegar, traditional vinegar is not pasteurized. Therefore, many traditional vinegars have health, as well as medicinal benefits. When shopping for vinegar, look for "unfiltered," "unpasteurized," "traditionally fermented," or "aged in wood." Vinegar is sensitive to heat and utensils made of reactive materials. Because it is sour, babies are usually not interested in the vinegar taste for their first one or two years. Used sparingly, it can help break up excess fats in food and congestion in the body.

The Yin and Yang of Fermented Foods 🏠

Finding fermented foods that do not have high sodium content can be challenging in feeding your baby. The fermented foods in this chart aid in digestion and nourish intestinal bacteria. They have varying amounts of sodium. Time, salt, cooking, and pressure are yang influences used in food processing. Some other determinants are the amount of liquid and the texture of the food. Because of the many variables, many foods have both yin and yang influences. Yogurt may have been fermented for a less than a day; while miso and cheese may have been fermented for one to two years.

On the yin side are the soft dairy products, such as kefir and yogurt, which are salt-free. Tempeh is more solid, with minimal sodium, but usually it is seasoned with a salty ingredient when cooked. The amount of salt and time used in the fermentation process influences

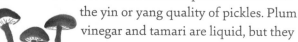

the yin or yang quality of pickles. Plum vinegar and tamari are liquid, but they

Yin-Yang Spectrum of Fermented Foods

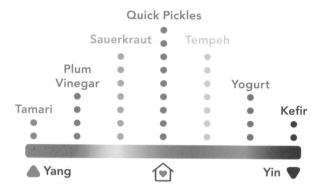

have high sodium content. Miso is more of a thick paste and is available in a range of flavors, with varying sodium contents. Listed in the chart above are balanced foods toward the center for daily use and foods on a wider spectrum for occasional use.

Fermented Foods for Your Baby

If your baby had a vaginal birth, he should start receiving the benefits of probiotics immediately because they are present in the birth canal. Breast milk also contains probiotics to help him develop his immune system. Colostrum, the first form of breast milk, is composed of 40 percent probiotics. If your baby did not have a vaginal birth, is not nursing, or if you had antibiotics during birth, you can offer him probiotic booster under the guidance of your health care provider. If you are nursing, you can take a probiotic booster and eat fermented foods to increase you and your baby's immunity.

It may be challenging to find fermented foods for your baby before he is one year old. Many of these foods are salty—such as miso, tamari, *umeboshi* plums, and fermented pickles—or are made with dairy products, such as yogurt and kefir. I have developed some recipes for fermented foods for babies and toddlers that are dairy-free and low in sodium.

If your child is experiencing digestive issues, fermented foods can help him get back on track with a stronger community of intestinal flora. If your child has to take antibiotics or stay in the hospital, he can benefit from eating naturally fermented foods and taking probiotic booster. These are also helpful for traveling or while at, when he may be exposed to a variety of new pathogens. Your baby can start eating some fermented foods between six and eight months. At six months, you can soak his grains for porridge to achieve a slight fermentation. He can try a small amount of sweet potato mash, and you can put probiotic booster in his grain or vegetable purees. At around seven months, he can enjoy pureed soups or vegetable broths with a very small amount of miso or tamari mixed in, and pickles or pickle juice can be added to a meal, as a digestive aid. These foods have salt, but the sodium is not as concentrated as when using straight salt. However, take care to use very little salt at this age. Water kefir, yogurt, or kefir can be introduced at around nine months. Offer tempeh

sandwiches, stews, or casseroles at around one year old, and you can continue to integrate fermented foods into his diet during cooking and with condiments, such as pickles, tamari, miso, and plum vinegar.

As your child grows and changes his diet, his gut flora also changes. By the age of two or three years old, most children have a fairly stable intestinal balance. At that time, your child's immune system has also matured considerably. The first two to three years are an opportunity to help him develop a strong colony of microbes to help build his immunity.

The chart below gives an overview of which fermented or probiotic foods to start feeding baby and when. The chart also includes how frequently to feed these foods.

When to Introduce Fermented Foods

Fermented Foods	Age Range	Frequency
 Sprouting grains	6 to 8 months	Daily
 Sweet potato mash	6 to 8 months	Occasionally
 Probiotic booster	6 to 12 months	Daily
 Miso • low sodium	7 to 9 months	Daily
Plum vinegar	7 to 9 months	Daily
 Tamari • low sodium	7 to 9 months	Daily
 Pickles • no sodium	7 to 9 months	Daily
 Water kefir	7 to 9 months	Occasionally
 Yogurt or dairy kefir • optional	9 to 12 months	Occasionally
 Tempeh	12 to 18 months	Occasionally
 *Umeboshi* plums	12 to 18 months	Occasionally
 Sourdough bread	12 to 18 months	Occasionally
 Cheese	12 to 18 months	Occasionally
 Probiotic snacks	12 to 18 months	Occasionally

Occasionally: 2–3 times a week

Miso or Tamari Soup

♡ 7 months+

🥄 8 (2-ounce) servings

V Vegetarian

GF Gluten-free

Miso or tamari soup is very calming and settling for the stomach and soul. The *Lactobacillus* has many properties to aid digestion and neutralize an acidic condition. Because of miso and tamari's high sodium content, start with a small amount, and increase the amount gradually, as your child grows.

1-inch square kombu sea vegetable or 1 teaspoon wakame flakes

3 cups water

1 cup diced vegetables

½ teaspoon miso or tamari for 7–12 months, 1 teaspoon for 12–18 months, 2 teaspoons for 18 months+

1 tablespoon water for mixing miso

Options:

Onions, carrots, yellow squash, zucchini, broccoli, cabbage, bok choy, kale, beets, string beans

Method

1. Boil sea vegetable in water for 5 minutes.

2. Add vegetables and cook for 20 to 25 minutes.

3. Mix miso paste in 1 tablespoon water in a small dish, until it has a smooth consistency, and add to soup. To retain the *Lactobacillus* in miso, do not boil soup after miso has been added.

4. For 7 to 9 months, strain or puree together with vegetables, for 9 months+ leave in small pieces of vegetables according to your baby's chewing ability.

5. Serve warm.

Variations

- Add ¼ teaspoon minced fresh or dried herbs while cooking, such as fennel, bay, basil, thyme, dill, cilantro, or parsley.

- Add tiny strips of nori sea vegetable as a garnish, making sure that the nori is moist, so that it is easy to swallow.

- Add cubes of tofu while cooking, and cook for at least 5 minutes.

Sweet Potato Mash

♡ 7 months+

🥄 8 (2 ounce) servings

V Vegetarian

GF Gluten-free

The small amount of *Lactobacillus* in unpasteurized yogurt acts as a starter to make a very low-sodium fermented food, without the negative effects of dairy. There should be a slightly fermented, tangy taste.

3 cups cooked sweet potatoes
(1–2 raw potatoes)

⅛ teaspoon sea salt for
6–12 months, ¼ teaspoon for
12–24 months, 1 teaspoon for
2 years+

1 tablespoon plain, unsweetened,
unpasteurized yogurt

Method

1. Preheat oven to 400°F.

2. Bake whole sweet potatoes for 1 hour.

3. Peel and mash cooked sweet potatoes with a fork.

4. Add salt and yogurt.

5. Spread the vegetable puree in a glass or ceramic container.

6. Fill a strong plastic bag with water and zip or tie with a knot. Make sure the seal is secure, and place over the sweet potato puree. The water-filled bag should spread out and cover the puree to prevent air contact.

7. Place a lid over puree with weight.

8. Leave in a warm place for 48 hours and taste.

9. Refrigerate to keep fresh.

Pickles with Sea Vegetables

♡ 7 months+

🥄 16 (1 ounce) servings

V Vegetarian

GF Gluten-free

This recipe is helpful for babies and toddlers because of its important probiotic qualities. The wakame provides minerals and the minimal amount of salt that is needed for the pickling process. The enzymes in naturally fermented pickles help secrete digestive juices, destroy pathogenic bacteria, and boost the growth of useful bacteria, such as *Lactobacillus bifidus*.

½ teaspoon sea salt

1 tablespoon wakame flakes, soaked in 2 tablespoons water for 10 minutes

2 cups vegetables, cut into thin slices

1 tablespoon plain, unsweetened, unpasteurized yogurt or whey

Water to cover vegetables

Options:

Cabbage, carrots, yellow squash, purple cabbage, cucumbers, zucchini, beets

Method

1. Add salt to wakame and soaking water in a glass measuring cup or bowl. Mix in yogurt or whey.

2. Put vegetables into a ceramic or glass bowl, or pickle crock.

3. Pour liquid mixture over vegetables and mix together.

4. Put a plate on top of the vegetables. Add a weight on top of the plate. A clean jar of water or beans can provide the pressure necessary to squeeze the liquid out of the vegetables.

5. Press the plate down onto the vegetables, and cover with a cotton towel.

6. After one day, if there is not enough liquid from the vegetables to cover them, add water to prevent air from contacting vegetables.

7. Place bowl in a warm, dark place for 3 to 4 days, depending on the weather.

8. Take off cover and weight. Press vegetables with your hand to squeeze out the liquid to make brine.

9. Pour the pickled vegetables and brine into two 8-ounce or one 16-ounce wide-mouth jar. Store in the refrigerator for up to 2 weeks.

10. Pour some of the juice onto your baby's grains, vegetables, or beans, or offer pureed or whole pickled vegetable for a side dish.

Fruit Pickles

♡ 9 months+

🥄 16 (1-ounce) servings

V Vegetarian

GF Gluten-free

This recipe is similar to the vegetable pickles, but made with fruit for an unusual taste and for probiotic qualities. Again, a minimal amount of salt is used for the pickling process. Fermented pickles help your child build his immunity naturally.

½ teaspoon sea salt

1 tablespoon plain, unsweetened, unpasteurized yogurt or whey

1 tablespoon water to mix with yogurt

2 cups fruit, cut into thin slices

Water to cover fruit

Options:

Apples, pears, plums, peaches, blueberries, strawberries, raspberries, mangos

Method

1. Mix salt, yogurt, and water in a small bowl.

2. Put fruit into a ceramic or glass bowl, pickle crock, or jar.

3. Pour yogurt, salt, and water mixture over fruit. Press down fruit with your hands. If using a bowl or pickle crock, transfer mixture to a jar.

4. Cover with cotton towel or jar lid.

5. Place container in a warm, dark place for 2 to 3 days, depending on the weather.

6. Add water until the liquid is above the level of the fruit, to prevent air from contacting fruit.

7. Store in the refrigerator for up to 2 weeks.

8. Pour some of the juice onto your baby's grains, vegetables, or beans, or puree the pickles for a side dish.

Water Kefir

♡ 6 months+

🥄 32 ounces

V Vegetarian

GF Gluten-free

This simple drink has many probiotic qualities that promote a healthy immune system, without dairy or salt. It is made with sweetener, but the beneficial bacteria metabolize the sugars, and the drink does not have the negative effects of a sugared drink. Water kefir has a wide variety of more than forty different bacteria and yeast, while the average supplement has only ten.

Water kefir starter is not the same as milk kefir starter. It is a white "grain" that resembles small chunks of gelatin and must be either purchased or shared by a friend when you make your first batch. The grains will grow, and they can then be saved and used indefinitely for repeated batches. The starter can be stored in the refrigerator for up to two weeks between batches.

4 cups water, boiled and cooled

¼ cup maple syrup, brown rice syrup, or organic sugar

½ lemon, cut cross-wise

1 tablespoon unsulfured raisins

1-inch square kombu or 1 teaspoon wakame flakes sea vegetable, or ⅛ teaspoon sea salt

¼ cup water kefir starter grains

Method

1. Pour into a large glass or ceramic container, such as a quart glass jar with a screw-on lid.

2. Mix in sweetener, lemon, raisins, and sea vegetable. Slowly add kefir grains.

3. Make sure that there are at least 2 to 3 inches of space between the kefir mixture and the rim of the glass container.

4. Cover the container with a loosely woven cotton cloth, using a rubber band to keep the cloth on. Contact with oxygen aids the beginning of the fermentation process.

5. Keep out of sunlight, ideally at a temperature between 65° and 82°F for 24 to 72 hours. Seal the container with a lid, and place in the refrigerator for another 24 to 48 hours.

Factors for Preparing Water Kefir Successfully:

❀ Metal can react with the kefir culture, so use ceramic, glass, wood, silicone, or plastic utensils.

❀ Chlorine kills beneficial bacteria in tap water that are necessary for fermentation. Even filtered water can sometimes contain chlorine and fluoride, so boil and cool water before using.

❀ Because the minerals are distilled from filtered water, add either a piece of sea vegetable, an egg shell, or a small amount of sea salt to replace minerals.

❀ Fermentation causes expansion, so water kefir should not be covered with a tight lid, because the lid can burst.

❀ Water kefir needs sugar to activate the grains for fermentation. Maple syrup, brown rice syrup, and organic cane sugar are healthy options. Non-carbohydrate or artificial sweeteners will not ferment. Honey has antimicrobial properties that can affect the growth of kefir grains, so it is not recommended as a sweetener for fermentation.

6. Strain the grains through a nonmetal strainer, such as cheesecloth or a nylon strainer. Discard the lemon and fruit, reserving kefir grains for a new batch.

7. Transfer the strained mixture to bottles for drinking and refrigerate.

8. To increase carbonation for older children, store strained mixture in airtight bottles at room temperature for two days to allow carbonation before refrigerating.

9. Repeat the process with the grains to make a new batch of water kefir.

10. Water kefir grains starter is also available in dehydrated form, which requires time for rehydrating. For maintaining kefir grains in between batches, they need added sweetener every two or three days to prevent them from turning to vinegar. It may take a few batches to get the starter grains completely activated, and they will grow with repeated use.

Fats and Seasonings

In Kyoto, Japan, near Muso Yochien (Dream Window Kindergarten) there is a temple that serves *kaiseki* cooking, which is both a method of food preparation and an art form. *Kaiseki* cooking displays the taste, texture, color, and arrangement of food to create fresh, local dishes that reflect the natural world. I enjoyed lunch there several times and remember the sensory experience and calm satisfaction I felt after my meals. These lunches reminded me of the colorfully arranged baby food photos in Japanese mothering magazines. Even for a six-month-old baby, eating in Japan is a sensual experience that includes taste, sight, smell, and texture.

Your baby explores through his senses, and each time he uses these senses, a neural connection is made in his brain. At around six months old, he discovers an exciting new world of sensory stimulation through food. His senses are sensitive, so foods that may taste bland to you may offer new sensations for him. Whole, organic, and fresh foods have subtle flavors by themselves, and these flavors can be enhanced with natural seasonings, such as oils, sea salt, sweeteners, herbs, and spices. Initially, just the simple taste of whole, fresh food is stimulating and satisfying to him, but as he grows and develops, he can enjoy a variety of seasonings that offer more than sensory satisfaction. These seasonings provide nutritional value, create emotional responses, and can stimulate his brain growth.

Your baby gets all the nutrition he needs while breast-feeding or taking formula. When introducing him to solid foods, he will also need good-quality oils or fats, natural sweeteners, and a moderate amount of salt for healthy growth and development. Herbs and spices add flavor and zest to his food.

This chapter identifies healthy fats; takes a look at the importance of, and sources for, balanced salt intake; explores natural sweeteners; and suggests herbs for flavor, health, and healing. Here, you can discover ways to introduce these new flavors to help your child develop a palate with varied tastes.

Fats

Essential fatty acids (EFAs) are vital to the healthy function of your baby's immune and nervous systems and heart. Healthy fats help his body absorb vitamins, aid in hormone production, and insulate his nerves. They also create energy and are essential for the growth and development of his brain and body. Essential fatty acids refer to fats and oils that need to be included in your baby's diet, because his body must have them but cannot produce them.

The Power of Fats

Essential fatty acids regulate body functions, such as heart rate, blood pressure, blood clotting, fertility, conception, and immunity. They are particularly important for children in relation to their neural development and the maturation of their sensory systems. They also stimulate skin and hair growth, maintain bone health, and regulate metabolism. Omega-3 and omega-6 are two important EFAs that support many biological functions, such as the manufacture and repair of cell membranes and expulsion of harmful waste products. Omega-9 is not considered an EFA because the body can produce it, as long as omega-3 and omega-6 are present. A deficiency in EFAs can lead to slow growth in infants and children, susceptibility to infection, and slow healing of wounds.

Omega-3 fatty acids are found in flaxseeds, chia seeds, cod-liver oil, walnuts, freshly ground wheat germ, and salmon. Omega-6 fatty acids are found in a variety of oils, including sesame oil, safflower oil, and sunflower oil. Dried beans, such as Great Northern, kidney, navy, and soybeans, contain small amounts of both omega-3 and omega-6 fatty acids.

Healthy fats support your baby's physical, emotional, and mental growth and development. These fats supply essential nutrients through nature's most concentrated source of energy. They build the membranes around every cell in his body, they are critical for the development of the brain, and they play a role in the formation of hormones. Fats keep skin, joints, and blood vessels lubricated; they hold vital organs in place, providing insulation and warmth during temperature changes. Healthy

fats offer vitamin E, which is important in promoting blood flow, preventing clotting, and boosting your baby's immune system. Eating healthy fats also provides sustained energy and creates a soothing, satisfied feeling. Cooking with fats adds a depth of flavor to food.

Fat Considerations

Despite the many health benefits of fats, there is a difference between healthy and unhealthy sources of fat. Unhealthy fats can cause digestive problems, raise insulin levels, and decrease metabolism and the absorption of vitamins and minerals. They increase the body's "bad" cholesterol, or low-density lipoprotein (LDL), which builds up in arteries and blocks blood flow, and decrease the "good" cholesterol, or high-density lipoprotein (HDL), which helps maintain low LDL levels. Unhealthy fats raise triglycerides, as well, which can increase the risk of a stroke. The following is a list of the groups of good- and poor-quality fats and how they are identified.

Unsaturated fats are usually liquid at room temperature and are divided into two groups: polyunsaturated fats and monounsaturated fats. Polyunsaturated fats play a key role in brain development and growth, and they have a beneficial effect on health, when eaten in moderation. They include omega-3 and omega-6 fatty acids and can be found in a variety of vegetable oils, as well as fatty fish and some nuts. Monounsaturated fats, found in olive oil, avocados, and oily fish can lower bad cholesterol and support good cholesterol. They also support your baby's immune system and the reduction of insulin resistance.

Saturated fats are found primarily in animal-based foods, including meat, eggs, butter, and other dairy products. These fats are typically solid at room temperature, hard to digest, and high in cholesterol. Examples of these saturated fats include butter (usually made from cows' milk), lard (from pork), tallow (from beef), and schmaltz (from poultry). Some plant-based sources of saturated fats are palm oil and coconut oil, which are healthier and easier to digest than their animal-based counterparts.

Hydrogenated and partially hydrogenated oils (trans fats) are made by injecting hydrogen into liquid oil to make it stable and solid at room temperature. Hydrogenation prevents oil from becoming rancid and keeps it from separating into a solid and a liquid, the way that

natural peanut butter separates. Many manufacturers started using hydrogenated vegetable oil, because it is cheaper, and it offers appealing characteristics to commercially baked and processed foods, such as structure, texture, and flavor to baked goods. Hydrogenated fats are often used for frying fast foods and in restaurants because they can withstand high heat and last longer. These fats raise levels of bad cholesterol and lower levels of good cholesterol.

Labeling laws regarding trans fats have become stricter and more transparent, but they allow companies to label their food as being trans fat-free if they contains less than 0.5 grams of trans fat per serving. As a result, many manufacturers switched to refined oils, such as cottonseed and soy oils, which are not much healthier. Most producers that sell to natural food stores have replaced partially hydrogenated oils with higher quality oils, but check the labels to be sure. If a label states that it contains fully hydrogenated oil, then it should be trans fat-free; if a food contains partially hydrogenated oils, then it contains trans fats.

Trans Fats	
The Top 10 Foods Most Likely to Have Trans Fats	Tips for Monitoring Trans Fat Consumption
• Margarine, processed peanut butter, and other non-butter spreads • Packaged cakes, cookies, and baking mixes • Instant ramen noodles and soups • Fried fast food • Frozen food • Commercial baked goods • Chips and crackers • Breakfast cereal and energy bars • Cookies and candy • Toppings and dips	• Read labels, and choose foods made without hydrogenated oils. • Cook your own meals. • Avoid chain restaurants and fast food establishments. • Shop at a local bakery. • Buy nut butters that are freshly ground. • Use natural oils, such as olive oil and sesame oil. • Order fish or meat broiled or baked in a restaurant. • Pop your own popcorn.

Oxidation of oils

Oils oxidize and become rancid through a chemical reaction when they are exposed to air, light, and high heat. Consuming rancid oils can lead to digestive distress, the introduction of free radicals into the body, the depletion of vitamins B and E, and damage to DNA in cells. You know oil is becoming rancid by smelling or tasting it and looking at its color—if it is darker than normal, it may be turning rancid.

Each type of oil has a temperature at which it oxidizes and breaks down in both nutrition and flavor. This temperature is called its smoke point. At this point, a bluish smoke is produced that is irritating to the eyes and throat, and it can emit harmful fumes and free radicals. The smoke point of oils varies according to the type of oil and the degree to which it has been refined. Refining oil raises the smoke point, and lighter colored oils are usually more refined so they can be used for high-heat cooking like deep-frying.

The method of storing oils determines the speed at which it can go rancid. Store oils in an opaque container, because it deteriorates quicker when exposed to light. A glass, rather than plastic, container gives you the assurance that the plastic is not dissolving into the oil. Storing them near the stove for convenience shortens the life span of the oil due to exposure to the heat of the stove. High temperatures increase the speed of deterioration, so store oils in a cool, dark place.

Smoke Points of Unrefined Oils

Oil	Smoke Point
Almond oil	420°F
Butter	250–300°F
Coconut oil	350°F
Flaxseed oil	225°F
Olive oil	375°F
Sesame oil	350°F
Safflower oil	255°F
Sunflower oil	255°F

Types of Fats

Whether your baby eats his fats through your cooking, prepared foods, or from restaurants, the type of oils and fats he consumes every day impacts his physical and mental growth and development. Vegetable oils can be extracted by pressing the food, such as olives, or through the use of chemical solvents. Pressing maintains most of the flavor and nutrition, whereas extraction via high heat and chemical processing removes many of the nutrients. Degumming, bleaching, and deodorizing are other processes that increase the shelf life of refined oils, while simultaneously removing the fatty acids, smells, flavors, and colors. Unrefined vegetable oils provide more nutrition without negative side effects for daily use; however, refining vegetable oils increases their smoke point. Ghee and butter are options for quality fats that are made with animal fats.

Sesame oil

Sesame oil is made from pressed sesame seeds and comes in two varieties: light, which is made from raw seeds, and dark, which is made from toasted seeds. Dark sesame oil has a stronger flavor, so light sesame oil is better for babies. Sesame oil contains antioxidants, vitamin B6, vitamin E, calcium, copper, iron, and magnesium. It is very high in the plant-based essential fatty acid, linoleic acid, which helps prevent inflammation and chronic disease. Sesame oil has a soothing, healing quality, resists oxidation, and is more stable than other oils. It can be used in cooking on high heat. Sesame oil has traditionally been used in Japan and China for skin care and cosmetics. Because of healing properties, I used sesame oil on my babies' bottoms and for skin care, as well as in their food.

Extra virgin olive oil

Extra virgin olive oil is the purest and most natural form of olive oil. It comes from the first cold pressing of the olives, so it contains the highest amount of vitamin E and other antioxidants, and has extremely low acidity. The processing of olive oil does not require heat and is the only oil that can be truly cold-pressed, which is a chemical-free process using only pressure, and produces a higher quality of olive oil that is naturally lower in acidity. Virgin olive oil is equally nutritious and produced in the same way as extra virgin oil, but from lower grade olives; it has 0.5 percent higher acidity than extra virgin. You can cook with olive oil at low to medium heat or add it to raw or cooked foods.

Flaxseed oil

Flaxseed oil and ground flaxseed meal provide the highest concentration of omega-3 fatty acids next to fish. It has soluble fiber, protein, omega-6 and omega-9 EFAs, B vitamins, and minerals. Almost all of your baby's body systems benefit from flaxseed oil. It supports healing, builds immunity, increases energy and stamina, and protects against high blood pressure and inflammation. Flaxseed oil makes a healthy supplement, or you can give it to your baby medicinally for constipation. Add flaxseed oil to cooked or raw food, rather than cooking with it because it is expensive and should not be used at high heat, because it has a low smoke point.

Chia oil

Chia oil is made from chia seeds that are second to flaxseeds in their omega-3 content. Besides having a rich amount of these fats, chia seeds also have a healthy ratio of omega-3s to omega-6s. The seeds and oil are known for lubricating dryness, relieving constipation, reducing nervousness, treating insomnia, and improving mental focus.

Almond oil

Almond oil is a rich source of minerals and vitamins B and E; it also helps lower cholesterol. It has a high smoke point and can serve as a cooking oil, you can serve it raw on already prepared foods, or use it in baking. You can also use it on your baby's skin for a massage or as a moisturizer. However, if your baby has an allergy or intolerance to nuts, he may have a reaction to almond oil.

Coconut oil

Coconut oil is a healthy fat, despite its classification as a saturated fat. It contains lauric acid, which is found in breast milk, has antiviral qualities and supports brain function and the immune system. Lauric acid has been associated with increasing good (HDL) cholesterol. Coconut oil can be used in baking at temperatures up to 375°F without becoming destabilized. Like almond oil, coconut oil has high amounts of vitamin E and is good for nourishing the skin.

Safflower Oil

Safflower oil is extracted from the seeds of the safflower plant. There are two types of safflower oil; one is rich in monounsaturated fats (MUFA) and the other is rich in polyunsaturated fats (PUFA). Both types are used for cooking, but (MUFA) is more prevalent, because it has a higher smoke point and is ideal for deep-frying. Safflower oil contains omega-6 fatty acids, and has a high content of linolenic acid, vitamin E, and vitamin K.

Ghee

Ghee is clarified butter that looks like liquid gold, and is commonly used in Indian cooking. It has a healthy ratio of omega-3s to omega-6s. With a high saturated fat content, ghee does not oxidize easily, and it has a high smoke point. Some lactose-intolerant people can consume ghee because it is low in lactose. Ghee has a long shelf life and does not need refrigeration.

Butter

Butter is a saturated fat that contains vitamins A and D. Organic, cultured, unsalted butter is easier to digest than salted butter, and it does not contain coloring or milk from cows treated with growth hormones. Conventional butter may contain food coloring, but the FDA does not allow butter to have other preservatives or additives. Butter's lactose can cause allergic reactions in babies who are lactose intolerant. Therefore, it is recommended to wait until your baby is one year old to introduce butter.

Lard

Lard is pig fat that has been used as a shortening due to its high smoke point and its ability to produce flaky, moist pie crusts. To improve shelf stability, lard is often hydrogenated and treated with bleaching, deodorizing agents, emulsifiers, and antioxidants, such as butylated hydroxytoluene (BHT, or a chemical preservative). Many packaged baked snacks, including breakfast bars, cakes, and cookies contain lard as a shortening.

Canola oil

Canola oil is extracted from the rapeseed plant, which has been genetically modified for culinary purposes. A relatively new oil, canola was developed in Canada in the 1970s. Canola oil is a monounsaturated fat with a small amount of omega-3 fatty acids, but it goes through an intensive refining process that can raise the trans fat level as high as 40 percent. Even though canola oil is commonly used in cooking and many food products, it has also been used as an insect repellent and for other industrial applications. Due to the low cost of production, canola oil is used in many prepared foods. Check labels to see whether it is listed as an ingredient, and I suggest to avoid giving your baby foods made with canola oil in exchange for other, healthier alternatives.

Fats for Your Baby

During the time you are breast-feeding or feeding your baby infant formula, you do not need to supplement his diet with oils. When he is ready for solid foods at six to eight months, you can introduce him to small amounts of healthy, unrefined oils by adding a few drops to grains, vegetables, and bean purees. Unrefined sesame oil, olive oil, and flaxseed oil are excellent oils to provide essential fatty acids for your baby. Beans, avocados, tofu, tahini, ground toasted seeds and nuts, and fish provide healthy fats in a whole food form. Watch for signs of possible allergies, especially to nuts, as you introduce each element into your baby's diet.

Your baby is ready to start eating some fats between six and eight months. The chart below gives an overview of which fats to start feeding baby and when. It also includes how frequently to offer them and which ones to avoid.

When to Introduce Fats		
Fats	**Age Range**	**Frequency**
 Sesame oil	6 to 8 months	Daily
 Flaxseed oil	6 to 8 months	Daily
 Extra virgin olive oil	7 to 9 months	Daily
 Chia seed oil	12 to 18 months	Daily
 Almond oil	12 to 18 months	Daily
 Coconut oil	12 to 18 months	Daily
 Safflower and sunflower oil	12 to 18 months	Occasionally
 Ghee	12 to 18 months	Occasionally
 Butter	12 to 18 months	Occasionally
Lard	All ages	Avoid
 Canola oil	All ages	Avoid

Occasionally: 2–3 times a week

Salt

Salt gives strength, vitality, and energy to power your baby's body movement. Salt is so essential that it has been used throughout history as a valuable trading commodity and even as a currency for wages. In its whole form, salt has tremendous healing properties and nutritional benefits. When it is refined and stripped of its minerals, excess sodium is known for its relationship to health risks. There is a difference in the quality of refined salt and whole sea salt. The quantity of the salt you give your child can affect his physical, emotional, and mental health.

Babies and children are very sensitive to salt, and monitoring salt intake is one of the most powerful ways you can influence your child's diet. Beyond its independent nutritional importance, the quality and amount of salt a child consumes determines his attraction to other foods. For example, eating salty foods makes him thirsty and creates a craving for sweets or fruits, and too much salt can cause irritability, insomnia, constipation, tension, and general discomfort.

Even though salt is necessary, it is a very challenging ingredient to manage in cooking and eating for your baby. Determining a balanced quantity can be difficult, considering salt's addictive properties. Snack and restaurant foods have significantly higher levels of refined salt than home-cooked whole foods, so it is difficult to manage the amount of salt your baby consumes when eating out. Preparing meals at home allows you to regulate your baby's salt intake and develop a stronger awareness of his physical and emotional responses to it.

The Power of Salt

Sodium is the compound that makes salt taste "salty." Your baby's body needs sodium to function properly, as it controls fluid balance, regulates his blood pressure and volume, supports the transmission of his nerve impulses, and influences the contraction and relaxation of his muscles. Salt helps your baby's body maintain a healthy acid-alkaline balance, acts as a digestive agent, and soothes his joints. Sea salt's high amounts of trace minerals also help his body heal through their response to cell

damage and inflammation. Certain salts can sharpen his brain functions and improve his mental clarity, as well. Despite the need for salt in carrying out bodily functions, too much salt can affect your baby in detrimental ways, including raising his blood pressure or compromising his kidney function. Your baby can become irritable and tense from excess salt. Salt can be addictive, too, creating a cyclical dependency on salty foods, which then cause cravings for sweets, and back again.

Salt Considerations

Once salt has been cooked into food, it is not visible, so it can be easy to underestimate the power of this concentrated substance. It is often hidden in unexpected places that can have an influence on your baby without your knowing it. Being aware of your baby's sodium intake is one of the most difficult food ingredients to manage. When you cook your own baby food, you know how much salt is in his food, and you can observe his condition and behavior and make adjustments of more or less to help him balance. When you offer him food that is prepared, you do not know how much sodium he is taking in, so his salt intake is more difficult to monitor. You can monitor your baby's salt intake by observing his bowel movements.

Salt in School Lunches

The majority of sodium from food service meals comes from refined salts, and not the nutritious whole salts that children's bodies need. In January of 2012, the USDA revised nutrition standards for school food programs and included new restrictions on sodium. They created a goal to reduce the amount of sodium in school meals by 50 percent over the next 10 years.

Processed and prepared foods

The vast majority of sodium in the average diet comes from foods that are processed, canned, frozen, and packaged. These foods include store-bought bread and packaged snacks and sweets, as well as condiments like soy sauce, tomato sauce, ketchup, mayonnaise, mustard, olives, and pickles. Ready-made meals like pizza, instant cereals, noodles, rice or potatoes, frozen dinners, and soups also contain high levels of sodium. If your baby eats processed and packaged foods or food served in restaurants often, he is probably consuming higher levels of sodium than he needs.

You can check the sodium per serving on the Nutrition Facts label when purchasing packaged foods. This label also lists whether the ingredients include salt or sodium compounds. When reading labels, you can calculate that a ¼ teaspoon of salt equals 600 milligrams of sodium. You may see products marketed as "sodium-free" or "reduced salt," but these may still contain too much salt for your child. The following are explanations of sodium marketing terminologies:

- ❄ **Sodium-free or salt-free:** Contains less than 5 mg of sodium per serving.

- ❄ **Very low sodium:** Contains 35 mg of sodium or less.

- ❄ **Low sodium:** Contains 140 mg of sodium or less.

- ❄ **Reduced or less sodium:** Contains at least 25 percent less sodium than market standards. (Compare these to other products in the same category.)

- ❄ **Lite or light in sodium:** Sodium content has been reduced by at least 50 percent from competing brands. (Compare these to others in the same category.)

- ❄ **Unsalted or no salt added:** No salt is added during the processing of a food that normally contains salt. (Some foods may still be high in sodium because of other ingredients.)

Salt in breast milk or formula

Everything a mother eats during breast-feeding affects her baby's nutritional balance, and salt is no exception. Formula also contains salt, and trying out different formulas could have an effect on your baby's sodium levels as well.

One way to monitor your baby's daily salt intake is to check his bowel movements. For a breast-fed baby, a healthy bowel movement is golden brown or yellow and soft. Dark brown or hard stools may mean your breast milk or his formula is too salty. If his bowel movement is green, loose, and watery, you or your baby may be consuming too much fruit, juice, liquid, or oil, or not enough salt.

Types of Salt

Sodium is the main ingredient in refined table salt and sea salt, but there are differences in the methods of processing, their trace minerals, tastes, and effects on your baby's body. The following list outlines the main sources of salt.

Refined salt

Table salt is mined from rocks in the earth and is 99.5 percent sodium chloride, with the addition of anti-caking chemicals, potassium iodine, and sugar to stabilize the iodine. Naturally occurring trace minerals are extracted during the high-heat refining process. The warnings against high levels of sodium consumption typically refer to this form of salt, which is most commonly found in processed and mass-produced foods. Refined salts lack minerals and have added chemicals. These factors make table salt an unhealthy seasoning for babies.

Sea salt

Naturally harvested sea salt has approximately 98 percent sodium content. Sea salt is evaporated from the ocean, where trace minerals are concentrated, rather than stripped out or diluted, as is the case with the refined rock salt. Some of these trace minerals include: chloride, calcium, magnesium, potassium, and iodine. However, the iodine found in sea salt is significantly less compared to the added iodine in table salt. The chloride component of sea salt activates amylase, which is needed to effectively digest carbohydrates. Minerals in

sea salt boost your baby's immune system and facilitate the functions of his liver, kidneys, and adrenal glands. Sea salt enhances the natural sweetness of grains, vegetables, and legumes, and it can stimulate your baby's appetite. The USDA currently certifies plant- or animal-based foods as organic and does not offer a certification process for minerals, such as salt. Look for other countries' organic certifications or companies that harvest salt using "organic compliant" methods.

Salt for Your Baby

Adding salt to everyday cooking is not necessary until after your baby is one year old. Before then, he spends most of his time sitting or lying down, and his body cannot process it. Once he becomes physically active, he can expel salt through perspiration. Cooking with oil, flour, and large quantities of water may need a small amount of salt for balance. Fermented foods, such as tamari, plum vinegar, miso, and pickles, contain sodium that is easier to assimilate than sea salt, so you can introduce very small amounts of these foods earlier, around seven to nine months. However, they are still salty, so take care, and pay attention to your baby's reaction. At one to two years, your child can start eating the same food as the rest of the family, with less salty seasoning. You can prepare food with a pinch or ⅛ teaspoon of salt, take out a portion for your child, and then add extra salt and seasonings for other family members. As an alternative to salt, you can add a small, one-inch piece of wakame or kombu for digestion support and added flavor. After age two, your toddler can eat almost all of the same foods as adults. The more salt your child has, the more likely he will crave fats and sugars. Although fats and sugars are important for healthy growth and development, too much salt may cause strong cravings.

Salt metabolizes more easily when it is cooked into food rather than added after cooking. The season or temperature also affects your baby's salt needs. In cold weather, salt is necessary for creating body heat; conversely, less salt is required on a hot day. Each child is different, so discovery through trial and error and paying attention to his responses are the keys to helping him make balance.

Sweeteners

When Emi was a toddler, we were active in a local church that often held social events after services. The church hall had tables set with punchbowls and rows of cookies. One Sunday after church, Emi remembers reaching up for a cookie, and at the same time, felt someone on the other side of the table pull the cookie out of her hand. That someone was me. From her toddler perspective, she could not understand why those sugar cookies were off-limits. As a parent, I found it challenging to monitor and maintain a no-sugar diet for my girls because sugar temptations seemed to be everywhere!

Although I tried to monitor their sugar intake, I wish I had been a little more relaxed and allowed my girls to enjoy occasional sugar treats at birthday parties and social events. That would have given them the opportunity to feel the effects of sugar, and then I could have prepared remedies afterward to bring them back to balance. They say now that the restriction of not having sugar made them want it more as they grew older. Sweets in social situations can be a temptation for your child, as well as part of "fitting in." As a parent, you may find it tough to balance between that temptation and discipline to find a harmonious and healthy equilibrium.

However, I do believe that a daily no-sugar diet and cultivating your baby's taste for natural sweetness is one of the most valuable gifts you can give him. Offering natural snacks and desserts can help satisfy your child's desire for sweets without the detriments of refined sugar. If you build a foundation that orients your child's taste buds toward whole foods, he can feel the pleasures, as well as the discomforts of sugar, and learn by experiencing nature's law of cause and effect. You can also help manage your child's sugar cravings by monitoring his salt intake.

The Power of Sweeteners

Refined white sugar contains over 99.9 percent sucrose and has no nutritional value—no complex carbohydrates, dietary fiber, proteins, vitamins, or minerals. Sugar contributes to weight gain and obesity and can upset your baby's insulin levels. Unlike a whole grain or protein-rich food, which offers sustained energy, refined sugar converts into an immediate burst of energy. This high is followed by an energy dip once all of the sugars have been processed, which ultimately feels like energy is being taken away from his body.

Refined sugars can depress the immune system, making your baby susceptible to colds and infections. This is because glucose and vitamin C have similar chemical structures. When sugar levels go up, glucose blocks vitamin C transport to white blood cells, which diminishes their ability to protect against viruses and bacteria.

Another negative effect of refined sugar is tooth decay, which can begin at an early age. Young children who have prolonged exposure to refined sugar are much more prone to tooth decay. According to the American Dental Association, as soon as sugar comes into contact with the mouth, bacteria produce acid that facilitate the decay process.

Babies and children need natural sweetness, and they can find it in complex carbohydrates like grains and beans, as well as sweet vegetables like carrots, sweet potatoes, and winter squash. In addition to these foods, you can introduce your baby to sweets with brown rice syrup and *amazake*, a Japanese drink made from fermented rice. Richer sweeteners, like honey and maple syrup can be used in baking and desserts.

Sweetener Considerations

Research confirms that refined sugars are a leading contributor of the obesity epidemics sprouting up across the world. The Centers for Disease Control says that as of 2012, 35.7 percent of U.S. adults over 20 are obese. This trend is permeating into early childhood, with overweight babies as young as six months. Overweight and obese children are at increased risk for developing chronic conditions, such as heart disease, high blood pressure, hypertension, high cholesterol, type 2 diabetes, and asthma.

Robert Lustig, MD, a pediatrician from the UC San Francisco School of Medicine, specializing in childhood obesity, conducted a study in 2009 that linked the high consumption of refined sugar to increasing rates of childhood obesity. His studies concluded that sugar is an addictive toxin, and he advocated for refined sugar regulation. At this point, the FDA has not regulated sugar, nor has it issued a recommended daily intake for nutrition labels.

White, brown, raw, and cane sugars, corn syrup, and fructose are all refined sugars. Organic or conventional growing and packaging processes do not distinguish whether a sugar is refined or not. Aspartame, sucralose, saccharine, and other artificial sweeteners are marketed for sugar-free diets and weight control, but are significantly sweeter than regular sugar, and they are not recommended for pregnant and nursing mothers or babies and young children.

High-fructose Corn Syrup

High-fructose corn syrup (HFCS), sometimes called corn sugar, has become a popular ingredient in sodas and fruit-flavored drinks. Despite being the most commonly added sweetener in processed foods and beverages, it is an additive that is associated with many health concerns. A team of Princeton University researchers found that when lab animals consumed the same amount of sugar, those with access to high-fructose corn syrup gained significantly more weight than those with access to regular table sugar. They also found a higher spike in body fat and triglycerides in the animals consuming high-fructose corn syrup. Thus, evidence suggests that the increased use of high-fructose corn syrup in soft drinks and processed foods coincides with the increased rate of obesity and obesity-related health problems. High-fructose corn syrup usually contains genetically modified organisms.

Glycemic index of sugars

When carbohydrates are digested, glucose is released into your baby's bloodstream and becomes his body's main source of energy. The glycemic index (GI) is a comparative measurement of the amount of glucose released by a particular food over a two- to three-hour period. Foods, such as complex carbohydrates and legumes release glucose slowly, providing sustained and steady energy. These foods rate low on the glycemic index. Fruit and foods containing refined sugar release glucose rapidly, which causes a short-lived energy spike followed by a dive. Foods with this effect rate high on the glycemic index scale.

Glycemic Index of Sugars

Agave nectar	15–30
Fructose	17
Brown rice syrup	25
Raw honey	30
Coconut palm sugar	35
Apple juice	40
Barley malt syrup	42
Amazake	43
Sugarcane juice	43
Organic sugar	43
Maple syrup	47
Evaporated cane juice	54
Black strap molasses	55
Raw sugar	55
Cola and soda	65
Corn syrup	70
Refined honey	75
Refined table sugar	75
High-fructose corn syrup	87
Glucose (aka dextrose)	100
Maltodextrin	150

Types of Sweeteners

Whole sweeteners offer natural and delicious sweetness that is not harsh or jolting for your baby's digestive and nervous systems.

Brown rice syrup

Brown rice syrup is one-third as sweet as refined white sugar and has a mildly sweet taste similar to butterscotch. It has a long shelf life, and does not crystallize, like honey can. It can be used as a sweetener in porridge and desserts, and it adds a crispy texture in baking. Babies can enjoy this syrup as a first introduction to sweeteners.

Amazake

Amazake is a traditional sweet Japanese drink made from fermented rice and is high in complex carbohydrates, fiber, and the B vitamins niacin and thiamin. *Amazake* can be blended into a thick, creamy liquid that can be eaten like a pudding or used as a sweetener.

Mari and Emi

Maple syrup

Maple syrup is the liquid form of the sap boiled down from the maple tree. This syrup is a good source of manganese, zinc, and fifty-four beneficial compounds, including antioxidants that inhibit enzymes correlating to type 2 diabetes. Despite maple syrup's natural sweetness, many commercial pancake syrups add high-fructose corn syrup; check the label to make sure the syrup you purchase is real maple syrup. As far as quality and nutrition, there are no known nutritional distinctions between consuming different grades of maple syrup, but organic maple syrup eliminates the possibility of pesticides or chemical fertilizers used on the maple trees. Because the method for making maple syrup involves intense boiling, botulism spores cannot thrive under the sustained high temperature used in processing the sap into syrup. You can offer your baby maple syrup before he is one year old.

Honey

Honey has more calories than refined white sugar and is assimilated directly into the bloodstream very quickly. With its acidity, high glycemic conversion rate, and the potential exposure to botulism, honey should be avoided until your child is at least one year old, when his intestines have matured to handle the possibility of botulism spores. Honey can be used as a sweetener in baking or desserts.

Molasses

Molasses is a thick, strong-flavored syrup that has long been used as a sweetener in traditional recipes. Some grades of molasses can be used as "table syrup" or poured onto cooked food, while other types of molasses are used in baking. Molasses has a strong flavor that affects the taste of the food. The dark blackstrap molasses is rich in calcium, iron, and potassium. Molasses also may contain botulism spores and is not recommended before your child is one year old.

Coconut palm sugar

Coconut palm sugar is an unrefined brown sugar with a caramel flavor. It is produced by tapping the nectar from the coconut palm tree flower, then condensing and drying the juice to make a whole brown sugar. It can be sprinkled on cereal, in desserts, and in baking. It has a low glycemic index, is highly nutritious, ecologically beneficial, and provides sustained energy.

Organic cane sugar

Organic cane sugar is made from organically grown sugarcane. This brownish sugar is still a refined sugar and therefore should be used in moderation after your baby is two years old. It is used in many products on the shelves of natural food stores, so check the labels carefully.

Brown sugar

Brown sugar is processed sugar with molasses added. Brown sugar is more likely than other sugars to undergo significant processing, such as extra refinement to keep it moist. The dyes and chemicals that are often added make this sweetener one of the unhealthier options for children.

Agave

Agave is a type of plant, native to Mexico and the southwestern United States, and some varieties grow in Southern Africa. Agave contains several edible parts, and its sap is used as a sweetener. However, most agave nectar products found in stores are not made from the plant, but are rather chemically produced sweeteners that are far more processed and devoid of nutritional value than even high-fructose corn syrup.

Stevia

Stevia is made from a plant indigenous to South America and has been used as a sweetener for hundreds of years. Only one, highly refined portion of the plant has been approved for use as a commercially available food sweetener in the United States. No specific studies have been done around the safety of stevia for infants or children.

Refined white sugar

Refined white sugar is 99.9 percent sucrose and is chemically refined from cane, beets, or corn with an intensely sweet flavor. White sugar is an ingredient found in many processed foods and lacks any nutritional value.

The Yin and Yang of Sweeteners

Chemicals, processing methods, and glycemic index are determinants for a yin or yang influence of sweeteners. Artificial sweeteners and high-fructose corn syrup contain chemicals and are more processed than refined white sugar, so they have an extremely yin influence. Next are refined sugars, especially when they are refined with a chemical process. Organic sugar is less refined than refined white sugar, so it has more of a yang influence. Maple syrup and molasses are next because they are more whole in liquid form. Honey comes from the nectar in flowers and has more of a yang influence

Yin-Yang Spectrum of Sweeteners

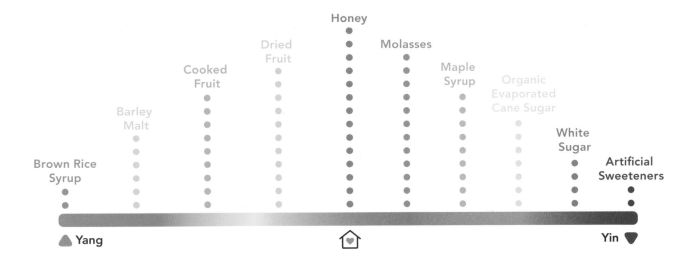

because bees add their enzymes. Brown rice syrup is a mild sweetener made from grain with a lower glycemic index; it metabolizes more evenly than other sweeteners, so it has more of a yang influence. *Amazake* is made from whole brown rice, so it has the most yang influence of the sweeteners. Listed in the chart are balanced foods toward the center for daily use, foods on a wider spectrum for occasional use, and extreme foods to avoid.

Sweeteners for Your Baby

Brown rice syrup is a mild natural sweetener to start with, and you can put a small amount in his grain cereals at around six months. *Amazake* can be added to grains for extra sweetness at the same age. You can introduce maple syrup around nine months. It is tapped from trees in a cold region, and has a sweeter taste than brown rice syrup for baking cookies, muffins, pies, and cakes. Honey could be considered an "animal food" because it is made by bees. It has a sweet-tasting, distinctive flavor that makes a good natural sweetener for baking or desserts. It should not be introduced before one year because of the possibility of botulism for young babies. Molasses can also be offered after his first birthday.

The chart below gives an overview of which sweeteners to start feeding at which age. It also includes how frequently to feed these sweeteners and which ones to avoid.

When to Introduce Sweeteners		
Sweeteners	**Age Range**	**Frequency**
 Rice syrup	6 to 8 months	Daily
 *Amazake*	6 to 8 months	Daily
 Maple syrup	9 to 12 months	Occasionally
 Honey	12 to 18 months	Occasionally
 Molasses	12 to 18 months	Occasionally
 Coconut palm sugar	12 to 18 months	Occasionally
 Organic cane juice	All ages	Avoid
 Agave	All ages	Avoid
 Stevia	All ages	Avoid
 Brown sugar	All ages	Avoid
Refined white sugar	All ages	Avoid

Occasionally: 2–3 times a week

Herbs and Spices

Every culture relies on plants for seasonings and for their therapeutic, healing properties. Culinary herbs, such as basil, cilantro (coriander), parsley, mint, dill, and garlic (although botanically closer to vegetables, such as onions and shallots, garlic is often used as a culinary herb), are used in different cultures to add flavor to food. European herbal traditions, East Asian medicine, and Ayurveda (the traditional healing system of India) are some of the primary philosophies used for herb-based healing. Many essential oils use herbs for fragrances, healing, cleansing, and purifying the body and soul.

Herbs are vitamin- and mineral-rich leaves of herbaceous (non-woody) plants. They tend to grow in more temperate climates. Spices, which are more commonly native to hot, tropical climates, are extracted from other parts of the plant, such as the root, stem, flower, bark, or seed. Herbs and spices add flavor and nutritional value, such as vitamins, minerals, and other healing properties to food. In many countries, herbs and spices are a part of baby food from the beginning. In Thailand, for example, babies are fed coconut milk, lemongrass,

and tamarind, while Indian babies have curry. Italian babies are exposed to basil and oregano, and French babies enjoy thyme and rosemary.

When you cook your own baby food at home, you can experiment with different herbs and spices for variety and enjoyment. Younger babies usually are satisfied with very simple cooking, but after your baby's first birthday, he may become bored with food and respond well to herbs and spices that make it more interesting to him.

The Power of Herbs and Spices

Herbs provide sensory and health benefits in cooking and for healing all kinds of illnesses. Herbs and spices can provide lightness, flavor, and variety to balance grains, vegetables, beans, and fish dishes. They can also help your baby's body fight against germs and toxins and build immune defenses. Herbs and spices can reduce cholesterol and blood pressure, as well as blood sugar levels for diabetics. Because your baby's body is small, he will be more sensitive than adults to the effects of these herbs and spices. Experiment with small amounts in the food that you cook for him and watch for his reaction. Herbs and spices make eating more interesting for him, and it can help him be satisfied with seasonings that do not include large amounts of salt and sugar.

Types of Herbs

All herbs have properties that affect food in some way. All herbs have properties that affect food in some way. Fresh herbs can range from very mild to a stronger taste, and most of them provide medicinal effects, in addition to enhancing the flavor of food.

Fennel

Fennel has a slightly sweet, earthy taste. The fresh plant or dried seeds can be made into a tea to increase milk production for nursing mothers, or to relieve colic or digestive upset for your baby. Fennel is known for relaxing muscles, and it also is helpful for relieving digestive issues. Fresh fennel can be cooked in with grains or vegetables for both taste and general health.

Bay

Bay aids in digestion, and is an herb mostly used in its dry form. Add bay leaves to grains, soups, and beans at the start of cooking and remove them before you serve the dish. Place dried bay leaves on a shelf or in a drawer of any cabinet to keep bugs out.

Basil

Basil is an herb that tastes similar to its cousin, mint. Basil comes in a number of varieties, each with distinct flavors and aromas. Used fresh or dried, basil combines nicely with grain, vegetable, bean, and fish dishes. Unlike many herbs, its flavor intensifies when cooked, so use it in moderation.

Thyme

Thyme, a member of the mint family, is a rich, aromatic herb that enhances the flavors of soups, vegetables, and sauces. Add thyme to a dish toward the end of preparation to preserve its flavor. It is often used in winter dishes because it has warming properties.

Mint

Mint is used as a cooling herb with its fresh, aromatic, and sweet flavor. The two most common cooking mints are peppermint and spearmint. Although fresh mint's menthol flavor can overpower certain foods, it makes a refreshing addition to grain, fruit, and vegetable dishes—especially cooler meals in the summertime.

Lemongrass

Lemongrass is an aromatic, sweet herb that adds zest to vegetable dishes, soups, and teas. Lemongrass tea is also used as a decongestant and to relieve diarrhea.

Cilantro

Cilantro is a flavorful antioxidant and digestive aid. Made into a weak tea, it can be used as a remedy for colic. Older children can chew cilantro to aid digestion. It can also enhance the production of breast milk.

Parsley

Parsley is a member of the carrot and celery family. It is a source of chlorophyll, vitamin A, vitamin C, and iron. Finely chopped pieces can be added to steamed vegetables or soups.

Types of Spices

Very strong spices, such as chile peppers, may be unappealing to your baby in the early months, but there are a number of mild spices that you can incorporate into your cooking that will be appealing to him.

Cinnamon

Cinnamon is a sweet spice that is often added to desserts or grains. Its warming effect helps aid digestion and circulation, and it offers a high dose of antioxidants. Medicinally, it has been used to combat bloating and diarrhea.

Curry

Curry is a blend of various spices that is warming to the body and stimulates digestion. A small amount of curry has a mild and sweet taste, so toddlers usually enjoy it. When I worked at Muso Yochien (Dream Window Kindergarten), *karē raisu*, or curry rice, was a popular dish in Japan, and a favorite dish for both the students and me. I learned to read the name in Japanese so that I could look forward to curry rice day. Most curry consists of cumin, turmeric, coriander, red pepper, and fenugreek. Depending on the recipe, additional ingredients include ginger, mustard seed, fennel seed, cinnamon, nutmeg, caraway, clove, cardamom, and other spices.

Garlic

Garlic is full of vitamins and minerals. With its antibacterial and antifungal properties, it helps fight infection and is cleansing to the system. Because it has a strong taste and is potent, make sure that it is fully cooked for your baby and wait until he reaches 12 months to introduce it.

Ginger

Ginger is warming and stimulating. It can be used as a digestive aid for stomach upset, motion sickness, or nausea. It can help make oils in fish or fried foods more digestible. The taste may be too strong for your child, so introduce it in small amounts blended into juices or add as a seasoning in cooking.

Vanilla

Vanilla comes from the fruit of an orchid plant, which grows in the form of a bean pod. The green bean goes through a fermentation process that takes about six months. Vanilla beans are soaked in hot water, rolled in blankets and dried, and then stored to ferment. This fermentation process creates the alcohol in vanilla extract. This alcohol has been used as a remedy for teething by rubbing vanilla extract on sore gums. Vanilla has been used to cure stomach distress, reduce anxiety, and promote feelings of well-being. There is nonalcoholic vanilla, but the taste may be weaker. Vanilla is a sweet tasty flavor for babies and children, and it can be used in baking, puddings, and desserts.

Brewer's Yeast

While not an herb, brewer's yeast is a flavorful nutritional supplement that is found in powdered, flaked or liquid form. It is a live culture that is full of protein, B vitamins, and minerals. Brewer's yeast reduces cholesterol, helps build healthy flora in the gut, and helps digest and process sugars and starches. It can be sprinkled on porridge for a nutritional boost.

Condiments

Mayonnaise, mustard, ketchup, and vinegar are all commonly used condiments for sandwiches and snacks.

Commercial mayonnaise recipes typically contain soybean oil mixed together with egg yolks, sugar, preservatives, and flavorings. Some natural brands include organic ingredients that substitute honey for sugar and olive oil for soybean oil. Check the list of ingredients to make sure mayonnaise does not include canola oil. Wait until 12 to 18 months to offer mayonnaise to your child.

Although ketchup has no fat, most commercial recipes include significant amounts of sugar, and more specifically, high-fructose corn syrup. A pediatrician I knew years ago suggested removing ketchup from a child's diet as the first step to treating a wide variety of ailments. He attributed ketchup's sugar content to many of children's physical and behavioral problems. Although some organic ketchup replaces corn syrup with organic cane sugar, the sugar content may still be high. Check the label before you purchase a bottle.

Mustard contains mustard seeds and turmeric, but may also contain salt, preservatives, spices, sugar, and flavorings. Mustards made with whole food, natural ingredients are available at gourmet shops and natural food stores, and they can add variety to your child's dishes. At 12 to 18 months, you can try mustard on sandwiches or in sauces to see if he likes the taste.

Herbs and Spices for Your Baby

If you breast-feed, then your baby tastes the herbs and spices that you eat through your breast milk. Some herbs, such as fennel and chamomile, are medicinal and can help digestion or colic by making an herbal infusion for your baby at six or seven months. If you give him herbal infusions before that age, make the infusion very diluted and give it in small doses. Check with your health care provider about herbal infusions for colic or digestive concerns.

When he is nine months old, you can add mild herbs to grain or vegetable dishes for seasoning, flavor, and health purposes. When you introduce your child to a new herb or spice, follow the same guidelines you would for other foods: introduce the herb or spice one at a time and wait three days to ensure that he has no allergic reaction. At around twelve months, you can try stronger tasting herbs and spices, paying attention to his response.

The following chart gives an overview of which herbs and spices to start feeding your baby and when. It also includes how frequently to offer them.

When to Introduce Herbs and Spices		
Herbs and Spices	Age Range	Frequency
Fennel	6 to 8 months	Daily
Bay	9 to 12 months	Daily
Basil	9 to 12 months	Daily
Thyme	9 to 12 months	Occasionally
Mint	9 to 12 months	Daily
Lemongrass	9 to 12 months	Daily
Cilantro	9 to 12 months	Occasionally
Vanilla	9 to 12 months	Occasionally
Parsley	12 to 18 months	Occasionally
Cinnamon	12 to 18 months	Occasionally
Curry	12 to 18 months	Occasionally
Garlic	12 to 18 months	Occasionally
Ginger	18 to 24 months	Occasionally

Occasionally: 2–3 times a week

Desserts and Snacks for Your Baby

Healthy desserts provide pleasure that can satisfy your child, without refined sugars. Natural sweeteners, such as fruit juice, rice syrup, maple syrup, and honey have a different effect on your child's body than refined sugars do. Cooked, frozen, and fresh fruit can satisfy a sweet tooth, but it is fun to have occasional baked goods, such as cookies, muffins, pies, and cakes. The recipes for rice pudding and couscous cake are quick and easy, and because they are moist, they are easier to digest than dry, baked desserts. When your child can chew, rice crispy treats are fun and simple to make. These desserts have a natural sweet taste, and without the intense sweetness of refined sugars. They are a good introduction to developing your baby's healthy sweet tooth.

Rice Pudding

♡ 12 months+

🥄 12 (4 ounce) servings

V Vegetarian

GF Gluten-free

Rice pudding is a tasty way to turn leftover rice into a healthy dessert, or you can cook extra rice with this pudding in mind. If a batch of rice turned out too wet or too dry, this is a good way to use it, making adjustments to the moisture level.

1 tablespoon tahini

2 tablespoons water for mixing tahini

2 ½ cups cooked short-grain brown rice

1 ½ cups water

½ cup rice syrup

½ teaspoon vanilla extract

¼ cup raisins

¾ teaspoon sea salt

1 teaspoon ground cinnamon

Method

1. Preheat oven to 350°F.

2. Mix tahini and 2 tablespoons water in a separate bowl or a grinding bowl.

3. Mix all ingredients together in a casserole or glass dish that has a cover, or use aluminum foil to cover.

4. Put casserole in oven, and bake for 50 minutes.

5. Remove cover, return pudding to oven, and bake for 15 minutes to cook off excess liquid.

6. Allow 15 minutes to cool and set before serving. This pudding can be served warm or at room temperature.

Variation

- For a sweeter taste, use ¼ cup maple syrup instead of rice syrup.

Applesauce Muffins

♡ 12 months+

🥣 12 to 15 muffins

V Vegetarian

Muffins are healthy, yummy, and comforting. Because they are made in individual servings, they make less mess, and are easy to carry out for snacks or bentos. Muffins are tasty when fresh, but if they are a few days old, you can cut them in half and toast them.

1 ½ cups whole wheat pastry flour

1 ½ cups unbleached flour

¾ teaspoon salt

2 teaspoons baking powder

2 eggs, whisked

2 cups applesauce

¼ cup honey

⅓ cup sesame or almond oil

⅓ cup water

1 cup apple, peeled and grated

Method

1. Preheat oven to 400°F, and grease muffin tins with a generous amount of oil.

2. Sift flours together with salt and baking powder.

3. In a separate bowl, mix eggs, applesauce, honey, oil, and water. Stir together.

4. Add grated apple to wet mixture.

5. Add dry ingredients to wet ingredients and stir to combine.

6. Spoon into oiled muffin tins ⅔ full.

7. Bake for 20 to 25 minutes, or until toothpick inserted into center comes out clean.

8. To reheat, wrap in aluminum foil and put into oven for 5 minutes.

Oatmeal Cookies

♡ 12 months+

⚱ 24 cookies

V Vegetarian

GF Gluten-free

Homemade oatmeal cookies are a traditional American treat, and these are extra crispy and delicious, considering they are so healthy. Make ahead for easy desserts or snacks—for home or on the go.

½ cup brown rice flour

½ teaspoon salt

¼ teaspoon ground cinnamon

2 cups quick gluten-free rolled oats

½ cup maple syrup or honey

¼ cup sesame or almond oil

1 teaspoon vanilla extract

¾ cup water

¼ cup raisins, soaked in 3 tablespoons hot water for 20 minutes

Method

1. Preheat oven to 350°F. Lightly oil a cookie sheet.

2. Sift together flour, salt, and cinnamon in a bowl, and then add oats.

3. Mix maple syrup, oil, vanilla, and water in a separate bowl, then stir in raisins with soaking water.

4. Pour the flour mixture into the wet ingredients, and stir.

5. Add more water if necessary. The cookie dough should be very wet but still thick.

6. Use a spoon to drop 1 tablespoon of dough for each cookie onto the cookie sheet.

7. Bake for 15 minutes, or until golden brown around edges and set in the middle.

Variations

• Substitute unbleached white flour for rice flour, if there is no concern about wheat allergies.

• Substitute 2 eggs and ¼ cup water for ¾ cup water.

Shape Cookies

♡ 12 months+

⚗ 24 cookies

V Vegetarian

This recipe is versatile for impromptu occasions or holidays, and you can adapt it with different cookie cutter shapes. Use cutters for Christmas, Halloween, Valentine's Day, or use animals to make these fun cookies all year round.

1 ½ cups unbleached flour

1 cup whole wheat pastry flour

½ teaspoon salt

1 teaspoon baking powder

2 eggs, whisked

1 teaspoon vanilla extract

½ cup maple syrup

⅓ cup sesame or almond oil, chilled

Method

1. Sift flours, salt, and baking powder into one bowl.

2. In a separate bowl, whisk the eggs, vanilla, maple syrup, and oil.

3. Stir wet ingredients into dry ingredients.

4. Use your hands to form a ball in the mixing bowl. Cover with a damp towel and refrigerate for 1 hour.

5. Preheat the oven to 375°F and grease cookie sheet with oil.

6. Remove dough from refrigerator. Divide dough into 2 parts and flatten one piece with your hand onto a floured cutting board.

7. Roll the dough with a rolling pin to ¼ inch thick.

8. Use as little extra flour as possible to avoid toughening the dough. Use cookie cutters to make shapes, and transfer them to cookie sheet. Re-roll dough and cut out more shapes.

9. Bake for 12 to 18 minutes, until lightly browned.

Fruit Pie

♡ 12 months+

🥄 2 (8-inch) pie crusts

V Vegetarian

Pies made with a fruit filling are a light and healthy dessert that the whole family can enjoy. You can make your own crust if you enjoy baking and have time; if not, frozen whole wheat or gluten-free crusts are quick and convenient. For this recipe, chilled oil and cold water are essential for getting a flaky crust. Experiment with single fruits or fruit combinations for variety and according to the occasion. This recipe makes enough for 2 pies with a bottom crust, or 1 pie with a lattice top. For pies with a bottom crust, either make 2 pies at one time, or freeze one of the crusts for later. Another option is to make several smaller pies.

Pie Crust:

2 cups unbleached flour, plus more for sprinkling

½ teaspoon salt

⅔ cup chilled coconut or sesame oil

¼ cup cold water

For pie filling, double Fruit Kuzu Recipe on page 453 with your choice of fruit

Method

1. Preheat oven to 450°F.
2. To make pie crust, sift flour and salt into a mixing bowl.
3. Use a fork to work in the chilled oil.
4. Start with adding 2 tablespoons of the cold water, and add more of the remaining 2 tablespoons water as needed.
5. Form dough into a ball, handling as little as possible.
6. Roll the dough onto a lightly floured cutting board or piece of wax paper.
7. Carefully lift rolled dough into the pie plate, and trim away excess dough using your fingers to pinch edges for a decorative finish.
8. Sprinkle flour over pie crust so that juices from fruit do not make crust soggy.
9. Bake unfilled piecrust for 15 minutes, or until golden brown. Let cool.
10. After crust cools, add filling and chill until set.

Variations

- For a savory pot pie, substitute vegetables for fruit, using water instead of juice. Add 2 tablespoons tamari and minced herbs to taste. Proteins such as tempeh, tofu, beans, fish, or chicken can also be added. Pour vegetable sauce into uncooked pie crust, cover with dough of second crust, and bake for 45 minutes.

Couscous Cake

♡ 12 months+

🥣 1 (8-inch) cake

V Vegetarian

This cake is very easy to make. Because couscous is not as refined as flour, and because the cake is moist instead of dry, it is more digestible than baked cakes or cookies. Couscous is a wheat product, so wait until 12 months to offer your child to prevent risk of gluten allergies.

2 ½ cups apple juice

¼ teaspoon sea salt

1 cup couscous

¼ cup unsulfured raisins

Method

1. Bring juice to a boil in pot, and add raisins and sea salt.

2. Stir in couscous, and boil for 2 to 3 minutes.

3. Remove from heat, and pour into an 8-inch round or square cake pan.

4. After couscous cools, the grains gel together so you can cut the cake into pieces for serving.

Variations

- Leave out the raisins and serve with a fruit kuzu sauce.
- Substitute dried fruits, such as apricots, cherries, or blackberries

Party Cake

♡ 12 months+

🥣 2 (8-inch) round or square cake layers, 12 to 16 cupcakes

V Vegetarian

For birthdays, holidays, and celebrations, I have made this cake countless times over many years. It is always popular, plain or with a sauce, made in a cake pan or as cupcakes. This is still my favorite cake recipe for special occasions. Fruit kuzu with fresh fruit is delicious, colorful, and festive.

Cake:

3 eggs

⅔ cup sesame, almond, or safflower oil

1 cup maple syrup or honey

2 cups whole wheat pastry flour

1 cup unbleached pastry flour

1½ teaspoons baking soda

¾ teaspoon salt

1 cup yogurt or almond milk

Water, if needed

1 teaspoon vanilla extract

Icing:

Double the Fruit Kuzu Recipe on page 453 for Cake Icing

Method

1. Preheat oven to 375°F. Oil and flour two 8-inch round or square cake pans.

2. To make cake, mix eggs, oil, and maple syrup or honey in a large bowl.

3. Sift flours, baking soda, and salt into a separate bowl.

4. Mix a small portion of the dry ingredients into the wet ingredients.

5. Mix in part of yogurt or almond milk. Continue mixing, alternating between adding dry ingredients and yogurt or almond milk. If needed, add extra water for a cake batter consistency.

6. Stir in vanilla.

7. Pour batter into prepared pans and bake for 30 minutes, or until cake tester inserted into center comes out clean. Let cool.

8. Spread fruit kuzu on each cake, then stack.

Variations

• For fruit shortcake, cut a 4 x 4-inch square piece of cake, and top with cut pieces of fresh fruit and *amazake* cream or yogurt sweetened with maple syrup.

• Substitute cream cheese icing for one or both layers. Mix together 12-ounces of cream cheese (softened) with ⅓ cup maple syrup and 1 teaspoon vanilla extract. For a special option, add ⅓ cup powdered cocoa to cream cheese icing for a chocolate flavor.

• Use a muffin tin to make cupcakes and top with cream cheese icing.

Crispy Rice Snack

♡ 18 months+

◡ 24 (2-inch) square bars

V Vegetarian

GF Gluten-free

This recipe is simple and delicious, and it can easily become a family favorite for snacks, holidays, and parties. Toddlers enjoy helping when cooking this recipe, because it is so easy.

1 cup brown rice syrup

1 cup almond butter, tahini, or sesame butter

¼ teaspoon sea salt

¼ teaspoon vanilla extract

6 cups crispy rice cereal

Method

1. Mix together brown rice syrup, nut butter, sea salt, and vanilla in a large saucepan over medium heat.

2. Remove from heat and let cool for 5 minutes.

3. Stir in cereal.

4. Spread mixture in a 12 x 8-inch pan, and press with your hands.

5. Let cool for 10 to 15 minutes, and then cut into 2-inch squares.

Beverages

AT MUSO YOCHIEN (Dream Window Kindergarten) where I taught in Japan, the "fix-all" remedy was *ume-sho-ban*, which is a mixture of *bancha* (a low-caffeine green tea) with shoyu (tamari) sauce and a salty pickled *umeboshi* plum. For every kind of upset, from a fall to a stomachache to an emotional disturbance, this traditional Japanese medicinal remedy calmed the children at the kindergarten. *Ume-sho-ban* is much like chicken soup in Western cultures. While customs are different around the world, beverages play an essential role in keeping fluid levels balanced.

During his first year, the primary nourishment for your baby is breast milk or formula. He does not need a lot of additional fluids, because they can make his stomach full, reducing his consumption of milk, which is his essential food for growth and development. If he is drinking formula, small amounts of other fluids may be necessary for his kidneys to excrete the extra salt found in the formula. When he starts solids, there is also liquid in the foods that he eats, such as, pureed grains, vegetables, and fruits.

The amount of fluids your baby drinks gradually increases as he approaches one year old, but your breast milk or formula is the primary beverage he needs for his first year.

Formula-fed babies consume water from their first day, and breast-fed babies consume water second-hand. If you are nursing, make sure to keep yourself hydrated with plenty of water and other fluids without added sweeteners, yeasts, or caffeine. Healthy, clean water is essential; beverages, such as soup broth and pureed soup, offer additional vitamins and minerals, as well as provide fluids for hydration. Barley tea, along with the majority of other herbal teas, have an alkaline-producing effect on your baby's system. Coconut water, rice milk, nut milk, soy milk, cow's milk, goat's milk, *amazake*, and vegetable and fruit juices have nutrients, as well as hydrating qualities.

The Power of Beverages

Water and fluids are necessary for healthy functioning of your baby's body—for hydration, to keep his body at the proper temperature, to move waste through his system, and to support joints and muscles. Fluids are easily and quickly absorbed and released through waste and sweat.

Water may contain trace minerals, depending on the source. However, each water source varies in its concentration, so water is not a dependable source for any specific mineral. Make sure that the water your baby consumes does not contain contaminants.

When your baby becomes more active through walking, he also begins to eat more solid foods and decrease his consumption of breast milk or formula. Because he is more active and drinking less milk at this age, around a year old, he needs more fluids. Activity and movement require energy that he gets from fluids, calories, and nutrients. He also may lose fluids,

nutrients, and electrolytes, or electrically charged salts that are necessary for cellular function, through sweating. Beverages help replenish nutrients and keep him hydrated. Dehydration can happen quickly at times of extreme heat, diarrhea, fever, vomiting, or airplane travel, so be especially aware of keeping your baby hydrated, especially at those times.

Temperature of Drinks

According to East Asian medicine, drinking cold drinks on an empty stomach can lead to digestive problems. Beverages that are at room or body temperature create less of a jolt on your baby's digestive system.

Types of Beverages

Once your child is drinking beverages other than breast milk or formula, there are different options to consider. Most beverages are largely made up of a high percentage of water, so establishing good-quality water in your home is necessary for his basic health. Most water sources in the United States are fairly safe. You can check your home's water quality and make adjustments as needed.

Water

Although water does not contain calories or nutrients, it is essential for life because your baby's body is made of 70 percent fluids. Your baby does not need extra water until he starts eating solid foods, at which time the water supports his kidney function. Your baby's kidneys filter his blood and eliminate cellular waste, including acids, minerals, and excess fluid. Each baby has different needs for water, and these needs vary with his level of activity, the weather, seasons, foods, and drinks. Your baby needs enough to prevent dehydration, but not too much that it fills him up and decreases his desire for milk.

If your baby is very thirsty, check his salt intake. The amount of sodium used in cooking and in processed foods can determine your baby's needs for fluids. Excess water can lead to a rare condition known as water intoxication, which can interfere with digestion and the absorption of nutrients. As little as 3 ounces a day could be too much water for a child under a year old, says Allen J. Walker, MD, head of the Emergency Department at Johns Hopkins Children's Center. If your baby goes swimming, make sure he is not swallowing too much water. Some symptoms of water intoxication in an infant include: low body temperature, facial swelling, drowsiness, irritability, and seizures.

Spring water

Spring water is bottled water that comes from an underground formation where water bubbles up or flows naturally to the surface of the earth. Commercial spring water can also be extracted from a spring below ground.

Purified water

Purified water has been treated with a cleansing or filtering process, such as charcoal, distillation, or reverse osmosis, to remove bacteria and to dissolve solids. Many bottled waters are purified drinking water.

Mineral water

Mineral water contains minerals and trace elements that occur naturally at its source.

Municipal or tap water

Municipal or tap water is water piped into your home. This water supply is legally required to meet the primary standards of the U.S. Environmental Protection Agency. According to the Environmental Working Group, many chemical pollutants can be found in tap water supplies, including trace levels of aluminum, arsenic, asbestos, cadmium, lead, and mercury. Understanding where your local water supply comes from, and what potential exposure the water may be subject to, is vital to ensuring your baby's water is of the highest quality. If there is any concern or question about the quality of your local water, have the water tested for metals, inorganics, disinfectant by-products, and volatile organic compounds.

 To check your area for pollutants visit ewg.org

Boiling and filtering water

Boil or filter tap water for drinking and cooking, especially for infants and small children, or if you are pregnant or breast-feeding. You can boil tap water for one minute to ensure it is safe from bacteria or viruses, and then store it in the refrigerator for up to two days. You can warm the water (make sure that it is not too hot), or leave it outside the refrigerator until it is at room temperature, before giving it to your baby.

If you use filtered water, boiling is not necessary, unless a pipe has broken. The National Sanitation Foundation (NSF) is a nonprofit organization that facilitates the development of safety standards and conducts testing to certify drinking water systems for a variety of standards. Some of the standards are for the safety of the material used in a product, and others relate to the performance of a product. When purchasing water filters and water filter systems, look for products that meet NSF material safety certifications, and explore performance certifications for a product. There are two basic locations for a water filter system: point of use, which is at the kitchen sink, and the point of entry, which is a filter for the water used throughout the whole building.

Point-of-use filters are used above or below the kitchen sink for drinking and cooking. Most point-of-use systems use carbon filters to adsorb impurities. The filters need to be changed periodically, but these are easy to change because they are easy to access. This is the least expensive and most practical system for most households.

Reverse osmosis filters are a point-of-use system that works by filtering the water through a carbon pre-filter that removes sediment, volatile organic

compounds, and chlorine. Water is then forced through a semipermeable membrane, which traps minerals in a housing. These minerals are then flushed out of the housing and down the drain with a large amount of water used for this purpose, and the filtered water is then sent to a storage tank. Storing the water is necessary in order to provide enough water flow to meet the demand when the faucet is turned on. Once the water leaves the tank, the water is filtered again by a post-carbon filter to remove any bad taste left from non-harmful bacteria growth in the tank. The filter removes pesticides, herbicides, insecticides, chlorine, iron, lead, fluoride, and other toxic ingredients. It also removes the good minerals, such as calcium and magnesium, but there is no waste in this system.

Point-of-entry filters are whole-house systems located at the point where the main water line enters the building. They are designed to remove a larger quantity of contaminants to provide better water quality at every fixture and water-using appliance within the home. Whole-house systems remove anything from sediment to uranium, but they are commonly used for everything that affects health. You can filter the water used in baths, showers, and bathroom sinks to ensure a final barrier between you and the source.

If you know there are health-threatening contaminants in your water, consult a certified water specialist in your area. After testing your water, you can match your particular needs to a system. You can improve most city water with a simple water filter at the kitchen sink. Follow the manufacturer's recommendation for changing the filter for optimal contaminant reduction.

 To find a certified specialist, visit the Water Quality Association wqa.org

Concerns about tap water

Water is one of the most natural and plentiful resources in the world, and yet, modern tap water can have chemicals that were added deliberately, like chlorine and fluoride, or unintentionally, like pesticides and herbicides from agricultural runoff, personal care products, or pharmaceuticals. Tap water, or municipal water, can vary by location. In developed countries, tap water is typically "safe," although using a water filter system provides a final barrier against known and unknown contaminants. If you live in an area with intensive commercial farming, mining, or industrial manufacturing, you may wish to investigate your local water situation more thoroughly.

Fluoride is commonly added to tap water to protect tooth enamel, and it is also in many toothpastes. Most people do not use a filtration system and do not know whether their water is fluoridated. However, municipalities are required to inform the public in their annual water report if they fluoridate the water supply. You can also have your water tested at a local laboratory at a low cost to find out the levels of fluoride in your water.

In 2006, the American Dental Association (ADA) advised parents against using fluoridated water in their infant formula, because of the risk of fluorosis, or mottled tooth enamel, due to overexposure to fluoride. Babies are vulnerable to fluoride toxicity, due to their small size, and because their kidneys cannot excrete fluoride. All water filters do not remove fluoride; the two types of filters that reliably remove fluoride are reverse osmosis and activated alumina filters.

Chlorine and chloramine are also routinely added to municipal tap water to prevent the spread of water-borne diseases. Although they prevent mass outbreaks of waterborne diseases, they are not healthy for your baby to drink every day. Most water filter systems can easily remove chlorine.

Because private well water may not have been treated, and is not regulated by authorities, it should be tested periodically. Check with your country extension service or with your regional EPA office, or call your state's Safe Drinking Water Hotline for information. The EPA offers information about possible contaminates in tap water.

 To read about safe drinking water visit water.eps.gov

Concerns about bottled water

There are very few benefits to choosing bottled water over filtered or public water, and there are many drawbacks associated with bottled water. Although some bottled water is pure and healthy, many tests have found contaminates in bottled water. Also, the plastic bottle, itself, has its own undesirable qualities: higher risk of chemicals that can leach into the water, greater pollution of the environment from plastic bottles, and higher transportation costs. One toxin in plastic, bisphenol A (BPA), can leach directly into drinking water. Plastic water bottles may also contain polyvinyl chloride (PVC) or polystyrene (PS).

Plastics that are known to be safer are polyethylene terephthalate (PETE), which is for one-time use, but not for refilling, high-density polyethylene (HDPE), and polypropylene (PP). Even though a certain plastic has been called safe, it still may present health concerns. Plastics all increase in molecular activity under high heat or exposure to light, fats, and acids, and can release petroleum-based toxins, in the form of liquids or gases, into their immediate surroundings.

Vegetable Broth

Vegetable broth and pureed vegetable soup are beverages that have nutrients, as well as hydrating qualities. This broth is made from boiled and strained vegetables and makes a nutritious first beverage. It has the benefits of water, with added nutrients from vegetables. It is an easy way to introduce your baby to the taste of vegetables and to incorporate nutrients into his diet. Start with one vegetable at a time and gradually add several kinds to get a variety of root, upward-growing, and ground vegetables. For extra vitamins and minerals, add wakame flakes, kombu, or leafy greens.

Vegetable Puree Soup

Vegetable puree soup is another easy way to provide vegetables to your baby. It is different than vegetable broth, in that it contains the whole vegetable fiber. Boil or steam the vegetables with water, then puree them to make a creamy, soup-like beverage. Serve slightly warm or at room temperature.

Herbal and Barley Teas

When my children were young, I often gave them a drink made with barley or herbal tea. Sometimes, I added a small amount of apple juice for sweetener.

These teas are alkaline-producing and balancing to digestion and the nervous system. They can also be prepared as a medicinal remedy. Iced beverages can chill your baby's digestive system, so serve him tea that is at room temperature or slightly warm, for easy digestion. Chamomile and fennel tea soothe digestion and can help your child sleep better. Roasted barley tea has an alkaline-producing effect, but it does have gluten, so you may wish to wait until he is one year old before offering it to your baby. Mint tea is cooling and can help an upset stomach.

Amazake

Amazake is a traditional Japanese sweet drink made from fermented sweet rice. *Koji* is a yeast starter, or an enzyme, used to break down the carbohydrates to bring out the natural sweetness of the rice. It can be eaten as a pudding, diluted to make a warm drink, or used as a sweetener in baking. For mothers, *amazake* is helpful in the production of breast milk. For babies and children, it is a delicious beverage. It is high in complex carbohydrates, fiber, and the B vitamins niacin and thiamin.

Rice Milk

Rice milk is made from brown rice and has many of the properties and nutritional benefits of the whole grain. It is free of casein and lactose and is considered the most hypoallergenic of all the milk alternatives. Rice milk is a good choice for people with allergies to nuts.

Like rice itself, rice milk is rich in B vitamins, especially B3, or niacin, and B6, which are essential for metabolism and nervous system function. It is also a source of magnesium, which promotes healthy blood pressure and bowel function. The fat in rice milk is unsaturated and has been shown to lower blood cholesterol.

Rice milk is rich in carbohydrates, with three or four times that of soy milk. Whenever possible, choose an organically grown rice milk. Dilute rice milk with water, because of the high glucose content. Rice milk can be used as a beverage, but it is not a substitute for breast milk or formula.

Coconut Water

Coconut water is the watery liquid found inside young coconuts and is high in antioxidants, amino acids, enzymes, B-complex and C vitamins, and the primary electrolytes needed for complete hydration: sodium, potassium, calcium, magnesium, and phosphorus. Coconut water has a sweet and refreshing taste that children like, and it provides rehydration on hot days or after a lot of activity. It has been marketed as a natural energy or sport drink due to its high electrolyte content and low levels of calories, carbohydrates, and fat. Coconut water can be served fresh from the coconut, or packaged in steel cans, Tetra Paks, or plastic bottles.

Vegetable Juice

Because vegetable juice is raw, it is not predigested the way cooked vegetables are. It is also not a whole food, because the fiber is stripped out, and drinking the juice alone is more concentrated than eating the whole vegetable. However, carrot juice, with the naturally sweet taste of carrots, makes a delicious vegetable juice, either alone or combined with another vegetable juice. Raw vegetable juice can be a refreshing and healthy treat occasionally, especially in warmer weather. You may wish to make your own vegetable juices with an electric juicer. As an alternative to extracting the juice, you may want to use a high-powered blender to create a thicker, smoothie-like juice that includes the fiber, rather than stripping it out—this would be closer to a whole food.

Fruit Juice

When your child eats a piece of whole fruit, such as an apple or an orange, he gets fiber, water, antioxidants, and other nutrients along with the fruit's sugars, which break down in his intestines and digest slowly. Typically, it takes six to eight whole apples to make one cup of apple juice, which is made by extracting the liquid and leaving out the fiber. The remaining juice has a concentrated fruit sugar content, which can be absorbed rapidly into his bloodstream and elevate his insulin levels. High blood sugar and insulin levels are known to cause mood swings and contribute to many serious illnesses, including diabetes and obesity.

Drinking apple juice can reduce your baby's appetite for other nourishing foods and desensitize his palate, so that he wants all of his foods to be as sweet as the juice. While your child can still absorb calories from apple juice, they will mostly be calories from sugars or carbohydrates, instead of calories from proteins or fats. This can lead to cravings, or an addiction to sweets, and it can cause other imbalances.

According to the American Academy of Pediatrics, drinking too much juice can contribute to obesity, the development of cavities, diarrhea, and other gastrointestinal problems, such as excessive gas, bloating, and abdominal pain.

American Academy of Pediatrics Juice Recommendations

- When you give your child juice, it should be 100% fruit juice that has been pasteurized or flash pasteurized, and not fruit drinks with added colors or sweeteners.

- Infants under 6 months of age should not be given juice, although many pediatricians do recommend small amounts of juice for children who are constipated.

- Infants between 6 and 12 months can drink up to 4 to 6 ounces of juice a day, but should do so only from a cup, not a bottle as drinking sweet beverages from a bottle can cause early tooth decay.

- Younger children aged one to six years should have only four to six ounces of juice a day, if at all.

- Older children should be limited to eight to 12 ounces of juice a day.

- Instead of juice, children should be encouraged to eat whole fruits.

Recent studies have found arsenic in apple juice in amounts that surpass the FDA's recommendations for heavy metals in juices. To be safe about arsenic in juice, choose juice that is organic and from a country of origin that has high safety regulations. Read labels to make sure the juice does not have added sugar, high-fructose corn syrup, food coloring, or chemical ingredients.

On the positive side, fruit juice is a refreshing drink and can be diluted with water or tea to reduce the sugar content per serving. It can be used as a sweetener in gelo or other desserts. It is also helpful for constipation, and fruit juice can help your baby relax if he is tense.

Almond and Sesame Milks

Almond and sesame milks are nutritionally rich, high-protein, plant-based alternatives to animal milk. They provide high concentrations of vitamin E, calcium, copper, iron, magnesium, manganese, phosphorus, potassium, selenium, and zinc. These nutrients occur naturally in homemade nut milks; some commercial nut milk varieties are fortified. Nut milk is also a rich source of omega-3 fatty acids and flavonoids, which act as powerful antioxidants that boost immunity and protect against heart disease, many forms of cancer, and other degenerative diseases. It is exceedingly low in saturated fat and calories and contains no cholesterol. Nut milk is both lactose- and casein-free. It does not cause a dramatic rise in blood sugar.

Almond and sesame milks are easy to make. Simply soak ⅓ cup of nuts or seeds in 1 cup of water overnight, cook for 15 to 20 minutes, and then blend until creamy. The primary concern with nut milk is nut allergies. Introduce a small first serving to make sure your child does not have a nut allergy. Choose or make organic nut milk when possible, and do not substitute it for breast milk or formula.

Soy Milk

Soy milk is a popular cow's milk alternative because it is low in saturated fat and has no cholesterol. It is also free of lactose and casein, which means it does not cause the allergic reactions that are common with cow's milk. However, there is some debate about whether soy milk is a healthy alternative, especially for boys, because soy proteins contain isoflavins that can mimic estrogen. Soybeans made into a liquid form have different properties of balance than do miso, tamari, and even tofu, which have been processed with salt or *nigari* (a coagulating agent for tofu). It is possible that soy milk can be hard to digest for some babies and children. Soy milk can be used as an occasional beverage, but should not be substituted for breast milk or formula.

Comparing Milks

per 8oz serving	Milk (Whole)	Soy (Unsweetened)	Almond (Unsweetened)	Rice (Unsweetened)	Coconut (Unsweetened)
Calories	148	131	30	90	70
Total fat	8 g	4.2 g	2.5 g	2.5 g	4.5 g
Saturated fat	4.6 g	0.5 g	0 g	0 g	4 g
Cholesterol	24 mg	0 mg	0 mg	0 mg	0 mg
Sodium	105 mg	124 mg	160 mg	130 mg	15 mg
Carbohydrates	12 g	15 g	<1 g	15 g	8 g
Dietary fiber	0 g	1.5 g	<1 g	0 g	1 g
Sugars	12 g	10 g	0 g	<1 g	7 g
Protein	8 g	8 g	1 g	<1 g	0 g
Vitamin A	7%	0%	10%	10%	10%
Vitamin C	0%	0%	0%	0%	0%
Calcium	27%	6%	45%	30%	10%
Iron	0%	8%	2%	0%	4%

*Percent Daily Values are based on a 2,000 calorie diet. Values are based on common brand name products.

Cow's Milk

Cow's milk is high in protein, sodium, and potassium. One of the proteins in milk, casein, can cause allergies, excess mucus, and chronic constipation in children. Cow's milk has a combination of low vitamin C and moderately high calcium, which prevents the body from absorbing iron, and can lead to anemia. Early exposure to cow's milk has also been linked to type 1 diabetes and obesity in children.

In his book *Eat, Drink, and Be Healthy*, Walter C. Willett, MD, the dean of nutrition at Harvard Medical School, points out that 75 percent of the world's adult population, including 50 million Americans, cannot digest lactose. The presence of lactose in the diet can cause a variety of digestive problems, including cramping, diarrhea, constipation, nausea, and bloating. The American Academy of Pediatrics recommends that parents do not introduce cow's milk, or cow's milk products, to children younger than 12 months of age. Furthermore, respected American "baby doctor" Benjamin Spock, MD, revised his recommendations on milk in the final book he published before his death, recommending no cow's milk for children under the age of two.

Cow's milk has the chemical makeup that meets the nutritional needs of a baby calf, but it does not replace the nutritional needs of breast milk or formula for the first year of a baby's life. If you choose to introduce cow's milk to your child after the age of one, make sure you choose organic whole cow's milk. Skim milk and low-fat milk are high in salt and protein and lack fats and nutrients that create a sense of satiation. Non-organic milk and milk products also contain recombinant bovine growth hormone (rBGH) to promote milk production and antibiotics to fight infections in the cows.

Goat's Milk

Goat's milk is less allergenic than cow's milk, and it has higher quantities of health-supporting fatty acids, such as linoleic fatty acid. Goat's milk can be a healthy, nutritional liquid food for babies over the age of six months, but goat's milk has drawbacks, too. Infants should not consume goat's milk as a replacement for breast milk or formula.

The primary concern about goat's milk is its protein content, which is even higher than that of cow's milk. Once in the bloodstream, protein turns into acid, which must be processed and eliminated by the kidneys. The high protein content of goat's milk can put stress on the immature kidneys of babies and young children.

Goat's milk may be a supplement to the diets of toddlers and adolescents, but it is not recommended for infants as a substitute for breast milk or infant formula. Most goat farmers do not use antibiotics and growth hormones, but you still may want to look for goat's milk that is organic or certified antibiotic- and growth hormone-free.

Sodas

Most sodas contain refined sugar, caffeine, and artificial colors that are completely unnecessary and damaging for young children. They have no nutritional value, and they can lead to obesity and diabetes, so they should be avoided. Natural sodas, sweetened with fruit juice, could be a refreshing treat for special occasions—read the label because many "natural" sodas still contain refined sugars.

The Yin and Yang of Beverages

Beverages are liquid so their basic nature has more of a yin influence. However, some determinants that affect the yin or yang effect of beverages include the actual content of the food, the sugar, salt, or fat content, as well as the preparation method—cooked or raw.

Sodas usually contain refined sugar and possibly chemicals or artificial sweeteners, so they are on the extreme yin side of the spectrum. Next is the juice of concentrated raw fruits with high sugar and low fiber content. Soy milk is next because it has a high fat content, and it is a plant-based milk. Then is cow's milk, which is animal food that is high in fats and lactose sugars. Coconut water is tropical (yin influence) but is whole, rather than concentrated and has trace minerals (yang influence). Raw vegetable juice is concentrated, but does not have the same sugar content of raw fruit juice. Almond and rice milk are higher in fat, but low in sugar content. Herbal teas vary according to the herb, but they usually have more of a balanced influence. Cooked vegetable juice has more of a yang influence, because the whole vegetables have been cooked. Barley tea is a roasted grain, so it has more of a yang influence and an alkaline-producing effect than herbal teas. Goat's milk has the most yang influence, because it has a lot of sodium and less fat than other milks. Listed in the chart are balanced foods toward the center for daily use, foods on a wider spectrum for occasional use, and extreme foods to avoid.

Beverages for Your Baby

After he starts eating solid food, you can supplement your baby's food and breast milk or formula with a small amount of water from a spoon or sippy cup. If your water is not filtered, the safest water to begin with is water that has been boiled and cooled to room temperature.

At six months, some other beverage options that provide nutritional value, as well as hydration are vegetable broths, vegetable puree soup, *amazake*, rice milk, barley tea, and herbal tea. Serve these beverages at room temperature or at about the same temperature of breast milk or formula.

At twelve months, when breast milk or formula is not the sole source of fluids, other beverages can be introduced in small amounts, such as coconut water, diluted fruit juice without added sugar, raw vegetable juice, almond and sesame milks (check to make sure he does not have an allergic reaction to nuts), and soy milk (sparingly). If you choose to introduce cow's or goat's milk to your child after the age of one, make sure you choose whole organic milk.

The chart below gives an overview of which beverages to introduce and when. The chart also includes how frequently to serve these beverages and which ones to avoid.

Yin-Yang Spectrum of Beverages

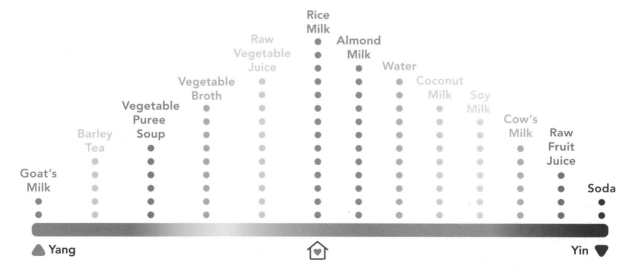

Yang · Yin

When to Introduce Beverages		
Beverages	Age Range	Frequency
Water	6 to 8 months	Daily
Vegetable broth	6 to 8 months	Daily
Vegetable puree and soup	6 to 8 months	Daily
Barley, chamomile, or fennel tea	6 to 8 months	Daily
Amazake	6 to 8 months	Daily
Rice milk	6 to 8 months	Occasionally
Coconut water	12 to 18 months	Occasionally
Raw vegetable juice	12 to 18 months	Occasionally
Fruit juice, diluted	12 to 18 months	Occasionally
Almond or sesame milk	12 to 18 months	Occasionally
Soy milk	12 to 18 months	Occasionally
Cow's milk	12 to 18 months	Occasionally
Goat's milk	12 to 18 months	Occasionally
Sodas	All ages	Avoid

Occasionally: 2–3 times a week

Beverage Recipes

Breast milk or formula is the main beverage that your baby needs for his first twelve months. If he is formula-fed, then he may need more fluids than if he is breast-fed. Filtered water can be a first beverage, and he may enjoy a broth made from cooked vegetables as a beverage. Roasted barley and herbal teas are alkaline-forming drinks that are healthy for daily use. *Amazake* is a traditional Japanese beverage that is naturally sweet and can be served as a drink or added as a sweetener. If you do not have time to make homemade *amazake*, then it is available to buy pre-made, either frozen or vacuum-packed.

Veggie Broth

♡ **6 months+**

🥣 **16 ounces Broth and 4 (2-ounce) servings Mixed Veggie Puree**

V Vegetarian

GF Gluten-free

This broth is packed with nourishment and one recipe makes two foods for serving: a clear broth and pureed veggies. Serve the broth with a spoon, trainer, or sippy cup.

1 cup mixed vegetables, cut into 1-inch pieces.

4 cups water

1-inch square kombu or 1 teaspoon wakame seaweed

⅛ teaspoon sea salt for 9–12 months, ¼ teaspoon for 12 months+

Options:

One to three of the following: broccoli, carrots, yellow squash, onions, peas, cabbage, kale, sweet potatoes, butternut squash, Japanese pumpkin

Method

1. Bring all ingredients to a boil in a pot over high heat, reduce heat, and simmer for 20 to 25 minutes.

2. Strain for a clear broth.

3. Puree the veggies in a blender, food processor, or food mill for serving separately.

Roasted Barley Tea

♡ 7 months+

🥣 8 ounces Tea

V Vegetarian

Roasted barley tea has antioxidant properties, is a good source of phytonutrients, and creates a soothing and comforting feeling. It contains eight essential amino acids and it is rich in vitamins, fiber, and minerals. Barley tea helps with cold symptoms and fever because it cleanses the system and inhibits the growth of bacteria. Make some barley tea and keep it in the refrigerator for several days. If your baby is not eating gluten for his first year, wait to give him this tea until his first birthday, because barley contains gluten.

2 tablespoons roasted barley tea

2 cups water

Method

1. Put barley and water in pan and bring to a boil.

2. Reduce heat and simmer for 5 minutes.

3. Cool, strain, and serve in a trainer bottle, sippy, or regular cup.

Herbal Tea

♡ 7 months+

🥣 16 ounces Tea

V Vegetarian

2 cups water

1 tea bag, 1 teaspoon herbs, or 1 tablespoon minced fresh herbs

Options:

Mint, lemongrass, lemon balm, chamomile, fennel, raspberry leaf

Tea is an alkaline-producing, everyday beverage for your baby and toddler, and does not have the sugars found in fruit juice that can cause tooth decay and other health concerns. Herbal teas have different properties with different effects. Alternate teas for variety.

Method

1. Put water in pan and bring to a boil.

2. Turn off heat, add tea bag or herbs, and steep for 5 minutes.

3. Cool, strain, and serve in a trainer bottle, sippy, or regular cup.

Amazake

♡ 6 months+

🥣 16 (2 ounce) servings

V Vegetarian

GF Gluten-free

Amazake is a creamy drink with a rich, sweet taste that is popular in Japan with children and adults. It is served warm or cool. *Amazake* can be purchased refrigerated, frozen, or vacuum packed at a natural foods store. *Amazake* bought in the store is probably pasteurized, which kills the *Lactobacillus,* but it still has a natural sweet flavor that is delicious. Homemade *amazake* is made with the simple ingredients of cooked sweet rice and *koji,* which starts a fermentation process. *Koji* is rice that has been inoculated with *Aspergillus* and is used for making sake, miso, and other traditional Japanese fermented foods. It can be purchased online.

1 cup sweet brown rice

Water for soaking rice

2 cups water for cooking rice

½ cup *koji*

½ cup water for *koji* mixture

⅛ teaspoon sea salt

Planning ahead

Cover grains with water and soak for 8 to 24 hours. If you do not have time to soak for the longer time span, soak for at least 1 hour, if possible.

Method

1. Strain soaking water, add rice and cooking water to pot, and bring to a boil.

2. Reduce heat and cook for 45 minutes to 1 hour, until all water has been absorbed.

3. Use a heat diffuser to keep grains from sticking to the bottom of the pot, and to prevent burning.

4. Transfer rice to a glass casserole dish and stir to break up grains. Let cool.

5. After the rice has cooled, mix in *koji* thoroughly, and add ½ cup water.

6. Preheat oven at 115º to 135ºF . If your oven will not go that low, preheat at oven's lowest temperature, and then turn it off. Wrap rice and *koji* mixture in a towel to keep warm, and place in oven.

7. Periodically, take the mixture out of the oven, and turn it back on, to raise the temperature. Then turn the oven off again and repeat until the *amazake* has a sweet taste. This may take 6 to 10 hours.

8. Stir every 2 hours.

9. After *amazake* has finished incubating, add sea salt and blend for a smooth, creamy consistency.

Variations:

• For a beverage, mix together 2 tablespoons *amazake* puree and ¼ cup water. *Amazake* is refreshing served slightly chilled during warm weather, and is comforting served warm in cold weather.

• For *amazake* pudding, in a small pot, heat 1 cup *amazake* in ¼ cup water. Dissolve 1 tablespoon kuzu or arrowroot flour in 1 tablespoon water in a separate bowl or a grinding bowl. Use a fork or pestle to dissolve thoroughly. Add kuzu or arrowroot liquid to simmering *amazake*, and stir until it turns transparent. Add ¼ teaspoon vanilla extract and/or 1 teaspoon raisins while cooking, for added flavor. *Amazake* can be used as a sweetener in other desserts.

CHAPTER 7
Menu Plans

PLANNING YOUR BABY'S FOOD may take some thought in the beginning. However, after you have had some experience with cooking and feeding your baby, you can easily take cues from her and follow your own intuition to make balanced and healthy meals that will satisfy her.

Your baby can start with very basic, simple, almost liquid foods, then try more of a variety of ingredients, textures, and tastes over time. This is a time of rapid growth for her, physically, emotionally, and mentally, so the quality of her food is very influential in her development.

From six to nine months, there are many ways your baby may approach her first feedings, so the charts have overlapping ages: 6 to 8 months and 7 to 9 months. Some babies have a big appetite and eat everything with gusto, while others just play and learn with food for several months before actually absorbing nutrition from meals. There are also many variables, such as whether she is breast- or bottle-feeding, whether she is weaning, and her age, sex, size, and condition. In the first stage, she may not be eating very much and may just be learning textures and the mechanics of how to swallow, while still getting most of her nourishment from breast milk or formula. In the next stages, food becomes more of a source of nutrition for her.

The menu plan offers examples for feeding your baby for her first three years. I have included the following age ranges: 6–8 months, 7–9 months, 9–12 months, 12–18 months, 18–24 months, 24–36 months.

Feeding Your Baby at 6 to 8 months

Development
Your baby sits up in a high chair, reaches for food, and starts cutting teeth

Meal Frequency and Consistency
2–3 meals
Soft, thin puree mixed with liquid on fingertip or spoon

Food Percentages
The chart below shows generally how much of each food group your baby needs at this stage.

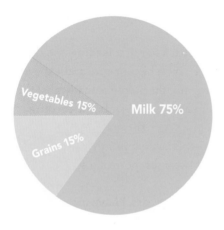

At the age of 6 to 8 months, begin by cooking one ingredient at a time. Usually a whole grain, either brown rice or millet, makes a good first meal, because grains cooked with a soupy consistency are similar to breast milk and formula. Next are single ingredient vegetables, followed by combinations of two grains, such as sweet brown rice and millet cooked together. Although allergies to single grains or single vegetables are unusual, it is easier to detect an allergy by starting out with single ingredients and observing responses or reactions your baby may have. First vegetables include sweet vegetables, such as butternut squash or pumpkin, yellow squash, sweet potatoes, peas, and nori sea vegetable.

In the beginning, foods should be cooked thoroughly, with a very smooth, soupy consistency to make the transition from liquids to solids. You can adjust the consistency as your baby grows by reducing the amount of liquid. Be sure to save extra water used in cooking to add to the puree, serve as a beverage, or for soup stock, so that your baby gets the most nutrients.

Offering vegetables before fruits helps establish an appreciation for savory tastes, as well as the simple sweetness found in vegetables. Also, fruits combined with grains and protein-rich foods can create gas, so waiting for four to six weeks after starting solids gives the digestive system a chance to start functioning with solids before bringing in another complication. After grains and vegetables, introduce protein-rich foods, starting with soft protein-rich foods, such as cooked tofu and tahini or sesame seeds added to grains before cooking. Soaking grains and pouring off the water is a process that mildly ferments and predigests the grains, providing a form of "good bacteria," which helps with digestion. Sweet potato mash is a fermented food that is not salty. At this time, you can mix probiotic booster into her pureed grain or vegetable to support her immune system. Check with your health care provider for guidance.

Natural oils, such as sesame, olive, coconut, and flaxseed oil added to food purees daily can supplement

Purees of rice, carrots, green peas, and tofu

fats in breast milk or formula. Unrefined, quality oils are healthy for babies, and they have a very different effect on the body than refined or over-processed oils, such as hydrogenated fats and canola oil. Occasionally, stir small amounts of natural grain sweetener, such as brown rice syrup or *amazake*, into grain cereals for a sweet taste and for a calming effect. You can add fennel for flavor and as a digestive aid. Herbal teas or cooked vegetable juices are alkaline-forming beverages that your baby can sip from a spoon or cup as a first beverage. Small amounts of water help your baby stay hydrated, especially on hot days. Start with one meal a day at the beginning of the day, and gradually increase the number of feedings and the quantity of food. Depending on your baby's appetite and readiness, the amount of food she eats gradually increases from ½ teaspoon, to 1 teaspoon, to 1 tablespoon, to 2 tablespoons and more as she grows. If you offer foods, your baby can lead the way to find her eating rhythm and the amount of food she needs as she grows.

Foods for Your Baby at 6 to 8 months

Milk	Breast milk or formula is still a source of many nutrients	**Fruits** 0 servings	Vegetables before fruits to develop savory taste buds
Grains 1–2 oz. per serving, 2–3 servings per day	Whole-grain puree—brown rice, sweet brown rice, quinoa, millet, gluten-free oats; one grain at a time; water-to-grain ratio 7:1	**Fermented Foods**	Probiotics from breast milk or formula; soak grains, low-sodium miso or tamari soup; juice of pickles; probiotic booster
Vegetables 1–2 oz. per serving, 2–3 servings per day	Sweet vegetables; avoid cruciferous and onions in the beginning; vegetable broth, puree soups, cooked vegetable juice	**Seasonings** ¼ teaspoon 1–2 servings per day	Mild sweet taste (no refined sugar or salt); brown rice syrup, *amazake*; fennel for seasoning, sesame oil, olive oil, flaxseed oil
Upward	Green peas, green beans		
Root	Carrot, sweet potato		
Ground	Japanese pumpkin, acorn squash, butternut squash, yellow squash, zucchini squash, green peas, green beans, sugar snap peas	**Beverages** 1–2 oz. per serving, 1–2 servings per day more on hot days	Water, vegetable broth, herbal tea, pureed soups, *amazake*
Sea	Nori 4-inch square or flakes		
Protein-Rich Foods	Protein sources: breast milk or formula, whole grains, soft, cooked tofu; toasted and ground sesame seeds, tahini		

2 tbsp = 1 oz. = ⅛ cup | 4 tbsp = 2 oz. = ¼ cup | 16 tbsp = 8 oz. = 1 cup

These are general guidelines that vary with each individual child, the constitution, size, and gender of the baby, the climate, location, season, and situation. Breast-feeding or bottle-feeding and time of weaning will also affect the amount of food needed.

6–8 Months	Week 1	Week 2	Week 3	Week 4 (M-W)
Early Morning	• Breast milk or formula	• Breast milk or formula	• Breast milk or formula	• Breast milk or formula
Breakfast	• Breast milk or formula	• Breast milk or formula	• 1–2 oz. Brown rice puree mixed with breast milk or formula • Breast milk or formula	• 1–2 oz. Sweet brown rice/millet puree mixed with breast milk or formula • Breast milk or formula
Lunch	• 1 oz. Brown rice puree mixed with breast milk or formula • Breast milk or formula	• 1 oz. Brown rice puree mixed with breast milk or formula • Breast milk or formula	• 1 oz. Sweet brown rice/millet puree mixed with breast milk or formula • 1–2 oz. Butternut squash puree • Breast milk or formula	• 1–2 oz. Sweet brown rice/millet puree mixed with ¼ t. sesame oil, ¼ t. brown rice syrup, or *amazake* • 1–2 oz. Butternut squash puree • 1–2 oz. Green bean puree • 1–2 oz. Vegetable broth, water, or herbal tea • Breast milk or formula
Midafternoon	• Breast milk or formula	• Breast milk or formula	• Breast milk or formula	• Breast milk or formula
Dinner	• Breast milk or formula	• 1 oz. Brown rice puree mixed with breast milk or formula • 1–2 oz. Butternut squash puree • 1 oz. Butternut squash broth or water • Breast milk or formula	• 1 oz. Sweet brown rice/millet puree mixed with breast milk or formula • 1–2 oz. Butternut squash puree • 1–2 oz. Green beans puree • 1–2 oz. Vegetable broth or water • Breast milk or formula	• 1–2 oz. Sweet brown rice/millet puree mixed with ¼ t. sesame oil & ¼ t. brown rice syrup or *amazake* • 1–2 oz. Carrot puree • 1–2 oz. Sugar snap pea puree • 1–2 oz. Vegetable broth, water, or herbal tea • Breast milk or formula
Bedtime	• Breast milk or formula	• Breast milk or formula	• Breast milk or formula	• Breast milk or formula

Week 4 (Th-Sun)	Week 5 (M-W)	Week 5 (Th-Sun)	Week 6 (M-W)	Week 6 (Th-Sun)
• Breast milk or formula	• Breast milk or formula	• Breast milk or formula	• Breast milk or formula	• Breast milk or formula
• 1–2 oz. Brown rice/millet puree mixed with breast milk or formula • Breast milk or formula	• 1–2 oz. Brown rice/millet/quinoa puree mixed with breast milk or formula • Breast milk or formula	• 1–2 oz. Sweet brown rice/millet puree mixed with breast milk or formula • Breast milk or formula	• 1–2 oz. Sweet brown rice/millet puree mixed with breast milk or formula • Breast milk or formula	• 1–2 oz. Sweet brown rice/millet puree mixed with breast milk or formula • Breast milk or formula
• 1–2 oz. Brown rice/millet puree mixed with ¼ t. sesame oil & ¼ t. brown rice syrup or *amazake* • 1–2 oz. Carrot puree • 1–2 oz. Sugar snap pea puree • 1–2 oz. Vegetable broth, water, herbal tea, or water kefir • Breast milk or formula	• 1–2 oz. Brown rice/millet/quinoa puree mixed with ¼ t. & ¼ t. brown rice syrup or *amazake* • 1–2 oz. Yellow squash puree • 1–2 oz. Vegetable broth, water, herbal tea, or water kefir • Breast milk or formula	• 1–2 oz. Brown rice/millet/quinoa, puree mixed with ¼ t. sesame Oil & ¼ t. brown rice syrup or *amazake* • 1–2 oz. Sweet potato puree • 1–2 oz. Vegetable broth, water, or herbal tea • Breast milk or formula	• 1–2 oz. Brown rice/millet/quinoa puree mixed with ¼ t. tahini & 2–3 drops of plum vinegar • 1–2 oz. Carrot puree • 1–2 oz. Zucchini puree • 1–2 oz. Vegetable broth, water, or herbal tea • Breast milk or formula	• 1–2 oz. Sweet brown rice/millet puree mixed with ¼ t. sesame oil • 1–2 oz. Sweet potato puree • 1–2 oz. Green pea puree • 1–2 oz. Tofu • 1–2 oz. Vegetable broth, water, or herbal tea • Breast milk or formula
• Breast milk or formula	• Breast milk or formula	• Breast milk or formula	• Breast milk or formula	• Breast milk or formula
• 1–2 oz. Brown rice/millet puree mixed with ¼ t. sesame oil & ¼ t. brown rice syrup or *amazake* • 1–2 oz. Yellow squash puree • 1–2 oz. Vegetable broth, water, herbal tea, or water kefir • Breast milk or formula	• 1–2 oz. Brown rice/millet/quinoa puree mixed with ¼ t. sesame oil & ¼ t. brown rice syrup or *amazake* • 4"-square Nori sea vegetable • 1–2 oz. Sweet potato puree • 1–2 oz. Vegetable broth, water, herbal tea, or water kefir • Breast milk or formula	• 1–2 oz. Brown rice/millet/quinoa puree mixed with ¼ t. sesame oil & ¼ t. brown rice syrup or *amazake* • 4"-square Nori sea vegetable • 1–2 oz. Carrot puree • 1–2 oz. Zucchini puree • 1–2 oz. Vegetable broth, water, or herbal tea • Breast milk or formula	• 1–2 oz. Brown rice/millet/quinoa puree mixed with ¼ t. sesame oil & ¼ t. brown rice syrup or *amazake* • 4"-square Nori sea vegetable • 1–2 oz. Sweet potato puree • 1–2 oz. Green pea puree • 1–2 oz. Vegetable broth, water, or herbal tea • Breast milk or formula	• 1–2 oz. Brown rice/millet puree mixed with ¼ t. sesame oil & ¼ t. brown rice syrup or *amazake* • 4"-square Nori sea vegetable • 1–2 oz. Yellow squash puree • 1–2 oz. Green beans puree • 1–2 oz. Mild miso, vegetable broth, water, or herbal tea • Breast milk or formula
• Breast milk or formula	• Breast milk or formula	• Breast milk or formula	• Breast milk or formula	• Breast milk or formula

Feeding Your Baby at 7 to 9 months

Development
Your baby tries to stand up, reaches for food and utensils, holds her bottle and spoon, and may drink from a cup

Meal Frequency and Consistency
2–3 meals, 1 snack
Soft, thick grainy puree with small chunky lumps

Food Percentages
The chart below shows generally how much of each food group your baby needs at this stage.

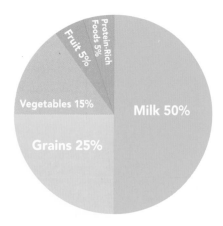

At around 7 to 9 months, broccoli, cauliflower, green beans, kale, cabbage, and bok choy expand her list of vegetables. These cruciferous vegetables have many nutrients, but they need to be cooked thoroughly for digestion and to retain iodine. A variety of vegetables of different colors and shapes ensure that your baby receives a wide range of vitamins and minerals. Sea vegetables, such as nori, wakame flakes, and kombu, offer extra minerals, digestibility, and flavor in grains, soups, vegetables, and beans.

You can mix in ½ teaspoon of sesame or olive oil to provide essential fatty acids for brain development. After introducing whole-grain cereals and vegetables, offer salt-free and gluten-free teething biscuits, as her teeth start coming in, which is usually around seven or eight months. Be sure and watch her while she eats crackers, so that she does not choke.

First fruits include cooked fruits, such as apples, pears, and peaches, and dried fruits that are cooked and pureed. Serve fruit separately from grains, vegetables, and protein-rich foods to aid digestion. Introduce beans, such as lentils, adzukis, pintos, black turtle, and white beans around eight or nine months of age. The concentrated protein of dried beans and bean products, such as tofu and tempeh, provide the necessary amino acids from a plant-based source. Nori sea vegetable is also a source of protein, as well as minerals, and you can cut up pieces and blend it in the puree for an extra nutrient boost. Offer fermented foods, such as low-sodium sweet white miso or tamari soup, juice of pickled vegetables, or water kefir to help build a strong immune system.

Alan Greene, MD, a clinical professor at Stanford University School of Medicine and author of *Raising Baby Green*, says that at around 12 months, babies develop neophobia, which is a suspicion and fear of new flavors, food sources, and styles of eating. Before their first birthday, they put anything in their mouths as they learn and explore. This stage is the chance to help develop food tastes for many different foods, so offer a variety of grains, vegetables, legumes, and seasonings while the window of opportunity is open.

Purees of broccoli, millet and rice, adzuki beans, and sweet potato

Foods for Your Baby at 7 to 9 months

Milk	Breast milk or formula is still a source of many nutrients	**Fruits** 1–2 oz. per serving, 1 serving per day	Small amounts of cooked fruit puree or dried fruit puree for dessert at least 30 minutes after grains, vegetables, or protein-rich food
Grains 2–3 oz. per serving, 3 servings per day	Whole-grain puree—brown rice, sweet brown rice, quinoa, millet, gluten-free oats, amaranth; mix grains for variety and nutrition; water-to-grain ratio 6:1; gluten-free bread and teething biscuits	**Cooked Temperate**	Apples, pears, apricots, cherries, peaches, plums, nectarines, strawberries
		Dried, Cooked, and Pureed	Apples, raisins, currants, apricots, peaches, pears
Vegetables 1–2 oz. per serving, 3–4 servings per day	Sweet vegetable puree; puree soups, cooked vegetable juice	**Fermented Foods** 2 oz. per serving, 1 serving per day	Probiotics from breast milk or formula; soak grains, low sodium miso or tamari soup; juice of water kefir, pickles; probiotic booster
Upward	Kale, collards, brussels sprouts, broccoli, cauliflower, cabbage, watercress, Chinese cabbage, bok choy, turnip greens, purple cabbage, celery; cruciferous vegetables should be well-cooked		
Root	Carrot, sweet potato, parsnips, onions	**Seasonings** ¼ teaspoon 2–3 servings per day	Mild sweet taste (no refined sugar or salt); brown rice syrup, *amazake*; small amount of sesame, olive or flaxseed oil, fennel
Ground	Japanese pumpkin, acorn squash, butternut squash, pumpkin, yellow squash, zucchini squash, green peas, green beans, sugar snap peas		
Sea	Nori flakes, wakame flakes, kombu, agar		
Protein-Rich Foods 1–2 oz. per serving, 2 servings per day	Main Protein source; breast milk or formula, cooked tofu, whole grains, ground & toasted sesame seeds, sunflower seeds, flaxseeds; tahini, pureed chestnuts, lentils, chickpeas, black beans, adzuki beans	**Beverages** 1–2 oz. per serving, 2–3 servings per day more on hot days	Water, vegetable broth, puree soups, fennel tea, chamomile tea, lemon balm tea, *amazake*

2 tbsp = 1 oz. = ⅛ cup | 4 tbsp = 2 oz. = ¼ cup | 16 tbsp = 8 oz. = 1 cup

These are general guidelines that vary with each individual child, the constitution, size, and gender of the baby, the climate, location, season, and situation. Breast-feeding or bottle-feeding and time of weaning will also affect the amount of food needed.

7–9 Months	Sunday	Monday	Tuesday
Early Morning	• Breast milk or formula	• Breast milk or formula	• Breast milk or formula
Breakfast	• 2–3 oz. Sweet brown rice/millet puree mixed with ¼ t. tahini, ¼ t. brown rice syrup, or *amazake* • 2 oz. Water kefir or miso soup • Breast milk or formula	• 2–3 oz. Sweet brown rice/millet puree mixed with ¼ t. tahini, ¼ t. brown rice syrup, or *amazake* • 2 oz. Water kefir or miso soup • Breast milk or formula	• 2–3 oz. Brown rice puree mixed with ¼ t. tahini, ¼ t. brown rice syrup, or *amazake* • 2 oz. Water kefir or miso soup • Breast milk or formula
Lunch	• 2–3 oz. Sweet brown rice/millet puree mixed with ¼ t. sesame oil and 2–3 drops of plum vinegar • 4"-square Nori sea vegetable mixed in rice puree • 1–2 oz. Carrot puree • 1–2 oz. Green beans puree • 1–2 oz. Adzuki bean puree • 1 oz. Pickles, vegetable broth, water, or herbal tea • Breast milk or formula	• 2–3 oz. Sweet brown rice/millet puree mixed with ¼ t. sesame oil and 2–3 drops of plum vinegar • 4"-square Nori sea vegetable mixed in rice puree • 1–2 oz. Sweet potato puree • 1–2 oz. Broccoli • 1–2 oz. Adzuki bean puree • 1–2 oz. Vegetable broth, water, or herbal tea • Breast milk or formula	• 2–3 oz. Brown rice puree mixed with ¼ t. sesame oil and 2–3 drops of plum vinegar • 4"-square Nori sea vegetable mixed in rice puree • 1–2 oz. Yellow squash and onions puree • 1–2 oz. Kale puree • 1–2 oz. Chickpea puree • 1–2 oz. Vegetable broth, water, or herbal tea • Breast milk or formula
Midafternoon	• 1–2 oz. Applesauce • Breast milk or formula	• 1–2 oz. Applesauce • Breast milk or formula	• 1–2 oz. Applesauce • Breast milk or formula
Dinner	• 2–3 oz. Sweet brown rice/millet puree mixed with ¼ t. sesame oil, and ¼ t. brown rice syrup or *amazake* • 1–2 oz. Sweet potato puree • 1–2 oz. Broccoli puree • 1–2 oz. Vegetable broth, water, or herbal tea • Breast milk or formula	• 2–3 oz. Sweet brown rice/millet puree mixed with ¼ t. sesame oil, and ¼ t. brown rice syrup or *amazake* • 1–2 oz. Yellow squash and onions puree • 1–2 oz. Kale puree • 1–2 oz. Vegetable broth, water, or herbal tea • Breast milk or formula	• 2–3 oz. Brown rice puree mixed with ¼ t. sesame oil, and ¼ t. brown rice syrup or *amazake* • 1–2 oz. Parsnip puree • 1–2 oz. Purple cabbage puree • 1–2 oz. Mild miso or tamari vegetable broth, water, or herbal tea • Breast milk or formula
Bedtime	• Breast milk or formula	• Breast milk or formula	• Breast milk or formula

Wednesday	Thursday	Friday	Saturday
• Breast milk or formula	• Breast milk or formula	• Breast milk or formula	• Breast milk or formula
• 2–3 oz. Brown rice puree mixed with ¼ t. tahini, ¼ t. brown rice syrup, or *amazake* • 2 oz. Water kefir or miso soup • Breast milk or formula	• 2–3 oz. Brown rice/millet/quinoa puree mixed with ¼ t. Tahini, ¼ t. brown rice syrup, or *amazake* • 2 oz. Water kefir or miso soup • Breast milk or formula	• 2–3 oz. Brown rice/millet/quinoa puree mixed with ¼ t. tahini, ¼ t. brown rice syrup, or *amazake* • 2 oz. Water kefir or miso soup • Breast milk or formula	• 2–3 oz. Sweet brown rice/millet puree mixed with ¼ t. tahini, ¼ t. brown rice syrup, or *amazake* • 2 oz. Water kefir or miso soup • Breast milk or formula
• 2–3 oz. Brown rice puree mixed with ¼ t. sesame oil and 2–3 drops of plum vinegar • 4"-square Nori sea vegetable mixed in rice puree • 1–2 oz. Parsnip puree • 1–2 oz. Purple cabbage puree • 1–2 oz. Chickpea puree • 1–2 oz. Vegetable broth, water, or herbal tea • Breast milk or formula	• 2–3 oz. Brown rice/millet/quinoa puree mixed with ¼ t. sesame oil and 2–3 drops of plum vinegar • 4"-square Nori sea vegetable mixed in rice puree • 1–2 oz. Sweet potato puree • 1–2 oz. Cauliflower puree • 1–2 oz. Tofu • 1–2 oz. Vegetable broth, water, or herbal tea • Breast milk or formula	• 2–3 oz. Brown rice/millet/quinoa puree mixed with ¼ t. sesame oil and 2–3 drops of plum vinegar • 4"-square Nori sea vegetable mixed in rice puree • 1–2 oz. Carrots puree • 1–2 oz. Green beans puree • 1–2 oz. Tofu • 1–2 oz. Vegetable broth, water, or herbal tea • Breast milk or formula	• 2–3 oz. Sweet brown rice/millet puree mixed with ¼ t. sesame oil and 2–3 drops of plum vinegar • 4"-square Nori sea vegetable mixed in rice puree • 1–2 oz. Butternut squash puree • 1–2 oz. Broccoli puree • 1–2 oz. Adzuki bean puree • 1–2 oz. Vegetable broth, water, or herbal tea • Breast milk or formula
• 1–2 oz. Applesauce • Breast milk or formula	• 1–2 oz. Dried fruit puree • Breast milk or formula	• 1–2 oz. Dried fruit puree • Breast milk or formula	• 1–2 oz. Dried fruit puree • Breast milk or formula
• 2–3 oz. Brown rice puree mixed with ¼ t. sesame oil and ¼ t. brown rice syrup or *amazake* • 1–2 oz. Sweet potato puree • 1–2 oz. Cauliflower puree • 1–2 oz. Vegetable broth, water, or herbal tea • Breast milk or formula	• 2–3 oz. Brown rice/millet/quinoa puree mixed with ¼ t. sesame oil and ¼ t. brown rice syrup or *amazake* • 1–2 oz. Carrots puree • 1–2 oz. Green beans puree • 1–2 oz. Vegetable broth, water, or herbal tea • Breast milk or formula	• 2–3 oz. Brown rice/millet/quinoa puree mixed with ¼ t. sesame oil and ¼ t. brown rice syrup or *amazake* • 1–2 oz. Butternut squash puree • 1–2 oz. Broccoli puree • 1–2 oz. Vegetable broth, water, or herbal tea • Breast milk or formula	• 2–3 oz. Sweet brown rice/millet puree mixed with ¼ t. sesame oil and ¼ t. brown rice syrup or *amazake* • 1–2 oz. Yellow squash puree • 1–2 oz. Green beans puree • 1–2 oz. Vegetable broth, water, or herbal tea • Breast milk or formula
• Breast milk or formula	• Breast milk or formula	• Breast milk or formula	• Breast milk or formula

Feeding Your Baby at 9 to 12 months

Development

Your baby stands up, tries to use toddler utensils, holds her trainer cup, plays with her food, and throws it on the floor; she is messy

Meal Frequency and Consistency

3 meals, 1 snack

Soft, thick grainy puree with small chunky lumps

Food Percentages

The chart below shows generally how much of each food group your baby needs at this stage.

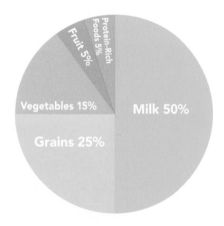

At 9 to 12 months, continue purees, adjusting the ratio of water to make a lumpier consistency as your baby starts learning to "gum" and chew her food.

Your baby's digestive system has become more developed and can process soft, mashed raw fruits such as cantaloupes, grapes cut into quarters, avocados, and bananas. If you offer fruits with seeds or pits, remove them before serving. Around this time your baby may be ready for gluten-free pasta or other soft-cooked vegetable pieces of "finger foods" that she can pick up and feed herself. Try beets, rutabagas, carrots, broccoli, green peas, and yellow squash. Offer her small pieces of nori as a garnish on grains, making sure that it is moist so that it does not stick to the back of her mouth. Kefir and yogurt can provide probiotic benefits on occasion. Be aware of choking hazards, and be sure to keep an eye on her while she is eating.

First finger foods

For the first few months it is necessary to keep food out of your baby's reach as you feed her. After she has eaten smooth purees, and purees with a lumpy texture, around eight months, the next step is to offer her soft foods in bite-sized pieces that she can pick up and eat by herself. Finger foods help develop manual dexterity and encourage your baby to eat independently, which gives her a measure of control in learning how to self-regulate her eating.

For first finger foods, give your baby very small pieces of food that are about the size of a pea. For nutritional needs, you can continue to feed purees from a bowl that is kept out of reach, but once she begins to feed herself, you can put finger foods directly onto the high chair tray or a place mat, or use a dish that is not breakable. Gradually increase different varieties and textures of food that are shredded and minced pieces, pea-sized pieces, sticks or chunks, hard pieces of crackers and toast, fruits, beans, and pasta.

The first phase of self-feeding is a very messy time to experiment and learn. My daughter, Mari, started self-feeding solid foods during the summer months, so I took her high chair outside in the backyard and fed her there, which saved me from cleaning up big messes.

Purees of kale, adzuki beans, and butternut squash; noodles, vegetable broth, with cantaloupe for dessert

Foods for Your Baby at 9 to 12 months

Milk	Breast milk or formula is still a source of many nutrients	**Fruits** 2 oz. per serving, 1–2 servings per day	Cooked puree or dried fruit puree or fresh fruit for dessert 30 minutes after grains, vegetables, or protein-rich food	
Grains 2–4 oz. per serving, 3–4 servings per day	Whole-grain puree—brown rice, sweet brown rice, quinoa, millet, oats, amaranth, gluten-free pasta or bread & teething biscuits; mix grains for variety and nutrition; water-to-grain ratio 5:1	**Cooked Temperate**	Apples, pears, apricots, cherries, peaches, plums, nectarines, strawberries	
		Dried, Cooked, and Pureed	Apples, raisins, currants, apricots, peaches, pears	
Vegetables 2 oz. per serving, 3–4 servings per day	Sweet vegetables; vegetable broth, pureed soups	**Fresh Temperate Mashed**	Apples, pears, apricots, cherries, peaches, plums, nectarines, grapes, cantaloupe, watermelon, honeydew melon	
Upward	Kale, collards, brussels sprouts, broccoli, cauliflower, watercress, Chinese cabbage, bok choy, turnip greens, purple cabbage	**Fresh Tropical Mashed**	Avocados, bananas, papayas, mangos	
Root	Carrot, sweet potato, parsnips, onions	**Fermented Foods** 1–2 oz. per serving, 1–2 servings per day	Probiotics from breast milk or formula; soak grains, low sodium miso or tamari soup; juice of pickles; 2–3 drops of plum vinegar, kefir or yogurt; probiotic booster, water kefir	
Ground	Japanese pumpkin, acorn squash, butternut squash, yellow squash, zucchini, green peas, green beans, sugar snap peas, celery	**Seasonings** ¼ teaspoon 3–4 servings per day	Mild sweet taste (no refined sugar or salt); brown rice syrup, *amazake*; small amount of sesame, olive, coconut or flaxseed oil, pinch of salt; basil, bay leaves, dill, fennel, lemongrass, or mint	
Sea	Nori flakes, wakame flakes, kombu, agar	**Beverages** 2 oz. per serving, 3–4 servings per day more on hot days	Water, vegetable broth, pureed soups, fennel tea, chamomile tea, lemon balm tea, rice milk, *amazake*	
Protein-Rich Foods 2–4 oz. per serving, 2–3 servings per day	Breast milk or formula, whole grains, ground sesame seeds, sunflower seeds, flaxseeds or tahini, pureed chestnuts, lentils, chickpeas, black beans, adzuki beans, pinto beans			

2 tbsp = 1 oz. = ⅛ cup | 4 tbsp = 2 oz. = ¼ cup | 16 tbsp = 8 oz. = 1 cup

These are general guidelines that vary with each individual child, the constitution, size, and gender of the baby, the climate, location, season, and situation. Breast-feeding or bottle-feeding and time of weaning will also affect the amount of food needed.

9–12 Months	Sunday	Monday	Tuesday
Early Morning	• Breast milk or formula	• Breast milk or formula	• Breast milk or formula
Breakfast	• 3 oz. Brown rice puree mixed with ¼ t. tahini and ¼ t. brown rice syrup or *amazake* • 2 oz. Water kefir or miso soup	• 3 oz. Brown rice puree mixed with ¼ t. tahini and ¼ t. brown rice syrup or *amazake* • 2 oz. Water kefir or miso soup	• 3 oz. Oatmeal puree with ¼ t. ground toasted seeds and ¼ t. brown rice syrup or *amazake* • 2 oz. Water kefir or miso soup
Lunch	• 2–4 oz. Brown rice/millet puree mixed with ¼ t. oil and ¼ t. brown rice syrup or *amazake* • 2 oz. Yellow squash • 2 oz. Green beans • 2 oz. Avocado • 1 oz. Pickles • 2 oz. Vegetable broth, water, or herbal tea • Breast milk or formula	• 2–4 oz. Spaghetti, mixed with ¼ t. olive oil and 2–3 drops of plum vinegar • 4"-square Nori sea vegetable flakes • 2 oz. Steamed carrot sticks • 2 oz. Steamed broccoli • 2 oz. Lentils • 1 oz. Juice of pickles • 2 oz. Vegetable broth, water, or herbal tea • Breast milk or formula	• 2–4 oz. Brown rice/millet puree • 2 oz. Fish (vegetarians—substitute fish for cooked tofu or tempeh) • 2 oz. Steamed asparagus • 2 oz. Sauteed mushrooms • 1 oz. Pickles • 2 oz. Vegetable broth, water, or herbal tea • Breast milk or formula
Midafternoon	• 2 oz. Baked apple • 2 oz. Dry whole grain gluten-free O's cereal • Breast milk or formula	• 2 oz. Banana mashed • 2 oz. Yogurt • Breast milk or formula	• 2 oz. Carrot juice • 2 oz. Puffed rice • Breast milk or formula
Dinner	• 3 oz. Spaghetti, mixed with ¼ t. olive oil and 2–3 drops of plum vinegar • 4"-square Nori sea vegetable flakes • 2 oz. Steamed carrot sticks • 2 oz. Steamed broccoli • 2–4 oz. Lentils • 1 oz. Juice of pickles • 2 oz. Vegetable broth, water, or herbal tea • Breast milk or formula	• 3 oz. Brown rice/millet • 2–4 oz. Fish (vegetarians—substitute fish for cooked tofu or tempeh) • 2 oz. Steamed asparagus • 2 oz. Sauteed mushrooms • 2 oz. Vegetable broth, water, or herbal tea • Breast milk or formula	• 1 Corn on the cob • 2 oz. Mashed potatoes • 2 oz. cabbage • 2–4 oz. Black bean soup • 1 oz. Pickles • 2 oz. Miso soup, water, or herbal tea • Breast milk or formula
Bedtime	• Breast milk or formula	• Breast milk or formula	• Breast milk or formula

Wednesday	Thursday	Friday	Saturday
• Breast milk or formula	• Breast milk or formula	• Breast milk or formula	• Breast milk or formula
• 3 oz. Oatmeal puree with ¼ t. ground toasted seeds and ¼ t. brown rice syrup or *amazake* • 2 oz. Water kefir or miso soup	• 3 oz. Brown rice/millet/quinoa puree mixed with ¼ t. ground flaxseeds and ¼ t. brown rice syrup or *amazake* • 2 oz. Water kefir or miso soup	• 3 oz. Brown rice/millet/quinoa puree mixed with ¼ t. ground flaxseeds and ¼ t. brown rice syrup or *amazake* • 2 oz. Water kefir or miso soup	• 3 oz. Sweet brown rice puree mixed with ¼ t. tahini and ¼ t. brown rice syrup or *amazake* • 2 oz. Water kefir or miso soup
• 1 Corn on the cob • 2 oz. Mashed potatoes • 2 oz. Cabbage • 2 oz. Black bean soup • 1 oz. Pickles • 2 oz. Miso soup, water, or herbal tea • Breast milk or formula	• 2–4 oz. Udon noodles with tamari broth • 2 oz. Baked sweet potato • 2 oz. Steamed watercress • 1 oz. Pickles • 2 oz. Water, or herbal tea • Breast milk or formula	• 2–4 oz. Brown rice • 2–4 oz. Tempeh and carrots • 2–3 oz. Green beans • 1 oz. Pickles • 2 oz. Tamari soup, water, or herbal tea • Breast milk or formula	• 2 Rice balls • 2–4 oz. Steamed mixed vegetables with plum vinegar and sesame or olive oil • 1 oz. Pickles • 2 oz. Kidney bean soup • 2 oz. Miso soup, water, or herbal tea • Breast milk or formula
• 2 oz. Cooked blueberries • 1 Oatmeal cookie • Breast milk or formula	• 2 oz. Cooked pear sauce • 2 oz. Yogurt • Breast milk or formula	• 2 oz. Coconut water • 1 Oatmeal cookie • Breast milk or formula	• 2 oz. Diluted fruit juice • 2 oz. Yogurt • 1 Rice cracker • Breast milk or formula
• 3–4 oz. Udon noodles with tamari broth • 2 oz. Baked sweet potato • 2 oz. Steamed watercress • 1 oz. Pickles • 2 oz. Water, or herbal tea • Breast milk or formula	• 3–4 oz. Brown rice • 2–4 oz. Tempeh and carrots • 2 oz. Green beans • 1 oz. Pickles • 2 oz. Miso soup, water, or herbal tea • Breast milk or formula	• 1–2 Rice balls • 4–6 oz. Steamed mixed vegetables with plum vinegar and sesame or olive oil • 1 oz. Pickles • 2–4 oz. Kidney bean soup • 2 oz. Miso soup, water, or herbal tea • Breast milk or formula	• 3–4 oz. Pasta salad with mixed vegetables • 2 oz. Avocado • 2 oz. Miso soup, water, or herbal tea • Breast milk or formula
• Breast milk or formula	• Breast milk or formula	• Breast milk or formula	• Breast milk or formula

Feeding Your Baby at 12 to 18 months

Development

Your baby begins walking and self-feeding with utensils; she holds them better, tilts her cup, spills less, and does not want to sit still and eat

Meal Frequency and Consistency

3 meals , 1–2 snacks

Soft table food cut into small bites, finger foods, soups

Food Percentages

The chart below shows generally how much of each food group your baby needs at this stage.

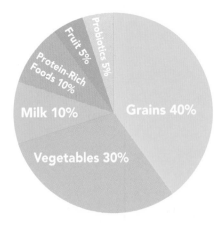

- Grains 40%
- Vegetables 30%
- Milk 10%
- Protein-Rich Foods 10%
- Fruit 5%
- Probiotics 5%

At 12 to 18 months your baby can eat many of the same foods that you eat, made with less salt and cut into smaller pieces. Since her digestive system is more developed and is not as sensitive, you can gradually introduce new foods, while continuing to monitor her condition for allergies.

When she is one year old, she can slowly try many of the foods that are common allergens, such as wheat, corn, barley, honey, fruit juice (diluted at 50 percent water and 50 percent juice in the beginning), citrus foods, and nut butters. New vegetables include mushrooms, potatoes, and asparagus. Offer other animal foods such as fish, eggs, and cow's milk products, if that is your preference. Tempeh is a good source of protein, and because it is a fermented food, it has probiotic properties. Maple syrup and honey offer a sweeter taste for making baked goods and served on pancakes.

Butter, almond oil, safflower oil, and sunflower oil can be used in baked goods or occasionally as seasonings in cooking. See whether she likes different herbs and spices, such as garlic, curry, and cinnamon. Barley tea is a healthy and alkaline-forming tea that children in Japan enjoy. I recommend waiting until 12 months before introducing it, because barley contains gluten. As you introduce new foods, pay attention to your child's reaction both physically and emotionally.

When cooking for the family, your toddler's seasonings need to be added separately and prior to seasoning the family's foods—especially salt and salty seasonings—so that you can control the amount of salt that she consumes. When she is crawling and walking, her system can metabolize salt more easily, and as she consumes less breast milk or formula that contains sodium, she needs some sea salt for brain and physical development. Salt is important for growth, but too much salt can cause cravings of extreme foods, as well as cause creating physical and behavioral problems. Processed and fast foods, such as pizza, chips, and chicken nuggets contain high amounts of sodium. To make sure that your child does not get too much salt at this early age, offer her healthy meals and snacks made at home.

Yellow squash, tempeh, fritters, and bok choy finger foods with peach gelatin for dessert

Foods for Your Baby at 12 to 18 months

Milk	Breast milk or formula becomes less central to nutrition; mostly for emotional support	**Fruits** 2 oz. per serving, 1–2 servings per day	Cooked puree, dried fruit puree, or fresh fruit for dessert 30 minutes after grains, vegetables, or protein-rich food
Grains 4 oz. per serving, 3–4 servings per day	Whole grains—brown rice, sweet brown rice, quinoa, millet, oats, amaranth, barley, corn grits, polenta, pasta, bread and teething biscuits, bread, couscous, dry cereals, muffins, crackers, toast sticks, spaghetti; mix grains for variety and nutrition; try introducing wheat; water-to-grain ratio 4:1	**Cooked Temperate**	Apples, pears, apricots, cherries, peaches, plums, nectarines, strawberries
		Dried, Cooked, and Pureed	Apples, raisins, currants, apricots, peaches, pears
		Fresh Temperate Mashed	Apples, pears, apricots, cherries, peaches, plums, grapes, cantaloupe, watermelon, honeydew melon
Vegetables 2 oz. per serving, 4–5 servings per day	Sweet vegetables; vegetable broth, pureed soups	**Fresh Tropical Mashed**	Avocados, bananas, papayas, mangos, oranges, tangerines, pineapple
Upward	Kale, collards, brussels sprouts, broccoli, cauliflower, watercress, Chinese cabbage, bok choy, turnip greens, purple cabbage, asparagus, mushrooms	**Fermented Foods** 2–3 oz. per serving, 1–2 servings per day	Soaked grains, miso, or tamari soup; low salt pickles; 2–3 drops of plum vinegar or low sodium tamari; small amounts of *umeboshi*; kefir or yogurt; probiotic booster
Root	Carrot, sweet potatoes, parsnips, rutabagas, beets, white potatoes	**Seasonings** ¼–½ teaspoon 2–3 servings per day	Mild sweet taste (no refined sugar or salt); brown rice syrup, *amazake*, maple syrup, honey, molasses; small amount of sesame, olive, coconut or flaxseed oil; basil, bay leaves, dill, fennel, lemongrass or mint, small amounts of salt
Ground	Japanese pumpkin, acorn squash, butternut squash, yellow squash, zucchini squash, green peas, green beans, sugar snap peas, celery		
Sea	Nori, wakame flakes, kombu, agar	**Beverages** 2–4 oz. per serving, 3–4 servings per day more on hot days	Water, vegetable broth, pureed soups, barley tea, fennel tea, chamomile tea, lemon balm tea, rice milk, *amazake*, fruit juice (diluted 50% water), raw vegetable juice, almond milk, soy milk (sparingly), coconut water
Protein-Rich Foods 2–3 oz. per serving, 1–2 servings per day	Whole grains, ground sesame seeds, sunflower seeds or flaxseeds, tahini; chestnuts, tempeh, lentils, chickpeas, black beans, adzuki beans, pinto beans, almond butter; white fish or salmon		

2 tbsp = 1 oz. = ⅛ cup | 4 tbsp = 2 oz. = ¼ cup | 16 tbsp = 8 oz. = 1 cup

These are general guidelines that vary with each individual child, the constitution, size, and gender of the baby, the climate, location, season, and situation. Breast-feeding or bottle-feeding and time of weaning will also affect the amount of food needed.

12–18 Months	Sunday	Monday	Tuesday
Breakfast	• 4 oz. Brown rice puree mixed with ½ t. tahini and ½ t. brown rice syrup or *amazake* • 2–3 oz. Water kefir or miso soup	• 4 oz. Brown rice puree mixed with ½ t. tahini and ½ t. brown rice syrup or *amazake* • 2–3 oz. Water kefir or miso soup	• 4 oz. Oatmeal puree with ½ t. ground toasted seeds and ½ t. brown rice syrup or *amazake* • 2–3 oz. Water kefir or miso soup
Lunch	• 4 oz. Brown rice/millet puree mixed with ¼ t. oil and ¼ t. brown rice syrup or *amazake* • 2 oz. Yellow squash • 2 oz. Green beans • 2 oz. Avocado • 1 oz. Pickles • 3–4 oz. Vegetable soup, water, or barley tea	• 4 oz. Spaghetti, mixed with ¼ t. olive oil and 2–3 drops of plum vinegar • 4"-square Nori sea Vegetable • 2 oz. Steamed carrot sticks • 2 oz. Steamed broccoli flowers • 2–3 oz. Lentils • 1 oz. Juice of pickles • 3–4 oz. Vegetable soup, water, or herbal tea	• 4 oz. Brown rice/millet puree • 2 oz. Fish, steamed (vegetarians—substitute fish for cooked tofu or tempeh) • 2 oz. Sauteed asparagus • 3–4 oz. Sauteed mushrooms • 1 oz. Pickles • 3–4 oz. Miso vegetable soup, water, or barley tea
Midafternoon	• 2 oz. Baked apple • 2 oz. Dry whole grain gluten-free O's cereal • 2–3 oz. Water or barley tea	• 2 oz. Banana mashed • 2 oz. Yogurt • 2–3 oz. Water or barley tea	• 2–3 oz. Carrot juice • 2 oz. Puffed rice
Dinner	• 4 oz. Spaghetti, mixed with ¼ t. olive oil and 2–3 drops of plum vinegar • 4"-square Nori sea vegetable flakes • 2 oz. Steamed carrot sticks • 2 oz. Steamed broccoli flowers • 2–3 oz. Lentils • 1 oz. Juice of pickles • 3–4 oz. Vegetable soup, water, or barley tea	• 4 oz. Brown Rice/Millet • 2–3 oz. Fish (vegetarians—substitute fish for cooked tofu or tempeh) • 2 oz. Steamed asparagus • 2 oz. Sauteed mushrooms • 3–4 oz. Miso, vegetable soup, water, or barley tea	• 1 Corn on the cob • 2 oz. Mashed potatoes • 2 oz. cabbage • 2–3 oz. Black bean soup • 1 oz. Pickles • 3–4 oz. water or herbal tea

Wednesday	Thursday	Friday	Saturday
• 4 oz. Oatmeal puree with ½ t. ground toasted seeds and ½ t. brown rice syrup or *amazake* • 2–3 oz. Water kefir or miso soup	• 4 oz. Brown rice/millet/ quinoa puree mixed with ½ t. ground flaxseeds and ½ t. brown rice syrup or *amazake* • 2–3 oz. Water kefir or miso soup	• 4 oz. Brown rice/millet/ quinoa puree mixed with ½ t. ground flaxseeds and ½ t. brown rice syrup or *amazake* • 2–3 oz. Water kefir or miso soup	• 4 oz. Sweet brown rice puree mixed with ½ t. tahini and ½ t. brown rice syrup or *amazake* • 2–3 oz. Water kefir or miso soup
• 1 Corn on the cob • 2 oz. Mashed potatoes • 2 oz. Cabbage • 2–3 oz. Black bean soup • 1 oz. Pickles • 3–4 oz. Water or barley tea	• 4 oz. Udon noodles with tamari broth • 2 oz. Baked sweet potato • 2 oz. Steamed watercress • 1 oz. Pickles • 3–4 oz. Water or herbal tea	• 4 oz. Brown rice • 2–4 oz. Tempeh and carrots • 2–3 oz. Green beans • 1 oz. Pickles • 3–4 oz. Miso soup, water, or barley tea	• 2 Rice balls • Steamed mixed vegetables with plum vinegar and sesame or olive oil • 1 oz. Pickles, kidney bean soup • 3–4 oz. water or barley tea
• 2 oz. Cooked blueberries • 1 Oatmeal cookie • 2–3 oz. water or herbal tea	• 2 oz. Cooked pear sauce • 2 oz. Yogurt • 2–3 oz. Water or herbal tea	• 2–3 oz. Coconut water • 1 Oatmeal cookie • 2–3 oz. Water or herbal tea	• 2–3 oz. Diluted fruit juice • 2 oz. Yogurt • 1 Rice cracker • 2–3 oz. Water or herbal tea
• 4 oz. Udon noodles with tamari broth • 2 oz. Baked sweet potato • 2 oz. Steamed watercress • 1 oz. Pickles • 3–4 oz. Water or barley Tea	• 4 oz. Brown rice puree • 2 oz. Tempeh and carrots • 2–3 oz. Green beans • 1 oz. Pickles • 2 oz. Miso soup • 3–4 oz. Water or barley tea	• 4 oz. Brown rice puree • 2–3 oz. Steamed mixed vegetables with plum vinegar and sesame or olive oil • 1 oz. Pickles, • 1–2 oz. Kidney bean soup • 3–4 oz. Water or herbal tea	• 4 oz. Pasta salad • 2 oz. Avocado • 3–4 oz. Miso soup, water, or barley tea

Feeding Your Baby at 18 to 24 months

Development

Your child's molars appear; she begins chewing and self-feeding; she loses attention for eating and wants to move during mealtimes

Meal Frequency and Consistency

3 meals, 1–2 snacks
Soft, chewable table food cut into small bites, finger foods, soups, dips, spreads

Food Percentages

The chart below shows generally how much of each food group your baby needs at this stage.

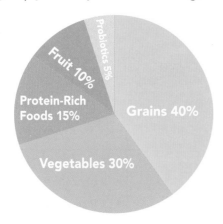

Probiotics 5%
Fruit 10%
Protein-Rich Foods 15%
Grains 40%
Vegetables 30%

At 18 to 24 months, your child can eat most of the same food you cook for your family, but with less salt and seasoning. Continue to take out a portion for your toddler before adding more seasoning for others. You will still need to monitor your child's salt intake and continue to observe any unusual responses to specific foods. By now, she can concentrate on eating and integrate with family mealtime. Her chewing skills should be maturing, so there is less concern for choking, and she can eat a wider variety of treats, such as sandwiches, cakes, and other desserts.

New foods to introduce are corn, buckwheat, raw vegetables, and nightshades, including tomatoes, peppers, spinach, and okra. You can introduce almonds and other nuts, along with small fruits such as blueberries, blackberries, raisins, and currants that still need to be monitored as choking hazards. If you plan to feed your child poultry, her teeth are probably developed enough to chew it at this age. Citrus fruit is acidic, and is best enjoyed occasionally.

You are your toddler's role model, so being positive and enthusiastic about healthy foods can influence her feelings about food. As she eats together with the family, it is natural for her to be interested in eating the food that you eat, so if some of your food is different from hers, it may be difficult to continue to feed her separate foods.

If your child began with simple, natural foods for her first foods, it is easy at this age to continue to feed her natural foods, because her taste buds have probably become discerning and sensitive. Until now, if your child has been eating packaged, processed foods that contain refined sugars, high sodium levels, and other additives, you may need to transition to natural foods gradually if you want to make a change at this stage.

At around the age of 18 months, many toddlers become picky eaters, which may be neophobia, or she may have just developed tastes for her favorite foods. A regular schedule and routine that does not include grazing or multiple snacks helps cultivate a healthy appetite. Do not force your child to eat or bribe her with dessert. If she has trouble gaining weight or is overweight, talk to your health care provider.

Chopped avocado, beans, and corn on the cob; with cantaloupe for dessert

Foods for Your Baby at 18 to 24 months

Milk	Weans from breast milk as source of food; gets all nutrients from food; may continue nursing for emotional comfort	**Fruits** 2 oz. per serving, 1–2 servings per day	Cooked puree, dried fruit puree, or fresh fruit for dessert 30 minutes after grains, vegetables, or protein-rich food
Grains 4 oz. per serving, 4–5 servings per day	Whole grains—brown rice, sweet brown rice, quinoa, millet, oats, amaranth, barley, corn grits, rice flakes, pasta, bread, couscous, dry cereals, muffins, buckwheat pancakes, crackers, pasta, corn on the cob; offer wheat if there are no allergic reactions; water-to-grain ratio 3:1	**Cooked Temperate**	Apples, pears, apricots, cherries, peaches, plums, nectarines, strawberries, blueberries, raspberries, blackberries
		Dried, Cooked	Apples, raisins, currants, apricots, peaches, pears
Vegetables 2 oz. per serving, 4–5 servings per day	Variety of vegetables	**Fresh Temperate**	Apples, pears, apricots, cherries, peaches, plums, nectarines, grapes, blackberries, raspberries, blueberries, strawberries, cantaloupe, watermelon, honeydew melon
Upward	Kale, collards, brussels sprouts, broccoli, cauliflower, cabbage, watercress, Chinese cabbage, bok choy, turnip greens, purple cabbage, asparagus, mushrooms, okra, spinach, peppers	**Fresh Tropical**	Avocados, bananas, papayas, mangoes, oranges, tangerines, pineapple
Root	Carrot, sweet potatoes, parsnips, rutabagas, beets, white potatoes, onions	**Fermented Foods** 2–3 oz. per serving, 1–2 servings per day	Soaked grains, miso, or tamari soup; pickles; 2–3 drops of plum vinegar or tamari as a seasoning; *umeboshi* plums, pickles; kefir or yogurt; probiotic booster
Ground	Japanese pumpkin, acorn squash, butternut squash, yellow squash, zucchini squash, green peas, green beans, sugar snap peas, celery	**Seasonings** 1–2 teaspoons occasionally 2–3 servings per day	Mild sweet taste (no refined sugar or salt); rice syrup, *amazake*, maple syrup, honey, molasses; sesame, olive, coconut or flaxseed oil; basil, bay leaves, dill, fennel, lemongrass or mint; observe baby's condition
Sea	Nori, wakame, kombu, agar		
Raw	Cucumbers, lettuce, tomatoes		
Protein-Rich Foods 3–4 oz. per serving, 2–3 servings per day	Whole grains, ground sesame, sunflower, or flaxseeds; tempeh, tahini; chestnuts, almonds, lentils, chickpeas, black beans, adzuki beans, pinto beans, almond butter; white fish or salmon	**Beverages** 4 oz. per serving, 3–4 servings per day more on hot days	Water, vegetable broth, barley tea, fennel tea, chamomile tea, lemon balm tea, rice milk, *amazake*, fruit juice (diluted 50% water), raw vegetable juice, almond milk, soy milk (sparingly), coconut water

2 tbsp = 1 oz. = ⅛ cup | 4 tbsp = 2 oz. = ¼ cup | 16 tbsp = 8 oz. = 1 cup

These are general guidelines that vary with each individual child, the constitution, size, and gender of the baby, the climate, location, season, and situation. Breast-feeding or bottle-feeding and time of weaning will also affect the amount of food needed.

18–24 Months	Sunday	Monday	Tuesday
Breakfast	• 4 oz. Brown rice puree mixed with ¼ t. tahini and ¼ t. brown rice syrup or *amazake* • 4 oz. Water kefir or miso soup	• 4 oz. Brown rice puree mixed with ¼ t. tahini and ¼ t. brown rice syrup or *amazake* • 4 oz. Water kefir or miso soup	• 4 oz. Oatmeal puree with ¼ t. ground toasted seeds and ¼ t. brown rice syrup or *amazake* • 4 oz. Water kefir or miso soup
Lunch	• 6 oz. Pasta salad • 2 oz. Avocado • 4 oz. Miso soup, water, or barley Tea	• 4 oz. Brown rice/millet • 2 oz. Butternut squash • 2 oz. Broccoli • 3–4 oz. Tempeh • 1 oz. Pickles • 4 oz. Miso soup, water, or barley tea	• 4 oz. Couscous • 2 oz. Beets • 2 oz. Brussels sprouts • 3–4 oz. White beans • 1 oz. Pickles • 4 oz. Tamari broth soup, water, or barley tea
Midafternoon	• 3 oz. Rice pudding • Barley tea • 4 oz. Water or barley Tea	• 2 oz. Banana • 2 oz. Yogurt • 4 oz. Water or barley Tea	• 4 oz. Carrot juice • 2 oz. Puffed rice
Dinner	• 4 oz. Brown rice/millet • 2 oz. Butternut squash • 2 oz. Broccoli • 3–4 oz. Tempeh • 1 oz. Pickles • 2 oz. Miso soup, water, or barley tea • 3 oz. Rice pudding	• 4 oz. Couscous • 2 oz. Beets • 2 oz. Brussels sprouts • 3–4 oz. White beans • 1 oz. Pickles • 2 oz. Tamari broth soup, water, or barley Tea • 2 oz. Banana	• 3–4 oz. Salmon salad sandwich (vegetarians—substitute cooked tofu or tempeh for salmon) • 3–4 oz. Steamed vegetables • 1 oz. Pickles • 2 oz. Vegetable soup • 4 oz. Water or barley tea • 2 oz. Applesauce

Wednesday	Thursday	Friday	Saturday
• 4 oz. Oatmeal puree with ¼ t. ground toasted seeds and ¼ t. brown rice syrup or *amazake* • 4 oz. Water kefir or miso soup	• 4 oz. Brown rice/millet/quinoa puree mixed with ¼ t. ground flaxseeds and ¼ t. brown rice syrup or *amazake* • 4 oz. Water kefir or miso soup	• 4 oz. Brown rice/millet/quinoa puree mixed with ¼ t. ground flaxseeds and ¼ t. brown rice syrup or *amazake* • 4 oz. Water kefir or miso soup	• 4 oz. Sweet brown rice puree mixed with ¼ t. tahini and ¼ t. brown rice syrup or *amazake* • 4 oz. Water kefir or miso soup
• Salmon salad sandwich (vegetarians— substitute cooked tofu or tempeh for salmon) • 3–4 oz. Steamed vegetables • 1 oz. Pickles • 2 oz. Vegetable soup, water, or barley tea	• 2 Rice balls • 2 oz. Acorn squash • 2 oz. Chinese cabbage • 2 oz. Adzuki beans • 1 oz. Pickles • 4 oz. Miso soup, water, or barley tea	• 6 oz. Spaghetti with vegetable sauce • 1 oz. Juice of pickles • 4 oz. Miso soup, water, or barley tea	• 6 oz. Curry rice • 2 oz. Turnip greens • 1 oz. Pickles • 4 oz. Miso soup, water, or barley tea
• 2 oz. Kanten gelo • 1 Oatmeal cookie • 4 oz. Water or herbal tea	• 2 oz. Cooked pear sauce • 2 oz. Yogurt • 4 oz. Water or herbal tea	• 4 oz. Coconut water • 1 Oatmeal cookie • 2 oz. Apple slices	• 4 oz. Diluted fruit juice • 2 oz. Yogurt • Rice cracker
• Rice balls • 2 oz. Acorn squash • 2 oz. Chinese cabbage • 3–4 oz. Adzuki beans • 1 oz. Pickles • 4 oz. Miso soup, water, or barley tea • 2 oz. Kanten gelo	• 6 oz. Spaghetti with vegetable sauce • 1 oz. Pickles • 4 oz. Water or barley tea • 2 oz. Cooked pear sauce	• 6 oz. Curry rice • 2 oz. Steamed turnip greens • 1 oz. Pickles • Water or barley tea • 4 oz. Water or barley tea • 2 oz. Applesauce	• 4 oz. Brown rice • 2 oz. Sweet potatoes • 2 oz. Steamed kale • 1 oz. Pickles • Pinto bean soup • 4 oz. Water or barley tea • 2 oz. Avocado

Feeding Your Baby at 24 to 36 months

Development
Your child now eats the same food as the rest of your family

Meal Frequency and Consistency
3 meals, 1–2 snack
Soft, chewable table food cut into small bites, finger foods, soups, dips, spreads

Food Percentages
The chart below shows generally how much of each food group your baby needs at this stage.

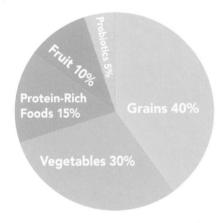

Probiotics 5%
Fruit 10%
Protein-Rich Foods 15%
Grains 40%
Vegetables 30%

At 24 to 36 months, your toddler can eat most of the same foods as other family members. She is independent and wants to do everything for herself, including self-feeding. She may have opinions about tastes and refuse certain foods that she previously enjoyed, or she may prefer to eat the same foods repeatedly. She is discovering and learning, as her individual self develops.

From two until three years, your child will probably encounter social situations in which it may be challenging to keep her from eating salty and sugary treats. After three years old, she can explore different foods, recognize results, and understand the connection between the two. However, before three years old, she does not have the cognitive, analytical abilities to comprehend the correlation between eating certain foods and the resulting physical reaction. Therefore, it is important to provide healthy desserts and treats to keep her satisfied and to do your best to protect her from extreme foods. If she does eat unfamiliar foods and gets off balance, then you can provide foods and remedies to guide her back to the center.

Encourage your child to help in the kitchen and grow some plants as she gets older, so that she can learn about cooking and where food comes from. Having her participate in the preparation of food is a way to occupy her while you are busy, to offer her the opportunity to experience the tastes and smells of cooking, and to enjoy being together.

Celebrations, such as birthdays and holidays become more meaningful and significant as your child gets older. Dishes, lunchboxes, cutlery, and cups in bright colors with animal designs are stimulating and interesting to engage her in eating. Funny face sandwiches and animal-shaped rice balls can help make eating more fun. At this age the ingredients do not change very much, so it is more how they are put together. You can still provide tasty and delicious meals with simple foods and cooking methods, using some creativity in their presentation.

Salmon, pasta with vegetables, pickles, and miso soup, with berry gelatin for dessert

Foods for Your Baby at 24 to 36 months

Milk	Weans from breast milk as source of food; gets all nutrients from food; may continue nursing for emotional comfort	**Fruits** 2 oz. per serving, 1–2 servings per day	Cooked, dried, or fresh fruit for dessert 30 minutes after grains, vegetables, or protein-rich food
Grains 4 oz. per serving, 4–5 servings per day	Whole grains—brown rice, sweet brown rice, quinoa, millet, oats, amaranth, barley, corn grits, polenta, rice flakes, pasta, bread, buckwheat pancakes, rye and wheat bread, couscous, dry cereals, muffins, crackers, dumplings, toast sticks, buckwheat pancakes, udon noodles, spaghetti, corn on the cob, soba noodles; mix grains for variety and nutrition; water-to-grain ratio 3:1	**Cooked Temperate**	Apples, pears, apricots, cherries, peaches, plums, nectarines, strawberries, blueberries, raspberries, blackberries
		Dried, Cooked	Apples, raisins, currants, apricots, peaches, pears
		Fresh Temperate	Apples, pears, apricots, plums, cherries, peaches, nectarines, grapes, blackberries, raspberries, blueberries, strawberries, cantaloupe, watermelon, honeydew melon
Vegetables 2 oz. per serving, 4–5 servings per day	Sweet vegetables; vegetable broth, pureed soups	**Fresh Tropical**	Avocados, bananas, papayas, mangoes, oranges, tangerines, pineapple
Upward	Kale, collards, brussels sprouts, broccoli, cauliflower, cabbage, watercress, Chinese cabbage, bok choy, turnip greens, purple cabbage, celery, mushrooms, asparagus	**Fermented Foods** 2–3 oz. per serving, 1–2 servings per day	Soaked grains, miso, or tamari soup; pickles; 2–3 drops of plum vinegar or tamari as a seasoning; small amounts of *umeboshi* or pickles; kefir or yogurt; probiotic booster
Root	Carrot, sweet potatoes, parsnips, rutabagas, beets, white potatoes, onions	**Seasonings** 1–2 teaspoons occasionally 2–3 servings per day	Mild sweet taste (no refined sugar or salt); rice syrup, *amazake*, maple syrup, honey, molasses; small amount of sesame, olive, coconut, or flaxseed oil; basil, bay leaves, dill, fennel, lemongrass or mint, salt
Ground	Japanese pumpkin, acorn squash, butternut squash, yellow squash, zucchini squash, green peas, green beans, sugar snap peas		
Sea	Nori, wakame, kombu, agar	**Beverages** 4 oz. per serving, 3–4 servings per day more on hot days	Water, vegetable broth, barley tea, fennel tea, chamomile tea, lemon balm tea, rice milk, *amazake*, fruit juice (diluted 50% water), raw vegetable juice, almond milk, soy milk (sparingly), coconut water
Raw	Cucumbers, lettuce		
Protein-Rich Foods 3–4 oz. per serving, 2–3 servings per day	Whole grains, ground sesame, sunflower, or flaxseeds; tempeh, tahini; chestnuts, almonds, lentils, chickpeas, black beans, adzuki beans, pinto beans, almond butter; white fish or salmon		

2 tbsp = 1 oz. = ⅛ cup | 4 tbsp = 2 oz. = ¼ cup | 16 tbsp = 8 oz. = 1 cup

These are general guidelines that vary with each individual child, the constitution, size, and gender of the baby, the climate, location, season, and situation. Breast-feeding or bottle-feeding and time of weaning will also affect the amount of food needed.

24–36 Months	Sunday	Monday	Tuesday
Breakfast	• 4 oz. Brown rice puree mixed with ¼ t. tahini and ¼ t. brown rice syrup or *amazake* • 3–4 oz. Water kefir or miso soup	• 4 oz. Brown rice puree mixed with ¼ t. tahini and ¼ t. brown rice syrup or *amazake* • 3–4 oz. Water kefir or miso soup	• 4 oz. Oatmeal puree with ¼ t. ground toasted seeds and ¼ t. brown rice syrup or *amazake* • 3–4 oz. Water kefir or miso soup
Lunch	• 4 oz. Brown rice • 2 oz. Sweet potatoes • 2 oz. Steamed kale • 1 oz. Pickles • Pinto bean soup • Water or barley tea	• 4 oz. Quinoa • 2 oz. Yellow squash and onions • 2 oz. Green beans • 2 oz. Chickpeas • 1 oz. Pickles • 2 oz. Miso soup, water, or barley tea	• 4 oz. Brown rice • 2 oz. Carrots • 2 oz. Watercress • 2 oz. Tempeh • 1 oz. Pickles • 2 oz. Vegetable soup, water, or barley tea
Midafternoon	• 1 Muffin • Herbal Tea	• ¼ Sliced fresh apple • 2 oz. Yogurt • 4 oz. Water	• 2 oz. Carrot Juice • Rice crispy treat • 4 oz. Barley tea
Dinner	• 4 oz. Quinoa • 2 oz. Yellow squash and onions • 2 oz. Green beans • 2 oz. Chickpeas • 1 oz. Pickles • 2 oz. Miso soup, water, or barley tea	• 4 oz. Brown rice • 2 oz. Carrots • 2 oz. Watercress • 2 oz. Tempeh • 1 oz. Pickles • 2 oz. Vegetable soup, water, or barley tea	• 4 oz. Pasta salad • 2 oz. Salmon (vegetarians—substitute cooked tofu or tempeh for salmon) • 2 oz. Miso soup • Water or barley tea

Wednesday	Thursday	Friday	Saturday
• 4 oz. Oatmeal puree with ¼ t. ground toasted seeds and ¼ t. brown rice syrup or *amazake* • 3–4 oz. Water kefir or miso soup	• 4 oz. Brown rice/millet/quinoa puree mixed with ¼ t. ground flaxseeds and ¼ t. brown rice syrup or *amazake* • 3–4 oz. Water kefir or miso soup	• 4 oz. Brown rice/millet/quinoa puree mixed with ¼ t. ground flaxseeds and ¼ t. brown rice syrup or *amazake* • 3–4 oz. Water kefir or miso soup	• Pancakes with maple syrup • 4 oz. Water • 3–4 oz. Water kefir or miso soup
• 4 oz. Pasta salad • 2 oz. Fish (vegetarians—substitute fish for cooked tofu or tempeh) • 2 oz. Miso soup, water, or barley tea	• 6 oz. Polenta with tomato sauce • 4 oz. Green salad • 2 oz. Vegetable soup, water, or barley tea	• 4 oz. Sweet brown rice • 2 oz. Zucchini • 2 oz. Broccoli • 3–4 oz. Black beans • 1 oz. Pickles • 2 oz. Miso soup, water, or barley tea	• 1 Almond butter and jam sandwich • Green salad • Vegetable soup • Pickles • 2 oz. Water or barley tea
• Banana slices • 1 Oatmeal cookie • 4 oz. herbal tea	• 2 oz. Cooked pears • 2 oz. Yogurt • 4 oz. Water	• 3–4 oz. Coconut water • 1 Oatmeal cookie	• Fresh fruit popsicle • 2 oz. barley tea
• 6 oz. Polenta with tomato sauce • 4 oz. Green salad • 2 oz. Vegetable soup, water, or barley tea	• 4 oz. Sweet brown rice • 2 oz. Zucchini • 2 oz. Broccoli • 2 oz. Black beans • 1 oz. Pickles • 2 oz. Miso soup, water, or barley tea	• 1 Almond butter and jam sandwich • 4–6 oz. Green salad • 2 oz. Vegetable soup • 1 oz. Pickles • Water or barley tea	• 4 oz. Brown rice/Barley • 2 oz. Baked root vegetables • 2 oz. Kale • 2 oz. Tofu • 1 oz. Pickles • 2 oz. Miso soup, water, or barley tea

CHAPTER 8

At Home in the World

WHEN EMI WAS 14 months old, we moved from Japan to the United States, traveling through Europe for six weeks. The trip was a test of our ability as parents to adapt and adjust, while also challenging Emi's flexibility and endurance. We could not take a lot of gear because we were on the move—I remember putting Emi in the carrier on our backs and the suitcase in the stroller because luggage did not have wheels back then. We used a combination of disposable diaper inserts, along with cloth diapers and covers, and somehow we made her baby food along the way. We moved leisurely and visited Hyde Park in London rather than museums. When we got to the Louvre in Paris, we contemplated an afternoon there, decided that I had already seen the Mona Lisa and Naoki had seen many photos of her, and enjoyed a sidewalk café instead. We did not have intense tourist agendas, but we enjoyed the people, the food, and the culture in a relaxed way, and we had a fun time.

Traveling with young children requires moving at a slower pace and rearranging priorities. Today's world offers endless options of how to put together a lifestyle that may include out-of-the-ordinary situations, even to the point that they become routine. Having children does not mean that you are homebound and stuck in a rigid schedule, and with such an array of "on-the-go" equipment available, it is easy to be mobile with your baby. Local excursions, visits to see family and friends, restaurant outings, camping trips, travel, holidays, and parties can be an integral part of daily life for your family. These experiences that are not in his daily routine teach him to be flexible, while discovering the world.

This chapter offers suggestions on getting out with your baby for local outings and various kinds of out-of-town travel. At the end of the chapter are suggestions for coming back to balance when the party is over or upon returning home. Recipes for outings, travel, holidays, and special events are included.

Food at Home and in the World

Food is a social and emotional experience that brings family and friends together to share and bond, while creating understanding. "You are what you eat," means that food impacts the quality of your cells, so that when a family eats the same foods, they experience another level of intimacy and connection. Eating meals together and developing celebrations around food establishes traditions that are pleasurable, satisfying, and joyful, and they also provide enduring memories. Because family members often eat out, due to busy lifestyles, creating family unity through food may require an extra effort.

One father I know ate the same foods he fed to his child, so that he could understand his child's experience of how the food tasted, along with its physical and emotional effects. Even if you do not eat dinner at the same time as your child, taking time to sit with him to share food can help him have a social sense of eating, rather than eating his food alone. A commitment to the regular sharing of food and conversation for some mealtimes each week teaches your child social skills and allow everyone in your family to connect up and share their various activities outside your home.

Daily food adds up to make your child's condition; therefore, simple, homemade, quality foods help build his health and temperament. However, making dishes for special occasions with a wider range of ingredients that are still healthy can provide enjoyment and cultural experiences for your family. If you share a holiday or birthday meal with friends or family, go on a picnic, or take a trip to the beach together, you can create your own family traditions and celebrations that help your child develop his sense of identity and belonging.

Planning Ahead for Travel

Planning ahead helps you to be prepared to meet your child's needs in out-of-the-ordinary situations. When you have the equipment that you need, healthy food and snacks available at routine times, and toys to keep your child entertained at the right moment, both you and your child will have a better time and experience less stress, while keeping cheerful temperaments. If you can find a balance between routines and relaxing, everyone will have more fun. When visiting friends or relatives, plan the foods that you need for your child, so that you are prepared and do not impose on your host. Check to see if the host has special equipment, such as a high chair or blender, or space in the freezer or refrigerator for your baby's food. Be clear and considerate when explaining your needs.

Consider your child's sleep and eating routines when planning the departure and arrival times for your excursions, trips, and social events. You may schedule his naptime for the ride across town, car trips, or an airplane flight. For birthday parties, holidays, and social gatherings, you can either plan the event to match his routine, if you have control of the time schedule, or adjust his nap so that he is rested and fresh for the event.

Take extra care of your child's health before going on a trip. Make sure that he gets plenty of sleep, exercise, and healthy foods beforehand, so that he will be strong and can adjust to the different schedule. Kuzu with brown rice syrup makes a calming pudding that travels well and can help relax your little one.

One of my travel rules that has developed from my own experience of leaving many things behind is: *Wasuremono wa nai desu, neh!* which means, "No forgotten things!" I try to keep the habit of looking behind me while getting up from a restaurant, airplane, or taxi seat, or when checking out of a hotel room. When you are traveling, you usually need everything you have with you, or you would not be carrying it. If you are on the move, retracing your steps to look for something can take time and may not be an option. Once something is left behind, it may be difficult to recover. I have never gotten back anything from the airlines that I have lost, including sweaters, glasses, e-readers, and telephones. The inconvenience of losing one of your basic essentials is difficult when traveling, along with the hassle of trying to replace it while on the road. Remember to always "look behind."

Equipment Essentials for Being On-the-go

There are many options for equipment that make traveling and on-the-go experiences with your baby easy and convenient. Below is a list of items that you may need for excursions.

Eating—Bottles with nipples if using formula or pumping and storing breast milk, breast pump, bottle brush, bowl, spoon, bibs, burp cloths, wipes, sippy cup, food mill or mini food processor, food scissors for cutting and mashing food, insulated bag, ice packs, dry snacks, frozen food cubes, jars of organic baby food, powdered formula (if using formula), disposable or reusable place mats, high chair cover, cooler. You can store frozen food cubes in an insulated food bag for 8 to 12 hours, or in a cooler for up to 24 hours. Make sure that they are not stored without refrigeration or insulation for over 4 hours. If you are overlapping breast-feeding with solid foods, you may rely more on breast-feeding during travel.

Sleeping—Crib sheet, blanket, pack and play (if going by car), night-light, sleeping bag.

Diapering—Diaper covers and cloth or disposable inserts or disposable diapers, wipes, changing pad, bags to hold dirty diapers.

Bath time—Nonskid bath mat, bath or beach towels, washcloths, soap.

Health and safety—Toothbrush, toothpaste, herbs, remedies or medications, lotions, oil, sunscreen, electrical outlet covers, tissues, bandages, ointment, first-aid kit, essential oils for calming.

Clothes—Two or three outfits per day, jacket, hat, mittens, raincoat, pajamas, sunhat, sunglasses, swim diaper, swim shoes, cover-up, beach towel.

Carrying—Sling or carrier, stroller, car seat, head support.

Toys—Teething rings, books, favorite toys that have multiple uses for bath, pool, and sand, toys with loops that fasten and are interchangeable, music player and headphones.

Local Outings

Planning your time schedule will help you be more efficient, even for nearby excursions, such as running errands, playdates, or going to child care. You can keep a bag prepared with the basics ready, in case you need to go out unexpectedly—a bottle or sippy cup, a bottle of water, food or snacks, one or two diapers, wipes, changing pad, bib, burp pad, blanket, a change of clothes, and toys. Fresh food can be added at the last minute.

Eating in Restaurants

Eating in restaurants can be a balancing act between taking care of a baby or toddler and giving parents a break. It helps to stick with your child's eating schedule, as much as possible, or feed him beforehand. When the weather is mild, eating at open-air cafés can be easy for your child to move around. If there are several adults, everyone can take turns holding your baby or walking around with your toddler.

For eating in a restaurant, you can take food you have prepared, or you can order at the restaurant, and use a food mill to puree food, or use food scissors for

cutting food. Sharing bites of food from your own plate is an option for toddlers who are eating adult food. Most restaurant food has more salt and seasoning than home-cooked food, or it may contain hydrogenated oils, high-fructose corn syrup, or MSG. Some restaurants offer steamed vegetables for the weight-watcher's diet that are lightly steamed without salt, which you can puree in a food mill. In many restaurants you can order fresh fruit, toast, plain noodles, brown or white rice, or oatmeal without seasoning. Here are some other tips:

- Look for restaurants that are family-friendly and welcome children.
- Make reservations ahead if the restaurant is a busy place so that you will not have to wait to be seated.
- Call ahead to confirm that a high chair or booster seat is available.
- Plan to go at a time that your baby will not be tired or grumpy.
- Take food, spoon, bowl, bib, bottle or sippy cup, snacks, and toys.
- Take your baby's car seat carrier inside the restaurant so that he can sleep.
- Make sure the table has adequate room for everyone.
- Remove condiments from the table to keep your child from grabbing them.
- Use a disposable or reusable place mat for protection.
- Be mindful of other eaters in the restaurant so that he is not disruptive to their meal.
- Keep your child out of the way of waitstaff to avoid accidents.
- Clean up any mess or food thrown on the floor before leaving.

Child Care and Preschool

While working at Muso Yochien (Dream Window Kindergarten) in Kyoto, Japan, the cook, Takehara-sensei, cooked brown rice lunches every day for 350 students, but when we went on field trips, the children took their lunches from home. At those times, I loved to walk around and take a look at the imaginative lunches that the students' mothers had prepared for them that morning. I wondered how early they had gotten up to make the bunny-shaped rice balls and flower-shaped sandwiches. Japanese packed lunches are called "bento," which is short for *obento*, the honorific form. Mothers make them for their children to take to school or outings, and they prepare them for their husbands to take to work. In Japan, you can buy premade bentos in bamboo or plastic boxes at restaurants, supermarkets, convenience stores, or stalls in the train stations. Bentos can be complicated with garnishes and decorations, or simple with the previous meal's leftovers arranged in an artistic way. Bentos are a way to make healthy food more appealing and to provide portion control for your baby or toddler.

Some child care centers and preschools provide meals and snacks, and others rely on the parents to provide their child's food, so you may need to research to find out the options available. Especially when my children were younger, I preferred to prepare their food myself, so that I could know what they were eating. For babies and toddlers at child care, you can pack bottles, food cubes of puree, finger foods, and teething biscuits in an insulated bag or backpack with the diapers, clothes,

bibs, and other essentials. Toddlers at preschool like to have a fun backpack to carry their lunch, extra clothes, raincoat, books, and toys. Below are some tips on making healthy and easy bentos.

- Use foods like salted pickled plums and plum vinegar for preserving rice and other foods.

- Use a variety of colors for visual appeal, as well as for health and balance.

- Do not mix cold and hot foods together because it can make them spoil. Also, eating hot and cold foods at the same time is disruptive to your baby's digestive system and can cause gas.

- Make a balanced meal with a grain, vegetable, protein-rich food, and fruit or cookie for dessert.

- Use a variety of tastes and seasonings that include salty, sweet, sour, spicy, and herb flavorings. Cold food requires more seasoning than hot food does.

- Keep it simple for everyday lunches—basic tasty food with three to five items is enough. Occasionally, you can add decorations for variety and fun.

- Use organic, local, and seasonal food, if possible, and avoid processed foods.

- Plan ahead when cooking meals by making extra so that you have leftovers.

- Shop for bento-friendly foods such as grains, noodles, bread for sandwiches, vegetables, beans, tempeh, fruit, healthy crackers, and snacks.

- Cookie cutters or molds will make different shapes of rice balls or sandwiches. Garnishes and decorations add color and taste for visual appeal.

- For packing, small containers or dividers help keep dishes separate. Snack and sandwich bags are lightweight and convenient for carrying crackers, cookies, and sandwiches. Thermoses keep food warm; ice packs keep food cold in insulated lunch bags.

Picnics

Walking through a park in Japan during springtime, you can often see groups of people enjoying *hanami*, or flower viewing under cherry blossom trees. Families, friends, and coworkers set up straw mats under the flowering trees and enjoy elaborate dishes along with tea or sake. When I saw these *hanami* picnics, I was touched by the beauty of the flowers and the spirit of the participants, as they laughed and sang songs celebrating spring.

Everyday picnics can be spontaneous and quick ways to alter routines and get outdoors. You can even have a picnic in your backyard, in your neighborhood, or in a nearby park. If you live near waterfalls, a zoo, or a park that has special plants and room to run and explore, you can enjoy picnics throughout the seasons there, and observe nature's changes in those familiar places.

Sandwiches, snack foods, crackers, chips, fruits, and desserts that are easy to transport and easy to eat with fingers are convenient for picnics. Take cool beverages for hot, sunny days, and thermoses of warm drinks for frosty temperatures.

Beach or Pool

As toddlers, Emi and Mari loved to go to the beach, where they swam in the ocean, and played for hours digging, sifting, and building structures from sand. Swimming in the pool or ocean can help your baby get cool and refreshed on a hot, summer day. Being in the water or walking on the beach in the sunshine offers him vitamin D, while connecting him to nature. In addition, swimming is a natural exercise that works his cardiovascular system, builds his muscles, and provides an opportunity to stretch his body.

Aside from providing exercise and fun, swimming lessons can help your child become confident and familiar with the water. In addition, they can teach him to float, rest, and breathe to be safe in the water. When you are around water with your child, keep your safety antenna up, and make sure he is supervised at all times.

In addition to the regular baby travel gear, you will need another list of items for beach or pool excursions.

Sun protection—Sunscreen (only if your baby is 6 months or older), sun hat, rash guard, sunglasses, tent or umbrella, lightweight blanket.

Swimming—Beach towel, float or arm bands, sand and water toys.

Eating—Cooler or cool bags, snacks, food, drinks.

Clothing—Swim diaper, swimsuit, beach cover-up, spare clothes, swim shoes.

Trips and Travel

Whether by car, train, or plane, traveling for more than a couple of hours usually upsets daily routines. A good night's sleep before going on a trip can help give both you and your child a good start. Make a checklist and pack ahead of time, so that you remember everything and are not in a rush right before you leave. Pack feeding supplies, diapers, clothes, some toys and books for entertainment along the way, skin care items, first-aid remedies, and essential oils for calming him. An umbrella stroller that is small can be helpful because it takes up less space. Make sure you have your travel documents, such as maps, travel guides, tickets, passports, and reservations. Save your travel checklists for future trips.

Car Travel

An advantage of traveling by car is that you usually have the flexibility to move in your own time, rather than the set schedules of airplanes, trains, or buses. You also have the luxury of space and freedom to put loose items that are not packed in the back seat or trunk. Because of this convenience, you may be tempted to take more than you need. Everything you pack will need to be carried into your destination, and unpacked when you return home.

You may need to consider arranging space for big equipment, like strollers, pack and plays, and luggage, so clean out unnecessary items beforehand to allow for space and ease of movement.

If you map out your itinerary, then you can plan for feeding and diaper changes. Organize essentials that you will need along the way, such as food, drinks, wipes, and so on, so that they are easily accessible. Toys, music, and singing can help entertain children while riding. A luxury of car travel is to be able to make noise without bothering others. When Emi and Mari were toddlers, I made special "car boxes" from long flat containers with snap-on lids that included art supplies, toys, and games.

If you have two adults traveling, then one person can sit in the back seat with your child, especially if he is in a rear-facing car seat; you can also use a rear-facing mirror. Make sure that he is buckled in and comfortable with a neck support and has a blanket for warmth in winter, or that he is cool enough in warm weather. Check to be certain that your car is in good condition and tuned up to circumvent unnecessary car troubles along the way. Other basic equipment to pack include a GPS system, maps, and emergency car items.

Airplane Travel

When traveling by airplane, you are at the mercy of the airlines—with their mechanical breakdowns and flight delays. Flying is a quick way to go a long distance, but the comfort and convenience can be challenging with a little one because of the unpredictability of air travel. In addition, more people are traveling these days, and airports and flights are busy and packed.

Plan ahead before the trip. Try to schedule your trip at times that are not peak travel times, such as before or after July 4th, Thanksgiving, or Christmas, if possible. Also, direct flights can reduce travel time, decrease the possibility of missing connections, and make the trip less stressful overall. If you live in a small town, this may not be an option. Check regulations for luggage and carry-on items, because they change often. Pack lightly, or at least take small items; you will have to carry everything you take. Take a change of clothes and extra food, in case there is a flight delay. See if it is possible to borrow a car seat, stroller, or pack and play at your destination to avoid having to travel with so much gear.

To prepare for your plane trip, give your baby healthy food, and for a few days beforehand, avoid foods that can cause gas or bloating, such as cruciferous vegetables, carbonated beverages, and artificial sweeteners. The pressure in the airplane causes restriction, so feed him calming and relaxing foods that are low in salt and sugar, and decrease the amount of animal foods when traveling to help him relax. You may wish to take your own baby food purees, finger foods, and bentos, because airport food is not predictable and not usually suited to meet the needs of young children.

Here are a few tips to help air travel go smoothly:

- ✳ When checking in, see if there is an extra seat for your baby, if he is under two years old and you did not buy him a ticket. It will be helpful to have the extra space for him to move around.

- ✳ Going through security may be a challenge because you will probably have a lot of gear. Check to see if there is a special line for families.

- ✳ Waiting for your flight to leave is a good chance to help your baby or toddler get as much movement or exercise as possible. Rolling or crawling on a blanket, walking, or running can help release extra energy before taking off.

- ✳ Buy some water before getting on the plane so that you have it when you need it.

- ✳ Usually, families are first for boarding, so you can get on the airplane and get settled with your child before others board.

- ✳ Gate check your stroller, car seat, and any other special baby gear that you are carrying.

- ✳ Make friends with your neighbors so that you can have their support for taking care of your baby, whether they are actually lending a hand or just offering moral support.

- ✳ Even a short flight can seem like a long time for a wiggly baby, so pace yourself with your tool kit, which can include toys and books for entertainment, diapers, extra clothes, essential oils, acupoint pressure, and calming foods.

- ✳ Babies are sensitive to changes in pressure. Give your baby something to suck on or drink when taking off to help relieve pressure on his ears.

- ✳ Make sure that he drinks plenty of fluids, as the cabin pressure can dehydrate him.

- ✳ The more you stay calm and cheerful, the better for everyone.

Train and Bus Travel

Traveling on trains and buses has some of the same limitations as air travel, with variations. You have to meet their schedule, and you do not have the control to make stops for feedings or diaper changes. For local bus rides, subways, or short train trips, you need to move quickly, carry everything without delay, and keep your child in tow. However, there are some advantages to traveling by train. Even though you are traveling in a more limited and confined space than a car, seat belts are not necessary, so you and your baby can have more freedom to move about. For long-distance travel by train, you can get a sleeper or family car (the price is lower if you reserve farther in advance), and the dining car provides a diversion for eating or playing games at the table. As with air travel, you carry everything that you need, so pack compactly and thoughtfully.

Visiting Family and Friends Overnight

Taking your first overnight trip to visit other family members or friends can feel daunting when you think about all the equipment and gear that is needed to take care of your baby for just one 24-hour period. However, planning and preparation will make you more confident, and as you have your own experiences, you will learn which supplies you really need, and how to make adjustments for others. Staying overnight with family and friends can be a good way to start getting out traveling with your baby, because you can have your first outings with their support. If your host has children, then you can borrow gear without having to take everything from home. Also, they will be sensitive to and understanding of your needs.

If your child has grandparents, family, or friends nearby, sleepovers for your child may start at an early age. Make sure your child is comfortable before going out on a sleepover, and make sure that the person in charge is familiar with your child's needs, normal schedule, food preferences, and diapering routines. If you start with first sleepovers for your child at the house of a neighbor or a friend nearby, you can easily bring him home if he has an emotional upset.

Hotel Stays

In the cold winter, my family sometimes took a family night to a motel in a nearby town that had an indoor pool for a getaway and relief from cabin fever. A change of scenery can lift your family's spirits. The chance to break away from routine with new adventures can be a time to bond and connect. Some economical and interesting options allow you to rent vacation lodging directly from the owners. These options are a way to stay in unique accommodations, such as a cabin, an apartment, or a house in a residential area. Many hotels or motels have suites or kitchenettes that provide extra space for relaxing and the convenience of cooking. Here are some suggestions for researching vacation accommodations:

❋ Look for family-friendly places.

❋ Check for a crib or pack and play, and bring your own sheets, if you feel that it is necessary.

❋ Check to see if a swimming pool is open in the season that you will be traveling.

❋ Confirm reservations before you go to make sure there are no waits while checking in.

❋ Consider other equipment you will need, such as a food mill, extra containers, and bibs.

❋ If you will be staying in a hotel, cabin, or rent-by-the-week apartment, ask about high chairs or any other baby-friendly features, or hazards, such as stairs or decks without safety rails.

Camping

Camping with your baby or toddler is a great way to get him outdoors and enjoy nature firsthand. If you do not have a lot of camping experience yourself, then you may prefer to start simply by camping from the car so that you have your essentials nearby. Being in the fresh air, playing in the woods, looking for wildlife, hiking, cooking in the outdoors, and sleeping in a tent can offer a break from city life that sends you back refreshed. Camping is an economical way to take a family vacation or short break from your daily routine and spend some time together outdoors.

Safety first

Make sure you have what you need, so your child is comfortable and safe, including sun protection items and warm clothing. Check out the camping area for bodies of water, leftover trash, animals, or sharp objects. Your baby or child needs to be supervised at all times, so divide up the duties with your partner or other adults, so that someone is in charge of him at all times. In addition to the regular baby travel gear, you will need these items for camping.

Shelter—Tent, tarp, sleeping bags, pillows, flashlights, lanterns and headlamps, folding chairs, trash bags.

Eating—Camping stove and fuel, cooler, pots and pans, kitchen utensils, water, kitchen towels, dish soap, sponges, silverware, aluminum foil, can and bottle opener, food.

Clothing—Comfortable and durable clothing that can get dirty, rain gear, pajamas, underwear, jackets.

Basics—Swiss army knife, paper towels, toilet paper, Ziploc bags, bandana, water bottles, buckets for collecting nature objects.

Getting around—Backpack carrier, jogging stroller, bike trailer, day pack.

Health—First-aid kit and remedies, bug repellent, soap, toothpaste and toothbrushes, towels.

Emi and Mari out camping

Birthday Parties

I grew up in Mississippi, where social events are an integral part of daily life. My mother organized many wonderful themed birthday parties for me that I, in turn, passed along to my girls. One summer, Emi had a Hawaiian luau for her birthday party, and we unloaded a dump truck of sand in the backyard for an instant beach. Her friends dressed up in Hawaiian skirts and leis, and we had fresh pineapple with other Hawaiian foods (minus the roasted pig). Mari had a Mexican fiesta with enchiladas, sombreros, ponchos, a piñata, and llama rides in the backyard. Mari loved hamsters, so one year we had a birthday party with a hamster theme, including large brown boxes for the kids to crawl around in, pretending to be hamsters. When Emi was older, we had a ladies' luncheon with a plate of food that looked like a girl's face, with macaroni and cheese for hair. You do not have to spend a lot of money to have a fun and creative party that children can enjoy and feel special on their day. When you make the food yourself, you can be sure that it is healthy, and you can take the opportunity to introduce other children to healthy treats.

First Birthday

A baby's first birthday is a milestone that brings a warm sense of progress and accomplishment, an excitement about reflecting on the past year, and an opportunity to look forward to future years. Between birth and his first birthday, your baby has grown physically and matured at a faster pace than he will during any single year for the rest of him life.

On his first birthday your baby will not really understand the meaning of a birthday, but he can enjoy a simple celebration that is dedicated to him. He may enjoy his own small cake that he can dig into all by himself and eat with his fingers. Some parents throw a big first birthday party for their child, inviting many family members and friends. However, if you consider your child's point of view and what is fun for him, then a simple party with less stimulation is probably what he would enjoy best.

A first birthday party also honors parents, who are naturally proud of their child. It is a good time for parents to celebrate their own good fortune, and to congratulate themselves for their hard work over the past year. It is also a time to thank grandparents, other relatives, and caregivers who have contributed to his well-being.

Second and Third Birthdays

By the time your child celebrates his second or third birthday, he knows how to say how old he is, and he can get excited about having a party and the anticipation of presents. Before you start planning, you may want to reflect on your strategy for keeping the party focused, so that you do not get sidetracked with the excitement of planning. This is your child's special day and his party, and you can help him celebrate and have a good time, while creating an event for his guests to enjoy. If you keep it simple with a personal touch, your child will have a special occasion that is meaningful.

Party planning—Sharing in the planning and decision making process with your child can be part of the fun. If you give him choices as much as possible, then he will feel more empowered and excited about his party. If you take an active part in the planning and activities together, then he will feel a shared experience. Plan ahead so that you are not in a rush at the last minute.

Guests—A good rule of thumb for the number of guests is to invite as many children as the child's age. A one-year-old has one guest, two for a two-year-old, and so on. Small groups make it easier to give each child the attention he needs. Make sure your child's special friends are on the list. Children under three years old need a parent or caretaker with them during the party time.

Party-planning Stages

There are several party stages to plan:

1. Arrival of guests

2. Activities

3. Honor your child with "Happy Birthday," cake, candles, and presents

4. Wind down, give party favors, and say good-byes

5. Clean up and put away gifts

Themes—Theme parties can be fun and a way to generate excitement. You can build a theme around a certain animal, like Mari's hamster party, serve food that animal eats, and create activities around the animal. Colors can be a theme—your toddler chooses the color, and everyone dresses accordingly with decorations and balloons in the respective color. Mari had a pink party during the year that she would only wear pink clothes. Other simple themes for two-year-olds are stuffed animals and stories. For three-year-olds, themes can be more complex, such as magic, the beach, art, safari, baseball, decorate-a-tricycle, outer space, pirates, dress-up, ballet, swimming pool, the Olympics, and different cultures.

Get help—There are cookie cutter-type parties set up for kids, where all the details are taken care of. However, if you decide to have a party with a personal touch, it does not mean that you have to do all the work. Ask family members and friends for help. If the birthday child has an older sibling, he can get involved in helping by greeting guests or collecting and recording presents for thank-you notes.

Emi and Mari

Food—If you are planning around a theme, then you may have certain inspirations, such as "hamster food". On special occasions, you may wish to widen the food options, while still keeping it healthy. Birthday cake (made either with maple syrup or honey) and ice cream with natural ingredients are birthday foods that can help make a fun party with special memories.

Decorations—Children love color and enjoy the special attention that decorations bring—streamers, balloons, birthday hats, plates, napkins, and cutlery help create a party mood. Music can add some auditory color.

Favors—Party favors can add to your theme, if you have one, or they can be simple inexpensive gifts, such as a box of crayons, or activities from the party. Painted T-shirts, hats, headbands, bags, or small toys make happy party favors. Here is a chance for you to get creative.

Photos—Take photos and videos for remembering your child's special event. If you take a video, you can show it at the end of the party as the children are leaving. Or you can print photos of the children for them to take home along with a homemade picture frame.

Entertainment—Plan activities that are age-appropriate, such as simple crafts, games, or toys with markers, paper, tape, clay, origami, puzzles, blocks, or items for stacking and sorting. Music for singing, playing games, or dancing can be an energizing activity. Games that involve physical exercise outdoors can be fun in warmer weather. Plan games that regulate your children's energy up and down so that you can adjust the party atmosphere, as needed. Some noncompetitive games are: Follow the Leader, Do the Hokey Pokey, and Simon Says.

Party time—Limit party time to one and a half to two hours for children under three years old, and make sure that the timing is not during your child's naptime.

Be flexible and adjust to the unexpected—The important thing to remember in party planning is that the main purpose is to have fun. Even if all the plans do not come out perfectly, keeping a positive attitude can help your child feel good about his special day. Chances are, something will not go as planned, so be prepared for the unexpected with a rainy day backup plan, a first-aid kit, extra games, food, and party favors.

Holidays

If your family has holiday traditions established, your baby or child's presence will make those celebrations more joyful for everyone. Holidays are wonderful opportunities to begin your own family traditions, break away from daily routines, and make memories. Religious holidays are times to observe and respect sacred traditions, but they are often combined with special foods and gatherings for the pleasure of sharing time together and strengthening the bonds of your family and friendships. For holidays when your baby is young, make sure you have food items planned and prepared in advance, so that you can relax and enjoy a special day. Family gatherings sometimes bring up past memories; planning ahead can help alleviate stress and keep gatherings comfortable and fun.

Holidays are usually associated with traditional dishes that have memories and emotional connection. I like to take family or other recipes and substitute ingredients, such as maple syrup or honey for sugar, vegetable oil for butter, and tempeh or beans for meat to create a similar, yet healthier experience. From southern soul food to burritos and spaghetti, there are many options for exploring a wide world of culinary opportunities and discovering favorites that can become traditions for your family.

Adjusting a recipe to your tastes and dietary standards can be easy, and sometimes you need more than one experiment to get it right. Familiar stews, stir-fried dishes, and casseroles can usually be made with vegetarian ingredients, possibly substituting tempeh or tofu for meat. To create a sauce or a creamy texture in a casserole, use kuzu, arrowroot, or a gravy made with flour or pureed grains instead of dairy products. In baking, I often substitute water, almond milk, or rice milk for cow's milk, and either water, applesauce, or yogurt for eggs. As I mentioned before, I use sea vegetables, such as kombu, for a savory umami flavor that pork, chicken, or beef might provide in soup stock, beans, and other dishes. You can balance acidic foods, such as tomato sauce, by adding miso to neutralize it; similarly, a few grains of salt can help bring out the natural sweetness of fruit and make it more digestible. By using a few basic principles for substitutions, you can adjust your favorite traditional family recipes to be healthy and satisfying. Holidays can be a time for relaxing your usual routine and giving your child more permission to widen his food boundaries.

New Year's Day

In the United States, New Year's Eve is considered a holiday for most adults. Hopefully your baby or toddler will not be awake at midnight when the clock turns over to a new calendar year. For the Japanese, New Year's is the most important family holiday, much the same as Christmas is for many in the West. In preparation, the last week of December is spent cleaning, paying debts, reflecting on the past year, looking toward a fresh start, and cooking special foods for the first three days of the year. On New Year's Eve, long buckwheat noodles are served at dinner as a symbol of longevity, and New Year's Day may begin with a viewing of the first sunrise or a trip to a temple or shrine to welcome the gods of the new year. *Mochitsuki*, or a *mochi*-making gathering, is a New Year's tradition that is associated with good fortune, health, and success. It is usually toasted over a hibachi to eat with vegetables and fish that are made and stored in stacked, lacquered bento boxes. Children look forward to the special treats and gifts that they receive on this annual holiday. The whole family enjoys the first three days of the year eating together, telling stories, playing games, and sitting around the *kotatsu*, a Japanese table that has a blanket that goes over the top with a space heater underneath.

The Chinese New Year occurs on a different date each year, set by the lunar calendar. It is usually at the second new moon following the winter solstice, between late January and early to mid-February. Central to the cycle of planting new crops, this celebration is the most important holiday in many parts of Asia. This is a time for families to get together in a spirit of joy, optimism, and feasting. Cultures that celebrate Chinese New Year have many special foods on this occasion, especially those that promise good fortune, prosperity, and an optimistic outlook.

Valentine's Day

A flower bouquet, a special toy, fresh fruit, or heart-shaped cookies are an alternative to chocolate for celebrating Valentine's Day for your little one. If your baby has older siblings, you can share time together and talk about what makes you love and appreciate each other. Tell your baby how much you love him, and give him extra hugs and kisses. Phone calls to grandparents will make their Valentine's Day special.

Spring Holidays

Spring is the time of renewal, with sprouting plants, first flower blooms, and birds returning from winter habitats. Eggs are age-old symbols of new life, and your toddler can enjoy boiling and painting eggs to celebrate spring or for Easter. You can fill plastic eggs with hidden surprises, like non-sugar treats or small toys, and hide the eggs again and again, indoors or outdoors.

There are many ways that children can participate in the seder festivities, from songs and games to artwork. Before the seder dinner, they can have a Passover scavenger hunt by searching your house for hametz, or leavened crumbs. During the seder, they can look for the *afikoman*, a small piece of matzo hidden in your home.

Children's Day

The Japanese have special holidays to respect and honor their children. Girls' Day, sometimes called Dolls' Day, and Boys' Day have been combined into one national holiday on May 5th called Children's Day. These holidays have been observed by the Japanese for many centuries to celebrate a child's unique character. Parents and relatives take time for prayer and gratitude for their children's healthy growth and happiness. Many Japanese still observe Girls' Day on March 3rd, and bring out ceremonial dolls that are bought when a baby girl is born. These dolls wear elaborate Japanese clothing and include the emperor and empress, along with their attendants and musicians. Small vases of peach blossoms are used for decoration. Obā-san, Emi and Mari's grandmother, gave them a set of Japanese dolls when they were born, and they enjoyed dressing up in Japanese *yukatas* (summer kimonos) and inviting their friends over for a tea party to celebrate Dolls' Day.

The symbol for Boys' Day is the carp, which stands for strength and determination, because carps swim against the river's current. On Boys' Day families take time to honor their sons and dedicate wishes that they grow up with good characteristics, including bravery and perseverance. On Boys' Day, most households fly one kite for each son that are made in the shape of a colorful carp fish. *Amazake* is a traditional drink enjoyed on Children's Day holidays.

Emi

Cinco de Mayo

Cinco de Mayo translates as the 5th of May, when Mexico won the 1862 Battle of the Puebla over the French. Surprisingly, this holiday is celebrated more in the United States and other countries than it is in Mexico. Whether you have Hispanic roots or just want to connect with Hispanic culture, this day is an opportunity to celebrate with traditional Mexican clothing, hats, music, food, and decorations.

Independence Day

July 4th is associated with summer fun in the United States—picnics, cookouts, pool parties, outings to nearby lakes and parks, and gatherings with neighbors or friends. By July, seasonal vegetables are plentiful, and corn on the cob is a favorite food to celebrate this holiday. Other healthy choices are noodle or pasta salads, green salads, veggie burgers, or tofu hot dogs. Fresh fruit, including blueberries, peaches, cantaloupe, and watermelon, are usually ripe and tasty in July.

Fireworks are a signature feature of the Fourth of July. Because they do not start until after dark, which is a late hour in midsummer for babies or toddlers, plan a restful afternoon if you attend firework festivities with your child. Keep in mind that the loud noises and explosions can be frightening to very young children. Take extra care if you do your own fireworks.

Halloween

When Japanese people asked me about Halloween customs, I was at a loss for words. I did not know anything about the history of the tradition, and I felt silly trying to explain them. Costumes, jack-o'-lanterns, witches, and black cats? Now, I easily find information on the internet—the Druids believed that they were surrounded by strange spirits, ghosts, witches, fairies, and elves on the night before November 1st. They saw this as a time to make a sacrifice to their gods for protection. The custom of trick-or-treating came from Ireland, where farmers went from house to house begging for food; they promised good luck to those who gave them food and made threats to those who refused to give.

Halloween is now a favorite holiday for children for the sheer fun and excitement of dressing up, followed by trick-or-treating or a costume party. Carving pumpkins into jack-o'-lanterns can create a festive atmosphere, and choosing a costume and a new identity for your little one can be exciting. Whether your child goes trick-or-treating door to door in a neighborhood or goes to a private gathering, Halloween is a holiday that is associated with sugary excess. I planned ahead about how to substitute, limit, or ration the Halloween bags of candy. In recent years, neighborhood and private Halloween parties have become increasingly popular. You could search out or host your own gathering that does not go overboard with candies and drinks made with sugar, food colorings, and other additives. For a neighborhood or community party, parents often enjoy dressing up, too.

When Emi and Mari were old enough for trick-or-treating, I did not want them to miss the fun, so they dressed up and I took them around with their bags to trick-or-treat. When we returned home, we sat on the living room floor with their bags of candy in the middle of the room. I blindfolded them and made some eerie sounds, while quickly switching their bags of sugar candy for ones with natural treats. When they took off their blindfolds, they had a new bag of goodies that they could enjoy without bellyaches and headaches.

Thanksgiving

In America, Thanksgiving is a holiday centered around food and family traditions. It is associated with the completion of the autumn harvest, which is a good time to acknowledge appreciation for food and other blessings, while sharing a spirit of gratitude. Thanksgiving can be a relaxed holiday without high expectations. It is easy to make healthy dishes that include whole grains, vegetables, plant-based or animal food proteins, fruits, and healthy desserts.

Christmas and Hanukkah

For the majority of Americans, and increasingly for people all over the world, even those who are not of the Christian faith, Christmas is the biggest holiday of the year. Christmas is associated with religious observance, gifts, decorations, singing both secular and religious songs, and other festivities. Most families enjoy elaborate meals, along with Christmas cookies and other special foods, during the Christmas season. Christmas cookies and snacks can be made ahead of time and stored in airtight containers or the freezer.

With a baby or toddler, you have a chance to create your own family's traditions. Most children enjoy decorating a tree, making gifts, cards, or cookies and taking them to relatives and friends. Christmas is a chance to teach your children about respecting sacred traditions.

Hanukkah, the Jewish traditional Festival of Lights, lasts for eight days and sometimes coincides with Christmas. Hanukkah has religious rituals, especially lighting the menorah each night, traditional foods, games for children, and small gifts.

These holidays often include many social events that have sugary deserts and out-of-the-ordinary dishes. It is fun to enjoy connections with friends and family and expand your daily routine. However, it may be challenging to keep your family healthy and balanced during the holidays. Planning ahead and making natural treats can help satisfy your child when the plate of sugary cookies is passed around.

Return Home to Balance 🏠

The fun and adventures of travel, social events, and holidays are exciting to plan for and to enjoy. They help your child broaden his world of people, places, and learning experiences. However, they often involve foods that include refined sugar and other extremes, along with disruptions of your child's routine. Returning home and getting back into a routine of ordinary day-to-day life is usually a welcome relief after travel, holidays or events. Home sweet home. Once you return, if your baby or child got off balance, you may need to prepare remedies to help bring him back to center and create some quiet time for settling back in.

Parents are role models, and the way you manage yourself communicates your priorities and principles to your child. The example you set teaches him to self-regulate and balance discipline and pleasure for himself on special occasions.

The following recipes offer foods, such as rice balls and sandwiches that are easy to take when traveling with your child, as well as some options for family meals. When going out, you can make individual bentos, or you can pack food in family size containers and carry small plates for serving. When your baby starts eating solid foods, you can integrate your family meals to coordinate with his meals, reducing your time spent shopping and in the kitchen. When you cook whole grains and vegetables for your baby, you can also cook the same foods for your family, either separately or together, and make seasoning adjustments at the end.

The family recipes below are simple dishes that you and your child can enjoy together, after he is chewing well. They are soft and easy to eat for a toddler, and they are all inclusive main course dishes that include grains, vegetables, and protein-rich foods. Recipes included are pasta salad, spaghetti, curry rice, and vegetable casserole. You can adjust your favorite soups, stews, and casseroles to meet your child's needs as he makes the transition to adult food. Eating the same quality of food together helps build a family bond.

Family Meals

WHEN YOUR BABY STARTS eating solid foods, you can integrate his meals to coordinate with the family's, reducing your time spent shopping and in the kitchen. When you cook whole grains and vegetables for your baby, you can also cook the same foods for your family, separately or together, and make seasoning adjustments at the end.

The recipes listed here are simple dishes that you and your child can enjoy together, after she is chewing well. They are soft and easy to eat for a toddler, and they are all-inclusive main course dishes that include grains, vegetables, and protein-rich foods. Recipes included are pasta salad, spaghetti, curry rice, and vegetable casserole. You can adjust your favorite soups, stews, and casseroles to meet your child's needs as she makes the transition to adult food. Eating the same quality of food together helps build a family bond.

Rice Balls

♡ 12 months+

🥄 12 (1-ounce) rice balls

V Vegetarian

GF Gluten-free

Rice balls are a traditional travel food in Japan in bentos for school, work, excursions, or long-distance trips. They are the Japanese version of a sandwich that is easy to eat as a finger food for all ages.

Because *umeboshi* plums have a high salt content, they help preserve rice balls for 2 or 3 days. Other fillings may be lower in sodium, making them more perishable, so they need to be eaten within several hours, or placed in an insulated bag or in the refrigerator. A breathable container helps keep rice balls fresh longer.

¾ cup short-grain brown rice

¼ cup sweet brown rice

Water to cover for soaking

2 cups water for cooking

⅛ teaspoon sea salt

Nori sea vegetable

Small dish of water

Umeboshi paste for filling for 12 months+

Planning ahead:
Cover grains with water and soak for 8 to 24 hours. If you do not have time to soak for the longer time span, soak for at least 1 hour, if possible.

Method
Cook Rice
1. Strain soaking water, add grains and cooking water to pot, and bring to a boil over high heat.

2. Reduce heat and cook for 45 minutes to 1 hour, until all water is absorbed.

3. Use a heat diffuser to keep grains from sticking to bottom of pot, and to prevent burning.

4. Transfer rice to a large or flat bowl so that air circulates around rice. Do not refrigerate rice before making into balls, or it will not stick together.

Make the Rice Balls

1. Cut nori into strips approximately 3 x 4 inches.

2. Place a small bowl of water near work area for dipping hands to keep rice from sticking.

3. When rice is cool enough to handle, wet hands, and take approximately ½ cup of rice in your hand (photo a).

4. Press the rice together to form round or oblong balls (photo b).

5. Press a hole in the center of ball, add ¼ teaspoon *umeboshi* plum paste for filling, and press rice to cover hole, shaping ball.

6. Wrap nori around rice ball (photo c).

7. Stick loose end to roll with a few drops of water (photo d).

Variations

Substitute single or multiple fillings:

*   Cooked or canned salmon or tuna pieces

*   Tempeh pieces

*   Almond butter or tahini

*   Sautéed or steamed vegetable pieces

*   Pickles

Sprinkle the outside with:

*   Toasted seeds or nuts, either ground or whole

*   A few drops of plum vinegar

*   A few drops of sesame, olive, or flaxseed oil

You can also use this recipe to make nori rolls.

*   Use a sushi mat and place a sheet of nori on the mat.

*   Spread rice on half of sheet horizontally.

*   Spread a strip of filling across the rice and roll up with the sushi mat, moistening across the edge.

*   Slice into rounds for simple sushi.

Sandwiches

Sandwiches are convenient for a quick lunch, at home or on the go. At nine months, your baby may enjoy a piece of bread or toast with a thick puree spread on it; at 12 months, he may find a single layer sandwich with soft ingredients manageable; and by 18 months, he can probably handle a two-layer sandwich with different fillings.

The ingredients can be prepared ahead of time, and sandwiches can be assembled with efficiency. See suggested combinations for sandwich ingredients, then mix and match for variety and according to your toddler's personal favorites.

For best taste, sandwiches should be served at room temperature, rather than chilled. Most vegetable sandwiches can stay fresh for several hours, even without refrigeration. Or you can put sandwiches in an insulated lunch bag and include a small freezer pack.

Choose bread made from whole grains, with simple, natural ingredients, and use gluten-free bread before your child is 12 months old and for those with a gluten intolerance. Fresh bread is most delicious, but you can also freeze bread to have it on hand when needed. Pita bread is a convenient option for children, because the pocket holds the fillings without as much mess.

Tempeh Sandwich

18 months+, 2 sandwiches, Vegetarian

1 teaspoon tamari

3 tablespoons water

2 teaspoons sesame oil

1 tablespoon mayonnaise, made without canola oil or eggs

1 tablespoon mustard, stone-ground without preservatives or additives

2 slices bread

Carrot slices, lightly steamed

2 tablespoons clover sprouts for 18 months+

Method

1. Cut tempeh into 2 pieces and slice down the middle.

2. Place the pieces in a small dish.

3. Mix tamari and water, pour the mixture over the tempeh, and marinate for 30 minutes.

4. Heat a skillet with the oil, place the tempeh slices in the skillet, and brown on one side for 5 minutes, then brown on the other side for 5 minutes.

5. Transfer to a plate, and let cool before making sandwiches. If you prepare tempeh ahead of time, it can be stored for 2 or 3 days in the refrigerator.

6. Spread mayonnaise and mustard on bread, and add carrot slices and sprouts.

7. Press sandwich lightly so that the ingredients stick together.

8. Cut sandwich in half.

Variations

• Add pickle slices or sauerkraut.

• Substitute sautéed greens or lettuce for sprouts.

• Substitute onions for carrots.

• Substitute tofu for tempeh. Eating raw tofu is not recommended.

Hummus Sandwich

12 months+, 1 sandwich, vegetarian

Hummus is an easy protein spread that is tasty for all ages. If you buy prepared hummus, check for salt content. For younger babies, it is easy to make your own with home-cooked or canned beans or chickpeas. Other beans make delicious spreads for variety.

2 tablespoons hummus or other bean spread

2 slices bread

Lettuce leaves

3 black olives, sliced

Method

1. Spread hummus on bread.

2. Add lettuce and olive slices.

3. Press sandwich lightly so that the ingredients stick together.

4. Cut sandwich in half.

Variations

• Substitute other bean spreads.

• Add cucumbers, tomatoes, or avocados.

Salmon Sandwich

18 months+, 2 sandwiches, animal protein

Canned salmon is an easy way to make a sandwich full of omega-3 fatty acids. When buying canned salmon, check the label for wild salmon instead of farm raised.

1 (6-ounce) can wild salmon, drained

1 teaspoon lemon juice

½ teaspoon fresh parsley or dill, minced

½ teaspoon olive oil

3 tablespoons mayonnaise, made without canola oil or eggs

2 slices bread

Cucumber slices

Method

1. Mix together salmon, lemon juice, herbs, and olive oil. Salmon salad can be prepared a day ahead, and kept in the refrigerator.

2. Spread mayonnaise on bread, add salmon mixture on one side, and top with cucumbers.

3. Press sandwich lightly so that the ingredients stick together.

Pasta Salad

♥ 12 months+

🥄 5 or 6 servings

V Vegetarian

GF Gluten-free option

Pasta salad is a crowd-pleaser and an easy dish for many occasions. Set aside a portion for your toddler if you need to add more seasoning for others. Use seasonal vegetables when possible for a colorful and tasty dish. Use gluten-free pasta for children under 12 months and if serving persons with gluten intolerance.

Pasta:

9 cups water

2 teaspoons sesame or olive oil

¼ teaspoon sea salt

2 cups whole-grain pasta
(shells, elbow macaroni, penne,
or bow tie)

Vegetables:

1 cup water

¼ teaspoon sea salt

1 cup carrots, cut into rounds

1 cup yellow squash, cut into ½-inch
pieces

1 cup onion, peeled and cut into
¼-inch pieces

2 cups broccoli, cut into
1-inch florets

Dressing:

2 teaspoons fresh cilantro, basil,
or parsley, minced

¼ cup sesame, olive, or coconut oil

1 tablespoon plum vinegar

1 tablespoon lemon juice

Types of pasta

Method

Pasta

1. Bring water to a boil in large pot.

2. Add oil and sea salt and stir to combine.

3. Add pasta to boiling water and cook according to package directions until tender.

4. Drain and rinse with cold water.

5. To make the vegetables, bring water to a boil in large pot; add salt.

6. Add vegetables, cover with a lid, and cook until tender, 10 to 20 minutes (photo a).

7. Use a heat diffuser to keep vegetables from sticking to the bottom of the pot, and to prevent burning.

8. Drain vegetables, while keeping leftover water for soup or other dish. Let cool (photo b).

Dressing

1. Mix together dressing ingredients.

2. Add more seasoning for older family members, if desired (photo c).

Assemble salad

1. When vegetables are cool, combine with the pasta in a large bowl.

2. Toss with dressing (photo d).

Variations

- Add or substitute other vegetables, such as cooked cauliflower, green beans, sugar snap peas, or zucchini, or raw avocados or cucumbers

- Add soaked wakame sea vegetable flakes.

- Substitute cooked brown rice or quinoa for pasta.

- Add a protein-rich food, such as cooked beans or pieces of fish, either cooked or canned.

Spaghetti with Sauce

♡ 18 months+

🥄 5 or 6 adult servings

V Vegetarian

GF Gluten-free option

Spaghetti is a favorite and fun food for meals, or for a quick snack. It can be cooked ahead of time and served at room temperature, and the noodles can be rinsed in hot water to serve with sauce. Spaghetti is convenient for a toddler, because you can make a large amount and use as needed. Wait until your child is 18 months before serving tomato sauce, because of the acidity and for controlling mess. Miso complements the acidity of tomatoes and creates a hearty umami taste.

Spaghetti:

12 cups water

2 teaspoons sesame or olive oil

¼ teaspoon sea salt

1 (8-ounce) package spaghetti

Sauce:

1 tablespoon olive oil

2 teaspoons minced garlic

1 ½ cups onion, peeled and cut into ½-inch pieces

2 cups portobello mushroom, cut into ½-inch pieces

1 ½ cups carrots, cut into ½-inch pieces

2 cups zucchini, cut into ½-inch pieces

¼ teaspoon sea salt

1 (28-ounce) can diced tomatoes

¼ cup miso paste (dark, if available)

2 tablespoons water

1 teaspoon basil or parsley

Method

Spaghetti

1. Bring water to a boil in pot.

2. Add oil and sea salt and stir to combine.

3. Add pasta to boiling water and cook according to package directions until tender.

4. Drain and rinse with cold water.

Sauce

1. Heat oil in a stainless steel or enamel skillet. (Do not cook tomato sauce in cast iron, because the acidity in tomatoes will remove the pan's seasoning.)

2. Add 1 tablespoon water. Add garlic, onions, mushrooms, carrots, and zucchini and sauté until tender (photo a).

3. Add sea salt, and sauté for 5 minutes, and then add tomatoes. Simmer for 20 to 25 minutes (photo b).

4. Use a heat diffuser to keep vegetables from sticking to the bottom of the pot, and to prevent burning.

5. Mix miso with water in a small dish until it has a smooth consistency (photo c).

6. Stir miso into sauce. To retain the *Lactobacillus* in miso, do not boil sauce after miso has been added. Add herbs and simmer over low heat for 5 minutes (photo d).

Assemble dish

- Serve sauce over spaghetti.

Variations

- Substitute other vegetables, such as sugar snap peas, string beans, yellow squash, or celery.

- Add pieces of salmon or white fish, shucked clams, peeled and deveined shrimp, or scallops.

Vegetable Curry Over Rice

♡ 12 months+

🥣 4 or 5 adult servings

V Vegetarian

GF Gluten-free

This recipe is satisfying and full of rich flavor from both vegetables and curry. When I was at Muso Yochien (Dream Window Kindergarten), curry rice was my favorite meal, and I learned to read the Japanese characters so that I could see the scheduled date on the menu plan for this delicious dish. Curry rice is so popular among children in Japan that they have a fun song about the ingredients and cooking process called "*karē raisu*" or カレーライス in Japanese katakana.

Brown Rice:

2 cups short-grain brown rice

Water for soaking rice

4 cups water

¼ teaspoon salt

Curried Vegetables:

1 tablespoon sesame oil

1 cup onion, peeled and cut into ½-inch pieces

1 cup white potato, peeled and cut into 1-inch pieces

1 cup butternut squash, peeled and cut into 1-inch pieces

1 cup carrot, cut into 1-inch pieces

1 cup shiitake, cut into ¼-inch slices

½ teaspoon sea salt

1 cup cooked chickpeas, canned or homemade from dried beans

1-inch square kombu or 1 teaspoon wakame flakes, soaked for 10 minutes in 1 cup water and drained

½ cup water

1 tablespoon curry powder

1 tablespoon kuzu

⅓ cup water for dissolving kuzu

Planning ahead:

Cover rice with water and soak for 8 to 24 hours. If you do not have time to soak for the longer time span, soak for at least 1 hour.

Method

Cook rice

1. To make rice, strain rice. Add rice and cooking water to pot, then bring to a boil.

2. Reduce heat and cook for 45 minutes to 1 hour, until all water is absorbed.

3. Use a heat diffuser to keep grains from sticking to the bottom of the pot, and to prevent burning.

Cook curried vegetables

1. To make curried vegetables, heat oil in a large skillet.

2. Add onion, and then add potato, squash, carrots, and mushrooms. Sauté the vegetables, stirring for 5 to 10 minutes.

3. Add sea salt, chickpeas, sea vegetable, and ½ cup water.

4. Bring to a boil, and cover with a lid. Reduce heat, and simmer for 30 minutes.

5. Stir in curry powder.

6. Dissolve kuzu in ⅓ cup water in a separate bowl or grinding bowl. Use a fork or pestle to dissolve thoroughly. Kuzu must be dissolved in cool or room temperature water before adding to hot food or liquid.

Assemble dish

1. Add kuzu liquid to simmering curry and stir to combine.

2. Serve curry over brown rice.

Variations

- Substitute broccoli, sweet potatoes, yellow squash, zucchini, green beans, green peas, cabbage, kale, cauliflower, bok choy, Chinese cabbage, or tomatoes.

- Add slices of tempeh, tofu, fish, shrimp, or chicken.

- Substitute arrowroot flour for kuzu as a thickener.

Mashed Vegetable Casserole

♡ 12 months+

🥣 6 to 8 adult servings

V Vegetarian

GF Gluten-free

Blending grains and vegetables to a creamy consistency provides a texture that has a sentimental and comforting feeling. It also disguises the ingredients, and is a way to get children to eat a healthy variety of foods when they may have developed a negative image of certain foods. The following recipe has the look and feel of mashed potatoes but offers a balanced main dish of a whole grain with vegetables.

Mashed Vegetables:

1 cup millet

Water for soaking millet

2 cups water for cooking

¼ teaspoon sea salt

4 cups cauliflower, or 1 head, cut into 1-inch pieces

½ cup water for cooking

¼ teaspoon salt

1 cup water for pureeing

Gravy:

1 tablespoon sesame, olive, or coconut oil

2 teaspoons minced garlic

1 ½ cups shiitake mushrooms, sliced

1 cup water

¼ teaspoon sea salt

2 tablespoons tamari

2 tablespoons kuzu

2 tablespoons water for dissolving kuzu

Tempeh and Green Peas:

Tempeh, substituting onions for carrots. See recipe on page 440

1 (10-ounce) package frozen organic green peas

Planning ahead

Cover millet with water and soak for 8 to 24 hours. If you do not have time to soak for the longer time span, soak for at least 1 hour.

Method

Mashed Vegetables

1. Prepare tempeh recipe (page 440) (photo a).

2. Strain soaking water, place millet and cooking water into pot, and bring to a boil over high heat.

3. Reduce heat and cook for 40 minutes, until all water is absorbed.

4. Use a heat diffuser to keep grains from sticking to the bottom of the pot, and to prevent burning.

5. Add cauliflower, water, and salt to a separate pan and cook for 10–15 minutes until tender.

6. Puree millet and cauliflower together in a blender or food processor with extra water.

7. Preheat oven to 400°F.

Gravy

1. Heat oil in pan, add garlic and shiitake mushrooms, and sauté until tender.

2. Add 1 cup water, salt, and tamari and stir to combine.

3. Bring to a boil, reduce heat to a low simmer, and cook for 5 minutes.

4. Dissolve kuzu in 2 tablespoons water in a separate bowl or grinding bowl. Use a fork or pestle to dissolve thoroughly. Kuzu must be dissolved in cool or room temperature water before adding to hot food or liquid.

5. Add kuzu liquid to simmering gravy, and stir until the mixture turns transparent.

Assemble Casserole

1. Spread tempeh and peas in a larger casserole dish (photo b).

2. Spread mashed vegetable over tempeh and peas (photo c).

3. Pour gravy over top of casserole (photo d).

4. Bake for 20 minutes, or until heated through.

Whole Living

Whole Living

YOU CAN EASILY CREATE a home environment filled with healthy items that promote whole living for your child. When Emi was a baby in Japan, we did not have much money, and we had a tiny apartment with very little furniture. I made a cushion out of natural cotton for an old dresser that we found in the trash, and it served as a changing table. We all slept together in a futon that we folded and stored during the daytime in order to set up a small table for eating. We lived simply, but we were happy and Emi had everything that she needed: safety, security, healthy food, love, and support to explore and learn.

You can offer your baby the basics that she needs in her environment with simple products made from natural ingredients. If you take the approach that less is more, then you can give her the items that she needs even within a budget. Educating yourself on the ingredients and properties of products helps you understand priorities when making purchasing choices.

Part 3, "Whole Living" provides thorough information about products that you need for your baby, as well as their ingredients.

- Chapter 9—"Ingredients and Materials" gives you a reference list of significant properties of the ingredients in the products that you need for your baby. This chapter is divided into five sections: Feeding Gear and Toys, Skin Care, Food Additives, Around the Home, and Textiles. At the end of the chapter, I discuss product testing, certifications, and manufacturing processes.

- Chapter 10—"Product Guide" offers information about 250 products and their main features. These products are divided into Nursery, Baby Care, Clothing, On the Go, Feeding, and Toys. Finally the chapter provides a newborn shopping list.

CHAPTER 9

Ingredients and Materials

IN 1925, MY GRANDMOTHER made my mother's clothes with natural materials, and my grandfather made her baby bed. Baby care had to be natural; my mother was breast-fed and wore cloth diapers because formula and disposable diapers were not available. Her family ate organic vegetables from their garden and fresh eggs from the chickens in their backyard. My mother's toys were a homemade doll, wooden spoons, cups, pots, and pans.

During the post–World War II boom, U.S. manufacturers made baby products, such as bottles and sippy cups, mattresses, clothing, and toys, without testing and regulations. Much of that manufacturing has moved overseas since then, and it has taken years to put testing procedures in place for these products and to enact bans to make sure that all materials are safe. Even today, though, laws do not require testing or labeling in some products. In addition, some products are made in countries whose regulations have loopholes—including the United States.

Today, your baby's products are made and transported all around the world. Imagine all the places that her teddy bear, sippy cups, and teethers have traveled. Was the organic cotton for her bodysuit really grown in Turkey, shipped to Thailand for knitting and dying, and then sewn and shipped to the United States? As a parent, it can be overwhelming to identify safety concerns and to figure out how to respond to them. There are so many issues to consider that it can be hard to know where to start.

I began my company from my experiences as a mother, with concern for my children's health and for the health of all children, as if they were my own. With the goal of making high-quality baby products, I have dug deep to find materials that are as natural as possible. Along the way, I have managed manufacturing processes in many countries—the United States, Mexico, Central and South America, Thailand, China, South Korea, Vietnam, and India.

My philosophy from the very beginning—over 30 years ago—has been to ensure that our products are free of any substances that could pose a health risk to babies. When we begin our product-development process at i play., Inc., I ask, "Would I use this product with my own children or grandchildren? Is this safe enough for them?" If the answer to either of these questions is "No" or "I do not know," we either find a safer way to make the product or do not make it at all. We are always looking for better materials and processes and scouting for possible harmful ingredients.

The good news is that today, you have access to a great deal of information about ingredients, materials, and products. You also have access to many products that have safe materials and ingredients. This chapter is a resource to educate you about many common materials and ingredients as you go through the process of making healthy choices for the products you use with your baby.

The chapter is divided into six sections: feeding products and toys that your baby puts in her mouth, skin care products that are absorbed through her skin, food additives used in processed foods, environmental substances that she breathes, both indoors and outdoors, textiles in the clothing that she wears, and information about testing procedures, certifications, and manufacturing processes, based on my over 30 years of experience with i play., Inc.

Feeding Gear and Toys

YOUR BABY DEVELOPS NEURAL pathways—groups of connected neurons—by exploring and sensing with her mouth. When her teeth begin to emerge, she wants to chew on everything. Bottles, sippy cups, teethers, and toys go directly into her mouth, while dishes and cutlery hold food that goes inside her mouth. Because your baby may ingest some of the by-products of these items, it is natural for parents to consider the safety of the materials used to produce them.

In addition to safety, functionality, convenience, environmental friendliness, and affordability are high priorities for parents when it comes to products. Your baby needs cups that are waterproof and that screw on tight, bowls that are durable and do not break easily, bottles that are shatterproof and clear enough to see the amount of liquid inside, and container lids that snap on and off easily. Products that are disposable, dishwasher-safe, and easy to store often fit today's family lifestyles. At the same time, taking care of your child's generation means taking care of the environment. Finally, parents cannot ignore the bottom line: the cost of the multiple products that your baby needs must fit into your budget.

This is a lot to ask of a product. It is challenging, both for parents and for baby-product designers, even to imagine items that satisfy all of those requirements. The answer often involves research. When you have information, you can make informed choices based on your lifestyle priorities. Do you prefer a glass sippy cup that is breakable and somewhat expensive, or a plastic one that is unbreakable and inexpensive but is made of petroleum? Will you buy your baby sunglasses that are made of polycarbonate (which contains BPA) but are unbreakable and easy to see through? Or will you purchase sunglasses that are made of a safer plastic that does not break easily but is visually less clear? Will you use cloth diapers that feel good next to your baby's bottom and are economical, or is it easier to use more expensive disposables to save time in your busy day?

These decisions are not clear-cut. Every situation is different, and each family has unique needs. This section contains information about a variety of materials used in feeding products and toys. You can read about the properties, pros, and cons of each material. Because plastic is a material used in many baby products, I have included extra information that will help you use plastic in the safest possible way.

The following list of materials starts with petroleum plastics to look for in feeding gear and toys, starting with safer plastics. Next, you will find information about other types of plastics, as well as potentially harmful additives that are combined with plastics during the manufacturing process. Finally, you will find nonpetroleum ingredients and materials that are safe alternatives to plastics, such as glass, ceramic, wood, and metals, as well as potentially harmful additives associated with those materials.

Plastics

In the movie *The Graduate*, the title character, a recent college graduate played by a young Dustin Hoffman, receives one word of career advice from a businessman and friend of his parents: "Plastics." In 1967, when The Graduate was released, the onslaught of product choices made of this versatile and functional material had just begun. Today, plastic is used all over the world in many kinds of manufacturing as a durable, inexpensive material for products that function well.

Plastics have become an integral part of daily life in the majority of cultures. Because the material is so inexpensive to manufacture, it is easy to think of plastic products as disposable. For example, it is often less expensive to buy a new toaster oven than to repair an old one. Despite this cheapness and convenience, the abundant manufacturing of plastic products has negative consequences for the environment and, potentially, for your baby's health.

Plastics are made from petroleum, which is a nonrenewable resource. Because plastic is not biodegradable, it is an environmental hazard that affects bodies of water, as well as animals and plants both in the water and on land. In addition, the manufacture and disposal of plastics drains other resources, creates soil and water pollution that threatens land and marine

life, and takes up landfill space until it finally decomposes up to 1,000 years later. During the manufacturing process, additives are combined with plastics to improve product function. Two materials, PVC (a plastic) and BPA (an additive), have been found to disrupt hormones and to have other negative health effects.

In 2003, before plastics became a concern in the news, at my company, i play., Inc., we discovered the use of PVC in baby products. After researching PVC, we educated parents about its dangers and made sure that all of our products were PVC-free. In 2006 we learned about similar concerns with BPA, a petroleum-based hormone disruptor, and quickly eliminated it from our products. Now we are researching ways to take care of plastics so that they are safer and seeking to make products with petroleum-free materials.

Petroleum Plastics

Different kinds of plastics have different properties. The following list uses the seven classes of plastics that facilitate recycling or reprocessing, as developed by the Society of the Plastics Industry. Each class is assigned a code that is usually printed on the bottom of the product. The numbers are not in order by priority; rather, I have separated the plastics into my own two categories: Safer and Avoid. The primary plastics that are recycled are PET, HDPE, and LDPE. Generally speaking, the degree of environmental impact coincides with the degree of impact on your baby's health.

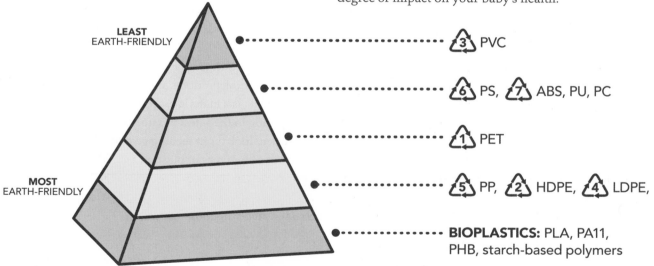

Safer Plastics

PP (polypropylene)
Medicine bottles, straws, cereal liners, reusable containers, sippy cups, dishes, cutlery, food containers, toys

PP

HDPE (high-density polyethylene)
Grocery bags, detergent bottles, milk and juice containers

HDPE

LDPE (low-density polyethylene)
Heavy-duty bags, squeezable bottles, plastic food wrap

LDPE

Plastics to Avoid

PVC (polyvinyl chloride)
Garden hoses, window frames, blister packs (for pills, batteries, etc.)

V

PS (polystyrene)
Plastic cutlery, foam packaging, foam egg cartons

PS

PC (polycarbonate), ABS (acrylonitrile butadiene styrene)
Baby bottles, water-cooler bottles, car parts

OTHER

PET or PETE (polyethylene terephthalate)
Plastic bottles (soft-drink and single-use water bottles), food jars, cosmetics containers

PETE

 PVC FREE Bibs

What is PVC? PVC, polyvinyl chloride, is a plastic that requires toxic chemicals to make it stable and soft for use in many baby items.

IS it harmful to your child?
- Vinyl chloride is a known human carcinogen.
- Lead and cadmium, common stabeilizers for PVC, are toxic—especially to young children.
- The plasticizers used to soften PVC, phthalates ("thay-lates"), have been shown to disrupt reproductive functions.
- Over time, PVC products break down, releasing these harmful chemicals into your child's environment.

Why take the risk? Babies develop by exploring through their senses and putting everything in their mouths. You can minimize the risk of ingestion by removing PVC products from your child's envirnment.

 i play.® is continually working to improve our products for children's health and safety, so all of our bibs are now PVC free.

Safer Plastics

Because plastics are made from petroleum, the existence of safe plastics is questionable. However, if you learn some of the basics about plastics and make informed, careful choices, I believe that you can use plastics in a safer way.

The polymers in plastic become more chemically volatile when they are exposed to extreme heat, extreme cold, saliva, detergents, oils, fats, and acids. Over time these substances melt the molecules in plastic containers, and they can leach into your baby's food. Think about the time when you put hot, oily tomato sauce into a plastic container, and the walls of the container turned orange and greasy. The different melting points of plastics affect their volatility. Products made with plastics that have a high melting point do not degrade as easily from contact with heat or with substances that cause them to decompose.

To use plastics in a safer way, choose products that are made from materials that have higher melting points. In addition, if you notice any wear and tear on your plastic containers—for example, bubbles, cracks, scratches, or residue buildup—recycle or discard them. To keep plastic from breaking down, take care not to put hot food or liquid in plastic containers, do not leave plastic items in the sun, and do not put them in the microwave.

The following list of safer plastics provides a description of the material, its appearance, where it is found, and things to consider when buying or using it.

Melting Points of Plastics

Plastic Type	Melting Point*
PP (polypropylene)	320° F to 338° F
HDPE (high-density polyethelyne)	250° F to 350° F
LDPE (low-density polyethelyne)	230° F to 248° F
PVC (polyvinyl chloride)	210° F to 500° F
PS (polystyrene)	347° F to 464° F
PC (polycarbonate)	302° F to 500° F
PET (polyethylene terphthalate)	500° F

* Melting points vary according to the density and exact formulation of the plastic.

Polypropylene (PP)

PP is durable and has a higher resistance to heat than many other plastics. PP is considered safer, as it is not known to leach any chemicals that are suspected of causing cancer or disrupting hormones. PP has a high melting point. It is translucent and provides a good moisture barrier. Its recycling code is (5).

Appearance: Matte or satin finish, transparent, semirigid or rigid

Found in: Reusable containers, baby bottles, food containers, such as yogurt and margarine tubs, disposable cups and plates, clothing, electronic equipment; because it is colorfast, it is also used in rugs, carpets, and mats

Considerations:
- Very strong, durable, and flexible
- Not prone to chemical leaching
- BPA-free and phthalate-free
- Can break down with prolonged heat and sunlight exposure
- Higher heat resistance than most plastics
- Resistant to fatigue and corrosion
- Not easily recycled

Safer Plastics

High-density polyethylene (HDPE)

HDPE is known for its strength and hardness. It is used in many home products because it does not shatter when dropped and is the most recycled plastic. It has a strong resistance to impact, is opaque, and provides a good moisture barrier. HDPE is considered a safer plastic, as it is not known to leach any chemicals that are suspected of causing cancer or disrupting hormones. Its recycling code is (2).

Appearance: Matte finish, usually opaque, semiflexible or rigid

Found in: Milk, water, and juice bottles; yogurt and margarine tubs; cereal-box liners; water pipes; grocery, trash, and retail bags

Considerations:
- Can be recycled and frozen
- Inexpensive
- Safer than PETE (less prone to breakdown/leaching)
- You cannot see contents clearly through plastic
- Does not hold up to some solvents (like PP does) so it is harder to sterilize

Low-density polyethylene (LDPE)

LDPE is often found in frozen-food bags, squeezable mustard and ketchup bottles, some plastic wraps, and flexible container lids. It has a strong resistance to impact, is translucent, and provides a good moisture barrier. LDPE is considered safer, as it is not known to leach any chemicals that are suspected of causing cancer or disrupting hormones. LDPE is more flexible than HDPE but not as strong. It is also petroleum-based and can be recycled with code (4) plastics.

Appearance: Matte finish, semitransparent, highly flexible

Found in: Squeezable condiment bottles, container lids, plastic wrap, sandwich bags, grocery bags

Considerations:
- Excellent resistance to acids, alcohols, and bases, so does not break down easily
- Not easily recycled

Ethylene vinyl acetate (EVA)

EVA is a durable, flexible, transparent copolymer plastic. It does not require a plasticizer to obtain its flexibility, so it is bisphenol A (BPA)- and phthalate-free. EVA can also be used as a fabric in bibs, a hard plastic in toys, or hard foam. As foam, it often requires formamides as to create stiffer, denser foam.

Appearance: Matte finish, semitransparent, highly flexible

Found in: Bibs, teethers, glue sticks, shoes, yoga mats, play mats, foam toys

Considerations:
- Waterproof, durable, and stain-resistant
- Very flexible
- UV stable
- Flammable and low heat resistance
- Foam EVA may contain formamide, which can cause reproductive damage and sinus or skin irritation

Safer Plastics

Polyhydroxybutyrate (PHB)

PHB is a version of polyester that is used in the textile industry. It is glucose or starch based and includes materials such as corn syrup and beet molasses.

Appearance: Matte or satin finish, transparent, semirigid or rigid

Found in: Medical sutures, gauzes, coatings for drugs, clothing, plastic wrap, disposable drinking cups

Considerations:
- Compostable and sustainable
- UV stable
- Water-resistant
- Nontoxic
- Expensive
- Flammable

Thermoplastic elastomer (TPE)

TPE combines plastic and rubber to create a flexible, stretchy, strong material.

Appearance: Matte finish, opaque, usually milky white, highly flexible

Found in: Teethers, toys, sippy cup spouts, shoes, kitchen utensils

Considerations:
- Has the structure and durability of plastics
- Has the high elasticity and flexibility of rubber
- Tear-resistant
- Recyclable, but not accepted at all recycling centers
- Petroleum product

Polyurethane (PU)

PU is one of the most versatile plastics and therefore one of the most utilized. It can be hard like fiberglass, squishy like upholstery foam, protective like varnish, bouncy like rubber, or sticky like glue. It can also be used as a lamination for fabric.

Appearance: Glossy finish, clear, flexible, or foam

Found in: Waterproof coatings, synthetic fibers like spandex, insulation, toys

Considerations:
- Flexible and durable
- Holds up to extreme temperatures
- Yellows over time
- Breaks down with sunlight
- Nonrecyclable

Polyamide (PA)

PA can occur naturally (wool and silk) or be made artificially (nylon and Kevlar®).

Appearance: Matte finish, opaque, flexible

Found in: Textiles, carpets, clothing, toothbrush bristles, seat belts

Considerations:
- Very flexible and durable
- Stain-resistant, mold- and mildew-resistant, and insect-resistant
- Nonrecyclable
- Melts instead of burning

Safer Plastics

Bioplastics

Bioplastics are safer plastics made from plant resins such as corn, bamboo, or potato. Bioplastics are often found in cutlery and dishes. Since this is new technology, there are many possibilities for these materials. Some bioplastics have small amounts of polypropylene as a binder and for flexibility. Some are compostable but often are nonrecyclable. Some examples of bioplastics are PLA (polylactic acid), PA 11 (polyamide 11), PHB (poly-3-hydroxybutyrate), and PSM (plastarch material, or starch-based polymers).

Polylactic acid (PLA)

PLA is the petroleum-free or less-petroleum-dependent version of PETE plastic, with which it shares many qualities. It is starch based, using primarily cornstarch, tapioca root, or sugarcane. It is considered a (7) (other) plastic for recycling purposes.

Appearance: Matte finish, semitransparent, semirigid

Found in: Food containers, including cups and bottles; utensils; packaging; toys

Considerations:
- Made from renewable resources
- Compostable and recyclable
- Very low heat tolerance
- Difficult to procure resin that is 100 percent GMO-free
- Not as flexible as PP

Plastics to Avoid

Polyvinyl chloride (PVC)

PVC can leach lead and phthalates into food and can emit toxic chemicals. This plastic can be found in juice bottles, plastic wraps, bibs, toys, and PVC piping. Vinyl (including PVC) is another plastic to avoid because it can leach lead and phthalates. Vinyl is found in juice bottles, plastic wraps, and PVC piping. PVC is petroleum based. In its regular form, it is used mostly for construction. Once manipulated into a flexible form by adding plasticizers (most often phthalates), it is more widely used in household items.

Hard PVC is safer than squishy PVC. PVC water pipes are made of hard PVC. Children's toys and teethers were once made with squishy PVC, using softeners such as DEHP and DINP (these are now two of the banned phthalates, so companies are required not to use them). Companies have replaced these two banned phthalates with DINCH (similar to DINP), which has not been banned yet, as its effects have not been researched thoroughly. It may be easiest to just avoid PVC, but if you find it important to use, look for citrate-based PVC instead of DINCH-based PVC. PVC uses the recycling code (3).

Appearance: Matte finish, naturally white and brittle, naturally rigid but becomes flexible if plasticizers are used

Found in: PVC pipes, shower curtains, playground equipment, plastic-wrapped foods, waterproof clothing, flooring, health care items (tubing, containers for liquids)

Considerations:
- Strong and durable
- Waterproof
- Fire-retardant
- Di(2-ethylhexyl) phthalate (DEHP), commonly found in PVC, is a suspected human carcinogen
- Phthalates and other plasticizers can leach into food that is stored in PVC
- Phthalates and lead can be toxic in toys

Plastics to Avoid

Polystyrene (PS)

PS is one of the most widely used plastics due to its low cost. It can leach carcinogens and is a potential hormone disrupter. It is found in egg cartons; packing peanuts; and disposable plates, cups, and takeout containers. It is hard to recycle and does not break down in landfills. The code is (6).

Appearance: Matte finish, transparent, rigid or foamed

Found in: Styrofoam cups and food containers, packaging, plastic cutlery, coolers, toys

Considerations:
- Insulating properties
- Benzene (material used in production) is a known human carcinogen
- Butadiene and styrene (the basic materials in polystyrene) are suspected carcinogens

Acrylonitrile butadiene styrene (ABS)

ABS is one of the strongest plastics made. It is commonly injected into molds to produce impact-resistant, tough, heat-resistant products. Its recycling code is (7) (other). It is a low hazard for humans.

Appearance: Glossy finish, opaque (translucent ivory or white), rigid

Found in: Toys, Legos, musical instruments, protective helmets, household appliances

Considerations:
- High resistance to extreme temperatures
- Insulating properties
- Lightweight
- Expensive
- Flammable

Polycarbonate (PC)

PC was once used with the additive BPA (bisphenol A). Newer PC bottles do not contain BPA, but most contain Tritan™, a new chemical softener designed to replace BPA. Tritan™ has not yet been proven to be toxin-free or toxic. Avoid BPA due to its estrogen-mimicker properties. PC is still often found in reusable water bottles, baby bottles, and electronic casings because it is strong, durable, lightweight, and transparent. PC's code (7) (other) is used when the product in question is made with a plastic other than the more commonly used first six categories, or when it is made of a combination of more than one plastic. Because this is a catch-all category, some plastics with this code are safe, while others should be avoided.

Appearance: Glossy finish, clear, rigid

Found in: Baby bottles, water bottles, CDs, DVDs, medical storage containers, eyewear lenses, electronic display screens

Considerations:
- Clearest of the plastics
- Flame-retardant
- May contain BPA, which exhibits hormone-like properties at high dosage levels that have been identified as possible hazards to fetuses, infants, and young children

Plastics to Avoid

Melamine

Melamine is a chemical used for kitchenware and industrial products. Dishes made of melamine are durable and shatterproof once they are hardened. However, they may release toxins when exposed to acidic foods or high heat, such as the heat of a micro-wave oven.

Appearance: Hard, glossy finish, maintains durable print or design

Found in: Dishes, cooking utensils, plastic products, industrial coatings

Considerations:
- Contains formaldehyde, which can be released when the melamine is heated or comes into contact with acidic food
- Contamination from melamine causes risk of kidney infection, irritability, blood in urine, little or no urine, and high blood pressure

Perfluorooctanoic acid (PFOA)

PFOA is a synthetic nonstick coating that provides a frictionless surface for pans and other cookware. Teflon® is a brand name by DuPont.

Appearance: Dark, shiny, smooth coating on pans

Found in: Cookware, wiring in aerospace industry, fabric and carpeting protectors for stain resistance, ski wax, computer chip processing equipment and systems

Considerations:
- Strong, tough, and self-lubricating
- Potential release of dangerous fumes from coated pans that are overheated can cause flu-like symptoms, such as headache, fever, chills, and nausea

Polyethylene terephthalate (PET or PETE)

PET or PETE is used in soft-drink, water, and salad-dressing bottles as well as in peanut-butter and jam jars. It used to be considered a safer plastic, but recent studies suggest that high temperatures can cause leaching of antimony, a regulated chemical that poses acute and chronic health effects in drinking water. PETE has a low melting point but is resistant to cold, sunlight, and impact.

All foods that contain acid must be packaged in a hot-water bath of 180°F in order to meet food-safety regulations that prevent botulism. Although PETE's melting point is 500°F, the plastic's polymer molecules can begin to change chemically at temperatures as low as 150°F. PETE is the most commonly used plastic, as well as the easiest and most commonly recycled plastic. It is petroleum based. Its recycling code is (1).

Appearance: Clear, glossy finish, semirigid to rigid

Found in: Soft-drink, water, sports-drink, ketchup, and salad-dressing bottles; peanut-butter, pickle, jelly, and jam jars; lotion and other cosmetics bottles

Considerations:
- Transparent
- Inexpensive
- Easily recycled
- Low heat resistance (200°F max)
- Not UV stable; should not be left in the sun
- Recent studies suggest that high temperatures can cause leaching of antimony, a regulated chemical that poses chronic health effects in drinking water

Additives to Plastics

Phthalates

Phthalates belong to a group of chemicals also known as phthalate esters. They are used primarily as plasticizers, which means they are added to a plastic to increase its flexibility, transparency, durability, and longevity. There are many different phthalates, and more than 25 kinds are commonly used. Six phthalates are banned for use in children's products in the United States and European Union: DEHP, DBP, BBP, DINP, DIDP, and DnOP.

If a product is labeled as "phthalate-free," it probably contains less than 0.1 percent of the six banned phthalates; the label does not mean that the product is actually free of all phthalates. Anything made from synthetic materials probably has some form of phthalates in it.

Phthalates are easily released into the environment because the bonds linking them to plastics are weak and easily broken. This also allows them to biodegrade easily. Some type 3 plastics (such as PVC) contain phthalates as plasticizers. However, manufacturers are not required to explicitly indicate their presence in a PVC product.

Children are more susceptible to phthalates than adults are because they explore with their mouths, so make sure your child's toys, teethers, and feeding prod-

ucts are phthalate-free. In August 2008, the Consumer Product Safety Improvement Act (CPSIA) became law in the United States. Under this law, "[I]t shall be unlawful for any person to manufacture for sale, offer for sale, distribute in commerce, or import into the United States any children's toy or child care article that contains concentrations of more than 0.1 percent of [DEHP, DBP, or BBP]," and "it shall be unlawful for any person to manufacture for sale, offer for sale, distribute in commerce, or import into the United States any children's toy that can be placed in a child's mouth or child care article that contains concentrations of more than 0.1 percent of [DINP, DIDP, or DnOP]."

Phthalates are found in personal-care products such as moisturizer and liquid soap (including baby lotion, powder, and shampoo), detergents, packaging such as water bottles and soft-drink bottles, children's toys, modeling clay, paints, pharmaceuticals, food products, PVC pipes and other products, and textiles.

Bisphenol A (BPA)

BPA is a liquid additive used to make plastics harder and less breakable. BPA is primarily found in polycarbonate plastic and in epoxy resins (many of which are used to line food cans). BPA has been used commercially since 1957. Manufacturers use at least 3.6 million tons each year. Currently, recycling codes (1), (2), (4), and (5) are very unlikely to contain BPA, as it is usually found in recycling code (7) plastics. The FDA, the European Union, and Canada have banned BPA from infant products (bottles, cups, and infant-formula packaging). BPA exhibits hormone-like properties at high dosage levels that have been identified as possible hazards to fetuses, infants, and young children. Plastics that are not used as recommended (for example, they are heated to high temperatures) are more likely to release BPA, which can then contaminate food and beverages. BPA is found in many clear, hard plastics, such as polycarbonate. It is also used in epoxy resins for coatings inside many food and beverage containers.

Additives to Plastics

Formamides

Formamides are industrial chemicals with many different uses, including use as a plasticizer in EVA products. Formamides have never been tested on humans, but a consumer study in Belgium (Test-Achats) and another in France (ANSES) showed reproductive issues and carcinogenic tumors in rats. When heated, formamides decompose to hydrogen cyanide and water vapor. Formamides can cause excessive burning of the skin and eyes, and they can be deadly if ingested. Products containing formamides pose the most health risks to children if they inhale the off-gassing of formamides from a product. This is especially true of newer products that have not had a chance to release all of their gases. Some parents choose to let all products off-gas for a period of time before letting their children handle them in order to prevent the inhalation of dangerous vapors. Formamides are found in softening agents used in foam toys and play mats as well as in the manufacturing process for paper.

Formaldehyde

Formaldehyde is a colorless, flammable, strong-smelling chemical that is used in building materials, fabrics, and many household products. Formaldehyde has been banned from manufacturing and import in the European Union under REACH (Regulation, Evaluation, Authorization and Restriction of Chemicals) regulations. Formaldehyde has been classified as a known human carcinogen (cancer-causing substance) by the International Agency for Research on Cancer and as a probable human carcinogen by the U.S. Environmental Protection Agency. Formaldehyde is used in pressed-wood products (such as particleboard and fiberboard); in flooring glues; as a coating on fabrics to make them wrinkle-free; in cigarette smoke; and via the use of unvented fuel-burning appliances, such as gas stoves, wood-burning stoves, and kerosene heaters.

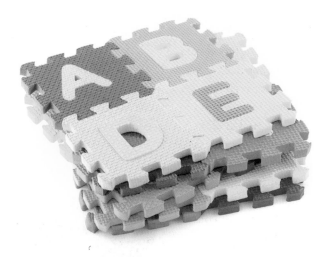

Nonpetroleum Ingredients and Materials

In our manufacturing process for containers and utensils at i play., we look for hard, nonporous materials, such as glass, ceramic porcelain, stainless steel, bioplastics, and safer petroleum plastics. If we could, I would rather make all of our products from petroleum-free materials at my company. However, as a manufacturer, it is challenging to find alternatives to plastic materials that are safe, healthy, practical, and affordable.

Natural rubber

Natural rubber (also called india rubber, latex, or caoutchouc) is harvested mainly in the form of the latex from certain trees. The process resembles the same setup for harvesting maple sugar from a maple tree, wherein the tree is tapped and the liquid is collected in a bucket as it flows out. The latex then coagulates into a workable material.

Appearance: Naturally matte finish, semiopaque, naturally milky white, highly flexible

Found in: Toys, pacifiers, balloons, rubber bands, erasers, rain boots

Considerations:

- Some babies have a latex allergy or other reaction to rubber
- Look for sustainably harvested rubber; the Forest Stewardship Council (FSC) issues certifications for sustainable harvesting techniques
- Very elastic and flexible
- All-natural
- Petroleum-free
- Biodegradable
- Nontoxic
- Affected by temperature change
- Expensive
- Nonrecyclable
- Can rip or tear
- Breaks down with heat, moisture, and sunlight

Silicone

Silicone was developed as an alternative to natural rubber and is silica (sand) based. It is an inert and stable material, which means it is unlikely to react with or leach into food, or to give off odors or vapors.

Appearance: Semigloss finish, transparent, clear, highly flexible

Found in: Toys, pacifiers, baby-bottle nipples, cups, bowls, storage containers, cutlery, kitchenware

Considerations:

- Very elastic and flexible
- All-natural
- Petroleum-free
- No known allergies to silicone
- Nontoxic and food-safe
- Easy to sterilize
- Stain/odor resistant
- Extreme temperature resistance
- Not accepted at all recycling centers
- Sometimes expensive
- Can turn yellow over time
- Can contain fillers; to check for fillers, pinch and twist a flat surface of the silicone item; if any white is present, this indicates a filler has been added and the silicone may not be uniformly heat resistant and may impart an odor to food

Nonpetroleum Ingredients and Materials

Glass

Glass, like silicone, has as its main component silica (sand). Other natural additives are mixed with the silica to form specific types of glass. Glass that is not thermal shock-resistant can break upon rapid reheating after freezing or upon rapid cooling after heating. Borosilicate glass (used for bottles) is the most thermal shock-resistant type of glass. Tempered soda-lime glass is used for green sprouts®'s glass food cubes, Mason jars, and Pyrex® food storage containers. They are usually not thermal shock-resistant.

Appearance: Glossy finish, transparent, clear, rigid

Found in: Food containers, dishes, cups, jars, sippy cups, baby bottles, bowls

Considerations:
- Transparent
- Nonporous, so does not absorb smells or flavors
- Easy to sterilize
- Does not have a reaction with its contents
- Food-safe
- Recyclable
- Dishwasher and oven-safe (when tempered)
- Breakable; however, tempered glass has been developed as a good shatterproof alternative to glass containers; sometimes referred to as safety glass, this glass is more shockproof and has greater resistance to extreme temperatures; when tempered glass does break, it breaks into tiny pieces all over rather than into sharp fragments
- Can be heavy
- Dangerous when cracked; if you use glass bottles or sippy cups with your baby, be sure not to leave your child unattended, and monitor the glass item for any signs of damage or cracks
- Colored glass can contain dangerous additives such as lead
- Can be expensive

Ceramic

Ceramic has been used to hold food for centuries. The traditional raw materials of ceramic include clay minerals, while more modern ceramic is made with aluminum oxide. Many ceramics have glazes to prevent the material from being porous and to make it easy to clean and sanitize.

Appearance: Flat finish, often coated in a glaze, opaque, usually neutral in color (white, beige, brown, tan), rigid

Found in: Plates, bowls, serving pieces, storage containers, art pieces, roof tiles, garden pots, bricks, tiles

Considerations:
- Some are oven-safe
- Made from an abundant and inexpensive resource
- Hard and durable, but heavy
- Chips and cracks easily
- Porous, so it absorbs smells, flavors, and does not sanitize easily unless it is glazed
- Some glazes and antique pottery could contain chemical toxins such as lead or cadmium; look for warning labels that say a product is not food-safe
- If you are concerned about the materials in ceramic coming into contact with food, you can buy lead-testing kits online or in hardware stores; in most cases, you will rub the swab from the test on the food-contacting surface of the pottery; with most kits, if the pottery contains lead that leaches onto the swab, the swab will change color; if you find that the pottery contains leachable lead, the FDA strongly advises against using the pottery for cooking, serving, or storing food or drinks

Nonpetroleum Ingredients and Materials

Wood

Wood is derived from the fibrous tissue of the stems and roots of trees and other woody plants. Sometimes wood also refers to other plant composites that have similar properties to wood, such as wood chips or fiber. Bamboo does not absorb water like other types of wood do, and some kinds of bamboo have antibacterial and antimicrobial properties.

Appearance: Naturally matte finish, often coated in varnish or oil, opaque, usually yellow/brown/red, rigid

Found in: Toys, cutting boards, dishware, utensils, kitchenware, flooring, furniture, hairbrushes, nailbrushes

Considerations:

- Strong and durable
- Inexpensive
- Derived from a renewable resource, but be sure to check for sustainable-growing practices; the Forest Stewardship Council (FSC) issues a sustainably harvested certificate; many companies post whether they are FSC certified
- Petroleum-free
- Not recommended for soaking
- Not dishwasher-safe
- Could contain splinters
- Subject to mold if not coated or sealed
- Wood from certain trees can trigger mild allergies
- Paints and stains applied to wood could contain harmful chemicals or VOCs (volatile organic compounds)

Stainless steel

Stainless steel is a combination of the elements iron, carbon, and chromium. The addition of chromium gives steel its stainless quality. Stainless refers to its ability to resist rust and to stain less than other forms of steel. Stainless steel is nonreactive, so you can cook any kind of food in it. It has low heat transfer and distribution, but high-quality stainless-steel cookware has an added core of aluminum or copper to mitigate that.

Appearance: Shiny finish, opaque, silver/gray, naturally semirigid (soft metal)

Found in: Home goods, cookware, bottles, cups, dishes, utensils, medical equipment

Considerations:

- Rust- and stain-resistant
- Easy to sanitize and sterilize
- Durable and heavy
- Does not hold odors
- Does not leach toxins
- Recyclable
- Does not require a protective coating
- Nontransparent
- Requires mining
- Affordable
- Dents easily

Nonpetroleum Ingredients and Materials

Aluminum

Aluminum is the third-most abundant element (after oxygen and silicon)—and the most abundant metal—in Earth's crust. In the 1960s, scientific studies showed that people with Alzheimer's disease have high levels of aluminum in their bodies; however, no study has been able to show a link between use of aluminum products and incidence of Alzheimer's. Aluminum is highly reactive to alkaline or acidic foods. Aluminum pans are thin and soft, and they tend to warp in high heat, which can lead to health concerns with long-term use.

Appearance: Shiny finish, opaque, silver/gray, naturally semirigid (soft metal)

Found in: Soda cans, foil wrap, cooking utensils, pots, food cans

Considerations:
- Lightweight and easy to manipulate
- 100 percent recyclable and recycled aluminum takes 6 percent of the energy it originally took to create; recycled aluminum gets stronger the more it is recycled
- Some people have skin allergies to aluminum
- Aluminum competes with calcium for absorption, so there is a chance that increased amounts of dietary aluminum (such as antacids) can contribute to reduced calcium intake.

Additives to Metals

This section provides information about potentially hazardous additives that are sometimes used in the manufacturing of metal products.

Cadmium is a chemical element that occurs naturally. Because it is highly resistant to corrosion, it is often used to coat other metals. Cadmium is a highly toxic carcinogen that is dangerous when inhaled as dust or fumes. Tobacco smoking is the single biggest source of cadmium exposure in the general population. Cadmium is restricted in Europe under REACH regulations. It is found in batteries, as a paint additive (cadmium yellow and orange), and as a stabilizing additive in plastics such as PVC.

Lead is a chemical element that occurs naturally. It is highly toxic. Lead causes nervous-system damage, blood disorders, and brain damage. It can accumulate in both soft tissues and bones. Although high-dose lead poisoning is possible, it is more common for lead poisoning to occur through exposure over time. Children can get lead poisoning by touching a lead object—or the dust or peelings of a lead object—and then putting their fingers in their mouth or eating food afterward. Read the labels of your child's art supplies and toys to ensure the product has been tested for lead. Do not give your child old or antique toys to prevent lead contact. Even if old paint is not peeling, it can still release lead particles into the air. Be sure that your house has had all old paint safely removed. You cannot see, taste, or smell lead. It is found in water pipes, paint additives (pre-1978), additives in plastics such as PVC, children's paint sets and art supplies, contaminated soil, painted toys and decorations made outside the United States, and toys (pre-1976). Lead in PVC can leach out when the plastic is cracked or peeling, so discard any PVC toys that are cracked or peeling.

Skin Care

YOUR BABY'S SKIN (integumentary system) holds her internal organs and bones together and protects her from external forces. As her skin breathes in and out, it takes in elements from the atmosphere and discharges internal excesses and wastes. She has a thousand types of microorganisms on her skin that provide immunity and protection from the sun. If she has a blemish or a rash, her skin generally heals on its own. For your baby's first three years, a few simple products made from pure ingredients are enough to protect your baby's skin from irritation, to prevent damage from extreme sun exposure, and to keep her healthy. In fact, protecting her from chemicals that exist in everyday skin care products is a greater challenge than securing lots of fancy and expensive skin care products. Most baby skin care products are unnecessary, and some can cause rashes and allergic reactions. Up to 45 percent of personal-care products in the United States contain undesirable ingredients, and close to 80 percent of the contents of these products have not been tested.

As with food, cosmetic labels must list all of the product's ingredients in descending order, with the ingredient that makes up the greatest amount of the product listed first and the ingredient that makes up the lowest amount listed last. You may see various claims on skin care packaging: "dermatologist-tested," "lab-tested," "hypoallergenic," and "designed for sensitive skin." However, because skin care and cosmetic products are not regulated in the United States, manufacturers can make claims without repercussions. If a product is approved by the American Academy of Dermatology, however, you can be assured that it meets high standards for safety. Otherwise, it is up to you to monitor your baby's skin care by reading ingredient lists to make sure that her products are free of potentially harmful chemical substances.

This section provides two lists. The first identifies chemical ingredients to avoid when purchasing skin care products for your baby. The second is a list of essential baby skin care items, each with a description of the product, ingredients to watch for, and considerations to think about.

Because the cosmetics industry is under-regulated, many baby products contain chemical preservatives, fragrances, thickeners, coloring agents, binders, and petroleum by-products that are meant to enhance the sensory experience of the product user. These chemicals may be colorless and invisible, but they can have a quiet and negative impact on your baby's health. You can keep your baby healthy by avoiding products that are made with these ingredients.

Ingredients to Avoid

Aerosol spray

Aerosol spray cans are designed to dispense a product quickly and easily. They can negatively affect the air quality as well as your baby's respiratory condition. If the ingredients in the aerosol contain harmful chemicals, your baby may ingest them from the air. Use a pump spray when possible to keep the air that your baby breathes fresh.

Alcohol

Alcohol is drying to your baby's skin, and it reduces vitamin A. It can cause dizziness, headaches, and digestive upset. For your baby or young child, avoid products with ethanol, ethyl alcohol, denatured alcohol, methanol, benzyl alcohol, methyl alcohol, isopropyl alcohol, and SD alcohol.

Aluminum

Aluminum by-products are used in foils, cans, trays, water, foods that absorb aluminum from the soil, medicines, vaccines, deodorants, and cosmetics. Excess amounts can be toxic and carcinogenic to your baby.

Artificial colors

Artificial colors are used in many skin care products. Most artificial colors are petroleum based. Soy-based coloring is safer.

Artificial fragrances

Artificial fragrances are often used to mask the smells of other chemicals in skin care products. They often have a strong, irritating scent, and they often contain alcohol, which may cause irritation and allergic reactions. In cosmetics, fragrances may contain phthalates, the same substances used in the production of plastics. Some phthalates are known hormone disrupters. On labels they appear as dibutyl phthalate(s), diethyl phthalate, 1,2-benzenedicarboxylic acid, dibutyl ester, dibutyl 1,2-benzenedicarboxylate, dibutyl ester1,2-benzenedicarboxylic acid, DBP, and Di-n-butyl phthalate. Natural oils (such as tea tree, lavender, and almond) offer a light, natural scent that sends healthy stimulation to your baby's brain.

Butylated Hydroxyanisole (BHA)

BHA is used as a preservative in some products. It is a proven carcinogen in lab animals.

Chlorides

Chlorides such as sodium chloride (table salt) and potassium chloride are frequently used as thickeners in lotions and other self-care products. While small amounts of these products are not harmful, when used excessively, they can irritate your baby's sensitive skin and eyes.

Diethanolamine (DEA) and Triethanolamine (TEA)

These ingredients are used as emulsifiers in skin care products, hair dyes, bubble baths, and dishwasher and laundry detergents. DEA and TEA can harm the skin and eyes, and they have been found to be carcinogenic.

Ingredients to Avoid

N,N-Diethyl-meta-toluamide (DEET)

DEET is an active ingredient in insect repellents for use against mosquitoes, ticks, and fleas. It is intended to be applied on clothing. Children's exposure to DEET is usually through the skin or ingestion. Results of toxicity include loss of muscle control, tremors, seizures, headaches, and convulsions. DEET is not recommended as an insect repellent for children.

Fluoride

Fluoride can result in fluorosis, a condition whereby teeth become mottled, then spotted with white areas, and eventually stained with yellow-black deposits. Some studies suggest that excessive fluoride actually weakens tooth enamel and can have a negative impact on ligaments, muscles, skin, and brain cells. Fluoride has been linked to a number of health problems, including dental deformity, allergic reactions, arthritis, and Crohn's disease. Look for fluoride-free toothpaste.

Formaldehyde

Formaldehyde is a carcinogen that can cause surface skin irritation. It is used as a preservative. On an ingredient list, it might appear as Germall II and Germall 115. Formaldehyde is also found in fabrics and toys.

Glycol

Glycol is used in cosmetics and comes in several forms: propylene glycol, ethylene glycol, diethylene glycol, and carbitol. Glycol has been linked to liver, kidney, and reproductive issues in laboratory animals. Propylene glycol is one of the most widely used ingredients in cosmetics. It helps skin and hair absorb moisture. This substance is also used as a lubricant in automotive antifreeze. It is a neurotoxin and can cause skin irritation.

Parabens

Parabens belong to a class of chemicals widely used as preservatives by the cosmetic and pharmaceutical industries. These compounds, as well as their salts, are used primarily for their bactericidal and fungicidal properties. They can be found in shampoos, commercial moisturizers, deodorants, shaving gels, personal lubricants, topical pharmaceuticals, spray-tanning solution, makeup, and toothpaste. They are also used as food additives. Parabens are absorbed through intact skin and through the gastrointestinal tract. Parabens have displayed the ability to mimic estrogen slightly. Permethrin is a pesticide in lice shampoo. It is used to kill lice and their eggs. The EPA classifies permethrin as a likely human carcinogen. You can make your own lice treatment without having to resort to highly toxic chemicals. Use a solution of tea tree, rosemary, lavender, peppermint, and eucalyptus essential oils combined with olive oil for natural lice removal.

Petroleum-based products

Petroleum-based products are used widely in the skin care industry. The process of taking crude oil and creating finished products is called distillation. Petroleum distillates, which are possible carcinogens, can be found in many everyday products such as sunblock, lip balm, hair conditioners, plastics, and household cleaners. Petrolatum, a semisolid mixture that is either colorless or pale yellow, is an ingredient in skin care products such as Vaseline and petroleum jelly. This by-product of the distillation of gasoline from crude oil is a core ingredient in many baby-care products. Petroleum jelly acts as a barrier when applied on the skin, but by itself, it has no moisturizing properties. It actually tends to interfere with the body's natural moisturizing mechanism, thus leading to dry skin. Since petroleum jelly forms a barrier on the skin, it traps moisture, bacteria, and heat within the skin.

Phthalates

Phthalates are used in many products—plastics for toys, dishes, and food packaging. In cosmetics, phthalates are used as dissolving agents and as plasticizers. DBP (dibutyl phthalate) is used in nail polish, and DEP (diethyl phthalate) and DMP (dimethyl phthalate) are used in other cosmetics and personal-care products. The American Academy of Pediatrics published an article stating that infants who are exposed to baby shampoos, lotions, and powders showed increased levels of phthalate in their urine. Phthalates are absorbed through the skin, ingested, or inhaled. Many phthalates are considered to be endocrine disrupters because of their complex effects on hormonal systems.

Sodium lauryl sulfate (sodium laureth sulfate)

Sodium lauryl sulfate, also called sodium laureth sulfate, is used as a foaming agent in shampoos and gels, as well as in pesticides. It is a common ingredient in skin care products and can cause allergic reactions, rashes, irritation, and hair loss. It is drying, so it can irritate skin and eyes. In addition, the production of this chemical is harmful to the environment, as it creates toxic particulate matter and VOCs (volatile organic compounds).

Titanium dioxide

Titanium dioxide is a white, opaque, odorless, absorbent, naturally occurring mineral. Titanium dioxide is chemically processed to remove impurities, thus leaving the pure, white pigment available for use. Titanium dioxide has a variety of uses and can be many found in products, ranging from paint to food to cosmetics. It is widely used to provide whiteness and opacity to products such as paints, plastics, papers, inks, foods, and toothpaste. Titanium dioxide is found in most sunblocks, in which it helps protect the skin from ultraviolet light. The International Agency for Research on Cancer (IARC) has determined titanium dioxide as a possible carcinogen. The titanium dioxide particles used in sunscreens have to be coated with other materials because titanium dioxide creates radicals in its photocatalytic reaction. These radicals are carcinogenic and can be damaging to the skin.

Toluene

Toluene helps nail polish goes on smoothly. Exposure to toluene can be toxic to your baby's nervous system, and it can impair breathing, cause nausea, and do developmental damage to a fetus. It is linked to malignant lymphoma.

Triclosan

Triclosan is an antibacterial compound used in antibacterial soaps, toothpaste, cosmetics, fabrics, and toys marketed to protect against harmful bacteria. This agent can actually lead to the creation of resistant strains of germs. Other adverse health effects include endocrine disruptions, skin irritation, and negative impact on thyroid hormones.

Safe Skin Care Essentials

Now that you know how to avoid potentially harmful chemicals in baby-care products, you can take care of your child's personal-care needs by following my suggestions below and using simple, pure ingredients and natural products. Below are my suggestions for healthy soaps and shampoos, lotions and oils, balms, powders, wipes, toothpaste, and sunscreen for your baby.

Soaps and shampoos

For the first few months, your baby does not need soap at all. When you start using soap, a natural liquid soap made with sesame, olive, almond, or calendula oil works for both body and hair.

Materials to avoid: Artificial fragrance, artificial colors, parabens, triclosan, sodium lauryl sulfate, diethanolamine (DEA), triethanolamine (TEA), propylene glycol

Lotions and oils

Only use lotions or diaper-rash ointments if your baby's bottom is irritated. When necessary, choose a natural version that contains sesame, olive, coconut, or other natural oil as a moisturizer. I used sesame oil on my babies' skin every day for nourishment and protection.

Materials to avoid: Mineral oil, petroleum jelly, artificial fragrance, artificial colors, parabens, diethanolamine (DEA), triethanolamine (TEA), propylene gel, butylated hydroxyanisole (BHA), chlorides

Diaper, lip, and cheek balms

Use products with vitamins A and E or natural oils, such as sesame, coconut, or almond, as an effective skin barrier and moisturizer.

Materials to avoid: BHA, petroleum jelly, artificial fragrance, parabens

Powders

The American Academy of Pediatrics recommends against using baby powder, as do many individual pediatricians. Talc-based powders have small particles that can dry your baby's mucous membranes and harm her breathing and lungs when they are inhaled. They can cause coughing, vomiting, and pneumonia. Corn-starch, baking soda, and bentonite clay work effectively as natural powders to prevent diaper rash by wicking away moisture from your baby's skin and reducing friction.

Materials to watch for: Talc, artificial fragrances

Wipes

Choose soft wipes for your baby's diaper care. Cotton cloths with water are an option, or if you use disposable wipes, look for aloe vera and vitamin E as healthy additives. The additives Bronopol (2-bromo-2-nitropropane-1, 3-diol) and DMDM hydantoin, which are found in fragrances, can release formaldehyde, which is a known carcinogen. You can make your own disposable wipes with unbleached paper towels and a solution of olive-oil soap and water mixed in a spray bottle. Store the wipes in a stainless steel or glass container. When you are on the go, you can keep them in a resealable bag.

Materials to avoid: Artificial fragrance, parabens, phthalates (fragrance), PEGs, propylene glycol, phenoxyethanol

Toothpaste

Children under the age of two do not need toothpaste. For her first two years, brushing with water is sufficient.

Materials to avoid: Triclosan, parabens, fluoride

Sunscreen

Before she is six months old, your baby's skin is too sensitive for sunscreen; instead, keep her out of direct sun and use sun hats and sun-protective clothing. After six months, make sure to get a sunscreen that protects against both UVA and UVB rays and that is made of natural ingredients.

Materials to avoid: Parabens, phthalates, oxybenzone, avobenzone, octisalate, octocrylene, homosalate, octinoxate

Food Additives

PART 2 OF THIS book, Whole Food, offers information about foods that nourish your baby's health and development. If you purchase an organic apple or carrot, you do not need to read a label about its ingredients or food additives, because those foods are whole foods. The more processed the food, the greater the chance that it will have substitutes and chemical additives.

Manufacturers add a variety of substances to foods for a number of reasons: to give them a long shelf life, to make them look more appealing, to enhance their flavor, and to add back nutrients that may have been taken out during processing. When you are educated about ingredients in food products and know how to read labels, you can more easily determine what you are buying.

This section of the chapter helps you navigate food ingredients and labels. When feeding your baby, be on the lookout for artificial additives as well as food allergens, trans fats, high-fructose corn syrup, and caffeine. The six main categories of food additives are as follows:

- Artificial sweeteners
- Artificial coloring
- Artificial flavors
- Preservatives
- Emulsifiers
- Visual Enhancers

Each additive includes a description, function, a list of foods that the additive is commonly used in, and special considerations to keep in mind. Chemical additives have a greater impact on children than they do on adults, so I recommend avoiding them as much as possible for your baby's first three years, when she is growing and developing rapidly.

Reading Labels

With the exception of very small food packets and unpackaged fresh foods (including produce and fish), all food sold in the United States is required to have a label. Items that contain more than one ingredient must have an ingredient list. Finally, anything that is added to a food whether it is a vitamin, a mineral, or an artificial preservative must be included on the nutrition label.

In general, when you read nutrition labels, look for foods that are high in fiber, vitamins, and minerals and low in sugar, sodium, cholesterol, fats (especially saturated fat and trans fat). In addition, pay attention to whether the product has chemical additives or food allergens, which you may want to minimize. In the United States, nutrition labels are divided into the following categories:

Serving size and number of servings

The nutritional information on a label is based on a single serving, but the container may include more than one serving. This information can be misleading unless you calculate the percentages of ingredients based on the total number of servings. For example, if a serving equals two cookies but your child eats four cookies, you must double the percentages of nutrients.

Calories

Again, be sure to calculate the total in relation to the actual number of servings consumed. A child's ideal daily calorie intake varies by age, gender, and level of activity, ranging from 1,000–1,400 in girl toddlers to 1,800–2,000 in boys and girls aged 9 through 13.

Fat, cholesterol, sodium, and carbohydrates

Pay attention to the percentages of the daily allowance rather than number of grams of each substance. On this part of the label, below 5 percent is preferable. Since your child's daily calorie intake is generally lower than that of an adult, high percentages of these ingredients have a stronger impact on her than they do on you.

Dietary fiber, vitamins, and minerals

Look for 20 percent or more of the daily allowance in these categories.

Nutrition Facts

Serving Size 1 cup (228g)
Serving Per Container 2

Amount Per Serving

Calories 250   **Calories from Fat** 110

	% Daily Value*
Total Fat 12g	18%
Saturated Fat 3g	15%
Trans Fat 3g	
Cholesterol 30mg	10%
Sodium 470mg	20%
Potassium 700mg	20%
Total Carbohydrate 31g	10%
Dietary Fiber 0g	0%
Sugars 5g	
Protein 5g	

Vitamin A	4%
Vitamin C	2%
Calcium	20%
Iron	4%

* Percent Daily Values are based on a 2,000 calorie diet. Your Daily Values may be higher or lower depending on your calorie needs.

	Calories	2,000	2,500
Total Fat	Less than	65g	80g
Sat Fat	Less than	20g	25g
Cholesterol	Less than	300mg	300mg
Sodium	Less than	2,400mg	2,400mg
Total Carbohydrate		300g	375g
Dietary Fiber		25g	30g

Ingredients

If an ingredient list is lengthy and full of unfamiliar words that you cannot pronounce, that is an indicator that it is not a whole food. Here are some tips for understanding ingredients lists:

- Ingredients are listed according to the percentage of the whole product that they represent. For example, if sugar is listed first, that means it is the main ingredient. If it is listed near the end, it represents a less significant portion of the total.

- The fewer ingredients, the better.

- If preservatives are added to a product, the manufacturer is required to explain what the preservative does. For example, it may say, "ascorbic acid to promote color retention."

- Subingredients do not have to be listed on an ingredient list. For example, bread may contain margarine that has been colored with a food coloring that is not mentioned on the label because it is not considered to have a "functional" effect on the bread; however, the oil in the margarine would be listed because it is considered to have a functional effect. Foods may also be treated with substances that prevent them from sticking to equipment. Those substances are not required to be included in the ingredients list.

Manufacturers protect their proprietary recipes by listing "natural ingredients" collectively. This term typically refers to a blend of herbs and spices.

Food Allergen Labels

Since 2006, U.S. food manufacturers have been required to declare on their packaging whether their product contains any of the eight major food allergens (which account for 90 percent of all food allergies) or an ingredient or protein derived from them: milk, eggs, fish, crustacean shellfish, tree nuts, wheat, peanuts, and soybeans. Particles in trace amounts, such as whey powder, may still make their way into a food. Food manufacturers are not required to declare potential allergens that may "accidentally" make it into a product (by being produced on the same machine or in the same factory), but many manufacturers do so voluntarily—for instance, you may see a label that states, "May contain traces of peanuts" or "Made in a factory that also produces peanuts." There is no standard that such labels must follow; according to the Food Allergy and Anaphylaxis Network, there are over 30 different ways that such trace allergens can be declared on a package. According to a 2007 study by the *Journal of Allergy and Clinical Immunology*, only 7 percent of products that provided the voluntary warning actually contain the allergen.

Chemical Additives

The U.S. Food and Drug Administration (FDA) designates some food additives as "generally recognized as safe" (GRAS). However, even though some additives appear to be safe, they may pose a risk or promote poor nutrition if they are consumed in large amounts. Young children may be sensitive, intolerant, and reactive to chemical additives. In addition, some additives need to be tested more thoroughly before they can truly be considered safe.

In the 1970s, Benjamin Feingold, MD, an allergist, proposed the following hypothesis: synthetic food additives can trigger hyperactivity in children who have certain genetic predispositions. To test his hypothesis, Feingold conducted research on approximately 600 children. He eliminated BHA (butylated hydroxyanisole) from their diet. The results showed that for 60 to 70 percent of the children tested, behavior associated with attention-deficit/hyperactivity disorder (ADHD) was eliminated. Although links between diet and ADHD are controversial, many parents have found that the Feingold Diet, which prohibits foods containing petroleum-based additives (including artificial colors and flavors) has benefited their children. You can learn more about the Feingold Diet at feingold.org.

When purchasing processed foods for your child, read the ingredients listed on food labels. If possible, I suggest avoiding the following ingredients in foods for your child: trans fats, high-fructose corn syrup, caffeine, and the six categories of chemical additives listed on the following pages.

Artificial Sweeteners

Artificial sweeteners are chemical sweeteners used as a substitute for the calories (and taste) of sugar. They are much sweeter than refined white sugar and are often combined with sodium to balance extreme sweetness.

Aspartame, acesulfame potassium, saccharin, and sucralose

Aspartame and acesulfame potassium are artificial sweeteners that are 200 times sweeter than table sugar, with a low-calorie and no-calorie content, respectively. Saccharin is a synthetic sweetener that contains zero calories. It is now the foundation for many low-calorie and sugar-free products. In the early 1970s, lab studies showed a correlation between saccharin and bladder cancer in rodents. This led to the Saccharin Study and Labeling Act of 1977, which mandated that all food containing saccharin be labeled with a warning. Sucralose is a synthetic sweetener that contains zero calories. It is approximately 320 to 1,000 times as sweet as table sugar, twice as sweet as saccharin, and three times as sweet as aspartame.

What are they used for? These sweeteners are low-calorie or zero-calorie substitutes for sugar in food and beverage products.

Found in: Diet soft drinks, fruit drinks, chewing gum, sugar-free candy, jams, canned fruit, baked goods, dry beverage mixes, gelatins, toothpaste

Considerations:

- Break down easily in extreme temperatures or high acidity, and therefore are not good for baking
- Sucralose and acesulfame potassium are stable under heat, so they can be used for baking
- People with phenylketonuria (PKU) must avoid phenylalanine, including aspartame
- Acesulfame potassium contains the carcinogen methylene chloride; long-term exposure can cause headaches, depression, nausea, liver effects, and cancer
- Although it passes through the body undigested, saccharin may trigger the release of insulin
- A recent Italian study links lifetime consumption of sucralose to higher risk for leukemia

Artificial Colorings

Artificial colorings are chemicals that are added to processed foods, drinks, and condiments to maintain or improve their appearance.

Food coloring

Food coloring consists of chemicals used to add color to food and beverages, especially processed foods. These chemicals can be artificial or naturally derived. Artificial colorings must be certified for safe consumption by the FDA. Currently, the FDA has approved seven artificial food colorings, which are preceded by "FD&C" on food labels. Natural food colorings are usually derived from plant sources such as seeds and spices. They are exempt from FDA certification.

What is it used for? To enhance colors in food products and to offset color loss due to light exposure and other environmental elements. Bright colors are often added to make foods look "fun" and attractive to children.

Found in: Many processed foods and beverages, including juices, candy, snack foods, breakfast cereals, baked goods, frozen desserts, flavored yogurt, ketchup, mustard, salad dressing

Considerations:
- Studies have linked artificial food-coloring agents to aggravated symptoms of ADD and ADHD; for more info, see: feingold.org
- Although most natural food colorings are derived from plants, some come from insects. For example, cochineal or carmine, a red dye, comes from the cochineal insect; make sure to check food labels carefully if your family follows a vegetarian or vegan diet

Color-retention agents

The most commonly used color-retention agents in food are potassium nitrite and sodium nitrate. Both nitrite and nitrates are used in curing meat and poultry.

What is it used for? Potassium nitrite and sodium nitrate are added to cured meat to preserve its color, to prevent fats from going rancid, and to stop bacteria from growing.

Found in: Most commonly used in cured meats (hot dogs, bacon, ham, lunch meat, sausage), but also occur naturally in vegetables and fruits, like spinach and celery; synthetic nitrogen fertilizers can also raise nitrate levels in crops grown in treated soil

Considerations:
- Removed from baby food in the 1970s
- When exposed to high heat during cooking, nitrites can convert to nitrosamines, which are known carcinogens
- Excessive consumption beyond a normal diet has been linked to numerous diseases and cancers; also known to cause infant health problems and pregnancy complications
- Eat organic foods and drink filtered water to prevent exposure to nitrates from synthetic fertilizers that have accumulated in the soil and groundwater

Artificial Flavorings

Artificial flavorings are chemical scents and fragrances that are added to processed foods, drinks, and condiments to maintain and improve flavor.

Monosodium Glutamate (MSG)

Classified by the FDA as GRAS, MSG is the sodium salt of glutamic acid. It has been used for over 100 years as a food flavor enhancer. Other ingredients that contain chemical glutamates are hydrolyzed proteins, yeast extracts, and protein concentrates. The Japanese name for MSG is *ajinomoto*.

What is it used for? Used as a flavor additive to chemically enhance savory and umami compounds and to create a savory flavor.

Found in: Many Asia food restaurants, ramen, canned vegetables, soups, processed meats, low-fat yogurt, ranch flavoring, cheese flavoring, Goldfish crackers, other snack foods

Considerations:

- Eliminated from baby food
- Now must be listed as a food additive in packaged foods
- The FDA does not require disclosure of the specific components and amounts of MSG used in "natural flavor"
- Believed to cause chest pain, headache, sweating, and numbness in certain people (1 percent of population), but researchers have found no definitive link
- Depression, irritability, and mood changes are a concern since glutamates are neurotransmitters in the human brain; neurologists continue to study possible side effects, but currently have established no conclusive connections
- Glutamates are neurotransmitters in the brain for learning and memory, and they can overstimulate the neurons; neurologists are concerned about side effects of MSG, but no conclusive studies show connections

Preservatives

Preservatives keep food shelf-stable for longer because they cause food to withstand heat, light, transportation, and time. Airtight packaging, vacuum packing, inert gases like nitrogen, and refrigeration can help preserve food. Manufacturers also use chemical additives to make food appear more attractive on the shelf. Natural methods of preserving food include fermentation, canning, drying, and freezing. Chemical preservatives include sodium benzoate, antioxidants, BHA, and BHT.

Sodium benzoate

A widely used food preservative, sodium benzoate is made from the salt of benzoic acid. Benzoic acid occurs naturally in low levels in cranberries, prunes, cinnamon, cloves, and apples.

What is it used for? Preserving food, especially highly acidic products

Found in: Salad dressings, carbonated drinks, jams, pickles, condiments, fruit juices

Considerations:
- When sodium benzoate is consumed in combination with ascorbic acid (vitamin C), benzene (a known carcinogen) is formed
- Heat, light, and shelf time increase the rate at which benzene is formed
- Research suggests that consumption of certain mixtures of artificial food colors and sodium benzoate are associated with increased hyperactivity in children

Antioxidant

An antioxidant is a molecule that blocks and neutralizes free radicals (the waste molecules produced when your body breaks down food). Antioxidants can be synthetic or can occur naturally in vegetables and fruits. Antioxidants are added to food to slow the rate of oxidation to keep it from spoiling or going rancid. Citric acid and ascorbic acid (vitamin C) are natural antioxidants used to preserve food, while BHA is a chemical antioxidant that prevents oxidation.

What are they used for? Antioxidants are used as preservatives in foods and cosmetics. They prevent food discoloration and help regulate pH in jams and jellies. Vitamin C can be added to food to replace nutrients that are lost in processing.

Found in: Jam, dried potatoes, canned fruit, cheese, dried soup; ascorbic acid occurs naturally in citrus fruits

Considerations:
- Artificial preservatives are made with synthetic chemicals and not recommended for babies
- Natural antioxidants aid in a healthy immune system, lower your risk of infection, and can assist in the prevention of certain diseases
- Studies show that overabundance of antioxidants can suppress key signaling mechanisms necessary for muscles to function effectively

Preservatives

Butylated hydroxyanisole (BHA)

BHA is a stabilizer, preservative, and an antioxidant. It prevents the oxidation of fats and oils, thus protecting them from spoilage.

What is it used for? Primarily used as a preservative in food, food packaging, and cosmetics.

Found in: Beverages, butter, ice cream, baked goods, chewing gum, snack foods, dry breakfast cereals, instant mashed potatoes

Considerations:

- Not permitted in infant food
- Listed as a carcinogen in California
- National Institutes of Health reports that BHA is "reasonably anticipated to be a human carcinogen" based on numerous animal tests.

Butylated hydroxytoluene (BHT)

BHT is a stabilizer, preservative, and an antioxidant. It prevents the oxidation of fats and oils, thus protecting them from spoiling.

What is it used for? BHT is primarily used to preserve food odor, color, and flavor. It is also utilized in food packaging and cosmetics.

Found in: Beverages, butter, ice cream, baked goods, chewing gum, snack foods, dry breakfast cereals, instant mashed potatoes

Considerations:

- BHT residues remain in human fat cells over extended periods
- Studies show possible negative developmental effects at high doses
- Extensive research shows that high doses of BHT lead to lung, liver, thyroid, and kidney damage
- Known human skin and respiratory toxicant and allergen
- Banned in U.S. baby food for potential association with hyperactivity in children

Emulsifiers

Emulsifiers keep water and oil mixed together without separating in products such as peanut butter, mayonnaise, ice cream, and homogenized milk. An emulsifier coats the oil droplets so that they can be dispersed in the water. Some natural emulsifiers used in foods are lecithin, egg yolks, and agar agar. Chemical emulsifiers that are commonly added to commercial food products include diglycerides and monoglycerides.

What are they used for? Used to keep oil and water-based ingredients from separating by interacting with fatty acids, protein, and water.

Found in: Processed foods such as extruded snacks, biscuits, bread, breakfast cereals, cakes, soft drinks, margarine, fruit preserves, "jelly" candy, ice cream, puddings, custards, dried potatoes, chocolate coatings

Considerations:

- May cause allergic reactions
- Monoglycerides and diglycerides (hydrogenated oils) are synthetic emulsifiers and contain trans fats

Visual Enhancers

In addition to artificial coloring, ingredients that enhance the visual appeal of foods include flour treatments and glazing agents. Packaging can be presented in an artistic way that enhances the look of food.

Flour-treatment agents

Flour-treatment agents are added to flour to improve baking functionality. There are three main types of agents: oxidizing agents (bleaching agents), reducing agents, and enzymes.

What are they used for? Oxidizing agents help strengthen the dough, while reducing agents weaken the flour by breaking the protein network and thus make the dough stronger. Enzymes speed up the reactions in dough for faster processing times.

Found in: Flour (natural flour without these additives is yellowish) and foods made with flour (breads, pastries, etc.)

Considerations:

• Potassium bromate, an oxidizing agent that bleaches baked goods, has been banned from use in food products in the EU, Canada, Nigeria, Brazil, South Korea, Peru, and China
• Potassium bromate is considered a category 2B (possibly carcinogenic to humans) by the International Agency for Research on Cancer (IARC)
• Currently, potassium bromate is not banned in the United States; however, the FDA has encouraged bakers to voluntarily stop using it in their products

Glazing agents

Glazing agents are natural or synthetic substances that coat and protect a food item. Common natural glazing agents include beeswax, carnauba wax, shellac, lanolin, paraffin, candelilla wax, and stearic acid. Common synthetic glazing, such as crystalline wax, is usually derived from petrolatum (a semisolid mixture of hydrocarbons obtained from petroleum) and mixed with natural agents.

What is it used for? Used to prevent water loss and to provide surface protection for food products. Makes fruit and vegetables appear shiny.

Found in: Fruit (coating), vegetables (coating), confections, chocolate, snack foods, cosmetics, chewing gum, soft drinks

Considerations:

• Some agents, such as carnauba wax and crystalline wax, can cause skin irritation
• If your family follows a vegetarian or vegan diet, note that beeswax and lanolin are animal products; lanolin usually contains pesticides from processing wool

Generally speaking, when making food choices for your baby, consider natural, whole foods compared to those with chemical additives. Foods with high amounts of synthetic ingredients can have a strong impact on your baby's small body. Read labels on the packages of processed foods for information that will help you make purchasing decisions.

Around the Home

PREPARING A NEST FOR your baby that is safe and comfortable can be fun and satisfying. When you put together her nursery or space, you may consider the colors and feeling for beautiful environment that is visually appealing and calm for her individual personality. Safety locks and gates help set parameters and furniture and storage containers help control the clutter to create order and allow space for her to move comfortably and discover.

You can nurture your baby to have a radiant life by being mindful of ingredients and materials in your home environment and in the outdoors that could be toxic or disruptive to her. Your baby is sensitive to ingredients in cleaning products, materials in furniture, and the fertilizers in your back yard. She absorbs them into her system through contact with her skin, by putting objects into her mouth, and by breathing.

The following list provides information for you to use as a reference to help keep the inside of your home toxin-free, and to help you be aware of concerns when exploring nature outside with your child.

Environmental Substances

It can be fun and satisfying to prepare a safe, comfortable nest for your baby. When you put together her nursery or other space, you may consider colors, shapes, and feelings that will create an environment that is visually appealing and suited to her personality. Safety locks and gates help set parameters, and furniture and storage containers control clutter, create order, and allow space for her to move comfortably and discover.

You can nurture your baby toward a radiant life by being mindful of ingredients and materials that could be toxic or disruptive to her, both in your home environment and outdoors. Your baby is most likely sensitive to ingredients in cleaning products, materials in furniture, and fertilizers in your yard. She absorbs these substances into her system through passive contact with her skin, putting objects into her mouth, and breathing.

You can use the following list as a reference for keeping the inside of your home toxin-free and safely exploring nature with your child.

Inside Your Home

For your baby's first few months, she will probably spend most of her time inside your house, unless she goes to child care. The air that she breathes is a form of nourishment for her. You can help maintain healthy air quality by looking around your home and considering the scent of your environment. Take stock of your baby's environment inside your home by looking at the cleaning products that you use, your home improvements and furnishings, and your electronics.

Air quality

Volatile organic compounds (VOCs) are emitted as gases from certain solids or liquids. They include a variety of chemicals, some of which may have adverse short- and long-term health effects. Because of their small size and rapidly developing bodies, babies and children are especially susceptible to VOCs. It is likely that you will find VOCs in chemical fragrances from room air fresheners and scented candles; odors from paints, furni-ture, cleaning supplies, dry-cleaning substances, copiers, and printers; and art supplies such as permanent markers. Other forms of air pollution inside your home may include tobacco smoke and indoor allergens such as pet dander, dust mites, and mold.

You can naturally freshen the air quality of your home with good ventilation, which is partly dependent on the weather. Open a window in warm weather, and use a humidifier in the winter. Bring in fresh flowers, herbs, and fruits to introduce a variety of natural fragrances. Use a diffuser for your favorite essential oils. You can reduce the effects of VOCs by washing new products to help dissolve residual chemicals, taking new items outside and letting them off-gas and air out, and using paints that are labeled "low VOCs" (milk- or soy-based paints do not involve the off-gassing that occurs with conventional paint).

Cleaning products

Choosing cleaning products and laundry detergents that are low on hazardous chemicals is an easy and inexpensive way to make a significant and direct impact on the quality of your baby's environment. Cleaning products that contain chemicals such as ammonia, bleach, and chlorine are effective for cleaning, but exposure to these chemicals can cause irritation to your baby's skin, eyes, and respiratory tract.

Available on the market today are cleaning products that are nontoxic, ammonia-free, petroleum-free, phosphate-free, and VOC-free. You can also dilute these products with water to make them more baby-friendly. Make your own cleaners using borax, lemon juice, hydrogen peroxide, white vinegar, or baking soda. Do your cleaning when your baby is not in the room to prevent exposure to cleaning products, and avoid using aerosol sprays so that you have better control of the ingredients in your products. If the weather allows, keep the windows open while you clean.

Home improvements and furnishings

Because your baby crawls around on the floor and puts everything she finds into her mouth, she is susceptible to ingredients and materials in your carpets and rugs, flame retardants on upholstery fabrics, mold, asbestos, and paint on the wall (old paint can contain lead or formaldehyde). Exposure to these substances can affect her nervous system and brain development. Following are some materials to look out for.

Fire retardants

A fire retardant is a substance that reduces flammability of fuels or delays their combustion. Fire retardants are found in fire extinguishers, surface coatings, textiles, rugs, carpets, furniture, mattresses, and toys. Some fire retardants contain chemicals that are potentially dangerous to the environment, such as PBDEs. Laboratory studies show that exposure to minute doses of PBDEs at critical points in development can damage the reproductive system and cause deficits in motor skills, learning, memory, and hearing, as well as changes in behavior. You can prevent the negative effects of fire retardants by using furniture, mattresses, and foam items that are PBDE-free. Consider alternative methods for fire retardants, including salt-water pretreatments and using baking soda to extinguish fires. Do not use stain guards, and avoid buying carpeting if possible. Use rugs made of natural materials, such as organic cotton or wool fibers that have vegetable-based dyes and no backing.

Formaldehyde

Formaldehyde is a colorless, flammable, strong-smelling chemical that is used in building materials and in the manufacturing of many household products. It is used to give a permanent press to clothing, to increase stain resistance, and to make fabrics colorfast. Formaldehyde is also used in foam insulation; pressed-wood products such as particleboard and fiberboard; carpeting; cigarette smoke; and unvented fuel-burning appliances, such as gas stoves, wood-burning stoves, and kerosene heaters. Formaldehyde has been banned from manufacturing and import in the EU under REACH regulation and has been classified as a known human carcinogen (cancer-causing substance) by the IARC and as a probable human carcinogen by the EPA. Exposure to formaldehyde can cause respiratory difficulties as well as eye, nose, and throat irritation. If you think you have formaldehyde insulation in your home, have the material professionally removed. Avoid cigarette smoke exposure, and make sure that all fuel-burning appliances in your house are properly vented. Wash clothing before wearing to prevent exposure of formaldehyde on your baby's skin. Check old wood for particleboard, and buy genuine wood if possible.

Inside Your Home

Lead

Lead is a chemical element with highly toxic effects. It causes damage to the nervous system as well as blood disorders and brain damage. Lead is also a neurotoxin that accumulates both in soft tissues and in bones. Although high-dose lead poisoning is possible, it is more common for lead poisoning to occur from gradual exposure. Lead is found in water pipes, additives in paints (pre-1978), additives in plastics such as PVC, children's paint sets and art supplies, contaminated soil, painted toys and decorations made outside the United States, and toys (pre-1976). Children can get lead poisoning by touching a lead object—or the dust or peelings of a lead object—and then putting their fingers in their mouth or eating food afterward.   You cannot see, taste, or smell lead. A calcium-rich diet can help protect against lead absorption. Read the labels of your child's art supplies and toys to ensure the products have been tested for lead. Do not give your child old or antique toys. Even if old paint is not peeling, it can still release lead particles into the air, so be sure that your house has had all old paint safely removed.

Asbestos

Asbestos is the commercial name given to a variety of six naturally occurring fibrous minerals. These minerals possess high tensile strength, flexibility, resistance to chemical and thermal degradation, and resistance to electricity. For many years asbestos minerals were used in commercial products, such as insulation and fire-proofing materials, automotive brakes and textile products, and cement and wallboard materials. Asbestos can separate into microscopic particles that remain in the air and are easily inhaled. People who have been constantly exposed to asbestos have developed several types of life-threatening diseases, including asbestosis, lung cancer, and mesothelioma. If you suspect there is asbestos in your home, have it professionally removed.

Mold

Mold grows in damp environments. By itself, mold is not toxic, but it can produce toxins that can be harmful if your baby eats, touches, or breathes them. Mold spores are commonly found in household dust, and when they are present in large amounts they can cause allergic reactions and respiratory problems. Remove mold by washing the area with soap and water. Throw away clothes that have mold on them. To handle mold issues in buildings, reduce moisture levels. Let in ventilation and sunlight, or turn on a heater or fan in the affected area to prevent mold growth. Wash dirty clothes and diapers so that they do not stay in the laundry hamper for a long time. Dust and clean often.

Electronics

Electrical appliances and wiring generate EMFs (electromagnetic fields), which are invisible lines of force that come from an electrical or wireless device. There are low- and high-frequency EMFs. Low-frequency EMFs are emitted by electricity and appliances. High-frequency EMFs are generated by wireless devices such as cell phones, devices with screens, and computers that use Wi-Fi. They are also found in radio receivers, televisions, MP3 players, video recorders, DVD players, digital cameras, and camcorders. To protect your baby from EMF stress, limit the number of appliances in her nursery and keep cords as far from her crib as possible.

When your baby is in nature, her body resonates with Earth's magnetic field and she is relaxed. Man-made low-frequency EMFs from electronics enter her body and create stress that affects her immune system and major organs, such as her brain and heart. EMFs can disturb sleep patterns. High-frequency EMFs are faster and create greater stress. Unplug appliances when they are not in use. Take your baby outside in nature, and relax with her. Limit your cell-phone time while taking care of your baby, and keep your phone away from her.

Outdoors

You have a certain amount of control over your baby's environment inside your house. Outside, you cannot monitor or change the weather, temperature, or air quality. When it comes to taking care of your baby in the outdoors, you can learn about the elements and flow with them. If your baby has an allergy to pollen, pets, mosquito bites, or bee stings, then you can do your best to avoid situations that could cause a reaction. When exploring with your baby outside, be on the lookout for poisonous plants such as poison ivy or poisonous mushrooms. If you have a garden or lawn, be aware of chemical fertilizers or pesticides that your baby could touch or ingest. If possible, use organic fertilizers or compost when growing vegetables, flowers, or shrubs. Sunlight provides valuable vitamin D, but exposure to too much direct sun can interfere with your baby's sensory development. Also, she needs protection from the sun on her skin when she is outside. Finally, toxic waste is an environmental substance that you cannot control, but you can be aware of it and limit your baby's contact with it.

Toxic waste is hazardous waste that comes from the discarded by-products of manufacturing, construction, farming, septic systems, batteries, computer equipment, disposable diapers, leftover paints, and hospital waste. The waste may be liquid or solid and can contain chemicals, heavy metals, and other toxins. The waste can spread rapidly and contaminate lakes, rivers, and the atmosphere. In the long term, they can accumulate in the groundwater that you drink and persist in the environment. For your baby's protection, avoid exposure to toxic waste and heavy metals. Manage your trash responsibly.

Textiles

OF SEVEN GRANDCHILDREN, I was my grandmother's only granddaughter. In the summers when I visited her and we sewed together, I developed my passion for fabric. I loved their colors and designs, textures and functions. When Emi and Mari were born, I made their cotton nightgowns, because, at that time, it was impossible to find cotton sleepwear. Since then, fabric technology has come a long way.

Over 30 years ago, when I started my business, i play., Inc., 100% cotton was the most natural fabric available. Then I discovered natural (or green) cotton, which was fabric that had not been bleached or dyed. Seamstresses worked in my basement making bodysuits, bibs, diapers, caps, blankets, and towels. Over the years, I introduced organic cotton several times, but no one knew what it was, or was interested in buying it at that time. Parents today are aware of the value in organic cotton for their babies.

Babies have many functional needs for comfort, breathability, absorbency, and for waterproof protection. There are many options in the market to create products for babies that are functional and comfortable with cute designs.

Now, when I attend fabric trade shows, I am fascinated by the array of options—functional fabrics with charcoal and bamboo, fabrics that wick away moisture, fabrics that have extra absorbency, and those that are waterproof and breathable. Although, I prefer natural fabrics, such as cotton, silk, and wool, I have come to accept the value of man-made fabrics, such as fleece, Lycra, and microfiber for the functions that they offer. The following list of fabrics gives you information about the primary textiles that you will find in your baby's clothing.

Plant-based Natural Fibers

Conventional cotton

Conventional cotton is the most common form of cotton used in consumer products.

Where does it come from? Cotton plants

Found in: Clothing, bedding, towels, plush toys

Considerations:
- Lightweight and breathable
- Bright colors available
- Inexpensive
- Contains some natural sun-protection properties (UPF 15)
- Could contain chlorine bleach for whitening or formaldehyde for dye fixing
- Could contain GMO cotton or fertilizers, pesticides, or other chemicals from the growing process

Green cotton

Green cotton is not necessarily organically grown; green or natural refers to the processing. The green cotton process uses no formaldehyde or bleach to strip the cotton of its natural colors.

Where does it come from? Cotton plants

Found in: Clothing, bedding, towels, plush toys

Considerations:
- Environmentally friendly processing
- Lightweight and breathable
- Softer than conventional cotton
- Does not fade or lose its natural color
- More expensive than conventional cotton
- Special harvesting techniques required
- Only colors available are natural off-white, cream, and khaki
- Does not contain chlorine bleach for whitening or formaldehyde for dye fixing
- Could contain GMO cotton or fertilizers, pesticides, or other chemicals from the growing process

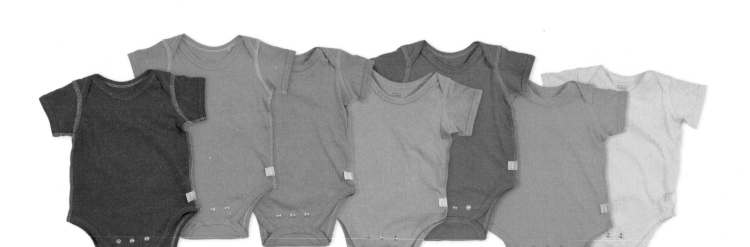

Plant-based Natural Fibers

Organic cotton

Organic cotton is grown from non-GMO seeds without chemical fertilizers or pesticides. It can be made into woven, knit, terry cloth, velour, or fleece fabrics.

Where does it come from? Cotton plants

Found in: Clothing, bedding, towels, plush toys

Considerations:
- Environmentally friendly
- GMO-Free
- Chemical fertilizer-free and pesticide-free
- Lightweight
- Breathable
- Hypoallergenic
- Softer than conventional cotton
- More expensive than conventional cotton
- Special harvesting techniques required
- Could contain chlorine bleach for whitening or formaldehyde for dye fixing

Jersey knit

Jersey knit is made with a single knitting that has one flat side and one piled side. It has a lighter weight and more stretch than interlock. Jersey knit can be made of cotton, polyester, or a blend.

Where does it come from? Wool, cotton, or synthetic fibers

Found in: T-shirts, bodysuits, knit caps, sheets, plush toys

Considerations:
- Very stretchy
- Lightweight and breathable
- Soft
- Easy to launder
- Inexpensive
- Wrinkle-resistant
- Can shrink
- Can stretch out

Plant-based Natural Fibers

Interlock knit

Interlock knit is thicker than jersey knit. Interlock knit is double knitted and has two rows of stitches, one directly behind the other, with the pile on the inside. This can create the impression that the fabric is made with two layers. It is used in footies, bodysuits, knit caps, sweaters, jackets, hoodies, and knit pants. Interlock knit can be made of cotton, polyester, or a blend.

Where does it come from? Wool, cotton, and synthetic fibers

Found in: Clothing, plush toys

Considerations:
- Holds shape better than jersey
- Thicker than jersey
- Breathable
- Soft
- Warm
- Easy to launder
- Inexpensive
- Wrinkle-resistant
- Can shrink
- Can stretch out

Woven terry cloth

Woven terry cloth is characterized by thick, uncut loops that form a soft pile on one or both sides of the fabric. The loops increase the fabric's absorbency. Woven terry cloth is not stretchy like knitted terry.

Where does it come from? Cotton and cotton/polyester blends

Found in: Bath and hand towels, washcloths, bathrobes, beach cover-ups, cloth diapers

Considerations:
- Highly absorbent
- Plush
- Breathable
- Soft and warm
- Easy to launder
- Very durable
- Wrinkle-resistant
- Can shrink
- Can unravel or pull

French terry cloth

French terry cloth is warp-knitted terry. It has more stretch than woven terry cloth.

Where does it come from? Cotton and cotton/polyester blends

Found in: Baby bath towels and washcloths, bathrobes, beach cover-ups, clothing

Considerations:
- Absorbent
- Breathable
- Soft
- Easy to launder
- Inexpensive
- Wrinkle-resistant
- Can shrink
- Can stretch out

Plant-based Natural Fibers

Velour

Originally designed as a stretchy alternative to velvet, velour is knitted, so it has a soft, fuzzy texture.

Where does it come from? Often made from cotton, but synthetic varieties are also available

Found in: Clothing, upholstery, car seats, plush toys, blankets

Considerations:
- Soft
- Stretchy
- Wrinkle-resistant
- Easier to care for than velvet
- Shrinks easily

Broadcloth

Broadcloth is a tightly woven plain-weave fabric that was originally made from wool but today is usually made from 100 percent cotton or a cotton blend. Its most common uses are in quilting and shirt making.

Where does it come from? Cotton, silk, wool, and polyester fibers

Found in: Clothing, quilts, upholstery

Considerations:
- Soft
- Durable
- Lightweight
- Can be expensive

Muslin

Muslin is a finely woven cotton material that is available in a large selection of weights and widths. Typically white or an undyed natural color, it absorbs dyes easily.

Where does it come from? Cotton

Found in: Clothing, bedding, wipes, blankets, stuffed toys

Considerations:
- Lightweight and breathable
- Easy to dye
- Inexpensive
- Easy to launder
- Softens over time
- Could contain chlorine bleach for processing or formaldehyde for dye fixing

Linen

Linen is a bast fiber textile made from the stalk of the flax plant. Known for its strength, even when wet, linen has been used since ancient times.

Where does it come from? Stalk of the flax plant

Found in: Clothing, bedding, hand towels, napkins, tablecloths

Considerations:
- Lightweight and breathable
- Highly absorbent
- Easy to dye
- Strongest known plant-based fiber
- Becomes stronger when wet
- Poor elasticity
- Presses and wrinkles easily
- Could contain chlorine bleach for processing or formaldehyde for dye fixing
- Processing can use enzymes or chemicals for turning the stalks into fibers; the enzymes are more natural and create less waste

Plant-based Natural Fibers

Bamboo fabric

Bamboo fabric is a natural textile made from the pulp of the hard bamboo trunk. After processing, its fibers resemble cotton fibers in their unspun form. Organic bamboo fabric is made from bamboo plants grown without the use of pesticides. It may be woven or knitted.

Where does it come from? Bamboo trunks

Found in: Clothing, bedding, towels, washcloths, bathrobes

Considerations:
- Lightweight
- Breathable
- Better absorption and wicking properties than cotton
- Hypoallergenic
- Renewable resource—bamboo grows rapidly and easily on marginal agricultural land
- Naturally antimicrobial
- Biodegradable
- Extremely soft
- Easy to launder
- Very durable
- Could contain chlorine bleach for processing or formaldehyde for dye fixing
- Bamboo bast fiber uses enzymes to process the hard bamboo trunks into soft fibers that can be spun into yarn
- Bamboo viscose fiber uses chemicals to achieve similar soft fibers

Rayon

Rayon is a man-made fiber, primarily made from tree wood pulp.

Where does it come from? Man-made cellulose fiber from wood pulp

Found in: Clothing, bedding

Considerations:
- Same comfort properties as natural fibers
- Can imitate the feel and texture of silk, wool, cotton, and linen
- Soft, smooth, cool, comfortable
- Highly absorbent
- Ideal for use in hot humid climates
- Biodegradable
- Many chemicals used for processing the cellulose fiber
- Low durability, especially when wet
- Dry-clean only
- Shrinks easily
- Could contain chlorine bleach for processing or formaldehyde for dye fixing

Animal By-product Natural Fibers

Silk

Silk fabric is made using protein filaments from the cocoons of silkworms. Since the fibers are so fine, often several strands are spun together to form a single thread.

Where does it come from? Silkworm cocoon filaments

Found in: Clothing, bedding

Considerations:

- Absorbent
- One of the strongest natural fibers
- Soft, smooth, and comfortable
- Cooling in hot weather and insulating in cool weather
- Expensive and labor-intensive
- Weakened with exposure to sunlight and perspiration
- Hand wash only
- Do not iron
- Often dry-clean only
- Wrinkles easily
- Not vegetarian/vegan in origin; the majority of silkworms are killed before they reach metamorphosis

Wool

Wool (merino, cashmere, mohair, angora, camel hair, alpaca) is made by combing or spinning the fleece, hair, or fur fibers of animals to form yarn. Wool can be woven, knitted, or felted.

Where does it come from? The fleece, hair, or fur of sheep, goats, rabbits, camels, llamas, and alpacas

Found in: Clothing, toys

Considerations:

- Cool in hot weather and highly insulating in cold weather
- Warm even when wet
- Resistant to bacteria, mold, and mildew
- Naturally flame-resistant
- Biodegradable
- Can feel scratchy
- Can shrink when washed
- Requires special laundering and care
- Not vegetarian/vegan in origin, but the fleece, hair, or fur is collected when the animals are shedding their coats; the animals stay alive

Synthetic Performance Fabrics

Elastane

Elastane (spandex, Lycra®, Elaspan®, Acepora, Creora®, Dorlastan®, Linel) is known for its elasticity and can be stretched up to 500 percent its original length and spring back without losing its integrity. When blended with natural fibers, it creates a lightweight and flexible fabric with high shape retention.

Where does it come from? Synthetic polymer made from polyurethane/polyurea

Found in: Sportswear and athletic apparel, leggings, swimwear, undergarments, socks and tights

Considerations:
- Lightweight
- Durable and abrasion-resistant
- Soft, smooth, and breathable
- Wrinkle-resistant
- Easy to launder
- Easy to dye, although can require formaldehyde for dye fixing
- Quick-drying
- Can be allergenic
- Fabric melts when in contact with flame or high temperatures

Nylon

Nylon is a synthetic fabric originally created as a replacement for silk. Nylon can be woven or knitted.

Where does it come from? Synthetic polymer made from plastic fibers (polyamides)

Found in: Clothing, upholstery, seat belts, thread, hairbrushes, toothbrushes, dental floss

Considerations:
- Exceptionally strong
- Elastic
- Easy to wash
- Resistant to damage from dirt, oil, chemicals, and perspiration
- Low moisture absorbency
- Lightweight
- Can melt at high temperatures
- Pealing can occur
- Can require formaldehyde for dye fixing

Synthetic Performance Fabrics

Polyester

Polyester (Polartec®, polar fleece, fleece, Capilene®, Coolmax®, wickaway) is a synthetic material made from petroleum derivatives. It has many high-performance qualities. Polyester can be highly insulating, breathable, and wicking. Combined with natural fibers such as cotton, rayon, or wool, polyester can provide strength and resistance to wrinkling and the elements.

Where does it come from? Synthetic polymer fibers derived from a petroleum resin

Found in: Clothing, bedding, upholstery, curtains, soft toys

Considerations:
- Durable and strong
- Insulating and warm
- Quick drying
- Lightweight
- Wicking
- Stain- and mildew-resistant
- Resistant to stretching and shrinking
- Wrinkle- and abrasion-resistant
- Easy to wash
- Can require formaldehyde for dye fixing
- Recycled polyester can be made by melting down postconsumer recycled PET bottles (generally water and soft-drink bottles) into a resin and then into a fiber; the result is as effective as polyester made from virgin petroleum resin

Polypropylene

Polypropylene is a thermoplastic polymer fiber used in insulating base-layer fabrics, thermal underwear, labeling, and nonwoven materials for diapers and sanitary products.

Where does it come from? Synthetic fibers made from petroleum derivatives

Found in: Insulating clothing, disposable diapers, sanitary products

Considerations:
- Insulating and warm
- Quick-drying
- Lightweight
- Repels water
- Easy to wash
- Holds odors
- Not flammable, but polypropylene melts when exposed to fire
- Formerly used widely in the U.S. military and outdoor industry, but has been mostly replaced by polyester base layers
- Can require formaldehyde for dye fixing

Synthetic Performance Fabrics

Microfiber

Microfiber is a manufactured fabric made from fiber strands less than one dernier. This can produce a soft, suede-like feel that is much stronger and more durable than real suede leather. Terry cloth made from microfiber is highly absorbent and antimicrobial.

Where does it come from? Synthetic polymer fibers of polyester, nylon, rayon, or acrylic

Found in: Clothing, upholstery, car interiors, cleaning cloths, cloth diapers, swim diapers

Considerations:
- Soft and suede-like
- Strong and durable
- Stain-resistant and easy to clean
- Highly absorbent and quick-drying
- Lightweight
- Antimicrobial
- Resists dust and lint
- Can require formaldehyde for dye fixing

Acrylic

Acrylic (acrilan, Orlon, Dralon) is a synthetic fiber that closely resembles wool in its character.

Where does it come from? Synthetic fibers made from the polymer polyacrylonitrile

Found in: Clothing, flame-retardant-protective clothing, yarns for knitting and crocheting, wigs, hair extensions

Considerations:
- Quick-drying
- Wicking
- Flexible esthetics for wool-like, cotton-like, or blended appearance
- Does not insulate well
- Easy to wash
- Retains shape
- Resistant to moths, oil, and chemicals
- Easy to dye and very colorfast
- Can irritate the skin of people with dermatological conditions such as eczema

Waterproof Fabrics and Coatings

Rubber

Rubber can be used as a waterproof coating. Natural rubber latex can be bonded to a fabric to create a waterproof barrier.

Where does it come from? Extracted from rubber trees

Found in: Raincoats, rain boots, shoe soles, waterproof gloves

Considerations:
- Waterproof
- Heavy-duty
- Heavy
- Expensive
- Requires vulcanizing to reduce smells, to increase flexibility, and to prevent melting in hot weather
- Exposure to extreme temperatures and humidity can cause disintegration
- Renewable resource
- Allergen to some

Thermoplastic rubber

Thermoplastic rubber is a synthetic rubber that can be used as a waterproof coating for fabrics.

Where does it come from? Synthetic polymer from petroleum derivatives

Found in: Rain boots, shoe soles

Considerations:
- Waterproof
- Heavy-duty
- Lighter weight than natural rubber
- Inexpensive
- When combined with natural rubber, can increase product's ability to withstand changes in temperature and humidity

Wax

Wax can be used as a water-resistant coating. Originally, sailors used linseed oil, but paraffin wax has generally replaced linseed oil due to higher water-resistance.

Where does it come from? Colorless, odorless solid derived from petroleum, coal, or shale

Found in: Coated canvas jackets and bags, sails

Considerations:
- Water-resistant
- Breathable
- Requires annual rewaxing to retain water resistance
- Not machine washable

Polyurethane

Polyurethane (PU) is a synthetic polymer bonded with fabric to create a single layer of waterproof material.

Where does it come from? Joining two petroleum-based reaction polymers

Found in: Raincoats, reusable cloth diapers, reusable swim diapers

Considerations:
- Waterproof
- Lightweight
- Flexible
- Not breathable
- Exposure to high temperatures can cause cracking and peeling of the laminate
- Cold-water wash and hang dry

Waterproof Fabrics and Coatings

Polytetrafluoroethylene

Polytetrafluoroethylene (PTFE) (Gore-Tex®, Omni-Tech®, waterproof/breathable fabric) is a synthetic polymer coating that allows fabrics to be both waterproof and breathable.

Where does it come from? Synthetic Teflon® membrane that is stretched to the point of allowing oxygen (but not water) to pass through and then bonded to a fabric

Found in: Waterproof and breathable outerwear, medical applications

Considerations:
- Waterproof
- Breathable
- Lightweight
- Flexible
- Wear and washing both reduce the durable water repellent (DWR) surface
- Cold-water wash and tumble dry or iron on low to reinvigorate the DWR surface
- Manufactured using perfluorooctanoic acid (PFOA), a known carcinogen; however, usually it does not come into direct contact with the skin

Polyvinyl chloride

Polyvinyl chloride (PVC) is a waterproof fabric coating.

Where does it come from? Synthetic polymer derived from petroleum derivatives, softened with the phthalates diethylhexyl phthalate (DEHP), dibutyl phthalate (DBP), and butyl benzyl phthalate (BBP) to increase plasticity and flexibility

Found in: Rainwear, soft insulated lunchboxes, backpacks, bibs

Considerations:
- Waterproof
- Not breathable
- High clarity
- Substantial feel
- Flexible
- Prone to peeling and cracking with exposure to heat, light, oils, acids, and time
- DEHP, DBP, and BBP are three of the banned phthalates for toys in the U.S. and EU
- PVC often contains high levels of lead, which is now regulated for children's products; should not leach unless PVC is peeling or cracking; if so, discard immediately

Polyethylene vinyl acetate (PEVA)

PEVA is a safer synthetic polymer alternative to PVC.

Where does it come from? Synthetic copolymer of polyethylene and vinyl acetate

Found in: Wipe-off bibs, reusable snack bags, shower curtains

Considerations:
- Inexpensive
- Waterproof
- Not breathable
- High clarity if desired
- Chlorine-free
- Petrochemical product
- Easy to clean

Waterproof Fabrics and Coatings

Ultraviolet protection factor

Ultraviolet protection factor (UPF) in textiles can be achieved through the construction of the fabric or through a special UPF coating. UPF ratings fall into ranges representing the percentage of UV radiation that the fabric is able to block:

Sun Protection in Textiles

UPF Rating	Protection Category	% UV Radiation Blocked
UPF 15–24	Good	93.3–95.9
UPF 25–39	Very good	96.0–97.4
UPF 40–50+	Excellent	97.5–99+

Where does it come from? For naturally occurring sun protection, darker colors, denser thread counts, and unique yarn-spinning techniques can all provide more protection than fabrics without these properties. Light-colored and lightweight fabrics for warm weather may require UPF coating to provide adequate sun protection.

Found in: Sun-protection clothing

Considerations:

- Fabrics that have naturally occurring UV protection are often too heavy to wear during hot weather (dark-colored denim, wool, silk)
- Fabrics that are lightweight and breezy often do not provide good UV protection (bleached cotton, polyester crepe, knits)
- UPF coatings are made from petrochemicals
- UPF coatings can wear off and lose some of their effectiveness over time
- Sunscreen is not recommended for babies under six months, so sun-protection clothing can help shield your baby during this time.

Formaldehyde

Formaldehyde for textiles is a resin that is used for wrinkle- and shrink-resistance and colorfastness. Under high heat or humidity, the resins can release formaldehyde. Japan and the EU have strict regulations for formaldehyde content, but at this point, there is no regulation to monitor the use of formaldehyde.

Where does it come from? Synthetic resin

Found in: Clothing, bedding, home textiles, furniture; used in cotton and cotton/polyester blends

Considerations:

- Can cause reaction for sensitive skin: allergic contact dermatitis, a form of eczema that can result in redness, swelling, blisters, itch, or burn

Testing, Certifications, and Manufacturing Processes

ALL OVER THE WORLD, countries have different testing requirements for products. When countries become more modernized, chemicals are used more often in manufacturing processes. At the same time, safety standards tend to increase, along with a desire to minimize the negative impact of chemicals in products.

It is impossible to lead a chemical-free life when the world around you does not. As a parent, you can learn to navigate the pros and cons in products as you set your priorities and make product decisions.

Different countries and states have their own regulating bodies that identify and control potentially harmful substances and protect the public by making sure that products are safe. California has its own set of regulations that ban many substances. With new discoveries, these standards are continually updating. When I was a baby, I sat on the front seat next to my mother as she drove her car, and she held her arm across my chest for safety when we came to a stop. When Emi and Mari were infants, they had car seats with minimal safety requirements. Today, a child is required to use a booster seat until she is eight years old.

In 2008, the Consumer Product Safety Commission (CPSC) had a major reform, and the result was the Consumer Product Safety Improvement Act of 2008 (CPSIA). CPSIA placed stricter limits on lead and other substances in children's products and restricted certain phthalates in toys and child care items. The act also made certain tests mandatory instead of voluntary. Since CPSIA went into effect, companies have been testing products according to more stringent safety requirements, and this improves the chance that your baby's products will be safe. Even with these new laws put into place, it is important to be aware of products manufactured before 2008, as they could contain higher limits of substances that are now banned.

There are two main types of testing for toys and other children's products:

Chemical testing Chemical testing of the base materials, including coatings, dyes, and paints. Examples are tests for heavy metals like lead and cadmium and tests for phthalates.

Safety Performance Tests This group includes tests that make sure products are physically safe and can withstand the use and abuse of a child, including looking for choking hazards, small parts, sharp points and edges, drop testing, torque and tension, and flammability. There are also more specific safety-performance tests for certain items like pacifiers and rattles. Hard-line gear such as cribs, car seats, strollers, jumpers, and backpacks are weight bearing and have a certain protocol, depending on the function.

The following list consists of U.S. and international agencies that are charged with ensuring product safety. You can use this list to find out about the products that you introduce to your child.

Product Safety Agencies

The United States Consumer Product Safety Commission (CPSC)

The CPSC is an independent agency that neither reports to nor is part of any other department or agency in the federal government. CPSC fulfills its mission by banning dangerous consumer products, issuing recalls of products already on the market, and researching potential hazards associated with consumer products. CPSC monitors the safety of consumer goods such as paint, child-resistant packages, and baby toys. You can get updates on their website for product recalls and the results of recent product and materials tests.

The United States Food and Drug Administration (FDA)

The FDA creates standards for regulating drugs, medical devices, cosmetics, and products that emit radiation, as well as food products. This agency also enforces compliance on products or packages that come into contact with food, and medical devices like infant teethers and toothbrushes. While the FDA regulates a large portion of the products that consumers purchase, the agency has no jurisdiction over many household goods.

The American Society for Testing and Materials (ASTM International)

ASTM International is an international standards organization that develops and publishes voluntary consensus technical standards for a wide range of materials, products, systems, and services. ASTM is responsible for setting the testing methods for toys and acceptable limits that companies follow to comply with toy regulations such as the Consumer Product Safety Improvement Act. These toy-safety specifications cover toys intended for use by children under 14 years old.

The European Committee for Standardization (CEN)

The CEN is a similar agency to the CPSC that regulates children's toys, furniture, and car seats. CEN sets European standards and other technical specifications. Compliance with CEN regulations is required, not optional, for all toys sold in the European Union for children under the age of 14 years.

Certifying Agencies

While they do not create enforceable laws, certifying agencies set and protect standards for a variety of products. When a product is certified, consumers can feel confident that a product has been produced according to stringent guidelines. Certifications can be first-party, second-party, or third-party.

First-party certifications are made by the company that produces the product. Examples include most marketing claims, product specifications, and material data-safety sheets declared by a company, such as Clorox® Green Works®. The Clorox Company claims that its Green Works® products are green, but the company does not do second- or third-party certifications.

Second-party certifications are made by trade associations that ensure the eligibility of products. An example of second-party certification is the American Textile Manufacturers Institute's Encouraging Environmental Excellence (E3) program, which has developed a set of standards and awards use of their logo if companies comply with these standards.

Third-party certifications are generated by nonprofit organizations or government bodies. The following certifications are examples of third-party certifications.

OEKO-TEX Standard

The OEKO-TEX® (or "eco-tex") Standard 100 monitors textile manufacturing by identifying and addressing issues regarding chemicals used in production, dyes, and postproduction, such as stain-resistant sprays.

The Better Cotton Initiative

The Better Cotton Initiative (BCI) promotes improvements in cotton cultivation. Working with organizations from across the cotton supply chain, the BCI aims to create "Better Cotton," which will benefit farmers and consumers.

The Organic Trade Association

The Organic Trade Association (OTA) promotes and protects organic trade to benefit the environment, farmers, the public, and the economy by working with businesses involved in producing anything organic, including food, fiber/textiles, personal-care products, and new sectors as they develop. OTA protects and advocates for organic standards so that consumers can have confidence in certified organic production.

The Global Organic Textile Standard

The Global Organic Textile Standard (GOTS) is the world's leading processing standard for textiles made from organic fibers. It defines high-level environmental criteria along the entire organic textile supply chain and requires compliance with social criteria as well.

Guidelines for Parents

Manufacturers are responsible for making products that are safe for consumers, but the responsibility of making safe product choices and using products safely still lies with the parent. Here are some basic things to remember.

- Glass bottles are an alternative to plastic, but they are breakable. Make sure your child is always fed or monitored by an adult when using a glass bottle. Regularly check to make sure that toys and feeding articles like cups and bottles are in good condition. If you see cracks, tears, or loose parts, toss the item in the trash.

- A baby or small child should never be put to bed with a bottle or sippy cup. It can be a safety hazard and can cause tooth decay, increased risk of ear infection, and choking.

- Do not tie a teether or pacifier around your baby's neck. This can easily get tangled or caught on a crib or other furniture and become a serious strangulation hazard. This includes necklaces. Babies want to put everything in their mouths, so avoid jewelry for your baby until she is over the age of three years.

- Do not leave an infant seat on a raised surface like a table or couch. This can result in a dangerous fall. These seats are considered safe only when your baby is secured in the seat in the car or on the floor.

- Plastic bags can be dangerous if the bag goes over your baby's head or near her mouth, because the film can cling to her mouth and nose and prevent breathing.

- Leave pillows, blankets, and stuffed animals out of your baby's crib for the first several months. Keep your baby's sleeping area clear of anything that can cover her face or prevent breathing.

- Consider natural fabrics whenever possible, and when you can, avoid acrylic, rayon, acetate, triacetate, and nylon. Choose products made with fabrics including cotton, linen, wool, cashmere, silk, or hemp, especially if they are worn next to the skin.

i play., Inc.'s Commitment to Safety and the Environment

I believe that it is the responsibility of the manufacturer to monitor safety standards for their products. Our position at i play., Inc. has always been to go above and beyond what is required for testing and product safety. We test to the highest denominator of testing standard. For instance, the standard for formaldehyde levels in Japan is higher than those in the European Union and the United States, so we test to the Japanese standard. Our international customers have helped us raise our standards, and they have taught us about ingredients to be aware of and to consider.

We are committed to testing all of our products at i play., Inc. for safety, durability, and quality. Following compliance with laws for children's products, we work in conjunction with the FDA as well as the CPSC to test for lead substrate, lead surface coating, phthalates, heavy metals, and cadmium. Feeding products are dishwasher tested for quality and durability, and textiles are tested for flammability, safety, choking hazards, formaldehyde, and truth in our labeling.

We do not use PVC, BPA, melamine, or nitrosamines. As much as possible, we use plant-based bioplastics, as well as natural materials such as wood, glass, and stainless steel. At i play., Inc., we pride ourselves on the thoroughness and thoughtfulness we bring to providing our customers with the safest baby products possible. We are continuously researching and testing our products for potential harmful substances and adding new requirements to our testing program.

Our mission and company values are based on the principles of nature and wholeness described at the beginning of this book. From there we strive to integrate those principles into our manufacturing processes. The following story tells how I learned about manufacturing and describes some of the challenges that I faced in founding my company.

i play., Inc.'s Manufacturing Story

In 1982, while I was pregnant with Mari, I started my mail-order business from a desire to provide natural products for babies. At that time, it was a one-woman operation. If I stood in the middle of the small spare bedroom, I could touch the laundry baskets filled with baby products with one hand, and my desk, where I processed orders, managed sales, and did accounting, with the other. Two to three years later, I expanded to the garage and hired my housekeeper as my first employee.

After 13 years of running the business in my home, I moved i play., Inc. to an industrial location, where I began manufacturing with home seamstresses. Every week we cut fabric, and women picked up the pieces in big black bags, sewed them at home, and returned the finished products in exchange for more cut pieces. At one point, they could sew 10,000 swim diapers a week!

As our product range grew, I developed in-house manufacturing with several women sewing. This was one of my most challenging times in business, as I learned that time is money, and labor and product costs could skyrocket without efficiency and controls. Dealing with the pressures and problems associated with manufacturing was not my personal strength, so I started outsourcing to small contractors around the United States—in North Carolina, Tennessee, Alabama, and Texas. These contractors required micromanaging, and it was difficult to control quality. I had to call them several times a day to keep them on track to meet deadlines.

At that time I was strongly against manufacturing outside the United States because of the same concerns that many people have today. In 1996, I had a change of heart when I went on a human-rights mission trip to Central America through the Center for Global Education. I saw poverty that I had never imagined, and I saw women begging for sewing work. It was very painful and sad for me to experience their desperation. That trip created a shift in my thinking: "People need work to make money to feed their families everywhere in the world." This changed my nationalistic thinking from believing in the value of only making products "Made in the USA."

As my business grew, I looked for larger-scale manufacturing in Latin America—Guatemala, Honduras, Mexico, and Colombia. At the time, the factories that I worked with did not have the capacity to print the fabric designs that we required, so we shipped fabric from Korea to Bogota, Colombia. They cut, sewed, and packaged the products and shipped them to us in North Carolina. We had lots of quality issues that required repairs and reworking. In addition, I did not appreciate the fact that the owner of the business was rarely available, and not at work, while the workers received low wages.

In 2002, a friend advised me of his experience of working in Asia with increased efficiencies. He introduced me to a factory in Thailand that improved product quality and gave me fewer headaches than I had experienced previously. Of course, I still had some problems with quality, scheduling, and communication, but that seems to be the nature of manufacturing. However, the overall efficiency and infrastructure for outsourcing were better than I had experienced in the past. Although costs were lower, I had added freight and duty costs, along with higher MOQs (minimum order quantities) and a longer lead time to receive the products. Because production thrives on making large amounts of the same thing over and over to reduce cost, I had to buy a large amount at one time.

Emi and Becky

As I traveled to Asia to work with our suppliers, I contemplated the complexity of the changing global situation. The United States has moved from an industrial era to an information age. Industrialization seems to move around the globe, chasing after cheap labor. As an economy strengthens, prices go up and companies move on to the factories that have the next-lowest price. I asked myself, "How does i play., Inc. fit into this global maze of product production?" Here were my considerations:

- Consumers are demanding lower prices. We are a small company, and we need to be price competitive with other juvenile products companies that outsource in Asia and offer low prices.

- We need suppliers that have the infrastructure to provide quality products in a timely and efficient manner. We must also be able to depend on and trust our suppliers.

- Domestic manufacturing is becoming less of an option for us, because many of the sources have disappeared.

- Owning and running a factory requires major capital equipment that my small business does not have, and production management is becoming a rare commodity.

- By outsourcing we have been able to diversify our product line to include apparel, feeding items, toys, and baby care. Next year we will carry dried ingredients for homemade baby food.

Meanwhile, I recognize that Americans have valid concerns about offshore manufacturing, particularly in China. My understanding is that the main concerns are quality, ecological concerns, social conditions, and U.S. jobs.

Quality

I believe that it is the responsibility of the company that owns the brand, instead of the contractor(s), to manage product quality as an integral process from start to finish. That means setting standards in design, raw material, construction, quality control, and testing.

Because of our international business, particularly in Europe and Japan, we have been alerted about material concerns sooner than other U.S. manufacturers

have been. We found out about PVC in 2003 and took it out of our product line. Years ago, we manufactured bibs with a PVC coating on fabric from New Jersey. When we discovered the dangers of PVC, we tested it and immediately took it out of our manufacturing process. In 2006, we petitioned against it and removed BPA before any regulations were enforced. We have now removed formamides from our products and are in the process of researching formaldehyde as a concern, even though there are currently no nationwide regulations regarding those chemicals in the United States.

Guoxu (Samuel) Zhu, a graduate of the University of Georgia, manages our office in China, overseeing production quality and factory conditions. Samuel has a son named River, and he shares our values for healthy baby products. He personally visits the factories regularly to check for quality and factory conditions.

Social conditions

In the past, labor practices in China have included child labor and unfair treatment of workers. However, our factory managers say that the demand for workers is higher than the supply, which means that workers currently have increased wages, power, and options. If workers do not like the conditions and pay at one factory, they can easily find a better job at another. These increased labor costs do affect our product costs.

Ecological concerns

Until recently there has been little concern for the environment in China. However, because the lack of concern for the environment has had negative effects, the government is starting to create environmental regulations and standards. At least they are taking some steps in that direction, but environmental issues are still a big problem for China. In our product-development processes, we choose materials that have a low negative environmental impact.

United States jobs

Many Americans say that outsourcing to other countries has reduced U.S. jobs. Factory skills such as cutting and sewing are not taught in technical schools or on the job site because today's youth who are going into the job market in our industry have little interest in factory work. i play., Inc. employs over 60 full-time staff, with around 25 in the office and 35 in the warehouse.

I have been to Asia a dozen times to work with suppliers—in China, Thailand, Taiwan, Vietnam, and Japan—and with each trip the changes seem to accelerate. I recognize that our global economy is not static; it is dynamic, ever changing, and complex. I cannot begin to understand all of the factors and how they fit together, how they affect each other, and what the implications will be in the next few years. I feel that it is impossible to find a clear-cut solution that is exactly right because of the complexity of the situation. The best I know to do is to try to be conscious and to try to make choices with intentionality and prioritization every day, while keeping our main purpose and values in mind.

Samuel, the manager of our office in China, says that because of the one-child policy, two parents and four grandparents place all of their resources into one child, and they want a better life for that child. They want her to have an education and do not expect that she will do factory work, the same as American parents wish for their children. The next generation is not entering the labor market as factory workers, so the majority of current factory workers in China are over 30 years old. The one-child policy also means there will be a reduction in China's population in the next generation, which is decreasing their labor force. Because of all these changes, it is hard to predict who will manufacture our products in the future.

Whatever the changes may be, we are always looking for a better way through sourcing in different countries and factories. We at i play., Inc. are committed to ongoing research and development for making healthy baby products, with the baby in mind, that are high quality and affordable.

CHAPTER 10
Product Guide

F ROM THE MOMENT YOU find out you are having a baby, friends and family members start making suggestions about what you need—a certain kind of nursing pillow, a stroller, a crib, and so on. If you are a first-time parent, it may be challenging to sift through all the product options to determine what you really need and when you need it. This guide is designed to introduce you to the myriad of products available for babies and toddlers. Knowing what types of products are available, you can more easily decide what you want to buy, make a shopping list, set a budget, and develop a registry.

When shopping for your baby, you can be extravagant, or you can be frugal and keep it basic. Either way, if you have an awareness of product functions and features, as well as the quality of materials and construction, then you can more easily determine your priorities. As I mentioned in chapter 9, it is unlikely that you will make the perfect product choice every time. With some education and forethought, however, you can choose safe and healthy baby products that are convenient for you, while considering the environment, too.

For each product in the following guide, you will find a description of the product's benefits and special features or considerations. In addition, you will find what age your child will be when you need to make a purchase and the quantity you will likely need. Some items require a one-time purchase that will last throughout your baby's early years and can be recycled to your next child or to a friend. You may be able to save money by borrowing or buying some items secondhand—for instance, a used crib or stroller. Other items, such as socks and T-shirts, require multiple purchases at each stage of growth. Finally, some items, such as lotion and disposable diapers, require repeated ongoing purchases. This chapter is divided into six categories of products:

- **Nursery**—Here you will find various options for big purchases like bedding and furniture, as well as small touches that you can add to your baby's nursery to create a warm feeling. You can design an elaborate nursery with matching accessories or simply add a co-sleeper next to your bed and a small dresser that doubles as a changing table.

- **Baby Care**—This section contains information about diapering, wellness, skin care, grooming, bath, and safety products.

- **Clothing**—Read this section for a big-picture look at essentials that take your baby through each season and accommodate his changing needs as he grows and develops.

- **On the Go**—This section guides you through carriers, strollers, car seats, and related accessories.

- **Feeding**—As your baby grows, so do his needs for feeding products. In this section I list all the necessary supplies from nursing to bottle-feeding and food preparation—throughout his first three years.

- **Toys**—Here I describe various toys and explain how they can be used to support your baby's development, based on Pathways of Whole Learning . The simplest toys—those made without all the blinking lights and buzzing noises—are often the ones that inspire a child's imagination. Simple toys made of wood and natural fibers allow your child to make his own fun.

Nursery

PRODUCTS FOR YOUR BABY'S nursery include furniture for sleeping and storage, containers and other organizational items, room decor, and keepsakes.

Sleep

Where will your baby sleep? Some parents prefer to have their baby stay in his own room in a crib so that he will develop the habit of sleeping alone. Other parents prefer the family bed, which means sleeping together with a co-sleeper during a baby's early months and, later, all sleeping in the same bed. Whatever you choose, you can make a safe and comfortable choice that fits your lifestyle.

You may prefer to start with a cradle, bassinet, or Moses basket when your baby is a newborn. If you choose a crib, you can plan ahead to convert it into a toddler bed later. When considering crib mattresses, make sure you find a firm one to prevent the risk of Sudden Infant Death Syndrome (SIDS). A mattress pad and sheet savers offer protection from diaper leaks and drool. Do not use crib bumpers, sleep positioners, or loose blankets in your baby's crib before he is 12 months old.

Furniture

In addition to a sleeping area, your baby will need a changing table for dressing and changing diapers, a changing pad, and a dresser or shelves for storing clothes. It is also convenient to sing and rock your baby to sleep with a rocking chair or glider and an ottoman that allows you to elevate your feet. Finally, as your child grows, a step stool will help him become more independent.

Organization

Baby care probably requires more time and energy than you imagined. The more organized you are, the more efficient and effective you can be in handling the logistics of diaper changes, feeding, bathing, and other tasks. Storage containers, drawer organizers, clothes hangers, a clothes hamper, a diaper stacker, and a diaper pail help you file away your baby's necessities in places where you can grab them quickly.

Decor

Whether or not you choose to research feng shui, a traditional Chinese system of room and furniture arrangement for optimal energy flow, when planning your baby's sleeping space, you can create a calm and peaceful retreat for your baby. Listen to your intuition, and follow your senses as you put it together. When possible, use soft colors and natural materials for your baby's bedding, curtains, rugs, decorations, and furniture. Think about light, airflow, and the location of your baby's crib. Minimize electrical objects near your baby. Essential oils, soft music, wall hangings, and other types of art can stimulate his senses.

Keepsakes

Document meaningful and important moments in your baby's life to create memories that you will treasure for a lifetime. Keepsakes display your baby's milestones and allow you to share these moments with him when he gets older.

Sleep

Crib
One-time purchase
Age needed: Newborn

 There is a wide range of cribs to choose from. Recent safety recommendations warn against cribs with drop sides, as well as vintage cribs that may have bars that are more than 2 ⅜ inches apart, could potentially pose a suffocation hazard. Cribs often come with adjustable mattress heights, which allows you to lower the height as your baby grows and starts standing up in his crib.

Function: Provides a safe sleeping space for your baby with built-in rails to prevent him from falling

Special Features or Considerations:
- Converts into toddler bed
- Built-in diaper storage
- Built-in changing table
- Adjustable mattress height

Mattress
One-time purchase
Age needed: Newborn

 A crib mattress is usually hypoallergenic and waterproof. Firm mattresses also support bone growth. To provide a waterproof layer many traditional mattresses use chemicals, such as PVC and polyurethane, along with toxic flame retardants to meet fire safety standards, which can be harmful. However, some mattresses do not use harmful chemicals. Use a secondhand mattress with caution. Some mattresses fit standard-size cribs and convert to a toddler bed for longevity.

Function: Provides a firm and safe surface in the crib for your baby to sleep on

Special Features or Considerations:
- Firmness—a soft surface can be a suffocation hazard.
- Hypoallergenic—latex can cause an allergic reaction.
- Waterproof—wipes clean with a damp cloth
- Organic, breathable, nontoxic materials
- Correct size for your crib certification

Cradle, Bassinet, or Moses Basket
One-time purchase
Age needed: Newborn

 In the early weeks and months when your baby is frequently nursing and napping, a bassinet or cradle may be a convenient option for day or night. Cradles take up less space than a standard-size crib and are easier to move. A Moses basket can also offer carrying handles made from soft cloth or wicker and is often lined with soft, cotton-based bumpers.

Function: Provides a small bed for your new baby

Special Features or Considerations:
- Easy to move
- Lightweight
- Weight limit

Sleep

Co-sleeper
One-time purchase
Age needed: Newborn

 Co-sleepers keep your baby close to you at night for more convenient nursing. With your baby in a co-sleeper, there is less chance of suffocation associated with co-sleeping in an adult bed. Co-sleepers generally have a side that drops down so that it can be attached to the side of an adult bed. Co-sleepers may also convert to a freestanding bassinet or a play yard, have a removable liner that can be machine washed, and often fold up into a carrying bag for easy storage and transportation.

Function: Helps make nursing during the night easy and improves your bond with your baby

Special Features or Considerations:
* Flame resistant
* Safety strap
* Removable liner
* Maximum weight of 30 pounds

Crib Mattress Pad
One-time purchase
Age needed: Newborn

 Crib mattress pads are designed to cover your baby's mattress. They are usually waterproof and help protect your baby's mattress from moisture and mildew buildup as well as stains.

Function: Protects your baby's mattress from moisture, mildew buildup, and stains

Special Features or Considerations:
* Waterproof
* PVC-free

Fitted Sheet
Multiple purchases
Age needed: Newborn

 Fitted sheets for cribs fit most standard crib mattresses. They tend to have a tighter fit than adult fitted sheets to avoid loose fabric that may pose a suffocation hazard.

Function: Provides a comfortable and protective layer between your baby and their mattress

Special Features or Considerations:
* Flannel, woven, or knit fabric
* Organic
* Machine washable

Sheet Savers
Multiple purchases
Age needed: Newborn

 Sheet savers are placed on top of bed sheets to help minimize washing and keep the mattress dry. They are often made with absorbent and waterproof layers.

Function: Protects your baby's bed sheet from moisture, mildew buildup, and stains

Special Features or Considerations:
* Waterproof
* Absorbent
* PVC-free

Sleep

Receiving Blanket
Multiple purchases
Age needed: Newborn

 Receiving blankets can be used for many purposes—covering your baby while nursing, for shade, or as a floor covering for tummy time.

Function: Provides coverage and warmth

Special Features or Considerations:
- Organic cotton
- Generous size
- Lightweight

Swaddle Blanket
Multiple purchases
Age needed: Newborn

 You can swaddle your baby by snugly wrapping him in a blanket to soothe him. Swaddle blankets are specifically designed for swaddling and may come with straps or sticky patches on the side to help keep the swaddle blanket in place. Another option is to use a square blanket.

Function: Helps reduce your baby's startle reflex

Special Features or Considerations:
- Organic
- Breathable
- Machine washable

Wearable Blanket
Multiple purchases
Age needed: Newborn

 A wearable blanket keeps your baby warm while he sleeps. He can still kick and move, and it does not cover his face or airways, preventing suffocation. They also reduce the risk of overheating. Usually sleep bags are sleeveless and have an opening at the bottom for easy diaper changes. You can adjust the level of warmth by layering clothing underneath, such as a short- or long-sleeved bodysuit or footed sleeper. Sleep bag come in different weights for summer or winter. If you are swaddling your baby, you may prefer to use a sleep sack after he can sleep without swaddling. Some larger sizes are available for up to five years, but they may be inconvenient after your baby is standing on his own.

Function: Keeps your baby warm and safe when sleeping

Special Features or Considerations:
- Weight of fabric
- Bottom opening for diaper changes

Heavy Blanket
Multiple purchases
Age needed: 18 months

 Thick blankets can be used when your baby is around 18 to 24 months, to keep him warm. Heavy blankets provide warmth in strollers and car seats during cold weather. Do not use heavy blankets in your baby's crib before 12 months old.

Function: Helps keep your toddler warm

Special Features or Considerations:
- Organic
- Machine washable

Sleep

Quilt
One-time purchase
Age needed: Newborn

You can use quilts when your baby is a toddler. A quilt provides warmth and may also be a keepsake item to pass down.

Function: Keeps your toddler warm when he is sleeping

Special Features or Considerations:
- 100% cotton
- Thickness
- Machine washable

Sound Machine
One-time purchase
Age needed: Newborn

Sound machines play a range of soothing sounds and music to help your baby get used to sleeping with noise in the background.

Function: Provides white noise to keep your baby from waking in the night from random household sounds.

Special Features or Considerations:
- On-off timer
- Volume control
- Crib attachment

Monitor
One-time purchase
Age needed: Newborn

Monitors help you hear your baby when you are not in the same room. Some monitors have a belt clip and are battery operated, allowing you to move about the house freely. Other monitors may have a video setting that lets you view your baby in addition to hearing him.

Function: Allows you to check on your baby while he is sleeping

Special Features or Considerations:
- Video monitors
- One-mile range
- Belt clip

Night Light
One-time purchase
Age needed: Newborn

Night lights provide comfort and convenience in the dark for your baby and your child. They can help light the way for your toddler when he is learning to toilet train during the night.

Function: Provides light during the night

Special Features or Considerations:
- LED or standard bulbs
- Design

Sleep

Toddler Bed
One-time purchase
Age needed: 18 months

Toddler beds come with removable guard rails to prevent your baby from rolling out of bed. They are often lower in height than standard beds, making it easy for your child to climb in and out of the bed. Some toddler beds may convert to an adult-sized bed with rails that are usually sold separately. Toddler beds come in many colors and themes to match your toddler's room.

Function: Built-in rails prevent your baby from rolling out of bed

Special Features or Considerations:
- 2 years and up
- Left and right removable guard rails
- Fun colors, animals, or characters

Furniture

Changing Table
One-time purchase
Age needed: Newborn

Changing tables provide an elevated surface for you to change your baby, allowing you to stand comfortably without having to bend. Most changing tables have a safety strap or rails to protect your baby from potential falls. You may find stand-alone changing tables that come with shelves for added storage or a dresser that provides a changing table on its surface. Some cribs have a built-in changing table.

Function: A place to change your baby's diaper

Special Features or Considerations:
- Safety harness
- Storage space

Changing Pad
Multiple purchases
Age needed: Newborn

Changing pads are placed directly on a changing table, providing comfort and stability for your baby during diaper changes. Unlike some portable changing pads, the pad that goes with a changing table often has raised sides and sometimes a safety strap to comfortably keep your baby from rolling. A removable and washable cover is convenient for accidents.

Function: Provides comfort and stability for your baby's diaper changes

Special Features or Considerations:
- PVC-free
- Machine-washable cover
- Absorbent
- Waterproof

Furniture

Dresser or Shelves
One-time purchase
Age needed: Newborn

A dresser or shelves helps you organize various items in your baby's nursery including: diapers, wipes, clothes, and toys. If your space is limited, some cribs and toddler beds have built-in storage which can be used for the same purpose.

Function: Provides storage

Special Features or Considerations:
- Shelves and drawers
- Built-in to crib or toddler bed

Rocking Chair or Glider
One-time purchase
Age needed: Newborn

Rockers or gliders provide a place to sit in your baby's nursery for feeding him or rocking him to sleep. Some rockers and gliders have cushions, head rests, and padded arms.

Function: A chair with a soothing motion to help your baby go to sleep

Special Features or Considerations:
- Organic
- Machine-washable cover

Ottoman
One-time purchase
Age needed: Newborn

An ottoman is a padded foot rest used along with a rocker or glider to elevate your feet while nursing or rocking your baby.

Function: Elevates your feet while rocking your baby

Special Features or Considerations:
- Organic cotton
- Machine-washable cover

Toddler Step Stool
One-time purchase
Age needed: 18 months

A toddler step stool can be helpful to have until your child is tall enough to reach different areas in the house on his own. The step stool helps him learn independence by reaching the potty during training and the sink to wash his hands and brush his teeth.

Function: Helps your child reach household items without your assistance

Special Features or Considerations:
- May come decorated with fun shapes, colors, animals, or even his favorite characters.
- For ages 2–7 years

Organization

Storage Containers
Ongoing purchase
Age needed: Newborn

 Having a few storage containers or baskets on hand to keep items like clothes, toys, and extra sheets will help you stay organized. Containers often have tight seals which prevents dust buildup. Storage containers come in a variety of materials, such as soft collapsible fabric, plastic, or wood. They come in different sizes as well.

Function: Helps find items quickly and efficiently

Special Features or Considerations:
• Lids
• Coordinates with nursery decor

Drawer Organizer
Multiple purchases
Age needed: Newborn

 Drawer organizers are sized to fit into drawers for organization and storage. They usually have multiple compartments and are especially convenient for small items like caps and socks.

Function: Helps store and find items quickly and efficiently

Special Features or Considerations:
• Collapsible
• Adjustable

Drawer Liners
Multiple purchases
Age needed: Newborn

 Line your baby's drawers to provide a barrier between the drawer bottom and your baby's clothes. Liners come scented and unscented; some stick to the drawer with adhesive backing.

Function: Keeps your child's clothes clean

Special Features or Considerations:
• Nonslip grip
• Scented or unscented
• May come decorated with designs to coordinate with room decor

Clothes Hangers
Ongoing purchase
Age needed: 6 months

 Baby clothes do not fit well on full-sized clothing hangers and can become stretched out. Smaller clothes hangers fit your child's clothes. Many options are available, including fabric coverings, wood, metal, or plastic, double hangers, and even collapsible.

Function: Hangers that fit small clothing

Special Features or Considerations:
• Covered with fabric
• Collapsible
• Coordinates with nursery decor

Organization

Clothes Hamper
One-time purchase
Age needed: Newborn

 Clothes hampers store soiled garments until you can launder them. They often come in breathable fabrics to minimize mildew buildup.

Function: Keeps dirty clothes together in a portable container

Special Features or Considerations:
- Breathable fabrics
- Fabric lined
- Design coordinates with your baby's room

Diaper Stacker
One-time purchase
Age needed: Newborn

 Diaper stackers are designed to store your baby's diapers for easy access during diaper changes. Many diaper stackers come with a built-in hook for you to hang it from a changing table. Some are decorative to coordinate with your baby's room decor.

Function: Provides easy access to diapers during diaper changes

Special Features or Considerations:
- Built-in hook
- Design coordinates with your baby's room

Toy Chest
One-time purchase
Age needed: Newborn

 A toy chest provides a place to store your baby's toys. Since toy chests are usually low to the ground, your baby can use it when he gets older to put away his own toys. Many toy chests double as a bench and may come with a padded seat on top.

Function: Helps store toys and keep your baby's room neat

Special Features or Considerations:
- Nursery space
- Padded seat

Decor

Decorative Pillow
One-time purchase
Age needed: Newborn

 Your baby will not be old enough to use a pillow until he is around 18 to 24 months. A decorative pillow in your baby's room can coordinate with his nursery and offer support for your back or arms when you are nursing.

Function: Provides comfort while nursing or sitting in your baby's room

Special Features or Considerations:
• Organic
• Machine washable
• Coordinates with your baby's room

Rug
One-time purchase
Age needed: Newborn

 Rugs provide a textured barrier on your floor and can be used for tummy time or as a designated play area. Many rugs have prints, fun shapes, or colors to match your baby's nursery theme. Rugs are easily changed, so they can be replaced as your child grows.

Function: Enhances your baby's nursery decor and can be used for tummy time or a play area

Special Features or Considerations:
• Made from natural fibers
• Nonslip

Decor

Wall Hanging
One-time purchase
Age needed: Newborn

 Wall hangings go on the wall for visual appeal. You can easily change wall hangings as your child grows.

Function: Provides art and beauty to your child's room.

Special Features or Considerations:
• Permanent or temporary attachment

Lamp
One-time purchase
Age needed: Newborn

 Lamps offer a softer light than overhead lighting, creating a calming atmosphere for your baby. Lamp bodies and shades come in colors that coordinate with your baby's nursery.

Function: Creates a calming atmosphere

Special Features or Considerations:
• Design
• Amount of light
• Safety—unbreakable material

Curtains or Blinds
One-time purchase
Age needed: Newborn

 Curtains or blinds over your baby's window offer privacy and allow you to control the natural light in the room. Be careful to keep cords up high where your baby cannot grab them.

Function: Helps your baby sleep by controlling the light let into nursery

Special Features or Considerations:
• Design you like
• Ability to control light

Wall Decal
One-time purchase
Age needed: Newborn

 Decals are stickers that go directly onto the wall for decoration. They are an economical way to brighten your baby's room.

Function: Adds design to your baby's nursery decor

Special Features or Considerations:
• Does not chip wall paint
• Designs you like

Switchplate Cover
One-time purchase
Age needed: Newborn

 Switch plate covers go over the light switch in your baby's room for decoration.

Function: Adds decoration to your baby's room

Special Features or Considerations:
• Design

Decor

Growth Chart
One-time purchase
Age needed: Newborn

 Growth charts help you keep track of your child's growth and height. Charts can be made of cloth, cardboard, or paper and have inches and feet measurements along the side. They sometimes hang from the wall and can be updated with new measurements with stickers, patches, markers, pens, or pencils.

Functions: Provides a fun way to track your baby's growth.

Special Features or Considerations:
*   Easy to use and read
*   Removable adhesive

Memories

Photo Frames
Multiple purchases
Age needed: Newborn

 You can display pictures of your baby in photo frames at home or in your office. They help protect the prints themselves, and you can easily change them as he grows. Many photo frames are designed for special occasions such as the day he was born, his first birthday, his first holiday celebration, etc. Digital photo frames are another option to store or display a number of photos on a rotating basis.

Function: Protects your baby's pictures and first memories

Special Features or Considerations:
*   Designs you like
*   Special occasion frames

Photo Album
Multiple purchases
Age needed: Newborn

Photo albums organize pictures of your baby, and protect the prints.

Function: Stores your baby's pictures and displays special moments

Special Features or Considerations:
- May come with space on the front for his picture to personalize the album
- May be engraved with baby's name and birth date

Birth Announcements
One-time purchase
Age needed: Newborn

Birth announcements are usually ordered after your baby is born and sent to friends and family within four to eight weeks after his birth.

Function: Announces the birth of your baby

Special Features or Considerations:
- Personalized with any theme

Handprint Kit
One-time purchase
Age needed: Newborn

Handprint keepsake kits provide a mold of your baby's hands or feet for a keepsake. They usually are made of plaster or clay and often come with a hook so it can be hung on the wall or made into a holiday ornament. You may also find kits that come with frames, to mount a photo of your baby next to his print.

Function: Saves a memory of your baby's feet and hands

Special Features or Considerations:
- Nonstick and nontoxic

Keepsakes

Baby Book
One-time purchase
Age needed: Newborn

Baby books record your baby's journey through his first few years. Many baby books are both a journal and a photo album to record memories and milestones. They often come preprinted with spaces for you to fill in accomplishments such as first foods, words, steps, weight, and height.

Function: Records your baby's milestones

Special Features or Considerations:
- Slip-in photo pockets to save pictured memories

Baby Care

PRODUCTS THAT YOU WILL use for daily baby care include items for bathing, skin care and grooming, diapering, wellness and health care, and safety around the home.

Bathing

Bath time is more than just washing your baby and getting him clean; it is a chance for the two of you to bond and for him to relax before sleeping. For a safe and fun bathing experience, make sure you have all the basics on hand, such as a spout cover, a tub thermometer, and a nonskid mat. Gather towels, washcloths, and skin care items before you put your baby in the bathtub. In addition, a bath kneeler can prevent back discomfort while you are bathing your baby. Finally, storage for toys helps keep them under control. Check the water temperature to be sure that it is not too hot or cold. Get a good grip on your baby to be sure that he does not slip under the water, and pay attention to him at all times while he is in the bath.

Skin care and grooming

Your newborn or infant does not need to be washed with soap every day, and shampooing his hair two to three times a week is plenty. As he gets older and starts to use soap and shampoo regularly, make sure that the brand you buy does not have perfumes, dyes, or chemicals that are likely to irritate his sensitive skin. Oil or lotion helps moisturize his skin, and diaper balm keeps his bottom healthy. Nail clippers and scratch mitts keep him from scratching himself. Basic grooming tools include a brush, comb, toothbrush, and toothpaste.

Diapering

There are many factors to consider when deciding how to diaper your baby: convenience, time, environmental impact, comfort, and money. Diapering involves a lifestyle choice, and it can vary with each situation and each child. Caregivers can choose from convenient, comfortable cloth-diapering options, including diaper covers, contoured or flat diapers, disposable inserts, diaper liners for minimizing mess, and all-in-one cloth diapers that go on your baby like disposables do. Eco-friendly disposable diapers are also available. You may decide to use one system completely or to combine different methods. Either way, keep in mind that your baby's diaper will probably be changed around 7,000 times before he is toilet trained.

Wellness and health care

Start your baby off on a wellness path by using a health care journal to record his visits to his health care provider and to note any illnesses that he experiences at home. To be prepared for accidents and illness, make sure you have the basics—a nasal aspirator, a thermometer, a medicine dispenser, and a first-aid kit. A humidifier can provide moisture in your home if the air is dry in winter.

Safety around the home

Baby care includes maintaining a safe environment for your child. Outlet covers, safety locks, and a safety gate provide protective boundaries. Cleaning supplies and laundry detergent made with nontoxic ingredients help you keep his world clean and safe at the same time.

Bathing

Sink or Bathtub Insert
One-time purchase
Age needed: Newborn

 An insert fits inside your kitchen sink or bathtub for bathing newborns. Once your baby can sit up, you can give him a bath in a standard bathtub. However, using a bathtub insert is faster to fill than the whole tub and provides more security for your baby by keeping him from slipping.

Function: Supports your baby in the bath

Special Features or Considerations:
*   BPA- and PVC-free

No-slip Bath Mat
One-time purchase
Age needed: Newborn

 No-slip bath mats provide a textured surface for traction in the bath tub. Place the mat directly onto the surface of your bathtub.

Function: Prevents your baby from slipping during bath time. Fits in most standard bathtubs

Special Features or Considerations:
*   Potential for mildew
*   BPA- and PVC-free

Bathing

Tub Thermometer
One-time purchase
Age needed: Newborn

 You can use a tub thermometer to test the temperature of water before putting your baby in the bathwater.

Function: Check temperature of bath water

Special Features or Considerations:
- Comes in fun shapes, colors, or characters
- Accuracy
- Ease of use and reading

Tub Spout Cover
One-time purchase
Age needed: Newborn

 A tub spout cover protects your baby's head from bumping the bathtub faucet during bath time. The tub spout cover slides over your tub's faucet. Most fit standard-size bathtubs. Tub spout covers often come in fun designs, which add to the fun of bath time with your baby.

Function: Provides cushion on the tub faucet to protect your baby's head

Special Features or Considerations:
- Fits in most standard bath faucets

Bath Toy Storage
One-time purchase
Age needed: Newborn

 A bath toy storage container makes toys accessible for your baby's bath time, and out of the way for other family members. Storage for bath toys comes in a variety of styles from pockets that hang from the shower head, to trays that span the top of a tub, and containers that attach to walls with suction cups.

Function: Stores and dries bath toys

Special Features or Considerations:
- Potential for mildew
- Attachable to bathroom wall or tile
- Built-in scoop
- PVC-free

Hooded Towels
Multiple purchases
Age needed: Newborn

 Hooded towels have a built-in hood to dry your baby's body and head and keep him warm at the same time. Small-sized towels are effective for your newborn baby. As he grows, he needs a larger towel. Animal designs can stimulate dramatic play.

Function: Dries your baby's body and head

Special Features or Considerations:
- Organic cotton
- Machine washable
- Generous sizing

Bathing

Washclothes

Multiple purchases
Age needed: Newborn

 Washclothes are usually made from knitted or woven terry. Woven terry makes a thick washcloth for washing larger areas of your baby's body, such as his legs, arms, torso, and head. Knitted terry washcloths are thin and are useful for cleaning small and delicate areas, such as his nose or ears. Use washclothes to wash him with shampoo or bath wash. You can also place a thick washcloth on your baby's belly during bath time to keep him warm.

Function: Helps you gently clean your baby

Special Features or Considerations:
- Organic cotton
- Machine washable

Rinse Cup

One-time purchase
Age needed: 6 weeks

 Rinse your baby's body and hair with a rinse cup. They are usually designed with a handle and spout for easy pouring. Rinse cups double as a toy for pouring water.

Function: Rinses soap off of your baby's body and hair

Special Features or Considerations:
- Nonslip grip handle
- PVC-free

Bath Kneeler

One-time purchase
Age needed: 3 months

 Bath kneelers help protect your knees with cushioned support for leaning over the tub to wash your baby during bath time.

Function: Provides cushion for your knees.

Special Features or Considerations:
- Waterproof
- Machine washable

Skin Care and Grooming

Shampoo and Wash
Ongoing Purchase
Age needed: 6 weeks

 Shampoo and wash keep your baby and his hair clean. Many shampoos and soaps contain chemicals that are toxic. Formaldehyde and dioxane are exempt from FDA labeling laws, so choose natural products with the shortest ingredients list.

Function: Keeps hair healthy and strong

Special Features or Considerations:
• Sodium lauryl sulfate-free

Oil or Lotion
Ongoing Purchase
Age needed: Newborn

 Use oil or lotion to moisturize your baby's skin and prevent symptoms of eczema, dry skin, and diaper rash.

Function: Moisturizes your baby's skin

Special Features or Considerations:
• Hypoallergenic
• Unscented

Diaper Balm
Multiple purchases
Age needed: Newborn

 Diaper balm protects and heals your baby's delicate skin. Rub diaper balm on your baby's bottom after each diaper change to create a moisture barrier and prevent diaper rash. You can also rub the diaper balm over a scrape, burn, or rash to help his skin heal.

Function: Prevents and heals diaper rash

Special Features or Considerations:
• Organic
• Nonpetroleum

Brush and Comb
Multiple purchases
Age needed: 6 weeks

 Baby brushes and combs remove tangles and help keep your baby's hair soft and healthy. A nonslip grip, helps prevent slipping and allows your child to comb his hair on his own. Brushes made with natural hair bristles are soft and gentle on his head.

Function: Loosens tangles and helps keep hair combed.

Special Features or Considerations:
• Nonslip grip
• Natural bristles

Toothbrush and Toothpaste
Ongoing Purchase
Age needed: 6 months

 Before your baby has teeth, it is still important to clean his gums. You can use a piece of gauze and your finger or a finger toothbrush to wipe his gums clean. Once he starts getting his teeth in, around six months of age, you can then use a small, soft-bristle brush twice a day. Toothpaste may contain fluoride. Do not give your child toothpaste before he is 24 months old, because he may swallow it. Once your baby is able to start brushing his own teeth, around 24 months, apply a pea-sized amount of toothpaste to his toothbrush to assist in getting rid of bacteria when cleaning.

Function: Provides care for your baby's teeth

Special Features or Considerations:
• PVC- and BPA-free toothbrushes
• Sodium lauryl sulfate-free

Skin Care and Grooming

Nail Clippers
One-time purchase
Age needed: Newborn

 Nail clippers trim your baby's fingernails safely, to help keep him free from scratches.

Function: Keeps nails trimmed

Special Features or Considerations:
- Nonslip grip
- Sized for trimming tiny nails
- Magnifier to increase precision

Scratch Mitts
One-time purchase
Age needed: Newborn

 Scratch mitts cover your newborn baby's hands to prevent him from scratching himself. Scratch mitts are often made with soft fabrics with no-pinch elastic to help the mitts stay on.

Function: Prevents scratches and keep hands warm

Special Features or Considerations:
- 100% cotton or organic cotton

Pacifier
Multiple purchases
Age needed: Newborn

 Pacifiers are nipple shaped for your baby to suck when he is not hungry but still needs the comfort of sucking. Pacifiers are not a substitute for nurturing or feeding your baby. If he is breast-feeding, using a pacifier may cause nipple confusion, so wait until he is well established in nursing. If you do use a pacifier, choose one that is made of quality materials and has an orthodontic design.

Function: Comforts your baby

Special Features or Considerations:
- BPA-free
- Orthodontic Design

Diapering

Diaper Cover
Multiple purchases
Age needed: Newborn

 Diaper covers are made from a waterproof or water-resistant material that goes over a cloth diaper and holds in moisture and solid matter. Many fabric options are available—polyester or cotton that is laminated with a waterproof coating, microfiber, or wool for breathability. Diaper covers come in a pull-up style with no side opening, side openings with hook-and-loop closures, and side opening with snap closures. You can insert different kinds of diapers in the diaper covers—flat pre-fold diapers, contoured diapers, biodegradable disposable inserts, or cloth inserts that fit into a pocket inside the diaper cover.

Function: Protects cloth diapers or disposable inserts from leaking

Special Features or Considerations:
- Fabric
- Waterproof
- Sizing
- Quantity needed
- Cost
- Design—colors or prints
- Comfort—soft material and elastic
- Convenience in changing diaper
- Trim fit
- Gussets for catching leaks
- Laundering requirements
- Umbilical cord notch

Diapering

Flat Pre-fold Cloth Diaper
One-time purchase
Age Needed: Newborn

Using pre-fold and flat diapers is economical. Usually, they are made of 100% cotton, but bamboo and hemp are also available. This style of diaper is convenient to use as a burp cloth or for cleaning spills. This style of diaper is adjustable as your baby grows from newborn to toddler—you can fold the diaper small when he is a newborn and when he is a toddler. You can double the diapers for extra absorbency and for nighttime use. These diapers dry quickly when laundered.

Function: Absorbs your baby's urine and solid matter

Special Features of Considerations:
- Fabric
- Absorbency
- Cost
- Convenience in changing diaper
- Laundering requirements
- Multipurpose
- Sizing
- Absorbency
- Material—cotton, bamboo, hemp, or microfiber

Contoured Fitted Diapers
Multiple Purchases
Age Needed: Newborn

Fitted diapers are contoured or shaped to fit inside a diaper cover. Some fitted diapers are flat with an hourglass shape and some have gussets and snaps or hook-and-loop closures. Fitted diapers do not require folding and they are easy to use. You can double the flat style as your baby grows for extra absorbency and for nighttime use. They come in 2–3 sizes from newborn to toddler.

Function: Absorbs your baby's urine and solid matter

Special Features or Considerations:
- Special Features and Considerations:
- Fabric
- Absorbency
- Cost
- Convenience in changing diaper
- Laundering requirements
- Sizing

Diaper Doubler
Multiple purchases
Age needed: Newborn

Diaper doublers are made to insert inside cloth diapers that are used with a diaper cover for extra absorbency. They are convenient to keep your baby from being disturbed during the night. As he grows, diaper doublers help prevent leaks for day-time use with toddlers. You can place the doubler next to your baby's skin or under the diaper next to the diaper cover.

Function: Provides extra absorbency with cloth diapers

Special Features or Considerations:
- Extra absorbent fabric for less bulk
- Standard size that can be used for different ages of baby

Diapering

All-in-one Diapers
Multiple purchases
Age needed: Newborn

All-in-one diapers are the easiest to use of cloth diapers but the most expensive. The diaper and cover are sewn together so that they function like a disposable diaper. Some styles have different sizes and some adjust as your baby grows. They take a long time to dry because of their thickness. All-in-one diapers are convenient for child care because of the simplicity of diaper changes.

Function: Absorbs and contains your baby's urine and solid matter

Special Features or Considerations:
*   Fabric
*   Waterproof
*   Sizing
*   Quantity needed
*   Cost
*   Design—colors or prints
*   Comfort—soft material and elastic
*   Convenience in changing diaper
*   Trim fit
*   Gussets for catching leaks
*   Laundering requirements
*   Umbilical cord notch

Diaper Liner
Ongoing purchase
Age needed: Newborn

Flushable diaper liners are a thin layer of nonwoven material that goes inside your baby's cloth diaper to contain solid matter. When changing your baby's diaper you can discard the liner and solid matter in the toilet.

Function: Contains solid matter to flush in the toilet

Special Features or Considerations:
*   Biodegradability
*   Soft and comfortable
*   Cost
*   Size—small and large

Disposable Inserts
Ongoing Purchase
Age Needed: Newborn

Disposable inserts are biodegradable rayon or bamboo inserts that fit inside a diaper cover. Usually, you can double them for extra absorbency as your baby grows and for nighttime use. You can use them exclusively or for traveling or camping.

Function: Absorbs your baby's urine and solid matter

Special Features or Considerations:
*   Material
*   Size
*   Cost
*   Absorbency
*   Biodegradability

Diapering

Disposable Diapers
Ongoing purchase
Age needed: Newborn

 All-in-one diaper made of disposable materials are the most expensive option of all diapering methods and the most convenient. They also have a negative impact on the environment because they are not biodegradable.

Function: Absorbs and contains your baby's urine and solid matter

Special Features or Considerations:
- Materials , waterproof
- Sizing
- Quantity needed
- Cost
- Design—colors or prints
- Comfort—gels or chemicals
- Convenience in changing diaper
- Trim fit
- Gussets for catching leaks
- Umbilical cord notch
- Color changing wetness indicator
- Biodegradability

Diaper Bag
One-time purchase
Age needed: Newborn

 Diaper bags organize and carry baby essentials when you are on the go. Most bags come with waterproof lining and multiple compartments to carry diapers, wipes, ointment/cream, a blanket or extra clothes, wet bags, burp pads, nursing or feeding supplies, and toys.

Function: Designed to organize and carry baby essentials on the go

Special Features or Considerations:
- Insulated bottle pockets
- Adjustable shoulder strap
- Changing pad and wipes case included
- Water-resistant
- Wipes clean with damp cloth
- May come with hooks to attach to stroller
- Basic, or fashion

BIODEGRADABLE DISPOSABLE DIAPERS THAT TAKE CARE ... NATURALLY

To order DOVETAILS® see page 4.

We made a disposable Dovetails Diapering System© back in 1990. Designed like diapers I found in Japan, they were biodegradable and were not made with plastic. I used them inside a diaper cover when traveling.

Diapering

Disposable Wipes
Ongoing purchase
Age needed: Newborn

 Disposable wipes clean your baby's bottom during diaper changes, wipe his face in between baths, or clean his runny nose. Disposable wipes are often sold in multipacks and are stored in a box container that keeps the wipes moist for later use.

Function: Easy for on the go

Special Features or Considerations:
- Unscented
- Alcohol-free
- Biodegradable

Wipe Warmers
One-time purchase
Age needed: Newborn

 A wipe warmer stores and warms disposable wipes.

Function: Make diaper changes more comfortable for your baby

Special Features or Considerations:
- Bacteria resistant
- Fits most standard refill packs

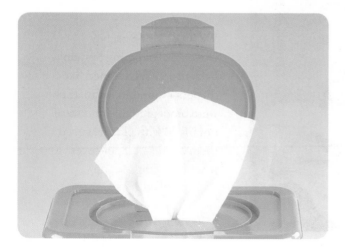

Diaper Pail
One-time purchase
Age needed: Newborn

 A diaper pail is a container to store soiled diapers until you are able to launder or dispose of them. You can designate any storage container as a diaper pail, as long as it is separate from other storage containers.

The type of pail you choose may depend on the system you use for cleaning diapers. In a wet system, fill pail with liquid mixture made with water, white vinegar, and baking soda to soak reusable diapers. A dry system is usually a pail with a plastic liner or a ventilated bag which can be used with any style of diaper. Some pails require special liners and filters, while others use regular garbage liners.

A well ventilated pail or bag will keep odors from building up inside, but if you do not have good ventilation in your home a tightly sealed pail may work better for you. A sturdy lid that locks can prevent your baby from playing in the pail and may be preferable if you are using a wet system.

When you are on the go, carrying a diaper pail is not convenient. A bag, often called a wet bag, can allow you to carry soiled diapers and keep them separate from clean diapers.

Function: Stores soiled diapers until laundering

Special Features or Considerations:
- Number of diapers the pail holds
- Wet or dry cleaning system
- Proprietary liners and filters
- Odor control
- May coordinate with your baby's room
- Machine washable
- Alternate bag for travel

Diapering

Diaper Changing Mat
One-time purchase
Age needed: Newborn

Diaper changing mats provide a flat surface to lay your baby on during diaper changes and can be used at home or on the go. Changing mats often fold or roll up to store in your diaper bag for easy portability. They are usually waterproof should an accident occur during the diaper change.

Function: Provides a clean surface to lay your baby on during diaper changes

Special Features or Considerations:
- Storage pockets
- Carrying handle
- Travel case for wipes included
- Nonskid backing

Potty Training

Potty Seat or Chair
One-time purchase
Age needed: 24 months

Potty training is a milestone in your toddler's life. Toddlers often shy away from standard adult toilets, so purchasing a potty seat or chair for your toddler may help him make the transition. Some potty chairs light up when your child presses the flush button, or a ring sound, which gives encouragement when he successfully uses the potty. Other options are a potty seat that fits on top of a standard toilet and may have handles on the sides to help your toddler from falling. As your child gets comfortable using the potty, you can remove the potty seat, so he can sit directly on the regular toilet seat.

Function: Toddler-sized seating to encourage potty use.

Special Features or Considerations:
- Splash Guard
- Nonskid

Reusable Training Pants
Multiple purchases
Age needed: 24 months

Training pants are underwear with a built-in pad to help with absorbency should your child have an accident when he is potty training.

Function: Helps your child transition into regular underwear

Special Features or Considerations:
- Machine washable
- Organic cotton

Potty Training

Disposable Training Pants
Multiple purchases
Age needed: 24 months

 Disposable training pants are constructed to mimic underwear, but they are made of the same materials as disposable diapers. This construction allows your child to pull the training pants on and off with ease. They have tabs on the side for opening if your child has a messy accident.

Functions: Minimizes messes during potty training

Special Features or Considerations:
- Multipacks
- Made from 100% unbleached cotton or flannel
- Reusable

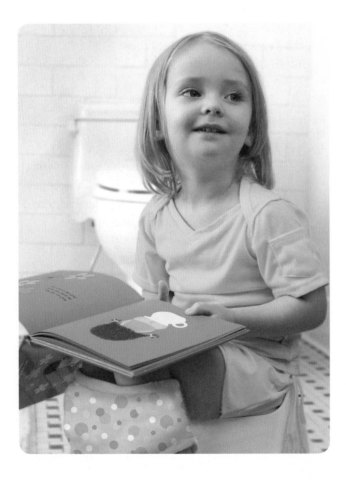

Wellness and Health Care

Health Journal
One-time purchase
Age needed: Newborn

 Keeping a health journal is a way to log information that can be helpful for you and your baby's health care provider. This information can be very useful for him, in case of illness or an accident.

Function: Keeps your baby's activities, nursing sessions, diaper changes, and health history

Special Features or Considerations:
- Space to store contacts for emergencies
- Expandable with room for additional pages

First-aid Kit
One-time purchase
Age needed: Newborn

 A first-aid kit is a place to store supplies for easy access during minor emergencies. You can make your own kit or purchase a prepackaged one. Prepackaged kits come in a carrying case that allows you to stay organized. It may also come with a step-by-step first-aid guide.

Function: Be prepared in the event of a minor emergency

Special Features or Considerations:
- First-aid guide
- Carrying case
- Refillable items
- Natural healing treatments

Wellness and Health Care

Medicine Dispenser
One-time purchase
Age needed: Newborn

 If your baby needs medication, a medicine dispenser with measurements can help you ensure the proper dosage.

Function: Feed your baby medication

Special Features or Considerations:
- Variety of types: Nipple, pacifier, syringe

Nasal Aspirator
One-time purchase
Age needed: Newborn

 When your baby is 18 months or younger, he may not be able to blow his nose effectively. Nasal aspirators help clear nasal passages through suction. They are designed with one end that provides suction and a soft tip that is gently inserted into your baby's nose.

Function: Alleviates blocked nasal passages

Special Features or Considerations:
- PVC-free
- Dishwasher safe
- Manual, bulb, and electric options
- Birth to 18 months

Thermometer
One-time purchase
Age needed: Newborn

 You can measure your child's body temperature to determine if he has a fever with a thermometer. There are a variety of thermometers available: rectal, ear, pacifier, temporal, and oral (oral thermometers are generally not recommended for children under five). Many thermometers are digital and come equipped with an alert feature; allowing for a quicker and more accurate read. You may also find thermometers with tip covers that help avoid cross contamination.

Function: Helps you monitor your child during illness

Special Features or Considerations:
- Available in fun shapes, colors, or characters
- Digital
- Mercury-free
- Protective case or storage bag
- 20-second response
- Memory recall
- Alerts when complete
- Tip covers

Humidifier
One-time purchase
Age needed: Newborn

 Humidifiers provide moisture to your baby's room to offer him relief from itchy skin, dry throat, and nasal congestion. This relief can help your baby sleep when he is not feeling well.

Function: Adds moisture to the air in the room

Special Features or Considerations:
- May come in designs, colors, animals, or characters
- Digital
- On-off timer
- Auto turn-off when tank is empty

Safety around the Home

Nontoxic Cleaning Supplies
Ongoing purchase
Age needed: Newborn

You can disinfect and clean your home safely with nontoxic cleaning supplies. There are a variety of nontoxic cleaners available that are eco-friendly.

Function: Cleans your home without harmful chemicals

Special Features or Considerations:
- Disinfecting
- Bleach-, ammonia-, and phosphate-free
- Eco-friendly

Gentle Laundry Detergent
Ongoing purchase
Age needed: Newborn

Gentle laundry detergents are specially formulated to be hypoallergenic and safe for your baby. These detergents gently clean your baby's clothes without the use of dyes that cause skin irritation.

Function: Cleans your baby's clothes without irritating his skin

Special Features or Considerations:
- Dye-free
- Color safe
- Removes soil, dirt, and stains
- Hypoallergenic

Outlet Covers
One-time purchase
Age needed: 9 months

As your child becomes mobile, he begins exploring his surroundings, which includes dangerous household items such as electrical outlets. You can easily place outlet covers into standard outlets to protect your child.

Function: Prevents electrical shock from outlets

Special Features or Considerations:
- Easy to install and use
- Fits your outlets

Safety around the Home

Safety Gates
One-time purchase
Age needed: 9 months

Safety gates block off an area of your home so your baby cannot gain access. Many safety gates come equipped with a swinging gate, so that you can securely lock it if necessary.

Function: Establish boundaries in your house for your baby's safety

Special Features or Considerations:
- 2-Way Door
- Wall Mounted
- Extra-wide opening

Safety Locks
One-time purchase
Age needed: 9 months

As your baby becomes mobile, he begins exploring his surroundings and opening doors. You can install safety locks on doors and bathroom or kitchen cabinets to keep out your child to protect him from potentially accessing dangerous household items such as medicines, cleaners, etc.

Function: Keeps doors and cabinets closed to protect your child

Special Features or Considerations:
- Easy to install and use
- Works on cabinets with handles or knobs

Clothing

CHOOSING CLOTHES FOR YOUR baby can be fun, as you think about his personality as well as his needs. What is the purpose of each clothing item? Are the fabric, construction, and design durable, breathable, and comfortable for him? What colors and styles match his style of expression and represent his best self? Most babies are tiny in the beginning, so it may be convenient to have two or three items in a preemie size. Because babies usually grow very fast in the first few months, however, you will probably not need many newborn-size clothes. If you opt for a size larger, then you'll know he can wear clothing comfortably as he grows. Generally speaking, basic, simple clothing made of natural materials feels good to your baby and performs well.

Layette

A layette is a baby's first wardrobe and essentials. It consists of versatile pieces such as bodysuits, socks, gowns, booties, shirts, pull-up pants, sleepers, footies, and caps. Newborns require frequent changes due to spit-up, dirty diapers, and spills. Clothing items made of combed or organic cotton are breathable and soft against your baby's sensitive skin, and they are especially beneficial before he is 12 months old.

Playwear

When your baby starts moving more, his clothing needs to change. Once he can get around, he needs play clothes that are more durable than layette items. Denim overalls and jeans, rompers, pants and shorts, short- and long-sleeved shirts, and dresses in basic mix-and-match colors offer flexibility. Once he is feeding himself, your baby makes more of a mess at mealtime and playtime, so when you are going out or traveling, take an extra outfit. In addition, he may need a light jacket or sweater to keep him warm. As he begins to cruise or walk, soft-soled shoes, and eventually tennis shoes and sandals, provide protection and support.

Swimwear and sun protection

Your child can enjoy physical activity as well as time outside at the pool or beach. Reusable swim diapers and swimsuits with built-in diapers are comfortable and let him move freely in the water. Swim diapers also eliminate the worry of solid waste entering a pool. Sun shirts, rashguards, sunglasses, and sun hats made with UV-protecting fabric offer sun protection. Other accessories for a trip to the beach or pool include a terry cover-up and some swim shoes or water sandals.

Outerwear

When purchasing outerwear, consider the intensity of the cold when choosing the thickness of your baby's outerwear. Buntings, which are warm sacks used before he can walk, come in lightweight and heavy-duty versions. Your child's needs partly depend on your daily activities and the location of your home (for example, in the city or in the country). Once he can walk, a bib and a warm, waterproof jacket protects your baby from the elements. While your new baby will probably not spend much time out in the rain, your toddler may need a raincoat or jacket with a hood and a zipper or snaps. Toddlers love to splash in puddles with a raincoat, rain boots, and an umbrella!

Layette

Homecoming Outfit
One-time purchase
Age needed: Newborn

If you had a hospital birth, you may dress your baby in a special homecoming outfit to mark the occasion and officially welcome him into your home.

Function: Welcomes your baby to the world

Special Features or Considerations:
- Organic cotton
- Machine washable

Bodysuits
Multiple purchases
Age needed: Newborn

Bodysuits are a one-piece garment that pulls over your baby's head and snaps together at the bottom. This bottom opening prevents slipping and allows easy access for diaper changes. Bodysuits come in both short-sleeved and long-sleeved versions.

Function: Covers your baby's torso neatly and allows easy diaper changes

Special Features or Considerations:
- Organic cotton
- Machine washable
- Outside seams
- Built-in extender

Garment Extenders
Multiple purchases
Age needed: Newborn

Garment extenders are a small rectangle piece of fabric that snaps into bodysuits, providing a few extra inches of length and extending the life of the garment. Garment extenders are often sold in multipacks that fit most standard bodysuit snaps.

Function: Increases the longevity of your baby's bodysuits, helping to save money

Special Features or Considerations:
- Organic cotton
- Machine washable

Gowns
Multiple purchases
Age needed: Newborn

Gowns are one-piece garments that pull over your baby's head or open on the side. They often open at the bottom for easy access for diaper changes and allow for air circulation. Knit gowns may also come with built-in hand mitts.

Function: Sleeping garment with easy access for diaper changes

Special Features or Considerations:
- Organic cotton
- Machine washable
- Built-in hand muffs

Layette

Knit Caps
Multiple purchases
Age needed: Newborn

 Knit caps keep your baby's head warm, assisting in regulating his body temperature. Knit caps often come in a layette set to match a bodysuit.

Functions: Covers your baby's head to keep him warm and regulate his body temperature

Special Features or Considerations:
- Organic cotton
- Machine washable
- Reversible
- Outside seams

Side Snap Knit Shirts
Multiple purchases
Age needed: Newborn

 Side-snap knit shirts are used from birth until around three months. You can change your baby's shirt with ease, because the side snaps offer easy access!

Function: Side snaps allow for easy changing

Special Features or Considerations:
- Organic cotton
- Machine washable
- Birth to 3 months
- Outside seams

Footed Knit Pants
Multiple purchases
Age needed: Newborn

 Footed knit pants have a built-in foot covering, so you do not need socks. These one-piece pants are convenient for your baby from birth until the time he is ready to walk. After your baby starts cruising and shows signs of being ready to walk, he will need his feet free. Footed knit pants pull on and off with ease, making diaper changes convenient.

Function: Covers your baby's lower body and feet

Special Features or Considerations:
- Organic cotton
- Machine washable
- Pull on
- Outside seams

Leggings
Multiple purchases
Age needed: 6 weeks

 Leggings cover your baby's legs for warmth and protection. They can be worn with short pants or under dresses and skirts.

Functions: Covers your baby's legs

Special Features or Considerations:
- Organic cotton
- Machine washable
- Relaxed fit

Layette

One-piece Footies
Multiple purchases
Age needed: Newborn

Footies are a one-piece full bodysuit that covers your baby's arms, body, legs, and feet. This one-piece garment comes with snap closures or a zipper to keep it securely closed and allow for easy dressing. Sleepwear regulations require footies over nine-months size to be treated with a flame retardant or to be snug-fitting.

Function: Keeps your baby warm while sleeping

Special Features or Considerations:
- Organic cotton
- Zipper or snap opening
- Outside seams

Socks
Multiple purchases
Age needed: Newborn

Socks help keep your baby's feet warm and protect his feet before he is old enough to walk and wear shoes. Once your baby starts to cruise and begins to walk on his own, socks that have a nonslip bottom prevent him from slipping.

Function: Covers your baby's feet and keeps them warm

Special Features or Considerations:
- Organic cotton
- Nonslip bottoms

Booties
Multiple purchases
Age needed: Newborn

Booties are made from soft materials, such as fleece, cotton, or wool. They slip on to help keep your baby's feet warm. Booties with no-pinch elastic at the top stay put around the ankles so they do not fall off.

Function: Protects your baby's feet

Special Features or Considerations:
- 100% cotton, fleece, or wool
- No-pinch elastic

Cardigan Sweaters
Multiple purchases
Age needed: Newborn

Layering your baby's clothes helps regulate his body temperature. Cardigan sweaters layer over a light T-shirt or bodysuit to help keep him warm. Closures include zippers or buttons.

Function: Layers over a shirt and helps keep your baby warm

Special Features or Considerations:
- Organic cotton
- Machine washable

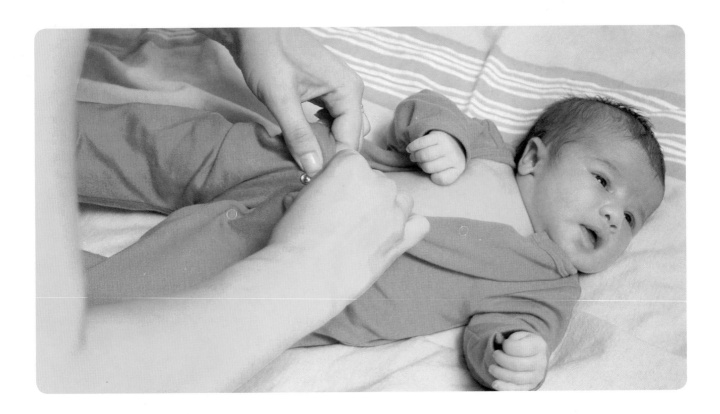

Layette

Pullover Sweaters
Multiple purchases
Age needed: Newborn

 Pullover sweaters layer over a light T-shirt, long-sleeved shirt, or bodysuit to help keep your baby warm. Check to see that the opening is wide enough to pull on and off your baby's head.

Functions: Layers over a shirt and helps keep your baby warm

Special Features or Considerations:
• Organic cotton
• Large neck opening
• Machine washable

Pajamas
Multiple purchases
Age needed: 9 months

 Pajamas are garments for your baby to sleep in. The style of pajamas you purchase may vary depending on your baby's age and season of the year. Choices include footed pajamas, two-piece sets, and gowns. Cotton pajamas are made to fit snugly or they are made of polyester to minimize fire risk, even though most modern homes do not have open furnaces. Make sure your baby does not overheat while sleeping.

Function: Keeps your baby warm while he is sleeping

Special Features or Considerations:
• Sizes range from 9 months to 5T
• Organic
• Machine washable

Playwear

Short and Long-sleeved Shirts
Multiple purchases
Age needed: 12 months

 Short-sleeved shirts are versatile in both warmer and cooler weather. They can be worn alone or layered under cardigans, jumpers, rompers, or outerwear.

Function: Covers your baby's upper body

Special Features or Considerations:
*   Large neck opening or snaps
*   Machine washable

Pants
Multiple purchases
Age needed: 12 months

 Long pants can be worn in both warm and cold weather. In summer and spring, lightweight and breathable fabrics keep your baby from overheating. In fall and winter, soft and thicker fabrics such as eco-fleece or microfiber keep him warm. Pants that have an elastic waistband or snaps are easier to get on and off for diapering.

Function: Covers your baby from the waist down

Special Features or Considerations:
*   Crotch and leg snaps
*   Pull-on waistband
*   Machine washable

Playwear

Rompers
Multiple purchases
Age needed: Newborn

 Rompers are one-piece garments that come in long or short pants and long or short sleeves. Many rompers offer snap closures around the legs or in the crotch area, allowing for easy access for diaper changes or potty training.

Function: Covers your baby's torso

Special Features or Considerations:
* Organic cotton
* Crotch snap
* Machine washable

Overalls
Multiple purchases
Age needed: 12 months

 Overalls are one-piece garments that are available in both long and short pants. They often are adjustable to fit your child. Overalls often have snaps on the pant leg as well as the side of the body, allowing for easy access for diaper changes.

Function: Covers your baby's body and legs

Special Features or Considerations:
* Adjustable shoulder straps
* Leg and side snaps

Shorts
Multiple purchases
Age needed: 12 months

 During warmer months, shorts are comfortable and convenient for daily wear and for easy diaper changes.

Function: Covers your baby's lower body in warm weather

Special Features or Considerations:
* Organic cotton
* Crotch/leg snap
* Pull-on waistband
* Durable fabric
* Machine washable

Dresses
Multiple purchases
Age needed: 6 weeks

 Dresses are comfortable and cute for your baby girl or toddler. Different styles are made with short or long sleeves. They can be worn with tights or leggings for formal occasions and for everyday wear.

Function: Clothing for your baby girl or toddler

Special Features or Considerations:
* Organic cotton
* Machine washable

Playwear

Jackets
Multiple purchases
Age needed: 12 months

 Jackets are designed for various seasons throughout the year. They are often made with water-resistant material to keep your baby dry. Some jackets are lined in fleece for warmth in the winter. A combination jacket lets you detach the warmer fleece-lined section from a lighter section, making it versatile for spring and early fall.

Function: Keeps your baby warm and dry

Special Features or Considerations:
• Water-resistant
• Machine washable
• Lined with fleece
• Design

Soft-soled Shoes
One-time purchase
Age needed: Newborn

 Soft-soled shoes protect your baby's feet and help keep them warm. They are intended for use before your baby learns to walk.

Function: Protects your baby's feet

Special Features or Considerations:
• Cushioned insole
• Flexible outsole
• Slip-on
• Machine washable

Tennis Shoes
One-time purchase
Age needed: 9 months

 Tennis shoes protect your baby's feet when he starts walking. Tennis shoes come with hook-and-loop closures, ties, and slip-on styles.

Function: Protects your baby's feet when he is walking

Special Features or Considerations:
• Cushioned insole
• Nonskid tread
• Design

Sandals
One-time purchase
Age needed: 9 months

Sandals are footwear with an open heel and open toe for warm weather. Many sandals come with a hook-and-loop closure, allowing for easy on-and-off access.

Function: Protects your baby's feet and provides air circulation in hotter weather

Special Features or Considerations:
• Cushioned insole
• Nonslip soles

Swimwear and Sun Protection

Reusable Swim Diaper
Multiple purchases
Age needed: 3 months

 Reusable swim diapers are designed to keep moisture away from your baby's delicate skin and are snug-fitting around the legs and waist to prevent leakage that may contaminate pool water. You may find swim diapers that offer side-snap closures which allow for quick changing and minimize the mess associated with diaper changes.

Function: Covers and protects your baby in the pool and keeps waste from leaking into the water

Special Features or Considerations:
- Waterproof
- Absorbent pad and wick-away lining
- Machine washable
- UPF 50+
- Side snaps
- May come in fun prints and bright colors

Swimsuit for Boys
One-time purchase
Age needed: 6 months

 Boys' swim trunks are available in different styles—drawstring, elastic, or snap options. Some boys' swim trunks for babies and toddlers have a built-in swim diaper.

Functions: Covers your baby in the pool or at the beach

Special Features or Considerations:
- Machine washable
- Built-in swim diaper
- Elastic leg opening
- Design

Swimwear and Sun Protection

Swimsuit for Girls
One-time purchase
Age needed: 6 months

 Girls' swimsuits are available in different styles—one-piece with straps or a two-piece that pairs a top with a swim bottom. Some girls' swimsuits designed for babies and toddlers have a built-in swim diaper.

Function: Covers your baby in the pool or at the beach

Special Features or Considerations:
*   Machine washable
*   Built-in swim diaper
*   Elastic leg opening
*   Design

Swim Shoes
One-time purchase
Age needed: 9 months

 Swim shoes protect your baby's feet from sand or rocks on the beach, which can be extremely hot and burn his feet. They also protect him from slipping on wet surfaces at a pool or waterpark. Swim shoes are designed to get wet and can be worn in the pool, ocean, or lake.

Function: Protects your baby's feet when he is walking on the beach or waterpark and also in the pool, ocean, or lake

Special Features or Considerations:
*   Hook-and-loop closure
*   Stretchy fabric that is adjustable
*   Adjustable strap
*   Water-resistant
*   Textured outsole

Sunglasses
One-time purchase
Age needed: 6 months

 Sunglasses protect your baby's eyes from the sun's UVA/UVB rays. Some sunglasses have a built-in flexible band that keeps the sunglasses from falling off your baby's head. Usually the band is adjustable.

Function: Protects your baby's eyes from the sun

Special Features or Considerations:
*   100% UVA/UVB protection
*   Flexible material
*   Color

Beach Towels
One-time purchase
Age needed: 3 months

 A beach towel is a summer essential for the beach or pool. A small beach towel or hooded bath towel for your baby eliminates the bulk of regular adult-size towels.

Function: Dries off your baby after swimming at the beach or pool

Special Features or Considerations:
*   Absorbent
*   Organic cotton
*   Machine washable
*   May come in fun prints and bright colors to coordinate with his swimwear

Swimwear and Sun Protection

Sun Hat
Multiple purchases
Age needed: Newborn

 A sunhat designed with a wide brim helps protect your baby from the sun's UV rays. Light-weight fabrics that wick away moisture help keep him cool and dry. Some hats come with an under-the-chin strap that ties, snaps, or closes in place with hook-and-loop closure to help the sunhat stay in place.

Function: Covers your baby's head and protects him from the sun

Special Features or Considerations:
- UPF 50+
- 100% cotton or microfiber
- Machine washable
- May be purchased as a set, matching your baby's swimsuit or trunks

Rashguard
Multiple purchases
Age needed: 3 months

 Rashguards protect your baby from the sun during outdoor water activities. They can be paired with a swim diaper or swim trunks for your baby to wear in the pool. UPF 50+ Lycra material can be worn in the water and is stretchy to go over his head. They come in both short- and long-sleeved options.

Function: Protects your baby's skin from the sun and rashes that may come with outdoor activities

Special Features or Considerations:
- UPF 50+
- May be purchased as a set, matching your baby's swimsuit or trunks

Sun Protection Shirt
Multiple purchases
Age needed: 6 months

 Sun protection shirts protect your baby's skin during outdoor activities in the sun. They are designed with lightweight, UV-blocking fabric.

Functions: Protects your baby's skin from the sun and rashes that may come with outdoor play activities

Special Features or Considerations:
- UPF 50+
- Machine washable

Cover-up
Multiple purchases
Age needed: 3 months

 Cover-ups made from absorbent materials such as cotton terry are designed to be worn after swimming in the pool or on the beach. They may pull over or zip up. Some have a hood and pockets.

Function: Keeps your baby dry and warm after being in the water or playing on the beach

Special Features or Considerations:
- UPF 50+
- Machine washable
- Cotton terry

Outerwear

Raincoat
Multiple purchases
Age needed: 6 months

 Raincoats keep your baby dry when it is raining. During warmer months, a lightweight fabric is cooler and in cooler months a heavier fabric with a lining keeps him warm. Raincoats usually come with a hood to keep his head dry, and those made with elastic help keep the hood in place.

Function: Covers your baby and keeps him dry in the rain

Special Features or Considerations:
*   Water-resistant material
*   Machine washable
*   Drawstring travel bag
*   Breathable material
*   PVC-free

Rain Boots
Multiple purchases
Age needed: 6 months

 Rain boots keep your baby's feet dry in wet weather. Rain boots designed for young children often come with loops on the top for easy on and off.

Function: Keeps your baby's feet dry when it rains

Special Features or Considerations:
*   Cushioned insole
*   Rubber material
*   Nonslip soles
*   May come designed in bright colors and designs

Umbrella
One-time purchase
Age needed: 6 months

 Mostly for fun, toddlers love being in the rain with an umbrella. Be aware of the points on the end of the umbrella.

Function: Keeps your toddler dry in the rain

Special Features or Considerations:
*   Soft handle
*   Easy open and close
*   Design

Winter Boots
Multiple purchases
Age needed: 12 months

 Warm boots with fur or insulation inside and waterproofing on the outside for cold weather in rain or snow.

Function: Keeps your child's feet warm in cold weather

Special Features or Considerations:
*   Special Features and Considerations:
*   Closures
*   Insulation
*   Waterproofing

Outerwear

Waterproof Jacket
Multiple purchases
Age needed:

Waterproof jackets offer protection from wind, rain, and cool or cold weather. A lightweight, windbreaker-style jacket with a hood or a heavier weight jacket can be layered over for warmth. Look for elastic-band hood openings to ensure maximum wind and water-resistance.

Function: Keeps your baby warm and dry in cool weather

Special Features or Considerations:
- Water and wind resistant
- Machine washable
- Elastic band hood
- Weight
- Design

Bunting
One-time purchase
Age needed:

A bunting is designed to keep your baby warm and dry during the winter. Some buntings have a hood, covered or fold-over hand openings, and covered feet.

Function: Covers your baby to keep him warm and dry

Special Features or Considerations:
- Water-resistant cover
- Crotch snap
- Warm or fleece lining
- Machine washable

Mittens
One-time purchase
Age needed:

Fleece mittens help keep your baby's hands dry and warm during the colder months. Mittens that come with elastic wrist openings help keep mittens in place.

Functions: Covers your baby's hands to keep him warm

Special Features or Considerations:
- Water-resistant
- Recycled fleece
- Machine washable

Caps
One-time purchase
Age needed:

Fleece caps keep your baby's head dry and warm. Some fleece caps pull over his ears and have under-the-chin straps that tie or snap to help keep the cap in place.

Function: Covers your baby's head to keep him warm

Special Features or Considerations:
- Water-resistant outer fabric
- Recycled fleece lining
- Machine washable

On the Go

OUTINGS WITH YOUR BABY require foresight and planning to make sure that you have everything to satisfy your baby's needs. After a few excursions, you will know what to anticipate. The essential items include carriers for short walks and younger babies, strollers for shopping or for longer outings with toddlers, and car seats and accessories for errands around town or road trips.

Carriers and strollers

When you wear or carry your baby, either at home or when going out, he stays close and connected to you. Backpack carriers are not as cozy, but they are convenient and comfortable for hikes or long walks. Although carriers are the most intimate way to carry your baby, a stroller is convenient for shopping excursions and for toddlers who have become too heavy to carry. Depending on your lifestyle and where you live, you may go through many different stages and types of strollers—the bassinet or stroller system used in the first months to a full-size stroller, a universal stroller that can be converted to carry a car seat, an umbrella stroller for an older child, or a jogging stroller designed for a smooth ride. If you are adding on to your family, and you already have a toddler, a double stroller can be convenient. Extra accessories include stroller netting, a travel bag to attach to the back of the stroller, and stroller hooks.

Car seats

Your baby's car seat needs to change as he grows. For a minimum of a year, or until he reaches a minimum of 20 pounds, use a rear-facing seat. Car seats with a detachable base work well when your child is light enough to carry, so that you can easily take him out of the car and use the seat as a baby carrier. At this age, it is convenient to have an extra base for a second car so that you do not have to move the base from car to car. Until the age of four, children must use a car seat with a five-point harness, and then they switch to a booster seat until age eight. Other car accessories include a car seat undermat, a head and body support, strap covers, a waterproof seat liner, a car mirror, and a car window shade.

Accessories

Products that can be helpful for specific excursions include a cover for your shopping cart, a play yard that can be used as a portable crib, and a bicycle seat for your baby.

Carriers and Strollers

Baby Sling or Rebozo
Multiple purchases
Age needed: Newborn

Modern baby slings, based on the traditional rebozo, from Mexico, come in different options. You can choose from wraps, ring slings, stationary over-the-shoulder carriers, backpack-style carriers, and many more. Wraps are usually made from stretchy fabric and are tied in a knot for a personalized fit. Ring slings (also called rebozos) are adjustable through a ring at the shoulder, allowing you to adjust the fabric up or down for a secure fit and comfort for you and your baby.

Slings allow for you to carry your baby in a variety of positions, such as semi-reclining, nursing position, front or rear facing, sideways Buddha, or kangaroo position. Most slings are adjustable, so they can be used by different family members. They are designed with shoulder padding for comfort and support. They have storage pockets to carry a few things with you on the go.

Function: Supports your baby for you to carry him

Special Features or Considerations:
- Machine washable
- Front storage pocket
- Recommended for babies from 8 to 25 pounds

Backpack Carrier
One-time purchase
Age needed: 6 months

Backpack carriers can be used for short excursions around town as well as for hiking trips. Most carriers are made to distribute your baby's weight evenly to lighten your load. Usually the carriers have storage compartments, sun or rain hoods and loops for carrying toys. Smaller carriers are convenient for everyday use. More complex ones are designed for the outdoors.

Function: Carries your baby and other gear comfortably on your back

Special Features or Considerations:
- Weight of carrier
- Padded waist or hip belt
- Built-in stand for loading your baby
- Changing pad
- Diaper bag
- Rearview mirror
- Detachable pillow

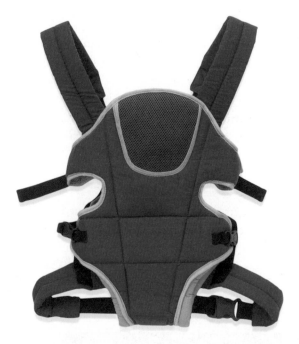

Carriers and Strollers

Stroller
Multiple purchases
Age needed: Newborn

When shopping for a stroller, consider your daily routine to help with your decision. Travel systems come equipped with a matching rear-facing car seat and car seat base, so you can move your baby's car seat directly from the base into the stroller and back with ease. Lightweight "umbrella" strollers may be all that you need once your baby is sitting up well and can hold his head up. A jogger stroller has special wheels designed for use while jogging. If you have multiple children, double, triple, and quad strollers are available to fit your needs.

Function: Holds your baby in a seated position while you walk and push him

Special Features or Considerations:
- Removable, machine-washable components
- Lockable wheels
- Multipoint safety harness
- Built-in/removable organizer tray
- Built-in cup holder
- Reclinable seat
- Collapsible

Stroller Muff
One-time purchase
Age needed: 6 months

Stroller muffs are usually made from soft, warm material and cover your baby's body, legs, and feet to keep him warm while he is riding in the stroller. Stroller muffs are closed at the bottom so the edges do not get caught in the stroller's wheels.

Function: Keeps your baby warm when he is in the stroller

Special Features or Considerations:
- Detachable
- Machine washable

Stroller Rain Cover and Sun Shade
One-time purchase
Age needed: Newborn

Most standard strollers come equipped with detachable covers that offer protection from the rain and provide shade from the sun while your baby is in the stroller.

Function: Covers and protects your baby from rain and the sun when he is riding in the stroller.

Special Features or Considerations:
- Detachable
- Machine washable

On-the-go Accessories

Stroller Netting
One-time purchase
Age needed: Newborn

Stroller netting attaches and covers most standard strollers, helping to protect your baby from the sun, wind, bugs, and rain.

Function: Covers your baby's stroller to protect him from the elements

Special Features or Considerations:
- Compatible with most standard strollers
- PVC-free and waterproof
- Wipes clean with soap and water

Travel Bag for Car Seat or Stroller
One-time purchase
Age needed: Newborn

Travel bags attach to a stroller or car seat to carry your essentials. Bags with short to medium straps do not get caught in stroller wheels as easily.

Function: Holds personal items and baby essentials on a stroller or car seat

Special Features or Considerations:
- Waterproof

Stroller Hooks
One-time purchase
Age needed: Newborn

Rather than having to hold everything in your hands, stroller hooks allow you to attach your purse, diaper bag, and shopping bags to your baby's stroller, helping you carry more when on the go.

Function: Attaches bags to your baby's stroller

Special Features or Considerations:
- Compatible with most standard strollers

Bicycle Seat
One-time purchase
Age needed: 9 months

Bicycle seats attach to most standard adult bikes, allowing you to bring your baby safely on a bike ride with you after he is at least 12 months old and sitting on his own.

Function: Attaches to your bike, so your baby can safely ride with you

Special Features or Considerations:
- Footrests for child
- Adjustable height
- Multipoint safety harness
- Locking safety lap bar
- Fits most standard adult bikes
- Safely holds children up to 50 pounds
- Removable/washable padding

On-the-go Accessories

Shopping Cart Covers
One-time purchase
Age needed: 6 months

Shopping cart covers drape over a store shopping cart for your baby to sit on directly. They protect your baby if he chews on the handles of the shopping cart. Shopping cart covers come in a variety of options, from small fold-up covers that fit inside your diaper bag to larger cushioned covers or those that have toys attached.

Function: Covers shopping cart handles to protect your baby from bumps, bruises, and germs

Special Features or Considerations:
- Machine washable
- Adjusts to fit on standard restaurant-style high chairs

Play Yard
One-time purchase
Age needed: 6 months

Play yards provide an enclosed space where your baby can play safely. They are easy to move from room to room or transport for traveling. Many play yards come equipped with a swinging gate and lock.

Function: Provides a safe place for your baby to play at home or when traveling

Special Features or Considerations:
- Rubber pads on bottom for stability and to prevent scratching of floors
- Locking gate
- Portable and movable (wheels)
- Removable bassinet and changer

Car Seats

Car Seat
One-time purchase
Age needed: Newborn

When shopping for a car seat, consider your baby's age and your lifestyle. There are a variety of styles to choose from, including an infant rear-facing car seat, a rear- and forward-facing toddler seat, a booster seat, and a convertible all-in-one seat. Rear-facing infant seats usually come with a detachable base and are designed to be used for approximately six to nine months. A rear- and forward-facing toddler seat can be used until your baby is about four years of age. It is recommended that you keep your baby rear facing as long as possible, with a minimum of two years. Once your toddler outgrows his toddler seat, he can graduate to a booster seat until he is around eight years old or 80 pounds. To avoid having to purchase multiple seats, you may opt for a convertible seat, which is usually designed to be used from birth through four years of age, when your toddler is ready to use a booster seat.

Function: Holds your baby and keeps him safe when riding in your car

Special Features or Considerations:
- Removable/machine-washable padding
- Multipoint safety harness
- Back closure
- Adjustable height
- Reclining seat
- Armrest
- Side impact protection
- Built-in cup and snack holder
- Meets the standards of Lower Anchors and Tethers for Children (LATCH) in the United States

Car Seats

Extra Car Seat Base
One-time purchase
Age needed: Newborn

 An extra car seat base for a rear-facing car seat can be convenient if your family has more than one vehicle. With an extra base you can use the same car seat with both cars. This avoids the cost of purchasing an extra car seat or having to uninstall and reinstall the same seat for different cars.

Functions: Provides an extra base for your car seat

Special Features or Considerations:
- LATCH equipped
- Car seat anchors
- Wipes clean with soap and water

Car Seat Undermat
One-time purchase
Age needed: Newborn

 Car seat undermats are designed to be placed under your baby's car seat, protecting the upholstery and keeping the car seat in position. Often these mats come equipped with a mesh bag for holding bottles, cups, or snacks.

Function: Protects the seat fabric under your baby's car seat

Special Features or Considerations:
Wipes clean with soap and water

Car Seats

Head and Body Support
One-time purchase
Age needed: Newborn

Head and body support inserts help your baby fit in the car seat snuggly and keep his head in place.

Function: Keeps your baby's head in place while in his car seat.

Special Features or Considerations:
*   Often comes with purchase of an infant car seat

Strap Covers
One-time purchase
Age needed: Newborn

Strap covers are usually made from a soft material, such as fleece. They go over the straps of your baby's car seat to protect him from irritation or chafing.

Function: Covers the straps on your baby's car seat

Special Features or Considerations:
*   Removable
*   Machine washable

Waterproof Seat Liner
One-time purchase
Age needed: Newborn

Waterproof seat liners fit in your baby's car seat to protect from diaper leaks and spills. These liners remove easily and are often machine washable.

Function: Protects your baby's car seat from spills

Special Features or Considerations:
*   Machine washable

Car Mirror
One-time purchase
Age needed: Newborn

Allows you to see your baby in a car seat while you drive.

Function: Helps you see your baby in the back seat of the car

Special Features or Considerations:
*   Fun shapes and colors to keep your baby's attention
*   Sturdy and convenient mounting
*   Visibility

Car Window Shade
Multiple purchases
Age needed: Newborn

Car window shades protect your baby by blocking the sun's dangerous UV rays and can keep him from overheating. Car window shades come in both stick-on strips and removable shades.

Function: Protects your baby from the sun

Special Features or Considerations:
*   UV protection
*   Stationary and removable options

Feeding

YOU START DECIDING WHAT to feed your baby as soon as he is born. Will you breast-feed, bottle-feed, or both? Once you have made that decision, what items do you need to support his feeding?

Nursing

Nursing requires less equipment and less money than bottle-feeding, but a few items can be helpful for nursing mothers. If you plan to go back to work or to spend a few hours away from your baby on a regular basis, you will need a breast pump to release and store your breast milk.

Bottles and cups

When bottle-feeding, you will need to decide which type of bottle to use. You may have to experiment with different bottles and nipple shapes before you find one that works for your baby. If your baby is not feeding well from one bottle, switch them until you find a successful combination. Check to see that nipples and bottles are BPA-free, PVC-free, and phthalate-free.

Bibs and burp pads

Before the age of six months, soft cotton bibs, wipes, and burp pads absorb your baby's spit-up and drool. If your baby drools a lot, a bib that is absorbent on one side but has waterproof backing prevents leaks on his clothes. When he begins eating solid foods, his mess increases, along with the need for waterproof material that wipes clean easily.

Food preparation

When you have the right tools, it is simple and economical to make your own baby food. You can easily make healthy and satisfying purees. It is helpful to consider the materials used in your food preparation items.

Furniture for feeding

High chairs come in many different styles that fit various homes and contexts. As your baby grows, he can sit at the table on a regular chair with a booster seat or a chair harness. A high-chair mat under his chair helps control the mess.

Dishes and utensils

When your baby starts eating solid foods, he will need plates and utensils. At first, you may use a long spoon to feed him from a bowl. As your child gets older and starts feeding himself, he will eat first with his fingers, and later with his own fork and spoon. When choosing these products, consider prioritizing natural materials, such as stainless steel, silicone, plant-based materials like corn, and plastics that are considered safe.

On the go

You will have to plan ahead for your baby's food needs when you go to a restaurant, send your baby to child care, or prepare for a picnic.

Nursing

Motorized Breast Pump
One-time purchase
Age needed: Newborn

Motorized breast pumps relieve pressure between feedings, stimulate lactation if you have a low milk supply, and store milk if you are away from your baby and cannot feed. A motorized pump is also helpful if you need to take medication that could be harmful for your baby and need to "pump and dump." Most motorized breast pumps are designed to fully disassemble for complete cleaning after each pumping session.

Function: Expresses breast milk efficiently

Special Features and Considerations:
- Includes milk storage bottles, extra flanges, sealing discs, cleaning brush, cleaning solution
- Bottle compatibility
- Travel carrying case included
- Battery operated or plugs into standard outlet
- Quiet operation

Manual Breast Pump
One-time purchase
Age needed: Newborn

With a hand-operated pump you can express breast milk without electricity. You can use it to relieve pressure between feedings or to build up a milk supply for future use. Manual pumps are lightweight and convenient for travel. Most pumps fully disassemble for complete cleaning after each pumping session.

Function: Expresses breast milk manually

Special Features and Considerations:
- Includes: milk storage bottles, extra flanges, sealing discs, cleaning brush, and cleaning solution
- Bottle compatibility
- Quiet operation
- No batteries or electricity required
- One-handed use
- Lightweight design travels well

Breast Milk Storage Bags
One-time purchase
Age needed: Newborn

Breast milk storage bags are convenient for storing and freezing breast milk. They are pre-sterilized and resealable with a pour spout for spill-proof transfer into a bottle. You can store bags in the freezer, and they are easily thawed. Most bags provide a place to write dates and other information.

Function: Space-saving breast milk storage for future use. Bags can be frozen or placed in the refrigerator

Special Features and Considerations:
- Pour spout
- Double-zip closure and tamper-evident safety seal

Nursing

Breast Pads
Multiple purchases
Age needed: Newborn

 Breast pads go inside a bra to prevent leakage. A contoured shape allows the breast pad to stay in place and helps keep nipples dry. Disposable options may have an adhesive strip to help them stay in place.

Function: Helps mom stay dry and comfortable in the case of breast milk leakage

Special Features and Considerations:
- Contoured
- Organic cotton
- Size and fit
- Waterproof
- Reusable—machine washable
- Disposable—cotton or paper material

Nursing Bra
Multiple purchases
Age needed: Newborn

 A nursing bra looks like a standard bra, but offers the extra support and functionality you need during breast-feeding. Bras that are 100% cotton, a blend of cotton and Lycra, or other stretchy fabrics provide flexibility and extra room for when your milk comes in.

Most women need a larger cup size during pregnancy and throughout breast-feeding. A tight bra can place pressure on your milk ducts, causing them to become clogged and possibly cause mastitis to set in.

Many nursing bras have added features such as cups that open or lower when you pull them aside or closures that unsnap, unzip, or unhook. Other convenient options allow you to open the cup for nursing easily with one hand.

Function: Provides support and allows easy access for nursing

Special Features and Considerations:
- 4-hook fastenings vs. standard two or three in the back provide added comfort
- Wide, nonslip shoulder straps provide extra support
- Cups that unclasp easily

Nursing

Nipple Cream
One-time purchase
Age needed: Newborn

 Nipple cream soothes and protects sore and cracked nipples. Many nipple creams contain lanolin. Lanolin is a greasy substance from sheep fur that is treated with pesticides and chemicals during processing. It is not recommended for babies to ingest lanolin. Lanolin-free and organic options are available for preventing and healing sore nipples.

Function: Soothe and protect nipples while breast-feeding

Special Features and Considerations:
- Lanolin-free
- Organic
- No taste, color, or perfume added
- No preservatives, chemicals, or other additives
- Hypoallergenic

Nursing Cover
One-time purchase
Age needed: Newborn

 A nursing cover provides full-coverage for discreet breast-feeding and cuts out surrounding distractions so your baby can feed quietly. They are also useful for bottle-fed babies. Nursing covers are lightweight and usually have a slightly raised edge, so you can watch your baby while nursing. They can also be used during breast-pumping sessions rather than going to a separate room.

Function: Provides full coverage for the nursing mom. Calms baby while nursing or bottle-feeding

Special Features and Considerations:
- Neck strap with adjustable height
- Folds easily and is lightweight
- Can be used as a shield from the sun in a stroller, front carrier, sling, or car seat
- Machine-washable options for easy cleaning

Nursing Pillow
One-time purchase
Age needed: Newborn

 Nursing pillows are crescent shaped to rest around your waist during nursing. This unique shape positions your baby for optimal feeding and provides added support to relieve back, neck, and shoulder stress during feeding. Nursing pillows are versatile and work with various nursing holds such as football, cradle, and cross-over. As your baby grows, nursing pillows can also be used for tummy time and provide additional support as he learns to sit.

Function: Positions your baby properly for optimal feeding. Helps relieve back, neck, and shoulder stress

Special Features and Considerations:
- Pillow is soft, comfortable, and firm enough to support your baby while nursing
- Machine-washable slip cover for easy cleaning
- Available in stylish prints
- Can also be used for tummy time, sitting support

Nursing Stool
One-time purchase
Age needed: Newborn

 Nursing stools provide leg support and alleviate stress on your back during breast-feeding. Although intended to be used during breast-feeding, they can also be used during pregnancy to prop your feet and avoid the onset of edema. Depending on height, stools can also be used as your baby grows, helping him reach the sink or the potty.

Function: Helps you comfortably position your baby for breast-feeding and alleviates stress on your back

Special Features and Considerations:
- Easy-to-use design
- Anti-slip base
- Use during pregnancy as a foot stool
- As your baby grows, it can be used as a step stool

Bottles and Cups

Feeding Bottles
Multiple purchases
Age needed: Newborn

 Feeding bottles come in various styles, shapes, sizes, and systems. Even if you are breast-feeding, you may need bottles for expressed milk. Choices of material include glass, plastic, or stainless steel. Do not put hot water into a plastic bottle or heat in a microwave, because the plastic can melt and leach into your baby's milk.

The size that works best for your baby depends on his age and eating level. Bottles have ounce markers on the side of the bottle so you can measure the exact amount you feed your baby. A travel cap keeps the nipple clean and provides extra leak protection when traveling. Some bottles are also breast-pump compatible so you can pump directly into the bottle, store your milk, and later feed directly out of the same bottle.

Function: Allows you to track your baby's daily intake in a bottle

Special Features and Considerations:
- BPA-free
- Breast-pump compatible
- Dishwasher safe
- Comes with extra bottle nipples
- Converts to sippy and straw cup
- Interchangeable with cups
- Leak proof
- Material—glass, plastic, or stainless steel

Bottle Nipples
Multiple purchases
Age needed: Newborn

 Bottle nipples are made from a variety of materials such as silicone or latex, and they usually come with the feeding bottle you purchase for your baby. Extra nipples are available for purchase separately.

As your baby grows, his needs change. Slow flow nipples are designed for your newborn until he is around 4 months old. From about four months of age to around 9 months, your baby may progress to a medium flow nipple. From about 9 months to 12 months, your baby may need a fast flow nipple. Babies have different, individual needs, so use the nipple that works best for your baby, regardless of his age.

Function: Attaches to your baby's bottle for feeding

Special Features and Considerations:
- BPA-free
- Dishwasher safe
- Ventilation to help reduce gas intake
- Mimics the shape of a mother's nipple

Bottles and Cups

Sippy Cup
Multiple purchases
Age needed: 6 months

 Sippy cups provide a transition from a bottle to a straw bottle or cup. They usually have a spill-proof valve built into the lid. Some sippys have wide, nonslip grips, making them easy for your baby to hold. Using a sippy spout after one year old may affect jaw and speech development. Material choices include glass, plastic, or stainless steel. Pay attention when he is drinking to be sure he does not choke.

Function: Helps your baby transition from a bottle to a cup

Special Features and Considerations:
• Material—glass, plastic, or stainless steel
• Valve to prevent spills
• Nonslip grip
• BPA- and PVC-free
• Dishwasher safe

Straw Bottle or Cup
Multiple purchases
Age needed: 12 months

 Straw bottles can help your baby transition from a sippy cup to a cup. Some babies skip sippy cups and go straight to a straw cup. Some straw cups have wide, nonslip grips, making them easy for your baby to hold. A pop-up straw helps keep the straw clean. A straw spout promotes healthy jaw and speech development. Material choices include glass, plastic, or stainless steel.

Function: Helps your baby transition from a sippy to a cup

Special Features and Considerations:
• Material—glass, plastic, or stainless steel
• Spill-proof straw system
• Nonslip grip
• BPA- and PVC-free
• Dishwasher safe

Bottle Brush
One-time purchase
Age needed: Newborn

 Bottle brushes have textured bristles to clean your baby's bottle and accessories. Some bottle brushes come equipped with a nipple brush that stores inside the handle.

Function: Cleans baby bottles

Special Features and Considerations:
• Includes nipple and bottle brush
• BPA-free
• Dishwasher safe
• Suction to the counter for easy storage

Bottles and Cups

Bottle Warmer
One-time purchase
Age needed: Newborn

Bottle warmers, used for both formula and breast milk, warm your baby's bottle evenly for a unified temperature. Some warmers come with an indicator light, which quietly alerts you that it is ready. Some may also have a removable basket and an automatic shutoff feature, which prevents overheating.

Function: Heats bottles easily

Special Features and Considerations:
• Heats evenly
• Removable basket
• Digital display
• Automatic shut-off
• Alarm sound

Bottle Sterilizer
One-time purchase
Age needed: Newborn

A bottle sterilizer's main function is to sterilize your baby's bottles. Many sterilizers can also be used on breast pump parts and accessories. Bottle sterilizers use steam for sterilization. Most sterilize 4–6 bottles at once, ranging in 2–10 minute cleaning times.

Function: Sterilizes your baby's bottles and accessories

Special Features and Considerations:
• Holds 4–6 bottles plus accessories
• Includes tongs
• Keeps components sterile for 24 hours
• Cycle time: 2–10 minutes
• Stay-cool handles
• Dishwasher safe

Dishwasher Basket and Drying Rack
One-time purchase
Age needed: Newborn

Dishwasher baskets contain small pieces and accessories while in a dishwasher. Some designs also serve as a drying rack.

Function: Holds small parts and accessories in the dishwasher

Special Features and Considerations:
• Basket capacity for small accessories
• Keeps straws upright
• Nipple sanitizing lid stores up to 14 nipples

Insulated Bottle Tote
One-time purchase
Age needed: Newborn

Insulated bottle totes provide insulation and storage when traveling to keep bottles cool or warm. Some styles have hooks for attaching to a diaper bag or stroller.

Function: Keeps milk or liquid cool or warm

Special Features and Considerations:
• Fits into diaper bags
• Attaches to stroller
• Interior or exterior mesh pockets for added storage
• Multiple compartments
• Accommodates various bottle sizes

Bibs and Burp Pads

Burp Pads
Multiple purchases
Age needed: Newborn

 Burps pads are made from absorbent cotton. Some have a waterproof layer for added protection. You can lay burp pads over your shoulder or lap when burping your baby to protect your clothes from spit-up and drool.

Function: Protects clothing from baby spit-ups

Special Features and Considerations:
- Organic cotton
- Contoured
- Waterproof inner layer
- Machine washable

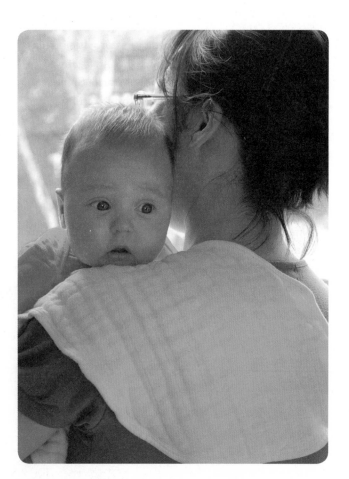

Cloth Wipes
Multiple purchases
Age needed: Newborn

Cloth wipes are convenient for wiping drips and drools as well as for cleaning your baby's bottom. Muslin or flannel cloth wipes are soft and absorbent. Cloth wipes are reusable and economical, and are often sold in multipacks.

Function: Wipes your baby

Special Features and Considerations:
- Organic cotton
- Soft
- Absorbent
- Size
- Multipacks

Newborn Bibs
Multiple purchases
Age needed: Newborn

 Newborn drool bibs are small absorbent bibs designed to protect your baby's clothes by catching drool and spit-ups.

Function: Protects your baby's clothes from drools and spit-ups

Special Features and Considerations:
- Organic cotton
- Absorbent
- Adjustable neck closure
- Machine washable

Bibs and Burp Pads

Infant Bibs
Multiple purchases
Age needed: 6 weeks

 Between 3 and 6 months, babies drool a lot and need a bib to keep their clothes from getting wet. Infant cloth bibs are usually made of absorbent material and may have a waterproof layer to help prevent leaks. They often come in multipacks for everyday use.

Function: Protects your baby's clothes from drips, drools, and messes

Special Features and Considerations:
- Absorbent cotton
- Waterproof inner layer
- Adjustable neck closure
- Machine washable

Waterproof Bibs
Multiple purchases
Age needed: 6 months

 Waterproof bibs are convenient when your baby starts eating solids, usually around 6 months. Waterproof fabric protects your baby's clothes from food messes . They are usually made from a stain-resistant material that can easily be wiped clean with a damp cloth. Some waterproof bibs also come with a pocket that catches excess food and crumbs.

Function: Provides a wipeable surface to keep your baby clean when he is eating solids

Special Features and Considerations:
- Waterproof
- Catch pocket
- Adjustable neck closure
- Easy to clean
- PVC-free

Full-coverage Waterproof Bibs
Multiple purchases
Age needed: 9 months

 Full-coverage bibs cover your baby's front, shoulders, and arms. They fit over your child's clothes and often come with a pocket to catch food. Full-coverage bibs can also serve as smock for toddlers during art projects.

Function: Protect your baby's clothes with extra coverage

Special Features and Considerations:
- Waterproof
- Catch pocket
- Full coverage for messy eating
- Adjustable neck closure
- Easy to clean
- PVC-free

Food Preparation

Reusable Pouch
One-time purchase
Age needed: 6 months

 You can fill your own reusable pouches with homemade baby food puree. With pouches, your baby can eat by himself without a lot of mess. When you use a reusable pouch, you reduce waste from disposable pouches.

Function: Stores pureed food for your baby

Special Features and Considerations:
- Dishwasher safe
- PVC-free
- Ease of use
- Attachments needed

Baby Food Storage Cubes
Multiple purchases
Age needed: 6 months

 You can store homemade baby food for future use in storage containers made of glass, silicone, or plastic. Most cubes come with a labeling system to keep track of what is in each container and when it was made. Secure locking lids help avoid spills.

Function: Stores homemade food for future use

Special Features and Considerations:
- BPA-free
- Storage tray for stacking
- Labeling system

Blender
One-time purchase
Age needed: 6 months

 A glass blender purees your baby's food when he starts eating solids without leaching plastics into it.

Function: Purees your baby's food

Special Features and Considerations:
- Size
- Speed
- Cost

Heat Diffuser
One-time purchase
Age needed: 6 months

 You can cook your baby's homemade food without scorching it by using a heat diffuser. Place the diffuser under your pot while cooking to reduce the risk of burning food.

Function: Evenly distributes heat to prevent hot spots while cooking baby food

Special Features and Considerations:
- Handle for holding

Food Preparation

Cooking Pot
One-time purchase
Age needed: 6 months

 Make your baby's grains, vegetables, beans, and fruits in a cooking pot that is made of stainless steel. You can cook two things at one time with a steamer basket at the top. A glass lid allows you to see the inside of the pot while cooking. Covered handles are convenient and protect you from burning yourself while cooking. A stainless steel covered aluminum bottom conducts heat evenly.

Function: Cooks your baby's food

Special Features and Considerations:
- Stainless steel
- Glass lid
- Thickness of pan
- Covered handles
- Steamer basket
- Size
- Stainless steel-covered bottom

Grinder Bowl
One-time purchase
Age needed: 6 months

 You can grind your baby's puree with a wooden pestle and ceramic bowl that is designed with grooves inside for grinding. Starchy vegetables such as squash, carrots, peas, and other vegetables as well as fruits are easy to grind without getting out the blender.

Function: Grinds your baby's puree quickly and easily

Special Features and Considerations:
- Ceramic material
- Grooves inside
- Wooden pestle
- Size
- Color

Furniture for Feeding

Standard High Chairs
One-time purchase
Age needed: 6 months

A baby high chair provides an elevated, safe space for you to feed your baby when he starts eating solids, around six months of age. Many high chairs offer safety options such as convertible harnesses and locking wheels to provide added stability. Some other features available are 4-in-1 systems so that the high chair can be used longer. The system works as a high chair, infant feeding booster, toddler booster, and youth chair. Some have an infant head and body support that keeps your baby in a comfortable position for feeding. Chairs have different height positions and reclining levels to help adjust your baby as he grows.

Function: Provides elevated seating to feed your baby

Special Features and Considerations:
- Converting 4-in-1 systems
- Convertible 3-and 5-point harness secures your baby
- Different height positions and reclining levels
- Removable, dishwasher-safe tray, pull-out insert makes cleanup quick and easy
- Machine washable
- Infant head and body support
- Front wheels and locking rear casters provide stability by keeping chair in place during meals

European-style High Chairs
One-time purchase
Age needed: 6 months

European-style high chairs are tray-less and generally do not have wheels. Most fit under the edge of standard dining tables, allowing your baby to sit at the dining table with you. Your baby can use European-style high chairs once they are able to sit well unassisted, around nine months.

Function: Provides safe elevation for your baby. Avoids the bulky design of the standard high chair and allows your baby to sit with you at the table

Special Features and Considerations:
- Your baby must be able to sit well unassisted
- Fits under the edge of most standard tables.
- Safety strap holds baby in place while eating
- Solid construction ensures long-lasting use

Furniture for Feeding

Booster Seat
One-time purchase
Age needed: 18 months

 At approximately 18 months of age, a booster seat allows your baby to sit in a regular dining chair with the rest of the family. Booster seats strap directly to the chair and provide a seat belt to prevent him from falling.

Function: Boosts your toddler to sit

Special Features and Considerations:
- Adjustable seat height
- Harness with straps to keep baby strapped in for safety
- Lightweight and easy to fold
- Used with any size chair
- Washable
- Weight limit: up to 50 lbs (most children stop needing booster seats at the table around 35–40 lbs, depending on your child's height and the table)

High Chair Mat
One-time purchase
Age needed: 6 months

 When your baby is learning to eat on his own, he can be very messy. High chair mats or splat mats are washable mats placed under his high chair or booster to protect the floor underneath and provide easy cleanup after mealtime.

Function: Easy mess cleanup and protected floors

Special Features and Considerations:
- Reusable and durable
- Easy to clean
- Compact for easy travel
- Wipe clean, line dry
- Multifunctional: during mealtime, picnics, and for art projects
- Protective barrier between your baby and bare floors

Chair Harness
One-time purchase
Age needed: 3 months

 Designed with a four-or five-point safety harness and adjustable straps, chair harnesses make feeding on-the- go simple and safe when a high chair is not available. Chair harnesses strap securely to adult chairs to accommodate your baby from around five months of age through his toddler years.

Function: Secures your baby in an adult chair when a high chair is not available

Special Features and Considerations:
- Machine washable
- Lightweight
- Easy travel

Food Journal
One-time purchase
Age needed: Newborn

 When your baby starts eating solid foods, keeping a food journal can be helpful to track his reactions to new foods and tastes.

Function: Records your baby's eating history

Special Features or Considerations:
- Age range
- Space for extra pages
- Complete information

Dishes and Utensils

Infant Spoons
Multiple purchases
Age needed: 6 months

 Infant spoons have long handles for feeding your baby first foods. They are made from soft materials that are gentle on your baby's gums. Infant spoons usually have shallow tips for small bites.

Function: Scoops baby food puree

Special Features and Considerations:
• BPA- and PVC-free
• Dishwasher safe
• Curved handle for guiding food
• Soft silicone scoop on end of spoon

Toddler Utensils
Multiple purchases
Age needed: 12 months

 Toddler utensils are usually rounded to prevent injury as your toddler learns to use them. They have shallow tips for toddler bites. Small forks, spoons, and knives help your toddler learn how to self-feed without using his hands.

Functions: Fit your toddler's hands to help him learn to self-feed

Special Features and Considerations:
• BPA-, PVC-, and melamine-free
• Dishwasher safe
• Nonslip grip

Plates and Bowls
Multiple purchases
Age needed: 6 months

 Small plates and bowls for your baby or toddler are sized to meet his needs. Many designs include dividers to separate foods and raised edges to help food stay in place. While your baby learns to self-feed, he may drop plates and bowls many times. Sturdy materials can help prevent breakage.

Functions: Provides a clean surface for your toddler at mealtime

Special Features and Considerations:
• BPA-, PVC-, and melamine-free
• Built-in dividers
• Dishwasher safe

Placemats
Multiple purchases
Age needed: 12 months

 Placemats help contain messes and provide a clean area for eating. They often have a nonslip grip to hold the mat securely in place.

Function: Provides a clean eating area for your baby

Special Features and Considerations:
• PVC-free
• Nonslip grip
• Dishwasher safe
• Waterproof

On-the-Go Feeding

To-go Containers
Multiple purchases
Age needed: 6 months

 To-go Containers are lightweight food containers for easy portability. You can use leftovers or make a lunch or snack for travel, child care, preschool, or picnics. Material choices include glass, plastic, stainless steel, bioplastic, and silicone.

Function: Carries homemade food and snacks easily

Special Features and Considerations:
- BPA-, PVC-, and melamine-free
- Dishwasher safe
- Secure grips
- Matching utensils
- Materials-glass, plastic, stainless steel, bioplastic, or silicone

Insulated Bags
Multiple purchases
Age needed: 6 months

 Bags with an insulated lining keep food and liquids warm or cool when you are on the go. They often have room for an ice pack on the side or bottom. Those with a waterproof coating help keep the outside of the bag dry from condensation buildup and from spills. These bags may have a carrying handle and a zip compartment to keep bottles secure.

Function: Holds food to maintain temperature control

Special Features and Considerations:
- Waterproof
- Multiple compartments

Ice Pack
Multiple purchases
Age needed: Newborn

 An ice pack is a plastic bag that has a nontoxic gel inside. After it is frozen, it keeps food and bottles inside an insulated bag cool when going out.

Function: Keeps food cool when going out

Special Features and Considerations:
- Nontoxic gel

Bento Box
One-time purchase
Age needed: 6 months

 A bento box is a container for packing healthy and visually appealing food for your child when he goes out. You can use leftovers or fresh foods to make a balanced meal. For a special treat, make sandwiches or rice balls in fun shapes.

Function: Stores your baby's food when going out

Special Features and Considerations:
- Natural materials
- Fun designs
- Closure
- Stacking or single layer
- Inserts for individual portions

Food Scissors
One-time purchase
Age needed: 6 months

 Food scissors are convenient to cut and mash table food into small, bite-sized-pieces for your baby at home or on the go.

Functions: Mashes table food into bite-sized pieces

Special Features and Considerations:
- For use at home or going out
- Durable ceramic blades

Toys

YOUR BABY LEARNS THROUGH play, and toys are his tools. I have identified seven pathways of learning that help him establish a foundation for development: senses, movement, interactive, communication, cognition, creativity, and nature. When you purchase toys, consider these different sources of learning. He may be especially strong in one or two areas, but you can help him develop all of his pathways so that they integrate and create balance. Some toys may stimulate your baby through several pathways. For example, a puppet encourages movement, interaction, and sensory stimulation at the same time. A book about nature can inspire his senses, communication, movement, interaction, cognition, nature, and creativity in one sitting.

Toys do not need to be complicated or expensive to stimulate your child. In fact, simple, open-ended toys and familiar items around the house offer opportunities for him to use his imagination and curiosity when playing. Visually appealing toys made of natural materials provide experiences that teach him about beauty and the qualities of objects. Versatile toys that can be used for different stages of learning save money and reduce clutter. Safety issues regarding toys include materials, construction, and potential choking hazards.

For his first year, your child learns mostly through his senses and movement. As he grows, he begins to interact with himself and you through language. As he develops higher mental functions, he engages in more complex thought processes, begins to solve problems, and masters cause and effect relationships. Then he develops his creativity through art, music, and imagination. All along the way, your baby learns through nature.

The toys in this section are listed in order of the age when he will start playing with them. Some toys, such as balls and plush toys, may be favorites throughout both infancy and toddlerhood.

Developmental Toys

Push
One-time purchase
Age needed: 6 months

 Push toys come in a variety of designs ranging from the classic "popcorn popper" to toys on wheels that are low to the ground. Push toys can help your baby balance as he is learning to walk.

Function: Encourages mobility for scooting, crawling, and walking. Develop gross- and fine-motor skills while promoting an understanding of cause and effect

Special Features or Considerations:
- Wheels for easy mobility
- Easy to grasp
- Additional features such as sound or movement

Pull
Multiple purchases
Age needed: 12 months

 Pull toys are more difficult to use than push toys, because your baby has to go forward while looking behind him. Pull toys have additional features when they are rolled across the floor, such as a wiggling tail or flapping wings.

Function: Encourages your baby to walk and engage in imaginative play. Builds gross- and fine-motor skills such as balance and coordination as well as an understanding of cause and effect

Special Features or Considerations:
- Wheels for easy mobility
- A short pull string that cannot loop for safety
- A familiar animal for imaginative play

Ball
Multiple purchases
Age needed: 6 months

 A soft ball made from fabric and other plush materials is a first ball for your baby. A ball can also function as a tactile toy that is safe for him to put in his mouth. You can progress to bouncier balls and games requiring more coordination when your baby is older.

Function: Advances gross-motor skills, and helps develop an understanding of sharing and cooperation when used in a game with others

Special Features or Considerations:
- Soft, interesting textures
- Lightweight
- Visually stimulating colors and patterns
- Inner chimes or rattles

Developmental Toys

Bath
Multiple purchases
Age needed: 6 months

 Bath toys make bath time more fun for your baby while he learns at the same time. He can play with bath toys in multiple ways including pouring, floating, and dunking in the water. Bath appliqués that stick to the side of the bathtub are textured for tactile sensation.

Function: Bath toys stimulate all seven pathways

Special Features or Considerations:
- Multifunctional
- Float, pour
- Mold and mildew resistant
- PVC-free

Doll
Multiple purchases
Age needed: 12 months

 A soft doll inspires interaction for your baby. Playing with and taking care of a doll encourages early role play for emotional and social development.

Function: Inspires your baby to mirror affection and emotions, develop verbal skills, and learn empathy and nurturing

Special Features or Considerations:
- Easy to hold and carry
- Machine washable

Attachable
Multiple purchases
Age needed: Newborn

 Attachable toys link to strollers, carriers, and other surfaces around your baby. They stimulate visual development, reaching and grasping. Attachable toys can be simple, colorful links or include features such as mirrors, sounds, plush pieces, and teethers.

Function: Encourages visual development, height and depth perception, gross-motor skills, and hand-eye coordination

Special Features or Considerations:
- Versatile
- Portable
- Easy transfer between surfaces

Transportation
Multiple purchases
Age needed: 6 months

 Transportation toys such as cars, buses, and planes develop fine-motor skills and imagination. They are usually small enough for your baby to grasp with his hand. Most transportation toys have wheels and roll along a hard surface.

Function: Inspires imaginative play while building fine-motor skills

Special Features or Considerations:
- Wheels for easy movement
- Multiple types of transportation

Developmental Toys

Rattles
Multiple purchases
Age needed: 3 months

 Rattles make sounds that stimulate your baby to learn when he listens and responds.

Function: Helps with auditory and visual development, fine-motor skills, and understanding cause and effect

Special Features or Considerations:
- Materials that are safe for baby such as wood, cornstarch, organic fabric, and polypropylene
- Different sounds

Puppets
Multiple purchases
Age needed: 3 months

 Puppets come sized for individual fingers or the entire hand. They often represent animals, people, or other characters. There are also puppets designed especially for the bath. Puppets can be used by you or your baby, depending on the size of the puppet and the age of your baby.

Function: Stimulates sensory, interactive play, mimicry, verbal development, and imagination

Special Features or Considerations:
- Soft and lightweight
- Portable
- Imaginative

Developmental Toys

Mobile
One-time purchase
Age needed: 3 months

 Mobiles offer visual stimulation for your baby. They often come with graphic shapes and bright colors that hang above your baby's head and may spin in a circular motion. Some mobiles also play soothing music.

Function: Helps your baby's eyes focus to develop his vision

Special Features or Considerations:
- Crib attachment
- On-off timer
- Volume control for music

Play Mat
One-time purchase
Age needed: 3 months

 A play mat allows your baby to explore on his stomach or lay on his back. It is usually made of soft materials so he is comfortable during tummy time. Play mats feature bright colors, fun characters, and different textures to engage your baby's senses.

Function: Provides a flat surface for your baby to explore

Special Features or Considerations:
- Bright, contrasting colors and patterns
- Fun motifs
- Different tactile elements
- Lightly padded and made of soft materials

Mirrors
Multiple purchases
Age needed: 3 months

 A safety mirror stimulates the interactive pathway. A regular mirror that is securely anchored also teaches your baby to recognize himself.

Function: Inspires self-awareness and self-discovery, helps develop vision (including tracking and depth perception), and promotes social and emotional growth

Special Features or Considerations:
- Unbreakable safe materials
- Nondistorted image

Exploration
Multiple purchases
Age needed: 3 months

 Exploration toys inspire your baby to discover the natural world around him. For younger babies, this may be as simple as putting objects in a bucket, while older babies may enjoy a safety magnifying glass or a net for chasing after butterflies.

Function: Encourages collecting and investigating in the natural world. Promotes curiosity and an interest in nature while using fine- and gross-motor skills and spatial awareness

Special Features or Considerations:
- Can grow with your baby
- Easy to use
- Engaging

Developmental Toys

Plush
Multiple purchases
Age needed: 3 months

 Plush toys provide sensory stimulation, imagination, and interaction. They can be soothing to your baby at bedtime and during other moments of stress or separation anxiety.

Function: Helps develop social skills and encourage tactile exploration

Special Features or Considerations:
* Soft textures
* Machine washable

Role Play
One-time purchase
Age needed: 12 months

 Role play toys include tools, garden tools, a play kitchen., toddler-sized grocery carts, lawnmowers, or vacuum cleaners.

Function: Encourages role play of activities

Special Features or Considerations:
* Grows with your baby and can last throughout his toddler years

Teethers
Multiple purchases
Age needed: 3 months

 Teethers come in a variety of sizes, shapes, and textures. Some are made from solid materials while others are filled with water and can be chilled.

Function: Helps alleviate pain associated with teething. Stimulates sensory development in your baby's mouth

Special Features or Considerations:
* PVC-free
* Wide variety of colors, textures, and shapes

Stacking
Multiple purchases
Age needed: 6 months

 Stacking toys include rings, cubes, boats, or cups. Bright colors, numbers, and nesting shapes help your baby stack and sort. Water-resistant toys can be fun in the bath, too.

Function: Develops fine- and gross-motor skills, problem solving, visual development, and cause and effect

Special Features or Considerations:
* Dual function: nesting and stacking
* Different colors for easy identification
* Bath toys

Developmental Toys

Sand Toys
Multiple purchases
Age needed: 6 weeks

 Sand toys are fun at the beach, in a sandbox, or for water play. Sand toys move sand around through sorting cups, a funnel, or with a bucket and shovel.

Function: Develops fine-motor and tactile skills, as well as hand-eye coordination. Playing outside in the sand inspires an appreciation for the natural world

Special Features or Considerations:
• Versatile—can also be used with water

Riding Toys
One-time purchase
Age needed: 24 months

 Your baby develops coordination and muscles as he learns to scoot along on a riding toy with his feet. Riding toys include balance bicycles, tricycles, wagons, cars, and other vehicles. There are also designs that grow along with your baby, transitioning from a tricycle you push for him to one he pedals himself.

Function: Develops gross-motor skills, balance, and coordination, while inspiring confidence, mobility, and exploration

Special Features or Considerations:
• Wide wheel base
• Easy-grasp handles
• Transitional

Dramatic Play
Multiple purchases
Age needed: 12 months

 Your child can develop his imagination by expressing himself in dramatic play. Simple dress-up accessories stimulate creativity.

Function: Teaches social and emotional skills

Special Features or Considerations:
• Versatile with endless options for characters
• Machine washable

Newborn Shopping List

Nursery (Quantity) Product

- ☐ (1) Crib
- ☐ (1) Mattress
- ☐ (1) Crib Mattress Pad
- ☐ (1) Fitted Sheet
- ☐ (4) Receiving Blanket
- ☐ (4-6) Swaddle Blanket
- ☐ (3-4) Wearable Blanket
- ☐ (1) Changing Table
- ☐ (1) Changing Pad
- ☐ (1) Dresser or Shelves

Optional (Quantity) Product

- ☐ (1) Cradle, Bassinet, or Moses Basket
- ☐ (1) Co-Sleeper
- ☐ (2-4) Sheet Savers
- ☐ (1) Quilt
- ☐ (1) Sound Machine
- ☐ (1) Monitor
- ☐ (1) Night-Light
- ☐ (1) Rocking Chair or Glider

- ☐ (1) Ottoman
- ☐ (1 set) Wall Decal
- ☐ (1) Switchplate Cover
- ☐ (1) Growth Chart
- ☐ (2-3) Photo Frames
- ☐ (1) Baby Book
- ☐ (3-4) Photo Album
- ☐ (1) 24pk Birth Announcements
- ☐ (1) Handprint Kit
- ☐ (1 per window) Curtains or Blinds

Babycare (Quantity) Product

- ☐ (1) Sink or Bathtub Insert
- ☐ (1) Tub Spout Cover
- ☐ (3-4) Hooded Towels
- ☐ (6-12) Washcloths
- ☐ (1 per month) Oil or Lotion
- ☐ (1 per month) Diaper Balm
- ☐ (1) Nail Clippers
- ☐ (1) Scratch Mitts
- ☐ (1) Diaper Cover
- ☐ (12-24) Flat Pre-fold Cloth Diaper
- ☐ (24-36) Contoured Insert
- ☐ (24-36) Fitted Diapers
- ☐ (1) 100pk Diaper Liner
- ☐ (12-18 per day) Disposable Inserts
- ☐ (24-36) All-in-one Diapers

- ☐ (12-18 per day) Disposable Diapers
- ☐ (18-24) Cloth Diapers
- ☐ (1-2) Diaper Bag
- ☐ (20 per week) Disposable Wipes
- ☐ (12-24) Diaper Pail
- ☐ (1-2) Diaper Changing Mat
- ☐ (1) Health Journal
- ☐ (1) First-Aid Kit
- ☐ (1) Nasal Aspirator
- ☐ (1) Medicine Dispenser
- ☐ (1) Thermometer
- ☐ (1 per month) Nontoxic Cleaning Supplies
- ☐ (1 per month) Gentle Laundry Detergent

Optional (Quantity) Product

- ☐ (1) Bath Toy Storage
- ☐ (1) No-slip Bath Mat
- ☐ (1) Tub Thermometer
- ☐ (1) Wipe Warmers
- ☐ (2-3) Pacifier
- ☐ (1) Humidifier

Download shopping lists at
growhealthygrowhappy.com

"Artificial Sweeteners and Cancer." National Cancer Institute at the National Institutes of Health. Last accessed June 13, 2014. http://www.cancer.gov/cancertopics/factsheet/Risk/artificial-sweeteners.

"Asbestos." U.S. Environmental Protection Agency. Last modified May 19, 2014. Last accessed June 16, 2014. http://www2.epa.gov/asbestos.

"Aspartame." American Cancer Society. Last modified May 28, 2014. Last accessed June 13, 2014. http://www.cancer.org/cancer/cancercauses/othercarcinogens/athome/aspartame.

ATSDR. "Arsenic." Centers for Disease Control and Prevention. Last modified March 3, 2011. Last accessed June 16, 2014. http://www.atsdr.cdc.gov/substances/toxsubstance.asp?toxid=3.

———. "Cadmium Toxicity: What Diseases Are Associated with Chronic Exposure to Cadmium?" Centers for Disease Control and Prevention. Last modified May 12, 2008. Last accessed June 16, 2014. http://www.atsdr.cdc.gov/csem/csem.asp?csem=6&po=12.

———. "Propylene Glycol." Centers for Disease Control and Prevention. Last modified March 3, 2011. Last accessed June 16, 2014. http://www.atsdr.cdc.gov/substances/toxsubstance.asp?toxid=240.

"Avoid Nitrates and Nitrites in Food." Healthy Child Healthy World. Last Modified April 1, 2013. Last accessed June 13, 2014. http://healthychild.org/easy-steps/avoid-nitrates-and-nitrites-in-food/.

Azad, Meghan B., et al. "Gut Microbiota of Healthy Canadian Infants: Profiles by Mode of Delivery and Infant Diet at 4 Months." *Canadian Medical Association Journal* 185:5 (2013): 385–394.

Baggish, Jeff. *How Your Immune System Works*. Emeryville, CA: Ziff-Davis, 1994.

Balch, Phyllis A. *Prescription for Nutritional Healing: A Practical A-to-Z Reference to Drug-Free Remedies Using Vitamins, Minerals, Herbs & Food Supplements*. New York: Avery, 2010.

Baldwin, Peyton. "Why Organic Cotton Is Better." *Mother Earth News*. Last modified June 3, 2008. Last accessed June 16, 2014. http://www.motherearthnews.com/nature-and-environment/organic-cotton-benefits.aspx#axzz32IGvn8Fy.

Baldwin Dancy, Rahima. *You Are Your Child's First Teacher: Encouraging Your Child's Natural Development from Birth to Age Six*. New York: Ten Speed Press, 2012.

Baron, Renee, and Elizabeth Wagele. *The Enneagram Made Easy: Discover the 9 Types of People*. San Francisco: HarperSanFrancisco, 1994.

Bartlett, Kelly. "Natural Discipline for the Early Years." *Green Child Magazine*. April 30, 2013. Last accessed March 12, 2014. http://www.greenchildmagazine.com/natural-discipline-for-the-early-years/.

"Basic Principles of Classical Adlerian Psychology." Alfred Adler Institutes of San Francisco and Northwestern Washington. Last accessed June 25, 2014. http://www.adlerian.us/.

Baumrind, Diana. "Child Care Practices Anteceding Three Patterns of Preschool Behavior." *Genetic Psychology Monographs* 75:1 (1967): 43–88.

Belic, Roko, dir. *Happy*. Film. Warren, NJ: Passion River Films, 2012.

Belleme, Jan, and John Belleme. *Cooking with Japanese Foods: A Guide to the Traditional Natural Foods of Japan*. Garden City Park, NY: Avery Pub. Group, 1993.

Bem, Sandra L. "The Measurement of Psychological Androgyny." *Journal of Consulting and Clinical Psychology* 42:2 (1974): 155–162.

Benaroch, Roy. *A Guide to Getting the Best Health Care for Your Child*. Westport, CT: Praeger, 2007.

Berman, Jenn. *Superbaby: 12 Ways to Give Your Child a Head Start in the First 3 Years*. New York: Sterling, 2010.

"BHT." Environmental Working Group. Last accessed June 25, 2014. http://www.ewg.org/skindeep/ingredient/700741/BHT/.

Birch, Stephen. *Shonishin: Japanese Pediatric Acupuncture*. Stuttgart, Germany: Thieme, 2011.

"Bisphenol A Frequently Asked Questions." BisphenolA. Last accessed June 25, 2014. http://www.bisphenol-a.org/about/faq.html?gclid=CMKUu-TLqbsCFdEWMgodOQIAjg.

Blackburn, Victoria, and Jessica Seminara. "What Is Formamide?" WiseGeek. Last accessed June 16, 2014. http://www.wisegeek.com/what-is-formamide.htm.

Bliss, Nishanga. *Real Food All Year: Eating Seasonal Whole Foods for Optimal Health & All-Day Energy*. Oakland, CA: New Harbinger Publications, 2012.

Bodrova, Elena, and Deborah J. Leong. *Tools of the mind: the Vygotskian approach to early childhood education*. 2nd ed. Upper Saddle River: Pearson Ed., 2007.

Boggeman, Sally, Tom Hoerr, and Christine Wallach. *Succeeding with Multiple Intelligences: Teaching through the Personal Intelligences*. St. Louis: New City School, 1996.

Bond, Annie B. "Which Plastics Are Safe?" Care2. Last accessed June 13, 2014. http://www.care2.com/greenliving/which-plastics-are-safe.html.

Bragdon, Liz. "4 Breathing Exercises for Kids to Empower, Calm, and Self-Regulate." Move with Me Action Adventures, January 30, 2012. Last accessed March 12, 2014. http://move-with-me.com/self-regulation/4-breathing-exercises-for-kids-to-empower-calm-and-self-regulate/.

Clothing (Quantity) Product

☐ (1) Homecoming Outfit	☐ (6-12 pairs) Socks	**Optional** (Quantity) Product
☐ (4-6) Bodysuits	☐ (2-4 pairs) Booties	☐ (1) Footed Knit Pants
☐ (6-9) Garment Extenders	☐ (3-4) Pullover Sweaters	☐ (1) Cardigan Sweaters
☐ (3) Gowns	☐ (2-4) Rompers	☐ (3-4) Bunting
☐ (4-6) Knit Caps	☐ (1 pair) Soft-soled Shoes	☐ (1 pair) Mittens
☐ (3-4) Side Snap Knit Shirts	☐ (2-3) Sunhat	☐ (1) Caps
☐ (3-4) One-Piece Footies		

On the Go (Quantity) Product

☐ (1-3) Baby Sling/Rebozo	**Optional** (Quantity) Product	
☐ (1) Stroller	☐ (1) Stroller Rain Cover and Sun Shade	☐ (1) Head and Body Support
☐ (1) Travel Bag for Car Seat or Stroller	☐ (1) Stroller Netting	☐ (1) Strap Covers
☐ (1) Car Seat	☐ (1) Stroller Hooks	☐ (1) Car Window Shade
	☐ (1) Extra Car Seat Base	☐ (1) Waterproof Seat Liner
	☐ (1-2) Car Seat Undermat	☐ (1) Car Mirror

Feeding (Quantity) Product

☐ (1) Motorized Breast Pump	☐ (12) Bottle Nipples	**Optional** (Quantity) Product
☐ (1-25pk) Breast Milk Storage Bags	☐ (6) Insulated Bottle Tote	☐ (1) Manual Breast Pump
☐ (1 per month) Breast Pads	☐ (6-12) Burp Pads	☐ (1) Bottle Brush
☐ (3) Nursing Bra	☐ (24) Cloth Wipes	☐ (1) Dishwasher Basket and Drying Rack
☐ (1 per month) Nipple Cream	☐ (6-12) Newborn Bibs	☐ (1) Nursing Cover
☐ (1) Nursing Pillow	☐ (1) Food Journal	☐ (1) Bottle Warmer
☐ (6) Feeding Bottles	☐ (3) Ice Pack	☐ (1) Nursing Stool
		☐ (1) Bottle Sterilizer

Developmental Toys (Quantity) Product

☐ (3) Attachable Toys

☐ Music

Bibliography

"3 Uses of Agar." *FitDay*. Last accessed June 25, 2014. http://www.fitday.com/fitness-articles/nutrition/healthy-eating/3-uses-of-agar.html.

"54 Beneficial Compounds in Pure Maple Syrup." Science Codex. Last accessed March 12, 2014. http://www.sciencecodex.com/uri_scientist_discovers_54_beneficial_compounds_in_pure_maple_syrup.

"2014 Recommended Immunizations for Children from 7 through 18 Years Old." Centers for Disease Control and Prevention. Last modified March 28, 2014. Last accessed June 25, 2014. http://www.cdc.gov/vaccines/who/teens/downloads/parent-version-schedule-7-18yrs.pdf.

"ABS Material." Last accessed June 25, 2014. http://www.absmaterial.com/.

"Acidulants." UnderstandingFoodAdditives.org. Last accessed June 13, 2014. http://www.understandingfoodadditives.org/pages/ch2p9-1.htm.

Acredolo, Linda P., and Susan Goodwyn. *Baby Hearts: A Guide to Giving Your Child an Emotional Head Start*. New York: Bantam, 2005.

———. *Baby Minds: Brain-Building Games Your Baby Will Love*. New York: Bantam, 2000.

———. *Baby Signs: How to Talk with Your Baby before Your Baby Can Talk*. Chicago: Contemporary, 1996.

"Activities to Promote Literacy." Raising Children Network. Last modified September 14, 2011. Last accessed June 25, 3014. http://raisingchildren.net.au/articles/activities_to_promote_literacy.html.

Adams, Casey. *Probiotics: Protection against Infection*. Wilmington, DE: Sacred Earth, 2009.

"Adult Obesity Facts." Centers for Disease Control and Prevention. Last modified March 28, 2014. Last accessed June 25, 2014. http://www.cdc.gov/obesity/data/adult.html.

Ainsworth, M. D. S., and S. M. Bell. "Attachment, Exploration, and Separation: Illustrated by the Behavior of One-Year-Olds in a Strange Situation." *Child Development* 41 (1970): 49–67.

Aist, Jennifer. *Babes in the Woods: Hiking, Camping, Boating with Babies & Young Children*. Seattle: Mountaineers Books, 2010.

Alfaro, Danilo. "Facts about Sodium Nitrate and Sodium Nitrite." About.com Culinary Arts. Last accessed June 13, 2014. http://culinaryarts.about.com/od/seasoningflavoring/a/nitrates.htm.

"Alpha-Linolenic Acid." University of Maryland Medical Center. Last modified June 19, 2013. Last accessed June 25, 2014. http://umm.edu/health/medical/altmed/supplement/alphalinolenic-acid.

American Dental Association. "Diet and Tooth decay." *Journal of the American Dental Association* 133 (2002): 527.

Ames, Louise Bates, and Frances L. Ilg. *Your Three-Year-Old: Friend or Enemy*. New York: Dell Pub., 1987.

———. *Your Two-Year-Old: Terrible or Tender*. New York: Dell, 1980.

Ames, Louise Bates, Frances L. Ilg, and Carol Chase Haber. *Your One-Year-Old: 12 to 24 Months, Fun-Loving and Fussy*. New York: Dell, 1983.

"Amino Acids." MedlinePlus. Last modified February 18, 2013. Last accessed June 25, 2014. http://www.nlm.nih.gov/medlineplus/ency/article/002222.htm.

Amsterdam, Beulah. "Mirror Self-Image Reactions before Age Two." *Developmental Psychobiology* 5:4 (1972): 297–305.

Angier, Natalie. "Insights from the Youngest Minds." *The New York Times*. April 30, 2012. Last accessed June 15, 2014. http://www.nytimes.com/2012/05/01/science/insights-in-human-knowledge-from-the-minds-of-babes.html?pagewanted=all&_r=0.

"Antibiotics and Antibiotic Resistance." U.S. Food and Drug Administration. Last modified May 6, 2013. Last accessed June 25, 2014. http://www.fda.gov/Drugs/ResourcesForYou/Consumers/BuyingUsingMedicineSafely/AntibioticsandAntibioticResistance/default.htm.

"Antibiotics Aren't Always the Answer." Centers for Disease Control and Prevention. Last modified December 16, 2013. Last accessed June 25, 2014. http://www.cdc.gov/features/getsmart/.

"Antioxidants." Medline Plus. Last accessed June 25, 2014. http://www.nlm.nih.gov/medlineplus/antioxidants.html.

"Antioxidants and Cancer Prevention." National Cancer Institute. Last accessed June 13, 2014. http://www.cancer.gov/cancertopics/factsheet/prevention/antioxidants.

"Antiperspirants Safety: Should You Sweat It?" WebMD. Last accessed June 16, 2014. http://www.webmd.com/skin-problems-and-treatments/features/antiperspirant-facts-safety?page=2.

"Anton van Leeuwenhoek: A History of the Compound Microscope." History of the Microscope. 2010. Last accessed June 23, 2014. http://www.history-of-the-microscope.org/anton-van-leeuwenhoek-microscope-history.php.

Arasaki, Seibin, and Teruko Arasaki. *Low Calorie, High Nutrition Vegetables from the Sea to Help You Look and Feel Better*. Tokyo: Japan Publications, 1983.

"Arsenic in Your Food." *Consumer Reports*. 2012. Last accessed June 25, 2014. http://consumerreports.org/cro/magazine/2012/11/arsenic-in-your-food/index.htm.

"Breastfeeding." American Academy of Family Physicians. Last accessed March 7, 2014.
http://www.aafp.org/patient-care/clinical-recommendations/all/breastfeeding.html.

"Breastfeeding." United Nations Children's Fund. Last accessed March 7, 2014. http://www.unicef.org/nutrition/index_24824.html.

"Breastfeeding." World Health Organization. Last accessed March 7, 2014. http://www.who.int/topics/breastfeeding/en/.

"Breastfeeding and Cancer." American Institute for Cancer Research. October 10, 2012. Last accessed June 25, 2014.
http://www.aicr.org/reduce-your-cancer-risk/tell-me-about/tellmeabout_breastfeeding.html.

"Breastfeeding Initiatives." American Academy of Pediatrics. Last accessed March 7, 2014. https://www2.aap.org/breastfeeding/index.html.

"Breastfeeding Your Baby." American College of Obstetricians and Gynecologists. Last accessed March 7, 2014.
http://www.acog.org/~/media/For%20Patients/faq029.pdf?dmc=1&ts=20140307T1444566960.

Brewer, Sarah. *Super Baby: Boost Your Baby's Potential from Conception to Year One*. London: Thorsons, 1998.

Bricker, Diane D. *AEPS Assessment, Evaluation, and Programming System for Infants and Children: Birth to Three Years and Three to Six Years*.
Baltimore: Paul H. Brookes Pub. Co., 2002.

———. *AEPS Assessment, Evaluation, and Programming System for Infants and Children: Curriculum for Birth to Three Years*.
Baltimore: Paul H. Brookes Pub. Co., 2002.

Brokaw, Meredith, and Annie Gilbar. *The Penny Whistle Party Planner*. New York: Weidenfeld & Nicolson, 1987.

Bronson, Martha. *Self-Regulation in Early Childhood: Nature and Nurture*. New York: Guilford Press, 2000.

Brown, Simon. *Modern-Day Macrobiotics: Transform Your Diet and Feed Your Mind, Body, and Spirit*. Berkeley, CA: North Atlantic, 2006.

Bruner, Jerome S. "The Organization of Action and the Nature of Adult-Infant Transaction" in D. d'Ydewalle and W. Lens,
Cognition in Human Motivation and Learning (Hillsdale, NJ: Erlbaum): 1–13.

———. "Toward a Sense of Community" in Gartner, et al. *Children Teach Children* (1971). *Saturday Review* 55 (1972): 62–63.

"Butylated hydroxytoluene (BHT)." Truth in Aging. Last accessed June 13, 2014.
http://www.truthinaging.com/ingredients/butylated-hydroxytoluene-bht.

"Caffeine during Pregnancy." BabyCenter. Last accessed June 13, 2014. http://www.babycenter.com/caffeine-during-pregnancy.

"Caffeine Myths and Facts." WebMD. Last accessed June 13, 2014. http://www.webmd.com/balance/caffeine-myths-and-facts.

Callahan, William J. *The Enneagram for Youth: Student Edition*. Chicago: Loyola University Press, 1992.

———. *The Enneagram for Youth: Counselor's Manual*. Chicago: Loyola University Press, 1992.

Calorie Control Council. "Sweet Facts about Acesulfame Potassium." Last accessed June 25, 2014. http://www.acesulfamek.org/.

Campbell, T. Colin, and Thomas M. Campbell. *The China Study: The Most Comprehensive Study of Nutrition Ever Conducted and the Startling
Implications for Diet, Weight Loss, and Long-Term Health*. Dallas: BenBella Books, 2005.

"Carbon Monoxide Questions and Answers." U.S. Consumer Product Safety Commission. Last accessed June 16, 2014. https://www.cpsc.gov/
en/Safety-Education/Safety-Education-Centers/Carbon-Monoxide-Information-Center/Carbon-Monoxide-Questions-and-Answers-/.

Carey, Susan, and Rochel Gelman. *The Epigenesis of Mind: Essays on Biology and Cognition*. Hillsdale, NJ: L. Erlbaum Associates, 1991.

Carson, Anne. *Caretaking a New Soul: Writing on Parenting from Thich Nhat Hahn to Z Budapest*. Freedom, CA: Crossing, 1999.

Celebrating Multiple Intelligences: Teaching for Success: A Practical Guide. St. Louis: School, 1994.

"Certified Products and Systems." National Sanitation Foundation. Last accessed March 17, 2014.
http://www.nsf.org/certified-products-systems.

César, Juraci A., et al. "Impact of Breast Feeding on Admission for Pneumonia during Postneonatal Period in Brazil: Nested Case-Control
Study." *BMJ* (1999): 318.

Challa, Shekhar. *Probiotics for Dummies*. Hoboken, NJ: Wiley, 2012.

"Chapter XXVII Environment: 15. Stockholm Convention on Persistent Organic Pollutants." United Nations Treaty Collection.
May 22, 2001. Last accessed March 10, 2014.
http://treaties.un.org/pages/ViewDetails.aspx?src=TREATY&mtdsg_no=XXVII-15&chapter=27&lang=en.

Charles, Cheryl, and Bob Samples. *Coming Home: Community, Creativity and Consciousness*. Fawnskin, CA: Personhood, 2004.

Charner, Kathy, Maureen Murphy, and Charlie Clark. *The Encyclopedia of Infant and Toddler Activities: For Children Birth to 3*.
Beltsville, MD: Gryphon House, 2006.

"Cheat Sheet: Safer Baby Wipes." SafeMama. Last accessed June 16, 2014. http://safemama.com/cheatsheets/safer-baby-wipes/.

"Chemical Cuisine." Center for Science in the Public Interest. Last accessed June 13, 2014. http://www.cspinet.org/reports/chemcuisine.htm.

Clare, and Douglas Godwin. *Is the Left Brain Always Right?: A Guide to Whole Child Development*.
Belmont, CA: D. S. Lake Publishers, 1989.

Chess, Stella, and Alexander Thomas. *Temperament: Theory and Practice*. New York: Brunner/Mazel, 1996.

Chevallier, Andrew. *Natural Health Encyclopedia of Herbal Medicine*. New York: DK Pub., 2000.

Chiron, C. "The Right Brain Hemisphere Is Dominant in Human Infants." *Brain* 120:6 (1997): 1057–1065. doi: 10.1093/brain/120.6.1057.

Chukovskiĭ, Korneĭ. *From Two to Five*. Berkeley: University of California, 1968.

"A Citizen's Guide to Radon: The Guide to Protecting Yourself and Your Family from Radon." U.S. Environmental Protection Agency. Last modified January 10, 2013. Last accessed June 16, 2014. http://www.epa.gov/radon/pubs/citguide.html.

Cline, Kyle. *Chinese Pediatric Massage: A Practitioner's Guide*. Rochester, VT: Healing Arts Press, 2000.

Cohen, Bonnie Bainbridge, and Lisa Nelson. *Sensing, Feeling, and Action: The Experiential Anatomy of Body-Mind Centering*. Northampton, MA: Contact Editions, 1993.

Cohen, Rebecca P. *Fifteen Minutes Outside: 365 Ways to Get out of the House and Connect with Your Kids*. Naperville, IL: Source, 2011.

Colbin, Annemarie. *The Book of Whole Meals: A Seasonal Guide to Assembling Balanced Vegetarian Breakfasts, Lunches, and Dinners*. New York: Ballantine, 1983.

———. *Food and Healing*. New York: Ballantine, 1986.

———. *The Natural Gourmet*. New York: Ballantine, 1989.

Cole, Michael. *The Development of Children*. New York: Worth, 2005.

Colwell-Lipson, Corey, and Lynn Hutner Colwell. *Celebrate Green!: Creating Eco-Savvy Holidays, Celebrations & Traditions for the Whole Family*. Renton, WA: Green Year LLC, 2008.

Committee on Nutrition. "The Use and Misuse of Fruit Juice in Pediatrics." *Pediatrics* 107:5 (2001): 1210–1213.

———. "The Use of Whole Cow's Milk in Infancy." *Pediatrics* 89:6 (1992): 1105–1109.

"Common Poisonous Plants and Plant Parts." Aggie Horticulture. Last accessed June 25, 2014. http://aggie-horticulture.tamu.edu/earthkind/landscape/poisonous-plants-resources/common-poisonous-plants-and-plant-parts/.

"Community Water Fluoridation." Centers for Disease Control and Prevention. Last accessed June 16, 2014. http://www.cdc.gov/fluoridation/faqs/.

"Consumer Reports Tests Juices for Arsenic and Lead." *Consumer Reports*. November 30, 2011. Last accessed June 25, 2014. http://www.consumerreports.org/cro/news/2011/11/consumer-reports-tests-juices-for-arsenic-and-lead/index.htm.

Cornell, Joseph Bharat. *Sharing Nature with Children: A Parents' and Teachers' Nature-Awareness Guidebook*. Nevada City, CA: Ananda Publications, 1979.

"Cotton and the Environment." Organic Trade Association. Last modified 2011. Last accessed June 16, 2014. http://www.ota.com/organic/environment/cotton_environment.html.

"Creating Environments for Healthy Human Development and a Healthy Biosphere for Generations to Come." Natural Learning Initiative. Last accessed January 13, 2014. http://naturalearning.org/.

"Cruciferous Vegetables and Cancer Prevention." National Cancer Institute at the National Institutes of Health. Last modified June 2012. Last accessed June 25, 2014. www.cancer.gov/cancertopics/factsheet/diet/cruciferous-vegetables.

Csikszentmihalyi, Mihaly. *Flow: The Psychology of Optimal Experience*. New York: Harper & Row, 1990.

Curtis, Deb, and Margie Carter. *Designs for Living and Learning: Transforming Early Childhood Environments*. St. Paul, MN: Redleaf, 2003.

Cusick, Lois. *Waldorf Parenting Handbook: Useful Information on Child Development & Education from Anthroposophical Sources*. Spring Valley, NY: St. George Publications, 1984.

Davies, Kim. *Natural Baby Care: Raising Your Child the Way Nature Intended*. London: Southwater, 2007.

Davis, William. *Wheat Belly: Lose the Wheat, Lose the Weight, and Find Your Path Back to Health*. Emmaus, PA: Rodale, 2011.

Day, Lin. "Babies and Mathematics." *Baby Sensory*. 2008. Last accessed March 14, 2014. http://www.babysensory.com/Downloads/Babies-and-MathematicsEN.pdf.

Day, Monimalika, and Rebecca Parlakian. *How Culture Shapes Social-Emotional Development: Implications for Practice in Infant-Family Programs*. Washington, DC: Zero to Three, 2004.

Denby, Nigel. "Food Additives." Sense about Science. Last accessed June 13, 2014. http://www.senseaboutscience.org/pages/food-additives.html.

Denham, Susanne A. *Emotional Development in Young Children*. New York: Guilford, 1998.

Dentzer, Susan. "The Positive and Negative Effects of Taking Antioxidants." PBS. Last modified April 11, 2000. Last accessed June 13, 2014. http://www.pbs.org/newshour/bb/health-jan-june00-vitamins_4-11/.

"Developmental Milestones: Understanding Words, Behavior, and Concepts." BabyCenter. Last accessed June 11, 2014.

http://www.babycenter.com/0_developmental-milestones-understanding-words-behavior-and-co_6575.bc.

Dewey, John. *Experience and Education*. New York: Macmillan, 1963.

"Dextromethorphan." MedlinePlus. Last modified July 8, 2011. Last accessed June 16, 2014.
http://www.nlm.nih.gov/medlineplus/druginfo/meds/a682492.html.

"Diethanolamine (DEA): A Carcinogenic Ingredient in Cosmetics & Personal Products." Cancer Prevention Coalition.
Last accessed June 16, 2014. http://www.preventcancer.com/consumers/cosmetics/diethanolamine.htm.

"Diseases & Topics: Safe Use of Insect Repellents." NC Department of Health and Human Services. Last modified April 22, 2013.
Last accessed June 25, 2014. http://epi.publichealth.nc.gov/cd/diseases/deet.html.

Dodt, Colleen K. *Natural Babycare: Pure and Soothing Recipes and Techniques for Mothers and Babies*. Pownal, VT: Storey Communications, 1997.

Doman, Douglas. *How to Teach Your Baby to Swim: From Birth to Age Six*. Garden City Park, NY: Square One, 2006.

Dominguez-Bello, Maria G., et al. "Delivery Mode Shapes the Acquisition and Structure of the Initial Microbiota across Multiple Body Habitats
in Newborns." *Proceedings of the National Academy of Sciences of the United States of America* 107:26 (2010): 11971–11975.

Dowling, Marion. *Young Children's Personal, Social, and Emotional Development*. London: Paul Chapman Pub., 2005.

Druckerman, Pamela. *Bringing up Bébé: One American Mother Discovers the Wisdom of French Parenting*. New York: Penguin Press, 2012.

Durani, Yamini. "Reye Syndrome." KidsHealth. Last accessed June 16, 2014. http://kidshealth.org/parent/infections/bacterial_viral/reye.html.

EFSA Panel on Food Additives and Nutrient Sources Added to Food (ANS). "Scientific Opinion on the Reevaluation of Carnauba Wax (E 903)
as a Food Additive." *EFSA Journal*. 2012. Last accessed June 25, 2014.
http://www.efsa.europa.eu/en/efsajournal/doc/2880.pdf. doi:10.2903/j.efsa.2012.2880.

"Egg Nutrition and Heart Disease: Eggs Aren't the Dietary Demons They're Cracked Up to Be." *Harvard Heart Letter*. July 2006.
Last accessed March 10, 2014. http://www.health.harvard.edu/press_releases/egg-nutrition.

Eliot, Lise. *Pink Brain, Blue Brain: How Small Differences Grow into Troublesome Gaps—and What We Can Do about It*.
Boston: Houghton Mifflin Harcourt, 2009.

———. *What's Going On in There?: How the Brain and Mind Develop in the First Five Years of Life*. New York: Bantam, 1999.

Elly, Jenivieve. "Can a Messy House Affect Behavior in Children?" TheBump.com Preschooler. Last accessed June 23, 2014.
http://preschooler.thebump.com/can-messy-house-affect-behavior-children-5412.html.

Elmer, Gary, Lynne V. McFarland, and Marc McFarland. *The Power of Probiotics: Improving Your Health with Beneficial Microbes*.
New York: Haworth, 2007.

England, Allison. *Aromatherapy and Massage for Mother and Baby*. Rochester, VT: Healing Arts, 2000.

"Ephedrine." RxList. Last accessed June 16, 2014. http://www.rxlist.com/ephedrine-drug/side-effects-interactions.htm.

Erhart, Shep, and Leslie Cerier. *Sea Vegetable Celebration*. Summertown, TN: Book Publishing Company, 2001.

Erikson, Erik H. *Childhood and Society*. New York: Norton, 1993.

Esko, Edward, and Wendy Esko. *Macrobiotic Cooking for Everyone*. Tokyo: Japan Publications, 1980.

Espeland, Pamela, and Elizabeth Verdick. *Knowing and Doing What's Right: The Positive Values Assets*. Minneapolis: Free Spirit Pub., 2006.

"Essential Fatty Acids." Linus Pauling Institute. Last modified January 2012. Last accessed June 25, 2014.
http://lpi.oregonstate.edu/infocenter/othernuts/omega3fa/.

Essential Oils: Pocket Reference. Orem, UT: Life Science Pub., 2011.

"EWG's 2013 Shopper's Guide to Pesticides in Produce." Environmental Working Group. Last accessed February 28, 2014.
http://www.ewg.org/foodnews/summary.php.

Eyre, Linda, and Richard M. Eyre. *Teaching Your Children Values*. New York: Fireside, 1993.

"Fabric Glossary." Fabric.com. Last accessed June 16, 2014. https://www.fabric.com/SitePages/Glossary.aspx.

"The Facts about Ammonia." N.Y. State Department of Health. Last modified May 2005. Last accessed June 16, 2014.
https://www.health.ny.gov/environmental/emergency/chemical_terrorism/ammonia_tech.htm.

"Facts about Chlorine." Centers for Disease Control and Prevention. Last modified April 10, 2013. Last accessed June 16, 2014.
http://www.bt.cdc.gov/agent/chlorine/basics/facts.asp.

Fallon, Sally, Mary G. Enig, Kim Murray, and Marion Dearth. *Nourishing Traditions: The Cookbook That Challenges Politically Correct Nutrition
and the Diet Dictocrats*. Washington, DC: NewTrends Pub., 2001.

Fan, Ya-li. *Chinese Pediatric Massage Therapy [Chung-kuo Hsiao Erh Tui Na Liao Fa]: A Parent's & Practitioner's Guide to the Treatment and
Prevention of Childhood Disease*. Boulder, CO: Blue Poppy, 1994.

Q: Probiotics." Danisco. Last accessed June 25, 2014. http://www.danisco.com/dietary-supplements/faq/.

Fassa, Lynda. *Green Babies, Sage Moms: The Ultimate Guide to Raising Your Organic Baby*. New York: New American Library, 2008.

Feder, Lauren. *Natural Baby and Childcare*. New York: Healthy Living, 2006.

———. *The Parents' Concise Guide to Childhood Vaccinations: Practical Medical and Natural Ways to Protect Your Child*. Long Island City, NY: Hatherleigh Press, 2007.

"Feed Additives." Food and Agriculture Organization of the United Nations. Last accessed March 17, 2014. http://www.fao.org/docrep/article/agrippa/660_en-06.htm.

Fenner, Pamela Johnson, and Karen L. Rivers. *Waldorf Education: A Family Guide*. Amesbury, MA: Michaelmas, 1995.

Ferre, Carl. *Acid Alkaline Companion*. Chico, CA: George Ohsawa Macroboitic Foundation, 2009.

Ferre, Julia. *Food and Intuition 101*. Vol. 1. Chico, CA: George Ohsawa Macrobiotic Foundation, 2012.

Fields, Denise, and Alan Fields. *Baby Bargains: Secrets to Saving 20% to 50% on Baby Furniture, Gear, Clothes, Strollers, Maternity Wear, and Much, Much More!* Boulder, CO: Windsor Peak Press, 2013.

Fiese, Barbara H., and Marlene Schwartz. "Reclaiming the Family Table: Mealtimes and Child Health and Wellbeing." *Social Policy Report* 22:4 (2008): 3–19. Last accessed June 25, 2014. http://www.yaleruddcenter.org/resources/upload/docs/what/reports/reclaimingfamilytable.pdf.

Finando, Donna. *Acupoint and Trigger Point Therapy for Babies and Children: A Parent's Healing Touch*. Rochester, VT: Healing Arts Press, 2008.

"Fire Retardants." Environmental Working Group. Last accessed June 16, 2014. http://www.ewg.org/key-issues/toxics/fire-retardants.

"Fish Consumption Advisories." U.S. Environmental Protection Agency. Last accessed June 25, 2014. http://water.epa.gov/scitech/swguidance/fishshellfish/fishadvisories/index.cfm.

"Flame Retardants." Green Science Policy Institute. Last accessed June 16, 2014. http://greensciencepolicy.org/topics/flame-retardants/.

Flaws, Bob. *A Handbook of TCM Pediatrics*. Boulder, CO: Blue Poppy Press, 2006.

Flaws, Bob. *Keeping Your Child Healthy with Chinese Medicine: A Parent's Guide to the Care and Prevention of Common Childhood Diseases*. Boulder, CO: Blue Poppy Press, 1996.

Flaws, Bob, and Honora Lee Wolfe. *Prince Wen Hui's Cook: Chinese Dietary Therapy*. Brookline, MA: Paradigm Publications, 1983.

"Fluoridation Facts." American Dental Association. Last accessed March 12, 2014. http://www.ada.org/sections/newsAndEvents/pdfs/fluoridation_facts.pdf.

"Foam Mats Health Risk: The Test Results Are In." Papalogic. Last modified August 1, 2011. Last accessed June 16, 2014. http://www.papalogic.com/foam-mats-health-risk-the-results-are-in/.

"Food Additives Guide (900-1520)." MBM.net. Last accessed June 13, 2014. http://www.mbm.net.au/health/900-1520.htm.

"Food Dye and ADHD: Food Coloring, Sugar, and Diet." WebMD. Last modified July 8, 2012. Last accessed June 13, 2014. http://www.webmd.com/add-adhd/childhood-adhd/food-dye-adhd.

"Formaldehyde and Cancer Risk." National Cancer Institute at the National Institutes of Health. Last modified June 10, 2011. Last accessed June 16, 2014. http://www.cancer.gov/cancertopics/factsheet/Risk/formaldehyde.

Fowler, James W. *Stages of Faith: The Psychology of Human Development and the Quest for Meaning*. San Francisco: Harper & Row, 1981.

Fratkin, Jake Paul. "Treating Infants and Small Children with Chinese Herbal Medicine." *Acupuncture Today*. September 2007. Last accessed June 25, 2014. http://www.acupuncturetoday.com/mpacms/at/article.php?id=31576.

"Frequently Asked TPE Questions." PolyOne. Last accessed June 16, 2014. http://www.glstpes.com/resources_faqs.php

Galinsky, Ellen. *Mind in the Making: The Seven Essential Life Skills Every Child Needs*. New York: HarperStudio, 2010.

Galland, Leo, and Dian D. Buchman. *Superimmunity for Kids*. New York: CopeStone, Inc., 1988.

Garabedian, Helen. *Itsy Bitsy Yoga: Poses to Help Your Baby Sleep Longer, Digest Better, and Grow Stronger*. New York: Simon & Schuster, 2004.

Gardner, Howard. *Frames of the Mind: The Theory of Multiple Intelligences*. New York: BasicBooks, 1993.

———. *Multiple Intelligences: New Horizons*. New York: BasicBooks, 2006.

———. *The Unschooled Mind: How Children Think and How Schools Should Teach*. New York: BasicBooks, 1991.

Gaskin, Ina M. *Ina May's Guide to Breastfeeding*. New York: Bantam, 2009.

Gates, Donna, and Linda Schatz. *The Body Ecology Diet: Recovering Your Health and Rebuilding Your Immunity*. Carlsbad, CA: Hay House, 2011.

Gavigan, Christopher. *Healthy Child, Healthy World: Creating a Cleaner, Greener, Safer Home*. New York: Dutton, 2008.

Gelman, Rochel and Ann L. Brown. "Changing Views of Cognitive Competence in the Young" in Neil Smelser and Dean Gerstein, eds., *Discoveries and Trends in Behavioral and Social Sciences* (Washington, DC: National Academy Press), 175–207.

Developmental Toys

Books
Multiple purchases
Age needed: 6 months

Books for your baby include paper books that you read to him, soft books, and sturdier books he can read himself. Interactive features such as mirrors, different textures, or places to insert family photos encourage sensory development.

Function: Strengthens hand-eye coordination and fine-motor skills, visual, and auditory skills

Special Features or Considerations:
*   Interactive features such as mirrors, different textures, and family photos
*   Simple storylines
*   Bright, contrasting colors

Texture
Multiple purchases
Age needed: 3 months

Texture toys vary widely and are often incorporated into other toys such as teethers and plush toys. Varied textures of different fabrics or firmer materials such as silicone with raised bumps provide tactile stimulation

Function: Improves your baby's tactile awareness

Special Features or Considerations:
*   Different fabrics and other varied materials
*   Incorporated into other toys

Cruising Toys
One-time purchase
Age needed: 9 months

Cruising toys provide stabilization while your baby explores his mobility. Your baby can stand behind a cruising toy and push it along as he learns to walk.

Function: Encourages new walkers while building confidence, cause and effect, and gross-motor skills

Special Features or Considerations:
*   Wheels for easy mobility
*   Tall, sturdy handle

Play Gym
One-time purchase
Age needed: 6 months

Play gyms allow your baby to play on his back, before he can sit up. They usually have a soft mat for him to lay on, with an attached overhead for hanging toys and objects.

Function: Encourages cause and effect and spatial awareness including reaching, and kicking. Also stimulates visual development and fine-motor skills

Special Features or Considerations:
*   Colorful with different patterns and textures
*   Comfortable for baby's back
*   Versatile hanging elements that move around easily

Developmental Toys

Music
Multiple purchases
Age needed: Newborn

 From birth, your baby enjoys rhythm and music. You can play children's songs and baby-friendly music for him while singing and dancing along.

Function: Develops and stimulates auditory and verbal skills

Special Features or Considerations:
- Variety of different types of music
- Easy to sing along and dance with
- Music that you enjoy

Instruments
One-time purchase
Age needed: 6 months

 Instruments for your baby include simple wooden maracas, rhythm sticks, keyboards, and xylophones.

Function: Develops fine- and gross-motor skills, cause and effect, and auditory function

Special Features or Considerations:
- Noise level
- Easy for baby to use
- No small parts

Art Supplies
Multiple purchases
Age needed: 18 months

 Art supplies for your child include crayons, markers, chalk, and paints. Look for art supplies that are designed for your baby's small hands with chunky designs, and paint that is nontoxic and nonstaining.

Function: Helps develop visual and fine-motor skills, and encourages creativity

Special Features or Considerations:
- Easy to hold
- Nonstaining
- Nontoxic

Puzzles
Multiple purchases
Age needed: 18 months

 First puzzles have simple shapes with 4–6 big pieces. Some puzzles have a picture of the piece on the puzzle board itself, since it is easier for your baby to match by pictures. As he grows, your child learns to put together more complex puzzles.

Function: Improves tactile skills, spatial awareness, and fine-motor skills

Special Features or Considerations:
- Large, simple pieces in limited numbers
- Easy to grasp

Gelman, Susan A., and Henry Wellman. "Cognitive Development: Foundational Theories of Core Domains."
    Annual Review of Psychology 43 (February 1992): 337–375.

Gerstein, H.C. "Cow's Milk Exposure and Type I Diabetes Mellitus: A Critical Overview of the Clinical Literature."
    Diabetes Care 17:1 (1994): 13–19.

Gibson, Leah. "Some Knit Fabric Basics." Oliver + S. Last modified December 8, 2010. Last accessed June 16, 2014.
    http://oliverands.com/blog/2010/12/some-knit-fabric-basics.html.

Giddens, Anthony, and John Bowlby. "Attachment and Loss, Volume I: Attachment." *The British Journal of Sociology* 21:1 (1970): 111.

Gillespie, Linda G., and Nancy L. Seibel. "Self-Regulation: A Cornerstone of Early Childhood Development." Beyond the Journal: Young
    Children on the Web. 2006. Last accessed February 28, 2014. journal.naeyc.org/btj/200607/Gillespie709BTJ.pdf.

Ginsburg, Kenneth R., and Martha M. Jablow. *Building Resilience in Children and Teens: Giving Your Child Roots and Wings.*
    Elk Grove Village, IL: American Academy of Pediatrics, 2011.

"Glazing Agents." UPC Food Search. Last accessed June 13, 2014. http://www.upcfoodsearch.com/ingredients/glazing-agents/.

"GMO Facts." Non-GMO Project. Last accessed February 28, 2014. http://www.nongmoproject.org/learn-more/.

Goetz, Terry. "Movement Matters: BrainDance Workshop." Lecture from Creative Dance Center.

Goleman, Daniel. *The Brain and Emotional Intelligence: New Insights.* Northampton, MA: More Than Sound, 2011.

———. *Social Intelligence: The New Science of Human Relationships.* New York: Bantam Books, 2007.

Gowen, Jean Wixson, and Judith Brennan Nebrig. *Enhancing Early Emotional Development: Guiding Parents of Young Children.*
    Baltimore: P. H. Brookes Pub., 2002.

Grace, Elizabeth. "Educational Toys for Babies." KidsDevelopment. October 31, 2012. Last accessed March 12, 2014.
    http://www.kidsdevelopment.co.uk/EducationalBabyToys.html.

———. "Language Development Stages in Young Children." KidsDevelopment. Last modified August 29, 2012. Last accessed June 25, 2014.
    http://www.kidsdevelopment.co.uk/LanguageDevelopmentStagesYoungChildren.html.

———. "Music and Cognitive Development." KidsDevelopment. Last modified October 29, 2010. Last accessed March 12, 2014.
    http://www.kidsdevelopment.co.uk/MusicAndCognitiveDevelopment.html.

———. "Understanding Babies' Emotions." KidsDevelopment. Last modified August 29, 2012. Last accessed March 12, 2014.
    http://www.kidsdevelopment.co.uk/understandingbabiesemotions.html.

———. "What Do Babies' Understand?" KidsDevelopment. Last modified May 12, 2012. Last accessed March 12, 2014.
    http://www.kidsdevelopment.co.uk/WhatBabiesUnderstand.html.

Greene, Alan R. *The Parent's Complete Guide to Ear Infections.* Allentown, PA: People's Medical Society, 1997.

———. *Raising Baby Green: The Earth-Friendly Guide to Pregnancy, Childbirth, and Baby Care.* San Francisco: Jossey-Bass, 2007.

———. "WhiteOut." Dr.Greene.com. Last accessed March 10, 2014. http://www.drgreene.com/whiteout/.

"GSFA Online Search: Food Additives." GSFA. Last modified 2013. Last accessed June 13, 2014.
    http://www.codexalimentarius.net/gsfaonline/additives/results.html?techFunction=10&searchBy=tf.

"A Guide to Polycarbonate in General." Polymer Technology and Services, LLC. Last accessed June 16, 2014.
    http://www.ptsllc.com/intro/polycarb_intro.aspx.

Haas, Elson M. *Staying Healthy with the Seasons [Si Ji Jian Kang Fa].* Millbrae, CA: CelestialArts, 1981.

"Hand Sanitizers: How Toxic Are They?" Texas Poison Center Network. Last accessed June 16, 2014.
    http://www.poisoncontrol.org/news/topics/dangerous-hand-sanitizer.cfm.

Hannaford, Carla. *Smart Moves: Why Learning Is Not All in Your Head.* Salt Lake City: Great River Books, 2005.

Hanson, Larch. *Edible Sea Vegetables of the New England Coast: A Forager's Guide with Recipes.* Steuben, ME: Maine Seaweed, 1983.

Harmon, Wardeh. *The Complete Idiot's Guide to Fermenting Foods.* New York: Alpha, 2012.

Hartley, Linda. *Wisdom of the Body Moving: An Introduction to Body-Mind Centering.* Berkeley, CA: North Atlantic, 1995.

Hazan, Cindy, and Phillip Shaver. "Romantic Love Conceptualized as an Attachment Process."
    Journal of Personality and Social Psychology 52:3 (1987): 511–524.

"Hazardous Substance Factsheet." New Jersey Department of Health and Senior Services. Last modified June 2003.
    Last accessed June 13, 2014. http://nj.gov/health/eoh/rtkweb/documents/fs/0947.pdf.

"Health Benefits and Nutritional Facts of Chicken Breast." Mayo Guide. Last accessed March 10, 2014.
    http://mayoguide.org/Health-Benefits-And-Nutritional-Facts-Of-Chicken-Breast.html.

"Health Benefits of Taking Probiotics." *The Harvard Medical School Family Health Guide*. September 2005. Last accessed June 25, 2014. http://www.health.harvard.edu/fhg/updates/update0905c.shtml.

"Health Concerns about Dairy Products." Physicians Committee for Responsible Medicine. Last accessed June 25, 2014. http://www.pcrm.org/health/diets/vegdiets/health-concerns-about-dairy-products.

"Health of the Planet and Its Inhabitants." Organic Trade Association. Last modified October 2008. Last accessed June 25, 2014. http://www.ota.com/organic/environment/health.html.

"Health Professionals Follow-Up Study." Harvard School of Public Health. Last accessed March 10, 2014. https://www.hsph.harvard.edu/hpfs/.

Healy, Jane M. *Your Child's Growing Mind: Brain Development and Learning from Birth to Adolescence*. New York: Broadway, 2004.

Helmenstine, Anne Marie. "Chemistry of BHA and BHT Food Preservatives." About.com Chemistry. Last accessed June 13, 2014. http://chemistry.about.com/od/foodcookingchemistry/a/bha-bht-preservatives.htm.

———. "What Makes Stainless Steel Stainless?" About.com Chemistry. Last accessed June 16, 2014. http://chemistry.about.com/cs/metalsandalloys/a/aa071201a.htm.

Hernandez, Mary. "9 Reasons You Want to Avoid Hand Sanitizers." Foods 4 Thought. Last modified January 27, 2013. Last accessed June 16, 2014. http://foods4thoughtblog.wordpress.com/2013/01/27/9-reasons-you-want-to-avoid-hand-sanitizers/.

Hill, Adam, and Bronwyn Harris. "What Is Phthalate?" WiseGeek. Last accessed June 16, 2014. http://www.wisegeek.com/what-is-phthalate.htm.

"History." Meatless Monday. Last accessed March 10, 2014. http://www.meatlessmonday.com/history.

Hollander, Annette. *How to Help Your Child Have a Spiritual Life*. New York: Bantam, 1982.

"Home Page." Aspartame Information Center. Last accessed June 13, 2014. http://www.aspartame.org/.

"Home Page." Enneagram.com. Last accessed June 25, 2014. http://www.enneagram.com.

"Home Page." Enneagram Institute. Last accessed June 25, 2014. http://www.enneagraminstitute.com/.

"Home Page." The Nurses' Health Study. Last accessed June 25, 2014. http://www.channing.harvard.edu/nhs/.

Hopgood, Mei-Ling. *How Eskimos Keep Their Babies Warm and Other Adventures in Parenting (from Argentina to Tanzania and Everywhere in Between)*. Chapel Hill, NC: Algonquin Books of Chapel Hill, 2012.

"How Is Glass Made?" GlassTopsDirect.com. Last accessed June 25, 2014. http://glasstopsdirect.com/news/how-is-glass-made.html.

"How Much Salt Do Babies and Children Need?" National Health Service. Last modified April 2013. Last accessed June 25, 2014. http://www.nhs.uk/chq/Pages/824.aspx?CategoryID=51.

"How to Save a Fortune on Infant Formula." *Consumer Reports*. October 30, 2008. Last accessed June 25, 2014. www.consumerreports.org/cro/news/2008/10/how-to-save-a-fortune-on-infant-formula/index.htm.

Hughes, Daniel A., and Jonathan F. Baylin. *Brain-Based Parenting: The Neuroscience of Caregiving for Healthy Attachment*. New York: W. W. Norton &, 2012.

"Hydrocortisone Topical." MedlinePlus. Last modified May 15, 2014. Last accessed June 16, 2014. http://www.nlm.nih.gov/medlineplus/druginfo/meds/a682793.html.

Hylander, Mary Ann, and Donna M. Strobino. "Human Milk Feedings and Infection among Very Low Birth Weight Infants." *Pediatrics* 102:3 (1998): E38.

Hyman, Mark. "5 Reasons High Fructose Corn Syrup Will Kill You." Dr. Mark Hyman. Last modified March 4, 2014. Last accessed June 13, 2014. http://drhyman.com/blog/2011/05/13/5-reasons-high-fructose-corn-syrup-will-kill-you/.

Iannelli, Vincent. "Probiotics for Kids: Child Nutrition Basics." About.com Pediatrics. Last modified May 28, 2014. Last accessed June 25, 2014. http://pediatrics.about.com/od/nutrition/a/0208_probiotics.htm.

"Immunization Schedule, Japan 2011 (For Those under 20 Years of Age)." IDSC. Last accessed March 14, 2014. http://idsc.nih.go.jp/vaccine/dschedule/Imm11EN.pdf.

"Immunization Schedules." Centers for Disease Control and Prevention. Last accessed February 6, 2014. www.cdc.gov/vaccines/schedules/easy-to-read/child.html.

Imus, Deirdre. *Growing Up Green: Baby and Childcare*. New York, NY: Simon & Schuster, 2008.

"Infant-Newborn Development." MedlinePlus. Last modified January 27, 2013. Last accessed June 25, 2014. http://www.nlm.nih.gov/medlineplus/ency/article/002004.htm.

"The Insect Repellent DEET." U.S. Environmental Protection Agency. Last modified June 16, 2014. Last accessed June 16, 2014. http://www.epa.gov/pesticides/factsheets/chemicals/deet.htm.

Institute of Medicine of the National Academies. "School Meals: Building Blocks for Healthy Children." October 2009. Last accessed June 25, 2014. http://www.iom.edu/~/media/Files/Report%20Files/2009/School-Meals/School%20Meals%202009%20%20Report%20Brief.pdf.

"Introduction to Polyurethanes." American Chemistry Council. Last accessed June 16, 2014. http://polyurethane.americanchemistry.com/Introduction-to-Polyurethanes.

Ivarsson, Anneli, et al. "Breast-Feeding Protects against Celiac Disease." *American Journal of Clinical Nutrition* 75:5 (2002): 914–921.

Jacks, Jimmy. *What Is Probiotics: Probiotic Side Effects*. Lexington, KY: CreateSpace, 2011.

James, Maia. "Safe Diaper Rash Cream Guide." Gimme the Good Stuff. Last accessed June 16, 2014. http://gimmethegoodstuff.org/safe-product-guides/diaper-rash-cream.

Jaret, Peter. "Safe Use of OTC Pain Relievers." WebMD. Last accessed June 16. 2014. http://www.webmd.com/pain-management/features/safe-use-otc-pain-relievers.

"Jean-Claude Lapraz: One of the First French Aromatherpists." The Herb Depot. Last modified March 17, 2013. Last accessed June 23, 2014. http://www.theherbdepot.com/famous-herbalists_jean-claude-lapraz-one-of-the-first-french-aromatherapists_452.html.

Jenkins, Peggy Davison. *Nurturing Spirituality in Children: Simple Hands-On Activities*. New York: Atria, 2008.

Johnson, Rachel K., et al. "Dietary Sugars Intake and Cardiovascular Health: A Scientific Statement from the American Heart Association." *Circulation* 120 (2009): 1011–1020.

The Joyful Child: Birth to Three. Arcata, CA: Michael Olaf Co., 2006.

Karen, Robert. *Becoming Attached: First Relationships and How They Shape Our Capacity to Love*. New York: Oxford Univ. Pub., 1998.

Karstadt, Myra L. "Testing Needed for Acesulfame Potassium, an Artificial Sweetener." *Environmental Health Perspectives*: A516-A516. Last accessed June 23, 2014. http://www.ncbi.nlm.nih.gov/pmc/articles/PMC1570055/.

Kastner, Jo. *Chinese Nutrition Therapy Dietetics in Traditional Chinese Medicine (TCM)*. Stuttgart, Germany: Thieme, 2004.

Katz, Sandor Ellix. *The Art of Fermentation: An In-Depth Exploration of Essential Concepts and Processes from around the World*. White River Junction, VT: Chelsea Green Pub., 2012.

———. *Wild Fermentation: The Flavor, Nutrition, and Craft of Live-Culture Foods*. White River Junction, VT: Chelsea Green Pub., 2003.

Keville, Kathi, and Mindy Green. *Aromatherapy: A Complete Guide to the Healing Art*. Berkeley, CA: Crossing, 2009.

"KidsHealth Comes from Nemours." KidsHealth. Last accessed March 13, 2014. http://kidshealth.org/parent/kh_misc/nemours.html.

Kim, Se-Kwon, ed. *Advances in Food and Nutrition Research*. Vol. 64. Waltham, MA: Academic Press, 2011.

King, Kendall A., and Alison Mackey. *The Bilingual Edge: Why, When, and How to Teach Your Child a Second Language*. New York: Collins, 2007.

Klement, Eyal, et al. "Breastfeeding and Risk of Inflammatory Bowel Disease: A Systematic Review with Meta-analysis." *American Journal of Clinical Nutrition* 80:5 (2004): 1342–1352.

Knowles, Sarah. "Why Over-Scheduling Children Can Backfire." KidsDevelopment. Last modified August 29, 2012. Last accessed March 12, 2014. http://www.kidsdevelopment.co.uk/why-overscheduling-children-can-backfire.html.

Kobylewski, Sarah, and Michael F. Jacobson. *Food Dyes: A Rainbow of Risks*. Washington DC: Center for Science in the Public Interest, 2010.

Kohl, MaryAnn F., Renee Ramsey, and Dana Bowman. *First Art: For Toddlers and Twos: Open-Ended Art Experiences*. Lewisville, NC: Gryphon House, 2012.

Kopp, Claire B. *Baby Steps: A Guide to Your Child's Social, Physical, Mental, and Emotional Development in the First Two Years*. New York: Henry Holt, 2003.

Kostelnik, Marjorie J. *Guiding Children's Social Development & Learning*. Clifton Park, NY: Delmar Cengage Learning, 2009.

Kushi, Aveline, and Wendy Esko. *Macrobiotic Family Favorites*. New York: Japan Publications, 1987.

Kushi, Michio, and Aveline Kushi. *Macrobiotic Pregnancy and Care of the Newborn*. Tokyo: Japan Publications, 1985.

Kushi, Michio, Edward Esko, and Marc Van Cauwenberghe. *Natural Healing through Macrobiotics*. Tokyo: Japan Publications, 1979.

Kushi, Michio, and Marc van Cauwenberghe. *Macrobiotic Home Remedies*. Tokyo: Japan Publications, 1985.

"Lactobacillus." WebMD. Last accessed June 25, 2013. http://www.webmd.com/vitamins-supplements/ingredientmono-790-lactobacillus.aspx?activeIngredientId=790&activeIngredientName=lactobacillus&source=1.

Lair, Cynthia, and Peggy O'Mara. *Feeding the Whole Family: Cooking with Whole Foods: Recipes for Babies, Young Children, and Their Parents*. Seattle: Sasquatch, 2008.

Landy, Sarah. *Pathways to Competence: Encouraging Healthy Social and Emotional Development in Young Children*. Baltimore: Paul H. Brookes Pub., 2009.

Lanigan, R. S., and T. A. Yamarik. "Final Report on the Safety Assessment of BHT(1)." National Center for Biotechnology Information. 2002. Last accessed June 13, 2014. http://www.ncbi.nlm.nih.gov/pubmed/12396675.

Lantieri, Linda. *Building Emotional Intelligence: Techniques to Cultivate Inner Strength in Children*. Boulder, CO: Sounds True, 2008.

Lara-Villoslada, Federico, et al. "Beneficial Effects of Probiotic Bacteria Isolated from Breast Milk." *British Journal of Nutrition* 98, suppl. 1 (2007): S96–100.

"Lead Poisoning." MedlinePlus. Last modified February 1, 2013. Last accessed June 16, 2014. http://www.nlm.nih.gov/medlineplus/ency/article/002473.htm.

"Learn about Chemicals around Your House." U.S. Environmental Protection Agency. Last modified January 27, 2014. Last accessed June 16, 2014. http://www.epa.gov/kidshometour/products/bleach.htm.

Levine, Janet. *Know Your Parenting Personality: How to Use the Enneagram to Become the Best Parent You Can Be.* Hoboken, NJ: John Wiley & Sons, 2003.

Levine, Laura E., and Joyce Munsch. *Child Development: An Active Learning Approach.* Thousand Oaks, CA: SAGE, 2011.

LeVine, Robert A. *Child Rearing as Cultural Adaptation.* New York: Academic Press, 1977.

Liebert, Mary Ann. "ABM Statements: Position on Breastfeeding." *Breastfeeding Medicine* 3:4 (2008): 269. Last accessed March 7, 2014. http://www.bfmed.org/Media/Files/Documents/pdf/Statements/ABM_Position_on_Breastfeeding%20bfm.2008.9988.pdf.

Liedloff, Jean. *The Continuum Concept.* New York: Knopf, 1985.

Lillas, Connie, and Janiece Turnbull. *Infant/Child Mental Health, Early Intervention, and Relationship-Based Therapies: A Neurorelational Framework for Interdisciplinary Practice.* New York: W. W. Norton, 2009.

Loo, May. *Pediatric Acupuncture.* Edinburgh, Scotland: Churchill Livingstone, 2002.

Louv, Richard. *Last Child in the Woods: Saving Our Children from Nature-Deficit Disorder.* Chapel Hill, NC: Algonquin Books of Chapel Hill, 2005.

Lustig, Robert. "Sugar: The Bitter Truth." University of California Television. YouTube. Last accessed June 25, 2014. http://www.youtube.com/watch?v=dBnniua6-oM.

Magnuson, Bernadene. "Relationship Between Aspartame, Methanol, and Formaldehyde Explained." Last modified 2008. Last accessed June 13, 2014. http://andevidencelibrary.com/topic.cfm?cat=4089&auth=1.

Mahler, Margaret S., Fred Pine, and Anni Bergman. *The Psychological Birth of the Human Infant: Symbiosis and Individuation.* New York: Basic Books, 2000.

Marin, Gilles. *Five Elements, Six Conditions: A Taoist Approach to Emotional Healing, Psychology, and Internal Alchemy.* Berkeley, CA: North Atlantic, 2006.

Martinez, Eliza. "Games That Encourage Physical Development in Infants." Globalpost. Last accessed March 12, 2014. http://everydaylife.globalpost.com/games-encourage-physical-development-infants-5888.html.

Martinez, Steve. "Local Food Systems: Concepts, Impacts, and Issues." *Economic Research Report* 97 (2010): iii. Last accessed February 28, 2014. http://www.ers.usda.gov/media/122868/err97_1_.pdf.

Masi, Wendy S. *Toddler Play.* San Francisco: Creative Pub. International, 2001.

Masi, Wendy S., and Roni Leiderman. *Baby Play.* San Francisco: Creative Pub. International, 2001.

Mason, T., et al. "Breast Feeding and the Development of Juvenile Rheumatoid Arthritis." *J Rheumatol* 22 (1995): 1166–1170.

Master, Allison, Ellen M. Markman, and Carol S. Dweck. "Thinking in Categories or Along a Continuum: Consequences for Children's Social Judgments." *Child Development* 83:4 (2012): 1145–1163.

Mayer, John D., and Peter Salovey. "The Intelligence of Emotional Intelligence." *Intelligence* 17:4 (1993): 433–442.

Mayhall, Yolanda. *The Sumi-e Book.* New York: Watson-Guptill, 1989.

McCall, Mindy Doyle. "Motor Development and Movement." USDB. Last accessed June 11, 2014. http://classic.usdb.org/deafblind/db/CIT%20Web%20Lessons/Motor%20Development%20and%20Movement/motordevelopmentGP_print.html.

McDonald, Libby. *The Toxic Sandbox: The Truth about Environmental Toxins and Our Children's Health.* New York: Penguin, 2007.

McKay, Tonya. "The Truth and Fiction about Propylene Glycol." Naturally Curly. Last modified March 1, 2009. Last accessed June 16, 2014. http://www.naturallycurly.com/curlreading/curl-products/curlchemist-the-truth-and-fiction-about-propylene-glycol/.

McMahon, Mary, and O. Wallace. "What Is Terrycloth?" WiseGeek. Last accessed June 16, 2014. http://www.wisegeek.com/what-is-terrycloth.htm.

McMains, S., and S. Kastner. "Interactions of Top-Down and Bottom-Up Mechanisms in Human Visual Cortex." *Journal of Neuroscience* 31:2 (January 12, 2011): 587–597.

"Meat and Poultry Labeling Terms." U.S. Department of Agriculture. Last accessed March 12, 2014. http://www.fsis.usda.gov/wps/wcm/connect/e2853601-3edb-45d3-90dc-1bef17b7f277/Meat_and_Poultry_Labeling_Terms.pdf?MOD=AJPERES.

Medina, John. *Brain Rules for Baby: How to Raise a Smart and Happy Child from Zero to Five.* Seattle: Pear, 2010.

Meggitt, Carolyn. *Understand Child Development.* London: Hodder Education, 2012.

Meier, Eric. "What Is Wood?" The Wood Database. Last accessed June 16, 2014. http://www.wood-database.com/wood-articles/what-is-wood/.

Mennella, J. A., C. J. Jagnow, and G. K. Beauchamp. "Pre- and Postnatal Flavor Learning by Human Infants." *Pediatrics* 107 (2001): e88.

Mercier, David. *A Beautiful Medicine: A Radical Look at the Essence of Health and Healing.* Easton, MD: Still Pond Press, 2012.

Mercola, Joseph M. "How Your Gut Flora Influences Your Health." Mercola.com. Last accessed June 25, 2014. http://articles.mercola.com/sites/articles/archive/2012/06/27/probiotics-gut-health-impact.aspx.

———. "MSG: Is This Silent Killer Lurking in Your Kitchen Cabinets." Mercola.com. Last modified April 21, 2009. Last accessed June 13, 2014. http://articles.mercola.com/sites/articles/archive/2009/04/21/msg-is-this-silent-killer-lurking-in-your-kitchen-cabinets.aspx.

Miller, Neil Z. *Vaccine Safety Manual for Concerned Families and Health Practitioners.* Santa Fe, NM: New Atlantean Press, 2010.

———. *Vaccines: Are They Really Safe and Effective?* Santa Fe, NM: New Atlantean Press, 2002.

Millward, D. Joe. "The Nutritional Value of Plant-Based Diets in Relation to Human Amino Acid and Protein Requirements." *Proceedings of the Nutrition Society* 58:2 (1999): 249–260.

Mischel, Walter, Ebbe B. Ebbesen, and Antonette Raskoff Zeiss. "Cognitive and Attentional Mechanisms in Delay of Gratification." *Journal of Personality and Social Psychology* 21:2 (February 1972): 204–218.

Moon, Jym. *Iron: The Most Toxic Metal.* Chico, CA: George Ohsawa Macrobiotic Foundation, 2011.

Mooney, Carol Garhart. *Theories of Attachment: An Introduction to Bowlby, Ainsworth, Gerber, Brazelton, Kennell, and Klaus.* St. Paul, MN: Redleaf Press, 2010.

———. *Theories of Childhood: An Introduction to Dewey, Montessori, Erikson, Piaget, and Vygotsky.* St. Paul, MN: Redleaf Press, 2000.

Morrisy, Beth. "Assisting Language Development." KidsDevelopment. Last modified August 29, 2012. Last accessed March 12, 2014. http://www.kidsdevelopment.co.uk/assisted-language-development.html.

———. "Babies and Crawling." KidsDevelopment. Last modified March 11, 2013. Last accessed March 12, 2014. http://www.kidsdevelopment.co.uk/babiescrawling.html.

———. "Brain Development in Young Children." KidsDevelopment. Last modified September 2, 2013. Last accessed March 12, 2014. http://www.kidsdevelopment.co.uk/BrainDevelopmentYoungChildren.html.

———. "A Child's Relationship with Their Mother." KidsDevelopment. Last modified December 6, 2012. Last accessed March 12, 2014. http://www.kidsdevelopment.co.uk/ChildsRelationshipWithMother.html.

———. "Encourage Your Child's Physical Development." KidsDevelopment. Last modified October 2, 2012. Last accessed March 12, 2014. http://www.kidsdevelopment.co.uk/EncourageChildsPhysicalDevelopment.html.

———. "Interactions between Babies." KidsDevelopment. Last modified August 29, 2012. Last accessed March 12, 2014. http://www.kidsdevelopment.co.uk/InteractionsBetweenBabies.html.

———. "Relationships among Siblings." KidsDevelopment. Last modified August 30, 2012. Last accessed March 12, 2014. http://www.kidsdevelopment.co.uk/RelationshipsAmongSiblings.html.

———. "Spatial Awareness in Young Children." KidsDevelopment. Last modified October 1, 2012. Last accessed March 12, 2014. http://www.kidsdevelopment.co.uk/SpatialAwarenessYoungChildren.html.

———. "Toilet Training and Children." KidsDevelopment. Last modified March 12, 2013. Last accessed March 12, 2014. http://www.kidsdevelopment.co.uk/ToiletTrainingChildren.html.

———. "What Do Babies Hear?" KidsDevelopment. Last modified May 11, 2012. Last accessed March 12, 2014. http://www.kidsdevelopment.co.uk/WhatBabiesHear.html.

———. "What Do Babies See?" KidsDevelopment. Last modified October 2, 2012. Last accessed March 12, 2014. http://www.kidsdevelopment.co.uk/BabiesVision.html.

———. "Your Child's First Steps." KidsDevelopment. Last modified October 2, 2012. Last accessed March 12, 2014. http://www.kidsdevelopment.co.uk/ChildrensFirstSteps.html.

Muhlenchemi. "Flour Treatment in Europe." May 1998. Last accessed June 13, 2014. http://www.nutrifood.eu/database/muehlenchemie/mc-fltr-e.pdf.

Muramoto, Noboru B. *Natural Immunity Insights on Diet and Aids.* Oroville, CA: George Ohsawa Macrobiotic Foundation, 1988.

Murphy, Suzanne P. and Rachel K. Johnson. "The Scientific Basis of Recent U.S. Guidance on Sugars Intake." *American Journal of Clinical Nutrition* 78:4 (2003): 8275–8335.

Murray, Michael T., Joseph E. Pizzorno, and Lara Pizzorno. *The Encyclopedia of Healing Foods.* New York: Atria, 2005.

Nagel, Michael C. *Nurturing a Healthy Mind: Doing What Matters Most for Your Child's Developing Brain.* Wollombi, N.S.W.: Exisle Publishing, 2012.

Nagel, Ramiel, and Sally Fallon. *Healing Our Children: Sacred Wisdom for Preconception, Pregnancy, Birth, and Parenting.* Los Gatos, CA: Golden Child Pub., 2009.

"Nail Polish 101." Goddess Huntress. Last accessed June 16, 2014. http://www.goddesshuntress.com/2012/03/29/nail-polish-101/.

Nelson, K. Jennifer. "What Is High-Fructose Corn Syrup? What Are the Health Concerns?" Mayo Clinic. Last modified September 27, 2012.
Last accessed June 13, 2014.
http://www.mayoclinic.org/healthy-living/nutrition-and-healthy-eating/expert-answers/high-fructose-corn-syrup/faq-20058201.

Nelson, Kendall, and Chris Pilaro. *The Greater Good*. Film. Hailey, ID: BNP Pictures, 2011.

"Neomycin/Bacitracin/Polymyxin: Topical, Mycitracin, Neosporin, Triple." MedicineNet. Last modified April 16, 2014.
Last accessed June 16, 2014. http://www.medicinenet.com/neomycinbacitracinpolymyxin-topical/article.htm.

Neustaedter, Randall. *The Vaccine Guide: Risks and Benefits for Children and Adults*. Berkeley, CA: North Atlantic Books, 2002.

"New Study Shows the Benefits of Eating Fish Greatly Outweigh the Risks." Harvard School of Public Health. October 17, 2006.
Last accessed July 25, 2014. http://archive.sph.harvard.edu/press-releases/2006-releases/press10172006.html.

Newcombe, Rachel. "Games That Encourage Learning and Thinking." KidsDevelopment. Last modified October 2, 2012.
Last accessed June 11, 2014. http://www.kidsdevelopment.co.uk/games-encourage-learning-thinking.html.

———. "At What Age Can Children Start Learning a Second Language?" KidsDevelopment. Last modified January 12, 2011.
Last accessed June 11, 2014. http://www.kidsdevelopment.co.uk/age-children-learning-second-language.html.

Newton, Ruth P. *The Attachment Connection: Parenting a Secure & Confident Child Using the Science of Attachment Theory*.
Oakland, CA: New Harbinger Publications, 2008.

Nolte, Dorothy. *Children Learn What They Live*. Lane Cove, N.S.W.: Finch, 2008.

Norris, Jeffrey. "Sugar Is a Poison, Says UCSF Obesity Expert." June 25, 2009. Last accessed June 25, 2014.
http://www.ucsf.edu/news/2009/06/8187/obesity-and-metabolic-syndrome-driven-fructose-sugar-diet.

Norris, Maggie, and Donna Rae Siegfried. *Anatomy & Physiology for Dummies*. Hoboken, NJ: Wiley Publishing, Inc., 2011.

"Nuts and Your Heart: Eating Nuts for Heart Health." Mayo Clinic. Last modified February 19, 2014. Last accessed June 25, 2014.
http://www.mayoclinic.com/health/nuts/HB00085.

Oaklander, Mandy. "Health Food Face-Off: Wild Salmon vs. Farmed Salmon." *Prevention*. Last accessed March 17, 2014.
http://www.prevention.com/which-healthier-wild-salmon-vs-farmed-salmon#.

Ogden C. L., M. D. Carroll, B. K. Kit, and K. M. Flegal. "Prevalence of Obesity in the United States, 2009–2010."
NCHS Data Brief no. 82. Hyattsville, MD: National Center for Health Statistics, 2012.

Okada, H. et al. "The 'Hygiene Hypothesis' for Autoimmune and Allergic Diseases: An Update."
Clinical and Experimental Immunology 160:1 (2010): 1–9.

Okamoto, Naomi. *Japanese Ink Painting: The Art of Sumi-e*. New York: Sterling Pub. Co., 1995.

Oktar, Nezih. "Theory of Neuroscience." *Journal of Neurological Sciences (Turkish)* 23:3 (2006): 155–158.

Olsen, Andrea, and Caryn McHose. *Bodystories: A Guide to Experiential Anatomy*. Barrytown, NY: Barrytown, 1998.

"Omega-3 in Fish: How Eating Fish Helps Your Heart." Mayo Clinic. Last modified February 7, 2014. Last accessed June 25, 2014.
http://www.mayoclinic.com/health/omega-3/HB00087.Ophardt, Charles E. "Saccharin: The oldest Sweetener Sweet' N Low, Sugar
Twin." Virtual Chembook. Last accessed June 13, 2014. http://www.elmhurst.edu/~chm/vchembook/549saccharin.html.

Oppenheimer, Sharifa. *Heaven on Earth: A Handbook for Parents of Young Children*. Great Barrington, MA: SteinerBooks, 2006.

Oswalt, Angela. "Infancy Physical Development: Gross Motor Skills." Seven Counties Services, Inc. Last accessed March 13, 2014.
http://sevencounties.org/poc/view_doc.php?type=doc&id=10109&cn=461.

"OTC Medications: Understanding the Risks." *University of Rochester Medical Center Health Encyclopedia*. Last accessed June 25, 2014.
http://www.urmc.rochester.edu/encyclopedia/content.aspx?ContentTypeID=1&ContentID=4531.

"Over 300 Pollutants in U.S. Tap Water." Environmental Working Group. Last accessed March 12, 2014. www.ewg.org/tap-water/home.

"Over-the-Counter Medicines." MedlinePlus. Last modified May 28, 2014. Last accessed June 16, 2014.
http://www.nlm.nih.gov/medlineplus/overthecountermedicines.html.

Palka, Yvonne. *Super Simple Sumi-e*. Langley, WA: HeartRock Press, 2012.

Pantley, Elizabeth. *The No-Cry Sleep Solution: Gentle Ways to Help Your Baby Sleep through the Night*. Chicago: Contemporary Books, 2002.

"Parabens." Safe Cosmetics Action Network. Last accessed June 25, 2014. http://safecosmetics.org/article.php?id=291.

"Parasites – Lice – Head Lice – Treatment." Centers for Disease Control and Prevention. Last modified September 24, 2013.
Last accessed June 16, 2014. http://www.cdc.gov/parasites/lice/head/treatment.html#otc.

Parker, Hilary. "A Sweet Problem: Princeton Researchers Find That High-Fructose Corn Syrup Prompts Considerably More Weight Gain."
Princeton University. Last modified March 22, 2010. Last accessed June 13, 2014. http://www.princeton.edu/main/news/archive/
S26/91/22K07/.

Parker, Steve. *The Human Body Book*. New York: DK Pub., 2007.

Parker-Pope, Tara. "Nutrition Advice from the China Study." *The New York Times*. January 7, 2011. http://well.blogs.nytimes.com/2011/01/07/nutrition-advice-from-the-china-study/.

Patterson, Charlotte J. *Infancy & Childhood*. Boston: McGraw-Hill Higher Education, 2009.

Payne, Kim John, and Lisa M. Ross. *Simplicity Parenting: Using the Extraordinary Power of Less to Raise Calmer, Happier, and More Secure Kids*. New York: Ballantine, 2010.

"PCBs in Farmed Salmon." Environmental Working Group. Last accessed March 10, 2014. http://salmonfarmscience.files.wordpress.com/2012/02/health_2003_ewg_report.pdf.

Pearson, Barbara Zurer. *Raising a Bilingual Child: A Step-by-Step Guide for Parents*. New York: Living Language, 2008.

Penley, Janet P., and Diane Eble. *Motherstyles: Using Personality Type to Discover Your Parenting Strengths*. Cambridge, MA: Da Capo LifeLong, 2006.

Perry A~. *Living Clay: Nature's Own Miracle Cure, Calcium Bentonite Clay: How to Treat and Cure 101 Ailments Naturally with Calcium Bentonite Clay*. Kyle, TX: Perry Productions, 2006.

"Pesticides and Food: Why Children May Be Especially Sensitive to Pesticides." U.S. Environmental Protection Agency. Last modified May 9, 2012. Last accessed June 16, 2014. http://www.epa.gov/pesticides/food/pest.htm.

Petrash, Jack. *Understanding Waldorf Education: Teaching from the Inside Out*. Beltsville, MD: Gryphon House, 2002.

"Physical Development: Age 0–2." CliffsNotes. Last accessed on March 13, 2014. http://www.cliffsnotes.com/sciences/psychology/development-psychology/physical-cognitive-development-age-02/physical-development-age-02.

"Physical Development in Infancy." Livestrong. Last modified January 30 2014. Last accessed June 25, 2014. http://www.livestrong.com/article/95858-physical-development-infancy/.

Pitchford, Paul. *Healing with Whole Foods: Oriental Traditions and Modern Nutrition*. Berkeley, MA: North Atlantic, 1993.

Plomin, R. "Chaotic Homes and Children's Disruptive Behavior: A Longitudinal Cross-Lagged Twin Study." *Psychological Science* 23:6 (2012): 643–650.

Pollan, Michael. *The Omnivore's Dilemma: A Natural History of Four Meals*. New York: Penguin, 2006.

"Polypropylene (PP)." *Plastipedia: The Plastics Encyclopedia*. Last accessed June 13, 2014. http://www.bpf.co.uk/plastipedia/polymers/pp.aspx.

"Prebiotics." International Life Sciences Institute. Last accessed March 17, 2014. http://www.ilsi.org/Europe/Pages/TF_Prebiotics.aspx.

"Prebiotics: A Consumer Guide for Making Smart Choices." International Scientific Association for Probiotics and Prebiotics. Last accessed March 11, 2014. http://www.isapp.net/Portals/0/docs/Consumer%20Guidelines%20prebiotic%202014.pdf.

Price, Weston A. *Nutrition and Physical Degeneration*. La Mesa, CA: Price-Pottenger Nutrition Foundation, 2008.

"Probiotics for Children." Galen's Watch: Probiotics for Children. Last accessed September 9, 2013. http://www.galenswatch.com/probiotics.html.

"Protein." Centers for Disease Control and Prevention. Last modified October 4, 2012. Last accessed June 25, 2014. http://www.cdc.gov/nutrition/everyone/basics/protein.html.

"The Protein Myth." Physicians Committee for Responsible Medicine. Last accessed March 10, 2014. http://www.pcrm.org/search/?cid=251.

Psaris, Jett, and Marlena S. Lyons. *Undefended Love*. Oakland, CA: New Harbinger Publications, 2000.

Ranzi, Karen. *Creating Healthy Children: Through Attachment Parenting and Raw Foods*. Ramsey, NJ: Super Healthy Children Pub., 2010.

Ratey, John. *Spark, the Revolutionary New Science of Exercise and the Brain*. New York: Little, Brown, 2013.

"Rayon Fiber." Fiber Source. Last accessed June 16, 2014. http://www.fibersource.com/f-tutor/rayon.htm.

Reichstein, Gail. *Wood Becomes Water: Chinese Medicine in Everyday Life*. New York: Kodansha International, 1998.

"The Report of the Dietary Guidelines Advisory Committee on Dietary Guidelines for Americans, 2005." U.S. Department of Health and Human Services. January 2005. Last accessed June 25, 2014. http://www.health.gov/dietaryguidelines/dga2005/report/.

Reverman, Susan. "Tactile Experiences for Infants for Brain Development." *Everyday Life*. Last accessed June 1, 2014. http://everydaylife.globalpost.com/tactile-experiences-infants-brain-development-3076.html.

Rhodes, Sharon Ann, and Patricia Zunic. *Cooking with Sea Vegetables*. Brookline, MA: Autumn, 1978.

Rico, Gabriele L. *Writing the Natural Way: Using Right-Brain Techniques to Release Your Expressive Powers*. New York: Tarcher/Putnam, 2000.

Ritchhart, Ron, and David Perkins. "Making Thinking Visible." Association for Supervision and Curriculum Development: 57–61. February 2008. Last accessed June 11, 2014.

Rivoli, Shelly. *Travels with Baby: Hundreds of Tips to Help During Travel with Your Baby, Toddler, and Preschooler*. Berkeley, CA: Travels with Baby Books, 2010.

———. *Travels with Baby: The Ultimate Guide for Planning Trips with Babies, Toddlers, and Preschool-Age Children*. Berkeley, CA: Travels with Baby Books, 2007.

Roehlkepartain, Jolene L., and Nancy Leffert. *What Young Children Need to Succeed: Working Together to Build Assets from Birth to Age 11.* Minneapolis: Free Spirit Pub., 2000.

Rogoff, Barbara. *The Cultural Nature of Human Development.* Oxford, UK: Oxford Univ. Pub., 2003.

Romm, Aviva Jill. *Naturally Healthy Babies and Children: A Commonsense Guide to Herbal Remedies, Nutrition, and Health.* Berkeley, CA: CelestialArts, 2003.

———. *Vaccinations: A Thoughtful Parent's Guide: How to Make Safe, Sensible Decisions about the Risks, Benefits, and Alternatives.* Rochester, VT: Healing Arts Press, 2001.

Rook, G. A. W. *The Hygiene Hypothesis and Darwinian Medicine.* Basel, Switzerland: Birkhäuser, 2009.

Ros, Emilio. "Health Benefits of Nut Consumption." *Nutrients* 2:7 (2010): 652–682.

Rossoff, Michael. "Immunization: Ally or Enemy? An Exclusive Talk with Keith Block, MD." *MarcoMuse* Feb.–Mar. 1983: 16–23.

Rovee-Collier, Carolyn. "The Development of Infant Memory." *Current Directions in Psychological Science* 8:3 (June 1999): 80–85. Last accessed June 25, 2014. http://bernard.pitzer.edu/~dmoore/psych199s03articles/r-collier_memory.pdf.

Royte, Elizabeth. "Corn Plastic to the Rescue." *Smithsonian Magazine.* Last modified August 2006. Last accessed June 16, 2014. http://www.smithsonianmag.com/science-nature/corn-plastic-to-the-rescue-126404720/?no-ist.

Ruffin, Novella J. "Human Growth and Development: A Matter of Principles." *Virginia Cooperative Extension* (2009): 1–2. Last accessed March 12, 2014. http://pubs.ext.vt.edu/350/350-053/350-053.html.

———. "Understanding Growth and Development Patterns of Infants." *Virginia Cooperative Extension* (2009): 1–6. Last accessed March 12, 2014. http://pubs.ext.vt.edu/350/350-055/350-055.html.

Ryan, Kathleen O., dir. *Infants: Social and Emotional Development.* Film. Chicago: Learning Seed, 2010.

Sadeharju, Karita, et al. "Maternal Antibodies in Breast Milk Protect the Child From Enterovirus Infections." *Pediatrics* 119: 5 (2007): 941–946.

"Safe Diaper Wipe Guide." Gimme the Good Stuff. Last accessed June 16, 2014. http://gimmethegoodstuff.org/safe-product-guides/diaper-wipes.

Saint Louis, Catherine. "Dental Group Advises Fluoride Toothpaste before Age 2." *The New York Times.* February 12, 2014. Last accessed June 25, 2014. http://well.blogs.nytimes.com/2014/02/12/dental-group-advises-fluoride-toothpaste-before-age-2/?_php=true&_type=blogs&_r=0.

Sanchez, Albert, et al. "Role of Sugars in Human Neutrophilic Phagocytosis." *American Journal of Clinical Nutrition* 26:11 (1973): 1180–1184.

Santrock, John W. "Emotional Development" in *A Topical Approach to Life-Span Development.* New York: McGraw-Hill, 2012.

Sassé, Margaret. *Active Baby, Healthy Brain: 135 Fun Exercises and Activities to Maximize Your Child's Brain Development from Birth through Age 5 1/2.* New York: Experiment, 2010.

Sax, Leonard. "Polyethylene Terephthalate May Yield Endocrine Disruptors." *Environmental Health Perspectives* 118:4 (April 2010): 445–448. Last accessed June 23, 2014. http://www.ncbi.nlm.nih.gov/pmc/articles/PMC2854718/.

Schaefer, Charles E., and Theresa Foy DiGeronimo. *Ages and Stages: A Parent's Guide to Normal Childhood Development.* New York: John Wiley, 2000.

Schiller, Pamela Byrne. *Seven Skills for School Success: Activities to Develop Social & Emotional Intelligence in Young Children.* Beltsville, MD: Gryphon House, 2009.

———. *Start Smart!: Building Brain Power in the Early Years.* Lewisville, NC: Gryphon House, 2012.

Schiller, Pam, and Pat Phipps. *The Daily Curriculum for Early Childhood: Over 1,200 Easy Activities to Support Multiple Intelligences and Learning Styles.* Silver Spring, MD: Gryphon House, 2011.

Schwarz, Eleanor Bimla, et al. "Duration of Lactation and Risk Factors for Maternal Cardiovascular Disease." Obstetrics & Gynecology 113:5 (2009): 974–982. doi: 10.1097/01.AOG.0000346884.67796.ca

Schwartz, Kevin, and Keith Garber. *Babysafe in Seven Steps: The Babyganics Guide to Smart and Effective Solutions for a Healthy Home.* New York: Ballantine Books Trade Paperback, 2014.

"Science of Early Childhood." Center on the Developing Child. Last accessed January 12, 2014. http://developingchild.harvard.edu/topics/science_of_early_childhood/.

Scott, Julian. *Natural Medicine for Children.* New York: Avon, 1990.

Scott, Julian, and Teresa Barlow. *Acupuncture in the Treatment of Children.* Seattle: Eastland, 1999.Sears, Robert. *The Vaccine Book: Making the Right Decision for Your Child.* New York: Little, Brown, 2011.

Sears, William. *The Baby Book: Everything You Need to Know about Your Baby—from Birth to Age Two.* Boston: Little, Brown, 2003.

———. *The Portable Pediatrician: Everything You Need to Know about Your Child's Health.* New York: Little, Brown, 2011.

Sears, William, and James M. Sears. *The Omega-3 Effect: Everything You Need to Know about the Supernutrient for Living Longer, Happier, and Healthier.* New York: Little, Brown, 2012.

Sears, William, and Martha Sears. *The Attachment Parenting Book: A Commonsense Guide to Understanding and Nurturing Your Baby.* Boston: Little, Brown, 2001.

———. *The Discipline Book: Everything You Need to Know to Have a Better-Behaved Child—from Birth to Age Ten.* Boston: Little, Brown, 1995.

———. *The Family Nutrition Book: Everything You Need to Know about Feeding Your Children—from Birth through Adolescence.* Boston: Little, Brown, 1999.

Sears, William, Martha Sears, and Elizabeth Pantley. *The Successful Child: What Parents Can Do to Help Kids Turn Out Well.* Boston: Little, Brown, 2002.

Seldin, Tim. *How to Raise an Amazing Child the Montessori Way.* New York: DK Pub., 2006.

"Self-Regulation." Tools of the Mind. Last accessed December 03, 2013. http://www.toolsofthemind.org/philosophy/self-regulation/.

Sethi, Anita. "The Real Difference Between Boys and Girls: What the Research Really Says about Gender And Babies." Parenting.com. Last accessed December 04, 2013. http://www.parenting.com/article/real-difference-between-boys-and-girls.

"Shaking the Salt Habit." American Heart Association. Last accessed on March 11, 2014. http://www.heart.org/HEARTORG/Conditions/HighBloodPressure/PreventionTreatmentofHighBloodPressure/Shaking-the-Salt-Habit_UCM_303241_Article.jsp.

"Shiitake Mushroom." American Cancer Society. Last modified November 2008. Last accessed June 25, 2014. www.cancer.org/treatment/treatmentsandsideeffects/complementaryandalternativemedicine/dietandnutrition/shiitake-mushroom.

Shino, Mika. *Smart Bites for Baby: 300 Easy-to-Make, Easy-to-Love Meals That Boost Your Baby and Toddler's Brain.* Boston, MA: De Capo, 2012.

Shonkoff, Jack P., and Deborah Phillips. *From Neurons to Neighborhoods: The Science of Early Child Development.* Washington, D.C.: National Academy, 2000.

Shopper's Guide to Natural Foods: A Consumer's Guide to Buying and Preparing Foods for Good Health. Garden City Park, NY: Avery Pub. Group, 1987.

Siegel, Daniel J., and Mary Hartzell. *Parenting from the Inside Out: How a Deeper Self-Understanding Can Help You Raise Children Who Thrive.* New York: J. P. Tarcher/Putnam, 2003.

Siegel, Daniel J., and Tina Payne. Bryson. *The Whole-Brain Child: 12 Revolutionary Strategies to Nurture Your Child's Developing Mind.* New York: Delacorte, 2011.

Silberg, Jackie. *Games to Play with Babies.* Beltsville, MD: Gryphon House, 2001.

"Silicone Tally: How Hazardous Is the New Post-Teflon Rubberized Cookware." *Scientific American.* Last modified May 5, 2010. Last accessed June 16, 2014. http://www.scientificamerican.com/article/earth-talk-silicone-tally/.

"Silk." *Encyclopedia Britannica.* Last accessed June 25, 2014. http://www.britannica.com/EBchecked/topic/544449/silk/283189/Elsewhere.

Silverstone, Alicia. *The Kind Diet: A Simple Guide to Feeling Great, Losing Weight, and Saving the Planet.* Emmaus, PA: Rodale, 2009.

Simple Botanicals. *Aromatherapy Guide to Essential Oils.* Sebastopol, CA: Simple Botanicals, N/A.

Siri-Tarino, Patty W. Qi Sun, Frank B. Hu, and Ronald M. Krauss. "Meta-Analysis of Prospective Cohort Studies Evaluating the Association of Saturated Fat with Cardiovascular Disease." *American Journal of Clinical Nutrition* 91:3 (2010): 535–546.

Sisson, Mark. "A Primal Primer: Prebiotics." Mark's Daily Apple. Last accessed June 11, 2014. http://www.marksdailyapple.com/prebiotics/.

Slater, Alan, and J. Gavin Bremner. *Infant Development.* Hillsdale, NJ L. Erlbaum, 1989.

Smith, Dana. "What's Keeping You Awake at Night?" Nature Education. Last modified June 7, 2013. Last accessed June 16, 2014. http://www.nature.com/scitable/blog/mind-read/what_keeps_you_awake_at.

Snel, Eline. *Sitting Still Like a Frog: Mindfulness Exercises for Kids (and Their Parents).* Boston: Shambhala Publications, 2013.

"Sodium and Salt." American Heart Association. Last accessed March 12, 2014. http://www.heart.org/HEARTORG/GettingHealthy/Nutrition-Center/HealthyDietGoals/Sodium-Salt-or-Sodium-Chloride_UCM_303290_Article.jsp.

Sole-Smith, Virginia. "Toxins Found in 'Toxin-Free' Nail Polish: Another Reason Beauty Regulation Needs a Makeover." *Slate Magazine.* Last modified April 13, 2014. Last accessed June 16, 2014. http://www.slate.com/blogs/xx_factor/2012/04/13/toxic_nail_polish_lies_found_on_beauty_industry_labels.html.

Solomon, Andrew. *Far from the Tree: Parents, Children, and the Search for Identity.* New York: Scribner, 2012.

"Some 'Lead-Free' Pottery Can Still Taint Food." Food and Drug Administration. Last modified November 19, 2010. Last accessed June 16, 2014. http://www.fda.gov/forconsumers/consumerupdates/ucm233531.htm.

Somer, Elizabeth. *Eat Your Way to Happiness: 10 Diet Secrets to: Improve Your Mood, Curb Your Cravings, Keep the Pounds off.* Don Mills, Canada: Harlequin, 2009.

"Sorting Out the Vinyls: When Is 'Vinyl' not PVC?" Healthy Building Network. Last modified April 28, 2005. Last accessed June 16, 2014. http://www.healthybuilding.net/pvc/SortingOutVinyls.html.

Sousa, David A. *How the Brain Learns.* Thousand Oaks, CA: Corwin, 2012.

"Soy Alert!" The Weston A. Price Foundation. Last accessed March 10, 2014. http://www.westonaprice.org/soy-alert.

Squires, Jane, and Diane D. Bricker. *Ages & Stages Questionnaires: A Parent-Completed Child Monitoring System.* Baltimore: Paul H. Brooks Pub. Co., 2009.

Stamm, Jill, and Paula Spencer. *Bright from the Start: The Simple, Science-Backed Way to Nurture Your Child's Developing Mind, from Birth to Age 3.* New York: Gotham, 2007.

Steckelberg, James M. "Should I Avoid Products That Contain Triclosan?" Mayo Clinic. Last modified April 15, 2014. Last accessed June 16, 2014. http://www.mayoclinic.org/healthy-living/adult-health/expert-answers/triclosan/faq-20057861.

Stein, Leslie J., et al. "The Development of Salty Taste Acceptance Is Related to Dietary Experience in Human Infants: A Prospective Study." *American Journal of Clinical Nutrition* 95:1 (2012): 123–129.

Steiner, Naomi, Susan L. Hayes, and Steven Parker. *7 Steps to Raising a Bilingual Child.* New York: AMACOM, American Management Association, 2009.

Steiner, Rudolf. *Practical Advice to Teachers: Fourteen Lectures Given at the Foundation of the Waldorf School, Stuttgart, from 21 August to 5 September 1919.* London: Rudolf Steiner, 1976.

Steiner, Rudolf, John Salter, and Pauline Wehrle. *Colour: Three Lectures Given in Dornach 6th to the 8th of May, 1921 Together with Nine Supplementary Lectures given on Various Occasions.* London: Rudolf Steiner, 1996.

"Study Examines Long-Term Health Effects of Soy Infant Formula." U.S. Department of Agriculture. Last accessed March 12, 2014. http://www.ars.usda.gov/is/ar/archive/jan04/soy0104.htm.

Sullivan, Karen. *The Parent's Guide to Natural Health Care for Children: How to Raise Happy, Healthy Children from Birth to 15.* Boston: Shambhala, 2004.

Summary Health Statistics for U.S. Children: National Health Interview Survey, 2011. Report no. 2013-1582, Series 10, Number 254. Hyattsville, MD: U.S. Department of Health and Human Services, 2013.

Szalavitz, Maia, and Bruce Duncan Perry. *Born for Love: Why Empathy Is Essential—and Endangered.* New York: HarperCollins, 2011.

"Talcum Powder and Cancer." American Cancer Society. Last modified May 13, 2014. Last accessed June 16, 2014. http://www.cancer.org/cancer/cancercauses/othercarcinogens/athome/talcum-powder-and-cancer.

Tara, William. *Macrobiotics and Human Behavior.* Tokyo: Japan Publications, 1984.

Teeguarden, Iona. *Acupressure: Way of Health, Jin Shin Do.* Tokyo, Japan: Japan Publications, 1978.

Teeguarden, Ron. *Radiant Health: The Ancient Wisdom of the Chinese Tonic Herbs.* New York: Warner Books, 1998.
"Thermoplastic Elastomers (TPE)." Timco Rubber. Last accessed June 16, 2014. http://www.timcorubber.com/rubber-materials/tpe.htm.

Thomas, Dan W., and Frank R. Greer. "Clinical Report—Probiotics and Prebiotics in Pediatrics." *Pediatrics* (2010). Last accessed March 11, 2014. doi: 10.1542/peds.2010-2548.

Thomson, John B., and Tim Kahn. *Natural Childhood: The First Practical and Holistic Guide for Parents of the Developing Child.* New York: Simon & Schuster, 1994.

Thorndike, Edward L. "Intelligence and Its Uses." *Harper's Magazine.* January 1920: 227–235.

Tian, Niu, et al. "Sodium and Potassium Intakes among U.S. Infants and Preschool Children, 2003–2010." *American Journal of Clinical Nutrition* 98:4 (2013): 1113–1122.

"Tobacco Products." U.S. Food and Drug Administration. Last modified May 21, 2014. Last accessed June 16, 2014. http://www.fda.gov/TobaccoProducts/default.htm.

"Toddler Development." About.com Toddlers and Twos. Last accessed June 23, 2014. http://babyparenting.about.com/od/childdevelopment.

Tough, Paul. *How Children Succeed: Grit, Curiosity, and the Hidden Power of Character.* Boston: Houghton Mifflin Harcourt, 2012.

"Trans Fat." American Heart Association. Last accessed March 12, 2014. http://www.heart.org/HEARTORG/GettingHealthy/FatsAndOils/Fats101/Trans-Fats_UCM_301120_Article.jsp.

"Trans Fat Is Double Trouble for Your Heart Health." Mayo Clinic. Last modified May 6, 2011. Last accessed June 13, 2014. http://www.mayoclinic.org/diseases-conditions/high-blood-cholesterol/in-depth/trans-fat/art-20046114.

"Triclosan: What Consumers Should Know." U.S. Food and Drug Administration. Last modified December 16, 2013. Last accessed June 16, 2014. http://www.fda.gov/forconsumers/consumerupdates/ucm205999.htm.

Trinidad, Trinidad P., et al. "The Potential Health Benefits of Legumes as a Good Source of Dietary Fibre." *British Journal of Nutrition* 103:4 (2010): 569–574.

"The Trouble with Sunscreen Chemicals." Environmental Working Group. Last accessed June 16, 2014. http://www.ewg.org/2014sunscreen/the-trouble-with-sunscreen-chemicals/.

Turner, Kristina. *The Self-Healing Cookbook: Whole Foods to Balance Body, Mind, and Moods.* Vashon Island, WA: Earthtones Press, 2002.

Twombly, Elizabeth, Ginger Fink, and Diane D. Bricker. *Ages & Stages Learning Activities*. Baltimore: P. H. Brookes Pub., 2004.

U.S. Department of Agriculture. "Nutrition Standards in the National School Lunch and School Breakfast Programs." *Federal Register* 77:17 (2012).vU.S. Department of Agriculture and U.S. Department of Health and Human Services. "Dietary Guidelines for Americans, 2010: Executive Summary." Last accessed June 25, 2014. http://www.cnpp.usda.gov/Publications/DietaryGuidelines/2010/PolicyDoc/ExecSumm.pdf.

U.S. Food and Drug Administration. "131.112 Cultured milk." *United States Code of Federal Regulations* 4–1–06 Edition: 292–294. Last accessed June 25, 2014. http://www.gpo.gov/fdsys/pkg/CFR-2006-title21-vol2/pdf/CFR-2006-title21-vol2-sec131-112.pdf.

U.S. Food and Drug Administration. "Guidelines for the Evaluation of Probiotics in Food and Agriculture Organization of the United Nations and World Health Organization. "Guidelines for the Evaluation of Probiotics in Food." Food and Drug Administration. April 30 and May 1, 2002. Last accessed June 25, 2014. http://www.fda.gov/ohrms/dockets/dockets/95s0316/95s-0316-rpt0282-tab-03-ref-19-joint-faowho-vol219.pdf.

Usui, Mikao, and Frank Arjava Petter. *The Original Reiki Handbook of Dr. Mikao Usui*. Twin Lakes, WI: Lotus Press, 1999.

"Vaccines, Blood & Biologics: Resources for You." U.S. Food and Drug Administration. Last accessed March 17, 2014. http://www.fda.gov/BiologicsBloodVaccines/ResourcesforYou/default.htm.

Varona, Verne. *Macrobiotics for Dummies*. Hoboken, NJ: John Wiley & Sons, 2009.

Vasey, Christopher. *The Acid-Alkaline Diet for Optimum Health: Restore Your Health by Creating PH Balance in Your Diet*. Rochester, VT: Healing Arts, 2006.

Verhasselt, Valérie. "Neonatal Tolerance under Breastfeeding Influence: The Presence of Allergen and Transforming Growth Factor in Breast Milk Protects the Progeny from Allergic Asthma." *The Journal of Pediatrics* 156:2 (2010): S16–S20.

Vilsack, Tom. "Secretary's Column: Healthier Meals for Our Nation's Children." February 3, 2012. Last accessed March 12, 2014. http://blogs.usda.gov/2012/02/03/secretarys-column-healthier-meals-for-our-nation%E2%80%99s-children/.

"Vitamin E." National Institutes of Health. Last modified October 2011. Last accessed June 25, 2014. http://ods.od.nih.gov/factsheets/VitaminE-QuickFacts/.

Vojdani, A. T., et al. "Immune Response to Dietary Proteins, Gliadin and Cerebellar Peptides in Children with Autism." *Nutritional Neuroscience* 7:3 (2004): 151–161.

Voorhies, Alicia. "What Is EVA and Why Is It in My Baby's Teether?" HubPages. Last modified November 26, 2008. Last accessed June 13, 2014. http://aliciavoorhies.hubpages.com/hub/What-is-EVA-and-Why-is-it-in-My-Babys-Teether.

Voss, Angie. *Understanding Your Child's Sensory Signals: A Practical Daily Use Handbook for Parents and Teachers*. Charleston, SC: CreateSpace Independent Publishing Platform, 2011.

Vulcan Productions. *Early Moments Matter: Small Steps, Long-Lasting Effects*. PBS, 2010.

Wagele, Elizabeth. *The Enneagram of Parenting: The 9 Types of Children and How to Raise Them Successfully*. San Francisco: HarperSanFrancisco, 1997.

Wagele, Elizabeth, and Judith Dome. *Finding the Birthday Cake: Helping Children Raise Their Self-Esteem*. Far Hills, NJ: New Horizon, 2007.

Wansink, Brian. *Mindless Eating: Why We Eat More Than We Think*. New York: Bantam, 2010.

Warren, Wendy, and Michael Gach. *Intermediate and Advanced Acupressure Course Booklet*. Berkeley, CA: Acupressure Institute, 2002.

Wassenaar, Trudy. "Bacteria and pH." Argonne National Laboratory. Last accessed March 17, 2014. http://newton.dep.anl.gov/askasci/mole00/mole00173.htm.

"Water Intoxication in Infants." Saint Louis Children's Hospital. Last accessed March 12, 2014. http://www.stlouischildrens.org/articles/wellness/water-intoxication-in-infants.

"Water on Tap: What You Need to Know." U.S. Environmental Protection Agency. Last accessed March 12, 2014. http://water.epa.gov/drink/guide.

Watson, Jane Werner, and Eloise Wilkin. *Wonders of Nature*. New York: Golden Book, 2010.

Way, Jenni. "The Development of Spatial and Geometric Thinking: 5 to 18." *NRICH*. Last accessed March 14, 2014. http://nrich.maths.org/2483/index.

Weil, Andrew. *Breathing: The Master Key to Self Healing*. Boulder, CO: Sounds True, 1999.

———. "Cooking with Silicone?" Weil Lifestyle. Last modified September 4, 2007. Last accessed June 16, 2014. http://www.drweil.com/drw/u/id/QAA400274.

———. "How Bad Is Baby Powder?" Weil Lifestyle. Last modified October 8, 2012. Last accessed June 16, 2014. http://www.drweil.com/drw/u/QAA401185/How-Bad-Is-Baby-Powder.html.

Wells, S. D. "Sodium Benzoate Is a Preservative That Promotes Cancer and Kills Healthy Cells." *Natural News*. Last modified September 29, 2011. Last accessed June 13, 2014. http://www.naturalnews.com/033726_sodium_benzoate_cancer.html.

———. "Sweetener Warning: Acesulfame Potassium Contains Methylene Chloride, a Known Carcinogen." *Natural News*. Last modified August 6, 2013. Last accessed June 13, 2014. http://www.naturalnews.com/041510_Acesulfame-K_methylene_chloride_carcinogen.html.

"What Are Germs?" KidsHealth. Last accessed April 2011. http://kidshealth.org/kid/talk/qa/germs.html.

"What Are the Six Common Air Pollutants?" U.S. Environmental Protection Agency. Last modified April 20, 2012. Last accessed June 16, 2014. http://www.epa.gov/air/urbanair/.

"What Are Trans Fats? Food Sources, Decoding Labels." WebMD. Last modified April 2, 2014. Last accessed June 13, 2014. http://www.webmd.com/food-recipes/understanding-trans-fats.

"What Is a Pesticide?" U.S. Environmental Protection Agency. Last modified May 16, 2014. Last accessed June 16, 2014. http://www.epa.gov/pesticides/about/.

"What Is Attachment Disorder? An Introduction." Last accessed January 12, 2014. http://www.attachmentdisorder.net.

"What Is Bamboo Fabric?" wiseGEEK. Last accessed June 16, 2014. http://www.wisegeek.org/what-is-bamboo-fabric.htm.

"What Is Polyhydroxybutyrate (PBH) and Is It Eco-Friendly?" Curiosity.com. Last accessed June 16, 2014. http://curiosity.discovery.com/question/what-polyhydroxybutyrate-pbh-eco-friendly.

"What Is Polyurethane?" wiseGeek. Last accessed June 16, 2014. http://www.wisegeek.org/what-is-polyurethane.htm.

White, Burton L. *The New First Three Years of Life*. New York: Fireside Book, 1995.

White, Chris, MD. "The Yin and Yang of Discipline." Essential Parenting. Last accessed June 25, 2014. http://www.essentialparenting.com/2012/01/26/the-yin-and-yang-of-discipline/.

"Why Go Fragrance Free?" Invisible Disabilities Association. Last accessed June 16, 2014. http://invisibledisabilities.org/educate/chemicalsensitivities/whygofragrancefree/.

"Why Is It Important to Eat Grains, Especially Whole Grains?" U.S. Department of Agriculture. Last accessed March 10, 2014. www.choosemyplate.gov/food-groups/grains-why.html.

Wikimedia Foundation. "Acesulfame Potassium." Wikipedia. Last modified June 6, 2014. Last accessed June 13, 2014. http://en.wikipedia.org/wiki/Acesulfame_potassium.

Wikimedia Foundation. "Acid." Wikipedia. Last modified June 9, 2014. Last accessed June 13, 2014. http://en.wikipedia.org/wiki/Acid.

Wikimedia Foundation. "Acrylic Fiber." Wikipedia. Last modified May 26, 2014. Last accessed June 16, 2014. http://en.wikipedia.org/wiki/Acrylic_fiber.

Wikimedia Foundation. "Acrylonitrile Butadiene Styrene." Wikipedia. Last modified May 14, 2014. Last accessed June 16, 2014. http://en.wikipedia.org/wiki/Acrylonitrile_butadiene_styrene.

Wikimedia Foundation. "Agar." Wikipedia. Last modified June 5, 2014. Last accessed June 13, 2014. http://en.wikipedia.org/wiki/Agar.

Wikimedia Foundation. "Allergy." Wikipedia. Last modified June 10, 2014. Last accessed June 16, 2014. http://en.wikipedia.org/wiki/Allergy.

Wikimedia Foundation. "Aluminium." Wikipedia. Last modified June 13, 2014. Last accessed June 16, 2014. http://en.wikipedia.org/wiki/Aluminium.

Wikimedia Foundation. "Ammonium Lauryl Sulfate." Wikipedia. Last modified June 16, 2013. Last accessed June 16, 2014. http://en.wikipedia.org/wiki/Ammonium_lauryl_sulfate.

Wikimedia Foundation. "Antioxidant." Wikipedia. Last modified June 8, 2014. Last accessed June 13, 2014. http://en.wikipedia.org/wiki/Antioxidant.

Wikimedia Foundation. "Aspartame." Wikipedia. Last modified June 12, 2014. Last accessed June 13, 2014. http://en.wikipedia.org/wiki/Aspartame.

Wikimedia Foundation. "Bioplastic." Wikipedia. Last modified June 1, 2014. Last accessed June 16, 2014. http://en.wikipedia.org/wiki/Bioplastics#Polylactic_acid_.28PLA.29.

Wikimedia Foundation. "Bisphenol A." Wikipedia. Last modified June 10, 2014. Last accessed June 16, 2014. http://en.wikipedia.org/wiki/Bisphenol_A.

Wikimedia Foundation. "Bleach." Wikipedia. Last modified June 15, 2014. Last accessed June 16, 2014. http://en.wikipedia.org/wiki/Bleach.

Wikimedia Foundation. "Borax." Wikipedia. Last modified June 8, 2014. June 16, 2014. http://en.wikipedia.org/wiki/Borax.

Wikimedia Foundation. "Butylated Hydroxyanisole." Wikipedia. Last modified March 15, 2014. Last accessed June 16, 2014. http://en.wikipedia.org/wiki/Butylated_hydroxyanisole.

Wikimedia Foundation. "Butylated Hydroxytoluene." Wikipedia. Last modified May 7, 2014. Last accessed June 13, 2014. http://en.wikipedia.org/wiki/Butylated_hydroxytoluene.

Wikimedia Foundation. "Cadmium." Wikipedia. Last modified June 2, 2014. Last accessed June 16, 2014. http://en.wikipedia.org/wiki/Cadmium.

Wikimedia Foundation. "Caffeine." Wikipedia. Last modified June 9, 2014. Last accessed June 13, 2014. http://en.wikipedia.org/wiki/Caffeine.

Wikimedia Foundation. "Ceramic." Wikipedia. Last modified June 15, 2014. Last accessed June 16, 2014. http://en.wikipedia.org/wiki/Ceramic.

Wikimedia Foundation. "Consumer Electronics." Wikipedia. Last modified June 7, 2014. Last accessed June 16, 2014. http://en.wikipedia.org/wiki/Consumer_electronics.

Wikimedia Foundation. "Diethanolamine." Wikipedia. Last modified December 22, 2013. Last accessed June 16, 2014. http://en.wikipedia.org/wiki/Diethanolamine.

Wikimedia Foundation. "E number." Wikipedia. Last modified June 9, 2014. Last accessed June 13, 2014. http://en.wikipedia.org/wiki/E_number.

Wikimedia Foundation. "Emotion." Wikipedia. Last modified June 24, 2104. Last accessed June 25, 2014. http://en.wikipedia.org/wiki/Emotion.

Wikimedia Foundation. "Emotional Self-Regulation." Wikipedia. Last modified May 21, 2014. Last accessed June 23, 2014. http://en.wikipedia.org/wiki/Emotional_self-regulation.

Wikimedia Foundation. "Ethylene-Vinyl Acetate." Wikipedia. Last modified May 27, 2014. Last accessed June 13, 2014. http://en.wikipedia.org/wiki/Ethylene-Vinyl_Acetate.

Wikimedia Foundation. "Fertilizer." Wikipedia. Last modified June 11, 2014. Last accessed June 16, 2014. http://en.wikipedia.org/wiki/Fertilizer.

Wikimedia Foundation. "Flour Treatment Agent." Wikipedia. Last modified January 16, 2014. Last accessed June 13, 2014. http://en.wikipedia.org/wiki/Flour_treatment_agent.

Wikimedia Foundation. "Foaming Agent." Wikipedia. Last modified June 16, 2014. Last accessed June 16, 2014. http://en.wikipedia.org/wiki/Foaming_agent.

Wikimedia Foundation. "Food Coloring." Wikipedia. Last modified June 6, 2014. Last accessed June 13, 2014. http://en.wikipedia.org/wiki/Food_coloring.

Wikimedia Foundation. "Formaldehyde." Wikipedia. Last modified June 7, 2014. Last accessed June 16, 2014. http://en.wikipedia.org/wiki/Formaldehyde.

Wikimedia Foundation. "Formamide." Wikipedia. Last modified June 14, 2014. Last accessed June 16, 2014. http://en.wikipedia.org/wiki/Formamide.

Wikimedia Foundation. "Glass." Wikipedia. Last modified June 14, 2014. Last accessed June 16, 2014. http://en.wikipedia.org/wiki/Glass.

Wikimedia Foundation. "Glazing Agent." Wikipedia. Last modified March 29, 2014. Last accessed June 13, 204. http://en.wikipedia.org/wiki/Glazing_agent.

Wikimedia Foundation. "Hdpe." Wikipedia. Last modified June 3, 2014. Last accessed June 13, 2014. http://en.wikipedia.org/wiki/Hdpe.

Wikimedia Foundation. "Health Effects of Tobacco." Wikipedia. Last modified June 12, 2014. Last accessed June 16, 2014. http://en.wikipedia.org/wiki/Health_effects_of_tobacco.

Wikimedia Foundation. "High Fructose Corn Syrup." Wikipedia. Last modified June 5, 2014. Last accessed June 13, 2014. http://en.wikipedia.org/wiki/High_fructose_corn_syrup.

Wikimedia Foundation. "Hydrogen Peroxide." Wikipedia. Last modified June 15, 2014. Last accessed June 16, 2014. http://en.wikipedia.org/wiki/Hydrogen_peroxide.

Wikimedia Foundation. "LDPE." Wikipedia. Last modified May 12, 2014. Last accessed June 13, 2014. http://en.wikipedia.org/wiki/LDPE.

Wikimedia Foundation. "Lead." Wikipedia. Last modified June 3, 2014. Last accessed June 16, 2014. http://en.wikipedia.org/wiki/Lead.

Wikimedia Foundation. "Lemon." Wikipedia. Last modified June 9, 2014. Last accessed June 16, 2014. http://en.wikipedia.org/wiki/Lemon.

Wikimedia Foundation. "List of Food Additives." Wikipedia. Last modified March 27, 2014. Last accessed June 13, 2004. http://en.wikipedia.org/wiki/List_of_food_additives.

Wikimedia Foundation. "List of Poisonous Plants." Wikipedia. Last modified June 1, 2014. Last accessed June 16, 2014. http://en.wikipedia.org/wiki/List_of_poisonous_plants.

Wikimedia Foundation. "Margaret Mahler." Wikipedia. Last modified April 28, 204. Last accessed June 23, 2014. http://en.wikipedia.org/wiki/Margaret_Mahler.

Wikimedia Foundation. "Mold." Wikipedia. Last modified June 1, 2014. Last accessed June 16, 2014. http://en.wikipedia.org/wiki/Mold.

Wikimedia Foundation. "Monosodium Glutamate." Wikipedia. Last modified June 8, 2014. Last accessed June 13, 2014. http://en.wikipedia.org/wiki/Monosodium_glutamate.

Wikimedia Foundation. "Natural Rubber." Wikipedia. Last modified June 9, 2014. Last accessed June 16, 2014. http://en.wikipedia.org/wiki/Natural_rubber.

Wikimedia Foundation. "Nitrate." Wikipedia. Last modified June 9, 2014. Last accessed June 13, 2014. http://en.wikipedia.org/wiki/Nitrate.

Wikimedia Foundation. "Nylon." Wikipedia. Last modified June 15, 2014. Last accessed June 16, 2014. http://en.wikipedia.org/wiki/Nylon.

Wikimedia Foundation. "Permethrin." Wikipedia. Last modified June 10, 2014. Last accessed June 16, 2014. http://en.wikipedia.org/wiki/Permethrin#Toxicology_and_safety.

Wikimedia Foundation. "Phthalate." Wikipedia. Last modified June 1, 2014. Last accessed June 16, 2014. http://en.wikipedia.org/wiki/Phthalate.

Wikimedia Foundation. "Piaget's Theory of Cognitive Development." Wikipedia. Last modified June 21, 2014. Last accessed June 25, 2014. http://en.wikipedia.org/wiki/Piaget%27s_theory_of_cognitive_development.

Wikimedia Foundation. "Polyamide." Wikipedia. Last modified April 10, 2014. Last accessed June 16, 2014. http://en.wikipedia.org/wiki/Polyamide.

Wikimedia Foundation. "Polycarbonate." Wikipedia. Last modified May 19, 2014. Last accessed June 16, 2014. http://en.wikipedia.org/wiki/Polycarbonate.

Wikimedia Foundation. "Polychlorinated biphenyl." Wikipedia. Last modified June 4, 2014. Last accessed June 16, 2014. http://en.wikipedia.org/wiki/Polychlorinated_biphenyl.

Wikimedia Foundation. "Polyethylene terephthalate." Wikipedia. Last modified June 3, 2014. Last accessed June 13, 2014. http://en.wikipedia.org/wiki/Polyethylene_terephthalate.

Wikimedia Foundation. "Polyhydroxybutyrate." Wikipedia. Last modified April 22, 2014. Last accessed June 16, 2014. http://en.wikipedia.org/wiki/Polyhydroxybutyrate.

Wikimedia Foundation. "Polypropylene." Wikipedia. Last modified June 13, 2014. Last accessed June 13, 2014. http://en.wikipedia.org/wiki/Polypropylene.

Wikimedia Foundation. "Polystyrene." Wikipedia. Last modified April 22, 2014. Last accessed June 13, 204. http://en.wikipedia.org/wiki/Polystyrene.

Wikimedia Foundation. "Potassium bromate." Wikipedia. Last modified June 13, 2014. Last accessed June 13, 2014. http://en.wikipedia.org/wiki/Potassium_bromate.

Wikimedia Foundation. "Probiotic." Wikipedia. Last modified June 25, 2014. Last accessed June 25, 2014. http://en.wikipedia.org/wiki/Probiotic.

Wikimedia Foundation. "Propylene Glycol." Wikipedia. Last modified June 15, 2014. Last accessed June 16, 2014. http://en.wikipedia.org/wiki/Propylene_glycol.

Wikimedia Foundation. "Pvc." Wikipedia. Last modified June 11, 2014. Last accessed June 13, 2014. http://en.wikipedia.org/wiki/Pvc.

Wikimedia Foundation. "Radiation." Wikipedia. Last modified June 9, 2014. Last accessed June 16, 2014. http://en.wikipedia.org/wiki/Radiation.

Wikimedia Foundation. "Saccharin." Wikipedia. Last modified June 5. 2014. Last accessed June 14, 2014. http://en.wikipedia.org/wiki/Saccharin.

Wikimedia Foundation. "Sodium Benzoate." Wikipedia. Last modified June 6, 2014. Last accessed June 13, 2014. http://en.wikipedia.org/wiki/Sodium_benzoate.

Wikimedia Foundation. "Sodium Bicarbonate." Wikipedia. Last modified June 12, 2014. Last accessed June 16, 2014. http://en.wikipedia.org/wiki/Sodium_bicarbonate.

Wikimedia Foundation. "Sodium Laureth Sulfate." Wikipedia. Last modified June 12, 2014. Last accessed June 16, 2014. http://en.wikipedia.org/wiki/Sodium_laureth_sulfate.

Wikimedia Foundation. "Sodium Nitrate." Wikipedia. Last modified May 22, 2014. Last accessed June 13, 2014. http://en.wikipedia.org/wiki/Sodium_nitrate.

Wikimedia Foundation. "Spandex." Wikipedia. Last modified May 31, 2014. Last accessed June 16, 2014. http://en.wikipedia.org/wiki/Spandex.

Wikimedia Foundation. "Splenda." Wikipedia. Last modified May 23, 2014. Last accessed June 13, 2014. http://en.wikipedia.org/wiki/Splenda.

Wikimedia Foundation. "Sucralose." Wikipedia. Last modified June 10, 2014. Last accessed June 13, 2014. http://en.wikipedia.org/wiki/Sucralose.

Wikimedia Foundation. "Terrycloth." Wikipedia. Last modified November 4, 2013. Last accessed June 16, 2014. http://en.wikipedia.org/wiki/Terrycloth.

Wikimedia Foundation. "Thermoplastic Elastomer." Wikipedia. Last modified May 8, 2014. Last accessed June 16, 2014. http://en.wikipedia.org/wiki/Thermoplastic_elastomer.

Wikimedia Foundation. "Toxic Waste." Wikipedia. Last modified June 16, 2014. Last accessed June 16, 2014. http://en.wikipedia.org/wiki/Toxic_waste.

Wikimedia Foundation. "Trans Fat." Wikipedia. Last modified May 28, 2014. Last accessed June 13, 2014. http://en.wikipedia.org/wiki/Trans_fat.

Wikimedia Foundation. "Ultraviolet." Wikipedia. Last modified June 11, 2014. Last accessed June 16, 2014. http://en.wikipedia.org/wiki/Ultraviolet.

Wikimedia Foundation. "Vinegar." Wikipedia. Last modified June 11, 2014. Last accessed June 16, 2014. http://en.wikipedia.org/wiki/Vinegar.

Wikimedia Foundation. "Wood." Wikipedia. Last modified June 9, 2014. Last accessed June 16, 2014. http://en.wikipedia.org/wiki/Wood.

Wilber, Ken. *The Atman Project: A Transpersonal View of Human Development*. Wheaton, IL: Quest, The Theosophical Pub. House, 1996.

Willett, Walter, P. J. Skerrett, Edward L. Giovannucci, and Maureen Callahan. *Eat, Drink, and Be Healthy: The Harvard Medical School Guide to Healthy Eating*. New York: Simon & Schuster Source, 2001.

Williamson, G. Gordon, and Marie E. Anzalone. *Sensory Integration and Self-Regulation in Infants and Toddlers: Helping Very Young Children Interact with Their Environment*. Washington, DC: Zero to Three, 2001.

Wing, Ali, and Mariella Krause. *Giggle Guide to Baby Gear*. San Francisco: Chronicle, 2008.

Wood, Rebecca Theurer. *The New Whole Foods Encyclopedia: A Comprehensive Resource for Healthy Eating*. New York: Penguin/Arkana, 1999.

"Wooden Toys and Child Development." KidsDevelopment. Last modified June 12, 2013. Last accessed June 11, 2014. http://www.kidsdevelopment.co.uk/wooden-toys-child-development.html.

Yamamoto, S. "Soy, Isoflavones, and Breast Cancer Risk in Japan." *Journal of the National Cancer Institute* 95:12 (2003): 906–913.

Yaron, Ruth. *Super Baby Food: Absolutely Everything You Should Know about Feeding Your Baby and Toddler from Starting Solid Foods to Age Three Years*. Archbald, PA: F. J. Roberts Pub., 1998.

———. *Traveling and Restaurants with Your Super Baby*. PDF e-book. Peckville, PA: F. J. Roberts Holdings, 2011."Yoga Poses for Developmental Movement." GoGo Babies. April 3, 2008. Last accessed June 11, 2014. http://www.gogobabies.net/2008/04/03/what-can-an-infant-learn-from-movement/.

Yoquinto, Luke. "The Truth about Food Additive BHA." *LiveScience*. Last modified June 1, 2012. Last accessed June 13, 2014. http://www.livescience.com/36424-food-additive-bha-butylated-hydroxyanisole.html.

Zand, Janet, Bob Rountree, and Rachel Walton. *Smart Medicine for a Healthier Child: A Practical A-to-Z Reference to Natural and Conventional Treatments for Infants and Children*. New York: Avery, 2003.

Zeitlin, Shirley, and G. Gordon Williamson. *Coping in Young Children: Early Intervention Practices to Enhance Adaptive Behavior and Resilience*. Baltimore: Brookes, 1994.

Zenn, J. Michael. *The Self-Health Revolution*. New York: Free, 2012.

Zeratsky, Katherine. "What Is MSG? Is It Bad for You?" Mayo Clinic. Last modified April 3, 2012. Last accessed June 13, 2014. http://www.mayoclinic.org/healthy-living/nutrition-and-healthy-eating/expert-answers/monosodium-glutamate/faq-20058196.

Zero to Three. "Still Face Experiment: Dr. Edward Tronick." U Mass Boston. YouTube. Last accessed June 25, 2014. http://www.youtube.com/watch?v=apzXGEbZht0.

Zhang, Yifang. *Using Traditional Chinese Medicine to Manage Your Emotional Health: How Herbs, Natural Foods, and Acupressure Can Regulate and Harmonize Your Mind and Body*. New York: Better Link, 2013.

Recipes at a Glance
A summary of recipes for quick reference.

Yin and Yang at a Glance

A summary of yin and yang, for quick reference, to help parents in nurturing their child.
Balance is not a permanent state. Your baby reaches out and explores, then returns back to center,
like coming home to his essence. Throughout this book are ways that you
can support your baby's balance, which are marked with: ⌂

Pathways of Whole Learning at a Glance

A quick reference to the developmental guide for parents to support whole learning.

Index

Gratitude and Thanks

I appreciate the opportunity to research and learn about the many topics as I created this "whole" book for babies and their parents. It has been a very stimulating and satisfying experience that has tapped in to my own passion, purpose, and potential. I express my heartfelt thanks to my team of supporters:

❋ *The Grow Healthy. Grow Happy.* design team:

- Julie Nunnally for her loyalty, hard work, and commitment to the vision of this book
- Norene Spencer for her beautiful *sumi-e* paintings
- Lynne Harty for her dedication to quality and perfection in her photography
- Chris Bryant for the creation of beauty and grace through his styling
- Lora Zorian for her creative direction and design
- Alison Hawkins for her flexibility, creativity, and sweetness in sharing her talents and designs
- Cynthia Potter for her meticulous and thoughtful design edits

❋ *The Grow Healthy. Grow Happy.* editorial team:

- Leonard Jacobs for his intelligence and knowledge, continual support, and belief in me and the value and purpose of this book
- Nikki Bruno Clapper for her professionalism, flexibility, and caring for quality editing
- Natalie Mortensen for her thoughtfulness and precision in proofreading
- Steve Hoffman for fact-checking to ensure that everything is correct
- Elizabeth Frankl for her thoughts and guidance
- Beth Brand for her sincerity, thoughtfulness, and hard work
- Elizabeth Shaw for her organization in producing the digital version of *Grow Healthy. Grow Happy.*

❋ *The Grow Healthy. Grow Happy.* research team:

- Garnett Hutchinson for her holistic thinking, wisdom, and insights in child development
- Michael Rossoff for his guidance in and knowledge of East Asian medicine
- Caren Bakkum for her ingenuity and precision in cooking and knowledge of natural foods
- John Belleme for his expertise in the benefits of traditional fermented foods
- Edward Cortright for his knowledge about healthy and clean water
- Sidney Setzer for her consistent willingness and her commitment to a job well done
- Claire Salinda for her thoughtful research, ideas, and reliable support
- Gilly Maccubbin for testing my recipes with openness and gusto

My support team of mentors, friends, and family:

- The i play. staff for their patience and their willingness to take responsibility for running our business
- Michio and Aveline Kushi, my mentors, for their inspiration and for sharing tools for healthy living
- Hideko Yoshida, my mentor, for her commitment to the health and happiness of young children
- Ron Walls, my friend, for his loyalty, dedication, and support through listening
- Vicki Rowe-Currence, my friend, for her emotional support, love of biking, and fun spirit
- Carol Bowman, my friend, for her ongoing support as a fellow mother and author
- Dan Fowler, my friend, for his steady and consistent friendship
- Joel Wollner, my friend, for his support, ideas, and concepts
- Fred Cannon, my late father, for teaching me to focus, to work hard, and to be persistent
- Evie Dillard, my grandmother, for teaching me how to sew and the value of integrity
- Erin Dillard, my grandfather, for sharing his spirit of entrepreneurship along with the resources to start my business
- Mike Cannon, my late brother, for inspiring me to play an active role as a parent
- David Cannon, my brother, for his research, sincere interest in this book, and overall support
- Bill Cannon, my brother, for his gracious acceptance of injustice
- Frederick Cannon, my brother, for allowing me to practice parenting skills early
- Naoki Kubota, my former husband, for his dedication to natural healing through acupuncture and whole foods
- Emi Kubota, my daughter, for sharing our dream to support parents and children in their pursuit of happy and healthy lives; for writing and editing with a desire for perfection; and for sharing our lives
- Mari Kubota, my daughter, for her support; for her knowledge of acupuncture and health; for feedback drawn from her multiple intelligences; for quality-assurance testing of the recipes; and for sharing our lives
- Zo Kubota-Johnson, my grandson, for recipe testing and modeling, and for being his sweet self